ALSO BY AMERICA'S TEST KITCHEN

The Perfect Pie

How to Cocktail

The Ultimate Burger

The New Essentials Cookbook

Cook's Illustrated Revolutionary Recipes

Vegetables Illustrated

Tasting Italy: A Culinary Journey

Spiced

How to Braise Everything

How to Roast Everything

Dinner Illustrated

The Complete Diabetes Cookbook

The Complete Slow Cooker

The Complete Make-Ahead Cookbook

The Complete Mediterranean Cookbook

The Complete Vegetarian Cookbook

The Complete Cooking for Two Cookbook

Cooking at Home with Bridget and Julia

Just Add Sauce

Nutritious Delicious

What Good Cooks Know

Cook's Science

The Science of Good Cooking

The Perfect Cake

The Perfect Cookie

Bread Illustrated

Master of the Grill

Kitchen Smarts

Kitchen Hacks

100 Recipes: The Absolute Best Ways to
Make the True Essentials

The New Family Cookbook

The America's Test Kitchen Cooking School Cookbook

The Cook's Illustrated Baking Book

The Cook's Illustrated Meat Book

The Cook's Illustrated Cookbook

The America's Test Kitchen Family Baking Book

The Best of America's Test Kitchen (2007–2020 Editions)

The Complete America's Test Kitchen TV Show Cookbook

Air Fryer Perfection

Instant Pot Ace Blender Cookbook

Cook It in Your Dutch Oven

Sous Vide for Everybody

Multicooker Perfection

Food Processor Perfection

Pressure Cooker Perfection

Vegan for Everybody

Naturally Sweet

Foolproof Preserving

Paleo Perfected

The How Can It Be Gluten-Free Cookbook: Volume 2

The How Can It Be Gluten-Free Cookbook

The Best Mexican Recipes

Slow Cooker Revolution Volume 2: The Easy-Prep Edition

Slow Cooker Revolution

The America's Test Kitchen D.I.Y. Cookbook

THE COOK'S ILLUSTRATED ALL-TIME BEST SERIES

All-Time Best Brunch

All-Time Best Dinners for Two

All-Time Best Sunday Suppers

All-Time Best Holiday Entertaining

All-Time Best Appetizers

All-Time Best Soups

COOK'S COUNTRY TITLES

One-Pan Wonders

Cook It in Cast Iron

The Complete Cook's Country TV Show Cookbook

FOR A FULL LISTING OF ALL OUR BOOKS

CooksIllustrated.com

AmericasTestKitchen.com

THE BEST OF

— AMERICA'S —

TEST KITCHEN

BEST RECIPES, EQUIPMENT REVIEWS, AND TASTINGS

2020

AMERICA'S TEST KITCHEN

— AMERICA'S — ®
TEST KITCHEN

AMERICA'S TEST KITCHEN
21 Drydock Avenue, Boston, MA 02210

THE BEST OF AMERICA'S TEST KITCHEN 2020
Best Recipes, Equipment Reviews, and Tastings

ISBN: 978-1-945256-89-9
ISSN: 1940-3925

Manufactured in the United States of America
10 9 8 7 6 5 4 3 2 1

Distributed by Penguin Random House Publisher Services
Tel: 800-733-3000

EDITORIAL DIRECTOR, BOOKS: Adam Kowit

EXECUTIVE MANAGING EDITORS: Debra Hudak and Todd Meier

DEPUTY EDITOR: Megan Ginsberg

EDITORIAL ASSISTANTS: Tess Berger and Sara Zatopek

ART DIRECTOR: Lindsey Timko Chandler

DEPUTY ART DIRECTORS: Allison Boales and Janet Taylor

PHOTOGRAPHY DIRECTOR: Julie Bozzo Cote

PHOTOGRAPHY PRODUCER: Meredith Mulcahy

FRONT COVER PHOTOGRAPH: Carl Tremblay

SENIOR STAFF PHOTOGRAPHERS: Steve Klise and Daniel J. van Ackere

STAFF PHOTOGRAPHER: Kevin White

ADDITIONAL PHOTOGRAPHY: Keller + Keller and Carl Tremblay

FOOD STYLING: Tara Busa, Catrine Kelty, Chantal Lambeth, Kendra McKnight,
Jessica Rudolph, Elle Simone Scott, and Kendra Smith

PHOTOSHOOT KITCHEN TEAM

    PHOTO TEAM AND SPECIAL EVENTS MANAGER: Timothy McQuinn

    ASSISTANT TEST COOKS: Sarah Ewald, Hannah Fenton, Jacqueline Gochenouer, and Eric Haessler

ILLUSTRATION: John Burgoyne

SENIOR MANAGER, PUBLISHING OPERATIONS: Taylor Argenzio

IMAGING MANAGER: Lauren Robbins

PRODUCTION AND IMAGING SPECIALISTS: Dennis Noble, Jessica Voas, and Amanda Yong

SENIOR COPY EDITOR: Jillian Campbell

COPY EDITORS: Christine Campbell and Rachel Schowalter

PROOFREADER: Pat Jalbert-Levine

INDEXER: Elizabeth Parson

CHIEF CREATIVE OFFICER: Jack Bishop

EXECUTIVE EDITORIAL DIRECTORS: Julia Collin Davison and Bridget Lancaster

PICTURED ON FRONT COVER: Torta Caprese (page 226)

CONTENTS

WELCOME TO AMERICA'S TEST KITCHEN

This book has been tested, written, and edited by the folks at America's Test Kitchen. Located in Boston's Seaport District in the historic Innovation and Design Building, it features 15,000 square feet of kitchen space including multiple photography and video studios. It is the home of *Cook's Illustrated* magazine and *Cook's Country* magazine and is the workday destination for more than 60 test cooks, editors, and cookware specialists. Our mission is to test recipes over and over again until we understand how and why they work and until we arrive at the best version.

We start the process of testing a recipe with a complete lack of preconceptions, which means that we accept no claim, no technique, and no recipe at face value. We simply assemble as many variations as possible, test a half-dozen of the most promising, and taste the results blind. We then construct our own recipe and continue to test it, varying ingredients, techniques, and cooking times until we reach a consensus. As we like to say in the test kitchen, "We make the mistakes so you don't have to." The result, we hope, is the best version of a particular recipe, but we realize that only you can be the final judge of our success (or failure). We use the same rigorous approach when we test equipment and taste ingredients.

All of this would not be possible without a belief that good cooking, much like good music, is based on a foundation of objective technique. Some people like spicy foods and others don't, but there is a right way to sauté, there is a best way to cook a pot roast, and there are measurable scientific principles involved in producing perfectly beaten, stable egg whites. Our ultimate goal is to investigate the fundamental principles of cooking to give you the techniques, tools, and ingredients you need to become a better cook. It is as simple as that.

To see what goes on behind the scenes at America's Test Kitchen, check out our social media channels for kitchen snapshots, exclusive content, video tips, and much more. You can watch us work (in our actual test kitchen) by tuning in to *America's Test Kitchen* or *Cook's Country* on public television or on our websites. Download our award-winning podcast *Proof*, which goes beyond recipes to solve food mysteries (AmericasTestKitchen.com/proof), or listen in to test kitchen experts on public radio (SplendidTable.org) to hear insights that illuminate the truth about real home cooking. Want to hone your cooking skills or finally learn how to bake—with an America's Test Kitchen test cook? Enroll in one of our online cooking classes. And you can engage the next generation of home cooks with kid-tested recipes from America's Test Kitchen Kids.

However you choose to visit us, we welcome you into our kitchen, where you can stand by our side as we test our way to the best recipes in America.

facebook.com/AmericasTestKitchen
twitter.com/TestKitchen
youtube.com/AmericasTestKitchen
instagram.com/TestKitchen
pinterest.com/TestKitchen

AmericasTestKitchen.com
CooksIllustrated.com
CooksCountry.com
OnlineCookingSchool.com
AmericasTestKitchen.com/kids

PASTA E FAGIOLI

◷ WHY THIS RECIPE WORKS Featuring various types of beans and shapes of pasta—and even inconsistent on the inclusion of meat—the iterations of this Italian American soup are endless. We wanted a soup that was savory, hearty, and brimming with creamy beans and soft bites of pasta. Starting with a base of pancetta, finely chopped vegetables, plenty of garlic, and tomato paste, we built a rich and flavorful broth as a backdrop for our soup. To thicken it, we pureed half the cannellini beans that we were adding to the soup. For ease, we added little ditalini to cook right in the simmering soup in the last moments before serving. Some grated Parmesan cheese for extra richness and a big handful of fresh basil for a blast of fragrant freshness were all that was needed to finish the dish.

When I was a kid, my family always celebrated milestone moments or special occasions with dinner at Il Villaggio. This Italian American restaurant, which was discreetly tucked into a northern New Jersey strip mall, might not have been well-known beyond my hometown, but its rendition of *pasta e fagioli* (or as we called it, "pasta fazool") made me swoon. It was deeply but gently savory, thick and hearty, and studded with creamy beans and soft little pieces of pasta—so good that I used to order one bowl as an appetizer and a second bowl for my entrée.

In Italy, every region has its own version of this pasta and bean soup, and versions vary greatly in America, too. Variables include pasta (fresh or dried; long noodles or short shapes), beans, vegetables, meat, tomato, and general thickness/brothiness. Having a specific version in mind—thank you, Il Villaggio—guided my choices in creating my own version.

Even though it didn't have any chunks of meat in it, I remember Il Villaggio's pasta e fagioli tasting rich and porky. So I started by sautéing chopped onions, celery, and carrots with pancetta, Italy's flavorful unsmoked bacon. Four cloves of minced garlic rounded out the savoriness and added a hint of sweetness, and a pinch of red pepper flakes provided a lively spark.

I moved on to the tomato component. We liked the flavor of fresh tomatoes, but they made the soup taste too acidic. To create a sweeter, full-bodied tomato flavor, I turned to tomato paste, taking time to brown it with the vegetables before adding liquid. Oh, and about that liquid—adding only chicken stock left me with a thin

bean soup. To build body, I pureed 1 cup of water and half the cannellini beans into a creamy paste and added it to the soup with the remaining whole beans. This technique provided the right amount of thickening.

Many recipes call for cooking the pasta separately and then adding it to the soup at the last minute. I understand the logic behind this: Pasta can easily overcook and bloat (soaking up the soup's broth) if kept in liquid for too long. But I really didn't want to get out an extra pot and boil water while I had a perfectly bubbling soup right in front of me. So I added one of my favorite small pastas, ditalini (small elbows work great, too), right to the pot and cooked it until just al dente. To complete the soup, I stirred in some Parmesan as well as chopped fresh basil, which brightened the flavors and contributed vibrant color. The soup was really, really good, perfect for a light supper or filling lunch—or your own special occasions.

—KATIE LEAIRD, *Cook's Country*

Pasta e Fagioli

SERVES 4 TO 6

You can use any small pasta shape, such as tubettini, elbow macaroni, or small shells, in place of the ditalini. To make this soup vegetarian, omit the pancetta and substitute vegetable broth for the chicken broth. If you do not have a food processor, you can use a blender to process the beans and water in step 1.

- 2 (15-ounce) cans cannellini beans, rinsed, divided
- 1 cup water
- 2 tablespoons extra-virgin olive oil, plus extra for drizzling
- 2 onions, chopped fine
- 2 carrots, peeled and chopped fine
- 1 celery rib, chopped fine
- 2 ounces pancetta, chopped fine
- ¾ teaspoon table salt
- ½ teaspoon pepper
- 2 tablespoons tomato paste
- 4 garlic cloves, minced
- ¼ teaspoon red pepper flakes (optional)
- 4 cups chicken broth
- 4 ounces (1 cup) ditalini
- 2 ounces Parmesan cheese, grated (1 cup), plus extra for serving
- ½ cup finely chopped fresh basil

PASTA E FAGIOLI

1. Process 1 can of beans and water in food processor until smooth, about 30 seconds. Set aside.

2. Heat oil in large saucepan over medium heat until shimmering. Add onions, carrots, celery, pancetta, salt, and pepper and cook until vegetables are softened, about 10 minutes.

3. Add tomato paste, garlic, and pepper flakes, if using, and cook until fragrant, about 2 minutes. Stir in broth, pureed bean mixture, and remaining can of beans. Bring to boil, reduce heat to medium-low, and simmer, stirring occasionally, until flavors have melded, about 10 minutes.

4. Increase heat to medium and bring to boil. Add pasta and cook, stirring occasionally, until pasta is al dente, about 12 minutes. Off heat, stir in Parmesan and basil. Serve, drizzled with extra oil and passing extra Parmesan separately.

TO MAKE AHEAD: At end of step 3, let soup cool completely. Refrigerate soup for up to 2 days or freeze for up to 1 month. If frozen, let soup thaw completely in refrigerator before reheating. To serve, bring soup to boil and continue with step 4.

HEARTY CABBAGE SOUP

✔ WHY THIS RECIPE WORKS Often a dieter's frenemy, cabbage has the bad reputation of being overbearing in taste, limp in texture, and smelly when cooked. But this humble vegetable has loads of potential for a healthy and satisfying soup. Too often, though, cabbage soup tastes weak and one-dimensional, consisting of little besides cabbage and broth. To create a version that would be as satisfying as it was healthy, we started with ground chicken, a great lean source of protein with much less sodium than sausage (a common pairing with cabbage). Sweating the aromatics helped amp up the flavor of the soup. Warm and slightly peppery caraway seeds paired perfectly with the cabbage while hot smoked paprika provided depth of flavor. Cooking the cabbage for about 30 minutes rendered it tender without turning it mushy. The addition of potatoes helped turn this soup into a hearty meal. Before serving we added ½ cup of low-fat sour cream for richness and tang.

Before creating *The Complete Diabetes Cookbook*, my fellow test cooks and I took it upon ourselves to learn about the science and management of the disease in order to inform our recipe development. As we worked with nutritionists and public health advocates, we learned that crafting healthy diabetes-friendly recipes wasn't quite as simple as cutting down on calories or eliminating certain foods; it's also important to have a balance of protein, healthy fats, carbohydrates, and plenty of fiber.

But we at the test kitchen firmly believe that food should nurture the soul as well as the body. In addition to promoting good health, a meal should provide comfort and enjoyment. As I thought about potential dishes that could accomplish all of the above, I decided to begin with a purely healthful canvas. That's how I zeroed in on cabbage soup. This humble soup may not be known for inspiring cravings, but you can't argue against its health factor. I was determined to produce a version of this soup that would turn healthful into hearty and drab into delicious.

The biggest challenge in making a diabetes-friendly soup is making it taste good while keeping sodium in check. Without adding more salt, I needed to figure out how to trick the palate into perceiving more flavor. Acid, I knew, can work to mimic saltier flavor in dishes. Fresh finishing herbs would also help brighten up the dish. But before I could think about garnishes, I had to develop a flavor-packed base for my soup.

To start, I bloomed some aromatics in oil and added green cabbage (tasters preferred it to napa or savoy cabbage), chicken broth, and just a bit of white wine (for its flavor-boosting acidity), cooking everything until the cabbage was tender but not soggy. To make my soup more substantial and satisfying, I decided to add potatoes; even though they're starchy, potatoes can be part of a nutritious diet when used in moderation. Russet potatoes released too much starch and became mealy during cooking, but red potatoes held their shape and transferred less starch to the broth; I also found that I liked the added texture of their skins, and leaving them on cut down on prep work. I cooked the potatoes with the broth-cabbage mixture until they were tender. The acidity and tang of low-fat sour cream also helped round out the flavor profile and make the soup more satisfying. Stirring the sour cream right into the soup caused it to curdle, but tempering it first worked well. I added a bit of the hot broth to the sour cream and whisked them together before adding the mixture to the rest of the soup, encouraging a pleasantly silky finish.

Since I'd added potatoes, I realized I was on my way to creating a soup that could be eaten as a nutritionally balanced meal. With that in mind, I decided to add a protein to enhance the soup's heartiness rather than keep it ultralean. Sausage and bacon were obvious options, both for their ease of preparation and their frequent pairing with cabbage. Unfortunately, both pork products are too high in sodium and nitrates for this recipe. Instead, I decided to re-create the effect of sausage using ground chicken, which has great flavor but is lower in fat, sodium, and nitrates. To bump up the sausage-y flavor even more, I browned the ground chicken in oil with onion, caraway seeds, and just a tiny bit of salt. Sweating the onion and caraway seeds gave them time to toast and thoroughly release their flavors. The caraway's delicate anise flavor also brought out the sweetness of the cabbage. I then cooked the remaining aromatics—garlic, thyme, and hot smoked paprika—for less than a minute to coax out their flavors before they had a chance to burn. The smoked paprika provided the savory smokiness that pork sausage would have contributed.

From there, I added the wine, broth, and cabbage plus a bay leaf and let the mixture simmer, keeping the pot covered to reduce evaporation and prevent the soup from becoming too thick. Next, in went the potatoes and eventually the tempered sour cream, which added some richness and tang. Aware that the timing with which food is seasoned plays an important part in how you perceive its flavor, I held off on stirring a final ½ teaspoon of salt into the pot until the end for maximum impact. Finally, I seasoned the soup with pepper and some dill for a fresh finish. One whiff of this healthy yet hearty meal confirmed that this was no average cabbage soup. With the meatiness from the chicken, the velvety-smooth consistency, and the complexity from the herbs, spices, and tangy sour cream, this was a nourishing soup I could get excited about.

—LEAH COLINS, *America's Test Kitchen Books*

Hearty Cabbage Soup
SERVES 8

If added directly to the soup, the sour cream may curdle and create unattractive lumps; adding a little hot broth to the sour cream (a technique known as tempering) raises its temperature and helps stabilize it so it can be slowly stirred into the soup without fear of curdling. Avoid red cabbage; it will discolor the soup.

- 3 tablespoons canola oil
- 1 pound ground chicken
- 1 onion, chopped fine
- 2 teaspoons caraway seeds, toasted
- ¾ teaspoon table salt, divided
- 5 garlic cloves, minced
- 1 teaspoon minced fresh thyme or ¼ teaspoon dried
- ½ teaspoon hot smoked paprika
- ¼ cup dry white wine
- 1 head green cabbage (2 pounds), cored and cut into ¾-inch pieces
- 8 cups unsalted chicken broth
- 1 bay leaf
- 12 ounces red potatoes, unpeeled, cut into ¾-inch pieces
- ½ cup low-fat sour cream
- 1 tablespoon minced fresh dill

1. Heat oil in Dutch oven over medium heat until shimmering. Add chicken, onion, caraway seeds, and ¼ teaspoon salt and cook, breaking up chicken with wooden spoon, until chicken is no longer pink and onion is softened, 7 to 9 minutes.

2. Stir in garlic, thyme, and paprika and cook until fragrant, about 30 seconds. Stir in wine, scraping up any browned bits, and cook until nearly evaporated. Stir in cabbage, broth, and bay leaf and bring to simmer. Reduce heat to medium-low, cover, and cook for 15 minutes. Stir in potatoes and continue to cook until vegetables are tender, 15 to 20 minutes longer.

3. Discard bay leaf. Stir few tablespoons of hot broth into sour cream to temper, then stir sour cream mixture and remaining ½ teaspoon salt into pot. Stir in dill and season with pepper to taste. Serve.

THAI HOT AND SOUR NOODLE SOUP WITH SHRIMP (GUAY TIEW TOM YUM GOONG)

THAI HOT AND SOUR NOODLE SOUP WITH SHRIMP

✔ **WHY THIS RECIPE WORKS** This authentic Thai soup contains generous amounts of shrimp and rice noodles—along with oyster mushrooms and cherry tomatoes—in a highly aromatic broth featuring classic hot, sour, salty, and sweet flavors. We created vibrancy by smashing galangal, scallions, lemon grass, makrut lime leaves, and Thai chiles to release their flavorful oils and then simmering them in store-bought chicken broth. Then we rounded out the classic flavor profile with more Thai ingredients: fish sauce, lime juice, cilantro, and Thai basil. Finally, we added a dollop of homemade *Nam prik pao*, a Thai chili jam that offers robust sweet, savory, and slightly spicy notes.

If you've ever eaten *tom yum* in a Thai restaurant, you'll know that this hot and sour soup is a bold example of the energetic flavors that Thai cuisine is famous for. The heat comes from chiles and galangal (also known as Thai ginger), the sour from lime juice and tamarind (a dark, tart fruit). But tom yum doesn't stop there: It also serves up saltiness courtesy of fish sauce and sweetness via a touch of sugar. Lemon grass, makrut lime leaves, cilantro, and Thai basil round out the fragrant bowl.

There are many versions of tom yum soup, but my favorite, known as *guay tiew tom yum goong*, is chock-full of shrimp, rice noodles, and sometimes mushrooms and/or tomatoes and topped with a deeply savory, sweet, and spicy chili jam. As a light main course, it's deeply satisfying.

Authentic recipes either start by simmering pork bones in water or they simply use plain water, whereas most modern versions call for store-bought chicken broth. A time-consuming stock didn't fit into my weeknight plans, so I tested chicken broth versus water. Broth was preferred for its depth.

Next, I looked to infuse the broth with some of Thailand's signature ingredients: lemon grass, makrut lime leaves, scallion whites, galangal, and Thai chiles. But when I simply sliced the aromatics and simmered them in the broth, it took more than an hour to extract sufficient flavor. On the other hand, pulsing the ingredients in a food processor not only made the broth unpleasantly intense but also required straining, which was a hassle. Ultimately, it made sense to do as Thai

cooks do: I sliced the aromatics and then lightly smashed them to partially break them down. With this approach, the broth developed a heady perfume after just 15 minutes of simmering, and the pieces could be removed using a slotted spoon. Sugar and fish sauce rounded things out with sweetness and saltiness.

To bulk up the soup, I stirred in fresh oyster mushrooms and the grassy green parts of the scallions. They would soften in the hot broth to add texture, and their mild flavors would offset the bold ones.

Next, I slipped a pound of peeled extra-large shrimp into the steaming broth off the heat for 5 minutes. The residual heat ensured that the shrimp gently cooked through with little risk of turning rubbery. Halved cherry tomatoes added pops of color and another layer of acidity and sweetness, and a healthy squeeze of lime juice delivered the sour flourish that is a hallmark of guay tiew tom yum goong.

As I ladled the soup over rice noodles that I had "cooked" by soaking them in boiling water, I was rewarded with a complex aroma rising from the bowls. Topped with fresh cilantro, Thai basil, and sliced Thai chiles, my soup was nearly ready.

In a final nod to authenticity, I topped each bowl with a crimson dollop of *Nam prik pao* (also known as Thai chili jam), a rich, sweet, savory, and slightly spicy condiment of fried garlic, shallots, and dried chiles cooked down with fish sauce and brown sugar. As I watched the smiling faces of my tasters slurping from their bowls, I knew my work was done.

—STEVE DUNN, *Cook's Illustrated*

Thai Hot and Sour Noodle Soup with Shrimp (Guay Tiew Tom Yum Goong)
SERVES 4 TO 6

Whole shrimp are traditional in this soup, but you can halve them crosswise before cooking to make them easier to eat. If galangal is unavailable, substitute fresh ginger. Makrut lime leaves (sometimes sold as kaffir lime leaves) add a lot to this soup, but if you can't find them, you can substitute three 3-inch strips each of lemon zest and lime zest. We prefer vermicelli made from 100 percent rice flour to varieties that include a secondary starch such as cornstarch. If you can find only the latter, soak them longer—up to 15 minutes.

4 ounces rice vermicelli

2 lemon grass stalks, trimmed to bottom 6 inches

4 scallions, trimmed, white parts left whole, green parts cut into 1-inch lengths

6 makrut lime leaves, torn if large

2 Thai chiles, stemmed (1 left whole, 1 sliced thin), divided, plus 2 Thai chiles, stemmed and sliced thin, for serving (optional)

1 (2-inch) piece fresh galangal, peeled and sliced into ¼-inch-thick rounds

8 cups chicken broth

1 tablespoon sugar, plus extra for seasoning

8 ounces oyster mushrooms, trimmed and torn into 1-inch pieces

3 tablespoons fish sauce, plus extra for seasoning

1 pound extra-large shrimp (21 to 25 per pound), peeled, deveined, and tails removed

12 ounces cherry tomatoes, halved

2 tablespoons lime juice, plus extra for seasoning, plus lime wedges for serving

½ cup fresh cilantro leaves

¼ cup fresh Thai basil leaves, torn if large (optional)

1 recipe Thai Chile Jam (Nam Prik Pao) (optional)

1. Bring 4 quarts water to boil in large pot. Remove from heat, add noodles, and let sit, stirring occasionally, until noodles are fully tender, 10 to 15 minutes. Drain, rinse with cold water, drain again, and distribute evenly among large soup bowls.

2. Place lemon grass, scallion whites, lime leaves, whole Thai chile, and galangal on cutting board and lightly smash with meat pounder or bottom of small skillet until mixture is moist and very fragrant. Transfer lemon grass mixture to Dutch oven. Add broth and sugar and bring to boil over high heat. Reduce heat and simmer for 15 minutes. Using slotted spoon, remove solids from pot and discard.

3. Add mushrooms, fish sauce, scallion greens, and sliced Thai chile and simmer for 3 to 4 minutes. Stir in shrimp. Cover and let sit off heat until shrimp are opaque and cooked through, 4 to 5 minutes. Stir in tomatoes and lime juice. Season with extra sugar, extra fish sauce, and extra lime juice to taste.

4. Ladle soup into bowls of noodles; sprinkle with cilantro and Thai basil, if using. Serve, drizzled with Thai Chile Jam, if using, passing lime wedges and extra sliced Thai chiles, if using, separately.

Thai Chili Jam (Nam Prik Pao)

SERVES 16 TO 20 (MAKES ¾ CUP)

Slice the shallots to a consistent thickness to ensure even cooking. For a spicier jam, add more chile seeds.

½ cup vegetable oil

2 large shallots, sliced thin

4 large garlic cloves, sliced thin

10 dried arbol chiles, stemmed, halved lengthwise, and seeds reserved

3 tablespoons lime juice, plus extra for seasoning (2 limes)

2 tablespoons packed brown sugar

2 tablespoons fish sauce, plus extra for seasoning

1. Set fine-mesh strainer over heatproof bowl. Heat oil and shallots in medium saucepan over medium-high heat, stirring frequently, until shallots are deep golden brown, 10 to 14 minutes. Using slotted spoon, transfer shallots to second bowl. Add garlic to hot oil and cook, stirring constantly, until golden brown, 2 to 3 minutes. Using slotted spoon, transfer garlic to bowl with shallots. Add arbols and half of reserved seeds to hot oil and cook, stirring constantly, until arbols turn deep red, 1 to 2 minutes. Strain oil through prepared strainer into bowl; reserve oil and transfer arbols to bowl with shallots and garlic. Do not wash saucepan.

2. Process lime juice, sugar, and shallot mixture in food processor until thick paste forms, 15 to 30 seconds, scraping down sides of bowl as needed.

3. Return paste to now-empty saucepan and add fish sauce and 2 tablespoons reserved oil. Bring to simmer over medium-low heat. Cook, stirring frequently, until mixture is thickened and has jam-like consistency, 4 to 5 minutes. Off heat, season with extra lime juice, extra fish sauce, and salt to taste. (Jam can be refrigerated for up to 1 month.)

NOTES FROM THE TEST KITCHEN

HOW TO COOK RICE VERMICELLI

Here's how we cook rice vermicelli that is destined for a soup bowl: Just boil water, turn off the heat, and add the noodles, stirring the noodles once or twice as they soak. The noodles are done when they're fully tender but not mushy; just taste one to check. Rinse the noodles with cold water to remove any starchy film and prevent clumping.

FREGULA WITH CLAMS AND SAFFRON BROTH

✔ **WHY THIS RECIPE WORKS** This soup of pasta and clams is a Sardinian classic that's all about simplicity. It relies chiefly on the flavors inherent in the soup's two main ingredients: chewy, toasty spherical *fregula*, and *arselle*, the small, briny, succulent hard-shell clams found along the coast. Broth enriched with tomatoes (in various forms depending on the recipe), parsley, garlic, a touch of fragrant saffron, pepper flakes, and olive oil traditionally constitutes the soup base. We cooked the pasta using the absorption method, right in our soup's base of chicken broth and water; this way, the fregula soaked up the flavorful broth during cooking. As a substitute for the Sardinian arselle, which aren't widely available in the United States, we landed on diminutive cockles, which are sweet and readily accessible. To cook the clams perfectly, we used our standard test kitchen method of steaming them in a shallow covered skillet and removing the clams as they opened. We chose sun-dried tomatoes, which are found in some traditional versions of this recipe, for our tomato product; given the soup's quick cooking time, their deep, concentrated flavor was a bonus. A sprinkling of parsley and lemon zest contributed a bright finish to a satisfying dish.

Derived from the Latin word *fricare*, meaning "to rub," *fregula* is an Italian pasta made by rubbing semolina flour and saffron-infused water together until the dough forms pasta pellets. These pellets, which resemble couscous, are then roasted in a wood-burning oven, giving them a delicate toasted flavor and a beautiful burnished hue. Originating in Italy's Mediterranean island of Sardinia, fregula is most traditionally prepared in *sa fregula con vongole*, a brothy soup with tiny clams called *arselle*, tomatoes, saffron, and aromatics. This dish's main appeal is its simplicity—as long as the pasta, clams, and tomatoes are prepared correctly, the handful of other simple ingredients will bring it all together. I wanted to build a complex-flavored soup that I could quickly and easily prepare while relaxing with a glass of crisp white wine.

I started by heating 2 tablespoons of extra-virgin olive oil in a Dutch oven over medium heat and adding garlic, pepper flakes, and crumbled saffron threads. A little goes a long way with saffron, so just ⅛ teaspoon was enough to add plenty of floral flavor without overwhelming the dish. Once it was fragrant, I added the

liquid. After playing around with different broths—chicken, fish, and vegetable—I settled on 2 cups each of chicken broth and water. This combination produced a well-balanced, neutral base for my soup.

This dish traditionally calls for tomatoes, but the tomato product (or products) vary from recipe to recipe—from canned tomatoes and fresh tomatoes to tomato paste and sun-dried tomatoes. Above all, I knew I wanted deep tomato flavor without turning this into a tomato-based soup. Canned diced tomatoes made the soup all about the tomatoes, and they also made it taste tinny; fresh plum tomatoes provided underwhelming tomato flavor. Oil-packed sun-dried tomatoes, a traditional Sardinian option, were my solution. They added concentrated tomato flavor without muddying the broth the way a dollop of tomato paste would. After patting the tomatoes dry, I roughly chopped them and tossed them in the pot with the chicken broth, water, and 2 tablespoons of fresh parsley.

I chose to cook the fregula directly in the broth rather than in a separate pot of water so that it could fully absorb the flavorful broth. Once I brought the broth to a boil, I added the fregula and cooked it to al dente, stirring it frequently to prevent sticking.

Although I wanted to keep this recipe as authentic as possible, arselle clams are nearly impossible to find in the States. Luckily, I found cockles to be a suitable, more readily available substitute. Small, sweet, and tender, they were reminiscent of the arselle; if unavailable, littlenecks are also a tasty swap.

While most recipes called for dumping the clams directly into the soup toward the end of cooking, this caused the cockles to become overcooked and rubbery. Cooking them in a 12-inch skillet proved beneficial in a number of ways. For one, they cooked faster in the heat of a shallow pan than in that of a deep Dutch oven. Also, I could easily spot any clams that didn't open up and quickly discard them instead of precariously digging them out of my soup pot. Finally, I could easily monitor the tiny bivalves to guarantee that they wouldn't overcook. I simply brought the cockles and 1 cup of dry white wine to a boil in a covered skillet, waited for the clams to just barely open up, and transferred them to a large bowl, which I then covered to keep them warm until serving. Because clams exude liquid as they cook, I was left with plenty of tasty, briny liquid that I didn't want to waste. To infuse the soup with a splash of deep-sea flavor, I strained the clam cooking liquid

FREGULA WITH CLAMS AND SAFFRON BROTH

through a fine-mesh strainer lined with a coffee filter directly into the Dutch oven. (The straining step is key because it prevents the soup from becoming unpleasantly gritty.)

At this point, the soup was delicious, and its three superstar ingredients—the tomatoes, the fregula, and the cockles—were shining. But how could I further highlight their flavors without detracting from them? Simple: I would stir in even more fresh parsley right before serving to reinforce its subtle, herbaceous flavor. And just ¼ teaspoon of aromatic lemon zest contributed a final note of brightness. Because the clam "juice" naturally contributed brininess, I waited to season my soup until right before serving—you may even find that you can forgo the salt altogether. For an elegant presentation, I ladled the soup into shallow bowls, floated a handful of cockles on top, and gave each serving a generous drizzle of extra-virgin olive oil for added richness and a rustic look.

—LAWMAN JOHNSON, *America's Test Kitchen Books*

Fregula with Clams and Saffron Broth

SERVES 4 TO 6

Cockles are traditional here and are our preferred choice, but if they are unavailable, you can substitute small littleneck clams.

2	tablespoons extra-virgin olive oil, plus extra for serving
2	garlic cloves, minced
⅛	teaspoon red pepper flakes
⅛	teaspoon saffron threads, crumbled
2	cups chicken broth
2	cups water
⅓	cup oil-packed sun-dried tomatoes, patted dry and chopped coarse
¼	cup minced fresh parsley, divided
1½	cups fregula
2	pounds cockles, scrubbed
1	cup dry white wine
¼	teaspoon grated lemon zest

1. Heat oil in Dutch oven over medium heat until shimmering. Add garlic, pepper flakes, and saffron and cook until fragrant, about 30 seconds. Stir in broth, water, tomatoes, and 2 tablespoons parsley and bring to boil. Stir in pasta and cook, stirring often, until al dente.

2. While pasta cooks, bring clams and wine to boil in covered 12-inch skillet over high heat. Cook, shaking skillet occasionally, until clams have just opened, 6 to 8 minutes. Using slotted spoon, transfer clams to large bowl. Discard any unopened clams. Cover to keep warm.

3. Strain clam cooking liquid through fine-mesh strainer lined with coffee filter into pot, avoiding any gritty sediment that has settled on bottom of skillet.

4. Stir in lemon zest and remaining 2 tablespoons parsley and season with salt and pepper to taste. Top individual portions with clams and drizzle with extra oil before serving.

MEXICAN CORN SALAD

✓ **WHY THIS RECIPE WORKS** Our Mexican Corn Salad (Esquites) features charred kernels whose nutty, slightly bitter flavor complements corn's natural sweetness. We achieved that charring on the stovetop by cooking kernels in a small amount of oil in a covered skillet. The kernels in contact with the skillet's surface browned and charred, and the lid prevented the kernels from popping out of the hot skillet. We cooked the corn in two batches to allow more kernels to make contact with the skillet and brown. After cooking the corn, we used the hot skillet to bloom chili powder and lightly cook minced garlic to temper its bite. We dressed the salad with a creamy and tangy mixture of sour cream, mayonnaise, and lime juice. Letting the corn cool before adding chopped cilantro and spicy serrano chiles preserved their bright colors and fresh flavors.

If you're enjoying grilled corn only with butter and salt, you're missing out. Take just one bite of Mexican street corn, called *elote*, and you'll know why it has become wildly popular in the United States. A charred ear of corn is slathered with rich, tangy crema; coated with salty cotija cheese; sprinkled with chili powder; and finished with a squeeze of lime. This smoky, creamy, bright, salty cob has just one catch: It's messy to eat.

Some vendors offer elote in salad form (*esquites*), with charred kernels layered or tossed with the garnishes. You get the ideal combination of flavors and textures in every bite but with the convenience of a fork. I wanted to find a way to make this flavor-packed side dish even when I'm not firing up the grill.

The broiler seemed a good place to start since its intense radiant heat is similar to that of a grill. I placed six ears of corn on a baking sheet and broiled them on the highest oven rack, rotating them every few minutes. Unfortunately, only the rows of kernels closest to the broiler browned; the rest turned dry and leathery. I thought that if I cut the kernels off the cob and spread them into an even layer, more of them might char, so I gave it a try. While more kernels browned, nearly all were overcooked. Because they were farther from the heating element, it had taken them much longer to develop any color.

It was time to try the stove. It seemed like cutting the kernels off the cob was still the way to go since it allows more kernels to come in contact with the heat. Plus, cut kernels release a starchy, sugary liquid that, in theory, would help with browning.

I grabbed a nonstick skillet and cooked the kernels in a little oil over high heat, without stirring them. The kernels touching the pan's surface charred beautifully and those in the middle were plump and perfectly cooked, but those on top remained raw and starchy. I was fine with some of the kernels not being charred so long as they were tender and plump, but what if I split the corn into two batches? This would put more kernels in contact with the hot skillet, and fewer kernels in the pan might lead to more even cooking.

NOTES FROM THE TEST KITCHEN

A NEAT WAY TO CUT CORN
The most common method of cutting corn from the cob involves standing the corn up vertically, which causes the kernels to scatter. Here's an alternative that keeps the kernels more contained.

Stand corn vertically and remove strip by slicing downward. Place corn horizontally on cut side. Use narrower front third of chef's knife to slice downward along cob and remove kernels.

I heated some oil in a fresh skillet, added half the kernels, and covered the skillet to trap steam. After 3 minutes, the corn on the bottom was perfectly charred and the rest was juicy and tender. After repeating the technique with the remaining kernels, I had plenty of charred corn to give my salad its signature flavor.

It was time to dress the dish. Mexican crema can be hard to find, but a combination of mayonnaise, sour cream, and lime juice produced a similar creamy tang and clung even better to the corn. To give my salad heat and bite, I stirred in some sliced serrano chile, chili powder, and garlic that I'd toasted in the empty skillet after cooking the corn. Finally, once the mixture had cooled, I tossed in cilantro, scallions, and some salty crumbled cotija cheese. The next time I'm craving my favorite way to eat corn, I can make a batch in less time than it takes to fire up the grill.

—LAN LAM, *Cook's Illustrated*

Mexican Corn Salad (Esquites)
SERVES 6 TO 8

Plain Greek yogurt can be substituted for the sour cream, if desired. We like serrano chiles here, but you can substitute a jalapeño chile that has been halved lengthwise and sliced into ⅛-inch-thick half-moons. Adjust the amount of chiles to suit your taste. If cotija cheese is unavailable, substitute feta.

- 3 tablespoons lime juice, plus extra for seasoning (2 limes)
- 3 tablespoons sour cream
- 1 tablespoon mayonnaise
- 1–2 serrano chiles, stemmed and cut into ⅛-inch-thick rings
- ¾ teaspoon table salt, divided
- 2 tablespoons plus 1 teaspoon vegetable oil, divided
- 6 ears corn, kernels cut from cobs (6 cups), divided
- 2 garlic cloves, minced
- ½ teaspoon chili powder
- 4 ounces cotija cheese, crumbled (1 cup)
- ¾ cup coarsely chopped fresh cilantro
- 3 scallions, sliced thin

1. Combine lime juice, sour cream, mayonnaise, serrano(s), and ¼ teaspoon salt in large bowl. Set aside.

2. Heat 1 tablespoon oil in 12-inch nonstick skillet over high heat until shimmering. Add half of corn and spread into even layer. Sprinkle with ¼ teaspoon salt. Cover and cook, without stirring, until corn touching skillet is charred, about 3 minutes. Remove skillet from heat and let stand, covered, until any popping subsides, about 15 seconds. Transfer corn to bowl with sour cream mixture. Repeat with 1 tablespoon oil, remaining corn, and remaining ¼ teaspoon salt.

3. Return now-empty skillet to medium heat and add remaining 1 teaspoon oil, garlic, and chili powder. Cook, stirring constantly, until fragrant, about 30 seconds. Transfer garlic mixture to bowl with corn mixture and toss to combine. Let cool for at least 15 minutes.

4. Add cotija, cilantro, and scallions and toss to combine. Season with salt and up to 1 tablespoon extra lime juice to taste. Serve.

BEET SALAD WITH GOAT CHEESE AND ARUGULA

WHY THIS RECIPE WORKS Roasting whole beets can take up to 2 hours (not including the time it takes for the oven to preheat and for the beets to cool before peeling). Instead, we peeled the beets, cut them into small chunks, and microwaved them in a covered bowl with a little water. Peeling them before cooking meant we didn't have to wait for them to cool before we proceeded. Cutting them into pieces exposed much more surface area so they cooked faster, and cooking them in the microwave caused water molecules inside the beets to boil rapidly and intensely, so they cooked through in less than 30 minutes. Beets work particularly well in a salad with cheese, greens, and nuts. Instead of tossing the components together (which usually results in muddy-looking cheese and beets that sink to the bottom of the bowl), we thinned the goat cheese with lemon juice and water, spread it on a platter, and topped it with lightly dressed beets and greens as well as toasted almonds for crunch.

If you aren't cooking beets, you should be. They're cheap, widely available, and nutritious; when properly cooked, they feature earthy sweetness and vibrant color.

If only they cooked faster. While roasting is easy (just wrap whole unpeeled beets in foil and throw them in the oven), even average-size beets need more than an hour to turn truly tender. Plus, you have to wait for the oven to preheat and then for the roasted specimens to cool before peeling. Also, beets cooked this way can't be seasoned; the salt merely sits on the skins.

I brainstormed ways to speed things up. Since water transfers heat more efficiently than air does, I tried boiling whole beets. This saved only 15 minutes. Peeling and cutting the beets into chunks shortened the cooking time to 25 minutes, but they leached flavor and color into the water and tasted washed-out. Steaming produced more flavorful results but took 50 minutes.

We often jump-start food in the microwave, so I gave that a whirl. I microwaved the beets for 20 minutes and then spread them on a baking sheet to finish in the oven, which took another 20 minutes. Not bad, but the cut surfaces browned, turning more savory than sweet—I wanted maximum sweetness.

Why not use the microwave to go all the way? Although it's a myth that microwaves penetrate all the way to the center of even the thickest food, they can easily penetrate to the interior of a beet chunk and heat the water molecules inside it, effectively steaming it from within. Indeed, the microwaved beets were tender in 25 minutes, the same as for boiling but without the washed-out flavor. Their surfaces were a tad dry, so I nuked another batch with ⅓ cup of water added to the bowl and covered it with a plate to trap steam.

These beets were silky and tender, and I could season them by adding a little salt to the water. And since I'd already peeled them, I could simply drain them and add them directly to a showstopping salad.

My hang-up with most beet salads—the kind tossed with goat cheese, nuts, and greens—is that the creamy cheese smears all over the other ingredients and turns muddy while the beets sink to the bottom of the bowl. So instead, I used the goat cheese as an anchor for the salad, thinning it with lemon juice and water; seasoning it with lemon zest, herbs, and spices; and spreading it across a serving platter. Then I topped it with a few handfuls of arugula and the beets (both lightly dressed with olive oil and more lemon juice), followed by toasted almonds for nutty crunch.

I now had a salad that looked as striking as it tasted. But I wasn't ready to say goodbye to this red root vegetable: Given the speed and convenience of my new cooking method, I'll be micro-steaming beets for just about any salad or side.

—STEVE DUNN, *Cook's Illustrated*

Beet Salad with Goat Cheese and Arugula

SERVES 6

Be sure to wear gloves when peeling and dicing the beets to prevent your hands from becoming stained. The moisture content of goat cheese varies, so add the water slowly in step 2. For the best presentation, use red beets here, not golden or Chioggia beets.

- 2 **pounds beets, trimmed, peeled, and cut into ¾-inch pieces**
- ½ **teaspoon plus ⅛ teaspoon plus 2 pinches table salt, divided**
- 4 **ounces goat cheese, crumbled (1 cup)**
- 2 **tablespoons minced fresh chives, divided**
- ½ **teaspoon grated lemon zest, plus 5 teaspoons juice, divided, plus extra juice for seasoning**
- ½ **teaspoon caraway seeds**
- ¼ **teaspoon pepper**
- 5 **ounces (5 cups) baby arugula**
- ¼ **cup sliced almonds, toasted, divided**
- 1 **tablespoon extra-virgin olive oil, divided**

1. In largest bowl your microwave will accommodate, stir together beets, ⅓ cup water, and ½ teaspoon salt. Cover with plate and microwave until beets can be easily pierced with paring knife, 25 to 30 minutes, stirring halfway through microwaving. Drain beets in colander and let cool.

2. In medium bowl, use rubber spatula to mash together goat cheese, 1 tablespoon chives, lemon zest and 2 teaspoons juice, caraway seeds, pepper, and ⅛ teaspoon salt. Slowly stir in up to ⅓ cup water until mixture has consistency of regular yogurt. Season with salt, pepper, and extra lemon juice to taste. Spread goat cheese mixture over serving platter.

3. In large bowl, combine arugula, 2 tablespoons almonds, 2 teaspoons oil, 1 teaspoon lemon juice, and pinch salt and toss to coat. Arrange arugula mixture on top of goat cheese mixture, leaving 1-inch border of goat cheese mixture. Add beets to now-empty bowl and toss with remaining 2 teaspoons lemon juice, remaining 1 teaspoon oil, and remaining pinch salt. Place beet mixture on top of arugula mixture. Sprinkle salad with remaining 2 tablespoons almonds and remaining 1 tablespoon chives and serve.

NOTES FROM THE TEST KITCHEN

WHY BEETS TAKE SO LONG TO COOK
Most vegetables turn to mush after being microwaved for half an hour because the pectin and hemicellulose that hold their cells together dissolve in the heat. But beets contain phenolic compounds that toughen their cellular cement. As a result, beet pectin is particularly heat-stable, which means it takes longer to soften beets during cooking.

MUSHY TURNIP

FIRM BEET

PAN-ROASTED PEAR SALAD

✔ **WHY THIS RECIPE WORKS** We can't get enough of juicy, sweet pears. They're great to eat all by themselves, but we think roasting them until their exteriors turn beautifully caramelized makes them even more irresistible. The caramelization gives the pears deeper sweetness to complement their floral notes, and the flesh turns perfectly tender. To celebrate peak pear season, we wanted to create a salad built around roasted pears. Using ripe-but-firm pears was a must, as this ensured that both their taste and texture were top-notch. Quartering the pears and then pan-roasting them allowed us to brown their exteriors without overcooking their centers. Tossing the pear slices with 2 teaspoons of sugar before we pan-roasted them intensified their sweetness and hastened their light caramelization. A vinaigrette made with maple syrup complemented the flavor of the roasted pears while chives, crispy bacon, and crumbled blue cheese added bold, salty counterpoints to the salad.

I love eating a juicy, ripe pear plain out of hand, but I find them more enticing when they're roasted until they're tender and creamy inside and lightly caramelized outside. I wanted to create a lush and satisfying salad built around the sultry appeal of roasted pears, something that wouldn't be out of place as part of a company-worthy dinner.

After researching recipes in our cookbook library, I assembled five promising versions of roasted pear salad and presented them to my colleagues. These

PAN-ROASTED PEAR SALAD

recipes were fine, but none of them blew us away. One thing they had in common: They all used the oven to roast the pears. Although this method did achieve a fair amount of caramelization, I wanted an alternative in case the oven was tied up with the main course. I wondered if I could free up the oven and achieve the same result in a skillet on the stovetop.

Through trial and error, I found that cutting the pears into quarters was ideal for allowing their exteriors to brown without overcooking the centers. As for the type of pear, I tried a few varieties. I settled on Bosc pears because they seared well and I didn't have to peel them. I tossed the quartered pears with 2 teaspoons of sugar before searing to intensify their sweetness and deepen the browning. Pears that were fully ripe started to break down in the skillet; ripe-but-firm fruit was the best choice.

To select the green that would accompany my pears, I tested every lettuce available at the supermarket. I finally choose mild, crunchy romaine, which would add nice texture without competing with the flavor of the pears. As for the dressing, my tasters thought that creamy dressings overwhelmed the pears, while simple vinaigrettes let the pear flavor shine. We also liked dressings with a little sweetness to echo that quality in the fruit, so I started with a simple mix of extra-virgin olive oil and fruity cider vinegar and tested sugar, honey, apple jelly, and maple syrup for the sweet component. Maple syrup's rich caramel flavor won my tasters' favor.

Chives contributed a subtle onion flavor and looked beautiful in the salad. To bring it all home, I added bits of crispy bacon and plenty of crumbled blue cheese for bold, salty counterpoints to the sweet pears and dressing. This salad looks and tastes festive enough for a special occasion, but it's easy enough for any day of the week.

—MORGAN BOLLING, *Cook's Country*

NOTES FROM THE TEST KITCHEN

PERFECTING PEAR PREP

1. Halve each pear and then scoop out core and seeds.

2. Halve each half to make quarters; keep peels on.

3. Sear quartered pears in skillet until well browned on cut sides.

Pan-Roasted Pear Salad

SERVES 6 TO 8

For the best texture, try to buy pears that are just shy of fully ripe; they should yield slightly when pressed.

- 4 slices thick-cut bacon, cut into ½-inch pieces
- 3 slightly underripe Bosc pears, quartered and cored
- 2 teaspoons sugar
- 5 tablespoons extra-virgin olive oil, divided
- ¼ cup cider vinegar
- 3 tablespoons maple syrup
- 1 teaspoon table salt
- ½ teaspoon pepper
- 2 romaine lettuce hearts (12 ounces), cut into 2-inch pieces
- ¼ cup chives, cut into 1-inch pieces
- 4 ounces blue cheese, crumbled (1 cup)

1. Cook bacon in 12-inch nonstick skillet over medium heat until crispy, 8 to 10 minutes. Using slotted spoon, transfer bacon to paper towel–lined plate. Discard fat and wipe skillet clean with paper towels.

2. Toss pears and sugar together in bowl. Heat 1 tablespoon oil in now-empty skillet over medium heat until shimmering. Cook pears, cut side down, until well browned, 2 to 4 minutes per side, redistributing as needed for even browning. Transfer pears to large plate and let cool completely, about 30 minutes.

3. Whisk vinegar, maple syrup, salt, pepper, and remaining ¼ cup oil together in large bowl. Add lettuce and chives and gently toss to combine. Season with salt and pepper to taste. Transfer to serving platter and top with blue cheese, bacon, and pears. Serve.

POTATO, GREEN BEAN, AND TOMATO SALAD

✓ **WHY THIS RECIPE WORKS** The secret to getting tender potatoes and vibrant green beans was to stagger the cooking. We cooked the potatoes in simmering water until just tender and then added the green beans so both vegetables finished cooking at the same time. We marinated the tomatoes in a bright, pungent dressing while the vegetables cooked and then tossed everything together before serving. A handful of parsley leaves and some chopped dill provided a refreshing pop.

After a full day of cooking and tasting food at work, I usually have just a simple salad for dinner. But since the typical combination of greens and vinaigrette can take you only so far, lately I've been looking to broaden my horizons by trying various salads that are still heavy on the vegetables but a bit more substantial. Why not create a hearty salad in the test kitchen that I'd be happy to eat for dinner at home?

Vegetables don't get much heartier than potatoes, so I knew I'd use spuds for my salad. I got to thinking about other ingredients that I don't usually add to my leafy greens and decided to give green beans a shot. And for a fresh, uncooked component that would add substance and acidity, I chose halved grape tomatoes. Now, how to bring it all together?

While cooking my way through a few salads made with these ingredients, I figured out an easy, efficient method to cook the potatoes and beans. I started by simmering the potatoes in salted water until they were just tender and then added 1-inch lengths of green beans to the same water. By the time the beans were done cooking, the potatoes were, too.

For a straightforward dressing, I whisked together the classic, simple combo of extra-virgin olive oil, white wine vinegar, salt, and pepper. Briny capers added punch, a sliced shallot contributed sweetness, and minced anchovies lent depth and salty complexity.

Briefly marinating the halved tomatoes in the dressing while the potatoes and beans cooked improved their flavor tremendously.

Fresh herbs added some pizzazz: After testing what seemed like an entire garden's worth, I landed on whole parsley leaves—their big size translated into more potent flavor—and chopped fresh dill. The final touch was to pour some of the dressing (just the seasoned oil and vinegar, without the tomatoes) over the potatoes and green beans immediately after draining them; the hot vegetables greedily soaked up the vinaigrette and tasted deeply seasoned in the finished salad.

—ASHLEY MOORE, *Cook's Country*

Potato, Green Bean, and Tomato Salad
SERVES 4

Make sure to scrub the potatoes well. High-quality extra-virgin olive oil makes a big difference here. You can substitute cherry tomatoes for the grape tomatoes, if desired. For the best results, use a rubber spatula to combine the ingredients in steps 3 and 4.

- 1½ pounds Yukon Gold potatoes, unpeeled, cut into ¾-inch chunks
- ¾ teaspoon table salt, plus salt for cooking vegetables
- 1 pound green beans, trimmed and cut into 1-inch pieces
- ½ cup extra-virgin olive oil
- ¼ cup white wine vinegar
- ¾ teaspoon pepper
- 6 ounces grape tomatoes, halved
- ¼ cup capers
- 1 shallot, sliced thin
- 2 anchovy fillets, rinsed and minced (optional)
- ½ cup fresh parsley leaves
- ¼ cup chopped fresh dill

1. Place potatoes and 2 teaspoons salt in large saucepan and cover with water by 1 inch. Bring to boil over high heat. Reduce heat to medium-low and simmer until potatoes are almost tender, about 7 minutes. Add green beans and continue to cook until both vegetables are tender, about 7 minutes longer.

2. While vegetables cook, whisk oil, vinegar, pepper, and salt together in large bowl; measure out ¼ cup dressing and set aside. Add tomatoes, capers, shallot, and anchovies, if using, to bowl with remaining dressing and toss to coat; set aside.

CAULIFLOWER SALAD WITH GOLDEN RAISINS AND ALMONDS

3. Drain potatoes and green beans thoroughly in colander, then spread out on rimmed baking sheet. Drizzle reserved dressing over potatoes and green beans and, using rubber spatula, gently toss to combine. Let cool slightly, about 15 minutes.

4. Add parsley, dill, and potato mixture to bowl with tomato mixture and toss to combine. Season with salt and pepper to taste. Serve.

CAULIFLOWER SALAD WITH GOLDEN RAISINS AND ALMONDS

✅ **WHY THIS RECIPE WORKS** Cauliflower's delicate flavor makes it an ideal canvas for a vibrant, fresh salad. We started by roasting florets from one head of cauliflower until caramelized. We then blitzed the core in the food processor and added it to the salad for a contrasting grain-like texture. A quick lemon vinaigrette and lots of chopped parsley and mint made this salad bright. To play up the cauliflower's natural sweetness, we stirred in a sweet and savory mix of minced shallot and golden raisins. Ground coriander added complex, lemony flavor, and toasted almonds provided a light crunch.

For decades, most Americans regarded cauliflower as an afterthought—a fine (if bland) choice for crudités or for a side dish when steamed with carrots and broccoli, but that was about it. But with this vegetable's recent surge in popularity, our eyes have been opened to newfound possibilities, most of them based on the enhanced appeal of roasted cauliflower. When it's roasted, the sugars in cauliflower caramelize, turning the flavor nutty and sweet. I wanted to dress up this once-neglected vegetable in a compelling salad.

To begin, I collected and prepared a handful of recipes for roasted cauliflower salads. Our favorite of the bunch, from acclaimed London-based chef and author Yotam Ottolenghi, was an herb-heavy salad that called for roasting two-thirds of a head of cauliflower until browned, soft, and sweet and then grating the remaining third on the large holes of a box grater and adding it to the salad raw. The contrasting flavors and textures of one vegetable treated two different ways were very appealing in the final dish.

Inspired by this success, I cut the florets into bite-size pieces and roasted them in a rimmed baking sheet on the lowest rack of a hot 475-degree oven. This oven rack position ensured that the bottoms of the florets caramelized while the tops retained a slightly firm texture. Rather than use one-third of the head, I roasted all the florets and blitzed just the raw core in the food processor until it was finely chopped. It took on an almost grain-like texture with a pleasant crunch. I whisked lemon juice and olive oil together for a quick vinaigrette and tossed in both types of cauliflower.

As for the herbs, parsley and mint added a cooling brightness that highlighted the subtle cauliflower flavor. Since I already had my food processor out, I used it to do the work of chopping the fresh herbs (about five pulses did the trick). This salad had a pleasing mix of sweet, roasted flavors balanced with freshness from the uncooked cauliflower and herbs.

Now, for the finishing touches. To play up the cauliflower's natural sweetness, I stirred in a minced shallot and some concentrated, fruity golden raisins, which I let soften in the vinaigrette while I assembled the salad. A little bit of coriander added a citrusy perfume and flavor. For a light crunch, I sprinkled on some toasted sliced almonds.

This salad was so good—savory, sweet, and complex—that I developed two additional versions: one with potent smoked paprika, apricots, and hazelnuts and a second with ground fennel, tart dried cranberries, and toasted pistachios. I'm sorry, cauliflower; I'll never call you boring again.

—MORGAN BOLLING, *Cook's Country*

Cauliflower Salad with Golden Raisins and Almonds

SERVES 4

When shopping, look for cauliflower with no leaves attached to the base of the head. Alternatively, if you can find only cauliflower with many leaves still attached, buy a slightly larger head (about 2¼ pounds). Kitchen shears make easy work of cutting the cauliflower florets away from the core, but you can use a paring knife if you prefer. For the best results, be sure to use a high-quality extra-virgin olive oil here. Toast the sliced almonds in a dry skillet over medium heat, stirring often, until browned and fragrant, 3 to 5 minutes.

1 head cauliflower (2 pounds)

5 tablespoons extra-virgin olive oil, divided

1¼ teaspoons table salt, divided

1 teaspoon pepper, divided

⅓ cup golden raisins

1 shallot, minced

1 teaspoon grated lemon zest plus 1 tablespoon juice

1 teaspoon ground coriander

1 cup fresh parsley leaves

½ cup fresh mint leaves

¼ cup sliced almonds, toasted

1. Adjust oven rack to lowest position and heat oven to 475 degrees. Trim outer leaves from cauliflower and cut stem flush with bottom of head; discard. Flip cauliflower stem side up. Using kitchen shears, cut around stem and core to remove florets. Chop core coarse and set aside. Cut florets through stems into 1-inch pieces (you should have about 6 cups florets).

2. Toss florets, 1 tablespoon oil, 1 teaspoon salt, and ½ teaspoon pepper together in bowl. Transfer to rimmed baking sheet and roast until florets are tender and browned on bottoms, 12 to 15 minutes. Let cool for 15 minutes.

3. While florets are roasting, combine raisins, shallot, lemon zest and juice, coriander, remaining ¼ cup oil, remaining ¼ teaspoon salt, and remaining ½ teaspoon pepper in large bowl; set aside.

4. Transfer core to food processor and process until finely chopped, 10 to 20 seconds, scraping down sides of bowl as needed; transfer to bowl with dressing. Add parsley and mint to now-empty processor and pulse until coarsely chopped, 5 to 7 pulses, scraping down sides of bowl as needed; transfer to bowl with dressing.

5. Add almonds and florets to bowl with dressing mixture and toss to combine. Season with salt and pepper to taste. Transfer to platter and serve.

VARIATIONS

Cauliflower Salad with Apricots and Hazelnuts
Substitute chopped dried apricots for golden raisins, ½ teaspoon smoked paprika for coriander, and hazelnuts, toasted, skinned, and chopped, for almonds.

Cauliflower Salad with Cranberries and Pistachios
Substitute dried cranberries for golden raisins, ground fennel for coriander, and chopped toasted pistachios for almonds.

SPANISH-STYLE MEATBALLS IN ALMOND SAUCE

✓ **WHY THIS RECIPE WORKS** To streamline the process of making tender tapas-style meatballs in a flavorful, thickened almond sauce, we processed ground pork, garlic, parsley, egg, and a panade of bread and water in a food processor. After shaping the mixture into 1-inch balls, we skipped browning, instead cooking the meatballs in a mixture of white wine, chicken broth, and softened onion flavored with paprika and saffron. This gentler method quickly cooked the meatballs through without our having to maneuver them much. To make the *picada*, which thickens and flavors the sauce, we ground blanched almonds and bread and then fried them in oil. We then mixed in minced garlic and parsley before stirring the picada into the sauce. A splash of sherry vinegar and a sprinkling of fresh parsley at the end added brightness to balance the flavors.

In Spain, *albóndigas*, or meatballs, are a quintessential tapas offering, enjoyed as part of a spread of shared dishes. Unlike Mexican albóndigas, which are simmered in a soup, these petite, saucy meatballs are typically served in a *cazuela* (a shallow clay baking dish) and eaten one by one using toothpicks.

I've enjoyed albóndigas coated in a robust tomato sauce, but I recently learned of another style. In this version, a saffron-and-paprika-infused wine sauce is flavored and thickened with *picada*, a lively mixture of fried ground nuts and bread, raw garlic, and often parsley. The ground nuts and bread in picada provide body as well as vibrant complexity. Frying the nuts and bread in olive oil brings richness and nuttiness that's accentuated by the grassy parsley and sharp garlic. I couldn't wait to give this style of meatballs a try.

I tested a handful of recipes, all of which followed a similar process. First, ground meat (pork alone or pork mixed with beef or veal) is combined with egg, garlic, parsley, and a panade—a paste of bread and liquid. The panade's liquid adds moisture while the bread starch interferes with the meat's proteins, preventing them from connecting too strongly and causing toughness. The meat mixture is then shaped into balls which are deep- or pan-fried until browned and then set aside while a sauce is created. To make the sauce, softened onion is cooked with broth and white wine. The

SPANISH-STYLE MEATBALLS IN ALMOND SAUCE (ALBÓNDIGAS EN SALSA DE ALMENDRAS)

meatballs are left to simmer in the sauce until it has reduced a bit and the meatballs are cooked through. Finally, the picada is stirred in.

Due to a range of cooking times and ingredient proportions, the sauces varied from porridge-like to brothy. And the meatballs? They were either too dry or so moist and tender that they failed to hold their shape. I envisioned moist, cohesive bite-size meatballs enveloped in a warmly spiced sauce, thickened and enlivened by a vivid picada. The petite meatballs would make an enticing appetizer that, along with rice or potatoes and a vegetable, could easily be served as a meal.

I wanted my albóndigas to have the tender yet sturdy quality of Italian meatballs. As for the flavor, I'd follow tradition and keep it relatively simple, which made sense since the sauce has so much depth.

I started with 1 pound of ground pork, one egg, two minced garlic cloves, 2 tablespoons of chopped parsley, and two slices of bread soaked in ¼ cup of water. Rather than stirring the ingredients together by hand, which can miss small pockets and leave bready spots in the meatballs, we've found that mixing the panade in the food processor and then pulsing it with the meat creates a more uniform blend.

After processing, I rolled the mixture into 1-inch meatballs—petite, but not so small that they would be tedious to shape. Deep frying can be a hassle, so I didn't even go there; I simply pan-fried the meatballs in a 12-inch nonstick skillet and then cooked them through in a placeholder sauce. The resulting meatballs were too tender: They failed to maintain a pleasing round shape and broke apart as I tried to scoop them into a serving dish.

It was clear that I'd added too much panade. For my next batch, I cut the amount in half. These meatballs had a better balance of moistness and structure, but the frequent turning required to brown them on all sides still caused some to split apart. I was also dealing with the usual challenges that accompany pan-frying meatballs, such as splattering oil and flattened, slightly tough sides where the meatballs touched the pan.

The benefits of deep frying were becoming clear: Submerging the meatballs in hot oil would not only quickly cook their exteriors so they wouldn't become tough but also set their surfaces so they would stay beautifully round and intact. I wondered if cooking the raw meatballs directly in the sauce, covered, so they would steam, would evenly cook them from all sides. I'd have to sacrifice browning, of course, but maybe that wouldn't matter since the saffron-, paprika-, and picada-laced sauce would be so packed with flavor.

Sure enough, meatballs cooked this way held their shape beautifully without developing the tough browned crust. They were also tender, moist, and perfectly round.

It was time for the critical final flourish: the picada. The nuts and bread are typically ground together and then fried, but I found it difficult to finely grind the almonds simultaneously with the bread. Instead, I first processed ¼ cup of slivered almonds (skins would be distracting in the sauce) and then pulsed in pieces of hearty white bread, which has just the right amount of heft and is widely available. Finally, I fried the mixture in extra-virgin olive oil before adding raw minced garlic and chopped fresh parsley.

During the last couple minutes of cooking, I stirred the picada into the sauce. It gave the dish richness, body, and some bracing sharpness, but I thought the sauce could be slightly thicker. So I ground the nuts finer, which gave them more volume. With more nut surface area exposed to the skillet, I was also able to fry the nuts more thoroughly for even richer flavor.

NOTES FROM THE TEST KITCHEN

THESE MEATBALLS ARE BETTER WITHOUT BROWNING

Browning can be detrimental to small meatballs like our *albóndigas* because of their high crust-to-interior ratio: As the exteriors of the meatballs darkened, they developed a tough crust, not to mention that the meatballs became misshapen. We got tender, perfectly spherical results—and eliminated messy splattering oil—by skipping the browning and simply simmering the meatballs in the sauce. Sure, we miss out on any flavor that browning normally provides, but our sauce is so deeply savory that it doesn't matter.

SIMMERED
Perfectly round and tender throughout

BROWNED
Misshapen, with slightly tough, thick crust

My sauce now had just the right amount of cling to coat the delicate, tender meatballs. Though it's not customary, I finished the sauce with a splash of sherry vinegar for acidity and a smattering of chopped parsley for color. I know tapas are meant to be shared, but as I dug into the albóndigas, I wasn't sure that I wanted to.
—ANNIE PETITO, *Cook's Illustrated*

Spanish-Style Meatballs in Almond Sauce (Albóndigas en Salsa de Almendras)

SERVES 6 TO 8

Sometimes fully cooked ground pork retains a slightly pink hue; trust your thermometer. These meatballs can be served as an appetizer with toothpicks or as a main course alongside a vegetable and potatoes or rice.

PICADA

- ¼ cup slivered almonds
- 1 slice hearty white sandwich bread, torn into 1-inch pieces
- 2 tablespoons extra-virgin olive oil
- 3 tablespoons minced fresh parsley
- 2 garlic cloves, minced

MEATBALLS

- 1 slice hearty white sandwich bread, torn into 1-inch pieces
- 1 large egg
- 2 tablespoons water
- 2 tablespoons chopped fresh parsley, divided
- 2 garlic cloves, minced
- 1 teaspoon table salt
- ½ teaspoon pepper
- 1 pound ground pork
- 1 tablespoon extra-virgin olive oil
- ½ cup finely chopped onion
- ½ teaspoon paprika
- 1 cup chicken broth
- ½ cup dry white wine
- ¼ teaspoon saffron threads, crumbled
- 1 teaspoon sherry vinegar

1. FOR THE PICADA: Process almonds in food processor until finely ground, about 20 seconds. Add bread and process until bread is finely ground, about 15 seconds. Transfer almond-bread mixture to 12-inch nonstick skillet. Add oil and cook over medium heat, stirring often, until mixture is golden brown, 3 to 5 minutes. Transfer to bowl. Stir in parsley and garlic and set aside. Wipe skillet clean with paper towels.

2. FOR THE MEATBALLS: Process bread in now-empty processor until finely ground, about 15 seconds. Add egg, water, 1 tablespoon parsley, garlic, salt, and pepper and process until smooth paste forms, about 20 seconds, scraping down sides of bowl as needed. Add pork and pulse until combined, about 5 pulses.

3. Remove processor blade. Using your moistened hands, form generous 1 tablespoon pork mixture into 1-inch round meatball and transfer to plate; repeat with remaining pork mixture to form about 24 meatballs.

4. Heat oil in now-empty skillet over medium heat until shimmering. Add onion and cook, stirring occasionally, until softened, 4 to 6 minutes. Add paprika and cook until fragrant, about 30 seconds. Add broth and wine and bring to simmer. Stir in saffron. Add meatballs and adjust heat to maintain simmer. Cover and cook until meatballs register 160 degrees, 6 to 8 minutes, flipping meatballs once.

5. Stir in picada and continue to cook, uncovered, until sauce has thickened slightly, 1 to 2 minutes longer. Off heat, stir in vinegar. Season with salt and pepper to taste. Transfer to platter, sprinkle with remaining 1 tablespoon parsley, and serve.

EASY EGG ROLLS

✓ **WHY THIS RECIPE WORKS** For a hot, fresh alternative to barely warm, soggy takeout egg rolls, we aimed to strike the right balance between supermarket shortcuts and from-scratch cooking. For egg rolls quick enough to make at home, we cut down on the knife work (pun intended) by using bagged coleslaw mix and ground pork, which made easy, delicious substitutes for the thinly sliced vegetables and minced fresh pork that traditional recipes call for. A simple mix of easy-to-find ingredients—garlic, ginger, soy sauce, and sugar—made a tasty sauce to flavor the filling. Shallow-frying the rolls in just ½ inch of oil in a skillet rather than in quarts of oil in a big Dutch oven made the cooking easier and the cleanup faster while still ensuring crispy, delicious egg rolls.

EASY EGG ROLLS

Crunchy, piping-hot Chinese restaurant egg rolls, with dipping sauces alongside, check off a bunch of the boxes that trigger the pleasure sensors in our brains: crispy, salty, sweet, savory, spicy, and meaty. But home versions seldom satisfy in a similar way. If I'm going to do the work of cooking the filling, wrapping the rolls, and frying them, I want the egg rolls to be great. And in making my own egg rolls, I also wanted to minimize the prep and mess and avoid hard-to-find ingredients.

After preparing and tasting five seemingly promising recipes, I realized I had my work cut out for me. To prep the filling alone, I had to mince pork, thinly slice a mound of cabbage, and laboriously cut carrots and mushrooms into matchsticks. I also had to find dark soy sauce, black vinegar, and Chinese rice wine. And that was just the start. I still had to cook and chill the filling ingredients, wrap and seal the rolls, and do the deep frying. I wanted tasty results with a lot less work.

To reduce the amount of prep work involved, I tried using bagged coleslaw mix—shredded cabbage and carrots—in place of the hand-chopped cabbage and carrot, and it worked great. Chopped shiitake mushrooms added a savory flavor to the vegetable mix. For the meat, I opted for ground pork, letting the supermarket grinder do the work for me. As for seasoning the filling, I knew from stir-fry recipes that I'd developed in the past that I could create a delicious, savory, and balanced sauce without hard-to-find ingredients. I started with a mix of garlic, ginger, soy sauce, and sugar. Using a measured ⅓ cup of filling per egg roll ensured that the rolls weren't overstuffed and wouldn't rupture in the oil.

These egg rolls were already better than takeout versions. But did they have to be deep-fried? I tried a move I hadn't seen in any other recipes: shallow-frying the egg rolls in just ½ inch (or so) of 325-degree oil in a skillet instead of a big Dutch oven. Using less oil made the cooking easier and the cleanup faster. With a single flip halfway through the roughly 6-minute cooking time, the egg rolls came out nicely crispy and perfectly cooked.

But the filling still needed something. My tasters remarked that it tasted a little too "flat" and "heavy." So in my next test I cooked the vegetables a little less (until just wilted), preserving their fresh flavor and crunch, and added a tablespoon of distilled white vinegar to brighten it all up. I also stirred in a bit of potent toasted sesame oil for depth and a hint of nutty sweetness.

Feeling confident while I waited for this batch of egg rolls to cool, I filled a couple of small serving bowls with duck sauce and Chinese hot mustard and set them out for my tasters. I knew I had landed on a good recipe when one of my colleagues stopped eating just long enough to exclaim that this was the best egg roll she'd ever had. The rest of them, still chowing down, nodded in agreement.

—MATTHEW FAIRMAN, *Cook's Country*

Easy Egg Rolls

MAKES 8 EGG ROLLS

This recipe can easily be doubled: Extend the cooking time of the pork mixture by about 5 minutes in step 1 and fry the egg rolls in two batches. We like to serve the egg rolls with duck sauce, Chinese hot mustard, and Soy-Vinegar Dipping Sauce (recipe follows).

- 8 ounces ground pork
- 6 scallions, white and green parts separated and sliced thin
- 3 garlic cloves, minced
- 2 teaspoons grated fresh ginger
- 3 cups (7 ounces) coleslaw mix
- 4 ounces shiitake mushrooms, stemmed and chopped
- 3 tablespoons soy sauce
- 1 tablespoon sugar
- 1 tablespoon distilled white vinegar
- 2 teaspoons toasted sesame oil
- 8 egg roll wrappers
- 2 cups vegetable oil, for frying

1. Cook pork in 12-inch nonstick skillet over medium-high heat until no longer pink, about 5 minutes, breaking up meat with wooden spoon. Add scallion whites, garlic, and ginger and cook until fragrant, about 1 minute. Add coleslaw mix, mushrooms, soy sauce, sugar, and vinegar and cook until cabbage is just softened, about 3 minutes.

2. Off heat, stir in sesame oil and scallion greens. Transfer pork mixture to large plate, spread into even layer, and refrigerate until cool enough to handle, about 5 minutes. Wipe skillet clean with paper towels.

3. Fill small bowl with water. Working with 1 egg roll wrapper at a time, orient wrappers on counter so 1 corner points toward edge of counter. Place lightly packed ⅓ cup filling on lower half of wrapper and mold it with your fingers into neat cylindrical shape. Using your fingertips, moisten entire border of wrapper with thin film of water.

4. Fold bottom corner of wrapper up and over filling and press it down on other side of filling. Fold both side corners of wrapper in over filling and press gently to seal. Roll filling up over itself until wrapper is fully sealed. Leave egg roll seam side down on counter and cover with damp paper towel while shaping remaining egg rolls.

5. Line large plate with triple layer of paper towels. Heat vegetable oil in now-empty skillet over medium heat to 325 degrees. Using tongs, place all egg rolls in

skillet, seam side down, and cook until golden brown, 2 to 4 minutes per side. Transfer to prepared plate and let cool slightly, about 5 minutes. Serve.

TO MAKE AHEAD: At end of step 4, transfer egg rolls to parchment paper–lined plate, wrap tightly in plastic wrap, and refrigerate for up to 24 hours. Alternatively, freeze egg rolls on plate, then transfer to zipper-lock bag and freeze for up to 1 month. Do not thaw before cooking; increase cooking time by about 1 minute per side.

Soy-Vinegar Dipping Sauce

MAKES ABOUT ¼ CUP

For the best results, be sure to use a good-quality soy sauce.

- 2 tablespoons soy sauce
- 1 tablespoon water
- 2 teaspoons distilled white vinegar
- 1 teaspoon sugar

Whisk all ingredients in bowl until sugar is dissolved.

SMOKY SHISHITO PEPPERS WITH ESPELETTE AND LIME

WHY THIS RECIPE WORKS Blistered Japanese shishito peppers—slender little peppers with thin skins, delicate flesh, and a fruity, grassy flavor that's neither sweet nor hot—are a popular bar snack. A sprinkling of coarse salt is a must, but these tame peppers are also the perfect base for showcasing bold finishing spices. For a burst of heat and acidity, we combined ground dried Espelette pepper, smoked paprika, and lime zest and then sprinkled the mixture over the cooked peppers.

There's a reason that shishito peppers have been a staple of bar menus and restaurant appetizer lists for years: They're extremely easy to make. Take some whole peppers—no need to stem or seed them—and throw them into a hot pan or deep-fryer for just a few minutes until their skins are appealingly blistered. Next, simply toss them with a quick spice blend and serve. From a restaurateur's point of view, shishito peppers are the perfect dish: Their name sounds

NOTES FROM THE TEST KITCHEN

ROLL THEM UP

1. PLACE AND SHAPE FILLING Place lightly packed ⅓ cup filling on lower half of wrapper. Use your fingers to shape filling into cylinder.

2. MOISTEN WRAPPER EDGE Dip your fingertips in water, then moisten entire border of wrapper with thin film of water.

3. FOLD UP BOTTOM, THEN FOLD IN SIDES Bring bottom corner of wrapper over filling and press it down on other side to seal. Then fold in sides.

4. ROLL INTO CYLINDER Roll into log shape and press edges to seal. Cover egg roll with damp paper towel while shaping remaining egg rolls.

intriguing, they're so quick to throw together that a single chef can prepare any number of orders while attending to other kitchen duties, and the markup (and thus the profit margin) on them can be significant.

That's not to say that shishito peppers are some kind of restaurant racket, or that you should never enjoy them again. These Japanese peppers are a joy to eat when prepared well. They're generally mild, with a fruity, grassy flavor reminiscent of jalapeño or serrano chiles minus the heat, making them an extremely versatile base for a wide array of spice combinations. Their thin skins easily take on a smoky char. And around one in 10 peppers packs a surprisingly spicy punch—not quite as hot as a jalapeño but enough to catch you by surprise—giving them an additional allure for those who like to have fun with their food. Shishitos are also popping up more and more frequently in farmers' markets and well-stocked supermarkets, making them an accessible option for home cooking. With this in mind, I set out to create a recipe that would prove just how versatile and easy charred shishito peppers can be.

As far as the recipe development process goes, this was one of my fastest ever. I learned that shishito peppers don't necessarily have to be deep-fried: Many of the recipes I found called for quickly cooking them in a small amount of oil over relatively high heat. My own tests confirmed that cooking the peppers in a hot skillet for just 3 minutes per side made for a perfect char without overcooking them.

For my finishing spice, I turned to the classic combination of spicy and sour in the form of chile powder and lime zest. I liked using Basque Espelette chile powder (made from ground dried Espelette chiles native to France) here due to its mild heat and subtle mix of smoke and sweetness. Even coated with a blend of Espelette, smoked paprika, salt, and lime zest, my first batch of peppers lacked punch; doubling the amounts of the spices in later tests proved the perfect solution. With a dash of lime juice at the end to brighten the flavors, my recipe was complete: Tasters devoured the peppers, and my fellow test cooks hovered nearby in case any were left over.

But I wasn't finished yet. With plenty of time left to experiment, I gave my creativity free rein and developed three additional spice blends. Straying a bit from the tried-and-true, I combined floral fennel pollen with spicy Aleppo pepper and sour lemon for a slightly more complex and elegant take on the traditional heat-and-acid approach. Next I tried mixing dried mint, poppy seeds, and orange zest. This combination didn't have the peppery kick of the others, but it brought a balanced sweetness to the dish that was especially nice when paired with the occasional spicy shishito. Finally, I wanted one more combination that would really stand apart from the rest. I began with dry mustard, which would provide the slightly spicy base. True inspiration came when I hit upon the idea of sprinkling bonito flakes over the peppers just before serving them. Bonito flakes are superthin, supersavory strips of dried, fermented, and smoked bonito fish that undulate gently when heated. The residual heat from cooking the peppers was just enough to make them wave around for a memorable presentation.

I was more than pleased with the array of flavor profiles I'd created. Whether classic, refined, or downright unusual, my spice mixes were sure to amp up any plate of shishitos. And with so many options that could be made in minutes, there was no longer any need to seek out a bar when I was in the mood for a smoky, savory snack.

—JOSEPH GITTER, *America's Test Kitchen Books*

Smoky Shishito Peppers with Espelette and Lime

SERVES 4

You can find shishito peppers at most well-stocked supermarkets or the farmers' market. If you can't find Basque Espelette chile powder, also referred to as Piment d'Espelette, you can substitute 1 teaspoon of Aleppo pepper or ¼ teaspoon of paprika plus ¼ teaspoon of red pepper flakes. The skillet will look full.

1 teaspoon ground dried Espelette pepper
1 teaspoon smoked paprika
½ teaspoon coarse finishing salt
¼ teaspoon grated lime zest, plus lime
    wedges for serving
2 tablespoons vegetable oil
8 ounces shishito peppers

1. Combine Espelette, paprika, salt, and lime zest in small bowl; set aside.

2. Heat oil in 12-inch skillet over medium-high heat until just smoking. Add shishitos and cook, without moving them, until first side is blistered, about 3 minutes. Using tongs, flip shishitos and continue to cook until blistered on second side, about 3 minutes longer. Transfer to serving platter and sprinkle with spice mixture. Serve with lime wedges.

VARIATIONS

Shishito Peppers with Fennel Pollen, Aleppo, and Lemon

If you can't find fennel pollen, you can substitute toasted cracked fennel seeds.

Substitute Aleppo pepper for Espelette pepper, fennel pollen for paprika, and lemon zest and wedges for lime zest and wedges.

Shishito Peppers with Mint, Poppy Seeds, and Orange

Substitute dried mint for Espelette pepper, poppy seeds for paprika, and orange zest and wedges for lime zest and wedges.

Shishito Peppers with Mustard and Bonito Flakes

Omit Espelette pepper. Substitute dry mustard for paprika. Sprinkle 2 tablespoons bonito flakes over shishitos just before serving.

BAKED GOAT CHEESE

WHY THIS RECIPE WORKS Warm goat cheese, broiled in a baking dish with lightly spiced tomato sauce, is a refreshing spin on the always-popular melted-cheese appetizer. Since goat cheese is so flavorful already, especially when served hot, we chose not to fuss with it, instead focusing on the sauce. For the marinara-like tomato sauce, we settled on a cooking time of 15 minutes, which falls right in between those of a fresh quick-cooked sauce and a deeper-flavored long-cooked sauce. Adding a mix of paprika, cumin, and red pepper flakes imparted a complex spiciness reminiscent of eastern Mediterranean and North African flavors. After about 10 minutes under the broiler, the sauce was bubbling and the goat cheese was nicely browned on top.

There is one thing you can count on at cocktail parties: Appetizers featuring melted cheese go fast. Put out a dish of cheesy buffalo dip, a bowl of *queso fundido*, or a wheel of baked Brie, and your guests will cluster around it, spooning soft, warm morsels onto chips or bread, tucking spiderweb strands of cheese into their mouths, and smiling and nodding in appreciation as they go. In short, cheese equals happy party guests. But its ubiquitousness at these kinds of events also means it's rare that a melted-cheese appetizer stands out.

But recently, I attended a party where the host served warm goat cheese broiled in a baking dish with a mildly spicy tomato sauce. The combination of tangy cheese, smoky and sweet sauce, and crunchy toast was great. While it didn't create those photo-op cheese strands, it delivered lively, festive flavor.

At the end of the evening, I congratulated the host on the delicious goat cheese. I then promptly went into my own kitchen to re-create it and, because I am competitive, improve on it.

Goat cheese was a given. And because it already has so much flavor, especially when served hot, I chose not to doctor it up at all and instead focus on the surrounding sauce.

I made a few versions of a marinara-like tomato sauce using a tried-and-true method: softening chopped onions in olive oil and then adding garlic and canned tomatoes. I cooked some sauces longer for deep flavor; others I cooked less for freshness. I settled on a cooking time of 15 minutes for the right counterpoint to the tangy goat cheese. But it needed another boost. I turned to the spice cabinet.

After auditioning everything from allspice to za'atar, I ultimately chose a mix of paprika, cumin, and red pepper flakes for a complexity that recalls eastern Mediterranean and North African flavors. I spooned my sauce into a baking dish and then formed a log of goat cheese into a 1-inch-thick circle for an appealing presentation, nestling it in the center of the sauce. After about 10 minutes under the broiler, the goat cheese was warmed through and nutty brown on top and the sauce was bubbling happily. Time to set out this appetizer for the party people to scoop onto toast points, smiling and nodding in appreciation all the while.

—BRYAN ROOF WITH HEATHER TOLMIE,
Cook's Country

BAKED GOAT CHEESE

Baked Goat Cheese
SERVES 8 TO 10

Goat cheese logs come in different sizes. Any size from 8 to 10 ounces will work in this recipe. Just press the log into a 1-inch-thick disk. If you can find only small logs of goat cheese (around 4 ounces), you can press two small logs together. Serve with crackers or toast points.

- 3 tablespoons extra-virgin olive oil, plus extra for drizzling
- 1 onion, chopped fine
- ¾ teaspoon table salt
- 3 garlic cloves, sliced thin
- 2 teaspoons smoked paprika
- 1 teaspoon ground cumin
- ¼ teaspoon red pepper flakes
- ¼ teaspoon pepper
- 1 (28-ounce) can crushed tomatoes
- 1 (8- to 10-ounce) log goat cheese, softened
- 2 tablespoons coarsely chopped fresh cilantro
- 1 teaspoon grated lemon zest

1. Heat oil in medium saucepan over medium heat until shimmering. Add onion and salt and cook, stirring occasionally, until golden brown, about 10 minutes. Add garlic, paprika, cumin, pepper flakes, and pepper and cook until fragrant, about 1 minute. Add tomatoes and bring to boil. Reduce heat to medium-low and simmer for 15 minutes. Season with salt to taste.

NOTES FROM THE TEST KITCHEN

FROM LOG TO DISK
Our shaping technique for the goat cheese just might take you back to your preschool days of sculpting shapes with Play-Doh. Here's how to do it.

Place sheet of plastic wrap on counter and stand log of cheese on its end in center of sheet. Place another sheet of plastic over column of cheese and press cheese with your palm into 1-inch-thick disk.

---

2. Adjust oven rack 6 inches from broiler element and heat broiler. Place goat cheese between 2 sheets of plastic wrap. Flatten goat cheese into 1-inch-thick disk, 3 to 4 inches in diameter, cupping your hands around exterior of disk as needed to make compact shape.

3. Transfer tomato sauce to shallow 2-quart broiler-safe baking dish. Place goat cheese in center. Broil until goat cheese is well browned, about 10 minutes. Sprinkle cilantro and lemon zest over sauce and drizzle with extra oil. Serve.

WHIPPED FETA DIP

✓ **WHY THIS RECIPE WORKS** We defied tradition with this lush, salty Greek-style dip by using cow's-milk feta instead of a true Greek feta made with sheep's or goat's milk or a combination of the two. The reason: Cow's-milk feta produced a firmer dip that held up well at room temperature. But we also wanted a dip that was loose enough to easily scoop up with soft pita. To achieve a more scoopable consistency, we processed the cow's-milk feta with a few tablespoons of milk in addition to the traditional extra-virgin olive oil. We also rinsed the feta in water to avoid an overly salty dip. A little garlic and lemon juice, along with 2 teaspoons of fresh oregano, rounded out the Greek flavor profile.

There's nothing wrong with serving feta on a cheese plate, but if you have a few minutes to spare, I suggest transforming it into the traditional Greek dip *tyrosalata*. Doing so is practically effortless: Just process the cheese with extra-virgin olive oil until it turns smooth, and then season it with additions such as lemon juice, garlic, and fresh herbs. It comes together in a matter of minutes, and as part of a meze spread (small plates served with drinks) with crudités or pita, the creamy, milky, salty dip is a real standout.

Feta varies widely depending on the type of milk it is made from—cow's, sheep's, goat's, or some combination thereof. I defaulted to our favorite high-quality cheese made from sheep's milk. Its richness and distinct tang are not only authentic (most Greek fetas are made from sheep's milk) but also the test kitchen's preferred feta profile.

But something strange happened when I buzzed together my first batch. The consistency was oddly loose—more like yogurt than dip—even though I'd added nothing more to the feta than the traditional couple of tablespoons of olive oil and splash of lemon juice. Stranger and more concerning still, the dip continued to thin as it sat at room temperature, as if it were melting before my eyes. So far, this dip was standing out for all the wrong reasons.

But here's the most surprising part of the story: The sheep's milk itself was to blame for the dip's drippy consistency, and the result was actually better—thicker and more stable—when I made it with cow's-milk feta. That's because sheep milk fat has a lower melting point than cow milk fat, so cheese made with sheep's milk softens at a lower temperature than cheese made with cow's milk. In the test kitchen, which runs a little warm, using cow's-milk feta was the only way to guarantee a consistently thick texture.

Of course, I assumed that cow's-milk feta would lack character and richness, but I needn't have worried. The subtleties of the sheep's-milk cheese were mostly obscured by the other flavors in the dip. After tasting my new cow's-milk feta version, I felt no compunction about making the substitution.

The only drawback was that the cow's-milk cheese actually made the dip a little too stiff, not to mention assertively salty (cow's-milk fetas tend to be saltier). Whipping in a few tablespoons of milk loosened its consistency enough that it could be swiped up with a piece of soft pita. And as for taming the salinity, I did what we often do with salty ingredients such as anchovies and capers: I rinsed it, which adequately tempered the saltiness.

With the base of the dip settled, I worked in some fresh oregano as well as a hint of minced garlic that I'd soaked in lemon juice to take the edge off its bite. It was a very traditional, very tasty take.

But the beauty of this dip—other than how easy it is to make—is that the tangy, milky-rich base takes well to lots of different flavors. It was just as easy to give the dip a smoky profile by adding roasted red peppers, smoked paprika, and a touch of cayenne as it was to pack it with grassy dill and parsley. With results this good, why wait to include this dip in a meze spread? I'll be whipping it up for a snack any old time.

—SANDRA WU, *Cook's Illustrated*

Whipped Feta Dip
SERVES 8

Cow's-milk feta makes a firmer dip that holds up well at room temperature; do not substitute sheep's-milk feta, which is softer. Because feta is quite salty, avoid serving this dip with salted chips; crudités and pita bread make great accompaniments.

1½ teaspoons lemon juice
¼ teaspoon minced garlic
8 ounces cow's-milk feta cheese
3 tablespoons milk
2 tablespoons plus 2 teaspoons extra-virgin olive oil, divided
2 teaspoons minced fresh oregano

1. Combine lemon juice and garlic in small bowl and set aside. Break feta into rough ½-inch pieces and place in medium bowl. Add water to cover, then swish briefly to rinse. Transfer to fine-mesh strainer and drain well.

2. Transfer feta to food processor. Add milk and lemon juice mixture and process until feta mixture resembles ricotta cheese, about 15 seconds. With processor running, slowly drizzle in 2 tablespoons oil. Continue to process until mixture has Greek yogurt–like consistency (some small lumps will remain), 1½ to 2 minutes longer, stopping once to scrape down sides of bowl. Add oregano and pulse to combine. Transfer dip to bowl. If serving immediately, drizzle with remaining 2 teaspoons oil. (Dip can be refrigerated for up to 3 days. If refrigerated, let sit at room temperature for 30 minutes and drizzle with oil before serving.)

VARIATIONS
Whipped Feta and Roasted Red Pepper Dip
Substitute red wine vinegar for lemon juice. Reduce milk to 2 tablespoons. Add ¼ cup jarred roasted red peppers, chopped; ½ teaspoon smoked paprika; and pinch cayenne pepper with milk. Omit oregano.

Whipped Feta Dip with Dill and Parsley
Substitute 1 tablespoon minced fresh dill (or mint, if desired) and 1 tablespoon minced fresh parsley for oregano.

VEGETABLE SIDES

CAESAR BRUSSELS SPROUTS

✓ WHY THIS RECIPE WORKS We were after tender Brussels sprouts coated in a pleasantly pungent Caesar dressing. However, thinly sliced sprouts left the dressing without anything to cling to, and whole or halved sprouts were too cumbersome. We landed on cutting the sprouts into quarters—they maintained their shape during cooking, and the dressing clung to each cut side. For the dressing, we went with a combination of lemon juice, Worcestershire sauce, mustard, garlic, and anchovy fillets along with some mayonnaise for a bright and punchy yet creamy Caesar dressing.

For several years now, Brussels sprouts have been enjoying a little time in the spotlight. Caesar Brussels sprouts—cooked or raw sprouts doused in the intense dressing—are just one of the many preparations showing up on restaurant menus and in cookbooks. I set out to craft the best version possible.

A few of the existing recipes I prepared featured raw Brussels sprouts (shredded or chopped), while others called for microwaving or roasting the sprouts before dressing them. Our favorite recipe called for roasting halved sprouts until browned and sweet before tossing them with the dressing. The Brussels sprouts got beautifully charred and were tender throughout.

While these sprouts were good, I wondered if I could get similar results without turning on the oven. So I tried cooking the sprouts in a skillet on the stovetop, and this method was just as successful. The sprouts, which I'd quartered so they'd cook quickly and have extra surface area to pick up browning and soak up dressing, got a pleasant dark char, which helped bring out their subtly sweet flavor. I found that it was best to cook the sprouts covered for the first 10 minutes until tender and then remove the lid to brown them, which took about 5 more minutes.

With the sprouts perfectly cooked, I turned my attention to getting the dressing just right. I didn't want it to be so strong that I couldn't taste the Brussels sprouts, but I wanted it to be bold and pungent like Caesar dressing should be. I used all the usual suspects—freshly squeezed lemon juice, mayonnaise (to cut the sharpness and provide a subtle creaminess), Worcestershire sauce, Dijon mustard, minced garlic, anchovies, salt, pepper, and extra-virgin olive oil—and tweaked the ratios until I had the balance I sought.

One last thing: A proper Caesar salad needs croutons. But I didn't want large hunks of crusty bread competing with the sprouts. Instead, after a bit of experimenting, I landed on topping the sprouts with crunchy Parmesan bread crumbs. They were the perfect complement to my boldly dressed, sweet, and tender Brussels sprouts.

—ASHLEY MOORE, *Cook's Country*

Caesar Brussels Sprouts

SERVES 4 TO 6

For the best results, be sure to choose Brussels sprouts with small, tight heads. We found that those measuring no more than 1½ inches in diameter were best. The skillet may seem very full at first in step 2, but the Brussels sprouts will shrink as they cook.

DRESSING

- 1½ tablespoons lemon juice
- 1 tablespoon mayonnaise
- 1 tablespoon Worcestershire sauce
- 1 tablespoon Dijon mustard
- 3 garlic cloves, minced
- 3 anchovy fillets, rinsed and minced
- ½ teaspoon pepper
- ¼ teaspoon table salt
- 3 tablespoons extra-virgin olive oil

BRUSSELS SPROUTS

- 2 pounds Brussels sprouts, trimmed and quartered
- 5 tablespoons extra-virgin olive oil, divided
- ½ teaspoon table salt, divided
- ¼ cup panko bread crumbs
- 1 ounce Parmesan cheese, grated (½ cup)

1. FOR THE DRESSING: Whisk lemon juice, mayonnaise, Worcestershire, mustard, garlic, anchovies, pepper, and salt in large bowl until combined. Slowly whisk in oil until emulsified; set aside.

2. FOR THE BRUSSELS SPROUTS: Combine Brussels sprouts, ¼ cup oil, and ¼ teaspoon salt in 12-inch nonstick skillet. Cover skillet, place over medium heat, and cook, stirring occasionally, until Brussels sprouts are bright green and have started to brown, about 10 minutes.

3. Uncover and continue to cook, stirring occasionally, until Brussels sprouts are deeply and evenly browned and paring knife slides in with little to no

CAESAR BRUSSELS SPROUTS

resistance, about 5 minutes longer. Transfer Brussels sprouts to rimmed baking sheet and let cool for 15 minutes. Wipe skillet clean with paper towels.

4. Combine panko, remaining 1 tablespoon oil, and remaining ¼ teaspoon salt in now-empty skillet and cook over medium heat, stirring frequently, until golden brown, 2 to 4 minutes. Transfer to small bowl and stir in Parmesan.

5. Add Brussels sprouts to dressing and gently toss to combine. Transfer to serving platter. Sprinkle with panko mixture and serve.

CHARRED SICHUAN-STYLE OKRA

✓ **WHY THIS RECIPE WORKS** Since okra stands up so well to the heat and punch of Creole cuisine, it makes sense that it would also pair well with a spicy Sichuan flavor profile. We started by making a concentrated chili oil, with the lip-tingling heat of Sichuan peppercorns. Broad bean chili paste gave the sauce heat and the distinct umami flavor of fermented beans. Hoisin sauce and rice wine brought sweetness, acidity, and body to the sauce. Last but not least, scallions provided a fresh contrast. Charring the okra pods whole before cloaking them with the sauce beautifully seared their exteriors while keeping good texture on their interiors. Altogether, this is a sumptuous showstopper of a dish.

Okra has a long culinary history, but it is probably best known as the quintessential vegetable of the American South. Even more than its Southern heritage, okra is known for one thing: its texture. When cooked properly, okra has a fresh vegetal flavor and delicate crunch. When cooked improperly, however, it becomes, for lack of a more appetizing description, slimy.

I'm a big fan of okra done right, so I wanted to give this unique vegetable a starring role in a dish with a different flavor profile than the ones it's usually associated with. Because okra is such a good match for the bold flavors of Cajun cooking, I decided to pair it with equally bold and spicy Sichuan-inspired flavors.

I started with my spice mixture, blooming fresh garlic and ginger and dried chiles in oil to bring out their flavors. Ground Sichuan peppercorns and star anise made the mixture's Sichuan flavor profile clear.

Rice wine and hoisin sauce contributed complexity and balancing sweetness. I also stirred in a few tablespoons of broad bean chili paste, a condiment of fermented beans and chiles that many consider to be the soul of Sichuan cuisine. Before long I had a thick, spicy, and multifaceted sauce.

So far, things had been pretty straightforward: I'd been combining classic Sichuan flavors, tinkering only slightly with amounts to get the balance of flavors just right. But now came the difficult part: marrying my sauce with the okra and, above all, ensuring that the okra turned out nicely charred and crisp-tender rather than limp and slimy. My first tests were massively disappointing: After mixing up my sauce, I cooked it together with the okra until the okra was tender. The flavors may have been there, but my okra was a viscous mess.

For cooking technique guidance, I delved into the science of why okra turns gummy when cooked. When heated, the starch molecules in the mucilage are loosened. They then rearrange to form a microscopic network that traps any available water to form a gel. However, temperatures above 190 degrees damage the starch molecules responsible for this transformation, making them less able to retain water. For this reason, cooking the okra over a high, dry heat seemed to be the way to go.

In my next tests, I seared the okra pods in a skillet with just a little bit of hot oil until they were beautifully charred. I stirred in my sauce only at the very end, once I'd removed the skillet from the heat. This was a huge improvement: My okra had developed much less of its signature gel, and it was beautifully crisp-tender.

But I still thought I could do even better. In the past, the test kitchen has found that frozen okra is less slimy than fresh okra, so next I tested whether there was a noticeable difference between using fresh or frozen okra in this dish. Frozen okra, as it turned out, was a little bit less slimy, but it also lacked the perfect crisp-tender texture and fresh flavor I wanted.

There was one last trick to explore in my quest for slime-free okra. In my research, I'd found that the way okra is cut can have a big impact on its texture. Keeping okra whole reduces the amount of mucilage that is directly exposed to heat and moisture, cutting down on sliminess. Until now I'd been cutting the okra into bite-size pieces, but going forward I decided to simply trim the woody stems and leave the pods

MAKING SICHUAN-STYLE OKRA

Okra is usually thought of in terms of Cajun or Creole recipes, or you might see it on the menu at Indian restaurants. Since it's such a natural pairing with the bold flavor profiles of those cuisines, why not use it in a spicy Chinese-inspired dish? Our version has ground dried red chiles, tongue-tingling Sichuan peppercorns, and broad bean chili paste for a trinity of flavorings that really bring the heat.

1. Trim stems from okra pods, making sure to leave top "cap" on each okra pod intact. This will prevent okra from becoming gooey as it cooks.

2. Use spice grinder (or mortar and pestle) to grind bird chiles and Sichuan peppercorns for spicy simmered sauce mixture.

3. Cook whole okra in hot oil over medium-high heat, stirring occasionally, until pods are well browned on most sides and still crisp-tender.

4. Add rice wine, water, and scallions to okra, lower heat, and cook until liquid is reduced by half and scallion greens are wilted.

5. Remove skillet from heat and stir Sichuan sauce into okra. Don't forget to remove star anise pod.

6. Transfer spicy charred okra to serving platter, sprinkle with chopped cilantro sprigs, and serve.

otherwise untouched. Immediately I saw a difference: My charred, sauce-covered okra was crisp, fresh-tasting, and wonderfully slime-free. Plus, leaving the pods whole made for a more striking presentation. At last, I had an unexpected take on okra that had even the most okra-shy of my tasters coming back for more.

—KATHERINE PERRY, *America's Test Kitchen Books*

Charred Sichuan-Style Okra

SERVES 4

If you can't find bird chiles (dried Thai red chiles), you can substitute ground red pepper flakes. Asian broad bean chili paste (or sauce) is readily available online; our favorite brand is Pixian. Lee Kum Kee brand is a good supermarket option. Use a spice grinder to grind the bird chiles and Sichuan peppercorns. Do not substitute frozen okra here.

⅓ cup plus 2 tablespoons vegetable oil, divided

2 garlic cloves, sliced thin

1 (½-inch) piece fresh ginger, peeled and sliced into thin rounds

5 bird chiles, ground fine (1½ teaspoons)

1 teaspoon Sichuan peppercorns, ground fine (½ teaspoon)

1 star anise pod

6 tablespoons Chinese rice wine or dry sherry, divided

¼ cup hoisin sauce

3 tablespoons Asian broad bean chili paste

1 pound okra, stemmed

6 scallions, white parts sliced thin on bias, green parts cut into 1-inch pieces

¼ cup water

12 sprigs fresh cilantro, chopped coarse

BROCCOLI AND CHEESE CASSEROLE

1. Combine ⅓ cup oil, garlic, ginger, chiles, Sichuan peppercorns, and star anise in small saucepan and cook over medium-high heat until sizzling, 1 to 2 minutes. Reduce heat to low and gently simmer until garlic and ginger are softened but not browned, about 5 minutes. Let cool off heat for 5 minutes, then stir in 2 table-spoons rice wine, hoisin, and chili paste until combined; set aside.

2. Heat remaining 2 tablespoons oil in 12-inch skillet over medium-high heat until just smoking. Add okra and cook, stirring occasionally, until okra is crisp-tender and well browned on most sides, 5 to 7 minutes.

3. Stir in scallions, water, and remaining ¼ cup rice wine; reduce heat to medium; and cook until liquid is reduced by half and scallion greens are just wilted, about 15 seconds. Off heat, stir in hoisin mixture until combined. Discard star anise and sprinkle with cilantro. Serve immediately.

BROCCOLI AND CHEESE CASSEROLE

✔ **WHY THIS RECIPE WORKS** In developing a recipe for broccoli and cheese casserole, we wanted to make a crowd-pleasing side dish that was ultracreamy and cheesy yet let the broccoli flavor shine. Microwaving fresh broccoli florets before assembling the casserole ensured evenly tender broccoli while cutting back on hands-on cooking time. For a creamy sauce with bold cheese flavor, we built a flour-thickened sauce and folded in extra-sharp cheddar cheese. To ensure that the extra-sharp cheddar didn't sep-arate, we also added a bit of American cheese to the sauce. American cheese contains stabilizers that kept the sauce silky and creamy even when it was exposed to high heat. Minced garlic and shallot, hot sauce, and dry mustard gave the sauce depth, and a crispy topping of buttery, Parmesan-enhanced panko bread crumbs provided a con-trasting crunch.

My mother used to make a dump-and-stir broccoli and cheese casserole with frozen broccoli, creamy con-densed soup, lots of melty cheese, and a buttery cracker topping. It was far from fancy, but I loved eating it as a kid. I wanted to serve an adult version of this classic side dish.

To start, I made a few existing recipes for broccoli and cheese casserole from a range of sources: family cookbooks, classics such as *Joy of Cooking*, and more. I learned a few things along the way. Fresh broccoli works much better than frozen, which tasted bland in this context. Casseroles that are built on flour-thickened white sauces are less gloppy than those made with stir-together sauces using cream cheese or condensed soup. And a crunchy topping is never a bad move.

I made a quick cheese sauce by cooking butter and flour before whisking in half-and-half and grated extra-sharp cheddar cheese, a process similar to the one you might use when making macaroni and cheese. I combined this sauce with 2 pounds of raw broccoli florets, sprinkled on some panko bread crumbs, and baked it. While it smelled delicious, this version fea-tured a curdled cheese sauce and a pool of bubbling fat—a common occurrence when you cook with aged cheeses such as sharp cheddar (the sharper the cheddar, the older it is), which tend to break under prolonged heat. What's more, the broccoli never got fully tender in the time it took to brown the crumbs.

First I dealt with the broccoli. I knew I'd have to precook it to reduce the oven time, which would help prevent the sauce from breaking. I tried blanching and roasting the broccoli, but microwaving was the easiest, fastest method and gave me consistent results. This step allowed me to reduce the oven time from 45 min-utes to 15 minutes while still fully cooking the broccoli. But even with just 15 minutes in the oven, my sauce was breaking into a greasy mess.

I was determined to stick with extra-sharp cheddar for its outsize flavor. A coworker suggested adding a bit of American cheese to the mix to help forestall the breakage I'd been experiencing; because American cheese contains emulsifiers, sauces made with it are more likely to stay together. A 1:3 ratio of American cheese to extra-sharp cheddar gave me a silky, creamy sauce with plenty of flavor, and additions of garlic, shallot, and dry mustard provided even more.

To take this broccoli and cheese casserole over the top, I mixed some grated Parmesan into the buttery bread-crumb topping before baking. This reinforced the nutty, cheesy flavors and helped the top crust turn extra-golden and crispy. I had a star side dish on my hands.

—MORGAN BOLLING, *Cook's Country*

Crunchy Broccoli and Cheese Casserole

SERVES 6 TO 8

If you do not have a bowl large enough to hold 2 pounds of broccoli, microwave it in two batches for 5 to 7 minutes each. Make sure the dry mustard is relatively fresh; its flavor starts to fade a few months after it's opened.

¾ cup panko bread crumbs

1 ounce Parmesan cheese, grated (½ cup)

3 tablespoons unsalted butter, melted, plus
    3 tablespoons unsalted butter

2¼ teaspoons table salt, divided

2 pounds broccoli florets, cut into 1-inch pieces

1 shallot, minced

2 garlic cloves, minced

3 tablespoons all-purpose flour

3 cups half-and-half

6 ounces extra-sharp cheddar cheese, shredded
    (1½ cups)

2 ounces American cheese, chopped (½ cup)

2 teaspoons hot sauce

1 teaspoon dry mustard

¼ teaspoon pepper

1. Adjust oven rack to upper-middle position and heat oven to 400 degrees. Combine panko, Parmesan, melted butter, and ¼ teaspoon salt in bowl; set aside.

2. Toss broccoli with ½ teaspoon salt in large bowl. Cover and microwave until broccoli is bright green and just tender, 8 to 10 minutes. Drain broccoli in colander, then transfer to 13 by 9-inch baking dish.

3. Melt remaining 3 tablespoons butter in medium saucepan over medium heat. Add shallot and garlic and cook until softened, about 2 minutes. Whisk in flour and cook for 1 minute. Slowly whisk in half-and-half. Increase heat to medium-high and bring mixture to boil. Off heat, quickly whisk in cheddar, American cheese, hot sauce, mustard, pepper, and remaining 1½ teaspoons salt until smooth.

4. Pour cheese sauce over broccoli and stir to combine. Sprinkle reserved panko mixture over top. Bake, uncovered, until casserole is bubbling around edges and golden brown on top, about 15 minutes. Let cool for 15 minutes. Serve.

TO MAKE AHEAD: Panko mixture and microwaved, drained broccoli can be refrigerated separately for up to 24 hours. To serve, continue with recipe from step 3, increasing baking time by 5 minutes.

SAUTÉED MUSHROOMS WITH RED WINE AND ROSEMARY

✓ **WHY THIS RECIPE WORKS** Sautéing mushrooms the usual way entails piling them in a skillet slicked with a couple of tablespoons of oil and waiting patiently for them to release their moisture, which then must evaporate before the mushrooms can brown. Instead, we accelerate the process by adding a small amount of water to the pan and steaming the mushrooms, which allows them to release their moisture more quickly. The added benefit of steaming them is that the collapsed mushrooms won't absorb much oil; in fact, ½ teaspoon of oil was enough to prevent sticking and encourage browning. And because we used so little fat to sauté the mushrooms, we were able to sauce them with a butter-based reduction without making them overly rich. Adding broth and simmering the buttery mixture ensured that the sauce emulsified, creating a flavorful glaze that clung well to the mushrooms.

You don't have to be a professional chef to know that "sauté" means to sear food in a small amount of hot fat so that it browns deeply and develops savory flavor. So you might wonder how I—a professional chef—came to conclude that the most important step when sautéing mushrooms is to first simmer them in water.

To explain, let me start by recounting what typically happens when you sauté mushrooms. You heat a little oil in a skillet, throw in the sliced fungi, and toss them around. Pretty soon, there's no oil left in the skillet, so you add a little more to lubricate the pan and encourage the browning that creates loads of new, rich-tasting flavor compounds. But mushrooms suck up oil like crazy, and you find yourself adding more and more. Then, just as browning seems to be getting underway, the mushrooms start to release their abundant moisture. Only once all of their jus has evaporated—which takes a lot of time and frequent stirring (to ensure even progress among all the slices)—can the mushrooms start browning in earnest. But by that time, you've already added so much fat to the pan that you may as well have deep-fried the mushrooms.

The problem is that mushrooms are full of air pockets that readily absorb oil. And all that water they contain thwarts browning. To yield meaty-tasting, well-browned mushrooms—not spongy oil receptacles—I'd have to start by quickly ridding them of all that air and water.

Thanks to our recipe for caramelized onions, I had a good idea of what to do: Start by adding water—not oil—to the skillet with the mushrooms. This might sound counterintuitive, since the whole idea of sautéing is to eliminate moisture and raise the food's temperature above 212 degrees so that the browning reactions can take place. But as with onions, surrounding the mushrooms with steam from the get-go would start cooking them all right away. Their cells would rupture sooner, allowing the mushrooms to rapidly exude moisture—the step that's the requisite precursor to browning.

So I loaded up my 12-inch nonstick skillet with a little more than a pound of sliced white button mushrooms and ¼ cup of water. I cranked the heat to high and, sure enough, within moments the liquid in the pan turned gray—proof that the mushrooms were giving up their jus. After only 5 minutes and just occasional stirring, that liquid had evaporated and the mound of mushrooms I'd started with had reduced enough to fit in a single layer across the skillet's cooking surface.

From there, I proceeded with a typical sauté method, drizzling several tablespoons of oil over the mushrooms to speed browning and letting them sizzle over medium-high heat until they developed good color.

But, surprisingly, multiple tablespoons of fat now seemed like way too much. Instead of readily soaking up the oil and leaving just enough to lubricate the pan and encourage browning, as they do when sautéed the typical way, the mushrooms didn't absorb much oil at all. In fact, much of the oil remained in the pan, so the mushrooms cooked up grease-slicked.

I ran a series of tests in which I incrementally decreased the amount of oil I added to the pan after the water evaporated, and I was stunned to discover that a mere ½ teaspoon was all I needed to prevent sticking and help accelerate browning. Why? Because while raw mushrooms contain air pockets that readily soak up oil, cooking the mushrooms before adding oil collapses those air pockets so that they can't absorb nearly as much.

Now that I had a method for sautéing mushrooms that was not only efficient but also downright lean, I felt justified in lavishing the mushrooms with a glossy butter-based glaze.

Once the mushrooms were well browned, I lowered the heat to medium and pushed the mushrooms to the sides of the pan to clear a space. In went a tablespoon of butter and some minced shallot and rosemary to give the dish depth and fragrance, followed by red wine and cider vinegar to deglaze the pan.

I gave the contents a stir to evenly coat the mushrooms with the sauce, but on closer inspection I noticed that the mushrooms were coated with droplets of fat—a clear sign that simply tossing the butter-wine mixture with the mushrooms hadn't thoroughly emulsified the sauce.

The problem was that there was very little sauce compared to the volume of mushrooms in the pan, which made it difficult to vigorously stir the mixture and incorporate the butter. So going forward I added ½ cup of chicken broth after the deglazing liquid had evaporated, and I let the buttery broth simmer until it had reduced by about half and the fat had emulsified into the liquid.

These were the dinner party–worthy sautéed mushrooms I'd had in mind: well browned, meaty textured, flavor packed, and lightly glossed with a buttery glaze. I checked that the recipe worked with portobello, cremini, and shiitake mushrooms and, to make it even more special, tried subbing in oyster and *maitake* mushrooms, varieties that are increasingly available in supermarkets. I also pulled together a few more simple sauces to give the dish some real bandwidth.

—LAN LAM, *Cook's Illustrated*

NOTES FROM THE TEST KITCHEN

EXPAND YOUR MUSHROOM UNIVERSE

Most people's go-to mushrooms are white, cremini, portobello, and maybe shiitake. These are all excellent mushrooms with deep earthy flavor, but our sautéed mushroom recipes present a good opportunity to try two other varieties that are increasingly available in supermarkets: oyster and *maitake*. Oyster mushrooms (second from right), recognizable by their fan-shaped caps, boast a savory flavor; they are often sold with their stems connected at the base. *Maitake* mushrooms (far right), which are also known as hen-of-the-woods mushrooms, have frilly caps; their stems may also be connected at the base. They feature a nutty, slightly smoky flavor. All these mushrooms can be used on their own or in combination in the recipes here.

Sautéed Mushrooms with Red Wine and Rosemary

SERVES 4

Use one variety of mushroom or a combination. Stem and halve portobello mushrooms and cut each half crosswise into ½-inch pieces. Trim white or cremini mushrooms; quarter them if large or medium or halve them if small. Tear trimmed oyster mushrooms into 1- to 1½-inch pieces. Stem shiitake mushrooms; quarter large caps and halve small caps. Cut trimmed *maitake* (hen-of-the-woods) mushrooms into 1- to 1½-inch pieces. You can substitute vegetable broth for the chicken broth, if desired.

1¼	pounds mushrooms
¼	cup water
½	teaspoon vegetable oil
1	tablespoon unsalted butter
1	shallot, minced
1	teaspoon minced fresh rosemary
¼	teaspoon table salt
¼	teaspoon pepper
¼	cup red wine
1	tablespoon cider vinegar
½	cup chicken broth

1. Cook mushrooms and water in 12-inch nonstick skillet over high heat, stirring occasionally, until skillet is almost dry and mushrooms begin to sizzle, 4 to 8 minutes. Reduce heat to medium-high. Add oil and toss until mushrooms are evenly coated. Continue to cook, stirring occasionally, until mushrooms are well browned, 4 to 8 minutes longer. Reduce heat to medium.

2. Push mushrooms to sides of skillet. Add butter to center. When butter has melted, add shallot, rosemary, salt, and pepper to center and cook, stirring constantly, until aromatic, about 30 seconds. Add wine and vinegar and stir mixture into mushrooms. Cook, stirring occasionally, until liquid has evaporated, 2 to 3 minutes. Add broth and cook, stirring occasionally, until glaze is reduced by half, about 3 minutes. Season with salt and pepper to taste, and serve.

VARIATIONS

Sautéed Mushrooms with Mustard and Parsley

Omit rosemary. Substitute 1 tablespoon Dijon mustard for wine and increase vinegar to 1½ tablespoons (liquid will take only 1 to 2 minutes to evaporate). Stir in 2 tablespoons chopped fresh parsley before serving.

Sautéed Mushrooms with Soy, Scallion, and Ginger

Substitute 1 thinly sliced scallion for shallot and grated fresh ginger for rosemary. Omit salt. Substitute 2 tablespoons soy sauce for wine and sherry vinegar for cider vinegar.

CHARRED GREEN BEANS

✔ **WHY THIS RECIPE WORKS** Deep-frying green beans evenly softens and blisters them, leaving them with a concentrated flavor and a soft, appealingly dense, satisfying chew. To achieve those results without the hassle of frying, we first softened the beans by steaming them in the microwave. Then we charred them in a skillet with just a couple tablespoons of hot oil. We didn't stir the beans for the first few minutes so that they developed deep color and flavor on one side; we then tossed them in the pan so that they blistered all over. Once they were charred, we seasoned them with a lemony salt-and-pepper mixture.

Sichuan cooks have a method for preparing green beans called "dry frying." It's a two-step approach in which the beans are deep-fried and then stir-fried with aromatics and maybe a little ground pork. There's not much sauce because the beans are the real draw: blistered, with a soft chew and concentrated flavor. It's a technique I would use regularly if dry frying didn't require the hassle of, well, frying. Especially because the beans could pair well with so many flavors beyond the typical Sichuan profile.

Instead, I tried shallow-frying a pound of beans in a couple of tablespoons of vegetable oil. They were only spottily blistered after 10 minutes because the ends of the raw beans curled up and didn't make full contact with the hot oil. They were still firm inside, too, and showed no signs of softening even after 20 minutes in the skillet.

GREEN BEANS ARE TOUGHER THAN YOU'D THINK

Green beans are rugged. Their cell walls are rich in hemicellulose and pectin that make them firm enough to snap when fresh. Those components, plus a substance called lignin, also make them very resistant to heat, which explains why they can be cooked for a long time or over high heat, as we do for our Skillet-Charred Green Beans, without turning to mush. Instead, prolonged heat exposure gives them a silky yet stable quality.

FIT TO BE TIED

It turns out that completely softening green beans is a lengthy process. That's because the components in the beans' cell walls that give raw green beans their snap also take a while to soften during cooking (see "Green Beans Are Tougher Than You'd Think").

The advantage of deep frying, I realized, is that the beans are fully submerged in the hot oil, which softens them more quickly than shallow frying, where only part of the bean is ever in contact with the oil. But what if I precooked the beans and wilted them enough to make greater contact with the oil in the pan?

Simmering the beans in water in a covered nonstick skillet was an obvious way to wilt them. Then I drained them, wiped the pan dry, got 2 tablespoons of oil smoking-hot, and added back the beans. This time, they blistered after 5 minutes. (I didn't move the beans for these first few minutes so they could develop an intense char on one side.) I shook the pan so that they would brown on the other sides, and after a few minutes they were downright charred. In fact, they boasted even richer flavor than typical dry-fried beans: The charring was deeper and more of the beans' water had been driven off, concentrating their flavor.

But simmering the beans left a residue that stuck to the pan during the frying stage, which meant I had to stop and wash the pan. I found it easier to soften the beans in a covered bowl in the microwave (but we provide a method for doing it in a skillet as well). If I rinsed but didn't dry them, there was just enough water clinging to the beans to produce steam that softened them

further. I stirred the beans every few minutes to redistribute them, which ensured even cooking. This nearly hands-off approach was my most successful yet.

Seasoning the beans with salt, pepper, and lemon (both zest and juice) was more than adequate. But considering how versatile these beans were, I wanted to mix up a couple exciting toppings that would complement their soft, slightly chewy texture. Fine-textured garnishes (such as the lemon salt) worked best because they stuck to the hot beans. For my first variation, I prepared a topping using seasoned panko bread crumbs—finely crushed so that they clung to the beans—to provide a pleasant textural contrast to the tender chew of the green beans. For another variation that would bump up the crunch factor and add a hit of spice, I mixed up a toasted panko–sesame seed topping bolstered with a handful of bold ingredients including ground Sichuan peppercorns, Korean red pepper flakes, grated orange zest, and toasted sesame oil.

Dry-fried beans will still be my go-to order when I visit a Sichuan restaurant. But I daresay my charred beans might have them beat—especially since they're hassle-free.

—ANDREW JANJIGIAN, *Cook's Illustrated*

Skillet-Charred Green Beans

SERVES 4

Microwave thinner, more tender beans for 6 to 8 minutes and thicker, tougher beans for 10 to 12 minutes. To make the beans without a microwave, bring ¼ cup of water to a boil in a skillet over high heat. Add the beans, cover, and cook for 5 minutes. Transfer the beans to a paper towel–lined plate to drain and wash the skillet before proceeding with the recipe.

½ teaspoon grated lemon zest plus 1 teaspoon juice
½ teaspoon kosher salt
¼ teaspoon pepper
1 pound green beans, trimmed
2 tablespoons vegetable oil

1. Combine lemon zest, salt, and pepper in small bowl. Set aside.

2. Rinse green beans but do not dry. Place in medium bowl, cover, and microwave until fully tender, 6 to 12 minutes, stirring every 3 minutes. Using tongs, transfer green beans to paper towel–lined plate and let drain.

SKILLET-CHARRED GREEN BEANS WITH CRISPY SESAME TOPPING

3. Heat oil in 12-inch nonstick skillet over high heat until just smoking. Add green beans in single layer. Cook, without stirring, until green beans begin to blister and char, 4 to 5 minutes. Toss green beans and continue to cook, stirring occasionally, until green beans are softened and charred, 4 to 5 minutes longer. Using tongs, transfer green beans to serving bowl, leaving any excess oil in skillet. Sprinkle with lemon-salt mixture and lemon juice and toss to coat. Serve.

VARIATIONS

Skillet-Charred Green Beans with Crispy Bread-Crumb Topping

Process 2 tablespoons panko bread crumbs in spice grinder or mortar and pestle until uniformly ground to medium-fine consistency that resembles couscous. Cook panko and 1 tablespoon vegetable oil in 12-inch nonstick skillet over medium-low heat, stirring frequently, until light golden brown, 5 to 7 minutes. Remove skillet from heat; add ¾ teaspoon kosher salt, ¼ teaspoon pepper, and ¼ teaspoon red pepper flakes; and stir to combine. Transfer panko mixture to bowl; set aside. Wash out skillet thoroughly and dry with paper towels. Proceed with recipe as directed, substituting panko mixture for lemon-salt mixture.

Skillet-Charred Green Beans with Crispy Sesame Topping

Korean red pepper flakes, called *gochugaru*, are also sold as Korean chili powder.

Grind 3 tablespoons sesame seeds, 1 tablespoon panko bread crumbs, and 1 teaspoon Sichuan peppercorns in spice grinder or mortar and pestle until uniformly ground to medium-fine consistency that resembles couscous. Cook sesame mixture and 2 teaspoons vegetable oil in 12-inch nonstick skillet over medium-low heat, stirring frequently, until light golden brown, 5 to 7 minutes. Off heat, stir in 1 teaspoon Korean red pepper flakes, 1 teaspoon toasted sesame oil, ¾ teaspoon kosher salt, and ½ teaspoon grated orange zest. Transfer sesame mixture to bowl; set aside. Wash out skillet thoroughly and dry with paper towels. Proceed with recipe as directed, substituting sesame mixture for lemon-salt mixture and sprinkling green beans with 2 thinly sliced scallion greens before serving.

GRILLED ZUCCHINI WITH RED PEPPER SAUCE

✓ WHY THIS RECIPE WORKS To avoid overcooked, watery zucchini, we cut them in half lengthwise and scored a crosshatch pattern into the cut sides with a sharp paring knife. We brushed the zucchini with olive oil and seasoned it with salt and pepper before charring it on the grill alongside a red bell pepper. We then steamed the bell pepper to remove its skin and blended it with red wine vinegar, garlic, and toasted almonds to create a tangy sauce. For an herbaceous touch, we finished the sauce by folding in chopped basil right before serving.

Someone should make a horror movie about a society overtaken by uncontrollable hordes of summer zucchini. In peak season, this vegetable is everywhere and home gardeners struggle to give it away. Attack of the killer zucchini, indeed. I wanted to write a happier script for this handsome vegetable, set in my favorite place for summer cooking—on the grill.

My early tests confirmed prior test kitchen findings: Big zucchini tasted dull and were much tougher and more fibrous than their smaller brethren. Medium zucchini (around 8 ounces each) were sweeter and more tender.

Since I wanted to avoid having to move lots of small pieces around the grill, I cut the zucchini in half lengthwise (as opposed to into spears or medallions) and began by marinating them in olive oil, salt, and pepper. I hoped the salty marinade would add flavor and help pull out some of the extra moisture before the vegetable hit the grill, thus reducing mushiness. And here was my first scary scene: The oil dripped off the grilling zucchini and caused flare-ups that resulted in a sooty taste. And the zucchini was bland and still mushy. Thumbs down.

An oily marinade was out. To encourage the zukes to give up their moisture on the grill, I tried cutting a shallow crosshatch pattern into the flesh side of each half. As long as I was gentle enough not to cut through the skin, this trick worked great and resulted in a firmer, nonmushy texture.

I now had perfectly cooked zucchini, but I still needed to jazz up the flavor. My mind immediately went to romesco sauce, a Spanish staple built on a puree of roasted red peppers, almonds, and olive oil. I threw a red bell pepper onto the grill with the zucchini and, once all the vegetables were cooked, headed inside to figure out the sauce.

After a bit of fiddling, I perfected my streamlined version of a romesco-style sauce. The grilled bell pepper provided a great foundation. Sliced almonds contributed a clean flavor and blended easily into the sauce. I added garlic for bite, red wine vinegar for tang, and basil for an intense herbal punch. The sauce came together in the food processor in a flash.

Beautifully charred zucchini paired with a summery sauce makes zucchini a less scary presence during the summer months. Stay tuned for the sequel.

—NATALIE ESTRADA, *Cook's Country*

Grilled Zucchini with Red Pepper Sauce

SERVES 4 TO 6

Look for zucchini that are no more than 2 inches in diameter and are about 8 ounces each to ensure correct grilling times. Clean and oil the cooking grate thoroughly to prevent the zucchini from sticking. We leave the bell pepper whole (minus the stem and core) and grill only two sides of it. Our favorite red wine vinegars are made by Laurent du Clos and Pompeian Gourmet.

  4 zucchini (8 ounces each), trimmed
  1 red bell pepper
1½ tablespoons plus ⅓ cup extra-virgin olive oil, divided
1¼ teaspoons table salt, divided
  ½ teaspoon pepper, divided
  2 tablespoons sliced almonds, toasted
1½ tablespoons red wine vinegar
  2 small garlic cloves, peeled
  2 teaspoons chopped fresh basil

1. Cut zucchini in half lengthwise. Using paring knife, cut ½-inch crosshatch pattern, about ¼ inch deep, in flesh of each zucchini half, being careful not to cut through skin. Cut around stem of bell pepper and remove core and seeds. Brush flesh sides of zucchini with 1 tablespoon oil and sprinkle with 1 teaspoon salt and ¼ teaspoon pepper. Brush bell pepper with 1½ teaspoons oil.

2A. FOR A CHARCOAL GRILL: Open bottom vent completely. Light large chimney starter filled with charcoal briquettes (6 quarts). When top coals are partially covered with ash, pour evenly over grill. Set cooking grate in place, cover, and open lid vent completely. Heat grill until hot, about 5 minutes.

2B. FOR A GAS GRILL: Turn all burners to high, cover, and heat grill until hot, about 15 minutes. Turn all burners to medium-high.

3. Clean and oil cooking grate. Place zucchini, flesh side down, and bell pepper, skin side down, on cooking grate. Cook (covered if using gas) until vegetables are well charred on first side, 7 to 9 minutes, rearranging zucchini as needed to ensure even browning.

4. Flip vegetables and continue to cook (covered if using gas) until fork inserted in zucchini meets little resistance and bell pepper is charred on second side, 8 to 10 minutes longer. Transfer zucchini to plate, flesh side up, as they finish cooking. Transfer bell pepper to small bowl, cover with plastic wrap, and let sit for 5 minutes.

5. Using spoon, remove skin from bell pepper (it's OK if some small pieces of skin remain; do not rinse bell pepper to remove skin); cut into coarse 1-inch pieces. Process bell pepper, almonds, vinegar, garlic, remaining ⅓ cup oil, remaining ¼ teaspoon salt, and remaining ¼ teaspoon pepper in blender until smooth, 30 to 60 seconds, scraping down sides of blender jar as needed. Transfer sauce to bowl and stir in basil. Season with salt and pepper to taste.

6. Spread half of sauce on platter. Arrange zucchini over sauce, flesh side up. Spoon remaining sauce over zucchini, as desired. Serve.

NOTES FROM THE TEST KITCHEN

WHEN IT COMES TO ZUCCHINI, GO SMALL
Larger zucchini can be bland, tough, and full of seeds. For this recipe, we call for zucchini that weigh about 8 ounces each.

A MEDIUM ZUCCHINI SHOULD BE ABOUT AS WIDE AS A BANANA

GRILLED ZUCCHINI WITH RED PEPPER SAUCE

THE EASIEST WINTER SQUASH

✓ **WHY THIS RECIPE WORKS** Roasting brings out the naturally sweet and toasty flavor of delicata squash. Its skin softens when cooked, so unlike many winter squashes, delicata squash doesn't need to be peeled. For this recipe, we spread squash slices on a rimmed baking sheet and covered the sheet tightly with aluminum foil to trap steam and ensure that each bite of squash cooked up creamy and moist. Placing the sheet on the oven's lowest rack put the slices close to the heating element and thus sped up cooking and browning. We dotted the slices with butter and let them brown during the final minutes of cooking to reinforce the delicata's subtle flavor.

A few years ago, we ran a tip on how to break down a large, dense winter squash such as a Hubbard: Place it in a zipper-lock bag and drop it onto asphalt from chest height, smashing it to pieces. It sounds severe, but taking a knife to a giant rock-hard squash (even a modest-size butternut can be a struggle) isn't for the faint of heart, never mind that peeling its tough skin is a real chore.

Allow me to suggest an alternative: crenellated, creamy yellow delicata squash. These beauties, which are available from late summer through early winter, boast thin, edible striped skin that softens when cooked. Their small size means they are relatively easy to cut and seed, which makes preparation a snap. What's more, they offer a delicate, nutty taste that's entirely different from the pronounced sweetness of most winter squashes.

Mild delicata is complemented by flavorful browning. That can be achieved by sautéing slices, but doing so requires cooking in multiple batches since each flat side needs to be touching the pan to pick up color. Oven roasting is a better option since you can prepare enough squash to serve four on a single baking sheet. Then, the squash can be topped with herbs or a simple sauce.

Most recipes call for simply arranging oiled squash slices on a baking sheet and roasting. But as the squash cooks, its water evaporates, leaving each piece with a leathery surface and a dry interior. I figured I'd have better luck with the technique that we use for other hard vegetables such as carrots: Oven-steam the squash until tender, and then brown the exterior.

I halved and seeded three squashes, sliced them ½ inch thick—skin and all—and tossed them with oil and salt. After spreading the slices into an even layer on a baking sheet, I covered the sheet with aluminum foil and placed it on the middle rack of a 425-degree oven. The foil trapped steam and helped the slices cook evenly without becoming desiccated. After half an hour, the slices were tender, so I removed the foil. Within minutes, any residual moisture evaporated and the starches and sugars on the surface of the squashes began to brown. After 15 minutes, I flipped the slices and then let the second sides turn deep golden brown, which took about 15 minutes longer.

These squash slices were tender and moist, but I was sure I could speed up the cooking and coax an even fuller, richer flavor from the delicata. I moved the oven rack to the lowest position so that the baking sheet would be closer to the heat source. This shaved 15 minutes off the total time and deepened the browning.

To reinforce the delicata's unique nuttiness, I dotted it with butter for the final 10 minutes—enough time for it to brown with no risk of burning. These tender, golden slices looked gorgeous, and each bite featured a slightly resilient strip of skin and toasty squash flavor—all without breaking a sweat.

—LAN LAM, *Cook's Illustrated*

Roasted Delicata Squash
SERVES 4 TO 6

To ensure that the flesh cooks evenly, choose squashes that are similar in size and shape. Delicata have thin, edible skins that needn't be removed; simply use a vegetable peeler to pare away any tough brown blemishes. You can substitute chives for parsley, if desired. Serve the squash as is or drizzled with Basque-Style Herb Sauce (Tximitxurri), Goat Cheese and Chive Sauce, or Spicy Honey (recipes follow).

3 delicata squashes (12 to 16 ounces each), ends trimmed, halved lengthwise, seeded, and sliced crosswise ½ inch thick
4 teaspoons vegetable oil
½ teaspoon table salt
2 tablespoons unsalted butter, cut into 8 pieces
1 tablespoon minced fresh parsley

1. Adjust oven rack to lowest position and heat oven to 425 degrees. Toss squash with oil and salt until evenly coated. Arrange squash on rimmed baking sheet in single layer. Cover tightly with aluminum foil and bake until squash is tender when pierced with tip of paring knife, 18 to 20 minutes.

2. Remove foil and continue to bake until sides touching sheet are golden brown, 8 to 11 minutes longer. Remove sheet from oven and, using thin metal spatula, flip squash. Scatter butter over squash. Return to oven and continue to bake until sides touching sheet are golden brown, 8 to 11 minutes longer. Transfer squash to serving platter, sprinkle with parsley, and serve.

Basque-Style Herb Sauce (Tximitxurri)
SERVES 4 TO 6 (MAKES ½ CUP)

For a sauce with some heat, substitute hot smoked paprika for the regular smoked paprika.

  ¼ **cup minced fresh parsley**
  ¼ **cup extra-virgin olive oil**
  2 **tablespoons sherry vinegar**
  2 **garlic cloves, minced**
  1 **teaspoon smoked paprika**
  ¼ **teaspoon table salt**

Stir all ingredients together in bowl and let sit for at least 15 minutes before serving.

Goat Cheese and Chive Sauce
SERVES 4 TO 6 (MAKES ⅓ CUP)

For the best results, use a good-quality goat cheese. The test kitchen's winning goat cheese is Laura Chenel's Pure Goat Milk Cheese Original Log.

  2 **ounces goat cheese, crumbled (½ cup)**
3–4 **tablespoons milk, divided**
  1 **tablespoon minced fresh chives**
  ½ **teaspoon grated lemon zest plus 1 teaspoon juice**

Whisk goat cheese, 3 tablespoons milk, chives, and lemon zest and juice in bowl until smooth. Add remaining milk, 1 teaspoon at a time, as needed to create sauce that is thick but pourable. Season with salt and pepper to taste and let sit for at least 15 minutes before serving.

Spicy Honey
SERVES 4 TO 6 (MAKES ½ CUP)

We prefer vinegary Frank's RedHot Original Cayenne Pepper Sauce here. Do not substitute a thick hot sauce, such as sriracha; it will make the honey too thick to drizzle. Microwaving in 20-second intervals will prevent the mixture from boiling over.

  ¼ **cup honey**
  2 **tablespoons hot sauce**

Stir honey and hot sauce together in liquid measuring cup. Microwave until sauce comes to boil, about 1 minute. Continue to microwave in 20-second intervals until sauce is reduced to ¼ cup. Let cool for at least 10 minutes before serving.

NOTES FROM THE TEST KITCHEN

MAKING PERFECT ROASTED DELICATA SQUASH
For a simple roasted squash side, we turned to delicata squash because it requires minimal prep compared to other winter squashes.

1. Halve and seed squashes (do not remove skins). Slice each half crosswise ½ inch thick.

2. Toss squash with oil and salt. Transfer to rimmed baking sheet and cover tightly with foil. Bake until squash is tender, about 20 minutes.

3. Uncover and continue to bake until squash is golden brown, about 10 minutes longer. Flip squash and scatter butter over squash. Return sheet to oven and bake for about 10 minutes. Serve.

CHEDDAR SCALLOPED POTATOES

CHEDDAR SCALLOPED POTATOES

✔ **WHY THIS RECIPE WORKS** We love scalloped potatoes, but most recipes call for more than an hour of oven time to soften the potatoes. We wanted a streamlined recipe that could be made any night of the week. We started by parboiling sliced russet potatoes in a combination of heavy cream and chicken broth on the stovetop. Then we stirred in some sharp cheddar cheese and transferred the gooey, cheesy potato mixture to a baking dish to finish cooking in the oven.

I love cooking for the holidays, but I have my limits. I'd also like to sit around the table listening to my Nana tell stories or to lounge on the sofa and watch my son toddle around the room. But my family loves soft, creamy scalloped potatoes and, hey, they deserve them. I wanted a recipe with a significantly shorter cooking time than traditional versions so I'd have more time to sit down and enjoy the company of my family.

For research, I tried a few existing recipes from cookbooks in our library. One version took almost 2½ hours to cook through in the oven. Some were made with only heavy cream, some with only milk, and some with a combination of cream and chicken broth. After these early tests, we liked the combo approach; the resulting potatoes were rich and satisfying but not so rich that we could eat only a few forkfuls.

I knew that I'd need to start my potatoes on the stovetop to cut down on overall cooking time. After many tests, I settled on a brief 8 minutes of simmering for 2 pounds of potatoes sliced ¼ inch thick. But rather than cook the potatoes in water and then drain off all that starch (which also helps thicken the sauce), I took a cue from earlier test kitchen recipes and simmered them in a mixture of broth and cream before baking them off in a casserole dish—no need for draining. My potatoes cooked up tender and soft. Just perfect.

Not every scalloped potato recipe calls for cheese, but my family loves it. So for my next round, I stirred a cup of shredded sharp cheddar into the potatoes after their stint on the stovetop—any earlier and the sauce was a broken mess. I then dumped the lot into a 13 by 9-inch baking dish, sprinkled another cup of shredded cheese over the top, and baked it for just 20 minutes. The top was a beautiful spotted brown, bubbling happily around the edges.

After waiting for the potatoes to cool (which was torture because they looked so good), my team and I dug in. Each thin potato slice was perfectly cooked; the cheesy, rich sauce coated every slice; and the whole thing was done in less than 45 minutes. I think I see some couch time in my future this holiday season.

—ASHLEY MOORE, *Cook's Country*

Cheddar Scalloped Potatoes
SERVES 6

Do not prepare the potatoes ahead of time or store them in water; the potato starch is essential for thickening the sauce. This recipe can easily be doubled. To do so, use a large Dutch oven instead of a large saucepan in step 1 and let the casserole cool for 30 minutes before serving in step 3.

- 2 pounds russet potatoes, peeled and sliced ¼ inch thick
- 1¼ cups heavy cream
- 1 cup chicken broth
- 1 teaspoon table salt
- ½ teaspoon pepper
- 8 ounces sharp cheddar cheese, shredded (2 cups), divided

1. Adjust oven rack to upper-middle position and heat oven to 425 degrees. Bring potatoes, cream, broth, salt, and pepper to simmer in large saucepan over medium-high heat.

2. Reduce heat to medium, cover, and cook, stirring occasionally, until paring knife can be slipped into and out of potatoes with no resistance, about 8 minutes, adjusting heat as necessary to maintain gentle simmer. Off heat, gently stir in 1 cup cheddar.

3. Transfer potato mixture to 13 by 9-inch baking dish, spread into even layer, and sprinkle with remaining 1 cup cheddar. Bake until bubbling around edges and top is golden brown, about 20 minutes. Let cool for 15 minutes. Serve.

TO MAKE AHEAD: At end of step 2, transfer potato mixture to 13 by 9-inch baking dish and let cool completely. Cover with aluminum foil and refrigerate for up to 24 hours. To serve, keep covered with foil and bake until heated through, about 20 minutes. Uncover, sprinkle with remaining 1 cup cheddar, and continue to bake, uncovered, until bubbling around edges and top is spotty brown, about 20 minutes longer.

CRUSHED RED POTATOES

✓ **WHY THIS RECIPE WORKS** Boiled and buttered red potatoes can be boring; all the flavor remains on the outsides of the potatoes, leaving the interiors bland. To fix that, we simmered 2 pounds of red potatoes until they were completely tender, drained them, and then melted some butter in the empty pot before adding minced garlic, minced fresh chives, minced fresh parsley, salt, and pepper. We then added the still-steaming potatoes, lightly pressed each with the back of a spoon until it broke apart, and gently stirred the potatoes with the buttery herb mixture to ensure that it worked its way into all the nooks and crannies (and every bite).

Boiled and buttered red potatoes are a reliable side dish—they're simple and satisfying, and the little spuds look great on the plate. But they can be a bit boring. Adding herbs to the butter can help, sure, but the seasonings and buttery goodness remain on the outsides of the potatoes, leaving the interiors tasting bland. How do you get flavor inside the spuds? By lightly crushing them so the seasonings can soak right in. Easy, right? Well . . .

To be clear, I wasn't looking to wind up for a fully smashed or mashed potato. My goal was to only lightly crush the potatoes so they just split apart; this way the melted butter (and other seasonings) could find its way into the nooks and crannies while the potatoes maintained some texture.

For my first test, I covered 2 pounds of golf ball–size red potatoes with cold water (we've found that potatoes cook more evenly when started in cold water) and added plenty of salt—a full 2 tablespoons—for deep seasoning. This may seem like a substantial dosage of salt, but it's the only way to evenly season the potatoes from the inside out. Plus, most of that salt will go down the drain with the cooking water. I brought the water up to a boil and then lowered the heat to cook the potatoes through gently. It took about 20 minutes of simmering until they were completely tender.

Then came the fun part: I transferred the drained potatoes to a serving platter and lightly crushed each steaming spud with the back of a wooden spoon—an act that, much like popping bubble wrap, was strangely satisfying. I poured on some seasoned melted butter and sprinkled some tender herbs on top—I found that

2 tablespoons each of minced parsley (for mild bitterness) and chives (for oniony bite) provided the balanced herbiness I was after. It was a solid first attempt at what I had in mind, but the butter and seasonings didn't penetrate or coat the potatoes quite as well as I'd hoped.

For the next batch, I tried returning the drained potatoes to the warm pot and stirring with a firm hand to break them up before adding the melted butter and herbs. But this method beat up the delicate potatoes too much, bringing them too close to mashed or smashed territory. It was better, I found, to drain the cooked potatoes and leave them in the colander while preparing a flavorful butter in the pot. I cooked a minced clove of garlic in melted butter until just golden and fragrant and then pulled the pot off the heat and added the minced herbs, plenty of salt and pepper, and finally the still-steaming cooked potatoes. Next, I lightly pressed each potato with the back of my spoon (a spatula offers similar control and feel, if you prefer) until it just broke apart and then gently stirred to ensure that all the buttery, garlicky, herby goodness worked its way into every bite.

Because potatoes are a blank canvas for flavor, I also mixed up two tasty variations. For the first, I swapped out butter for extra-virgin olive oil and added a sprinkling of smoked paprika. For the second, I substituted fresh oregano, briny capers, and bright lemon juice for the chives and parsley. It's time to say goodbye to boring, underseasoned spuds.

—CECELIA JENKINS, *Cook's Country*

Crushed Red Potatoes with Garlic and Herbs
SERVES 4 TO 6

Be sure to use small red potatoes measuring 1 to 2 inches in diameter. Use a gentle hand when crushing the potatoes.

2   pounds small red potatoes, unpeeled
½   teaspoon table salt, plus salt for cooking potatoes
6   tablespoons unsalted butter
1   garlic clove, minced
2   tablespoons minced fresh chives
2   tablespoons minced fresh parsley
¼   teaspoon pepper

1. Place potatoes and 2 tablespoons salt in Dutch oven and cover with water by 1 inch. Bring to boil over high heat. Reduce heat to medium-high and simmer until paring knife slips easily into and out of potatoes, about 20 minutes. (Potatoes should be very tender.) Drain potatoes in colander.

2. In now-empty pot, melt butter over medium heat. Add garlic and cook until fragrant, about 30 seconds. Off heat, stir in chives, parsley, pepper, and salt.

3. Add potatoes to pot. Press each potato with back of spoon or spatula to lightly crush (do not mash; potatoes should still have texture). Stir to coat potatoes with butter mixture (potatoes will break up slightly; this is OK). Transfer to platter. Serve.

VARIATIONS

Crushed Red Potatoes with Garlic and Smoked Paprika

Substitute extra-virgin olive oil for butter and heat until shimmering. Sprinkle 1 teaspoon smoked paprika over crushed potatoes on platter before serving.

Crushed Red Potatoes with Oregano and Capers

Substitute 1 tablespoon chopped fresh oregano, 1 tablespoon rinsed capers, and 1 tablespoon lemon juice for chives and parsley. Decrease salt in step 2 to ¼ teaspoon.

NOTES FROM THE TEST KITCHEN

GETTING THE TEXTURE JUST RIGHT

1. Press on cooked potatoes with wooden spoon until they crack open and are lightly crushed.

2. Stir gently to further break down crushed potatoes and distribute seasoned butter mixture.

GERMAN POTATO SALAD

✔ WHY THIS RECIPE WORKS A good German potato salad will have tender, not mushy, red potatoes; plenty of bacon; the tangy bite of mustard; and a sharp vinegary finish. For our version we found that the salad reached its full flavor potential in a skillet rather than in a traditional saucepan. Rendering bacon and incorporating the rendered fat into the dressing layered tons of flavor into the salad. Slicing the potatoes into ¼-inch-thick rounds ensured that they cooked to just tender in the time it took to reduce the cooking liquid to become part of the dressing. After sitting in the cider vinegar and mustard vinaigrette for a few minutes postboiling, these potatoes transformed into a delicious salad that was at once rich, smoky, and vibrant.

When I was a kid, every road trip to my grandmother's house resulted in a race to the refrigerator for the first helping of potato salad. Usually served as a side dish but often eaten as a snack, the boiled, dressed-up spuds always hit the spot.

Potato salad is a spectacularly flexible side dish. Ask one person to describe the perfect potato salad, and then ask another—you'll get two wildly different answers. I did just that, soliciting ideas from coworkers, but as soon as one described so-called German potato salad, with red potatoes, plenty of bacon, the tangy bite of mustard, and a sharp vinegary finish, I was intrigued. This style of potato salad has a velvety, almost creamy texture, which gives it an extra-comforting profile, especially in cooler months.

All potato salads start with potatoes, and I needed to figure out how to cut mine for the best ratio of potatoes to dressing and add-ins. I also wanted potatoes that were soft but not mushy. After testing chunks, halves, and slices of red potatoes, I found that ¼-inch-thick slices boiled for about 15 minutes were best.

Following a cue from some old recipes I found, I decided to add salt, sugar, and celery seeds to the boiling water to help flavor the potatoes.

Now I was ready for the dressing. All the research I'd done indicated that a strong dose of vinegar was essential here. So I whisked together a few dressings using varying styles and amounts of vinegar. Cider vinegar, with its strong tangy flavor and faint sweetness, won out over distilled white and wine vinegars. And

GERMAN POTATO SALAD

while some dressings called for olive oil or canola oil, the best just called for using the flavorful rendered fat from the bacon.

Tossing the warm potatoes with this dressing and then giving them a 15-minute rest to absorb it created an irresistible salad. A heaping handful of fresh scallions and chopped parsley finished it off. I had the creamy, bacon-enriched, supercomforting salad I'd set out to create.

—ALLI BERKEY, *Cook's Country*

German Potato Salad

SERVES 4 TO 6

We developed this recipe with Grey Poupon Harvest Coarse Ground Mustard. Use small red potatoes measuring 1 to 2 inches in diameter.

- 8 slices bacon, cut into ½-inch pieces
- 2 pounds small red potatoes, unpeeled, sliced ¼ inch thick
- 3 cups water
- 2 tablespoons plus 1 teaspoon sugar, divided
- 1¼ teaspoons table salt, divided
- 1 teaspoon celery seeds
- 3 tablespoons cider vinegar
- 2 tablespoons whole-grain mustard
- ¼ teaspoon pepper
- 4 scallions, sliced thin
- 3 tablespoons chopped fresh parsley
- 3 tablespoons finely chopped sweet green vinegar peppers (optional)

1. Cook bacon in 12-inch nonstick skillet over medium heat until crispy, 5 to 7 minutes. Using slotted spoon, transfer bacon to paper towel–lined plate. Pour bacon fat into liquid measuring cup. (You will need ¼ cup fat for dressing. If you have too much or too little, you can discard excess or add vegetable oil as needed to equal ¼ cup). Set aside.

2. Add potatoes, water, 2 tablespoons sugar, 1 teaspoon salt, and celery seeds to now-empty skillet and bring to boil over high heat. Cook, stirring occasionally, until potatoes are tender, about 15 minutes. Continue to cook until liquid is syrupy and just coats bottom of skillet, 3 to 5 minutes longer. Transfer potatoes and cooking liquid to large bowl.

3. Stir vinegar, mustard, pepper, remaining 1 teaspoon sugar, and remaining ¼ teaspoon salt into reserved bacon fat until combined. Add dressing to potato mixture and stir to thoroughly combine. Let sit for 15 minutes.

4. Add scallions; parsley; peppers, if using; and bacon to potato mixture. Using rubber spatula, firmly stir to partially break up potatoes and give salad creamy texture, about 20 strokes. Serve warm.

AIR-FRYER PARMESAN, ROSEMARY, AND BLACK PEPPER FRENCH FRIES

✔ **WHY THIS RECIPE WORKS** Once we learned how to make crave-worthy French fries in the air fryer, we thought that giving them a Parmesan-rosemary coating would be a cinch. We tossed the hot fries with grated cheese and minced herbs, but only some adhered; the rest fell to the bottom of the bowl. Switching gears, we added the cheese partway through cooking. Now the cheese clung and even crisped into a coating, but it lost some of its Parmesan flavor. The Goldilocks moment came when we cooked some cheese onto the fries for a crust and then tossed more with the cooked fries for flavor. (Adding the rosemary both during and after cooking also best highlighted the herb's aroma.) To gild the lily, we added black pepper and sprinkled a third handful of cheese onto the finished fry pile, which melted into a lacy coating. Frequently tossing the fries ensured the most even cooking and the best browning. We found that tossing the fries in a bowl, rather than in the air-fryer basket, yielded the best results and the fewest broken fries.

In recent years, air fryers have gained popularity as a no-fuss way to produce crispy, fried-tasting food with a fraction of the oil of deep-frying. When I think of fried food, French fries are the first thing to come to mind, so it's no surprise that recipes for air-fryer French fries abound. Many of these recipes not only claim to be healthier but also promise exceptional ease: Some call for doing nothing more than cutting potatoes into sticks and then placing them in the basket of the air fryer without any oil at all.

I was skeptical. The test kitchen has a recipe for deep-fried French fries that calls for a multistep process involving soaking the potatoes to remove excess starch, chilling the uncooked fries, and then frying them in two stages to produce crispy exteriors and fluffy interiors. Surely there was a reason for all those steps. Nevertheless, I tried a recipe for hands-off air-fryer fries to see if I was missing something. After I cooked the fries oil-free in the air fryer for 15 minutes, they emerged pale and tasteless. Clearly, the hands-off method was not the way to go. On the other end of the spectrum, some air-fryer recipes called for hours of prep work, including soaking the potatoes for up to 24 hours before frying. Although these labor-intensive renditions were more in line with the classic test kitchen recipe, they seemed to require a lot of work for fries made in a device designed for ease. I wanted to find a way to simplify the process without sacrificing taste and texture.

It turns out that air-fryer fries benefit from the same tricks as their deep-fried kin. Russet potatoes are high in starch, which makes them cook up fluffy and tender. But all that starch can also turn the exteriors gummy and unappealing when fried, so soaking the potatoes in water to wash away some of that starch is essential. Luckily, I found that rinsing the cut potatoes and then soaking them in hot water for 10 minutes was sufficient to rid them of extra starch. The air fryer also enabled me to use significantly less oil; a couple of tablespoons was all I needed. My fries still had a few problems, though. Classic deep-frying recipes call for two-stage frying: once at a lower temperature to cook the fries through and a second time at a higher temperature to crisp them up. I simulated this in the air fryer by setting it to a lower temperature initially and raising the temperature once the fries were about halfway done, but my fries were cooking unevenly and tasted lean despite the oil. The solution came to me when I decided to toss the fries in a bit of oil and salt a second time partway through cooking. This redistributed the fries, allowing them to cook more evenly, and the additional salt and oil they picked up helped them achieve a truly crispy, golden crust.

Now that I had cracked the code for great air-fryer French fries, I aimed even higher: I would toss them with Parmesan and rosemary for an extra punch of flavor. I started off with ¼ cup of grated Parmesan and 2 teaspoons of minced fresh rosemary. It turned out that this small amount of Parmesan wasn't enough to achieve the bold, nutty flavor and extra-crispy crust I was after. Also, cooking the Parmesan with the potatoes in the air fryer dulled some of its fruity notes, and I wanted more pronounced rosemary flavor. Going forward, I tripled the amount of Parmesan from ¼ cup to ¾ cup and tried adding it at the very end, tossing it in a bowl with the cooked fries. This time, the fries still lacked Parmesan flavor—not because I hadn't added enough, but because it was falling off the fries and ending up on the bottom of the bowl. I finally found success when I tried adding the Parmesan in batches. Adding ¼ cup of Parmesan and 1 tablespoon of rosemary to the fries halfway through cooking deepened the flavor of the herbs and allowed the cheese to melt and adhere to the potatoes, crisping up on the edges for a crackly coating. I tossed another ¼ cup of the Parmesan and 1 teaspoon of rosemary with the fries when they were done cooking. Sprinkling a final ¼ cup of Parmesan over the top before serving made for a pretty presentation.

While my recipe may not be the simplest way to make air-fryer fries, my colleagues agreed that my efforts were worth it: When they weren't busy gobbling the fries down, my tasters said they were "the best non-fried French fries" they'd ever had.

—KATHERINE PERRY, *America's Test Kitchen Books*

Air-Fryer Parmesan, Rosemary, and Black Pepper French Fries
SERVES 2 TO 4

Do not clean out the tossing bowl while you are cooking; the residual oil helps the crisping process.

1½	pounds russet potatoes, unpeeled
2	tablespoons vegetable oil, divided
1½	ounces Parmesan cheese, grated (¾ cup), divided
4	teaspoons minced fresh rosemary, divided
¼	teaspoon table salt
¼	teaspoon pepper

1. Cut potatoes lengthwise into ½-inch-thick planks. Stack 3 or 4 planks and cut into ½-inch-thick sticks; repeat with remaining planks.

2. Submerge potatoes in large bowl of water and rinse to remove excess starch. Drain potatoes and repeat process as needed until water remains clear. Cover potatoes with hot tap water and let sit for 10 minutes. Drain potatoes, transfer to paper towel–lined rimmed baking sheet, and thoroughly pat dry.

3. In clean, dry bowl, toss potatoes with 1 tablespoon oil, then transfer to air fryer basket. Place basket in air fryer, set temperature to 350 degrees, and cook for 8 minutes. Transfer potatoes to now-empty bowl and gently toss to redistribute. Return potatoes to air fryer and cook until softened and potatoes have turned from white to blond (potatoes may be spotty brown at tips), 5 to 10 minutes.

4. Transfer potatoes to now-empty bowl and toss with ¼ cup Parmesan, 1 tablespoon rosemary, salt, pepper, and remaining 1 tablespoon oil. Return potatoes to air fryer, increase temperature to 400 degrees, and cook until golden brown and crispy, 15 to 20 minutes, tossing gently in bowl to redistribute every 5 minutes.

5. Transfer fries to bowl and toss with ¼ cup Parmesan and remaining 1 teaspoon rosemary. Season with salt and pepper to taste. Transfer to larger plate and sprinkle with remaining ¼ cup Parmesan. Serve immediately.

WHOLE ROMANESCO WITH BERBERE AND YOGURT-TAHINI SAUCE

✔ **WHY THIS RECIPE WORKS** This fractal-looking vegetable is perfect for cooking whole, as we do in this showstopping dish. For a tender interior and nicely charred exterior, we started by partially cooking the romanesco in the microwave. Then we brushed melted butter over the romanesco and transferred it to the oven to finish cooking and develop some browning. We basted the broiled romanesco with more butter and our take on berbere, a warmly aromatic and highly flavorful Ethiopian spice blend. A bright, cooling yogurt sauce and crunchy pine nuts finished it off.

A true farmers' market gem, romanesco is a stunning, alien-like vegetable closely related to cauliflower and broccoli. Considering its bright chartreuse color and unique fractal shape, it's surprising that romanesco, a member of the Brassicaceae family, hasn't hit vegetable fame like some of its relatives—cauliflower, Brussels sprouts, and kale—have. While a simple Google search of "cauliflower recipe" produces about 70 million results, the same search for romanesco produces a wimpy 800,000 results. I wanted to come up with a recipe that takes advantage of romanesco's impressive appearance while letting its somewhat crunchy texture and delicate flavor shine.

I started by simply breaking down a head of romanesco into small florets and sautéing it with basic aromatics. While it was tasty, I quickly realized that the appeal of romanesco isn't just its flavor—its over-the-top presentation also makes it stand out. With that in mind, I decided to keep the romanesco whole. My biggest challenge would be figuring out how to cook it so that the interior wasn't complete mush by the time the outside caramelized.

My initial plan of attack was simply throwing the romanesco head in the oven and roasting it until it was nice and brown. But as I pulled the romanesco out of the oven and cut into it, I realized that what I feared most had come true: By the time the outside was well browned, the inside was overcooked. Plus, it spent upwards of an hour in the oven—and no matter how grand, I didn't want to invest that much time preparing a vegetable. Scratch that. I'd have to find a quick and reliable cooking method that gave me a perfectly tender interior and a well-browned exterior. In the test kitchen, we often turn to the humble microwave to accelerate the vegetable-cooking process—would that approach work with the bulky romanesco?

In a word, yes. The even and diffuse heat of the microwave gently cooked the romanesco through in about 10 minutes. To infuse the vegetable with flavor from the get-go, I added 3 tablespoons of unsalted butter to a large bowl with the romanesco and covered the bowl before zapping it in the microwave. This also meant I didn't have to melt the butter separately in the microwave or on the stove. Covering the bowl helped capture more steam, therefore cooking the romanesco faster.

But the romanesco was still missing its charred exterior, which would not only amp up its stunning appearance but also add a complex layer of flavor through caramelization. The intense heat of the broiler would be the perfect environment to achieve an evenly browned surface. After transferring the microwaved romanesco to an ovensafe skillet, I broiled it for about 10 minutes. This romanesco emerged perfectly done from the inside out—tender on the inside and burnished on the outside. It was time to pump up the flavor profile with some vibrant seasonings and a complementary sauce to drizzle over my masterpiece.

Wanting to give the dish a deeply complex flavor, I had the idea to season the romanesco with berbere, an Ethiopian spice blend with prominent spicy, bitter, and sweet notes. Commonly used as a dry rub for meats, a seasoning for hearty stews, and even a tableside condiment like salt and pepper, berbere can contain up to 15 spices—paprika, ground dried chiles, and cayenne pepper for heat; cumin, coriander, and fenugreek for bitterness; cloves, allspice, nutmeg, and cinnamon for sweetness; and a slew of additional spices to round out its flavor. But much like cooking the romanesco itself, I wanted to keep it simple. So I raided the test kitchen's spice cabinet and gathered all of berbere's signature spices with the goal of streamlining it to a few ingredients that would touch on its key flavors.

I was able to pare the laundry list of spices down to just six: paprika, cayenne pepper, coriander, allspice, cardamom, and cumin. I mixed this simplified berbere with 3 tablespoons of butter and popped the mixture into the microwave to let the spices bloom in the butter as it melted. After removing the broiled romanesco from the oven, I basted it with my berbere butter to infuse it with flavor.

To balance out the bold berbere and butter-basted, straight-out-of-the-oven romanesco, I needed to whip up a cooling, tangy sauce to serve on the side. I simply whisked together whole-milk yogurt, tahini, lemon zest and juice, a bit of minced garlic, and salt and pepper. The bright acidity from the yogurt and lemon juice cut through the rich romanesco without overpowering it.

Just before serving, I cut the romanesco into wedges and sprinkled it with toasted chopped pine nuts for crunch and minced cilantro for freshness. Watch out kale and cauliflower—this brassica is more than worthy of viral internet fame.

—TIM CHIN, *America's Test Kitchen Books*

Whole Romanesco with Berbere and Yogurt-Tahini Sauce

SERVES 4

If you can't find a 2-pound head of romanesco, purchase two 1-pound heads, and reduce the microwaving time in step 2 to 5 to 7 minutes. Our favorite tahini is Ziyad Tahini Sesame Paste.

YOGURT-TAHINI SAUCE

- ½ cup whole-milk yogurt
- 2 tablespoons tahini
- 1 garlic clove, minced
- ½ teaspoon grated lemon zest plus 1 tablespoon juice

ROMANESCO

- 1 head romanesco or cauliflower (2 pounds)
- 6 tablespoons unsalted butter, cut into 6 pieces, divided
- ¼ teaspoon table salt
- ½ teaspoon paprika
- ¼ teaspoon cayenne pepper
- ¼ teaspoon ground coriander
- ⅛ teaspoon ground allspice
- ⅛ teaspoon ground cardamom
- ⅛ teaspoon ground cumin
- ⅛ teaspoon pepper
- 2 tablespoons toasted and coarsely chopped pine nuts
- 1 tablespoon minced fresh cilantro

1. FOR THE YOGURT-TAHINI SAUCE: Whisk all ingredients in bowl until combined. Season with salt and pepper to taste. Set aside until ready to serve.

2. FOR THE ROMANESCO: Adjust oven rack 6 inches from broiler element and heat broiler. Trim outer leaves of romanesco and cut stem flush with bottom florets. Microwave romanesco and 3 tablespoons butter, covered, in large bowl until paring knife slips easily into and out of core, 8 to 12 minutes.

3. Transfer romanesco, stem side down, to 12-inch ovensafe skillet. Brush romanesco evenly with melted butter from bowl and sprinkle with salt. Transfer skillet to oven and broil until top of romanesco is spotty brown, 8 to 10 minutes. Meanwhile, microwave paprika, cayenne, coriander, allspice, cardamom, cumin, pepper, and remaining 3 tablespoons butter in now-empty bowl, stirring occasionally, until fragrant and bubbling, 1 to 2 minutes.

4. Using potholder, remove skillet from oven and transfer to wire rack. Being careful of hot skillet handle, gently tilt skillet so butter pools to 1 side. Using spoon, baste romanesco until butter is absorbed, about 30 seconds.

5. Cut romanesco into wedges and transfer to serving platter. Season with salt to taste and sprinkle pine nuts and cilantro over top. Serve with sauce.

WHOLE ROMANESCO WITH BERBERE AND YOGURT-TAHINI SAUCE

PASTA, PIZZA, SANDWICHES, AND MORE

FALAFEL

✓ **WHY THIS RECIPE WORKS** The best falafel are moist, tender, packed with flavorful seasonings such as onion and herbs, and sturdy enough to form and fry. We started by soaking dried chickpeas overnight to soften them slightly before grinding them into coarse bits along with onion, herbs, garlic, and spices. Instead of binding the dough with raw flour, which yields dry, bready fritters, we mixed in a cooked-flour paste that added moisture without making the dough too fragile to work with. Cooking the fritters at a relatively low 325 degrees allowed their moist interiors to fully cook by the time their exteriors were brown and crispy.

Rather than insert myself into the age-old debate over the origins of falafel, I prefer to think of it as a preparation with ancient roots and timeless universal appeal. But my recipe may prove to be divisive in another way: The key to its success comes from a technique associated with Asian bread baking. Before I explain how I landed there, however, it's important to understand why falafel is inherently tricky to make well.

Most falafel dough is nothing more than uncooked dried chickpeas or fava beans that have been soaked overnight so that they soften slightly before being coarsely ground in a food processor with onion, garlic, spices, and loads of fresh herbs. Grinding—not pureeing—the beans is what makes good falafel pleasantly nubbly and light, not pasty, and the abundant seasonings add freshness, warmth, and complexity. But both of those factors make forming and frying the fritters a real challenge. Binding the coarse bean bits is like trying to make gravel stick together. The onion and herbs help make the falafel appealingly moist, but that moisture also makes the dough wet and often too fragile to pack into cohesive rounds or patties, never mind fry in a pot of vigorously bubbling oil.

That's why many recipes call for mixing starch into the dough—flour, cornstarch, and chickpea flour are all common additions. It's a surefire way to soak up that moisture and create a paste that helps bind the components so that the mixture is easy to handle and sturdy enough to withstand cooking. But the drawback, as I discovered when I made falafel with each of the three starches, is that when you use enough starch to act as an effective binder, it can render the falafel dense, dull-tasting, and overly dry.

Those competing goals would be the focus of my testing. But before I jumped in, I wanted to give the admittedly rogue idea of using canned chickpeas a whirl. But these were a complete bust. Just a few spins in the food processor turned the drained canned beans into a sludgy puree that translated into falafel that were equally pasty and sludgy. I'd stick with the soaked dried chickpeas after all. But how to make cohesive dough out of coarsely ground beans and loads of watery onion and herbs without drying out or otherwise ruining the falafel's texture? That was another matter—and where that Asian bread-baking technique came in handy.

It's called *tangzhong*. The gist is that you whisk together a little flour and water and briefly cook the mixture until it forms a smooth, pudding-like paste, which you then combine with the rest of the ingredients. In breads, this cooked paste miraculously allows you to add extra water to the dough without making it too sticky or soupy to handle. Even more impressive is the exceptionally moist and tender final result.

A cohesive mixture that would cook up moist and tender was exactly what I needed for my falafel, so I experimented with the ratio of flour paste to chickpea base until the mixture was easy to form and stayed intact during frying. When I scooped a fritter from the hot oil and took a bite, I knew I was onto something: It was not only wonderfully moist and tender but also much lighter-textured than the batches I'd made with uncooked starches.

The tangzhong method was a keeper, and I was able to lighten the texture of the fritters even more by adding a couple of spoonfuls of baking powder—an addition I saw in some modern falafel recipes—to the flour paste after microwaving. The only hitch was that by the time their exteriors were brown and crispy, these fritters, with their added moisture from the paste, were a tad raw at their cores. So I lowered the temperature of the oil from 350 to 325 degrees, which allowed them to fry longer without burning.

These falafel were killer: crispy and mahogany on the outside, with pleasantly nubbly, moist, and assertively seasoned interiors. When I stuffed them into fresh Pita Bread (page 186) with traditional fixings such as a lemony tahini sauce and a zingy tomato-chile puree, I felt convinced that nobody would fault me for introducing an Asian technique into a Middle Eastern classic. It may even go down in falafel history.

—STEVE DUNN, *Cook's Illustrated*

FALAFEL

Falafel

SERVES 4 TO 6 (MAKES 24 FALAFEL)

This recipe requires that the chickpeas be soaked for at least 8 hours. Use a Dutch oven that holds 6 quarts or more. Chickpea flour can be substituted for the all-purpose flour; if using, increase the water in step 4 to ½ cup. Do not substitute quick-soaked or canned chickpeas; they will make stodgy falafel. Serve the falafel with the tahini sauce as an appetizer or in Pita Bread (page 186) with lettuce, chopped tomatoes, chopped cucumbers, fresh cilantro, pickled vegetables (such as carrots, cabbage, or turnips), and Tomato-Chile Sauce (recipe follows), if desired. Serve the first batch of falafel immediately or hold it in a 200-degree oven while the second batch cooks.

FALAFEL

- 8 ounces dried chickpeas, picked over and rinsed
- ¾ cup fresh cilantro leaves and stems
- ¾ cup fresh parsley leaves
- ½ onion, chopped fine
- 2 garlic cloves, minced
- 1½ teaspoons ground coriander
- 1 teaspoon ground cumin
- 1 teaspoon table salt
- ¼ teaspoon cayenne pepper
- ¼ cup all-purpose flour
- 2 teaspoons baking powder
- 2 quarts vegetable oil, for frying

TAHINI SAUCE

- ⅓ cup tahini
- ⅓ cup plain Greek yogurt
- ¼ cup lemon juice (2 lemons)
- ¼ cup water

1. FOR THE FALAFEL: Place chickpeas in large container and cover with water by 2 to 3 inches. Soak at room temperature for at least 8 hours or up to 24 hours. Drain well.

2. FOR THE TAHINI SAUCE: Whisk tahini, yogurt, and lemon juice in medium bowl until smooth. Whisk in water to thin sauce as desired. Season with salt to taste; set aside. (Sauce can be refrigerated for up to 4 days. Let come to room temperature and stir to combine before serving.)

NOTES FROM THE TEST KITCHEN

KEEP IT COARSE

To achieve falafel's desirably nubbly, open structure (right), it's crucial to grind the soaked dried chickpeas just until they're broken down into coarse bits (sesame seeds are a good visual reference). Processing them any further will result in a pasty dough and dense fritters.

COARSE GRIND   **COARSE INTERIOR**

3. Process cilantro, parsley, onion, garlic, coriander, cumin, salt, and cayenne in food processor for 5 seconds. Scrape down sides of bowl. Continue to process until mixture resembles pesto, about 5 seconds longer. Add chickpeas and pulse 6 times. Scrape down sides of bowl. Continue to pulse until chickpeas are coarsely chopped and resemble sesame seeds, about 6 more pulses. Transfer mixture to large bowl and set aside.

4. Whisk flour and ⅓ cup water in separate bowl until no lumps remain. Microwave, whisking every 10 seconds, until mixture thickens to stiff, smooth, pudding-like consistency that forms mound when dropped from end of whisk into bowl, 40 to 80 seconds. Stir baking powder into flour paste.

5. Add flour paste to chickpea mixture and, using rubber spatula, mix until fully incorporated. Divide mixture into 24 pieces and gently roll into golf ball–size spheres. Transfer spheres to parchment paper–lined rimmed baking sheet once formed. (Falafel can be refrigerated for up to 2 hours.)

6. Heat oil in large Dutch oven over medium-high heat to 325 degrees. Add half of falafel and fry, stirring occasionally, until deep brown, about 5 minutes. Adjust burner, if necessary, to maintain oil temperature of 325 degrees. Using slotted spoon or spider skimmer, transfer falafel to paper towel–lined baking sheet. Return oil to 325 degrees and repeat with remaining falafel. Serve immediately with tahini sauce.

Tomato-Chile Sauce

MAKES ABOUT 1½ CUPS

The test kitchen's favorite canned diced tomatoes are Hunt's Diced Tomatoes.

- 1 (15-ounce) can diced tomatoes, drained
- ½ cup fresh cilantro leaves and stems
- 3 garlic cloves, minced
- 1 tablespoon red pepper flakes
- 1 tablespoon red wine vinegar, plus extra for seasoning
- 1 teaspoon ground cumin
- 1 teaspoon ground coriander
- ¾ teaspoon table salt
- ½ teaspoon smoked paprika
- ⅛ teaspoon sugar
- 2 tablespoons extra-virgin olive oil

Process tomatoes, cilantro, garlic, pepper flakes, vinegar, cumin, coriander, salt, paprika, and sugar in food processor until smooth paste forms, 20 to 30 seconds. With processor running, slowly add oil until fully incorporated, about 5 seconds. Transfer to bowl and season with salt and extra vinegar to taste.

SLIDERS

✔ WHY THIS RECIPE WORKS Good sliders share four essential qualities: crispy, charred exteriors; tender, juicy interiors; gooey, melty cheese; and soft buns. To achieve all four of these objectives at once, we came up with a plan. To start, we carefully divided ground beef into 2-ounce portions, weighing each to ensure that the portions would cook evenly. We then pressed the portions into uniform patties before cooking them quickly in a skillet. As they cooked, we sprinkled some finely chopped onion onto the patties and then pressed them firmly so that the onion would adhere. Once we flipped the patties (the sides with the onion were now facing down), we immediately topped them with cheese and the bun tops, added some water to the pan, and covered it. The evaporating water created steam, which melted the cheese and softened the onion and buns as the sliders finished cooking. A quick burger sauce rounded things out.

The miniature burgers known as sliders (popularized by the White Castle hamburger restaurant chain) satisfy a lot of cravings in just a few bites. Tender, beefy burger? Check. Soft, steamy roll? Check. Gooey melted cheese and sweet browned onions? Check and check. So why don't more people make sliders at home?

It might be the perceived bother of shaping and cooking lots of little burgers versus fewer larger ones. Since the burgers are so small, it's extra-important that they're all the same size to prevent any runts from overcooking. To portion and shape the patties efficiently and precisely, I used three common kitchen tools—a digital scale, a zipper-lock plastic bag, and a clear pie plate. After weighing out a dozen 2-ounce balls of ground beef (1½ pounds of meat) on the scale, I cut through the sides of a heavy quart-size plastic bag, placed a single beef ball between the layers, and used the pie plate to push the beef into an even, tidy 4-inch-diameter patty. Easy. On to the cooking.

Classic sliders come topped with browned onions—they're part of the signature flavor. But I didn't want to add another step and a second pan to my recipe. The trick, I discovered, was to sprinkle some finely chopped onion on top of the patties when they first hit the skillet and then press the onion into the meat with the back of a spatula. After I flipped the patties to brown them on the onion side, I topped each with American cheese and the bun top. These sliders tasted fine but weren't quite perfect: The onion had too much crunch, the cheese was barely melted, and the bun was a little stiff.

I thought back to the classic sliders I'd devoured at many fast-food restaurants and remembered how soft the buns had been. One colleague suggested I add some water and cover the skillet for the last bit of cooking (with the bun tops on the sliders) to achieve a similarly soft, steamy texture. Genius. The steam not only softened the buns but also helped finish cooking the finely chopped onion and fully melted the cheese.

Excited by these successes, I made another batch of sliders—this time with the bun bottoms slathered with an easy stir-together burger sauce—and eagerly called my team to taste. Our corner of the kitchen became eerily quiet before a colleague finally said, "I feel like I should be eating these out of a sack in the back seat of my mother's station wagon." That's just about the best compliment a slider can get.

—ASHLEY MOORE, *Cook's Country*

Sliders

MAKES 12 SLIDERS

Plan ahead: This recipe moves quickly, so be sure to have everything ready before you begin cooking. We recommend using Martin's Dinner Potato Rolls in this recipe. It is important to weigh each portion of beef to ensure that the patties cook consistently.

SAUCE

¼ cup mayonnaise
2 tablespoons ketchup
1 teaspoon sweet pickle relish
1 teaspoon sugar
1 teaspoon distilled white vinegar
1 teaspoon pepper

SLIDERS

1½ pounds 85 percent lean ground beef
12 (2½-inch) slider buns or soft dinner rolls, halved horizontally
6 slices deli American cheese (6 ounces), divided
1½ teaspoons kosher salt
1 teaspoon pepper
2 teaspoons vegetable oil, divided
½ cup finely chopped onion, divided
¼ cup water, divided

1. FOR THE SAUCE: Whisk all ingredients together in bowl; refrigerate until ready to use.

2. FOR THE SLIDERS: Cut sides of 1-quart zipper-lock bag, leaving bottom seam intact. Divide beef into twelve 2-ounce portions, then roll into balls. Working with 1 ball at a time, enclose in split bag. Using clear pie plate (so you can see size of patty), press ball into even 4-inch-diameter patty. Remove patty from bag and place on baking sheet. Cover sheet with plastic wrap and refrigerate until ready to cook. (Patties can be shaped up to 24 hours in advance.)

3. Divide sauce evenly among bun bottoms. Arrange bun bottoms, sauce side up, on platter; set aside. Stack American cheese and cut into quarters (you will have 24 pieces). Combine salt and pepper in bowl.

4. Sprinkle both sides of patties with salt-pepper mixture. Heat 1 teaspoon oil in 12-inch nonstick skillet over medium heat until just smoking. Using spatula, transfer 6 patties to skillet. Sprinkle ¼ cup onion evenly over tops of patties and press firmly into patties with back of spatula.

5. Cook patties, uncovered and without moving them, for 2 minutes. Flip patties and top each with 2 pieces American cheese; add bun tops. Add 2 tablespoons water to skillet (do not wet buns), cover, and continue to cook until cheese is melted, about 90 seconds longer.

6. Transfer sliders to prepared bun bottoms and tent with aluminum foil. Wipe skillet clean with paper towels. Repeat with remaining 1 teaspoon oil, 6 patties, ¼ cup onion, American cheese, bun tops, and 2 tablespoons water. Serve immediately.

CROQUE MONSIEUR

✔ WHY THIS RECIPE WORKS We were looking for a truly impressive version of this French bistro favorite—one featuring crisp buttered bread; salty-sweet ham; a creamy white sauce; and nutty Gruyère cheese. We chose to amp up the béchamel sauce called for in traditional recipes by adding both Gruyère and Parmesan cheeses. To cut down on prep time and ensure that the sandwiches were ready to eat at the same time, we assembled all four of them on a baking sheet, layering on the cheese sauce and Black Forest ham before topping them all with more sauce and cheese. A quick trip under the broiler was all that was needed to meld the sandwich ingredients and create a bubbly-browned top.

To define the croque monsieur (loosely translated from French as "Mr. Crunch") as a grilled ham-and-cheese sandwich is to vastly understate it. This big bistro favorite—two slices of butter-brushed bread toasted and layered with sweet, salty ham; creamy white sauce; and plenty of nutty Gruyère cheese—is beautiful to behold and so rich, runny, and substantial that it requires a fork and knife to eat.

The traditional method calls for griddling the sandwiches individually, topping them with cheese, and then sliding them under a broiler to finish, but I wanted four sandwiches all at once. And I wanted to keep the crunch in the croque and not allow the sauce to turn everything soggy.

All good sandwiches start with good bread, and after auditioning baguette, sourdough, and others, I chose eight slices of white sandwich bread, which stayed tender while also taking on plenty of crunch. After

CROQUE MADAME

brushing each slice evenly on both sides with melted butter, I lined them up on an oiled baking sheet and slipped them into the oven to toast.

Most recipes for croque monsieur call for a simple white sauce (a béchamel, which is common in many macaroni and cheese recipes) as well as grated Gruyère. To simplify things, I decided to combine the two into a cheesy sauce (adding cheese to a béchamel turns it into a Mornay sauce). Getting the perfect ratio of ingredients for a spreadable but not runny consistency took some testing, but after a few rounds, the best formula revealed itself: 2 tablespoons each of flour and butter, cooked together briefly, and then 1 cup of whole milk stirred in along with 1¼ cups of shredded and grated cheeses—Gruyère, of course, plus a bit of Parmesan to add even more savoriness. A pinch of nutmeg (a classic addition) contributed warmth and complexity.

Choosing the ham was an easy task. Black Forest ham sliced to order (very thin) from the deli is tender, flavorful, and miles ahead of the presliced, packaged ham rectangles you get from the supermarket cooler. Delicately folding the ham over itself before laying it on the sandwich, rather than simply stacking it in flat sheets, made the sandwich easier to eat; no big sheets of ham came sliding out when I took a bite.

A bit more cheese sauce spread over the top of the sandwich and a final sprinkling of Parmesan and Gruyère before a trip under the broiler to meld it all together created a gorgeous, melty, bubbly-browned top. The result was a sandwich worth savoring with a knife and fork: crunchy, grand, satisfying, and worthy of the title "monsieur."

—BRYAN ROOF WITH MATTHEW FAIRMAN, *Cook's Country*

Croque Monsieur

SERVES 4

For the best results, be sure to use a good-quality Gruyère cheese here.

SANDWICHES

- 8 slices hearty white sandwich bread
- 4 tablespoons unsalted butter, melted
- 12 ounces thinly sliced deli Black Forest ham
- ¼ cup grated Parmesan cheese
- 4 ounces Gruyère cheese, shredded (1 cup)

MORNAY SAUCE

- 2 tablespoons unsalted butter
- 2 tablespoons all-purpose flour
- 1 cup whole milk
- 4 ounces Gruyère cheese, shredded (1 cup)
- ¼ cup grated Parmesan cheese
- ½ teaspoon table salt
- ¼ teaspoon pepper
   Pinch ground nutmeg

1. FOR THE SANDWICHES: Adjust oven rack 6 inches from broiler element and heat oven to 375 degrees. Line rimmed baking sheet with aluminum foil and spray with vegetable oil spray.

2. Brush bread on both sides with melted butter and place on prepared sheet. Bake until light golden brown on top, about 10 minutes. Remove sheet from oven and flip slices. Return sheet to oven and bake until golden brown on second side, about 3 minutes. Reserve 4 slices for sandwich tops; evenly space remaining 4 slices on sheet.

3. FOR THE MORNAY SAUCE: Melt butter in small saucepan over medium heat. Whisk in flour and cook for 1 minute. Slowly whisk in milk and bring to boil. Once boiling, remove saucepan from heat and quickly whisk in Gruyère, Parmesan, salt, pepper, and nutmeg until smooth.

4. Spread 1 tablespoon Mornay on each slice of toast on sheet. Then, folding ham slices over themselves multiple times so they bunch up, divide ham evenly among slices of toast. Spread 2 tablespoons Mornay on 1 side of each reserved slice of toast and place slices Mornay side down on top of ham.

5. Spread 2 tablespoons Mornay evenly over top of each sandwich, making sure to cover toast completely, including edges (exposed edges can burn under broiler). Sprinkle sandwiches with Parmesan, followed by Gruyère.

6. Bake until cheese on tops of sandwiches is melted, about 5 minutes. Turn on broiler and broil until cheese bubbles across tops of sandwiches and edges are spotty brown, about 5 minutes. Serve.

VARIATION

Croque Madame

Top each sandwich with fried egg.

PHILLY TOMATO PIE

✔ WHY THIS RECIPE WORKS This South Philadelphia specialty boasts a tender yet chewy crust topped with a bright, savory tomato sauce. We achieved the signature chewy-soft crust by using less water by weight in proportion to the weight of the flour. This yielded fine holes and a pleasantly spongy chew. Letting the dough rise twice—pressing it into the pan in between—gave it maximum yeasty flavor. For the invigorating, herby sauce, we started with a savory base of onion and garlic and then added a hefty amount of dried oregano along with red pepper flakes for kick. One can of tomato sauce contributed just the right tomato flavor and texture, and a tablespoon of sugar provided the sauce's signature sweetness.

As a lover of all things topped with gooey melted cheese, I found Philly tomato pie puzzling at first. A South Philadelphia specialty, Philly tomato pie evolved as a frugal and resourceful way for the area's Italian American family-owned bakeries to use up leftover bread dough. It has a thick crust similar to that of Sicilian-style pizza. It's sold by the rectangular slice like Sicilian-style pizza. And like all pizza, it has tomato sauce. But this Philly pie features no cheese.

Though I initially wondered where the fun was in that, I've also never met a pizza I didn't like, so I kept an open mind and gave it a try. Philly tomato pie's crust is thick and chewy-soft. The sauce is invigorating—sweet-tart and herby. This pie is generally eaten at room temperature. Cheese or no cheese, I was smitten at first bite and eager to craft a home version that would be no different.

The recipes I tried missed the chewy-crust mark, instead ranging from superlight to dense-yet-pliable (read: cardboardy). The sauces were one-note, with sweetness that trampled the tomato flavor, and most overcooked on the pies, leaving thin, raisiny spots of dried-out sauce. Many recipes caved to outsider expectations of cheese (albeit not the gooey kind) grated on top. I intended to stick to the script: chewy-soft crust, bright sauce, and no cheese.

To get the texture of the crust right, I needed to know how water affected the dough. Generally speaking, the higher the ratio of water to flour in a dough, the more "open" or airy the crumb. Experimentation helped me find the best ratio of water to flour to produce an open and chewy texture.

Once I'd mixed a dough of flour, yeast, water, and oil in my stand mixer, I let it sit for 10 minutes to hydrate before adding salt—if added sooner, it would draw moisture away from the flour (see "Wait on the Salt"). I then turned on the mixer and let it do the remaining kneading. When the dough was satiny and sticky, I scooped it directly into a greased baking pan to relax and rise. Once the dough had doubled in size, I could easily shape it to fit the pan using my hands. Side-by-side tests of a dough that had risen only once, before shaping, and a dough that had risen a second time after shaping illustrated that more rising time meant more flavor development.

For an assertive sauce, I started by sautéing a bit of onion in olive oil and then flavored it with a moderate amount of minced garlic, a hefty amount of herby dried oregano, and, for kick, ¼ teaspoon of red pepper flakes. For the classic tomato flavor and texture, I added one 15-ounce can of tomato sauce, and for the sauce's signature sweetness, 1 tablespoon of sugar. Simmering it for 10 minutes allowed the flavors to meld and yielded enough sauce to cover the pie in a thin layer that wouldn't overreduce in the oven. Letting the sauce cool before spreading it and baking the pie made even coverage easier to achieve.

In typical tomato-pie fashion, I let my version cool to room temperature before serving it, and as with pieces scooped up in a South Philly family bakery, no one—myself included—missed the cheese.

—CECELIA JENKINS, *Cook's Country*

NOTES FROM THE TEST KITCHEN

WAIT ON THE SALT

To produce a chewy pizza crust, we use a technique called autolyse; this simply entails mixing the flour, yeast, and liquid but withholding the salt for a short period (10 minutes in this case). Salt slows flour's absorption of water, so delaying the addition of salt allows the flour to soak up liquid and become more thoroughly hydrated. More hydration means more gluten formation, which leads to a chewier finished crust—exactly what we were after here.

Philly Tomato Pie

SERVES 4

When kneading the dough on medium speed, the mixer may wobble and shimmy. To keep it in place, position a dish towel or shelf liner beneath the mixer and keep a close watch on it. You will need a nonstick metal baking pan for this recipe.

DOUGH

2½ cups (12½ ounces) all-purpose flour

¾ teaspoon instant or rapid-rise yeast

1 cup water, room temperature

1½ tablespoons extra-virgin olive oil

1½ teaspoons table salt

SAUCE

2 tablespoons extra-virgin olive oil

¼ cup finely chopped onion

2 garlic cloves, minced

2 teaspoons dried oregano

¼ teaspoon red pepper flakes

1 (15-ounce) can tomato sauce

1 tablespoon sugar

1. FOR THE DOUGH: Spray 13 by 9-inch nonstick baking pan with vegetable oil spray. Using stand mixer fitted with dough hook, mix flour and yeast on medium speed until combined, about 10 seconds. With mixer running, slowly add room-temperature water and oil and mix until dough forms and no dry flour remains, about 30 seconds, scraping down bowl as needed. Turn off mixer, cover bowl with plastic wrap, and let dough stand for 10 minutes.

2. Add salt to dough and knead on medium speed until dough is satiny and sticky and clears sides of bowl but still sticks to bottom, 6 to 8 minutes. Transfer dough to prepared pan, cover pan tightly with plastic, and let dough rise at room temperature until doubled in size, about 1½ hours.

3. FOR THE SAUCE: While dough rises, heat oil in small saucepan over medium heat until shimmering. Add onion and cook, stirring occasionally, until softened and lightly browned, 3 to 5 minutes. Add garlic, oregano, and pepper flakes and cook until fragrant, about 30 seconds. Add tomato sauce and sugar and bring to boil. Reduce heat to medium-low and simmer until sauce is slightly thickened and measures about 1¼ cups, about 10 minutes. Let sauce cool completely.

4. Using your well-oiled hands, press dough into corners of pan. (If dough resists stretching, let it rest for 10 minutes before trying to stretch again.) Cover pan tightly with plastic and let dough rise at room temperature until doubled in size, about 1½ hours. Adjust oven rack to upper-middle position and heat oven to 450 degrees.

5. Spread sauce evenly over dough, leaving ½- to ¼-inch border. Bake until edges are light golden brown and sauce has reduced in spots, about 20 minutes. Let tomato pie cool in pan on wire rack for 5 minutes. Run knife around edges of pan to loosen pie. Using spatula, slide pie onto cutting board. Cut into 8 pieces and serve.

PIZZA AL TAGLIO WITH ARUGULA AND FRESH MOZZARELLA

✔ **WHY THIS RECIPE WORKS** Our *pizza al taglio* recipe uses a dough containing lots of water and olive oil to create a tender and airy crust with a crispy, light underside. Because the dough was so wet, we folded it by hand (rather than employ a stand mixer) to develop gluten. We placed the dough in a baking pan to proof overnight in the refrigerator to develop flavor and allow the dough to relax for easy stretching to its final dimensions. We then coated the top of the dough with olive oil, turned it out onto a baking sheet, and allowed it to proof for an hour until it was bubbly and risen. Finally, we topped the pizza and baked it on the lowest rack of a 450-degree oven until the bottom was crispy and the toppings were baked.

In an unassuming pizzeria in a shopping plaza on the outskirts of Rome, I ate the greatest slice of pizza I've ever had. It was rectangular, about ¾ inch high, slicked with a nearly imperceptible varnish of tomato sauce, and topped with *soppressata*, oozy provolone and mozzarella cheeses, and paper-thin slices of potato. The sauce, soppressata, and cheeses made for a salty-savory punch, and the potatoes—not something I would normally think to include on pizza—were lightly crisped, browned, and curled at the edges. But the best part was the crust: full of irregularly sized holes, tender and chewy in equal measure, with an audibly crispy yet delicate bottom and a yeasty, tangy, complex flavor.

This memorable slice turned out to be a Roman invention known as *pizza al taglio*. Though it's baked in rectangular pans and cut into slabs like Sicilian pizza, its bubbly crumb and delicately crispy bottom bear more of a resemblance to good focaccia. And though the toppings on the slice I enjoyed had been applied before the crust went into the oven so they could cook and brown, pizza al taglio can also resemble an open-faced sandwich, with fresh or uncooked items such as salad greens, soft cheeses, or cured meats piled on when the crust comes out of the oven. Roman pizzerias sell it by the length and cut it with scissors (*al taglio* means "by the cut").

The challenge to creating my own version of al taglio would be designing a crust that was substantial yet also tender and airy. The few recipes I found for al taglio dough aimed to do this through two interrelated approaches: high hydration and long fermentation.

Putting lots of water in the dough serves two functions. One, it aids in the gluten development necessary for good structure. Two, it makes the gluten strands more flexible, which allows them to stretch and expand during baking to produce an airy crumb full of large and small holes.

A long, cool fermentation of at least 16 hours also serves a couple of functions: At lower temperatures, the yeast produces more of the desirable acids that give bread better, more complex flavor than it does at room temperature. And though shorter rests help strengthen gluten, longer rests actually loosen the gluten structure, making it more flexible and the crust more tender.

With all that in mind, I put together a working recipe I settled on a 75 percent hydration level (meaning 75 grams of water for every 100 grams of flour), 1 tablespoon of olive oil, 1 teaspoon of instant yeast, and 1¼ teaspoons of salt.

All the al taglio recipes I found called for mixing the dough by hand. Furthermore, instead of kneading the dough, they called for folding it over itself several times, letting it rest, and then repeating the folds and the rest one or two more times. I loved how low-tech this approach was, and I followed suit: I stirred together bread flour, yeast, water, and oil until no dry flour remained. I covered the dough and let it rest for 10 minutes. This quick rest lets the flour absorb water and encourages gluten development to begin before the salt (which would inhibit both) is added. Then I stirred in the salt and let the dough sit for another 20 minutes.

HOW TO FOLD DOUGH

Instead of kneading the dough, our recipe calls for folding it in on itself, letting it rest, and then folding and letting it rest again. This allows gluten to develop. Here's how we do it.

1. Grasp edge of dough with your wet fingertips and gently lift.

2. Place edge down in middle of dough. Rotate bowl 90 degrees and repeat for total of 6 turns.

It was time to fold. After wetting my hands to prevent the dough from sticking to them, I gently lifted the edge of the dough and brought it to the middle, repeating these folds all the way around the dough. After 20 minutes, I gave the dough another set of folds. These simple movements, in combination with time, were a surprisingly effective way to build gluten in this wet dough. The dough was now smooth and supple; it was also starting to show plenty of yeast activity. I then covered the bowl with plastic wrap and placed it in the refrigerator to ferment overnight.

After its overnight rest, I turned the dough out onto a baking sheet liberally coated with vegetable oil spray and stretched it toward the corners of the sheet. I covered the dough, let it proof at room temperature until it was slightly puffy, and then brushed on a tomato sauce and baked it in the middle of a 450-degree oven instead of the usual 500-degree oven. I hoped a lower temperature (and thus a longer baking time) would crisp the bottom of the crust sufficiently without a baking stone. After about 25 minutes, the bottom was reasonably crispy and the top was browned.

The crust from this first go-round wasn't bad. It had great flavor, good stature, and a decent mix of large and small air pockets. But it wasn't quite as light and tender as I wanted it to be. There were also some mechanical

PIZZA AL TAGLIO

issues. Even after sitting in the baking sheet for an hour, the dough was a little elastic and thus hard to fully and evenly stretch over the surface of the sheet.

To improve the crust's texture, I started by increasing the amount of water. At 80 percent hydration, it was definitely lighter, airier, and more tender. And 85 percent was even better, but at that point it was a very sticky dough that was challenging to work with. So I settled on 82 percent—12 ounces of water and 14⅔ ounces of flour—as an easier-to-handle compromise. I also upped the olive oil in the dough from 1 to 2 tablespoons, since fat makes gluten strands more flexible during proofing, allowing larger air pockets to form without bursting.

All that remained was to improve my shaping and baking approach. Though the dough was plenty relaxed after its rest in the refrigerator, all the manhandling I did trying to stretch a round ball into a wide rectangle made the dough prone to springing back from the edges of the sheet. What if I started out with something more rectangular in shape? Instead of fermenting the dough in its mixing bowl overnight, I moved it to a baking pan and pressed it into an oval before wrapping the pan and placing it in the refrigerator.

The next day, I turned the dough out onto a baking sheet. Fully relaxed and more than halfway to its final dimensions, it was easy to stretch the rest of the way by dimpling the dough and dragging it toward the corners of the sheet. This gentle treatment helped it retain the air pockets that had formed during proofing, resulting in the best crust yet. (I avoided proofing the dough overnight in the baking sheet because the dough needs plenty of oil on its underside to prevent sticking and to help it crisp on the bottom. The oil also needs to go on shortly before baking so that it doesn't get absorbed by the dough.) Finally, to get the bottom to crisp up more, I moved the sheet from the middle of the oven to the lowest rack, closer to the heat source.

Nearly anything you might want to put on top of bread can work as an al taglio topping. I topped one version with arugula, fresh mozzarella, and Parmesan when it came out of the oven. I piled prosciutto, fresh figs, and ricotta salata on another. To re-create that epic slice from Rome, I layered a third version with soppressata, provolone, and potato slices.

I'd never pass up a chance to go back to that pizzeria in Rome. But now that I have my own "pizza by the cut," I don't have to.

—ANDREW JANJIGIAN, *Cook's Illustrated*

Pizza al Taglio with Arugula and Fresh Mozzarella
SERVES 4 TO 6

The dough for this pizza requires a 16- to 24-hour rest in the refrigerator. You'll get the crispiest texture by using high-protein King Arthur bread flour, but other bread flours will also work. Weigh your flour and water for the best results. Anchovies give the sauce depth, so don't omit them; they won't make the sauce taste fishy.

DOUGH
- 2⅔ cups (14⅔ ounces) bread flour
- 1 teaspoon instant or rapid-rise yeast
- 1½ cups (12 ounces) water, room temperature
- 2 tablespoons extra-virgin olive oil
- 1¼ teaspoons table salt
- Vegetable oil spray

SAUCE
- 1 (14.5-ounce) can whole peeled tomatoes, drained
- 1 tablespoon extra-virgin olive oil
- 2 anchovy fillets, rinsed
- 1 teaspoon dried oregano
- ½ teaspoon table salt
- ¼ teaspoon red pepper flakes

TOPPING
- ¼ cup extra-virgin olive oil, divided
- 4 ounces (4 cups) baby arugula
- 8 ounces fresh mozzarella cheese, torn into bite-size pieces (2 cups)
- 1½ ounces Parmesan cheese, shredded (½ cup)

1. FOR THE DOUGH: Whisk flour and yeast together in medium bowl. Add room-temperature water and oil and stir with wooden spoon until shaggy mass forms and no dry flour remains. Cover bowl with plastic wrap and let sit for 10 minutes. Sprinkle salt over dough and mix until fully incorporated. Cover bowl with plastic and let dough rest for 20 minutes.

2. Using your wet hands, fold dough over itself by gently lifting and folding edge of dough toward middle. Turn bowl 90 degrees; fold again. Turn bowl and fold dough 4 more times (total of 6 turns). Cover bowl with plastic and let dough rest for 20 minutes. Repeat folding technique, turning bowl each time, until dough tightens slightly, 3 to 6 turns total. Cover bowl with plastic and let dough rest for 10 minutes.

3. Spray bottom of 13 by 9-inch baking pan liberally with oil spray. Transfer dough to prepared pan and spray top of dough lightly with oil spray. Gently press dough into 10 by 7-inch oval of even thickness. Cover pan tightly with plastic and refrigerate for at least 16 hours or up to 24 hours.

4. FOR THE SAUCE: While dough rests, process all ingredients in blender until smooth, 20 to 30 seconds. Transfer sauce to bowl, cover, and refrigerate until needed. (Sauce can be refrigerated in airtight container for up to 2 days.)

5. FOR THE TOPPING: Brush top of dough with 2 tablespoons oil. Spray rimmed baking sheet (including rim) with oil spray. Invert prepared sheet on top of pan and flip, allowing dough to fall onto sheet (you may need to lift pan and nudge dough at 1 end to release). Using your fingertips, gently dimple dough into even thickness and stretch toward edges of sheet to form 15 by 11-inch oval. Spray top of dough lightly with oil spray, cover loosely with plastic, and let rest until slightly puffy, 1 to 1¼ hours.

6. Thirty minutes before baking, adjust oven rack to lowest position and heat oven to 450 degrees. Just before baking, use your fingertips to gently dimple dough into even thickness, pressing into corners of sheet. Using back of spoon or ladle, spread ½ cup sauce in even layer over surface of dough. (Remaining sauce can be frozen for up to 2 months.)

7. Drizzle 1 tablespoon oil over sauce and use back of spoon to spread evenly over surface. Transfer sheet to oven and bake until bottom of crust is evenly browned and top is lightly browned in spots, 20 to 25 minutes, rotating sheet halfway through baking. Transfer sheet to wire rack and let cool for 5 minutes. Run knife around rim of sheet to loosen pizza. Transfer pizza to cutting board and cut into 8 rectangles. Toss arugula with remaining 1 tablespoon oil in bowl. Top pizza with arugula, followed by mozzarella and Parmesan, and serve.

VARIATIONS

Pizza al Taglio with Potatoes and Soppressata

Decrease oil in topping to 3 tablespoons and omit arugula, mozzarella, and Parmesan. After spreading sauce over dough, lay 6 ounces thinly sliced soppressata in even layer over sauce, followed by 10 ounces thinly sliced provolone. Toss 1 pound peeled and thinly sliced small Yukon Gold potatoes with ½ teaspoon pepper and remaining 1 tablespoon oil. Starting in 1 corner, shingle potatoes to form even row across bottom of pizza, overlapping each slice by about one-quarter. Continue to layer potatoes in rows, overlapping each row by about one-quarter. Bake pizza as directed until bottom of crust is evenly browned and potatoes are browned around edges. Sprinkle pizza with 2 teaspoons chopped fresh parsley before serving.

Pizza al Taglio with Prosciutto and Figs

Omit sauce ingredients as well as arugula, mozzarella, and Parmesan in topping. Spread remaining 2 table-spoons oil evenly over dough. Bake pizza as directed until bottom of crust is evenly browned and top is lightly browned in spots. Let pizza cool, then cut as directed. Top slices of pizza with 4 ounces thinly sliced prosciutto, followed by 8 thinly sliced figs and 2 ounces thinly shaved ricotta salata.

CRISPY TACOS (TACOS DORADOS)

✓ **WHY THIS RECIPE WORKS** Commercial taco kits are convenient, but the seasoning packets taste flat and the shells are prone to cracking. Frying your own shells results in great taste and texture, but the process is tedious and messy. Instead, we made *tacos dorados*, a Mexican preparation in which corn tortillas are stuffed with a beef filling before being folded in half and fried. We first tossed ground beef with a bit of baking soda to help it stay juicy before adding it to a savory base of sautéed onion, spices, and tomato paste. Next, we stirred in shredded cheese to make the filling more cohesive. To build the tacos, we brushed corn tortillas with oil, warmed them in the oven to make them pliable, and stuffed them with the filling. Finally, we pan-fried the tacos in two batches until they were supercrispy and golden.

Maybe it's nostalgia—the first bite that cracks the shell, sending orange grease down your wrist. Or perhaps it's the satisfying combination of spiced meat, creamy cheese, and cool, crisp lettuce that makes hard-shell tacos so popular. Either way, Americans have an enduring love for this lunchroom and dinnertime staple.

Ease is a big part of the appeal: Relying on a packet of powdered taco seasoning and a sleeve of prefried taco shells means that dinner comes together in a flash. But when I recently prepared tacos using the contents of a supermarket kit, my middle school memories were obscured by a dust cloud of flat spices covering dry, nubbly meat.

I'd followed the kit's instructions for preparing the shells, baking them for a few minutes before serving, and they were fine, though not terribly flavorful. Frying your own shells into the proper U shape using corn tortillas produces better results—rich corn flavor and a light, crispy texture that's miles apart from the hard crunch of the prefab type—but the process is tedious and messy.

Not truly satisfied with either choice, I dug into the history of hard-shell tacos. It turns out that although commercially made hard-shell tacos are an American innovation, crispy-shell tacos have long existed in Mexico under the name *tacos dorados*, or "golden tacos." The way they're prepared is pure genius: Soft corn tortillas are filled, folded in half, and then deep-fried. At the table, the tacos are opened like a book and stuffed with garnishes.

After just one go-round with the filling-before-frying method, I was hooked. The fried shells were shatteringly crispy on their flat sides yet flexible at their spines, so they didn't break into a million pieces when I took a bite, and they boasted true corn flavor. This was what I had been craving; I just needed to come up with a low-fuss technique.

Before I tackled frying the filled tortillas, I wanted to revamp the usual beef taco filling to work in my tacos dorados. I started with 90 percent lean ground beef, figuring that 85 percent would be on the greasy side. To ensure that the meat stayed tender and juicy, I used a test kitchen trick: raising its pH with baking soda to help the proteins attract and retain more water. I combined ¼ teaspoon of baking soda with 1 tablespoon of water so it would distribute evenly. I then stirred it into the raw beef and let the mixture sit.

Meanwhile, I sautéed finely chopped onion and added modest amounts of common taco seasonings—chili powder, paprika, ground cumin, and garlic powder—to bloom in the oil and release their flavors. Then I added the treated beef and cooked it until it lost its pink color.

It was a fine start, but I wanted a bolder spice flavor and more meaty depth. I increased all the spices to a total ¼ cup, and to boost the savoriness, I cooked a couple of tablespoons of umami-rich tomato paste in the skillet with the onion before adding the beef. My filling was now well spiced and rich-tasting. It was time to stuff the meat into tortillas and fry them up.

To ensure that the tortillas were pliable enough to be filled without cracking or falling apart, I borrowed a technique that we use for enchiladas: brushing each side with oil and then briefly baking the tortillas until they become flexible.

But even with tortillas that cooperated nicely, my filling was a little loose and tended to spill out. I tried binding it with flour and even with mashed canned beans, but ultimately it was easier simply to stir in some of the cheddar cheese I was already using as a garnish. I mixed ½ cup of the shredded cheddar into the beef while it was still hot. The cheese melted seamlessly, helping the beef stay put in the tortilla and enriching the mixture as well.

Finally, instead of deep-frying, which seemed fussy for these slender tacos, I simply shallow-fried them in the same skillet I'd used to cook the beef. I was able to fry 12 tacos in just ¼ cup of oil, and with some strategic arrangement in the skillet, I could complete the job in two batches of six.

As my colleagues eagerly pried open the tacos, added garnishes, and crunched away, I knew I had upped my taco game for good.

—ANNIE PETITO, *Cook's Illustrated*

NOTES FROM THE TEST KITCHEN

SHELLS THAT DON'T SPLIT
We've all eaten tacos that shatter at the first bite. That's why we were happy to find that stuffing tortillas with filling before frying them not only produces great-tasting tacos but also creates crispy yet flexible shells that stay intact when you dive in.

TO WIT We pried our taco shells open to a 90-degree angle with no splitting or cracking, an impossible feat with store-bought shells.

CRISPY TACOS (TACOS DORADOS)

Crispy Tacos (Tacos Dorados)

SERVES 4

Arrange the tacos so they face the same direction in the skillet to make them easy to fit and flip. To ensure crispy tacos, cook the tortillas until they are deeply browned. To garnish, open each taco like a book and load it with your preferred toppings; close it to eat.

1	tablespoon water
¼	teaspoon baking soda
12	ounces 90 percent lean ground beef
7	tablespoons vegetable oil, divided
1	onion, chopped fine
1½	tablespoons chili powder
1½	tablespoons paprika
1½	teaspoons ground cumin
1½	teaspoons garlic powder
1	teaspoon table salt
2	tablespoons tomato paste
2	ounces cheddar cheese, shredded (½ cup), plus extra for serving
12	(6-inch) corn tortillas
	Shredded iceberg lettuce
	Chopped tomato
	Sour cream
	Pickled jalapeño slices
	Hot sauce

1. Adjust oven rack to middle position and heat oven to 400 degrees. Combine water and baking soda in large bowl. Add beef and mix until thoroughly combined. Set aside.

2. Heat 1 tablespoon oil in 12-inch nonstick skillet over medium heat until shimmering. Add onion and cook, stirring occasionally, until softened, 4 to 6 minutes. Add chili powder, paprika, cumin, garlic powder, and salt and cook, stirring frequently, until fragrant, about 1 minute. Stir in tomato paste and cook until paste is rust-colored, 1 to 2 minutes. Add beef mixture and cook, using wooden spoon to break meat into pieces no larger than ¼ inch, until beef is no longer pink, 5 to 7 minutes. Transfer beef mixture to bowl; stir in cheddar until cheese has melted and mixture is homogeneous. Wipe skillet clean with paper towels.

3. Thoroughly brush both sides of tortillas with 2 tablespoons oil. Arrange tortillas, overlapping, on rimmed baking sheet in 2 rows (6 tortillas each). Bake until tortillas are warm and pliable, about 5 minutes. Remove tortillas from oven and reduce oven temperature to 200 degrees.

4. Place 2 tablespoons filling on 1 side of 1 tortilla. Fold and press to close tortilla (edges will be open, but tortilla will remain folded). Repeat with remaining filling and remaining tortillas. (At this point, filled tortillas can be covered and refrigerated for up to 12 hours.)

5. Set wire rack in second rimmed baking sheet and line rack with double layer of paper towels. Heat remaining ¼ cup oil in now-empty skillet over medium-high heat until shimmering. Arrange 6 tacos in skillet with open sides facing away from you. Cook, adjusting heat so oil actively sizzles and bubbles appear around edges of tacos, until tacos are crispy and deeply browned on 1 side, 2 to 3 minutes. Using tongs and thin spatula, carefully flip tacos. Cook until deeply browned on second side, 2 to 3 minutes, adjusting heat as necessary.

6. Remove skillet from heat and transfer tacos to prepared wire rack. Blot tops of tacos with double layer of paper towels. Place sheet with fried tacos in oven to keep warm. Return skillet to medium-high heat and cook remaining tacos. Serve tacos immediately, passing lettuce, tomato, sour cream, jalapeños, hot sauce, and extra cheddar separately.

THREE-CHEESE RAVIOLI WITH BROWNED BUTTER–PINE NUT SAUCE

✔ **WHY THIS RECIPE WORKS** We started our ravioli by using a simple three-ingredient, egg-rich pasta dough that was quick to make in a food processor and was easily rolled thin by hand. We then developed a method for portioning the filling, cutting the dough into rectangles, and folding the dough over the filling that required no special equipment and made it easy to ensure that all air bubbles were removed from the ravioli so they didn't burst during cooking. Our three-cheese blend of ricotta, fontina, and Parmesan delivered nuanced flavor and a pleasantly smooth texture. We topped the ravioli with a classic—and simple—browned butter–pine nut sauce.

When I have the time, I relish the opportunity to slow down, roll up my sleeves, and turn to projects such as making ravioli the traditional way, without a pasta machine. There is something magical about mixing up a supple dough and then using only a rolling pin and a knife to create a stuffed pasta.

A few years ago, we designed a pasta recipe to be rolled without a machine. It relies heavily on egg yolks and oil to provide enough fat to limit gluten development so the dough can be rolled without springing back. Cut into strands, boiled, and tossed with a creamy tomato sauce, the pasta is a real winner.

To see how the dough would work as the wrapper for ravioli, I whipped up a batch in the food processor. After a resting period to allow the flour to hydrate and the gluten to relax, it was easy to roll into long sheets. Working with one sheet at a time, I brushed the lower half of the long side with egg white (this would help seal the ravioli) and then deposited six mounds of a simple ricotta filling on top of the egg white.

Covering the filling was tricky: I folded the top half of the sheet toward me and suspended the dough with one hand while using my other hand to enclose each mound in dough and press out air. (Trapped air would create pockets of steam during cooking that could cause the wrapper to burst.) Once the perimeter of each mound was sealed, I cut the sheet into individual ravioli and boiled them for 6 minutes.

The filling was lackluster, but I could easily fix that. I was more concerned that the pasta seemed underdone, especially at the edges where it was doubled.

To jazz up the ricotta, I folded in bits of creamy fontina and shreds of nutty Parmesan along with a little heady nutmeg. I also fine-tuned my shaping method: Instead of folding the entire 18-inch length of dough over the mounds of cheese, I cut the sheet into six rectangles and folded them individually.

Now to address the underdone doubled edges. Most ravioli recipes call for rolling the dough superthin, but that is incredibly difficult to do by hand. Instead, I just let the boiling water do the work for me: I cooked another batch and sampled the ravioli at the 7-minute mark and every minute thereafter until the pasta was supple yet resilient, which took a full 13 minutes.

Topped with an elegant sauce of browned butter studded with toasted pine nuts, these pillowy three-cheese ravioli were something to be savored.

—STEVE DUNN, *Cook's Illustrated*

Three-Cheese Ravioli with Browned Butter–Pine Nut Sauce

SERVES 4 TO 6 (MAKES 36 RAVIOLI)

If using King Arthur All-Purpose Flour, increase the egg yolks to seven. To ensure the proper dough texture, weigh the flour and make sure to use large eggs. The longer the dough rests in step 2, the easier it will be to roll out. When rolling the dough, don't add too much flour; it can cause excessive snapback. You can use a pasta machine if you prefer. If you don't have a pot that holds 6 quarts, cook the ravioli in two batches; toss the first batch with some sauce in a bowl, cover it with foil, and keep it warm in a 200-degree oven while the second batch cooks. Watch the pine nuts carefully while toasting to ensure that they don't burn.

PASTA DOUGH

- 2 cups (10 ounces) all-purpose flour, plus extra as needed
- 2 large eggs plus 6 large yolks
- 2 tablespoons extra-virgin olive oil

FILLING

- 8 ounces (1 cup) whole-milk ricotta cheese
- 4 ounces Italian fontina cheese, cut into ¼-inch pieces (1 cup)
- 2 ounces Parmesan cheese, grated (1 cup), plus extra for serving
- 1 large egg
- ½ teaspoon pepper
- ¼ teaspoon table salt
- ⅛ teaspoon ground nutmeg

RAVIOLI

- 1 large egg white, lightly beaten
- Table salt for cooking

SAUCE

- 8 tablespoons unsalted butter
- ½ cup pine nuts, toasted
- 2 tablespoons chopped fresh parsley
- ½ teaspoon table salt

1. FOR THE PASTA DOUGH: Process flour, eggs and yolks, and oil in food processor until mixture forms cohesive dough that feels barely tacky to touch, about 45 seconds. (Pinch dough between your fingers; if any dough sticks to your fingers, add up to ¼ cup extra flour, 1 tablespoon at a time. Process until flour is fully incorporated after each addition, 10 to 15 seconds, before retesting. If dough doesn't become cohesive, add up to 1 tablespoon water, 1 teaspoon at a time, until it just comes together; process 30 seconds longer.)

2. Turn out dough onto dry counter and knead until smooth, 1 to 2 minutes. Shape dough into 6-inch-long cylinder. Wrap in plastic wrap and let rest at room temperature for at least 1 hour or up to 4 hours. Wipe processor bowl clean.

3. FOR THE FILLING: Process all ingredients in now-empty processor until smooth paste forms, 25 to 30 seconds, scraping down sides of bowl as needed. Transfer filling to medium bowl, cover with plastic, and refrigerate until needed.

4. Line rimmed baking sheet with parchment paper. Cut dough cylinder crosswise into 6 equal pieces. Working with 1 piece of dough at a time (keep remaining pieces covered), dust both sides with flour, place cut side down on clean counter, and press into 3-inch square. Using heavy rolling pin, roll into 6-inch square.

5. Dust both sides of 1 dough square lightly with flour. Starting at center of square, roll dough away from you in 1 motion. Return rolling pin to center of dough and roll toward you in 1 motion. Repeat rolling steps until dough sticks to counter and measures roughly 12 inches long. Lightly dust both sides of dough with flour and continue to roll out dough until it measures roughly 20 inches long and 6 inches wide, frequently lifting dough to release it from counter. (If dough firmly sticks to counter and wrinkles when rolled out, carefully lift dough and dust counter lightly with flour.) Transfer dough sheet to prepared baking sheet and cover with plastic. Repeat rolling with remaining 5 dough squares and transfer to prepared sheet (2 dough sheets per layer; place parchment between layers). Keep dough covered with plastic.

6. FOR THE RAVIOLI: Line second baking sheet with parchment. Lay 1 dough sheet on clean counter with long side parallel to counter edge (keep others covered). Trim ends of dough with sharp knife so that corners are square and dough is 18 inches long. Brush bottom half of dough with egg white. Starting 1½ inches from left edge of dough and 1 inch from bottom, deposit 1 tablespoon filling. Repeat placing 1-tablespoon mounds of filling, spaced 1½ inches apart, 1 inch from bottom edge of dough. You should be able to fit 6 mounds of filling on 1 dough sheet.

7. Cut dough sheet at center points between mounds of filling, separating it into 6 equal pieces. Working with 1 piece at a time, lift top edge of dough over filling and extend it so that it lines up with bottom edge. Keeping top edge of dough suspended over filling with your thumbs, use your fingers to press layers together, working around each mound of filling from back to front, pressing out as much air as possible before sealing completely.

8. Once all edges are sealed, use sharp knife or fluted pastry wheel to cut excess dough from around filling, leaving ¼- to ½-inch border around each mound (it's not necessary to cut folded edge of ravioli, but you may do so, if desired). (Dough scraps can be frozen and added to soup.) Transfer ravioli to prepared baking sheet. Refrigerate until ready to cook. Repeat shaping process with remaining dough and remaining filling.

9. Bring 6 quarts water to boil in large pot. Add ravioli and 1 tablespoon salt. Cook, maintaining gentle boil, until ravioli are just tender, about 13 minutes. (To test, pull 1 ravioli from pot, trim off corner without cutting into filling, and taste. Return ravioli to pot if not yet tender.) Drain well.

10. FOR THE SAUCE: While ravioli cook, melt butter in 10-inch skillet over medium-high heat. Continue to cook, swirling skillet constantly, until butter is dark golden brown and has nutty aroma, 1 to 3 minutes longer. Off heat, add pine nuts, parsley, and salt. Using spider skimmer or slotted spoon, transfer ravioli to warmed bowls or plates; top with sauce. Serve immediately, passing extra Parmesan separately.

TO MAKE AHEAD: Freeze uncooked ravioli in single layer on parchment paper–lined rimmed baking sheet. Transfer frozen ravioli to zipper-lock bag and freeze for up to 1 month. Cook from frozen with no change to cooking time.

NOTES FROM THE TEST KITCHEN

TASTING WHOLE-MILK RICOTTA CHEESE

Ricotta should be creamy and dense, with a fresh dairy flavor. To find one that fit the bill, we tasted four whole-milk ricottas both plain and in baked manicotti. We found our favorite in **Belgioioso Ricotta con Latte Whole Milk Ricotta Cheese**. Tasters described this slightly sweet ricotta's consistency as "luscious." In manicotti, the ricotta added richness but didn't flatten the flavors of the herbs and tomato sauce.

CHEESY STUFFED SHELLS

✔ WHY THIS RECIPE WORKS For a quicker version of stuffed shells, we got right down to stuffing them—no parboiling first. We found that the quickest and easiest way to fill the raw pasta shells was to choose jumbo shells with wide openings and pipe in the filling using a pastry bag. For a supercheesy filling, we mixed creamy ricotta, shredded fontina, and grated Pecorino Romano cheeses with savory minced garlic, fragrant chopped fresh basil, and dried oregano. We stirred cornstarch into the filling to keep the ricotta from becoming grainy once it was baked. We also added two eggs to make the filling pipable and to keep it from oozing out of the shells during baking. Smothering the filled shells in a thin tomato sauce meant that the pasta cooked through properly during baking, absorbing liquid while still leaving behind a full-bodied—not chunky or dehydrated—sauce. We first baked the shells covered to trap as much moisture as possible and cook the pasta and then uncovered to brown the cheese sprinkled over the top and reduce the sauce.

My ultimate comfort food: jumbo pasta shells stuffed with cheese, topped with tomato sauce and more cheese, and baked until golden brown.

But stuffed shell recipes can be frustrating. Most call for precooking the shells and then using a spoon or pastry bag to fill them without ripping them to shreds. Some demand that you simmer a sauce for hours before it goes over the shells. Some cheater recipes don't even bother with stuffing the shells, instead instructing you to just stir everything together and bake for an hour or longer; in the end, you're left with a mess of torn pasta and grainy cheese. I wanted an easier process and better results.

I first focused on the parboiling step. Would uncooked shells, filled and sauced, soften enough in the oven? We've used a similar approach for other baked pasta dishes (such as baked ziti), so I headed into the test kitchen to see if this shortcut would work.

I picked 25 open raw shells from the box (to fill a typical 13 by 9-inch baking dish). Then I transferred some seasoned ricotta to a plastic zipper-lock bag, snipped off one corner, and piped the cheese into the shells. Once I'd added a quick marinara sauce and some shredded cheese, I covered the dish tightly with foil and baked it. But the sauce cooked down too far, leaving some pasta exposed and undercooked.

I needed a thinner sauce with more liquid. I added 2 cups of water; this time, the shells absorbed the liquid they needed and cooked through properly, leaving behind a rich but still fluid—not chunky and dehydrated—sauce.

After a great deal of testing, I landed on a flavorful filling that melted well: ricotta, fontina, Pecorino Romano, basil, dried oregano, and garlic. Two eggs stirred into the mixture helped the filling stay put as the stuffed shells baked and made the filling easier to pipe. And a bit of cornstarch helped the filling maintain a silky texture.

After 45 minutes of covered cooking in the oven, the shells were nearly done. I removed the foil and sprinkled more fontina over the top. After just 15 minutes more, I had a bubbling-around-the-edges, beautifully browned casserole of cheesy, saucy, superflavorful stuffed shells. Bonus: You can even assemble the dish in advance and bake it the next day.

—CECELIA JENKINS, *Cook's Country*

Cheesy Stuffed Shells

SERVES 6 TO 8

Shred the fontina on the large holes of a box grater. Be sure to use only open, unbroken shells here. We developed this recipe using Barilla Jumbo Shells and were able to find at least 25 open shells in each 1-pound box we used. Pipe each shell only about three-quarters full on your first pass, and then divide the remaining filling evenly among the shells.

SAUCE

- **2** tablespoons extra-virgin olive oil
- **1** onion, chopped
- **½** teaspoon table salt
- **½** teaspoon pepper
- **6** garlic cloves, minced
- **¼** teaspoon red pepper flakes
- **1** (28-ounce) can tomato puree
- **2** cups water
- **1** teaspoon sugar

CHEESY STUFFED SHELLS

FILLING

- 10 ounces (1¼ cups) whole-milk ricotta cheese
- 4 ounces fontina cheese, shredded (1 cup)
- 2 ounces Pecorino Romano cheese, grated (1 cup)
- 2 large eggs
- 3 tablespoons chopped fresh basil
- 1½ tablespoons cornstarch
- 2 garlic cloves, minced
- 1 teaspoon dried oregano
- ½ teaspoon table salt

SHELLS

- 25 jumbo pasta shells
- 8 ounces fontina cheese, shredded (2 cups)
- 1 tablespoon chopped fresh basil

1. FOR THE SAUCE: Heat oil in large saucepan over medium heat until shimmering. Add onion, salt, and pepper and cook, stirring occasionally, until softened and lightly browned, about 10 minutes.

2. Stir in garlic and pepper flakes and cook until fragrant, about 30 seconds. Stir in tomato puree, water, and sugar and bring to simmer. Reduce heat to medium-low and cook until flavors have melded, about 5 minutes. (Cooled sauce can be refrigerated for up to 3 days.)

3. FOR THE FILLING: Stir all ingredients in bowl until thoroughly combined. Transfer filling to pastry bag or large zipper-lock bag (if using zipper-lock bag, cut 1 inch off 1 corner of bag).

NOTES FROM THE TEST KITCHEN

FILLING STATION

We found that it was much easier to fill rigid uncooked pasta shells than it was to work with floppy boiled ones, so we designed a recipe that involved filling raw shells with the cheese mixture, assembling the casserole, and baking it—no precooking of the pasta required. Select shells with wide openings for easier filling.

Use a pastry bag (or a zipper-lock bag with one corner snipped off) to pipe in the cheese mixture until each shell is about three-quarters full (as shown at left), and then divide the remaining filling among the shells.

4. FOR THE SHELLS: Adjust oven rack to middle position and heat oven to 400 degrees. Place shells open side up on counter. Pipe filling into shells until each is about three-quarters full. Divide remaining filling evenly among shells.

5. Spread 1 cup sauce over bottom of 13 by 9-inch baking dish. Transfer shells, open side up, to prepared dish. Pour remaining sauce evenly over shells to completely cover.

6. Cover dish tightly with aluminum foil and place on rimmed baking sheet. Bake until shells are tender and sauce is boiling rapidly, about 45 minutes. Remove dish from oven and discard foil; sprinkle fontina over top. Bake, uncovered, until fontina is lightly browned, about 15 minutes. Let shells cool for 25 minutes. Sprinkle with basil. Serve.

TO MAKE AHEAD: At end of step 2, let sauce cool completely. At end of step 5, cover dish tightly with aluminum foil and refrigerate for up to 24 hours. When ready to eat, bake shells as directed in step 6.

AGNOLOTTI

✓ **WHY THIS RECIPE WORKS** There are many regional differences in Italian cuisine, but almost every region has a filled pasta. These stuffed specialties vary, with each containing the prized ingredients of its respective region. Piedmontese agnolotti, pillow-shaped pasta stuffed with a comforting, meltingly tender braised meat filling and simply tossed in browned butter, are a standout. Legend has it that after a victorious battle, a nobleman requested a celebratory meal from his chef. With little food on hand, the chef used leftover braised meat to fill egg pasta. But while the filling for agnolotti traditionally is made from leftovers, we don't usually have braised beef on hand, so we started from scratch. We chose boneless beef short ribs for their rich flavor and tender texture. Savoy cabbage, butter, and rosemary, common Piedmontese ingredients, enhanced the texture and flavor of the filling. The traditional way of shaping agnolotti is the simplest: Rather than having to cut, fill, and shape each piece, the filling is piped over long sheets of pasta and then pinched and cut into segments.

Hailing from Italy's northern region of Piedmont, agnolotti is a traditional pasta stuffed with both rich flavor and history. Legend has it that after a victorious battle, a Piedmontese nobleman requested a celebratory meal from his chef, Angeloto. The resourceful chef created this now-famed pasta using handy leftover meat. Nowadays, agnolotti can be filled with pretty much anything—from ricotta to pureed butternut squash—but the most traditional filling pays homage to that nobleman's quick-thinking chef. I wanted to re-create this quintessential Piedmontese recipe while highlighting a handful of ingredients that hail from northern Italy.

I first had to nail down the pasta, the filling, and the pasta-filling technique. For ease, I mixed up the pasta dough in the food processor. Six egg yolks, in addition to two whole eggs and a couple of tablespoons of olive oil, made the dough a dream to roll and gave it good flavor. Resting the dough for at least 30 minutes before forming the agnolotti allowed the gluten time to relax so the dough wouldn't contract after it was rolled out.

On to the filling. I knew I wanted to stick with a meat-based filling boosted with aromatics, a delicately flavored green vegetable, and freshly grated cheese. Recipes called for a range of meats, from ground pork and country-style pork ribs to ground beef and beef short ribs. While I liked the ease of ground meat, I decided it was worth the extra time and effort to go all out with traditional, meltingly tender braised meat.

I first cut a pound each of boneless country-style pork ribs and boneless beef short ribs into 1½-inch chunks and browned them in a Dutch oven with unsalted butter. I added a generous 1½ cups of chopped savoy cabbage for a subtle vegetal note and as a nod to Piedmontese ingredients. Then, I sautéed the aromatics (onion, garlic, and rosemary) and added my braising liquid, a combination of beef broth and red wine (Barolo is traditional, but any dry red will work). After simmering on the stove for about an hour, the pork-beef mixture was tender.

I then transferred the mixture to the food processor and blended it until it was finely ground. Bear with me here—this would allow me to avoid the labor-intensive process of shredding 2 pounds of meat and would also create a cohesive filling that I could dollop across the pasta sheets before shaping the agnolotti. After blitzing the meat, I stirred in ½ cup of grated Grana Padano cheese, a hard, nutty cheese made in Piedmont; one egg as a binder; and ¼ teaspoon of nutmeg to round out the meatiness.

I divided my pasta dough into five pieces, rolled out each piece into a transparent sheet, and cut each sheet into long rectangles. Using a 1-teaspoon measure, I scooped small balls of filling across the pasta sheets, leaving 1 inch between each dollop of filling; I then folded the sheets over the filling, formed the dough into pillow-like shapes, and trimmed the excess with a fluted pastry wheel. I cooked the pasta for just a few minutes in salted boiling water.

This filling was tasty, but there was too much of it, and what was more, it was soupy. I decided to nix the pork ribs—the short ribs were much more tender and moist, and sticking with one cut of meat simplified my ingredient list. I dialed the meat back to 1½ pounds of beef short ribs, and this time I drained the beef mixture in a fine-mesh strainer set over a bowl and added just ¼ cup of the braising liquid to the food processor. The flavors could stand to be tweaked a bit, too. I upped the cabbage to 2 cups and decreased the nutmeg to just ⅛ teaspoon.

I wondered if I could simplify the pasta-filling process. I already had this finely ground, scoopable filling—what if I just piped it across the pasta sheets? I transferred the room-temperature meat filling to a large zipper-lock bag, snipped off one corner, piped the filling lengthwise down the center of the sheet, and folded the sheet in half over the filling. Working my way down the sheet, I gently pinched together 1-inch segments of agnolotti, being careful not to burst the little "pillows," and then cut through the pinched sections to separate the pasta into individual pieces. To ensure that the agnolotti would hold their shape when boiled, I gave them a final pinch and let them dry on floured baking sheets for about 30 minutes.

The agnolotti needed a sauce that wouldn't overwhelm their rich and flavorful filling. I settled on a hazelnut–browned butter sauce and curbed the richness with a splash of red wine vinegar.

I combined the sauce, the cooked pasta, and 2 tablespoons of pasta cooking water—the starchy water created a more luxurious sauce—and gave it a quick toss. A sprinkling of minced fresh parsley further brightened up the dish. I think it's safe to say Angeloto and his nobleman would be impressed by my rendition of this special-occasion meal.

—LEAH COLINS, *America's Test Kitchen Books*

AGNOLOTTI

Agnolotti

SERVES 8 TO 10

Take care when shaping the agnolotti; pinching the pasta too tightly may cause the final shape to burst open. You can find Grana Padano at most well-stocked cheese counters; if you can't find it, you can substitute Parmigiano-Reggiano. Our favorite pasta machine is the Marcato Atlas 150 Wellness Pasta Machine.

PASTA

- 2 cups (10 ounces) all-purpose flour, plus extra as needed
- 2 large eggs plus 6 large yolks
- 2 tablespoons extra-virgin olive oil
  Table salt for cooking

FILLING

- 1½ pounds boneless beef short ribs, trimmed and cut into 1½-inch pieces
- ½ teaspoon table salt
- ¼ teaspoon pepper
- 2 tablespoons unsalted butter
- 2 cups chopped savoy cabbage
- 1 onion, chopped
- 3 garlic cloves, minced
- 2 teaspoons minced fresh rosemary
- ½ cup dry red wine
- 2 cups beef broth
- 1 ounce Grana Padano cheese, grated (½ cup)
- 1 large egg
- ⅛ teaspoon ground nutmeg

SAUCE

- 8 tablespoons unsalted butter
- ¼ cup hazelnuts, toasted, skinned, and chopped coarse
- ¼ teaspoon table salt
- ¼ teaspoon red wine vinegar

- 2 tablespoons minced fresh parsley

1. FOR THE PASTA: Process flour, eggs and yolks, and oil in food processor until mixture forms cohesive dough that feels soft and is barely tacky to touch, about 45 seconds. (If dough sticks to your fingers, add up to ¼ cup extra flour, 1 tablespoon at a time. Process until flour is fully incorporated after each addition, 10 to 15 seconds, before retesting. If dough doesn't become cohesive, add up to 1 tablespoon water, 1 teaspoon at a time, until it just comes together; process 30 seconds longer.) Transfer dough to clean counter and knead to form uniform ball. Wrap tightly in plastic wrap and let rest for 30 minutes or up to 4 hours.

2. FOR THE FILLING: Pat beef dry with paper towels and sprinkle with salt and pepper. Melt butter in Dutch oven over medium-high heat. Brown beef on all sides, 7 to 10 minutes; transfer to plate.

3. Add cabbage and onion to fat left in pot and cook over medium heat until softened, about 3 minutes. Stir in garlic and rosemary and cook until fragrant, about 30 seconds. Stir in wine, scraping up any browned bits, then stir in broth. Return beef and any accumulated juices to pot and bring to simmer. Reduce heat to medium-low, cover, and simmer until beef is tender, about 1 hour.

4. Drain beef mixture in fine-mesh strainer set over bowl. Reserve ¼ cup cooking liquid; discard remaining liquid. Transfer beef mixture and reserved liquid to food processor and process until finely ground, about 1 minute, scraping down sides of bowl as needed. Add Grana Padano, egg, and nutmeg and process until combined, about 30 seconds. Transfer filling to bowl; refrigerate for 30 minutes. (Filling can be refrigerated for up to 24 hours; let come to room temperature before proceeding with recipe.)

5. Transfer dough to clean counter, divide into 5 equal pieces, and cover with plastic. Flatten 1 piece of dough into ½-inch-thick disk. Using pasta machine with rollers set to widest position, feed dough through rollers twice. Bring tapered ends of dough toward middle and press to seal. Feed dough seam side first through rollers again. Repeat feeding dough tapered end first through rollers set at widest position, without folding, until dough is smooth and barely tacky. (If dough sticks to your fingers or to rollers, lightly dust dough with flour and roll again.)

6. Narrow rollers to next setting and feed dough through rollers twice. Continue to narrow rollers progressively, feeding dough through each setting twice, until dough is very thin and semitransparent. (If dough becomes too long to manage, halve it crosswise.) Transfer pasta sheet to well-floured sheet of parchment paper. Cover with second sheet of parchment, followed by damp dish towel, to keep pasta from drying out. Repeat rolling with remaining 4 pieces of dough, stacking pasta sheets between layers of floured parchment.

7. Liberally dust 2 rimmed baking sheets with flour. Transfer filling to 1-gallon zipper-lock bag. Cut ¾ inch off 1 corner of bag. Position 1 pasta sheet on lightly floured counter with long side parallel to counter edge (keep remaining sheets covered). Using pizza cutter or sharp knife, trim pasta into uniform 4-inch-wide sheet. Pipe filling lengthwise down center of sheet, leaving 1-inch border at each end. Lightly brush edges with water. Fold bottom edge of pasta over filling until flush with top edge. Gently press to seal long edge of pasta flush to filling; leave narrow edges unsealed. With index finger and thumb of both your hands facing downward, pinch filled portion of pasta together at 1-inch increments to create individual sections (you should have about 15 sections).

8. Using fluted pastry wheel or pizza cutter, trim excess dough from filled pasta strip, leaving ¼-inch border on ends and 1-inch border on top. Starting at bottom edge of strip, roll pastry wheel away from you

in 1 motion between pinched sections to separate agnolotti. Pinch edges of each agnolotto to reinforce seal, then transfer to prepared baking sheets. Repeat with remaining pasta sheets and filling (you should have about 75 agnolotti). Let agnolotti sit uncovered until dry to touch and slightly stiffened, about 30 minutes. (Agnolotti can be wrapped in plastic wrap and refrigerated for up to 4 hours or chilled in freezer until firm, then transferred to zipper-lock bag and frozen for up to 1 month. If frozen, do not thaw before cooking; increase simmering time to 4 to 5 minutes.)

9. FOR THE SAUCE: Cook butter, hazelnuts, and salt in 12-inch skillet over medium-high heat, swirling skillet constantly, until butter is melted, turns golden brown, and has nutty aroma, about 3 minutes. Off heat, stir in vinegar; set aside sauce. Bring 4 quarts water to boil in large pot. Add half of agnolotti and 1 tablespoon salt and simmer gently, stirring often, until edges of pasta are al dente, 3 to 4 minutes. Using slotted spoon, transfer agnolotti to sauce in skillet, gently toss to coat, and cover. Return water to boil and cook remaining agnolotti; transfer to sauce. Add 2 tablespoons cooking water and gently toss to coat. Sprinkle with parsley and serve immediately.

NOTES FROM THE TEST KITCHEN

SHAPING AGNOLOTTI

1. Fold bottom edge of pasta sheet over filling until flush with top edge. Gently press to seal long edge of pasta flush to filling.

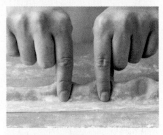

2. With index finger and thumb of both your hands facing downward, pinch filled portion of pasta together through filling at 1-inch increments.

3. Trim excess dough from pasta strip. Starting at bottom edge of strip, roll pastry wheel away from you in 1 motion between pinched sections to separate agnolotti. Pinch edges of each agnolotto to reinforce seal.

PORK, FENNEL, AND LEMON RAGU WITH PAPPARDELLE

✓ **WHY THIS RECIPE WORKS** Our white ragu skips tomatoes in favor of bright lemon and rich cream. We ensured plenty of savoriness by creating fond twice. We first browned chopped pancetta, onion, and fennel in a Dutch oven and then added water and a touch of cream to create a braising liquid. To this we added a pork butt roast, which we halved crosswise to make cooking faster and shredding easier, and transferred it to the oven, where a second fond formed on the sides of the pot. After scraping this second fond into the sauce, we brightened its flavor with plenty of lemon zest and juice before adding the pasta.

Mention the word "ragu," and a rich, meaty, tomatoey sauce typically comes to mind. But sauces containing tomato are a relatively recent addition to the Italian culinary repertoire, not appearing until the early 1800s. Long before then, *ragù bianco* (a simple, not-too-saucy mixture of any number of chopped or shredded meats, aromatics, and often white wine—but never tomato) was on the menu.

Ragu bianco started out as fare for nobility. Beef, pork, or game was stewed, and the deeply savory cooking liquid was used to dress pasta as one course. Meanwhile, the meat was carved and arranged on a platter for a subsequent course. Eventually, this style of eating was copied by the gentry, who used smaller, less expensive cuts. By the late 17th century, the practice had trickled down to commoners, who ultimately combined the meat and pasta into one dish.

Ragu bianco is still prevalent in Italy, and the sky's the limit in terms of how it can be flavored. I was eager to develop my own version after enjoying a stunning example at Maialino, a restaurant in New York City, featuring large shreds of meltingly tender braised pork punctuated by tart lemon, licorice-y fennel, and salty Pecorino Romano cheese. When tossed with pasta, the sauce formed a fresh-tasting and satisfying dish.

Almost all ragus, whether red or white, start with a soffritto—a sautéed mixture that typically includes finely chopped onion, carrot, and celery and sometimes meat. I kept the onion but ditched the carrot and celery since I planned on using a large fennel bulb. The fennel would offer an herbaceous sweetness instead of the earthy, mineral-y flavors of carrot and celery.

I softened my soffritto in a Dutch oven with a little olive oil and then added fresh thyme and garlic, stirring until the heady scents of the aromatics were released. Instead of loosening the fond with the usual white wine, I deglazed with lemon juice and water.

Next, I nestled a 1½-pound boneless pork butt roast—a deeply marbled, relatively inexpensive cut from the upper part of the pig's shoulder that we often use in pork braises—into the soffritto. I transferred the pot to a 300-degree oven, where the pork would spend more than an hour in the 140- to 190-degree zone. In that temperature range, collagen breaks down more rapidly than it does at lower temperatures, turns to gelatin, and enhances tenderness, but the muscle protein doesn't overcook.

Sure enough, about 2 hours later, the meat was supple and fork-tender. I removed the roast from the pot, let it cool a bit, and tried to shred it with two forks. That turned out to be quite a chore with such a large piece of meat, but I ignored that problem for the moment and tossed the sauce with pappardelle—wide egg noodles that would pair well with the chunky ragu—along with a bit of the pasta cooking water and a few handfuls of grated Pecorino Romano.

The large bites of pork were perfect, but the rest of the dish was far from it, with a dry texture and little to no lemon flavor. In the frank words of a colleague, I'd served up "the pork version of a bad tuna casserole."

I gave it another go, this time halving the pork butt against the grain before braising, expecting that the shorter fibers would be easier to shred.

Fixing the wan flavor required a multipronged approach. I considered searing the pork on the stovetop before braising to develop more meatiness, but a simpler solution came to mind: Adding a little cured pork to my soffritto would quickly provide tons of flavor without my having to sear the pork butt. I diced a couple of ounces of pancetta and simmered it in ⅔ cup of water to draw out its fat and juices. When the water evaporated, the meat started to sizzle in a layer of savory pork fat that had collected on the bottom of the pot. I sautéed the vegetables and aromatics in the fat and deglazed with just water, holding back the lemon juice until later so its delicate notes wouldn't be obliterated by the long braise.

To get color on the pork without adding any extra work, I turned up the oven to 350 degrees. Since most of the meat sat above the cooking liquid, I hoped that it would brown at this higher temperature. Indeed, the pork was tawny, tender, and juicy after just 1½ hours. What's more, increasing the temperature had caused the braising liquid to bubble and splatter onto the sides of the Dutch oven, forming a second layer of fond. I pulled the pork out of the pot to rest, put the lid on for a few minutes to let the steam loosen the fond, and then scraped the savory bits from the sides of the pot into the braising liquid.

To finish the sauce, I stirred in the juice of two lemons along with some of their floral zest. I then shredded the pork—it was indeed easier with two smaller roasts—and returned it to the pot. When I tossed the ragu with the pappardelle, I incorporated a little extra pasta cooking water. The intensified meatiness and citrusy complexity were just right, as were the tender shreds of meat. But the ragu now lacked body.

What was missing? How about butter? Whisking in a few tablespoons gives a pan sauce body, but with chunks of pork in the pot, the butter was difficult to whisk in and the sauce didn't emulsify properly. A colleague suggested trying cream instead. I put together another batch, adding just ⅓ cup of heavy cream to the pot along with ¾ cup of pasta cooking water. What a difference! The pappardelle was now coated with a cohesive, velvety sauce.

In fact, the cream was so stable that I found I could add it to the ragu at the beginning of cooking and get the same results—a boon since it had been cooling down the ragu a bit when added just before serving.

I stirred in plenty of Pecorino before garnishing the dish with the chopped fennel fronds. Here was a lively, luxurious ragu bianco—fit for royalty.

—LAN LAM, *Cook's Illustrated*

Pork, Fennel, and Lemon Ragu with Pappardelle

SERVES 4 TO 6

Pork butt roast is often labeled Boston butt in the supermarket. To ensure that the sauce isn't greasy, be sure to trim the roast of all excess surface fat. You can substitute tagliatelle for the pappardelle, if desired.

    4 ounces pancetta, chopped
    1 large onion, chopped fine
    1 large fennel bulb, 2 tablespoons fronds chopped,
       stalks discarded, bulb halved, cored, and
       chopped fine
    4 garlic cloves, minced
    2 teaspoons minced fresh thyme
 1½ teaspoons table salt, plus salt for cooking pasta
    1 teaspoon pepper
   ⅓ cup heavy cream
    1 (1½-pound) boneless pork butt roast, well
       trimmed and cut in half against grain
 1½ teaspoons grated lemon zest plus ¼ cup juice
       (2 lemons)
   12 ounces pappardelle
    2 ounces Pecorino Romano cheese, grated (1 cup),
       plus extra for serving

1. Adjust oven rack to middle position and heat oven to 350 degrees. Cook pancetta and ⅔ cup water in Dutch oven over medium-high heat, stirring occasionally, until water has evaporated and dark fond forms on bottom of pot, 8 to 10 minutes. Add onion and fennel bulb and cook, stirring occasionally, until vegetables soften and start to brown, 5 to 7 minutes. Stir in garlic, thyme, salt, and pepper and cook until fragrant, about 30 seconds.

2. Stir in cream and 2 cups water, scraping up any browned bits. Add pork and bring to boil over high heat. Cover, transfer to oven, and cook until pork is tender, about 1½ hours.

3. Transfer pork to large plate and let cool for 15 minutes. Cover pot so fond will steam and soften. Using spatula, scrape browned bits from sides of pot and stir into sauce. Stir in lemon zest and juice.

4. While pork cools, bring 4 quarts water to boil in large pot. Using 2 forks, shred pork into bite-size pieces, discarding any large pieces of fat or connective tissue. Return pork and any accumulated juices to Dutch oven. Cover and keep warm.

5. Add pasta and 1 tablespoon salt to boiling water and cook, stirring occasionally, until al dente. Reserve 2 cups cooking water, then drain pasta and add it to Dutch oven. Add Pecorino and ¾ cup reserved cooking water and stir until sauce is slightly thickened and cheese is fully melted, 2 to 3 minutes. If desired, stir in remaining reserved cooking water, ¼ cup at a time, to adjust sauce consistency. Season with salt and pepper to taste and sprinkle with fennel fronds. Serve immediately, passing extra Pecorino separately.

NOTES FROM THE TEST KITCHEN

DOUBLE THE FOND, DOUBLE THE FLAVOR

In our *ragù bianco*, two rounds of fond development ensure plenty of rich flavor. First, we simmer pancetta to extract its juices and fat and let that liquid turn into a deeply savory fond. Then, as the pork shoulder simmers in the oven, juices and fat splatter onto the sides of the pot, creating a second layer of fond. To loosen the fond on the sides, we simply cover the pot for a few minutes so that steam can soften it.

BROWNED PANCETTA CREATES FIRST LAYER

SPLATTERING PORK JUICES CREATE SECOND LAYER

PASTA ALLA GRICIA

✓ **WHY THIS RECIPE WORKS** *Pasta alla gricia* is a simple pasta dish based on cured pork, black pepper, and Pecorino Romano. The fat from the pork (*guanciale* is traditional, but easier-to-find pancetta works well) combines with starchy pasta cooking water and cheese to create a creamy sauce for the pasta. The traditional method is to let parcooked pasta finish cooking in the reserved cooking water so its starch can help the water and pork fat emulsify, but the technique can be finicky. For consistent results, we cooked the pasta to al dente in half the usual amount of water and then added the extra-starchy pasta cooking water to the rendered pork fat and reduced the mixture to a specific volume. The boiling further concentrated the starches in the water and emulsified the mixture before we mixed in the pasta.

Rome has four iconic—and outrageously good—pasta dishes: *cacio e pepe*, *amatriciana*, carbonara, and *gricia*. I've long been a huge fan of the more well-known first three but had never tried gricia, which features *guanciale* (cured hog jowls), ground black pepper, and tangy, salty Pecorino Romano. So when a former colleague who grew up in Rome offered to make it for lunch on a quiet day in the test kitchen, I couldn't refuse a taste.

My colleague put a pot of rigatoni on to boil while he sautéed chopped guanciale in a skillet. When the pork was deeply browned but still retained a tender chew, he removed it, leaving behind its rendered fat. In went the drained rigatoni, which was only halfway cooked (also known as *al chiodo*, or "to the nail"), along with a lot of pasta water—roughly 2 cups. As he let the rigatoni simmer until it was al dente, he stirred it with the starchy water and pork fat to form a creamy sauce, a technique known as *mantecare*. Finally, he returned the browned guanciale to the mix, along with a few more splashes of pasta water, lots of pepper, and plenty of grated Pecorino.

It was a memorable lunch: The porky guanciale was at the forefront, followed by the heat of the pepper and the tang of the cheese; it all formed a rich yet delicately creamy sauce to coat the rigatoni.

But when I made the dish (using pancetta since guanciale can be hard to find), it became clear that the technique was more art than science: As the al chiodo pasta cooks through, it absorbs some of the pasta water and releases starch to help emulsify the water and fat

THE ROMAN PASTA QUARTET
Four simple pasta dishes serve as pillars of Roman cuisine. Cooks debate the precise details, but the handful of ingredients that goes into each is well established.

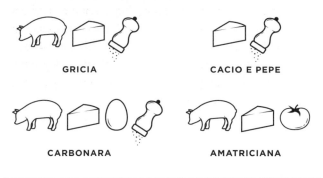

GRICIA   CACIO E PEPE

CARBONARA   AMATRICIANA

into a creamy sauce. How much pasta water to add depends on knowing how much more cooking the pasta needs and how much water it will absorb. And if there isn't enough pasta water to maintain the emulsion, the sauce will be broken and greasy. I wanted to remove the guesswork for those times when I can't give dinner my undivided attention.

That would mean using the more straightforward approach of adding al dente pasta to a finished sauce. But rather than use the standard 4 quarts of water to boil the pasta, I scaled the water to 2 quarts (unsalted since the pancetta and Pecorino contributed plenty of salt). This way, the water would have double the starch, helping ensure emulsification.

I added 2 cups of the starchy pasta water to the rendered fat and boiled the mixture for a few minutes. This not only caused some evaporation to further concentrate the starch but also broke the fat into smaller, more numerous droplets. I then stirred in the al dente pasta and the browned pancetta, followed by the Pecorino, transforming the liquid from thin and brothy to nicely emulsified.

This method was nearly foolproof, but I made a final tweak to guarantee consistent results. I boiled the fat-water mixture not for a specific time but to a specific volume: 1½ cups. This way, I'd always use the same amount of liquid to coat the pasta.

With this recipe for gricia at the ready, I couldn't wait until it was my turn to make lunch.

—ANNIE PETITO, *Cook's Illustrated*

Pasta alla Gricia (Rigatoni with Pancetta and Pecorino Romano)

SERVES 6

This pasta is quite rich; serve it in smaller portions with a green vegetable or salad. For the best results, use the highest-quality pancetta you can find. If you can find guanciale, we recommend using it and increasing the browning time in step 2 to 10 to 12 minutes. Because we call for cutting the pancetta to a specified thickness, we recommend having it cut to order at the deli counter; avoid presliced or prediced products.

- 8 ounces pancetta, sliced ¼ inch thick
- 1 tablespoon extra-virgin olive oil
- 1 pound rigatoni
- 1 teaspoon coarsely ground pepper, plus extra for serving
- 2 ounces Pecorino Romano cheese, grated fine (1 cup), plus extra for serving

1. Slice each round of pancetta into rectangular pieces that measure about ½ inch by 1 inch.

2. Heat oil and pancetta in large Dutch oven over medium-low heat, stirring frequently, until fat is rendered and pancetta is deep golden brown but still has slight pinkish hue, 8 to 10 minutes, adjusting heat as necessary to keep pancetta from browning too quickly. Using slotted spoon, transfer pancetta to bowl; set aside. Pour fat from pot into liquid measuring cup (you should have ¼ to ⅓ cup fat; discard any extra). Return fat to Dutch oven.

3. While pancetta cooks, set colander in large bowl. Bring 2 quarts water to boil in large pot. Add pasta and cook, stirring often, until al dente. Drain pasta in prepared colander, reserving cooking water.

4. Add pepper and 2 cups reserved cooking water to Dutch oven with fat and bring to boil over high heat. Boil rapidly, scraping up any browned bits, until mixture is emulsified and reduced to 1½ cups, about 5 minutes. (If you've reduced it too far, add more reserved cooking water to equal 1½ cups.)

5. Reduce heat to low, add pasta and pancetta, and stir to evenly coat. Add Pecorino and stir until cheese is melted and sauce is slightly thickened, about 1 minute. Off heat, adjust sauce consistency with remaining reserved cooking water as needed. Transfer pasta to platter and serve immediately, passing extra pepper and extra Pecorino separately.

HOT SESAME NOODLES WITH PORK

✔ **WHY THIS RECIPE WORKS** Chinese *dan dan* noodles feature long, tender noodles; salty-sweet pork; and a mildly spicy sauce. To capture the spirit of this dish without searching high and low for hard-to-find ingredients, we swapped the traditional noodles for spaghetti that we cooked beyond al dente until tender. A combination of dry sherry (a suitable substitute for Chinese rice wine), hoisin sauce, and soy sauce enhanced the flavor of the ground pork. Sesame oil and tahini contributed richness to the sauce, and Asian chili-garlic sauce and Sichuan peppercorns gave it a kick.

When my editors asked me to develop a recipe for Chinese-style sesame noodles, I knew exactly which dish I wanted to use for inspiration: *dan dan* noodles. The first time I had these noodles they opened up flavor possibilities I didn't even know existed. They were tossed with a lively, bright-red chili oil, but had a tempered spiciness that was enhanced and balanced with scallion, toasted sesame oil, meaty soy sauce, tangy vinegar, and pleasantly numbing Sichuan peppercorns. The noodles were also dotted with little bits of supersavory minced pork. I ordered another bowl before I finished the first.

For a home-cooked version of these noodles, I decided that my goal would not be to re-create an exact replica of an authentic Sichuan dish. Rather, I set out to develop a recipe that was true to the essential idea of the original but that didn't call for hard-to-find ingredients or a special wok.

Traditional dan dan noodles have four main components: long, tender noodles; a complex sesame-flavored sauce; a topping of salty-sweet, savory minced pork; and a punch of heat. (They usually also include pickled mustard greens, which would be too time-consuming to make for my version.) I wanted to create a delicious, foolproof recipe that stayed true to that basic framework. For a similarly shaped but commonly available noodle, I started with plain old spaghetti cooked beyond al dente until fully tender to mimic the softer noodles commonly used in traditional versions.

Using ground pork for the topping was a no-brainer, and to enhance its flavor, I knew I'd use two supermarket staples—hoisin and soy sauces—but many recipes also call for Chinese rice wine, which can be hard to

HOT SESAME NOODLES WITH PORK

find. Luckily, we've had good results substituting dry sherry for Chinese rice wine in other recipes, and it worked great here, too. With a pound of spaghetti setting the baseline, I found that 8 ounces of pork was the right amount; the heavily seasoned pork is an accent here, not the star.

For the heart of my rich sesame sauce, a combination of toasted sesame oil and tahini (sesame paste) worked as an excellent replacement for the traditional Chinese sesame paste. To achieve the bold but balanced heat provided by dried Sichuan chiles, I used a combination of crushed red pepper flakes—sautéed in oil with scallion whites and garlic to bloom their flavor—and Asian chili-garlic sauce. A little rice vinegar added brightness and spark. A sprinkling of ground Sichuan peppercorns, which have a heady citrusy aroma and a mild numbing effect, imparted the signature lip-tingling sensation that's characteristic of much Sichuan cuisine. (Don't worry if you can't find them and don't want to mail-order—the dish is still great without them.)

As I was putting the finishing touches on the recipe, I was happy to see that the noodles were becoming so popular in the test kitchen that I could hardly save any for myself. Luckily, I now had a simple recipe that was fast enough for me to whip up my own batch—no sharing—as soon as I got home.

—MATTHEW FAIRMAN, *Cook's Country*

Hot Sesame Noodles with Pork

SERVES 4 TO 6

We like to serve these noodles drizzled with Sichuan Chili Oil (recipe follows). Tahini is a Middle Eastern paste made from toasted sesame seeds; the savory paste is similar in texture to natural peanut butter. Look for it in the condiment section or the international section of the supermarket.

- 1 **pound spaghetti**
- ¼ **teaspoon table salt, plus salt for cooking pasta**
- 2 **tablespoons toasted sesame oil**
- 8 **ounces ground pork**
- ¼ **cup soy sauce, divided**
- 5 **teaspoons hoisin sauce, divided**
- 1 **tablespoon dry sherry**
- ¼ **cup tahini**
- 2 **tablespoons rice vinegar**
- 1 **tablespoon Asian chili-garlic sauce**

- 2 **teaspoons sugar**
- ¼ **cup vegetable oil**
- 6 **scallions, white parts sliced thin, green parts sliced thin on bias**
- 3 **garlic cloves, minced**
- 1 **teaspoon red pepper flakes**
- ½ **teaspoon ground Sichuan peppercorns, plus extra for serving (optional)**

1. Bring 4 quarts water to boil in large Dutch oven. Add pasta and 1 tablespoon salt and cook, stirring often, until tender. Drain pasta and return it to pot. Add sesame oil and toss to coat; cover to keep warm.

2. Cook pork in 12-inch nonstick skillet over medium-high heat until no longer pink, 3 to 5 minutes, breaking up meat with wooden spoon. Stir in 1 tablespoon soy sauce, 1 tablespoon hoisin, and sherry and cook until all liquid has evaporated and pork is well browned, 3 to 5 minutes. Transfer pork to bowl; set aside.

3. Whisk 1 cup hot water, tahini, vinegar, chili-garlic sauce, sugar, salt, remaining 3 tablespoons soy sauce, and remaining 2 teaspoons hoisin together in second bowl; set aside. Combine vegetable oil, scallion whites, garlic, pepper flakes, and peppercorns, if using, in now-empty skillet and cook over medium heat until fragrant, about 2 minutes.

4. Add oil mixture and tahini mixture to pot with pasta and toss to coat. Transfer pasta to platter and top with pork, scallion greens, and extra peppercorns, if using. Adjust consistency with additional hot water as needed. Serve.

Sichuan Chili Oil

MAKES ABOUT ¾ CUP

There's no need to peel the ginger. Make sure to use toasted sesame oil here.

- ½ **cup peanut or vegetable oil**
- 2 **tablespoons red pepper flakes**
- 1 **tablespoon Sichuan peppercorns**
- 2 **teaspoons smoked paprika**
- 2 **garlic cloves, smashed and peeled**
- 1 **(½-inch) piece ginger, smashed**
- 1 **cinnamon stick**
- 2 **tablespoons toasted sesame oil**

Heat peanut oil in small saucepan over medium heat to 350 degrees. Off heat, add pepper flakes, peppercorns, paprika, garlic, ginger, and cinnamon stick. Let cool completely, about 1 hour. Strain oil mixture through fine-mesh strainer into jar; discard solids. Stir in sesame oil. (Oil can be stored at room temperature for up to 3 weeks or refrigerated for up to 3 months.)

SHRIMP RISOTTO

✓ **WHY THIS RECIPE WORKS** For a simplified shrimp risotto, we started by making a quick stock: We seared shrimp shells to extract their flavorful compounds, added water and seasonings, and simmered for just 5 minutes. Next we sautéed onion and fennel and then added the rice to the pot, followed by white wine and almost all the stock. We simmered the risotto covered to help it cook evenly and stirred it only twice. Adding the salted shrimp off the heat ensured that they would cook very gently and retain their delicate texture, and cutting each shrimp into thirds meant every bite of risotto was studded with shrimp. Final additions of butter, lemon, chives, and Parmesan contributed complexity while keeping things light.

A risotto featuring creamy Arborio rice; plump, juicy shrimp; and light, bright seasonings is one of those slam-dunk dishes that every cook needs in their repertoire. Its subtle flavors are universally appealing, and it's luxurious enough for company.

A few years ago, we came up with a revolutionary risotto-making technique: Our Almost Hands-Free Risotto calls for gently boiling Arborio rice in stock in a covered Dutch oven so that the agitation of the grains (rather than the cook's spoon) sloughs the starch from the rice. Just before the rice is done, a final portion of stock is added and the risotto is stirred for just 2 to 3 minutes to maximize creaminess before the dish is finished with butter and cheese.

I was inspired by the ease of this recipe and wanted to build upon it to create a shrimp risotto bursting with briny seafood flavor. I started with the backbone of the dish: shrimp stock. For this crucial element, I knew that homemade was the only way to go; while I aimed to keep things as simple as possible, I was also determined to infuse my dish with maximum flavor. Luckily, I knew a fast and easy method for making my own. Crustacean shells contain tons of proteins, sugars, and flavor-boosting glutamates and nucleotides—just what I wanted to extract into the stock. Instead of ditching the shells after I peeled my shrimp, I seared the shells in oil; added water, bay leaves, salt, and peppercorns; and simmered—but only for 5 minutes. That's because we've found that some of the flavor compounds in the shells are volatile and release into the air with longer cooking times. The result was an ultrafast stock that would infuse my risotto with a taste of the sea.

Next, I sautéed finely chopped onion and fennel. The fennel's mild anise notes were lovely, but it took a long time to lose its crunch. A smidge of baking soda raised the fennel's pH, helping it (and the onion) break down faster. I then added the rice, cooked it until it turned translucent, and deglazed the pot with dry white wine before adding the stock.

Finally, I stirred in whole shrimp, but they were so big that I got a bite of shrimp in only every few forkfuls. Cutting the shrimp into pieces made for better distribution, but then they rapidly overcooked.

To solve the problem, I sprinkled the shrimp with salt before I prepared the risotto—the salt would be absorbed by the shrimp, helping keep them moist. Once the risotto was finished, I slid the pot off the burner and added the shrimp pieces, letting them cook to juicy, plump perfection in the residual heat. Parmesan, butter, chives, and lemon zest and juice enhanced the beautifully flavored, creamy rice.

—STEVE DUNN, *Cook's Illustrated*

NOTES FROM THE TEST KITCHEN

SEAFOOD AND CHEESE? YOU BET.

Italian tradition maintains that seafood and cheese should never appear on the same plate, lest the milky, salty dairy overwhelm the delicate seafood flavor. Yet the pairing is quite common—and delicious. Think lox and cream cheese, pizza with anchovies, tuna melts, and lobster mac and cheese. Likewise, our risotto just wasn't as complex without a small amount of Parmesan. Even this Sicilian fish recipe from around 400 BC advocated for the pairing: "Gut. Discard the head, rinse, slice; add cheese and oil." That's good enough for us.

SHRIMP RISOTTO

Shrimp Risotto

SERVES 4 TO 6

Accompanied by a salad, this risotto makes a great dinner, but it can also be served in eight smaller portions as a first course.

1	pound extra-large shrimp (21 to 25 per pound), peeled, deveined, and tails removed, shells reserved
1¾	teaspoons table salt, divided
1	tablespoon vegetable oil
7	cups water
15	black peppercorns
2	bay leaves
4	tablespoons unsalted butter, divided
1	onion, chopped fine
1	fennel bulb, stalks discarded, bulb halved, cored, and chopped fine
⅛	teaspoon baking soda
2	garlic cloves, minced
1½	cups Arborio rice
¾	cup dry white wine
1	ounce Parmesan cheese, grated (½ cup), plus extra for serving
¼	cup minced fresh chives
½	teaspoon grated lemon zest plus 1 tablespoon juice, plus lemon wedges for serving

1. Cut each shrimp crosswise into thirds. Toss with ½ teaspoon salt in bowl and set aside. Heat oil in Dutch oven over high heat until shimmering. Add reserved shrimp shells and cook, stirring frequently, until shells begin to turn spotty brown, 2 to 4 minutes. Add water, peppercorns, bay leaves, and 1 teaspoon salt and bring to boil. Reduce heat to low and simmer for 5 minutes. Strain stock through fine-mesh strainer set over large bowl, pressing on solids with rubber spatula to extract as much liquid as possible; discard solids.

2. Melt 2 tablespoons butter in now-empty pot over medium heat. Add onion, fennel, baking soda, and remaining ¼ teaspoon salt. Cook, stirring frequently, until vegetables are softened but not browned, 8 to 10 minutes (volume will be dramatically reduced and onion will have mostly disintegrated). Add garlic and stir until fragrant, about 30 seconds. Add rice and cook, stirring frequently, until grains are translucent around edges, about 3 minutes.

3. Add wine and cook, stirring constantly, until fully absorbed, 2 to 3 minutes. Stir 4 cups stock into rice mixture; reduce heat to medium-low, cover, and simmer until almost all liquid has been absorbed and rice is just al dente, 16 to 18 minutes, stirring twice during simmering.

4. Add ¾ cup stock to risotto and stir gently and constantly until risotto becomes creamy, about 3 minutes. Stir in Parmesan and shrimp. Cover pot and let stand off heat for 5 minutes.

5. Gently stir chives, lemon zest and juice, and remaining 2 tablespoons butter into risotto. Season with salt and pepper to taste. If desired, stir in additional stock to loosen texture of risotto. Serve, passing lemon wedges and extra Parmesan separately.

STUFFED PORTOBELLO MUSHROOMS

✓ **WHY THIS RECIPE WORKS** Just because it's a vegetable doesn't mean that the hearty portobello mushroom always has to be a side dish. To help it take center stage, we started by using a spoon to gently scrape the dark gills from the underside of each portobello cap. Removing the gills made for cleaner mushroom flavor and a more pleasant texture. Next, we marinated our mushroom caps in a concentrated combination of extra-virgin olive oil and red wine vinegar. After the mushrooms had absorbed all that bright flavor, we roasted them in a 475-degree oven until they were tender. Meanwhile, we made a creamy, flavorful stuffing of garlicky Swiss chard and goat cheese. We topped the mushrooms with some Parmesan-enhanced panko bread crumbs for crunchy textural contrast.

Portobello mushroom caps were made for stuffing. Why? For starters, their hefty size and circular shape make a perfect "dish" to hold stuffing. Plus, they have a brawny, earthy flavor that can stand up to potent stuffing ingredients, making the dish a potential tastebud-rocking powerhouse. I say "potential," though, because most stuffed portobellos I've had have been bland, spongy, and sad.

Determined to break the curse, I set out to create a recipe for truly memorable stuffed portobello mushroom caps. I began by preparing a handful of promising recipes for my tasters. The recipes called for stuffing the caps with various combinations of sautéed vegetables, meats, cheese, and beans. A few literally fell flat, emerging from the oven as thin, deflated disks. But one recipe gave me hope; it called for marinating and roasting the caps before stuffing them, which resulted in moist and tender 'shrooms.

I got busy developing my own version. In addition to stemming the mushrooms, I found that scraping out the dark brown gills from the underside of each cap made them taste much cleaner. Moving on to the marinade, I tested various ingredients and landed on a simple combination of olive oil and red wine vinegar. Letting the mushroom caps soak in the vinaigrette in a zipper-lock bag was efficient and easy; 30 minutes to 1 hour of soaking infused the caps with plenty of flavor. A 20-minute stint in a hot oven drove off excess moisture and cooked the mushrooms through, ensuring that they were tender and moist—not spongy or soggy.

I wanted to fill these caps with a vegetarian-friendly mixture, so for a rich, creamy base, I used tangy fresh goat cheese. For bulk and flavor, I tested spinach, kale, and Swiss chard; we preferred the milder flavor and tender texture of sautéed Swiss chard. Toasted Parmesan bread crumbs made for an irresistibly crunchy topping.

Once I'd filled the caps and topped them with the crumbs, they needed only a few more minutes in the oven to heat through. I let the mushrooms cool slightly and called my team to taste. Happy people all around.

—ASHLEY MOORE, *Cook's Country*

NOTES FROM THE TEST KITCHEN

PREPPING THE MUSHROOMS

Using a spoon to gently scrape the dark gills from the underside of each portobello cap not only makes for cleaner mushroom flavor but also improves the roasted mushrooms' texture.

Stuffed Portobello Mushrooms

SERVES 4

Use a spoon to remove the gills from the mushroom caps for the best texture.

- ½   cup plus 1 tablespoon extra-virgin olive oil, divided
- 3   tablespoons red wine vinegar
- ¾   teaspoon table salt, divided
- ½   teaspoon pepper
- 4   portobello mushroom caps (4 to 5 inches in diameter), gills removed
- ½   cup panko bread crumbs
- 1   ounce Parmesan cheese, grated (½ cup)
- 10 ounces Swiss chard, stems and leaves cut into ½-inch pieces
- 3   garlic cloves, minced
- ⅛   teaspoon red pepper flakes
- 4   ounces goat cheese, softened
- ½   cup torn fresh basil leaves
- 1½ teaspoons grated lemon zest

1. Adjust oven racks to upper-middle and lower-middle positions and heat oven to 475 degrees. Combine 6 tablespoons oil, vinegar, ½ teaspoon salt, and pepper in 1-gallon zipper-lock bag. Add mushrooms, seal bag, turn to coat, and let sit at room temperature for at least 30 minutes or up to 1 hour.

2. Line rimmed baking sheet with parchment paper. Arrange mushrooms gill side down on prepared sheet. Roast on lower rack until tender, about 20 minutes.

3. Combine panko and 2 tablespoons oil in 12-inch nonstick skillet and cook over medium heat, stirring frequently, until golden brown, about 5 minutes; transfer to bowl and stir in Parmesan. Wipe skillet clean with paper towels.

4. Heat remaining 1 tablespoon oil in now-empty skillet over medium-high heat until shimmering. Add chard and remaining ¼ teaspoon salt and cook until wilted and liquid has evaporated, 5 to 7 minutes. Stir in garlic and pepper flakes and cook until fragrant, about 30 seconds. Off heat, stir in goat cheese, basil, and lemon zest.

5. Flip mushrooms gill side up and distribute filling evenly among mushrooms. Sprinkle panko mixture evenly over top. Bake on upper rack until topping is golden brown, about 4 minutes. Serve.

STUFFED PORTOBELLO MUSHROOMS

CHAPTER 4

MEAT

BEEF TOP LOIN ROAST WITH POTATOES

✓ **WHY THIS RECIPE WORKS** To create a juicy, tender roast and creamy, beefy-tasting potatoes, we started with a top loin roast and trimmed the thick ribbons of fat that run along its sides. Browning the trimmings along with the roast yielded loads of rendered fat (and flavorful fond), which we then used to brown the potatoes. From there, we covered the potatoes with aluminum foil, which trapped steam that helped them cook through and allowed us to roast the beef on top of them (poking holes in the foil let the juices drip through). While the cooked roast rested, we flipped the potatoes cut side up; added broth that we fortified with flavor by simmering it with the seared beef scraps, herbs, and seasonings; and braised the spuds in a 500-degree oven—creating our own version of an old-school French classic called fondant potatoes. Finally, we strained and defatted the remaining broth to serve as a jus alongside the meat and potatoes.

Roasting beef with potatoes sounds as though it will produce the ideal holiday spread. While the meat cooks, the spuds sitting underneath or around it soak up the drippings and transform into a flavorful side dish that impresses just as much as (if not more than) the roast itself. But as smart and simple as that sounds, it's folklore. In my experience, cooking the meat and potatoes together rarely produces the best version of either one.

The problem is partly due to a lack of space. Most roasting pans can't accommodate a piece of meat large enough to feed a crowd plus enough potatoes to go alongside it. So the options are to cram the potatoes into the pan, which causes them to steam, thwarting flavorful browning, or to include only enough to feed a few guests.

The more fundamental issue is that the two components require radically different cooking methods. Low-and-slow heat is the best way to ensure a juicy, evenly cooked roast, but it also makes for sparse drippings and, thus, bland potatoes. On the other hand, the only way to really brown and crisp potatoes in the oven is to crank the heat way up. But who's willing to risk overcooking a pricey roast for the sake of the spuds?

Finding a way to roast enough beef and potatoes for a crowd while allowing the roast to cook up juicy and tender (and release flavorful drippings to infuse and crisp the potatoes) would require real strategy.

I often default to prime rib for the holidays because of its well-marbled meat and fat cap, which crisps up into a thick crust, making it feel festive. But there are other good options, such as top loin roast. This is the cut that produces strip steaks; like prime rib, it boasts well-marbled meat and a nice fat cap. Plus, it's boneless and uniform, which makes it easy to cook and slice.

I crosshatched the fat cap to help it render and crisp and then salted the meat overnight to ensure that it would be well seasoned and juicy. For the time being, I would cook the meat and potatoes separately (I'd tackle the merger later). I seared the roast, top and bottom, in a large roasting pan and then transferred it to a 300-degree oven, where it cooked gently until it reached 115 degrees. That's about 10 degrees shy of medium-rare, but the temperature of the meat would climb as it rested.

Potatoes won't crisp in a crowded pan even if the heat is blasting, so I scrapped that goal in favor of an old-school French preparation called fondant potatoes that creates marvelously flavorful results without crisping. To make fondant potatoes, you halve and brown the spuds on the cut side and then braise them in fat and stock. The potatoes absorb the flavorful liquid, turning so velvety that they practically dissolve in your mouth. Not worrying about crisping also meant that I could pack plenty of potatoes into the pan.

I browned 5 pounds of peeled, halved Yukon Gold potatoes (their starchy yet creamy consistency seemed ideal) in the rendered fat left in the pan, flipped them, poured beef broth around them, and returned them to a 500-degree oven. Thirty minutes later, they were plump and extremely tender. I transferred them to a platter and strained and defatted the remaining broth, which would make a nice jus for serving.

They tasted beefy on the outside but bland within— no surprise since commercial broth contains no fat and only moderate beef flavor. But the roast had those qualities in spades. Time for that merger.

One unique feature of top loin roast is the sinewy strips of meat and fat that run along either side of the roast. They're often left behind on the plate, but I decided to use them. I cut them off and sliced them into 1-inch pieces to brown alongside the roast.

The results were worth the minimal knife work: The trimmings gave up loads more fat and fond for the potatoes to soak up. (Starting the meat and trimmings in a cold pan maximized the amount of fat that was rendered, because the fat had time to melt thoroughly before the meat's exterior browned too much.) To maximize their efficacy, I simmered the browned scraps with the broth before using it to braise the potatoes, which amped up the broth's beefiness and the flavor of the spuds. Further doctoring the broth with garlic and herbs rounded it out; adding gelatin gave the reduced jus unctuous body.

Cooking the meat and potatoes together wasn't tricky once I had extracted all that flavor and fat from the trimmings. But it did require a strategic setup. After searing the meat and scraps, I laid the potatoes cut side down in the pan, keeping them in a single layer to ensure even cooking, and covered them with aluminum foil that I then poked holes in. That created a "rack" on which I placed the roast; it also allowed the juices to drip through to the potatoes and trapped steam that helped the potatoes cook through. When the roast hit 115 degrees, I set it aside to rest; gingerly flipped the potatoes; added my beef-enhanced, strained broth; and finished the potatoes in a 500-degree oven.

It was a success: juicy, tender meat and creamy potatoes that tasted truly beefy.

—ANDREW JANJIGIAN, *Cook's Illustrated*

Beef Top Loin Roast with Potatoes

SERVES 8 TO 10

Top loin roast is also known as strip roast. Use potatoes that are about 1½ inches in diameter and at least 4 inches long. The browned surfaces of the potatoes are very delicate; take care when flipping the potatoes in step 7. To make flipping easier, flip two potatoes and remove them from the pan to create space before flipping the rest.

    1   (5- to 6-pound) boneless top loin roast

    2   tablespoons plus 2 teaspoons kosher salt, divided

    2   teaspoons pepper, divided

    5   pounds Yukon Gold potatoes, peeled

    ¼   cup vegetable oil

    5   cups beef broth

    6   sprigs fresh thyme

    2   small sprigs fresh rosemary

    2   tablespoons unflavored gelatin

    4   garlic cloves, lightly crushed and peeled

BEEFING UP THE FLAVOR OF POTATOES

There are a few reasons that the potatoes in this dish are so darn full of beefy flavor: We introduce beefy goodness to them three different times and in three different ways over the course of cooking.

BROWN IN RENDERED FAT After searing the roast and the trimmings, we sear the potatoes, broad side down, in the rendered fat to create a deeply browned, beefy-tasting surface.

ROAST WITH BEEFY JUICES We cover the potatoes with a "rack" made from perforated foil and roast the beef on top so its juices drip down onto the potatoes.

BRAISE IN MEATY BROTH While the meat rests, we braise the potatoes, browned side up, in a quick enriched broth made from the trimmings, saturating them with more meaty flavor.

SHOPPING FOR STRIP STEAK IN ROAST FORM

Top loin roast, which comes from the short loin in the middle of the cow's back, is the roast that generates strip steaks (it's also called "strip roast"). The well-marbled, tender meat and ample fat cap make it a great alternative to other premium roasts, such as prime rib (it costs about $4 less per pound than prime rib, too). We trim off the strips of meat and fat that run along the sides of the roast and brown them with the roast to generate lots of flavorful juices for cooking the potatoes.

MEAT A DIFFERENT CUT
Top loin roast is a great alternative to prime rib.

1. Pat roast dry with paper towels. Place roast fat cap side down and trim off strip of meat that is loosely attached to thicker side of roast. Rotate roast 180 degrees and trim off strip of meat and fat from narrow side of roast. (After trimming, roast should be rectangular with roughly even thickness.) Cut trimmings into 1-inch pieces. Transfer trimmings to small bowl, wrap tightly in plastic wrap, and refrigerate.

2. Using sharp knife, cut ¼-inch-deep slits, ½ inch apart, in crosshatch pattern in fat cap of roast. Sprinkle all sides of roast evenly with 2 tablespoons salt and 1 teaspoon pepper. Wrap in plastic and refrigerate for 6 to 24 hours.

3. Adjust oven rack to lowest position and heat oven to 300 degrees. Trim and discard ¼ inch from end of each potato. Cut each potato in half crosswise. Toss potatoes with remaining 2 teaspoons salt and remaining 1 teaspoon pepper and set aside.

4. Place oil in large roasting pan. Place roast, fat cap side down, in center of pan and scatter trimmings around roast. Cook over medium heat, stirring trimmings frequently but not moving roast, until fat cap is well browned, 8 to 12 minutes. Flip roast and continue to cook, stirring trimmings frequently, until bottom of roast is lightly browned and trimmings are rendered and crispy, 6 to 10 minutes longer. Remove pan from heat and transfer roast to plate. Using slotted spoon, transfer trimmings to medium saucepan, leaving fat in pan.

5. Arrange potatoes in single layer, broad side down, in pan. Return pan to medium heat and cook, without moving potatoes, until well browned around edges, 15 to 20 minutes. (Do not flip potatoes.) Off heat, lay 18 by 22-inch sheet of aluminum foil over potatoes. Using oven mitts, crimp edges of foil to rim of pan. With paring knife, poke 5 holes in center of foil. Lay roast, fat side up, in center of foil. Transfer pan to oven and cook until meat registers 115 degrees, 1 to 1¼ hours.

6. While roast cooks, add broth, thyme sprigs, rosemary sprigs, gelatin, and garlic to saucepan with trimmings. Bring to boil over medium-high heat. Reduce heat and simmer for 15 minutes. Strain mixture through fine-mesh strainer into 4-cup liquid measuring cup, pressing on solids to extract as much liquid as possible; discard solids. (You should have 4 cups liquid; if necessary, add water to equal 4 cups.)

7. When meat registers 115 degrees, remove pan from oven and increase oven temperature to 500 degrees. Transfer roast to carving board. Remove foil and use to tent roast. Using offset spatula, carefully flip potatoes. Pour strained liquid around potatoes and return pan (handles will be hot) to oven (it's OK if oven has not yet reached 500 degrees). Cook until liquid is reduced by half, 20 to 30 minutes.

8. Carefully transfer potatoes to serving platter. Pour liquid into fat separator and let settle for 5 minutes. Slice roast and transfer to platter with potatoes. Transfer defatted juices to small bowl. Serve, passing juices separately.

BEEF BULGOGI

WHY THIS RECIPE WORKS For bulgogi at home we first had to pick the best cut of beef. Rib-eye steak offered a nice combination of marbled interior and rich beef flavor. To shave the meat superthin, we froze it in chunks so it firmed up enough to cleanly slice into bite-size pieces. Treating the meat with baking soda helped it stay tender, and because the meat was so thin, we found that there was no need to coat it with a marinade until just before cooking. For our version, we balanced the marinade's signature sweet flavor with soy sauce, garlic, sesame oil, pepper, and chopped onion, which brought savory undertones and diluted the marinade so the beef wasn't too intensely flavored. We cooked the beef in a moderately hot skillet before stirring it until it was fully cooked, which took just a few minutes. A quick, savory, spicy sauce (called *ssamjang*) and daikon pickles offered flavor and textural contrast to the sweet beef. Lettuce leaves, steamed rice, and other sides made it a complete meal.

When I first tried bulgogi (literally "fire meat") at a Korean barbecue restaurant not too long ago, I immediately fell in love—not just with the dish but with the whole experience. Diners used chopsticks to spread thinly sliced beef, wet with a sweet soy marinade, across a hot grill in the center of the table. The meat sputtered and hissed, and after a few minutes it was lightly browned and cooked through. Each diner then piled a few pieces into a lettuce leaf, spooned on a deeply savory chile sauce, wrapped up the lettuce into a package, and ate it. Steamed rice was served on the side to help balance the intense flavors, along with an array of different sauces and pickles collectively known as *banchan*.

KOREAN MARINATED BEEF (BULGOGI)

Eating in this communal way, with each person customizing their own bites of the dish, was fun and convivial. It's no wonder that bulgogi is one of the most popular dishes in Korea, at restaurants and at home. I couldn't wait to re-create the experience in my kitchen.

Tender and/or fatty cuts are commonly chosen for bulgogi so that the thin slices, which end up fairly well-done, don't turn tough or dry. Popular choices include rib eye, sirloin, tenderloin, and skirt steak. After tasting all the cuts side by side, we chose rib eye for its rich beefiness and generous marbling.

Traditionally, the steak for bulgogi is sliced razor-thin, and we've found that partially freezing the meat makes this task much easier. I divided a single rib-eye steak into 1½-inch-wide pieces and then froze them for 35 minutes before slicing them thin. As I worked, the steak was transformed into an impressively large, wispy pile of shaved meat. It was now time for the marinade.

The marinade for bulgogi skews sweet, but in addition to sugar, it contains a good amount of soy sauce and garlic. I put together a batch containing soy sauce, garlic, sugar, toasted sesame oil, and pepper; tossed it with the meat; and let it sit for 30 minutes.

I cooked the slices (without wiping off the marinade, per tradition) in a nonstick skillet over moderately high heat, let them sit for a minute to brown slightly, and then stirred until they were no longer pink, just a few minutes longer.

Unfortunately, this beef had a sweetness that screamed teriyaki, not bulgogi. I decreased the sugar from 6 tablespoons to 4, increased the soy sauce from 2 tablespoons to 3, and for savoriness, doubled the garlic cloves to four and added ¼ cup of chopped onion—an ingredient I had seen in some bulgogi recipes. I pureed the mixture (also common) and then marinated and cooked the beef as before. Much better: The sweetness was still apparent but much more tempered.

The meat tasted great and wasn't dry, but it was a bit chewy, since the thin pieces couldn't help but be cooked well beyond medium-rare. Many bulgogi recipes address this issue by including certain fruits such as pear for the enzymes they contain that supposedly tenderize meat. But I found that tossing the beef with baking soda (our go-to treatment for tenderizing meat) and letting it sit for a few minutes before marinating it was more effective, as pear and other fruits turned the surface of the meat mushy.

But I had one more question about the marinade: The test kitchen learned long ago that marinades do most of their work on the meat's surface, and my thin slices were nearly all surface. What's more, the beef was cooking directly in its marinade. Was soaking the slices for 30 minutes superfluous? When tasting three batches—one marinated for 30 minutes, one for 15 minutes, and another just before cooking—no one could detect a difference. A quick soak just before cooking was the way to go.

I cooked up another batch of meat, this time adding a handful of scallion greens during the last 30 seconds for freshness and a vibrant green color. The salty-sweet beef was ultratender and moist.

Finally, I turned to the banchan. First up was the traditional savory chile sauce *ssamjang* to dab onto the meat. I combined minced scallion whites with two potently flavored Korean pantry staples made from fermented soy beans: sweet, savory, and spicy gochujang and salty, rich *doenjang* (see "Punch Up Your Pantry with These Korean Staples"). I also added sugar, garlic, toasted sesame oil, and a little water to loosen its consistency. Then, for a crisp, pungent element, I soaked daikon radishes in vinegar, salt, and sugar for 30 minutes to create a quick pickle.

With steamed rice, lettuce leaves, and potent kimchi to go with the tender beef, spicy sauce, and tangy pickles, I had a fun, satisfying meal that I couldn't wait to share.

—ANNIE PETITO, *Cook's Illustrated*

Korean Marinated Beef (Bulgogi)
SERVES 4

To save time, prepare the pickles and chile sauce while the steak is in the freezer. You can substitute 2 cups of bean sprouts and one cucumber, peeled, quartered lengthwise, seeded, and sliced thin on the bias, for the daikon, if desired. It's worth seeking out the Korean fermented bean pastes *doenjang* and gochujang, which are sold in Asian markets and online. If you can't find them, you can substitute red or white miso for the doenjang and sriracha for the gochujang. You can eat bulgogi as a plated meal with steamed rice and kimchi or wrap small portions of the beef in lettuce leaves with chile sauce and eat them like tacos.

PICKLES

- 1 **cup rice vinegar**
- 2 **tablespoons sugar**
- 1½ **teaspoons table salt**
- 1 **pound daikon radish, peeled and cut into 1½-inch-long matchsticks**

CHILE SAUCE (SSAMJANG)

- 4 **scallions, white and light green parts only, minced**
- ¼ **cup doenjang**
- 1 **tablespoon gochujang**
- 1 **tablespoon water**
- 2 **teaspoons sugar**
- 2 **teaspoons toasted sesame oil**
- 1 **garlic clove, minced**

BEEF

- 1 **(1¼-pound) boneless rib-eye steak, cut crosswise into 1½-inch-wide pieces and trimmed**
- 1 **tablespoon water**
- ¼ **teaspoon baking soda**
- ¼ **cup chopped onion**
- ¼ **cup sugar**
- 3 **tablespoons soy sauce**
- 4 **garlic cloves, peeled**
- 1 **tablespoon toasted sesame oil**
- ¼ **teaspoon pepper**
- 2 **teaspoons vegetable oil**
- 4 **scallions, dark green parts only, cut into 1½-inch pieces**

1. FOR THE PICKLES: Whisk vinegar, sugar, and salt together in medium bowl. Add daikon and toss to combine. Gently press on daikon to submerge. Cover and refrigerate for at least 30 minutes or up to 24 hours.

2. FOR THE CHILE SAUCE (SSAMJANG): Combine all ingredients in small bowl. Cover and set aside. (Sauce can be refrigerated for up to 3 days.)

3. FOR THE BEEF: Place beef on large plate and freeze until very firm, 35 to 40 minutes. Once firm, stand each piece on 1 cut side on cutting board and, using sharp knife, shave beef against grain as thin as possible. (Slices needn't be perfectly intact.) Combine water and baking soda in medium bowl. Add beef and toss to coat. Let sit at room temperature for 5 minutes.

4. Meanwhile, process onion, sugar, soy sauce, garlic, sesame oil, and pepper in food processor until smooth, about 30 seconds, scraping down sides of bowl as needed. Add onion mixture to beef and toss to coat evenly.

5. Heat vegetable oil in 12-inch nonstick skillet over medium-high heat until shimmering. Add beef mixture in even layer and cook, without stirring, until browned on 1 side, about 1 minute. Stir and continue to cook until beef is no longer pink, 3 to 4 minutes longer. Add scallion greens and cook, stirring constantly, until fragrant, about 30 seconds. Transfer to platter. Serve with pickles and chile sauce.

NOTES FROM THE TEST KITCHEN

PUNCH UP YOUR PANTRY WITH THESE KOREAN STAPLES

Our bulgogi recipe features three mainstays of Korean cuisine that can be used in a variety of ways.

KIMCHI

In Korea, this accompaniment is on the table at breakfast, lunch, and dinner. There are hundreds of variations, but the best-known type, which is tangy and spicy, is made of salted fermented napa cabbage and seasoned with chili powder, garlic, ginger, and scallions. Add it to grain bowls, stir-fries, scrambled eggs, burgers, hot dogs, or grilled cheese.

GOCHUJANG

This thick, sweet, savory, and spicy paste is made from *gochugaru* (Korean chile flakes), dried fermented soybean powder, sweet rice powder, salt, and sometimes sugar. Use it when preparing Korean fried chicken, in marinades or dipping sauces, or to pep up soups, stews, and even deviled eggs.

DOENJANG

Fermented soybeans give this coarse-textured, miso-like, salty, rich paste a slight sourness. Use it as a replacement for miso in soups, stews, and dressings or as a coating on meat, fish, or tofu.

A POWERFUL TRIO
Keep kimchi, gochujang, and *doenjang* on hand
for authentic Korean flavor.

TEXAS BARBECUE BRISKET

TEXAS-STYLE SMOKED BRISKET

✓ **WHY THIS RECIPE WORKS** We wanted to develop a recipe for an authentic Texas-style smoked brisket with a tender, juicy interior encased in a dark, peppery bark. And we wanted to do it on a charcoal grill. We started with a whole 10- to 12-pound brisket (both the point and flat cuts). Seasoning the brisket overnight with kosher salt and pepper enhanced the flavor of the meat without masking any of its beefiness. To avoid drying out the meat as it cooked, we used a grill setup called a charcoal snake. This C-shaped array of smoldering briquettes provided low, slow, indirect heat to the center of the grill for upwards of 6 hours, so we needed to refuel only once during the exceptionally long cooking time. Cooking the brisket fat side down gave it a protective barrier against the direct heat of the fire. And wrapping the brisket in aluminum foil toward the end of its cooking time and letting it rest in a cooler for 2 hours before serving helped keep it ultramoist and juicy.

Settle in and get comfortable. Like drinking 18-year-old single-malt Scotch, smoking a whole brisket is a task best taken slow. But if you're willing to invest a bit of time, attention, and patience—and take a bold leap of faith—truly sublime eating is well within reach.

As any Texan worth their spurs will tell you, a properly smoked brisket holds irresistible appeal—it's ultrabeefy, tender, and juicy on the inside, with a dark, peppery, smoky crust (or bark) on the outside. Legendary Texas barbecue joints don't even offer sauce; instead they season the meat sparely and confidently with salt, pepper, and smoke.

Why cook a whole brisket? Most home cooks use just half a brisket, either the lean flat cut or the fattier point cut, because whole briskets are so large and take so long to cook. But a whole brisket feeds a crowd, looks and tastes incredible, and, for those who love a grilling challenge, is the crowning achievement of backyard barbecue mastery.

Texas brisket is traditionally smoked in commercial smokers that can handle hundreds of pounds of meat at once. Brisket is just about the least tender cut on the steer; it's laden with tough collagen and needs long, low, moist cooking to break down that collagen and become tender. Commercial smokers have fireboxes set away from the smoking chamber so the meat is never too close to the fire; this indirect cooking allows the meat to retain moisture while it slowly tenderizes and soaks up smoke flavor over the half-day cooking time. I set out to defy convention and smoke an entire brisket to Texas-level tenderness using just a regular charcoal grill.

But there were some challenges. Since charcoal grills are much smaller than commercial smokers, the brisket has to be closer to the fire on a grill, putting it in danger of cooking too hot and drying out or of becoming a victim of sooty flare-ups. Plus, refueling the grill with more charcoal means opening the grill lid, a step that makes it hard to maintain a steady temperature inside the grill.

I started at the butcher counter, ordering several 12-pound full briskets. I tried a handful of techniques from different experts that promised smoker-quality brisket using a charcoal grill. But at best these recipes and methods gave me mediocre brisket—and at worst, bone-dry, stringy meat. Seeing my frustration, a coworker sent me a link to a website that described something from the competitive barbecue circuit called the "charcoal snake." The what?

A charcoal snake is a C-shaped array of briquettes that slowly burns from one end to the other. With wood chips or chunks on top, it is supposed to provide hours of low, slow, smoky heat without the need to open the grill or refuel. It sounded a little ridiculous, but I figured it was worth a shot.

I carefully laid out the ring of charcoal, lit one end, threw on a big brisket (fat side up, per tradition), inserted a temperature probe in the meat, covered the grill, and waited until the inside of the brisket hit 200 degrees, which took about 8 hours. This brisket had a nice bark and was pretty moist (if a tad tough), and it gave me hope that this method would work.

Over several weeks, I honed my process and learned some valuable lessons. Wood chunks are preferable to chips because they burn more slowly and thus produce more constant smoke. Placing a disposable aluminum pan filled with water in the center of the snake helps moderate the grill temperature. Precisely configuring the briquettes and wood chunks into a snake provides about 5½ hours of slow, gentle heat (meaning I had to refuel only once). Rubbing the raw brisket with plenty of salt and pepper and refrigerating it for 12 to 24 hours before grilling ensures deep seasoning. Wrapping the brisket in foil once it reaches 170 degrees helps keep it juicy and speeds the last bit of cooking. And cooking the meat to an internal temperature of 205 degrees is best; any lower and the meat will be chewy, any higher and it can get too soft and begin to dry out.

I was making progress, but I wanted my brisket to be more tender. We know that the sweet spot for collagen to break down without overcooking the meat is between 180 and 200 degrees. I found that if I pulled the wrapped brisket from the grill at 205 degrees and let it rest, still tightly wrapped in foil, in a cooler for 2 hours, it stayed in this temperature range longer and emerged supremely moist and tender.

One last problem: The bottom of the brisket was coming out a bit dry. I reached out to Andy Husbands and Chris Hart, two nationally renowned barbecue experts. They suggested cooking the brisket fat side down. It was untraditional, but this way the fat would sit against the cooking grate and act as a protective barrier against the direct heat of the fire. It worked great, making for a brisket that was moist all the way through. And with the water pan below the grate, flare-ups weren't an issue.

After smoking 497 pounds of beef, I sliced up one last brisket. My tasters confirmed that I had finally achieved my goal: a gloriously tender brisket with deep smoke flavor and rich bark, all on a backyard charcoal grill. Texas, we've got news for you.

—MORGAN BOLLING, *Cook's Country*

NOTES FROM THE TEST KITCHEN

BUY THE RIGHT BRISKET

A full brisket is from the lower chest of the cow and ranges from 8 to 20 pounds in size. It's made up of both the point and flat cuts. While the flat alone is easier to find (it's what you're likely to find packaged in the meat case), special-ordering a full brisket from the butcher counter is well worth it. A full brisket allows you to offer diners both lean slices from the flat portion and moist (or fatty) slices from the point.

The ideal brisket will have an even, ½-inch-thick fat cap. If you can't get a whole brisket in the 10- to 12-pound range, it's better to buy a slightly larger brisket and trim it down to size (smaller briskets are more prone to drying out on the grill).

POINT
Thicker, fattier

FLAT
Thinner, leaner

Texas Barbecue Brisket
SERVES 12 TO 15

We developed this recipe using a 22-inch Weber Kettle charcoal grill. Plan ahead: The brisket must be seasoned at least 12 hours before cooking. We call for a whole beef brisket here, with both the flat and point cuts intact; you may need to special-order this cut. We recommend reading the entire recipe before starting.

- 1 (10- to 12-pound) whole beef brisket, untrimmed
- ¼ cup kosher salt
- ¼ cup pepper
- 5 (3-inch) wood chunks
- 1 (13 by 9-inch) disposable aluminum pan

1. With brisket positioned point side up, use sharp knife to trim fat cap to ½- to ¼-inch thickness. Remove excess fat from deep pocket where flat and point are attached. Trim and discard short edge of flat if less than 1 inch thick. Flip brisket and remove any large deposits of fat from underside.

2. Combine salt and pepper in bowl. Place brisket on rimmed baking sheet and sprinkle all over with salt mixture. Cover loosely with plastic wrap and refrigerate for 12 to 24 hours.

3. Open bottom vent completely. Set up charcoal snake: Place 1 layer of 58 briquettes, 2 briquettes wide, around perimeter of grill, overlapping slightly so briquettes are touching, leaving 8-inch gap between ends of snake. Place second layer of 58 briquettes, also 2 briquettes wide, on top of first. (Completed snake should be 2 briquettes wide by 2 briquettes high.)

4. Starting 4 inches from 1 end of snake, evenly space wood chunks on top of snake. Place disposable pan in center of grill. Fill disposable pan with 6 cups water. Light chimney starter filled with 10 briquettes (pile briquettes on 1 side of chimney). When coals are partially covered with ash, pour over 1 end of snake. (Make sure lit coals touch only 1 end of snake.)

5. Set cooking grate in place. Clean and oil cooking grate. Place brisket, fat side down, directly over water pan, with point end facing gap in snake. Insert temperature probe into side of upper third of point. Cover grill, open lid vent completely, and position lid vent over gap in snake. Cook, undisturbed and without lifting lid, until meat registers 170 degrees, 4 to 5 hours.

6. Place 2 large sheets of aluminum foil on rimmed baking sheet. Remove temperature probe from brisket. Using oven mitts, lift brisket and transfer to center of foil, fat side down. Wrap brisket tightly with first layer of foil, minimizing air pockets between foil and brisket. Rotate brisket 90 degrees and wrap with second layer of foil. (Use additional foil, if necessary, to completely wrap brisket.) Make small mark on foil with marker to keep track of fat/point side. Foil wrap should be airtight.

7. Remove cooking grate. Starting at still-unlit end of snake, pour 3 quarts unlit briquettes about halfway around perimeter of grill over gap and spent coals. Replace cooking grate. Return foil-wrapped brisket to grill over water pan, fat side down, with point end facing where gap in snake used to be. Reinsert temperature probe into point. Cover grill and continue to cook until meat registers 205 degrees, 1 to 2 hours longer.

8. Remove temperature probe. Transfer foil-wrapped brisket to cooler, fat side up. Close cooler and let rest for at least 2 hours or up to 3 hours. Transfer brisket to carving board, unwrap, and position fat side up. Slice flat against grain ¼ inch thick, stopping once you reach base of point. Rotate point 90 degrees and slice point against grain (perpendicular to first cut) ⅜ inch thick. Serve.

BACON-WRAPPED FILETS MIGNONS

✓ **WHY THIS RECIPE WORKS** The trick to these mouthwatering filets mignons is getting perfectly cooked steaks and crispy slices of bacon at the same time. Too often things don't pan out, and we're either left with perfectly cooked steaks and chewy, undercooked bacon or crispy bacon and overdone filets. So we reversed the usual method. By slowly cooking the wrapped filets in a low oven until they were just shy of medium-rare, we ensured that they were perfectly cooked before giving the bacon the attention it needed. After being rendered slightly in the oven, the bacon was ready for a quick trip to the skillet to finish crisping. Using the edges of the skillet to stand the steaks on their sides, we were able to get fully seared steaks with crispy, porky wrappers. A simple Gorgonzola vinaigrette acted as a tangy, creamy companion.

Filet mignon is a lean, lush cut of meat that, when cooked to pink perfection, has an unsurpassed buttery texture and clean, mild, beefy flavor. But for some, paying top dollar for a "mild" steak doesn't compute. Hence, bacon-wrapped filet mignon, a steakhouse favorite that ups the ante by wrapping each steak in a strip of salty, smoky goodness.

Great bacon-wrapped filets mignons can be a challenge to pull off not only because you have to get the bacon and beef correctly cooked on the same timetable but also because it can be hard to fully render and crisp the bacon while keeping it firmly attached to the perimeter of each steak. I set out to find a foolproof method for getting this impressive dish done right.

I gathered a handful of recipes to test. All followed a similar procedure: Secure the bacon around the sides of the beef with toothpicks or twine, sear the top and bottom in a skillet, and finish cooking in the oven. The recipes that called for removing the steaks from the oven once the bacon was crisp produced grossly overcooked beef—not OK. But those that called for removing the steaks at the proper temperature (about 125 degrees for medium-rare) were afflicted with flabby, under-rendered bacon. This method wouldn't do.

I knew that searing the beef was critical to enhancing this mild cut's flavor and to working some of the fat out of the bacon. I also knew that I couldn't rely on bacon crispiness as a cue to determine when the steaks were done—a digital thermometer was a must. Considering these two points, I turned to a test kitchen method that calls for first gently cooking the steaks to near-perfect doneness in a low oven and then searing them—either under the broiler or in a skillet on the stovetop—to brown the meat (and hopefully crisp the bacon).

Over several days of testing, I figured out each step in succession. First, secure the belt of bacon around each steak with a toothpick. Then, roast the steak in a low 275-degree oven until the meat reaches 115 degrees—I wanted the steaks to get to about 125 degrees for medium-rare, and pulling them from the oven a tad early allowed for a little carryover cooking plus searing time to get them up to temperature. (When the steaks emerge from the oven at their 115-degree target, the bacon is about halfway rendered but nowhere near crispy and browned.)

I tried heating the broiler and doing the searing there, but turning each steak to expose all sides of the bacon to the heat was too much work. It was better

BACON-WRAPPED FILETS MIGNONS

simply to sear the partially cooked steaks in a skillet on the stovetop. I started them on their sides and then turned each steak two or three times to crisp the bacon (see "Amazing Bacon-Wrapped Steaks in Four Easy Steps"). After the steaks had spent about 5 minutes total on their sides, I quickly seared the bacon-free flat surfaces to create a flavorful browned crust. At this point, the interiors of the steaks were a perfect 125 degrees. Success!

These filets mignons were juicy and well browned, with crispy, flavorful bacon wrappers. But since this was a special-occasion meal, I wanted a sauce to take it over the top. After playing around with all kinds of flavors and sauce textures, I ended up with a supergood gorgonzola vinaigrette; I know it sounds weird, but trust me when I say that this sauce is a game changer. It looks like an oddly chunky salad dressing, but the crumbles of potent blue cheese and bits of shallot create a bright, tangy concoction that perfectly complements the beef and bacon flavors. So save your steakhouse dollars and invest a little time and effort into creating an even better steak at home.

—ALLI BERKEY, *Cook's Country*

Bacon-Wrapped Filets Mignons

SERVES 4

To double this recipe, double all the ingredients except the oil and roast and sear the eight steaks as you would if you were preparing four steaks. You can serve the steaks with Gorgonzola Vinaigrette (recipe follows), if desired.

- 2 teaspoons kosher salt
- 1 teaspoon pepper
- 1 (2-pound) center-cut beef tenderloin roast, trimmed
- 4 slices bacon
- 1 tablespoon vegetable oil

1. Adjust oven rack to middle position and heat oven to 275 degrees. Set wire rack in rimmed baking sheet. Combine salt and pepper in bowl. Cut tenderloin crosswise into 4 equal steaks. Pat steaks dry with paper towels and sprinkle evenly with salt mixture.

2. Working with 1 steak at a time, wrap 1 slice bacon around circumference of steak, stretching as needed, and secure overlapping ends with toothpick inserted

AMAZING BACON-WRAPPED STEAKS IN FOUR EASY STEPS

1. SECURE BACON Wrap slice of bacon around each steak and secure with toothpick.

2. ROAST IN OVEN Cook steaks elevated on wire rack set in rimmed baking sheet in 275-degree oven.

3. SEAR BACON IN SKILLET Sear bacon with steaks on their sides in rounded corners of skillet.

4. SEAR MEAT Finally, sear top and bottom of each wrapped steak.

horizontally. Place steaks on prepared wire rack. Roast until steaks register 115 degrees (for medium-rare), about 40 minutes, or 125 degrees (for medium), 45 to 50 minutes.

3. Heat oil in 12-inch nonstick skillet over medium-high heat until just smoking. Position steaks on sides in skillet with bacon seam side down and nestled into rounded corners of skillet. Cook until bacon is evenly browned, rotating steaks as needed, about 5 minutes. Position steaks flat side down in center of skillet and cook until steaks are well browned on tops and bottoms, 1 to 2 minutes per side.

4. Transfer steaks to platter, tent with aluminum foil, and let rest for 10 minutes. Gently remove toothpicks, leaving bacon intact. Serve.

Gorgonzola Vinaigrette
MAKES ABOUT 1 CUP

For a creamier texture, buy a wedge of Gorgonzola cheese instead of a precrumbled product.

     2 tablespoons white wine vinegar
     2 teaspoons Dijon mustard
    ½ teaspoon kosher salt
    ⅛ teaspoon pepper
    ¼ cup extra-virgin olive oil
     2 ounces Gorgonzola cheese, crumbled (½ cup)
     1 small shallot, sliced thin
     2 tablespoons chopped fresh parsley

Whisk vinegar, mustard, salt, and pepper together in bowl. Slowly whisk in oil until emulsified. Stir in Gorgonzola, shallot, and parsley.

HAMBURGER STEAKS WITH ONION GRAVY

✓ **WHY THIS RECIPE WORKS** This classic comforting dish is ready in less than 30 minutes—perfect for a week-night dinner. To flavor the ground beef, we used convenient soup mix, which was packed full of garlic and onion. A bit of panko helped the meat retain moisture during cooking, keeping it tender and juicy. Searing the patties left behind a deeply seasoned fond, which we used to build a rich and slightly sweet onion gravy. We finished with a bit of butter to give the gravy richness and body and round out the intense meaty flavor.

The classic "Hamburg steak" first arrived stateside with German immigrants in the 19th century. This beef patty served with a rich onion-y gravy was a staple in the homes of German Americans who could afford to buy meat regularly. For those who couldn't, it served as a special-occasion supper.

But hamburger steak has devolved over the years into little more than a dense, dry burger without a bun. It should be juicy, laced with flavor throughout, and doused with a buttery brown gravy made from scratch. With those lofty goals in mind, I set out to restore some glory to this humble dish.

Don't confuse hamburger steak with Salisbury steak. Whereas Salisbury steak's gravy is distinctly peppery and heavy with mushrooms, the gravy served with hamburger steak leans on onions and garlic. These additions contribute just enough flavor for a bold, slightly sweet personality. But this restrained ingredient list can also be a quick trip to Dullsville.

My first experiments with existing recipes were a lesson in disappointment. The finished patties were dry, tough, and drastically underseasoned.

To tackle the dryness, I introduced a panade, a mixture of bread crumbs and liquid that's often incorporated into meatballs and meatloaf to help them retain moisture. Adding a panade made with fresh bread crumbs did just that, but it also gave my patties a gummy texture. I ditched the panade in favor of straight bread crumbs, in this case crunchy panko. These light, flaky bits didn't need a soak before being added to the beef, and they softened just enough as the beef cooked, soaking up all the liquid the meat released (and keeping it from seeping out).

The patties now had great texture but were lacking in flavor. Instead of cooking fresh garlic and onion, I simply added garlic powder, onion powder, and seasoned salt. Taking the convenience theme one step further, a colleague suggested replacing those ingredients with something her mom had used to make this dish in the 1980s: onion soup mix. It worked—the potent mix seasoned the meat throughout and added a complex oniony flavor.

Gravy time. A pan gravy, generally made while the meat is resting, requires some fond left in the skillet, so a hard sear was the way to go. Searing the patties for 4 minutes per side gave them great color and created a lovely fond. To that I added sliced onion to cook for about 4 minutes until softened, followed by flour. Finally, I stirred in some beef broth.

The steaks were done, but the gravy was too thin—nothing that a vigorous bubble, about 4 minutes, and a bit of butter couldn't fix. Finally, I topped the steaks with minced chives, which lent freshness and echoed the oniony flavors in the steak. Tender meat, flavorful gravy, and a comforting profile—this hamburger steak now had a place in my regular dinner rotation.

—ALLI BERKEY, *Cook's Country*

Hamburger Steaks with Onion Gravy

SERVES 4

The test kitchen's favorite panko bread crumbs are Ian's Panko Bread Crumbs, Original Style.

- 1½ pounds 85 percent lean ground beef
- ½ cup panko bread crumbs
- 2 tablespoons Lipton Onion Soup and Dip Mix
- ½ teaspoon pepper
- 3 tablespoons unsalted butter, divided
- 1 onion, halved and sliced thin
- 1½ tablespoons all-purpose flour
- 1½ cups beef broth
- 1 tablespoon minced fresh chives

1. In large bowl, mix beef, panko, soup mix, and pepper with your hands until fully combined. Form mixture into four 4-inch-diameter patties, about ½ inch thick. Using your fingertips, press down center of each patty to create slight indentation.

2. Melt 1 tablespoon butter in 12-inch nonstick skillet over medium-high heat. Cook patties until well browned and meat registers 130 degrees, about 4 minutes per side. Transfer to platter and tent with aluminum foil.

3. Reduce heat to medium, add onion to now-empty skillet, and cook until lightly browned and beginning to soften, about 4 minutes. Stir in flour and cook for 1 minute. Whisk in broth and bring to boil. Cook until thickened, about 4 minutes. Off heat, stir in remaining 2 tablespoons butter. Season with salt and pepper to taste. Spoon sauce over steaks and sprinkle with chives. Serve.

NOTES FROM THE TEST KITCHEN

TASTING BEEF BROTH

In the past, we've struggled to find a beef broth that delivers adequately beefy flavor. Hopeful that a better, truly beefy broth had come along since our last tasting, we rounded up 10 options. In the end, we had just one product to recommend: **Better Than Bouillon Roasted Beef Base**. This product stores easily, costs just $0.02 per reconstituted fluid ounce, and does a good job of boosting savory depth in soups and stews. Though it was lacking in actual beefy taste, its good amount of salt and multiple powerful flavor enhancers delivered "fuller flavor" than other products; it bested our previous favorite, from Rachael Ray, by far.

SOUS VIDE BUTTER-BASTED RIB-EYE STEAKS

✔ **WHY THIS RECIPE WORKS** Nicely cooked rib-eye steak is a culinary showstopper but is also a challenge to pull off. The risk of over- or undercooking—and therefore ruining an expensive cut of meat—can make cooking a thick-cut rib eye at home an intimidating endeavor. But with the help of the sous vide method, preparing steak at home is suddenly a sure bet. Cooking sous vide allows you to control the precise temperature (and therefore doneness) of a steak, cooking it to the exact same temperature throughout. This means your steak is perfectly cooked every time. Sous vide steaks are often seared in a hot pan after cooking in the water bath to give them the exterior Maillard browning that we love. For these rib eyes, we upped the ante with butter basting, which involved continuously spooning hot fat over the steaks to quickly create a nice deep-brown crust. Bonus: It gave the steaks the nutty flavor of browned butter. We reserved that butter to use as a rich sauce to drizzle over the top for a decadent steak dinner. Because these steaks cooked at a slightly lower temperature to allow enough time for them to butter-baste properly without overcooking, we also quickly seared them before they went into the water bath to reduce the risk of bacterial growth.

For most home cooks, the first test of their brand-new sous vide circulator is a steak. If you've made pan-seared steaks, you can understand why: It requires serious precision on the stovetop to achieve the ideal medium-rare center while also forming a beautifully burnished crust. And because regular stovetop cooking heats steak from the outside in, seared steaks often have an unappealing gray band of overcooked meat between their pinkish-red centers and browned exteriors. To keep my bone-in rib-eye steaks tender, juicy, and flavorful, I'd use a sous-vide-then-sear technique. To add even more flavor, I would put together some flavored butters to baste the steaks with at the end of cooking.

Before I'd dive into the recipe testing process, I had to understand exactly what sous vide cooking is and how it works. A sous vide machine preheats a water bath to a precise temperature; then, food is sealed in a plastic bag and immersed in the bath. Eventually, the food reaches the same temperature as the water, which is generally set to the desired serving temperature of the final dish. However, because you can't achieve a crisp crust in low, diffuse heat, most sous vide steak recipes will hold the water bath at a lower temperature, knowing that the necessary searing step will bring the steak to a higher final temperature.

In contrast, the conventional stovetop method sets the temperature of the heat source much higher than the serving temperature of the food, making it imperative to remove the food at just the right moment, when it's done but not overcooked. Given this narrow time frame, overcooking steak is almost always inevitable.

But while cooking sous vide, there's usually no risk of overcooking, which makes it a game-changing technique, especially for temperature-sensitive, expensive foods such as steak. The low cooking temperature ensures juicy meat, and dialing in the precise temperature creates exceptionally consistent results that can't be achieved with traditional steak-cooking methods.

With my newly acquired sous vide knowledge, it was time to head to the kitchen. First, I'd have to figure out the best temperature for the water bath. In our sous vide recipe for Perfect Seared Steaks, we set the sous vide to 130 degrees; after cooking the steaks for a few hours, we pat them dry (to encourage browning) and sear them over medium-high heat for just 1 minute per side— enough time for the steaks to form a crust without overcooking. Because I would be butter-basting the steaks for at least a few minutes post–water bath to infuse the rib eyes with buttery flavor, I'd have to sous vide at a slightly lower temperature to account for the additional cooking time in the hot skillet.

I decided to set the sous vide to 125 degrees, hoping that this slightly cooler temperature would allow me to baste the steaks without the concern of overcooking them. To avoid any potential bacterial growth in this cooler water bath, I first seasoned the steaks with salt and pepper and quickly seared them in 1 tablespoon of vegetable oil—just 1 minute per side brought them up to a food-safe temperature. Then, I placed each steak in a 1-gallon zipper-lock bag with another 2 tablespoons of oil each. I tightly sealed the bags, squeezing out as much air as possible to further encourage even cooking, lowered them into the 125-degree water bath, clipped each bag to the side of a 12-quart storage container (though you can also use a Dutch oven or a stock pot, as long as it has at least a 7-quart capacity), released any remaining air bubbles, and let them sous vide away from 2 hours up to 3 hours.

I transferred my evenly cooked steaks to a paper towel–lined plate, let them rest for 5 to 10 minutes, and patted them dry with paper towels—the dry surface would boost browning. I heated 3 tablespoons of vegetable oil in a skillet until it was just smoking (the hot oil guarantees a well browned crust), briefly cooked the rib eyes on each side, and slid them to the back of the skillet while I shifted my focus to the infused butter.

The first concoction I dreamed up was a classic combination of aromatic shallot, garlic, and thyme. I melted 3 tablespoons of unsalted butter in the front of the skillet, added the aromatics, and then basted the steaks for 3 minutes (flipping them every 30 seconds) until they were nicely browned on both sides. Because butter-basted steak is a true flavor playground, I thought up two simple but flavorful variations: one with green peppercorns, shallot, and star anise pods, and another with orange zest, shallot, and rosemary sprigs. I couldn't let the precious remaining butter go to waste, so I strained it into a small bowl, ditched the solids, and served it alongside the steaks.

Once I cut into my juicy, medium-rare steak and drizzled it with the fragrant butter, I was sure of one thing: I'd never attempt to perfect a pan-seared rib eye without my trusty sous vide again.

—SASHA MARX, *America's Test Kitchen Books*

Sous Vide Butter-Basted Rib-Eye Steaks

SERVES 4

This recipe moves quickly once you start searing in step 3, so have everything prepared and within arm's reach before you start.

- 2 **(2-pound) bone-in rib-eye steaks, about 2 inches thick, trimmed**
- 1 **teaspoon table salt**
- ½ **teaspoon pepper**
- ½ **cup vegetable oil, divided**
- 3 **tablespoons unsalted butter**
- 1 **large shallot, peeled and quartered lengthwise through root end**
- 2 **garlic cloves, smashed and peeled**
- 5 **sprigs fresh thyme**

1. Using sous vide circulator, bring water to 125°F/52°C in 7-quart container.

SOUS VIDE BUTTER-BASTED RIB-EYE STEAKS

2. Pat steaks dry with paper towels and sprinkle with salt and pepper. Heat 1 tablespoon oil in 12-inch skillet over medium-high heat until just smoking. Cook steaks, 1 minute per side. Place steaks in 2 separate 1-gallon zipper-lock freezer bags. Add 2 tablespoons oil to each bag. Seal bags, pressing out as much air as possible. Gently lower bags into prepared water bath until steaks are fully submerged, and then clip top corner of each bag to side of water bath container, allowing remaining air bubbles to rise to top of bag. Reopen 1 corner of each zipper-lock bag, release remaining air bubbles, and reseal bags. Cover and cook for at least 2 hours or up to 3 hours.

3. Transfer steaks to paper towel–lined plate and let rest for 5 to 10 minutes. Pat steaks dry with paper towels. Heat remaining 3 tablespoons oil in clean 12-inch skillet over medium-high heat until just smoking. Place steaks in skillet and cook, without moving them, for 30 seconds. Flip steaks and continue to cook for 30 seconds.

4. Slide steaks to back of skillet, opposite handle, and add butter to front of skillet near handle. When butter has melted, add shallot, garlic, and thyme sprigs. Holding skillet handle, tilt skillet so butter pools near base of handle. Using metal spoon, baste steaks with butter and aromatics, concentrating on areas where crust is less browned. Continuously baste steaks, flipping every 30 seconds, until well browned on both sides, about 3 minutes.

5. Reduce heat to medium and transfer steaks to cutting board. Using tongs, stand each steak on its side in skillet and cook, rotating as needed, until well browned on edges, about 1 minute; return to cutting board. Strain seasoned butter into small bowl; discard solids. Carve steaks off bones, then slice ¼ inch thick. Serve with seasoned butter.

VARIATIONS

Sous Vide Butter-Basted Rib-Eye Steaks with Green Peppercorn–Star Anise Butter
Substitute 2 teaspoons whole green peppercorns, cracked, for garlic and 5 star anise pods, cracked, for thyme.

Sous Vide Butter-Basted Rib-Eye Steaks with Rosemary-Orange Butter
Substitute 8 (2-inch) strips orange zest for garlic and 1 sprig fresh rosemary for thyme.

VIETNAMESE PORK WITH RICE NOODLES

✔ **WHY THIS RECIPE WORKS** Vietnamese *bun cha*—a vibrant mix of grilled pork, crisp salad, and delicate yet resilient rice vermicelli, united by a light yet potent sauce—is an ideal meal for a hot summer night. We started by boiling dried rice vermicelli, after which we rinsed the noodles well and spread them on a platter to dry. Then we mixed up the bold and zesty sauce known as *nuoc cham* using lime juice, sugar, and fish sauce. To ensure that every drop of the sauce was flavored with garlic and chile, we used a portion of the sugar to help grind the pungent ingredients into a fine paste. For juicy pork patties, we mixed baking soda into ground pork, which helped the meat retain moisture and brown during the 8-minute grilling time. Per tradition, we also seasoned the pork with shallot, fish sauce, sugar, and pepper. Briefly soaking the grilled patties in the sauce is a traditional step that further flavored the patties and imbued the sauce with grill flavor. We then plated the components separately to allow diners to combine them according to their taste.

I usually start the summer months dreaming about ambitious grilling projects such as ribs and brisket, but when the evenings turn hot and humid, I find myself seeking out lighter, fresher options that I can make more quickly. That's how I learned about *bun cha*, a vibrant Vietnamese dish of rice noodles, grilled pork, crisp vegetables, and a light yet potent sauce.

In the street-food stalls of Hanoi, where the dish originated, cooks prepare fatty cuts such as pork shoulder or belly in two ways: They slice some into thin strips and marinate it in fish sauce, sugar, black pepper, and maybe some minced shallots or onions, and they finely chop the rest, mix it with similar seasonings, and shape it into patties. Then they grill all the pork over hot coals and unload the sizzling meat into bowls of *nuoc cham*, an intensely flavored mixture of lime juice, fish sauce, sugar, water, and sometimes garlic and chile. The nuoc cham picks up the meaty char flavor while every inch of the pork is bathed in zesty sauce. Then the pork is plucked from the bowl and served with rice noodles; tender greens; leafy herbs; and crisp cucumbers or bean sprouts. Diners assemble bowls of the components to their taste and drizzle more of the meat–infused sauce over the top.

I headed to the test kitchen and, following the lead of a recipe I'd found, marinated pork belly strips in fish sauce, sugar, pepper, and minced shallots. I also finely chopped pork shoulder, folded in more of the seasonings, and shaped the mixture into patties. Then, I piled hot coals on one side of my grill, dropped the cooking grate in place, and arranged the meat over the coals.

The pork belly released lots of fat, causing flare-ups, so I had to move the strips around a lot and I lost about a quarter of them between the bars. Those that didn't fall through were nicely charred but chewy. Ultimately, I decided to skip the strips and stick with just the patties, making the recipe quicker to prepare. But the patties needed work. Though they were easier to maneuver and stayed more tender than the pork belly, they were dry inside by the time their exteriors had charred sufficiently. Besides, chopping the pork shoulder had taken longer than it did to actually cook it.

I'd seen a few recipes that called for supermarket ground pork in place of the chopped meat. It wouldn't be as authentic, but taking the shortcut would make this dish a snap to prepare. Besides, my goal for the pork would remain the same: deeply savory, well-charred, rich meat that balanced the bright tasting sauce, crisp vegetables, and noodles.

I mixed 1 pound of ground pork with the usual seasonings plus ½ teaspoon of baking soda—a favorite test kitchen trick. The baking soda boosts the meat's pH, which in turn enhances browning and inhibits the tendency of meat fibers to tighten up and squeeze out moisture as they cook. The result: patties that browned quickly and stayed juicy.

Nuoc cham, according to cookbook author Andrea Nguyen, is a dipping sauce that every Vietnamese cook needs to master and is the element that brings together all the components in this dish and many others in Vietnamese cuisine. It's also a cinch to make. The first trick is to balance the saltiness of the fish sauce with the brightness of lime juice or vinegar and the sweetness of sugar. The second is to add just enough water so that the sauce enlivens rather than overpowers whatever you're dressing. My placeholder version tasted balanced but spartan, so I tried incorporating the chile and garlic I had seen in some recipes.

However, I couldn't mince the chile and garlic finely enough to distribute their flavors evenly throughout the sauce, so some bites were fiery or pungent while others fell flat. But Nguyen makes a helpful suggestion in her version: Combine the aromatics with some of the sugar using a mortar and pestle. The granules act as an abrasive, helping reduce everything to a paste that makes every drop of the sauce taste more vibrant. (In lieu of a mortar and pestle, you can smear the sugar across the minced aromatics several times with the flat side of a chef's knife on a cutting board.)

When cooked, rice vermicelli should be fine and delicate yet resilient. After quickly boiling the noodles, I drained and rinsed them with cold water to halt their cooking and wash away surface starch to minimize stickiness. Then I drained them again and spread them out on a platter to air-dry while I made the salad.

I tore some Boston lettuce into bite-size pieces and, per Vietnamese tradition, arranged the nuoc cham–moistened pork, remaining sauce, noodles, greens, herbs (mint and cilantro), and cucumber slices separately so that diners could build their own salads.

Every bite was an extraordinary balance of smoky, juicy meat; tangy, salty-sweet sauce; cool, tender greens; and delicately springy noodles. And the kicker was that when I tallied up my over-the-heat cooking time—4 minutes to boil the noodles plus 8 minutes to grill the patties—it equaled just 12 minutes, making this an ideal dinner to cook on a sweltering summer night. Or on any night, for that matter.

—ANDREA GEARY, *Cook's Illustrated*

NOTES FROM THE TEST KITCHEN

A WORLD-CLASS CONDIMENT

Nuoc cham—a salty-sour-sweet combination of fish sauce, lime juice, and sugar that is often diluted with water and seasoned with garlic and/or chile—is as essential to Vietnamese cooking as salsa is to Mexican cuisine. It functions as a dipping sauce or dressing for countless dishes and is a snap to make. The key is flavor balance. We make sure to use hot water (which helps quickly dissolve the sugar) and to grind—not just mince—the garlic and chile so that their assertive flavors disperse evenly.

The salty, sour, sweet, and spicy flavors of nuoc cham enhance countless Vietnamese dishes.

VIETNAMESE GRILLED PORK PATTIES WITH RICE NOODLES AND SALAD (BUN CHA)

Vietnamese Grilled Pork Patties with Rice Noodles and Salad (Bun Cha)

SERVES 4 TO 6

Look for rice vermicelli in the Asian section of your supermarket. We prefer the more delicate springiness of vermicelli made from 100 percent rice flour to those that include a secondary starch such as cornstarch. If you can find only the latter, just cook them longer—up to 12 minutes. For a less spicy sauce, use only half the Thai chile. For the cilantro, use the leaves and the thin, delicate stems, not the thicker stems close to the root. To serve, place platters of noodles, salad, sauce, and pork patties on the table and allow diners to combine components to their taste. Use the sauce sparingly.

NOODLES AND SALAD

8 ounces rice vermicelli

1 head Boston lettuce (8 ounces), torn into bite-size pieces

1 English cucumber, peeled, quartered lengthwise, seeded, and sliced thin on bias

1 cup fresh cilantro leaves and stems

1 cup fresh mint leaves, torn if large

SAUCE

3 tablespoons sugar, divided

1 small Thai chile, stemmed and minced

1 garlic clove, minced

⅔ cup hot water

5 tablespoons fish sauce

¼ cup lime juice (2 limes)

PORK PATTIES

1 large shallot, minced

1 tablespoon fish sauce

1½ teaspoons sugar

½ teaspoon baking soda

½ teaspoon pepper

1 pound ground pork

1. FOR THE NOODLES AND SALAD: Bring 4 quarts water to boil in large pot. Stir in noodles and cook until tender but not mushy, 4 to 12 minutes. Drain noodles and rinse under cold running water until cool. Drain noodles very well, spread on large plate, and let stand at room temperature to dry. Arrange lettuce, cucumber, cilantro, and mint separately on large platter and refrigerate until needed.

2. FOR THE SAUCE: Using mortar and pestle (or on cutting board using flat side of chef's knife), mash 1 tablespoon sugar, Thai chile, and garlic to fine paste. Transfer to medium bowl and add hot water and remaining 2 tablespoons sugar. Stir until sugar is dissolved. Stir in fish sauce and lime juice. Set aside.

3. FOR THE PORK PATTIES: Combine shallot, fish sauce, sugar, baking soda, and pepper in medium bowl. Add pork and mix until well combined. Shape pork mixture into 12 patties, each about 2½ inches wide and ½ inch thick.

4A. FOR A CHARCOAL GRILL: Open bottom vent completely. Light large chimney starter filled with charcoal briquettes (6 quarts). When top coals are partially covered with ash, pour evenly over half of grill. Set cooking grate in place, cover, and open lid vent completely. Heat grill until hot, about 5 minutes.

4B. FOR A GAS GRILL: Turn all burners to high, cover, and heat grill until hot, about 15 minutes. Leave all burners on high.

5. Clean and oil cooking grate. Cook patties (directly over coals if using charcoal; covered if using gas) until well charred, 3 to 4 minutes per side. Transfer grilled patties to bowl with sauce and gently toss to coat. Let stand for 5 minutes.

6. Transfer patties to serving plate, reserving sauce. Serve noodles, salad, sauce, and pork patties separately.

CARNE ADOVADA

✔ **WHY THIS RECIPE WORKS** To make *carne adovada*, a classic New Mexican pork braise, we started by cutting boneless pork butt into large chunks and salting them (so that they would be well seasoned and retain moisture during cooking) while we prepared the chile sauce. We used dried red New Mexican chiles, which are fruity and relatively mild. But rather than toast them, as we often do with dried chiles, we simply steeped them in water to preserve their bright flavor. When they were pliable, we blended them with aromatics and spices (including garlic, oregano, cumin, cayenne, and cloves), as well as honey and white vinegar, to form a thick paste; then we added some of the soaking water to form a smooth puree. We tossed the pork with the puree in a Dutch oven and then braised it in a low oven until the meat was very tender.

Before I take you on a deep dive into *carne adovada*, one of New Mexico's most celebrated dishes and quite possibly the easiest braise you will ever make, I need to back up and explain how hugely significant chiles are in New Mexican cuisine.

For one thing, the state boasts its own unique chile cultivars. New Mexican chiles are relatively mild and are sold both fresh—either unripe and green or ripe and red—and dried. They were first developed at New Mexico State University in 1913 and have since become one of the defining ingredients in the local cuisine—not to mention the state's most lucrative cash crop. New Mexico even passed a law declaring that only chiles grown in the state may be labeled as such. Dishes that feature the chiles typically contain few other seasonings so that the chile flavor can shine.

Carne adovada is a perfect example. To make it, cooks simmer chunks of pork in a thick sauce made from dried red New Mexican chiles; garlic; dried oregano; spices such as cumin, coriander, or cloves; vinegar; and a touch of sugar or honey. (*Adobada*, the Mexican preparation on which the dish is based, refers to meat cooked in a sauce of chiles, aromatics, and vinegar.) When the meat is fall-apart tender, the rich, robust, brick red braise is served with tortillas or rice and beans.

That's the purist's version, anyway. But there are also plenty of recipes for carne adovada that complicate the flavors by adding superfluous ingredients such as raisins, coffee, and/or a mix of other kinds of chiles so that the final result is more like a mole sauce. Many of these recipes, I found, are also plagued by typical braise problems, such as dry meat and over- or underseasoned sauce that is either too scant or too soupy.

I got to work on a minimalist braise—one that would feature moist, tender pork in a simple, potent sauce that tasted first and foremost of chiles.

Most of the recipes I found called for boneless butt roast, which is affordable, streaked with flavorful fat, and loaded with collagen that breaks down during cooking, rendering the meat tender. I cut the roast into 1½-inch chunks, which would be equally easy to eat wrapped in a tortilla or with a fork, and tossed the pieces with kosher salt so that the meat would be deeply seasoned. I didn't sear it since the meat above the surface of the liquid would brown in the oven.

Most of the simpler sauce formulas went something like this: Toast whole dried New Mexican chiles—as much as 8 ounces—and then steep them in boiling water until their stems soften, which takes about 30 minutes. Then, puree the chiles with enough water to form a thick paste and season it with garlic, spices, vinegar, and a sweetener.

Eight ounces of chiles formed a massive pile that I wouldn't be able to toast or puree in a single batch, so I scaled down to a more manageable (but still generous) 4 ounces. After toasting and steeping them, I processed the chiles with 4 cups of the water they had soaked in, plus a couple of garlic cloves, Mexican oregano (less sweet than the Mediterranean kind), cumin, cloves, white vinegar, and sugar until it formed a loose puree. I poured the sauce over the meat in a Dutch oven, brought it to a boil on the stove, covered it, and transferred it to the oven, where it would simmer gently and evenly with no stirring.

After about 2 hours of braising, the meat was fork-tender. But the sauce was way off—so loose and thin that it didn't cling to the meat. And despite the load of chiles it contained, the flavor was washed-out.

Reducing the water by half thickened the puree and made its flavor more concentrated, albeit boring and one-dimensional. I'd have to think about tweaking the flavors. The bigger problem was that the chile seeds and skins hadn't broken down completely in the blender (New Mexican chile skins are particularly tough), and their texture was more noticeable now that there was less liquid.

Going forward, I made sure to seed the chiles before toasting them. As for the bits of skin, I tried straining them out to make the puree ultrasmooth, but it was a fussy step and the sauce suffered. Not only did the strained sauce lack vibrancy in both color and flavor—chile skins contain high concentrations of flavor and aroma compounds that give them much of their astringent, floral, and fruity notes—but I also found that the tiny insoluble particles of pureed skin and pulp were also responsible for making the sauce viscous enough to cling to the meat.

The trick to smoothing out the puree was refining my processing method. Instead of adding all the water at the start, which left the skins swimming in liquid, I started with just enough liquid to keep the blender running before adding the rest. That way there was more friction to grind the solids.

Back to refining the flavor of the sauce. Bumping up the amounts of garlic and vinegar, switching from sugar to the more nuanced sweetness of honey, and introducing a dash of cayenne pepper for subtle heat were all good moves. But the sauce still lacked the fruity brightness I was hoping for.

Toasting chiles is standard practice when you want to deepen their flavor; it can also add hints of char. But if I was after a sweeter, slightly acidic profile—which dried red New Mexican chiles naturally offer—maybe toasting them was the wrong move.

To find out, I held a side-by-side tasting of my *adovada* made with toasted and untoasted chiles. Sure enough, the untoasted batch boasted rounder flavor that was fruity, a touch sweet, and slightly astringent. Best of all, skipping the toasting step made the dish even easier to prepare.

The result was bright, rich, just a little spicy, and deeply satisfying—precisely the pure and simple adovada I'd had in mind. It's what I'll be making for dinner when I want a bold, hearty braise. And since its flavors also pair brilliantly with eggs and potatoes, I'll be sure to save the leftovers for breakfast.

—ANNIE PETITO, *Cook's Illustrated*

NOTES FROM THE TEST KITCHEN

ALL ABOUT NEW MEXICAN CHILES

Chiles are as fundamental to New Mexican cuisine as soy is to Japanese cooking or potatoes are to Irish food. In fact, New Mexico breeds and grows its own unique cultivars, which are sold both fresh and dried. Fresh chiles are used in everything from casseroles to burgers to rice; dried chiles are used in sauces for braised meats such as *carne adovada* or for enchiladas. Here's a rundown on the flavor and heat profile of the dried kind and how to substitute for them.

FLAVOR
Fruity, sweet, slightly acidic

HEAT
Relatively mild; Scoville rating: 0 to 7,000 (For reference: Bell peppers rate from 0 to 1,000; jalapeños rate from 1,000 to 50,000; and habaneros rate from 100,000 to 500,000.)

APPEARANCE
Wrinkly; dark red; particularly shiny, leathery skins

SUBSTITUTE
Dried California chiles

Braised New Mexico–Style Pork in Red Chile Sauce (Carne Adovada)

SERVES 6

Pork butt roast is often labeled Boston butt in the supermarket. For an accurate measurement of boiling water, bring a full kettle of water to a boil and then measure out the desired amount. If you can't find New Mexican chiles, substitute dried California chiles. Dried chiles should be pliable and smell slightly fruity. Kitchen shears can be used to cut them; we like Shun Multi-Purpose Shears. If you can't find Mexican oregano, substitute Mediterranean oregano. Letting the stew rest for 10 minutes before serving allows the sauce to thicken and better coat the meat. Serve with rice and beans, crispy potatoes, or flour tortillas with shredded lettuce and chopped tomato, or shred the pork as a filling for tacos and burritos.

1 (3½- to 4-pound) boneless pork butt roast, trimmed and cut into 1½-inch pieces

4 teaspoons kosher salt, divided

4 ounces dried New Mexican chiles, wiped clean, stemmed, seeded, and torn into 1-inch pieces

4 cups boiling water

2 tablespoons honey

2 tablespoons distilled white vinegar

5 garlic cloves, peeled

2 teaspoons dried Mexican oregano

2 teaspoons ground cumin

½ teaspoon cayenne pepper

⅛ teaspoon ground cloves

Lime wedges

1. Toss pork and 1 tablespoon salt together in bowl; refrigerate for 1 hour.

2. Place chiles in medium bowl. Pour boiling water over chiles, making sure they are completely submerged, and let stand until softened, 30 minutes. Adjust oven rack to lower-middle position and heat oven to 325 degrees.

3. Drain chiles and reserve 2 cups soaking liquid (discard remaining liquid). Process chiles, honey, vinegar, garlic, oregano, cumin, cayenne, cloves, and remaining 1 teaspoon salt in blender until chiles are finely ground and thick paste forms, about 30 seconds. With blender running, add 1 cup reserved liquid and process until smooth, 1½ to 2 minutes, adding up to

¼ cup additional reserved liquid to maintain vortex. Add remaining reserved liquid and continue to blend sauce at high speed, 1 minute longer.

4. Combine pork and chile sauce in Dutch oven, stirring to make sure pork is evenly coated. Bring to boil over high heat. Cover pot, transfer to oven, and cook until pork is tender and fork inserted into pork meets little to no resistance, 2 to 2½ hours.

5. Using wooden spoon, scrape any browned bits from sides of pot and stir until pork and sauce are recombined and sauce is smooth and homogeneous. Let stand, uncovered, for 10 minutes. Season with salt to taste. Serve with lime wedges. (Leftover pork can be refrigerated for up to 3 days.)

TUSCAN GRILLED PORK RIBS

✔ **WHY THIS RECIPE WORKS** To re-create juicy, deeply porky, chewy-tender Tuscan-style ribs, we started by removing the tough, papery membranes from two racks of St. Louis–style spareribs. Cutting the ribs into two-rib sections created more surface area for flavorful browning, and salting them for an hour prior to grilling ensured that they cooked up juicy and well-seasoned. Grilling the ribs over a medium-hot (rather than blazing) fire helped prevent the meat from drying out, as did removing them from the fire when their temperature reached between 175 and 185 degrees—and they still came off the fire in about 20 minutes. Drizzling the pork with a vinaigrette made from olive oil, minced rosemary, garlic, and lemon juice balanced its richness without obscuring its meaty flavor.

You probably know ribs as a low-and-slow affair featuring fall-off-the-bone meat that's been steeped in smoke and coated with a flavorful rub or sauce. Tuscan grilled pork spareribs, known as *rosticciana* ("RO-stee-chee-AH-na"), are not those ribs.

Their preparation falls in line with the less-is-more ethos of Tuscan cuisine, where foods are seasoned sparingly to allow their natural flavors to shine. In this case, it's all about the pork, so the seasonings are restricted to salt, pepper, and maybe a hint of garlic or rosemary. Then the ribs are grilled quickly over a hot fire until the meat is browned and crispy but still succulent with satisfying chew. Eating them with your hands is a truly primal experience.

That said, I couldn't wrap my head around the concept of ribs that weren't barbecue until I tasted these. The smoky meat was juicy in a way I never knew ribs could be and purely porky without the distraction of smoke and spices. I was hooked.

Spareribs are cut close to the belly of the pig. A full rack contains the brisket bone and surrounding brisket meat and often weighs about 5 pounds. To produce smaller, more rectangular racks, butchers remove the brisket portion; this cut is called St. Louis–style spareribs. Meaty, flavorful, and easy to work with, it has become our go-to cut for most rib recipes.

Stretched across the rack's underside is a tough, papery membrane that we sometimes leave intact when barbecuing since it softens during the long cooking time. But because these ribs would spend very little time over the fire, I stripped the membranes from two racks (see "How to Remove the Membrane from Spareribs") before brushing them with oil to jump-start browning, seasoning them with salt and pepper, and laying them meat side down over a medium-hot fire. Once they started to color, I flipped them every few minutes for about a half-hour until they were deeply browned. The ribs were relatively juicy because they retained much of their natural moisture during the brief cooking process. The surface browning was great, but could it be better?

I'd come across rosticciana recipes that called for cutting the racks into individual ribs before cooking, which seemed like a good way to expose more meat to the flavor of the grill. When I tried it, each rib became encased in a crisp crust; even better, the individual ribs cooked quickly, cutting the total time spent on the grill to about 20 minutes.

But managing 20-odd pieces over the hot fire was tricky. So instead of cutting the racks into individual ribs, I cut them into two-rib segments. This gave me pieces with plenty of surface area for browning but half as many pieces to shuffle and a thicker pocket of meat between each pair of bones that I hoped would stay juicy. That pocket also provided a place to check the meat's temperature, which needed to hit 175 to 185 degrees to allow just a little collagen breakdown and leave the ribs with a desirably meaty chew.

To ensure that the ribs would be as juicy as possible, I salted them an hour before cooking. Though not typical for rosticciana, salting altered the meat's protein structure so that it was better able to retain moisture during cooking—and helped season it, too.

Well-browned, well-seasoned, pleasantly chewy, and juicy as can be, these ribs were entirely satisfying. They didn't need any adornment, though I was intrigued by the light-handed finishes I saw in some rosticciana recipes: a sprinkling of chopped garlic and rosemary, a brush with an oil-dipped rosemary sprig, or a squeeze of lemon.

My take—a vinaigrette incorporating all three of those elements, which I drizzled over the meat at the table—started with minced garlic and fresh rosemary, which I briefly microwaved in olive oil to temper their harsh raw flavors. Stirring some fresh lemon juice into the warm infused oil created a vibrant, savory dressing that complemented the rich pork.

Take it from me, a skeptic at first: These ribs will be unlike any others you've had. In fact, with no barbecue sauce or spice rub, it might be like tasting ribs for the first time.

ANNIE PETITO, *Cook's Illustrated*

Tuscan Grilled Pork Ribs (Rosticciana)

SERVES 4 TO 6

When portioning the meat into two-rib sections, start at the thicker end of the rack. If you are left with a three-rib piece at the tapered end, grill it as such. Take the temperature of the meat between the bones.

RIBS

2 (2½- to 3-pound) racks St. Louis style spareribs, trimmed, membrane removed, and each rack cut into 2-rib sections
2 teaspoons kosher salt
1 tablespoon vegetable oil
1 teaspoon pepper

VINAIGRETTE

¼ cup extra-virgin olive oil
2 garlic cloves, minced
1 teaspoon minced fresh rosemary
2 tablespoons lemon juice

1. FOR THE RIBS: Pat ribs dry with paper towels. Rub evenly on both sides with salt and place on wire rack set in rimmed baking sheet. Let stand at room temperature for 1 hour.

2. FOR THE VINAIGRETTE: Combine oil, garlic, and rosemary in small bowl and microwave until fragrant and just starting to bubble, about 30 seconds. Stir in lemon juice and set aside.

3A. FOR A CHARCOAL GRILL: Open bottom vent completely. Light large chimney starter filled with charcoal briquettes (6 quarts). When top coals are partially covered with ash, pour evenly over grill. Set cooking grate in place, cover, and open lid vent completely. Heat grill until hot, about 5 minutes.

3B. FOR A GAS GRILL: Turn all burners to high, cover, and heat grill until hot, about 15 minutes. Turn all burners to medium-high.

4. Clean and oil cooking grate. Brush meat side of ribs with oil and sprinkle with pepper. Place ribs meat side down on grill. Cover and cook until meat side begins to develop spotty browning and light but defined grill marks, 4 to 6 minutes. Flip ribs and cook, covered, until second side is lightly browned, 4 to 6 minutes, moving ribs as needed to ensure even browning. Flip again and cook, covered, until meat side is deeply browned with slight charring and thick ends of ribs register 175 to 185 degrees, 4 to 6 minutes.

5. Transfer ribs to cutting board and let rest for 10 minutes. Cut ribs between bones and serve, passing vinaigrette separately.

NOTES FROM THE TEST KITCHEN

HOW TO REMOVE THE MEMBRANE FROM SPARERIBS
The papery membrane on the rack's underside is chewy and unpleasant to eat. Here's how to remove it.

1. LOOSEN Slip tip of paring knife under edge of membrane on each rack.

2. PULL Gripping loosened edge with paper towel, slowly pull off membrane. It should come off in one piece.

SWEET-AND-SOUR BABY BACK RIBS

✔ **WHY THIS RECIPE WORKS** For an any-season indoor take on this crowd favorite, we wanted something different from the classic Southern barbecued ribs. Enter these sticky, glossy, tropical sweet-and-sour baby back ribs. Since they cook quickly and pack loads of pork flavor, baby back ribs fit the bill perfectly here. For a dead-simple cooking method that would result in tender, juicy ribs with a beautiful burnished color, we found that roasting them for about 2 hours in a 325-degree oven was just right. As for the sticky, sweet-and-savory sauce, we added fresh garlic, ginger, and jalapeños to a base of orange juice, sugar, and cider vinegar and finished up with a bit of ketchup, soy sauce, and, surprisingly, fish sauce. These last three ingredients provided an intense savory complexity to balance the sweet-and-sour base. Applying the sticky sauce three times—brushing it on once at the outset, again before the last 10 minutes of roasting, and then tossing the cut ribs in the remaining sauce before serving—made these ribs beautifully irresistible.

Growing up in the South, I always associated ribs with sweet, tangy barbecue sauce. But for a midwinter game-day rib feast in my adopted hometown of Boston, I decided to make something a little more surprising: something sticky, glossy, and tropical, with sweet and spicy notes of citrus, ginger, and jalapeño.

My first decision was to use baby back ribs. I chose them because they cook relatively quickly and pack tons of pork flavor. A couple of 2-pound racks of baby backs would be plenty for a crew of four to six people, so I started there. Some people get finicky and pretreat their ribs with a rub, a marinade, or even a brine (I do that sometimes, too). But I wanted to give this a swing without the extra time and effort of those steps.

Instead, I simply spread the racks on a rimmed baking sheet, seasoned them with salt and pepper, brushed on a healthy coating of sauce (more on this later), and popped them into the oven. A few rounds of experimentation showed me that I would have to be precise about the temperature: Too low and the ribs didn't achieve a beautiful burnished color before drying out; too high and they turned black before cooking through.

A 325-degree oven was just right. After 2½ hours, the ribs turned a beautiful, rusty shade of brown. When I tugged at the meat with a pair of tongs, it slipped off the bone in juicy chunks. Perfect. A quick check with the digital thermometer identified this sweet-spot internal temperature: 205 degrees.

As for the sauce, getting the balance right—neither overly sweet nor harshly sour, with just enough heat and salt—took some doing. I relied on a cup of orange juice for a vibrant citrus base. For fresh, aromatic bite and bright, spicy heat, I sautéed garlic and ginger with sliced jalapeños. Adding ½ cup of white sugar and ⅓ cup of tart cider vinegar delivered the sweet and sour portions of the promise.

But I needed some complexity, so I turned to savory ketchup, salty soy sauce, and, surprisingly, fish sauce. This addition was a revelation. The fish sauce (a cousin of Worcestershire) introduced a strong savory background flavor that played well with the other ingredients, and it tasted nothing like fish on the ribs.

Brushing the sauce onto the ribs in two stages—once before roasting and again 10 minutes before they came out of the oven—gave me beautifully lacquered racks. I cut them into individual ribs and then, because I wanted supremely sticky ribs, tossed them in the remainder of the sauce.

With a final gilding of bright green scallions, these ribs were an irresistible sight. But take my advice: Hand out plenty of paper towels when you serve these ribs. They make the most beautiful kind of mess.

—MATTHEW FAIRMAN, *Cook's Country*

NOTES FROM THE TEST KITCHEN

TAKE THE TEMPERATURE
How do you know when the ribs are tender and ready to be glazed? Use a digital thermometer.

Simply insert the tip of the probe into the center of a rib in the middle of the rack at an angle that is parallel to the bones. If the temperature registers at least 205 degrees, the target temperature for tenderness, go ahead and glaze.

SWEET-AND-SOUR BABY BACK RIBS

Sweet-and-Sour Baby Back Ribs

SERVES 4 TO 6

Because we prefer a slightly spicier sauce, we leave the seeds in the jalapeños when slicing them. If you're averse to spice, remove the seeds from the jalapeños before slicing them.

SAUCE

- 1 cup orange juice
- ½ cup sugar
- ⅓ cup cider vinegar
- 2 tablespoons ketchup
- 2 tablespoons soy sauce
- 1½ tablespoons cornstarch
- 1 tablespoon fish sauce
- 2 tablespoons vegetable oil
- 2 jalapeño chiles, stemmed and sliced into thin rings
- 2 garlic cloves, minced
- 1 teaspoon minced fresh ginger

RIBS

- 2 (2-pound) racks baby back ribs, trimmed
- 1 tablespoon kosher salt
- 1 teaspoon pepper
- 4 scallions, sliced thin on bias, divided

1. FOR THE SAUCE: Whisk orange juice, sugar, vinegar, ketchup, soy sauce, cornstarch, and fish sauce together in bowl. Heat oil in medium saucepan over medium-high heat until shimmering. Add jalapeños, garlic, and ginger and cook until fragrant, about 30 seconds. Stir in orange juice mixture and bring to boil. Cook, stirring occasionally, until thickened, about 3 minutes. Transfer ½ cup sauce to bowl, leaving jalapeños behind, and set aside.

2. FOR THE RIBS: Adjust oven rack to middle position and heat oven to 325 degrees. Line rimmed baking sheet with aluminum foil and set wire rack in sheet. Sprinkle ribs all over with salt and pepper. Place ribs on prepared wire rack and brush all over with reserved sauce (use all sauce). Arrange ribs meat side up. Roast until tender (fork inserted into meat will meet no resistance) and middle of rib rack registers at least 205 degrees, 2 to 2½ hours.

3. Brush tops of ribs with ¼ cup remaining sauce. Return ribs to oven and roast until sauce sets, about 10 minutes. Let ribs cool for 5 minutes. Reheat remaining sauce over medium heat until hot, about 4 minutes. Cut ribs between bones. Toss ribs, half of scallions, and remaining sauce together in large bowl. Transfer to serving platter and sprinkle with remaining scallions. Serve.

STUFFED PORK TENDERLOIN

✔ **WHY THIS RECIPE WORKS** We wanted to create a recipe for ultraflavorful pork tenderloin by packing the meat with a pungent stuffing. To prevent leaking, we butterflied the meat, meaning we sliced the tenderloin nearly in half lengthwise. We then pounded the tenderloin to an even thickness before rolling it around a mixture of smoky bacon and sweet, tart apples and tying it with kitchen twine. Gruyère cheese bound the bacon-and-apple stuffing together while adding nutty richness.

Pork tenderloin—one of America's favorite cuts of pork—is supremely tender and fast-cooking. While I appreciate those attributes, this cut isn't exactly a flavor powerhouse. The test kitchen has addressed this lack of flavor by creating some great recipes that dress it up with crumb crusts, intense spice rubs, or fancy sauces. But, tasty as they may be, all of those solutions are superficial. For maximum impact, I decided to pack the inside of the meat with a bold stuffing.

But before I did, I had two big questions to answer: How, exactly, would I stuff the meat? And what would I stuff it with? For inspiration, I dug up six wildly diverse recipes for stuffed pork tenderloin and prepared them in the test kitchen. The techniques for stuffing entailed everything from tying two tenderloins together with filling between them to cutting a pocket in the meat to using the handle of a wooden spoon to bore a hole down the length of the tenderloin.

I found that butterflying held the stuffing in place most reliably. "Butterflying" means slicing the tenderloin almost in half down its length so you can open it up like a book. By doing this, I could lay stuffing on the pork and roll it up like a jelly roll. I found that pounding the butterflied meat to an even thickness made for tidier rolling and more even cooking; it also created a larger surface area that held more stuffing. Trussing the stuffed tenderloins with kitchen twine ensured that the stuffing stayed secure inside the pork.

Now it was time to nail down the stuffing itself. In my initial test recipes, stuffing that used bread or bread crumbs absorbed pork juices and turned gummy. Those based on herb pastes (basically riffs on pesto) tasted good but didn't feel substantial enough to warrant the work. I wanted a knockout stuffing.

Our favorite tenderloin from the initial recipes was stuffed with a simple mix of apple and bacon, a tasty duo that hit salty and sweet notes. But it lacked depth and cohesion. Softening the chopped apple in bacon fat added dimension, and adding a minced shallot and some fresh thyme to the skillet developed the background flavor. As for a binder, shredded Gruyère cheese proved perfect; the nutty cheese melted in the oven and united the bacon and apple into a cohesive filling.

For a final test, I butterflied and pounded two tenderloins, loaded on the tasty stuffing, rolled them up and tied them, and then seared the tenderloins in a hot skillet before finishing them in a 350-degree oven. Slicing through the gorgeously browned crust revealed the soft, cheesy, extremely flavorful stuffing. It smelled amazing—and tasted even better. I finally had pork tenderloin that packed a wallop of intense meaty, savory flavor.

—MORGAN BOLLING, *Cook's Country*

Pork Tenderloin Roulade with Bacon, Apple, and Gruyère

SERVES 4 TO 6

You will need an ovensafe nonstick skillet for this recipe. Our favorite Gruyère is 1655 Le Gruyère AOP.

STUFFING

- 3 slices bacon, cut into ½-inch pieces
- 1 Granny Smith apple, peeled, cored, and chopped
- 1 shallot, minced
- 1 teaspoon minced fresh thyme
- 3 ounces Gruyère cheese, shredded (¾ cup)

PORK

- 2 (1- to 1¼-pound) pork tenderloins, trimmed
- 1½ teaspoons kosher salt
- ½ teaspoon pepper
- 1 tablespoon extra-virgin olive oil

1. FOR THE STUFFING: Cook bacon in 12-inch ovensafe nonstick skillet over medium heat until crispy, 5 to 7 minutes. Add apple, shallot, and thyme and cook until

NOTES FROM THE TEST KITCHEN

STUFFING PORK TENDERLOIN

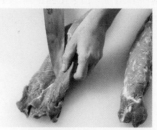

1. Slice tenderloins almost in half lengthwise, open flaps like book, and then pound each tenderloin to ¼-inch thickness.

2. Working with 1 tenderloin at a time, sprinkle half of stuffing over half of tenderloin, roll meat into tight log, and then secure with twine.

apple is softened, 4 to 6 minutes. Transfer to bowl and let cool for 10 minutes. Stir in Gruyère. Wipe skillet clean with paper towels.

2. FOR THE PORK: Adjust oven rack to middle position and heat oven to 350 degrees. Cut tenderloins in half horizontally, stopping ½ inch from edge so halves remain attached. Open up tenderloins, cover with plastic wrap, and pound to even ¼-inch thickness.

3. Working with 1 tenderloin at a time, trim and discard any ragged edges to create neat rectangle. With long side of tenderloin facing you, sprinkle half of stuffing (scant 1 cup) over bottom half of tenderloin, leaving 1-inch border around edges. Roll tenderloin away from you into tight log.

4. Position tenderloins seam side down and tie crosswise with kitchen twine at 1-inch intervals to secure. (Stuffed tenderloins can be wrapped individually in plastic wrap and refrigerated for up to 24 hours.)

5. Sprinkle each tenderloin with ¾ teaspoon salt and ¼ teaspoon pepper. Heat oil in now-empty skillet over medium-high heat until shimmering. Add tenderloins and brown on all sides, 6 to 8 minutes. Transfer skillet to oven and roast until center of stuffing registers 140 degrees, 16 to 20 minutes. Transfer tenderloins to carving board, tent with aluminum foil, and let rest for 10 minutes. Remove twine, slice into 1-inch-thick medallions, and serve.

GRILLED BONE-IN LEG OF LAMB WITH CHARRED-SCALLION SAUCE

GRILLED BONE-IN LEG OF LAMB

✓ **WHY THIS RECIPE WORKS** This grand cut has an iconic figure, impressive enough for any celebration, but its tapered shape also means that cooking it over a fire will result in uneven doneness. To combat this, we set up a half-grill fire and started the leg of lamb on the cooler side of the grill before searing it over the hotter side. This helped us avoid flare-ups while still giving the roast a charred exterior and a lovely medium-rare interior. Before grilling, we smeared a powerful paste of fresh thyme, dried oregano, garlic, lemon zest, and plenty of salt and pepper onto the leg of lamb and refrigerated it overnight to season the meat and add flavor to its exterior. And since a beautiful roast needs a beautiful sauce, we charred some scallions on the grill and stirred them into a rich mixture of olive oil, red wine vinegar, parsley, and garlic.

The grilling area at our Boston test kitchen sits next to a cruise ship terminal. This means that any test cook who grills on a Friday has a crowd of spectators eager to watch while they wait to set sail. It can be fun to have an audience when you're expertly crosshatching a thick-cut steak. Or it can mean that there are hundreds of people to bear witness when a beautiful 8-pound leg of lamb gets enveloped in flames from the grill. I should know. It happened to me.

I'd been thrilled to be assigned the task of developing a recipe for grilled leg of lamb. I love lamb's meaty, mildly gamy flavor, especially that of the leg. This grand cut has an iconic figure, impressive enough for any celebration, but its tapered shape also means that, over a fire, the meat will cook unevenly, ending up burnt on the narrow end and raw in the middle. My task: to highlight meaty lamb flavor while achieving more even doneness, from the charred exterior to a lovely medium-rare center.

To get started, I coated an 8-pound bone-in leg of lamb with salt and pepper. I got a charcoal grill ripping hot with smoldering coals spread evenly over its base and placed the lamb on the grate. It wasn't long before the lamb's fat began to render and drip onto the coals. The ensuing flames grew quickly, engulfing the leg and prompting oohs and aahs from my audience. The flames may have looked cool, but they resulted in a sooty flavor. My lamb tasted like a spent cigar.

I needed to contain the flames, so for my next test I built a half-grill fire, with all the coals on one side of the grill. I wanted to sear the lamb over the hotter side and then race to move it to the cooler side before the fat rendered and the flames licked up. I lost the race. I tried trimming the fat more aggressively and cooking the lamb entirely over the cooler side. There were no flare-ups, but the leg was pale and sad-looking.

Here in the test kitchen, we often turn to a technique called reverse searing when cooking big cuts of meat. You cook the meat through at a lower temperature first and then sear it to create a flavorful crust. Using this method, I figured, would allow the fat to gently render long before the meat saw the direct heat, minimizing flare-ups.

I placed the lamb on the cooler side of the grill and let it cook until it reached 120 degrees, which took about 1½ hours. I then moved it to the hotter side, where it seared perfectly, acquiring a gorgeous dark-brown crust to go with its nicely medium-rare center. Perfect.

To dress it up, I smeared my next leg of lamb with a paste of fresh thyme, dried oregano, coriander, garlic, lemon zest, and plenty of salt and pepper. I found that leaving this powerful paste on the lamb overnight before grilling helped season the meat and add flavor to the exterior.

A beautiful roast needs a beautiful sauce, so I charred some scallions on the grill before searing the lamb. I then chopped them and stirred them into a mixture of extra-virgin olive oil, parsley, red wine vinegar, and spicy red pepper flakes.

The cruise ship passengers watched wistfully as I took that leg back into the kitchen. And as I sliced off a bit of that juicy meat with its dark-brown, flavor-packed crust and dipped it in some charred-scallion sauce, I started making plans to cook another for an upcoming dinner party. I'd finally mastered the flames.

—MORGAN BOLLING, *Cook's Country*

Grilled Bone-In Leg of Lamb with Charred-Scallion Sauce
SERVES 10 TO 12

The seasoned meat must be refrigerated for at least 12 hours before cooking. For an accurate temperature reading in step 5, insert your thermometer into the thickest part of the leg until you hit bone, then pull it about ½ inch away from the bone.

FOUR STEPS TO JUICY LAMB WITH A FLAVORFUL CRUST

1. RUB WITH PASTE
Massage spice paste into lamb, cover lamb with plastic wrap, and refrigerate for at least 12 hours.

2. GRILL LOW AND SLOW
Set up grill with hotter and cooler zones and grill lamb, fat side up, over cooler side until it's almost done.

3. SEAR OVER HIGH HEAT Move lamb to hotter side of grill, fat side down, to create flavorful seared crust.

4. CARVE INTO THIN SLICES Starting at widest part of lamb, thinly slice at 45-degree angle toward exposed bone end.

THE CASE FOR BONE-IN

Would a boneless leg of lamb be easier to cook evenly and carve perfectly? Yes. So why go bone-in here? The practical reasons are that boneless roasts come in netting that you have to cut away (it is not grill-safe), necessitating tying with twine, and a bone-in leg gives you a range of doneness levels throughout the roast to please all tastes. But mostly it comes down to the grand, festive look of a whole bone-in leg. The cut is also a nod to earlier times when animals were butchered more simply and large cuts were cooked over a live fire, as in this recipe. Go all out—go for a bone-in leg of lamb.

LAMB

- 12 garlic cloves, minced
- 2 tablespoons vegetable oil
- 2 tablespoons kosher salt
- 1½ tablespoons pepper
- 1 tablespoon fresh thyme leaves
- 1 tablespoon dried oregano
- 2 teaspoons finely grated lemon zest
- 1 teaspoon ground coriander
- 1 (8-pound) bone-in leg of lamb, trimmed

SCALLION SAUCE

- ¾ cup extra-virgin olive oil
- ¼ cup chopped fresh parsley
- 1 tablespoon red wine vinegar
- 2 garlic cloves, minced
- 1 teaspoon pepper
- ¾ teaspoon kosher salt
- ¼ teaspoon red pepper flakes
- 12 scallions, trimmed

1. FOR THE LAMB: Combine garlic, oil, salt, pepper, thyme, oregano, lemon zest, and coriander in bowl. Place lamb on rimmed baking sheet and rub all over with garlic paste. Cover with plastic wrap and refrigerate for at least 12 hours or up to 24 hours.

2. FOR THE SCALLION SAUCE: Combine oil, parsley, vinegar, garlic, pepper, salt, and pepper flakes in bowl; set aside.

3A. FOR A CHARCOAL GRILL: Open bottom vent completely. Light large chimney starter filled with charcoal briquettes (6 quarts). When top coals are partially covered with ash, pour evenly over half of grill. Set cooking grate in place, cover, and open lid vent completely. Heat grill until hot, about 5 minutes.

3B. FOR A GAS GRILL: Turn all burners to high, cover, and heat grill until hot, about 15 minutes. Leave primary burner on high and turn off other burner(s). (Adjust primary burner [or, if using 3-burner grill, primary burner and second burner] as needed to maintain grill temperature between 350 and 400 degrees.)

4. Clean and oil cooking grate. Place scallions on hotter side of grill. Cook (covered if using gas) until lightly charred on both sides, about 3 minutes per side. Transfer scallions to plate.

5. Uncover lamb and place fat side up on cooler side of grill, parallel to fire. (If using gas, it may be necessary to angle thicker end of lamb toward hotter side of grill to fit.) Cover grill (position lid vent directly over lamb if using charcoal) and cook until thickest part of meat (½ inch from bone) registers 120 degrees, 1¼ hours to 1¾ hours.

6. Transfer lamb, fat side down, to hotter side of grill. Cook (covered if using gas) until fat side is well browned, 7 to 9 minutes. Transfer lamb to carving board, fat side up, and tent with aluminum foil. Let rest for 30 minutes.

7. Cut scallions into ½-inch pieces, then stir into reserved oil mixture. Season sauce with salt and pepper to taste. Slice lamb thin and serve with sauce.

SPICED LAMB POT ROAST WITH FIGS

WHY THIS RECIPE WORKS Less common (and less expensive) than leg of lamb, a lamb shoulder roast is an intensely flavorful cut. It's ideal for slow braising, which breaks down the collagen and fats that add flavor and body to the cooking liquid and produces fall-apart tender meat. We found that braising the shoulder in the oven—and turning it once halfway through braising—provided more even heat than cooking on the stovetop, and browning the shoulder first added complex flavors. What really elevated this dish, however, was simmering the lamb in ruby port along with rosemary and aromatics. After the long braise, the liquid turned rich and developed a deep flavor. While the lamb rested, we defatted the liquid, reduced it, and then stirred in figs, creating a balanced sauce with salty, sweet, and tart notes. For even more flavor, and to help the lamb stay juicy, we seasoned the roast with ground coriander, ground fennel seed, and salt. A sprinkling of parsley added pleasant freshness.

The meaty foundation of Middle Eastern cuisine, lamb is beloved in all sorts of preparations, from rich and hearty stews to *kofte* (grilled lamb kebabs) either served over rice pilaf or nestled in pita bread with fresh, crisp vegetables and a creamy sauce. Both dishes have their virtues: A comforting bowl of lamb stew can warm you up on the coldest of days, and kofte is a more unexpected and exciting choice than chicken or steak for a mid-summer cookout. I wanted to create a stunning Middle Eastern-inspired lamb centerpiece suitable for year-round feasting.

Before I experimented with the flavor profile, I'd have to decide on a cut of meat. Bone-in leg of lamb would certainly be a showstopper, but its unwieldy shape makes it difficult to handle and produces uneven doneness. Buying a boneless shoulder roast and rolling it into a cylinder would give me more foolproof results. I could also fit this more compact roast in the Dutch oven, meaning I wouldn't have to lug out a roasting pan. Boneless cuts also have another benefit: Most of lamb's signature gamy flavor is packed in the fat, not the muscle. Removing the leg bone and butterflying the meat opens it up like a book, allowing you to trim excess fat that can make lamb roast too gamy for some.

On to the cooking method. Like most roasts, I would brown the shoulder in a bit of oil to develop flavorful fond, add aromatics, deglaze the pot with a complementary cooking liquid, and then roast the lamb until it became tender. To infuse the roast with Middle Eastern flavors from the get-go, I covered it with salt, pepper, and an assortment of spices before browning it. But after 10 minutes of browning, the spice crust had burnt, resulting in a bitter-tasting final product.

How could I encourage the spice rub to penetrate the meat without burning it? I recalled that in some of our recipes for boneless roasts tied with twine, we season the cut side of the meat before rolling it up and tying it. The benefits are threefold: Putting the spices inside the roast prevents them from burning. The cut side is a bit craggier, so the seasonings can soak into the meat more readily. And finally this method encourages flavor development from the inside out rather than superficially. Before trying it out, I pared down the spices to ground coriander for nutty, citrusy notes and ground fennel for a sweet anise flavor.

I rolled up my new and improved lamb roast and seared it in 2 tablespoons of extra-virgin olive oil, further highlighting its Middle Eastern flavors. After it was browned on all sides, I transferred it to a plate while I sautéed the aromatics in the leftover fat—an onion and five minced garlic cloves kept it simple but flavorful. I perused the cooking liquid options, and while beef broth and red wine were fine additions, I was on the hunt for something a bit different. Maybe a fortified wine would add more depth of flavor. I opted for ruby port, a fruity fortified wine from Portugal that, when reduced, would complement the savory lamb. I added 2 cups of ruby port, scraping up the flavorful browned bits from the pot, tossed in 2 sprigs of

SPICED LAMB POT ROAST WITH FIGS

rosemary for an herbal note, returned the lamb to the pot, and roasted it in a 300-degree oven for about 2½ hours.

The lamb emerged fragrant and fork-tender, but the braising liquid was too thin, and it was missing a textural element. Fresh figs would be the perfect addition; like ruby port, they're slightly sweet, and their sugars and natural pectins would help thicken the braising liquid into a luxurious sauce. After defatting the braising liquid, I brought it to a simmer, added quartered figs, and let it reduce for about 10 minutes. Because the figs had broken down considerably, this sauce was thick and gloppy—not the pourable reduction I imagined. I remedied this by stirring in the figs during the last few minutes of cooking time. These figs were tender and saucy with the right amount of resistance. Finally, some parsley added much needed freshness. This unexpected yet elegant lamb roast could rival even the most mainstream dinner party showstoppers.

—RUSSELL SELANDER, *America's Test Kitchen Books*

Spiced Lamb Pot Roast with Figs

SERVES 8 TO 10

We prefer the subtler flavor and larger size of lamb labeled "domestic" or "American" for this recipe.

- 1 tablespoon ground coriander
- 2 teaspoons ground fennel
- 1½ teaspoons table salt
- 1½ teaspoons pepper
- 1 (4- to 5-pound) boneless lamb shoulder, trimmed
- 2 tablespoons extra-virgin olive oil
- 1 onion, chopped fine
- 5 garlic cloves, minced
- 2 cups ruby port
- 2 sprigs fresh rosemary
- 12 ounces fresh figs, stemmed and quartered
- ¼ cup chopped fresh parsley

1. Combine coriander, fennel, salt, and pepper in bowl. Place lamb with rough interior side (which was against bone) facing up on cutting board and sprinkle with 4 teaspoons spice mixture. Starting from short side, roll lamb tightly and tie with kitchen twine at 1-inch intervals. Sprinkle exterior with remaining spice mixture. Transfer to plate, cover, and refrigerate for at least 1 hour or up to 24 hours.

2. Adjust oven rack to lower-middle position and heat oven to 300 degrees. Pat lamb dry with paper towels. Heat oil in Dutch oven over medium-high heat until just smoking. Brown lamb on all sides, 8 to 10 minutes; transfer to plate.

3. Pour off all but 1 tablespoon fat from pot. Add onion and cook over medium heat until softened, about 5 minutes. Stir in garlic and cook until fragrant, about 30 seconds. Stir in port, scraping up any browned bits, and bring to simmer. Return lamb to pot, adding any accumulated juices. Add rosemary sprigs, cover, and transfer pot to oven. Cook until lamb is tender and fork slips easily in and out of meat, 2¼ to 2¾ hours, flipping roast halfway through cooking.

4. Remove pot from oven. Transfer lamb to carving board, tent with aluminum foil, and let rest while finishing sauce. Discard rosemary sprigs and strain braising liquid through fine-mesh strainer into fat separator; reserve solids. Allow braising liquid to settle for 5 minutes. Add defatted braising liquid and reserved solids to now-empty pot and bring to simmer over medium-high heat. Cook until slightly thickened and reduced to 1½ cups, about 10 minutes. Stir in figs and cook until heated through, about 2 minutes. Season with salt and pepper to taste.

5. Discard twine, slice lamb ½ inch thick, and transfer to serving platter. Spoon sauce over lamb and sprinkle with parsley. Serve.

NOTES FROM THE TEST KITCHEN

TYING A BONELESS LAMB ROAST

1. Place roast on counter with rough side (which was against bone) facing up. Starting from short side, roll roast tightly into cylinder.

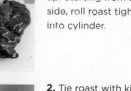

2. Tie roast with kitchen twine at 1-inch intervals.

BEST GRILLED CHICKEN THIGHS

BEST GRILLED CHICKEN THIGHS

✓ **WHY THIS RECIPE WORKS** We found that the best way to grill chicken thighs was also the easiest. Cooking the thighs over indirect heat until they registered 185 to 190 degrees, which took about 40 minutes, allowed collagen in the meat to break down into gelatin, which ensured moist and silky chicken. And grilling the thighs skin side down thoroughly rendered the fat under the skin's surface, turning the skin paper-thin, and broke down and softened the skin's collagen—both of which allowed the skin to get nicely crispy once we seared it over direct heat for the last few minutes of cooking. We coated the thighs with a bold-flavored paste, applying most of it to the flesh side so as not to interfere with crisping by introducing too much extra moisture to the skin. Briefly searing the flesh side of the chicken thighs before serving took the raw edge off the paste on that side.

One of my earliest cooking memories is of my dad positioned at the grill, squirt bottle in one hand and grill tongs in the other, working furiously to rescue chicken thighs from a three-alarm blaze. In a rush to get dinner on the table, he would position the thighs directly over the fire to cook them quickly. Within minutes, their rendering fat dripped into the flames, ignited, and grew into a blaze that forced him to shuffle the chicken around the grate while he simultaneously tried to quell the fire with water from his squirt bottle. I can't lie: The pyrotechnics were pretty thrilling to watch as a kid. But eating the chicken was less thrilling—the chewy meat tasted of acrid smoke and was covered with rubbery, badly charred skin.

Chicken thighs have a lot going for them: They're more flavorful and less prone to overcooking than leaner breasts, boast a relatively high ratio of meat to bone, and have a flat layer of skin that is prime for browning and crisping. What makes them challenging to cook, especially over a live fire, is that they tend to have more subcutaneous fat than other parts of the chicken, which can cause flare-ups on the grill. This also means the fat is at risk of not thoroughly rendering and remaining chewy and flabby.

My goal was to create a recipe that would produce juicy, flavorful meat, rendered fat, and crispy skin—minus the inferno.

My colleague Andrea Geary recently developed a recipe for spice-rubbed chicken drumsticks that I thought might be a good blueprint for thighs, too. The key in her recipe is to cook the chicken over indirect heat for about an hour, during which time fat and collagen in the meat and skin render and break down, respectively. Patience is rewarded with meat that's tender and juicy and skin that's primed for crisping. She also arranges the drumsticks in two rows alongside the fire and rearranges them halfway through cooking—those closer to the heat go to the outside, and those on the outside go closer to the heat—so that they all have even exposure to the heat and finish cooking at the same time. Then she moves the drumsticks directly over the heat to brown them briefly and crisp the skin, which takes only a few minutes thanks to all the rendering that took place earlier.

I got started by arranging eight thighs skin side up on the cooler side of a grill, thinking that the fat in the skin would lubricate the meat as it rendered. After 20 minutes, I rearranged the pieces and then let them cook for another 15 to 20 minutes until they registered between 185 and 190 degrees. That's well past the point of doneness for white meat (160 degrees), but previous tests have found that dark meat benefits from being cooked much more thoroughly, especially if it also cooks slowly. That's because the longer the meat spends cooking at temperatures above 140 degrees, the more of its abundant collagen breaks down and transforms into gelatin that lubricates the meat, making it seem juicy and tender.

The method was dead easy, and all seemed to be going well until I moved the thighs to the hotter side of the grill and flipped them skin side down to crisp. Fat poured out from under the skin, dripped into the fire, and sent flames shooting up. I managed to salvage some of the thighs from the flames and was pleased that the meat was, indeed, quite tender and moist after the lengthy stint over indirect heat. But the skin wasn't nearly as nice to eat—not just because it was burnt in spots, but because it was still flabby and chewy beneath the surface.

Crispy, evenly bronzed chicken skin is a real treat, but it takes both ample time and heat to produce those results. That's partly because chicken skin—particularly the skin on thighs—is padded with fat that must render before the skin can crisp. But fat isn't the only factor that makes chicken skin flabby and chewy; skin, like meat, contains collagen that must break down in order for it to turn tender. Only once the skin is tender can it then crisp.

The thighs were already spending a long time on the grill, but maybe the skin wasn't getting hot enough to shed fat. So I spent the next several tests exposing the skin to more heat. Making a hotter fire helped render the fat and crisp the skin, but it did so at the expense of the meat, which moved too quickly through the collagen breakdown zone and was thus not as tender. I had better luck turning the thighs skin side down midway through cooking instead of at the end; more direct (but still gentle) heat melted the fat, which now dripped out of each piece instead of puddling under the skin. But I got the best results yet when I cooked the chicken skin side down from start to finish. By the time the meat was tender, much of the skin's fat had rendered and the skin had become paper-thin and soft, so all I had to do to crisp it up was slide the thighs over to the hotter side for about 5 minutes. The method was so easy, and the results were perfectly cooked—if a bit plain—thighs.

I wanted to add more flavor to the mix, but I didn't want to thwart my skin-crisping efforts by dousing the thighs with a wet marinade. Instead, I came up with a couple of robustly seasoned pastes to rub onto the chicken: a version that tapped into my love of Korean fried chicken with gochujang and soy sauce, and a mustard and tarragon paste with loads of garlic.

The trick was applying the paste strategically, since even moderate moisture could soften the skin. I found that spreading two-thirds of the paste on the flesh side of each thigh worked best; there were lots of nooks and crannies to capture the paste, and the remaining third that I rubbed over the skin seasoned and flavored it without adding enough moisture to inhibit crisping. The only hitch: Since the chicken cooked skin side down the whole time, the paste on the flesh side looked and tasted a bit raw. So after the skin crisped over the hotter side of the grill, I flipped the pieces onto the flesh side for a minute or two to take the raw edge off the paste.

Perfectly tender, juicy meat; thin, crispy skin; bold flavor; and a method that requires practically zero work. Dinner's in the bag—not in the fire.

—STEVE DUNN, *Cook's Illustrated*

NOTES FROM THE TEST KITCHEN

APPLY THE PASTE STRATEGICALLY
Our pastes add potent flavor, but it's important to apply them strategically. We found that too much paste on the skin prevented it from crisping, so we applied two-thirds of the paste to the flesh side and the remaining one-third to the skin side to ensure that the skin was seasoned but not wet.

⅔ FOR THE FLESH SIDE
Nooks and crannies in the flesh hold on to paste and capture bold flavors.

⅓ FOR THE SKIN SIDE
Minimal moisture means skin can crisp.

Best Grilled Chicken Thighs
SERVES 4 TO 6

In step 1, the chicken can be refrigerated for up to 2 hours before grilling. It is important to allow the chicken thighs to reach 185 to 190 degrees before removing them from the grill; otherwise, they will taste dry and overcooked.

- 8 (5- to 7-ounce) bone-in chicken thighs, trimmed
- ½ teaspoon kosher salt
- 1 recipe paste, divided (recipes follow)

1. Place chicken, skin side up, on large plate. Sprinkle skin side with salt and spread evenly with one-third of spice paste. Flip chicken and spread remaining two-thirds of paste evenly over flesh side. Refrigerate while preparing grill.

2A. FOR A CHARCOAL GRILL: Open bottom vent halfway. Light large chimney starter mounded with charcoal briquettes (7 quarts). When top coals are partially covered with ash, pour evenly over half of grill. Set cooking grate in place, cover, and open lid vent halfway. Heat grill until hot, about 5 minutes.

2B. FOR A GAS GRILL: Turn all burners to high, cover, and heat grill until hot, about 15 minutes. Leave primary burner on high and turn off other burner(s). (Adjust primary burner [or, if using 3-burner grill, primary burner and second burner] as needed to maintain grill temperature around 350 degrees.)

3. Clean and oil cooking grate. Place chicken, skin side down, on cooler side of grill. Cover and cook for 20 minutes. Rearrange chicken, keeping skin side down, so that pieces that were positioned closest to edge of grill are now closer to heat source and vice versa. Cover and continue to cook until chicken registers 185 to 190 degrees, 15 to 20 minutes longer.

4. Move all chicken, skin side down, to hotter side of grill and cook until skin is lightly charred, about 5 minutes. Flip chicken and cook until flesh side is lightly browned, 1 to 2 minutes. Transfer to platter, tent with aluminum foil, and let rest for 10 minutes. Serve.

Gochujang Paste

MAKES ABOUT ⅓ CUP

Gochujang, or Korean red chili paste, can be found in Asian markets or in the Asian or international section of large supermarkets.

    3 tablespoons gochujang
    1 tablespoon soy sauce
    2 garlic cloves, minced
    2 teaspoons sugar
    1 teaspoon kosher salt

Combine all ingredients in bowl.

Mustard-Tarragon Paste

MAKES ABOUT ⅓ CUP

Rosemary or thyme can be substituted for the tarragon, if desired. When using this paste, we like to serve the chicken with lemon wedges.

    3 tablespoons Dijon mustard
    5 garlic cloves, minced
    1 tablespoon finely grated lemon zest
    2 teaspoons minced fresh tarragon
    1½ teaspoons kosher salt
    1 teaspoon water
    ½ teaspoon pepper

Combine all ingredients in bowl.

KUNG PAO CHICKEN

WHY THIS RECIPE WORKS We started our spicy, tingle-inducing Kung Pao Chicken by toasting peanuts in a skillet to maximize their crunch before setting them aside to cool. Next we toasted coarsely ground Sichuan peppercorns and arbol chiles that we'd halved lengthwise to release their heat. We stirred in plenty of garlic and ginger and then added marinated diced chicken thighs. We covered the skillet to facilitate quick and even cooking of the chicken. When it was almost cooked through, we added some celery for crisp freshness and then a quick and concentrated sauce mixture that cooked down to a glaze. Stirring in the scallions and toasted peanuts last ensured that they retained their all-important crunch.

If you haven't eaten kung pao chicken in the past 10 years, there's a good chance you've never had the real thing. I hadn't, until recently.

In the '90s, the dish was my go-to Chinese restaurant order. The diced chicken and vegetables, peanuts, and vaguely sweet-and-sour sauce were familiar, while the fiery dried chiles scattered throughout supplied an appealing undercurrent of heat. But eventually the novelty wore off, as did any urge to make it myself.

Then, a few months ago, I ordered kung pao in a restaurant and was delighted by the addition of Sichuan peppercorns, which imbued the dish with a woodsy fragrance and citrusy tang and created an intriguing tingling sensation on my lips and tongue, a perfect complement to the chiles' heat. In fact, the interplay of peppercorns and fiery chiles is so foundational to Sichuan cuisine that it has a name: *ma la*, which means "numbing heat." Sichuan peppercorns were banned in the United States from 1968 to 2005 because they might carry a disease that could endanger the American citrus crop, so these tiny dried fruits of the prickly ash tree had been tragically absent from my '90s kung pao. But now, back where they belonged, they snapped the flavors of kung pao chicken into focus.

With my interest in the dish reawakened, I was eager to devise my own version of kung pao chicken. I knew that chiles and buzzy peppercorns weren't enough to ensure success, though. The chicken would have to be juicy and the peanuts crunchy, with a crisp, cooling vegetable for contrast. And I wanted a potent glaze that lightly coated—not heavily sauced—each piece but still delivered flavor to every bite.

Most recipes called for boneless, skinless chicken breasts or thighs. I went with thighs because they're not only more resistant to overcooking but also more flavorful, so they'd make a better match for the strong flavors of kung pao. I tossed the diced thighs in a marinade that, based on my research, appeared to be pretty universal: savory soy sauce; sweet rice wine; floral, earthy white pepper; and a bit of cornstarch that would help the marinade cling to the meat and give some body to the glaze when cooked.

Vegetables aren't a major player in kung pao chicken, but a small amount adds welcome color and crunch. Celery and scallions are common, so I diced them to match the size of the smallest element of the dish: the peanuts. Cutting everything to the same size is a hallmark of kung pao chicken. It provides visual harmony and allows the diner to experience multiple flavors and textures in every bite. I also grated some ginger, minced some garlic, and whisked up a quick glaze composed of a bit more soy; complex, fruity black vinegar; dark brown sugar; and some toasted sesame oil. I kept the volume small so I'd end up with just enough glaze to coat all the components.

To start, I heated a tablespoon of vegetable oil in a nonstick skillet and added a generous handful of dried arbol chiles (a fine substitute for the traditional bright-red *chao tian jiao*, or "facing heaven" chiles) and some ground Sichuan peppercorns. When they were fragrant and just starting to darken, I added the peanuts and then the garlic and ginger. The last two clumped up in the hot skillet, but I figured they'd disperse once I added the chicken.

Because the chicken pieces were a pain to turn constantly, I introduced an innovation: I covered the skillet. This way, the pieces cooked from the top as well as the bottom. When the chicken was mostly cooked, I added the celery. After pouring in the sauce and reducing it to a glaze consistency, I stirred in the scallions, killed the heat, and took a taste.

Let's start with the positives: The chicken thighs were tender and juicy throughout, the celery and scallions were crisp, and the dark glaze coated everything nicely. On the negative side, the peanuts were soggy and soft. And those sticky clumps of garlic and ginger hadn't spread out as I had hoped; they had instead collected all the Sichuan peppercorn dust, forming sneaky sensory bombs. As for the heat, despite my free hand with the chiles, it was almost nonexistent.

I had a hunch about why my arbol chiles, which I knew to be impressively spicy, weren't imparting much "pow" to my kung pao. To test it, I touched an intact chile to my tongue. Nothing. Then I opened up a chile and tasted the interior. Ouch. There was plenty of heat on the inside since most capsaicin resides in the ribs and seeds of chiles, but there wasn't enough time or moisture in my recipe to coax that flavor through the tough skin.

So for my next batch, I halved the chiles lengthwise to expose as much of their spicy interiors as possible. (But to ensure that I didn't overwhelm my tasters with heat, I jostled the chiles until all the seeds fell out.) And to aid the distribution of the grated ginger and minced garlic, I put them in a small bowl and stirred in 1 tablespoon of oil.

I also tweaked the order of operations a bit. Because I wanted the peanuts to be as toasty and crunchy as possible, I first cooked them in a teaspoon of oil and then transferred them to a plate, where they would continue to crisp as they cooled. Then I stir-fried the halved chiles and the ground peppercorns and added the ginger and garlic, which dispersed with minimal persuasion thanks to their coating of oil. I added the chicken, covered the skillet, and, once the chicken was mostly cooked, tossed in the celery. I then stirred in the sauce, and only when it was fully reduced did I add the peanuts and scallions, so both would be coated but maintain their texture.

With its lightly glazed components and characteristic sensations of spice, tingle, crunch, crispness, and juiciness in every bite, this version of kung pao was as real as it gets.

—ANDREA GEARY, *Cook's Illustrated*

Kung Pao Chicken

SERVES 4 TO 6

Kung pao chicken is typically quite spicy. To adjust the heat level, use more or fewer chiles, depending on the size (we used 2-inch-long chiles) and your preference. Have your ingredients prepared and your equipment in place before you begin to cook. Use a spice grinder or mortar and pestle to grind the Sichuan peppercorns coarse. Sherry vinegar can be substituted for the Chinese black vinegar, if desired. Serve with white rice and a simple vegetable side such as broccoli or bok choy. Do not eat the chiles.

KUNG PAO CHICKEN

CHICKEN AND SAUCE

- 1½ **pounds boneless, skinless chicken thighs, trimmed and cut into ½-inch cubes**
- ¼ **cup soy sauce, divided**
- 1 **tablespoon cornstarch**
- 1 **tablespoon Chinese rice wine or dry sherry**
- ½ **teaspoon white pepper**
- 1 **tablespoon Chinese black vinegar**
- 1 **tablespoon packed dark brown sugar**
- 2 **teaspoons toasted sesame oil**

STIR-FRY

- 1 **tablespoon minced garlic**
- 2 **teaspoons grated fresh ginger**
- 2 **tablespoons plus 1 teaspoon vegetable oil, divided**
- ½ **cup dry-roasted peanuts**
- 10–15 **dried arbol chiles, halved lengthwise and seeded**
- 1 **teaspoon Sichuan peppercorns, ground coarse**
- 2 **celery ribs, cut into ½-inch pieces**
- 5 **scallions, white and light green parts only, cut into ½-inch pieces**

1. FOR THE CHICKEN AND SAUCE: Combine chicken, 2 tablespoons soy sauce, cornstarch, rice wine, and white pepper in medium bowl and set aside. Stir vinegar, sugar, oil, and remaining 2 tablespoons soy sauce together in small bowl and set aside.

2. FOR THE STIR-FRY: Stir garlic, ginger, and 1 tablespoon oil together in second small bowl. Combine peanuts and 1 teaspoon oil in 12-inch nonstick skillet over medium-low heat. Cook, stirring constantly, until

peanuts just begin to darken, 3 to 5 minutes. Transfer peanuts to plate and spread into even layer to cool. Return now-empty skillet to medium-low heat. Add remaining 1 tablespoon oil, arbols, and peppercorns and cook, stirring constantly, until arbols begin to darken, 1 to 2 minutes. Add garlic mixture and cook, stirring constantly, until all clumps are broken up and mixture is fragrant, about 30 seconds.

3. Add chicken and spread into even layer. Cover skillet, increase heat to medium-high, and cook, without stirring, for 1 minute. Stir chicken and spread into even layer. Cover and cook, without stirring, for 1 minute. Add celery and cook uncovered, stirring frequently, until chicken is cooked through, 2 to 3 minutes. Add soy sauce mixture and cook, stirring constantly, until sauce is thickened and shiny and coats chicken, 3 to 5 minutes. Stir in scallions and peanuts. Transfer to platter and serve.

SKILLET-ROASTED CHICKEN BREASTS WITH GARLICKY GREEN BEANS

✓ WHY THIS RECIPE WORKS This recipe is a twofer from one skillet. First, we seasoned bone-in, skin-on chicken breasts under the skin with salt. We placed them skin side down in a cold skillet and then turned on the heat to render the fat and brown the skin slowly without overcooking the delicate flesh just beneath it. Once the skin was well browned, we flipped the breasts and placed them in a 325-degree oven to cook through. While the cooked chicken breasts rested, we added garlic and red pepper flakes to the skillet and cooked them until the chicken juices reduced and the aromatics began to sizzle in the chicken fat and release flavor. We then added green beans along with a little water to the pan, covered the pan, and let the beans cook through. With the skillet uncovered, the savory, chicken-y liquid thickened to coat the green beans.

When you roast bone-in, skin-on chicken breasts in a skillet, fat renders from the skin, juices seep from the flesh, and bits of meat stick to the pan. These tidbits crackle and brown, creating a concentrated, chicken-y infusion. Tradition dictates that you use these drippings to whip up a pan sauce. But that's wasting an

---

NOTES FROM THE TEST KITCHEN

LUBRICATE YOUR AROMATICS

Small pieces of garlic and ginger can clump up when you add them to the pan, preventing some bits from blooming in the oil and their flavors from evenly permeating the dish. Here's our solution to the problem.

Combine aromatics with 1 tablespoon oil before adding mixture to pan. Oil helps distribute garlic and ginger evenly throughout dish.

opportunity to make a one-pan meal. Why not cook a vegetable in them to create a rich, savory side? Add crusty bread and a bottle of wine and you're done—with just one pan to wash.

I started by peeling back the chicken skin so I could season the flesh directly with salt; I then repositioned the skin. To ensure that the fat would end up fully rendered, I wanted to kick-start that process by searing the chicken on the stove before transferring it to the oven. I turned to a technique the test kitchen has used successfully in the past: I placed the chicken skin side down in a cold skillet and then turned on the burner. This cold-start method allows fat to render gently with little risk of overcooking the meat just below the surface. By the time the pan gets blazing hot, the fat is well rendered and the skin is thin, flat, and ready to begin crisping and browning.

I also spritzed the skin with vegetable oil spray to keep it from sticking to the bottom of the skillet and pierced it with a skewer to encourage the fat to escape. Once the skin was well browned, I flipped the breasts and transferred the skillet to a 325-degree oven. After 30 minutes in the oven, the breasts were perfectly cooked, the skin was crispy, and the savory drippings were plentiful.

I had a couple of requirements for the vegetable. First, it had to come together in the 10 minutes that the chicken needed to rest. Second, it had to showcase the deeply flavorful juices, fond, and fat. I decided on easy, quick-cooking green beans—they have plenty of surface area for the drippings to cling to.

But the drippings alone wouldn't be enough to flavor the beans; I also needed aromatics and seasonings. Sliced garlic and red pepper flakes were a natural fit. I added both to the pan, cranked up the heat, and scraped up the fond. When the garlic and pepper flakes started to sizzle, that was my cue that all the moisture had evaporated and the ingredients were blooming and releasing flavor into the chicken fat.

I added the beans along with ⅓ cup of water and covered the pan so they could steam. After 8 minutes or so, I removed the lid and continued simmering just long enough to reduce the liquid to coat the beans, which were now infused with the essence of chicken.

I transferred the beans to a platter and showered them with Parmesan cheese before placing the juicy, crispy-skinned chicken on top. Dinner was served.

—ANDREW JANJIGIAN, *Cook's Illustrated*

Skillet-Roasted Chicken Breasts with Garlicky Green Beans
SERVES 4

Trim excess fatty skin from the thick ends of the breasts before cooking.

- 4 (10- to 12-ounce) bone-in split chicken breasts, trimmed
- 2¼ teaspoons kosher salt, divided
- Vegetable oil spray
- 3 garlic cloves, sliced thin
- ¼ teaspoon red pepper flakes
- 1¼ pounds green beans, trimmed
- ⅓ cup water
- 1½ ounces Parmesan cheese, shredded (½ cup)

1. Adjust oven rack to lower-middle position and heat oven to 325 degrees. Working with 1 breast at a time, use your fingers to carefully separate skin from meat. Peel back skin, leaving skin attached at top and bottom of breast and at ribs. Sprinkle 1½ teaspoons salt evenly over chicken (⅜ teaspoon per breast). Lay skin back in place. Using metal skewer or tip of paring knife, poke 6 to 8 holes in fat deposits in skin of each breast. Spray skin with oil spray.

2. Place chicken, skin side down, in 12-inch ovensafe skillet and set over medium-high heat. Cook, moving chicken as infrequently as possible, until skin is well browned, 7 to 9 minutes. Carefully flip chicken and transfer skillet to oven. Roast until chicken registers 160 degrees, 25 to 30 minutes.

3. Transfer chicken to plate; do not discard liquid in skillet. Add garlic, pepper flakes, and remaining ¾ teaspoon salt to skillet and cook over medium-high heat, stirring occasionally and scraping up any browned bits, until moisture has evaporated and mixture begins to sizzle, 2 to 4 minutes. Add green beans and water and bring to simmer.

4. Cover skillet, reduce heat to medium, and cook until green beans are tender, 8 to 10 minutes, stirring halfway through cooking. Uncover and continue to cook, stirring frequently, until sauce begins to coat green beans, 2 to 4 minutes longer. Add any accumulated chicken juices to skillet and toss to combine. Season with salt to taste. Transfer green beans to serving platter and sprinkle with Parmesan. Top with chicken and serve.

BRAISED CHICKEN WITH MUSTARD AND HERBS

Skillet-Roasted Chicken Breasts with Harissa-Mint Carrots

Substitute 1 thinly sliced shallot for garlic and 2 teaspoons harissa for pepper flakes. Substitute 1½ pounds carrots, peeled and sliced on bias ¼ inch thick, for green beans. Increase salt for vegetables to 1 teaspoon, water to ½ cup, and covered cooking time to 10 to 12 minutes. Add 2 teaspoons lemon juice and 1½ teaspoons chopped fresh mint with accumulated chicken juices. Substitute additional 1½ teaspoons chopped fresh mint for Parmesan.

BRAISED CHICKEN WITH MUSTARD AND HERBS

✔ WHY THIS RECIPE WORKS For well-seasoned, juicy braised chicken pieces, we started by brining about 4 pounds of bone-in, skin-on drumsticks, thighs, and cut chicken breasts. We then browned the drumsticks, thighs, and larger breast pieces to create a flavorful fond, to which we added aromatics and just enough flour to emulsify the fat and make the sauce silky. Then we deglazed the pot with water and wine to create a braising liquid. Staggering the cooking of the dark and white meat ensured that the tough collagen in the dark meat broke down before the white meat dried out. Adding the broad pieces of the breasts first gave them a quick jump start before the thinner tapered pieces went into the pot. Finally, we transferred the pot to the oven and let the chicken pieces simmer gently until tender. We finished the sauce with a handful of fresh herbs and lemon juice or vinegar for brightness.

Remember the Corn Flakes slogan that Kellogg's ran in the late '80s, "Taste them again for the first time"? This braising story is my culinary equivalent of that campaign—a pitch to rediscover an old classic. I recently spent some time reacquainting myself with the basic tenets of braising chicken parts—both white and dark meat—and learned several ways to make a good dish a whole lot better.

Before we dig in, a refresher on what exactly braising is and why it's an ideal way to cook chicken: It involves browning food and then partially covering it with liquid in a lidded pot and simmering it gently until the meat is tender. As it simmers, the cooking liquid takes on the meat's flavor to create a luxurious, deeply savory sauce that you spoon over the meat.

Chicken is great for braising. It's got skin that renders loads of fat as well as collagen, which add flavor and lush body to the sauce, and meat that turns tender and gives up savory juices. But those assets can become liabilities if not handled properly. Chicken skin can stick to the pot and tear away from the meat, or its fat can make the sauce greasy. And then there's the age-old issue when cooking chicken parts: Dark meat takes longer to cook than white meat does.

My goal wasn't to reinvent the wheel. Rather, I put the classic method under the microscope to see if there were any improvements to make that would allow this technique to live up to its full potential.

I started with 4 pounds of split breasts and leg quarters. To shorten the cooking time and make it easier to arrange everything in the pot, I separated the leg quarters into drumsticks and thighs.

After patting the chicken dry, I browned the skin side of each piece in a Dutch oven to create a deeply savory fond. Some recipes call for discarding the skin at this point, but I left it on so that its fat and collagen would contribute to the braising liquid as the meat simmered (it could be discarded before serving). The fat would add savory flavor, and the collagen would transform into gelatin, suffusing the liquid with silkiness.

I set aside the skin-on chicken and sautéed finely chopped onion with garlic, thyme, and pepper in the rendered chicken fat, stirring a tablespoon of flour into the softened aromatics before deglazing with white wine and water. The starch in the flour would keep the chicken fat emulsified and thicken the sauce, as a roux does for gravy. *Voilà*— braising liquid.

Now for the timing issue. White meat is done at 160 degrees, and we've determined that dark meat turns ultratender and succulent at 195 degrees, which is perfect for a braise. We also know that as it heats up, the chewy collagen in dark meat turns into soft gelatin, and this reaction continues as the temperature climbs.

Most recipes for braised chicken call for starting all the pieces together and removing the breasts as they come up to temperature. Instead, I opted for a staggered method, which would require less monitoring. I placed the browned legs and thighs in the simmering liquid and cooked them to 140 degrees, which took about 8 minutes. The breasts went in next, at which point I moved the pot to the oven, where everything cooked at a leisurely pace until the dark meat and the thickest parts of the breasts hit 195 degrees and 160 degrees, respectively. I was happy to have nailed those temperatures, but the breast meat—particularly the tapered ends—was dry and chalky.

The next time around, I cut the breasts crosswise, separating the thinner tapered ends from the thicker broad ends so that I could add the thin pieces to the pot last. I also brined the chicken before cooking. Meat destined for braising is not typically brined, but this unorthodox step greatly improved the white meat, keeping it moist and tender, and offered extra insurance that the thighs stay moist.

It took a few tries to find the final order of operations, but I eventually came up with the following routine: Give the dark meat an 8-minute head start, nestle the broad ends of the breasts into the pot skin side down, flip them 5 minutes later (I found that they needed to cook on both sides since they were so thick), and finally, add the tapered ends. (Try as I might, I couldn't prevent the tapered ends from overcooking if I browned their skin, so I left them unbrowned.) Finally, I covered the pot and transferred it to a 300-degree oven, where the enveloping heat finished cooking the chicken at a bare simmer. After roughly 20 more minutes, all three cuts of chicken were as tender and juicy as could be.

The only thing that remained was to give the sauce some oomph. Fresh parsley, whole-grain mustard, and lemon juice perked things up. The recipe was easily adaptable by swapping out the mustard and herbs for other ingredients, such as tomato and basil for a Mediterranean version. These recipes will remind you why this technique is a classic.

—LAN LAM, *Cook's Illustrated*

Braised Chicken with Mustard and Herbs

SERVES 4 TO 6

Chicken breasts are broader at one end than the other, so cut more than halfway up each breast to create two pieces of equal mass. There's no need to take the temperature of the dark meat; it will be properly cooked by the time the white meat reaches its target temperature. If you prefer not to serve the skin, wait until step 6 to remove it; browning the skin produces flavorful compounds that add complexity to the sauce, and braising it releases gelatin, which gives the sauce a rich texture.

½ cup table salt, for brining

1½–2 pounds bone-in split chicken breasts, trimmed and each cut crosswise into 2 pieces of equal mass

1½–2 pounds chicken leg quarters, separated into drumsticks and thighs, trimmed

1 tablespoon vegetable oil

1 onion, chopped fine

3 garlic cloves, minced

1 tablespoon minced fresh thyme

1 teaspoon pepper

1 tablespoon all-purpose flour

⅓ cup dry white wine

3 tablespoons minced fresh parsley

1½ tablespoons whole-grain mustard

2 teaspoons lemon juice

1. Dissolve salt in 2 quarts cold water in large container. Submerge chicken in brine, cover, and refrigerate for 30 minutes to 1 hour. Remove chicken from brine and thoroughly pat dry with paper towels. Set aside tapered breast pieces.

2. Adjust oven rack to middle position and heat oven to 300 degrees. Heat oil in Dutch oven over medium-high heat until just smoking. Place all chicken except reserved tapered breast pieces skin side down in pot and cook until skin is well browned, 5 to 8 minutes. (Reduce heat if pot begins to scorch.) Transfer chicken to plate. Pour off all but 2 tablespoons fat from pot, then reduce heat to medium.

3. Add onion and cook, stirring occasionally, until softened, 5 to 7 minutes. Stir in garlic, thyme, and pepper and cook until fragrant, about 30 seconds. Stir in flour and cook, stirring constantly, for 1 minute. Stir in wine and 1¼ cups water, scraping up any browned bits.

4. Place thighs and drumsticks skin side up in pot and bring to simmer over medium heat. Cover and cook for 8 minutes. (Sauce will have consistency of thick gravy but will thin as chicken cooks.) Add broad breast pieces, skin side down, along with any accumulated juices. Cover and cook until broad breast pieces register 105 to 115 degrees, 3 to 5 minutes. Remove pot from heat.

5. Using tongs, flip broad breast pieces skin side up. Add tapered breast pieces, skin side up, to pot and cover. Transfer pot to oven and cook until breast pieces register 160 to 165 degrees, 15 to 30 minutes.

6. Transfer chicken to serving dish. Discard skin from tapered breast pieces (or all skin, if desired). Sauce should thinly coat back of spoon; if necessary, simmer until slightly thickened, 1 to 2 minutes. Stir parsley, mustard, and lemon juice into sauce. Season with salt and pepper to taste. Pour sauce over chicken and serve.

VARIATION

Braised Chicken with Basil and Tomato

Increase garlic to 4 cloves and add ¼ teaspoon red pepper flakes with garlic. Substitute 2 tablespoons tomato paste for thyme and dried oregano for pepper. Substitute chopped fresh basil for parsley and red wine vinegar for lemon juice. Sprinkle chicken with additional 1 tablespoon chopped fresh basil before serving.

INDIAN BUTTER CHICKEN (MURGH MAKHANI)

✔ **WHY THIS RECIPE WORKS** Butter chicken (*murgh makhani*) should taste rich and creamy but also vibrant and complex, so we started by softening lots of onion, garlic, ginger, and chile in butter, followed by aromatic spices such as garam masala, coriander, cumin, and black pepper. Instead of juicy chopped or crushed tomatoes, we opted for a hefty portion of tomato paste and water, which lent the sauce bright acidity, punch, and deep color without too much liquid. A full cup of cream gave the sauce (we pureed it to make it smooth) lush, velvety body, and we finished it by whisking in a couple more tablespoons of solid butter for extra richness and body. To imitate the deep charring effect of a tandoor oven, we broiled chicken thighs coated in yogurt—its milk proteins and lactose browned quickly and deeply—before cutting them into chunks and stirring them into the sauce.

Murgh makhani, also known as "butter chicken," is a rich and wildly popular northern Indian dish. But according to most sources, it was actually originally intended to solve a rather pedestrian problem: how to prevent leftover meat from tandoor-roasted chickens from drying out. The solution—bathing the charred meat in a lush, tomato-based gravy that's enriched with butter (and often cream, too) and scented with ginger, garlic, and spices such as garam masala, coriander and cumin—turned out to be utterly magnificent. In fact, butter chicken has since helped spawn a major restaurant franchise and become one of the most popular Indian preparations in the world.

It's also a popular dish to make at home, as the sauce itself is a snap to prepare: Soften some onion, garlic, and ginger in melted butter; add the spices so that their flavors bloom; stir in chopped tomatoes (canned is fine); enrich the pot with cream and possibly more butter; and finish it with a sprinkle of chopped cilantro for color and freshness.

It's the chicken that poses a challenge, because the most important element—the charred exterior that provides an essential point of contrast for the rich sauce—is not easy to achieve without the intense heat of a tandoor oven, the traditional beehive-shaped clay vessel that fires up to 900 degrees.

Some recipes skip the charring altogether and call for simply braising chicken pieces in the sauce, but the meat lacks the charred flavor that makes this dish complex, not just rich. Other recipes approximate the tandoor's effect by marinating the chicken (usually boneless, skinless breasts or thighs to make eating the meat easier) in yogurt and then roasting or broiling it, which seemed like a more promising idea.

Lean white meat would require careful monitoring in a hot oven to prevent it from drying out, so I started with thighs, which contain more fat and collagen and would thus be more forgiving.

Marinating the chicken in yogurt for several hours is a traditional first step when making tandoori chicken, the claim being that the acidic dairy tenderizes and flavors the meat. But the test kitchen has found that acids like yogurt don't actually tenderize; over time, they simply make the meat's surface mushy.

Instead, we prefer to coat chicken in yogurt just before cooking it. The yogurt gives the exterior of the meat tangy flavor even without a long marinating time and, more important, its proteins and lactose brown faster than the chicken does, making it easier to imitate the desirable char flavor of tandoor-roasted birds.

To be sure it was worth the extra step, I cooked two batches of thighs, one plain and one coated in yogurt (the Greek kind, since it's a more concentrated source of milk proteins than regular yogurt), and the difference was clear: After about 15 minutes under the broiler (its intense heat would be the closest replica of the tandoor oven), the plain chicken was spottily browned while the yogurt-coated batch boasted fuller, more flavorful browning. Yogurt was in, and to make the most of it, I stirred in a little salt that would help season the chicken.

As for the sauce, it should be similar to chicken *tikka masala* (a close relative of butter chicken), but richer and more concentrated; think of it as a tomatoey cream sauce rather than a creamy tomato sauce. The trick to making it well is adding enough richness that the sauce is lush, but not so much that it dulls the vibrancy of the tomato and tastes cloying. But getting that balance just right took some work.

The first consideration was how to incorporate the butter into the sauce. Melting a couple tablespoons to soften the aromatics and bloom the spices was a fine way to start, but by the time I added a can of tomatoes, the sauce was neither rich nor creamy. An additional 2 tablespoons made the sauce richer, but only when half the butter was left solid and whisked in at the end of cooking did the sauce turn silky. Why? For the same reason we often finish pan sauces by thoroughly whisking in cold butter: Doing so allows it to emulsify as it melts, becoming suspended in the liquid by the casein proteins that naturally surround each fat globule. If the butter is melted and then whisked in, its fat is already separated from the protein, so it breaks into large droplets that don't incorporate evenly.

But while the solid butter made it more luxurious, the sauce lacked its characteristic creaminess. Adding even more butter caused the sauce to break because the emulsion can hold only so much fat. This made me realize why many recipes add cream, too. After a few tests, I'd worked in a full cup, though every extra tablespoon of cream dulled the tomato's brightness. Adding more chopped tomatoes wasn't the answer, since their juice would only thin the sauce's creamy body. Instead, I switched to a combination of tomato paste—a whopping ½ cup—and water, taking advantage of the paste's superconcentrated, punchy flavor and vibrant color that gave the sauce an attractive rust-red tint. I also added a little heat (a minced serrano chile and some black pepper) and sweetness (sugar), and buzzed the mixture with an immersion blender until the sauce was thick and silky smooth.

At that point, all I had to do was cut up the chicken into chunks, stir it into the creamy, bright-tasting sauce, and sprinkle on a handful of chopped cilantro. All told, the dish came together in about 30 minutes—faster than a takeout order from my favorite Indian restaurant—and could be made in half the time if I made the sauce in advance.

—ANDREW JANJIGIAN, *Cook's Illustrated*

Indian Butter Chicken (Murgh Makhani)

SERVES 4 TO 6

Traditionally, butter chicken is mildly spicy. If you prefer a spicier dish, do not remove the ribs and seeds from the chile. The sauce can be refrigerated for up to four days in an airtight container and gently reheated before adding the hot chicken. Serve with basmati rice and/or warm naan.

- 4 tablespoons unsalted butter, cut into 4 pieces and chilled, divided
- 1 onion, chopped fine
- 5 garlic cloves, minced
- 4 teaspoons grated fresh ginger
- 1 serrano chile, stemmed, seeded, and minced
- 1 tablespoon garam masala
- 1 teaspoon ground coriander
- ½ teaspoon ground cumin
- ½ teaspoon pepper
- 1½ cups water
- ½ cup tomato paste
- 1 tablespoon sugar
- 2 teaspoons table salt, divided
- 1 cup heavy cream
- 2 pounds boneless, skinless chicken thighs, trimmed
- ½ cup plain Greek yogurt
- 3 tablespoons chopped fresh cilantro, divided

1. Melt 2 tablespoons butter in large saucepan over medium heat. Add onion, garlic, ginger, and serrano and cook, stirring frequently, until mixture is softened and onion begins to brown, 8 to 10 minutes. Add garam masala, coriander, cumin, and pepper and cook, stirring frequently, until fragrant, about 3 minutes. Add water and tomato paste and whisk until no lumps of tomato paste remain. Add sugar and 1 teaspoon salt and bring to boil. Off heat, stir in cream. Using immersion blender or blender, process until smooth, 30 to 60 seconds. Return sauce to simmer over medium heat and whisk in remaining 2 tablespoons butter. Remove saucepan from heat and cover to keep warm. (Sauce can be refrigerated for up to 4 days; gently reheat sauce before adding hot chicken.)

2. Adjust oven rack 6 inches from broiler element and heat broiler. Combine chicken, yogurt, and remaining 1 teaspoon salt in bowl and toss well to coat. Using tongs, transfer chicken to wire rack set in aluminum foil–lined rimmed baking sheet. Broil until

INDIAN BUTTER CHICKEN (MURGH MAKHANI)

chicken is evenly charred on both sides and registers 175 degrees, 16 to 20 minutes, flipping chicken halfway through broiling.

3. Let chicken rest for 5 minutes. While chicken rests, warm sauce over medium-low heat. Cut chicken into ¾-inch chunks and stir into sauce. Stir in 2 tablespoons cilantro and season with salt to taste. Transfer to serving dish, sprinkle with remaining 1 tablespoon cilantro, and serve.

CAST-IRON OVEN-FRIED CHICKEN

✓ WHY THIS RECIPE WORKS Many of us crave fried chicken more often than we're willing to put in the time and effort to make it. We wanted to find an easier way to get that crunchy, deeply seasoned exterior and juicy meat we all love—without going to the trouble of deep frying. This meant using the oven instead of the stovetop. We started by preheating a 12-inch cast-iron skillet in a 450-degree oven. Next, we dredged the chicken in a well-seasoned flour mixture; added just ½ cup of vegetable oil to the preheated skillet; placed the chicken, skin side down, in the skillet; and returned the skillet to the oven to fry the chicken. We then flipped the chicken halfway through cooking to achieve an all-over crispy exterior. Is this oven-fried chicken absolutely indistinguishable from true deep-fried chicken? Not quite. But because it is fried in just ½ cup of oil, it is quite a bit easier to make and has many of the same attributes.

Fried chicken is a perennial favorite in the test kitchen. Between all the regional styles, the recipes passed down through generations, and the memories of gathering around a table with loved ones and fighting over the drumsticks, fried chicken has a cultural and emotional resonance few foods can match. But, for better or for worse, dread of the effort it takes to make fried chicken at home (and of the cleanup required afterward) usually outweighs my desire to eat it. Unwilling to let this stand, I wondered if turning to the oven might yield a method for producing chicken that was juicy and crispy enough to satisfy my fried-chicken craving.

Many oven-fried chicken recipes (including some of our own) instruct the cook to coat the chicken pieces in bread crumbs before baking them. This makes for good eating, but the crumb coating has a different texture than the crispy exterior of chicken that's coated in seasoned flour and fried in hot oil. I wanted something closer to the genuine article and thus settled on coating my chicken in seasoned flour.

Knowing that I'd need plenty of heat to transform that flour coating into a crispy crust, I grabbed a 12-inch cast-iron skillet (cast iron is great at holding on to heat), tossed the chicken pieces in flour that I'd seasoned with salt and pepper, poured a few tablespoons of vegetable oil into the skillet, and baked the chicken in a hot oven. What a disaster that was. The flour coating got soggy, and the chicken was totally overcooked and bone-dry by the time it picked up any exterior color.

That result made me take a new approach. If I wanted chicken that tasted like it had been cooked in a good amount of hot oil, logic said I'd have to cook it in a good amount of hot oil. Through a series of tests over a period of several days, I came up with the following method: Preheat the skillet in a 450-degree oven. When the skillet is nice and hot, pour in ½ cup of vegetable oil (it should measure roughly ⅛ inch deep), slip the floured chicken in skin side down, bake the chicken until the skin side is crispy and golden brown (which takes about 15 minutes), and then flip the chicken. Fifteen minutes later, the chicken is cooked through but still moist, with a crispy coating that crunches like deep-fried chicken. As a bonus, it makes your kitchen smell amazing.

With my basic cooking method down pat, I could polish up the details. To season the flour, I added paprika, granulated garlic, cayenne pepper, salt, and plenty of black pepper (freshly ground is best). To make sure the flour adhered, I dipped the chicken pieces in beaten egg before coating them in the flour mixture and used my fingers to press the coating onto the pieces. And to create an extra-crunchy coating, I added some water to the seasoned flour and rubbed it with my fingers until little shaggy pieces formed; these pieces added extra physical mass to the coating that, when fried, became very crunchy.

While my oven-fried chicken may not fool a deep-fryer die-hard, I was more than pleased with the results. Using a fraction of the oil and with much less mess, my recipe yielded golden-brown chicken with excellent crunch. For me, this means I can make—and happily eat—fried chicken at home each and every week.

—ASHLEY MOORE, *Cook's Country*

Cast-Iron Oven-Fried Chicken

SERVES 4

To fit 3 pounds of chicken pieces, you will need a 12-inch cast-iron skillet for this recipe. Note that the cast-iron skillet should be preheated along with the oven in step 1. One 4½- to 5-pound whole chicken will yield the 3 pounds of parts called for in this recipe.

- 3 **pounds bone-in chicken pieces (split breasts cut in half crosswise, drumsticks, and/or thighs), trimmed**
- 1 **tablespoon plus ¼ teaspoon pepper, divided**
- 2¾ **teaspoons table salt, divided**
- 3 **large eggs**
- 2 **cups all-purpose flour**
- 2 **teaspoons baking powder**
- 1 **teaspoon paprika**
- 1 **teaspoon granulated garlic**
- ⅛ **teaspoon cayenne pepper**
- 3 **tablespoons water**
- ½ **cup vegetable oil, for frying**

1. Adjust oven rack to middle position. Place 12-inch cast-iron skillet on rack and heat oven to 450 degrees. Set wire rack in rimmed baking sheet and line half of rack with triple layer of paper towels. Sprinkle chicken with ¼ teaspoon pepper and ¼ teaspoon salt.

2. Lightly beat eggs and 1 teaspoon salt together in medium bowl. Whisk flour, baking powder, paprika, granulated garlic, cayenne, remaining 1 tablespoon pepper, and remaining 1½ teaspoons salt together in second medium bowl. Add water to flour mixture; using your fingers, rub flour mixture and water until water is evenly incorporated and shaggy pieces of dough form.

3. Working with 1 piece of chicken at a time, dip in egg mixture, allowing excess to drip off; then dredge in flour mixture, pressing firmly to adhere. Transfer coated chicken to large plate, skin side up.

4. When oven temperature reaches 450 degrees, carefully remove hot skillet from oven (skillet handle will be hot). Add oil to skillet and immediately place chicken, skin side down, in skillet. Return skillet to oven and bake for 15 minutes.

5. Remove skillet from oven and flip chicken. Return skillet to oven and continue to bake until breasts register 160 degrees and drumsticks/thighs register 175 degrees, about 15 minutes longer.

NOTES FROM THE TEST KITCHEN

HOW TO MIMIC STOVETOP FRYING IN THE OVEN

We pour a good amount of oil into the bottom of the skillet to cover it in a thin layer, ensuring that the chicken crisps up on each side. The oil heats quickly in the preheated skillet, preventing the flour coating from turning gummy.

1. HEAT SKILLET Place cast-iron skillet on middle rack in 450-degree oven so it gets nice and hot.

2. ADD OIL Once skillet is heated through, carefully remove it from oven and add ½ cup vegetable oil.

3. ADD CHICKEN Carefully place chicken, skin side down, in hot oil and return skillet to oven.

4. FLIP After 15 minutes, flip chicken and continue to cook until chicken is done, about 15 minutes longer.

6. Using tongs, transfer chicken, skin side up, to paper towel–lined side of prepared wire rack to blot grease from underside of chicken, then move chicken to unlined side of rack. Let chicken cool for about 10 minutes. Serve.

CHICKEN SCAMPI

✔ **WHY THIS RECIPE WORKS** To re-create this Italian restaurant favorite for home cooks, we shallow-fried chicken tenders in a 12-inch skillet and just 2 tablespoons of oil and paired them with a garlicky sauce that we embellished with strips of tender red bell pepper. Just before tossing all the components together, we finished the sauce with a bit of butter to give it the proper consistency—ideal for mopping up with crusty bread or pouring over a bowl of pasta.

Recently a friend of mine, knowing that I worked in the test kitchen, asked if I had ever had chicken scampi from Olive Garden. He grew up eating this dish and said he still craves it to this day. But wait—"chicken scampi"? *Scampi* means "langoustine" in Italian, and there are no langoustines anywhere near this dish. Rather, my friend described fried chicken tenders served in the style of shrimp scampi, the classic lemony, garlicky, saucy dish often found on Italian American menus. It sounded promising, so we ordered some takeout to try in the kitchen.

It was pretty good, but not great. The cream-based sauce felt a little heavy and unusual for something in the "scampi" style. And the red onions in the dish looked odd and tasted unpleasantly strong. But we liked the breaded chicken tenders and garlicky sauce studded with strips of colorful bell pepper. The dish definitely held promise, and I was determined to fulfill it.

I started with the chicken. To emulate the golden, crispy coating of the restaurant dish, I seasoned chicken tenderloins (you can use strips of chicken breast, too) and dredged them first in beaten egg and then in flour. Then I seared the chicken in oil in a nonstick skillet until it was browned on both sides and removed the golden tenders so I could build the sauce in the same skillet for maximum efficiency.

To get the sauce going, I added a little more oil to the hot skillet and tossed in some sliced red bell pepper. When it was soft and browned, I added a few cloves of sliced garlic. After about a minute, the garlic smelled amazing and was just starting to color, so I stirred in some flour (for thickening) and then a combination of chicken broth and white wine. I let the sauce bubble away until it was slightly reduced, and then I finished it with lemon for brightness and butter for richness and a glossy sheen. Finally, I returned the fried chicken

tenders to the pan to warm through and meld with the flavorful sauce. It was good, but my tasters wanted more garlic and less sourness, so I upped the number of garlic cloves to eight and held the lemon from the sauce, instead serving the chicken with lemon wedges on the side.

When all was said and done, I was really happy with the straightforward flavors of this simple, comforting dish, which I liked best served with crusty bread for mopping up the tasty sauce. But the real test was my Olive Garden–loving friend. "It's not exactly the same," he said as he pondered his first few bites. "It's definitely better." Check, please!

—ASHLEY MOORE, *Cook's Country*

Chicken Scampi

SERVES 4 TO 6

If you can't find chicken tenderloins, slice boneless, skinless chicken breasts lengthwise into ¾-inch-thick strips. You can use torn basil in place of the parsley, if desired. Serve with crusty bread and lemon wedges.

- 2 large eggs
- 1¼ teaspoons table salt, divided
- ¾ cup plus 1 tablespoon all-purpose flour, divided
- 2 pounds chicken tenderloins, trimmed
- ¼ teaspoon pepper
- 6 tablespoons extra-virgin olive oil, divided
- 1 red bell pepper, stemmed, seeded, and sliced thin
- 8 garlic cloves, sliced thin
- 1¼ cups chicken broth
- ¾ cup dry white wine
- 4 tablespoons unsalted butter, cut into 4 pieces
- 2 tablespoons chopped fresh parsley

1. Lightly beat eggs and ½ teaspoon salt together in shallow dish. Place ¾ cup flour in second shallow dish. Pat chicken dry with paper towels and sprinkle with pepper and ¼ teaspoon salt. Working with 1 piece of chicken at a time, dip in egg mixture, allowing excess to drip off, then dredge in flour, shaking off any excess. Transfer to large plate.

2. Heat 2 tablespoons oil in 12-inch nonstick skillet over medium-high heat until just smoking. Add half of chicken and cook until golden brown and registering 160 degrees, about 3 minutes per side. Transfer chicken to clean plate and tent with aluminum foil. Wipe skillet clean with paper towels and repeat with 2 tablespoons oil and remaining chicken.

3. Wipe skillet clean with paper towels. Heat remaining 2 tablespoons oil in now-empty skillet over medium-high heat until just smoking. Add bell pepper and remaining ½ teaspoon salt and cook until softened and well browned, 5 to 7 minutes. Add garlic and cook until fragrant and golden brown, about 1 minute. Stir in remaining 1 tablespoon flour and cook for 1 minute.

4. Stir in broth and wine and bring to boil, scraping up any browned bits. Cook until mixture is reduced to about 1½ cups, 5 to 7 minutes. Reduce heat to low and stir in butter until melted. Return chicken to skillet and cook, turning to coat with sauce, until heated through, about 2 minutes. Season with salt and pepper to taste. Transfer to shallow serving platter and sprinkle with parsley. Serve.

CHICKEN IN ADOBO

✔ **WHY THIS RECIPE WORKS** The intense depth of flavor in this adobo comes from a balanced mixture of dried chiles. We combined guajillo and ancho chiles to create a complex and vibrant red sauce to coat tender pieces of chicken. Lightly toasting the chiles muted their bitterness; after toasting them, we soaked the chiles in water until they were softened and then blended them with vinegar and a bit of orange juice to enhance their sweetness. Once we stirred in the browned chicken pieces and brought the adobo to a simmer, we transferred the pot to the oven to braise. We finished the dish with a splash of lime juice to brighten things up. Warmed flour tortillas helped wipe up any extra sauce.

Adobo, the potent, pleasantly bitter sauce made from dried chiles, plays many roles in the cuisines of Mexico and the American Southwest: marinade, braising sauce, baste, and tableside condiment for all kinds of meats. (In Filipino cuisine, adobo is something else altogether.) Making adobo should be relatively easy: Toast dried chiles to activate their flavor, soak them, and then pulverize them in a blender with vinegar, herbs, and garlic. The best versions are simultaneously complex and deeply comforting. I set out to make a recipe for chicken in adobo that was easy and tasted amazing.

The recipes I found each called for different chiles—chipotle, guajillo, ancho, arbol, and pasilla chiles were all in play. My tasters thought that chipotle (smoked and dried jalapeño) and arbol chiles brought too much heat to the party and pasilla chiles were a little too rich in this dish; fruity ancho and guajillo chiles, which are available in the Latin American section of most supermarkets, were the best way forward.

Next, I tested various methods to help the chiles reach their fullest potential. Some recipes called for frying the dried chiles in oil to bloom their flavor; this was messy and heightened the chiles' bitterness in an unpleasant way. I found that it was much better and easier to quickly dry toast them on a baking sheet in the oven; this brought out the chiles' multifaceted flavors but not their bitterness.

Once I'd soaked the toasted chiles in hot tap water for 5 minutes, they were soft and pliable and ready to be buzzed in the blender. Some recipes call for adding the soaking water, but again, we found the results unpleasantly bitter. I used a little chicken broth instead; the broth added savoriness and, along with a bit of cider vinegar and orange juice, thinned the blended chiles into a flavorful sauce. A little brown sugar helped deepen the adobo's enchanting flavors.

Once the adobo sauce was ready, I seared bone-in chicken pieces in a Dutch oven and then transferred the pieces to a plate while I sautéed some chopped onion in the rendered chicken fat. I added garlic, tomato paste, oregano, cumin, cinnamon, and orange zest and then the potent adobo from the blender. I nestled the chicken pieces back into the pot, skin side up, and moved the pot to the oven so the chicken could gently cook through in the flavorful sauce.

By this time the kitchen smelled incredible, and my hungry colleagues were starting to hover around my workstation. I plated some chicken, spooned the sauce on top, sprinkled on some chopped cilantro, and stepped back as my tasters converged. Some of my coworkers made little tacos with the tortillas I'd warmed, and others ate the saucy chicken with a knife and fork, but they all had one thing in common: They asked for seconds.

—ALLI BERKEY, *Cook's Country*

Chicken in Adobo
SERVES 4

One ounce of guajillo chiles is about eight chiles; ½ ounce of ancho chiles is about one chile. Remove the strips of orange zest with a vegetable peeler. You can use all white-meat or all dark-meat chicken pieces, if desired. Serve with rice or warm flour tortillas.

1	ounce dried guajillo chiles, stemmed and seeded
½	ounce dried ancho chiles, stemmed and seeded
1½	cups chicken broth
¼	cup cider vinegar
2	(3-inch) strips orange zest plus 2 tablespoons juice
1	tablespoon packed brown sugar
1¾	teaspoons table salt, divided
1	teaspoon pepper, divided
3	pounds bone-in chicken pieces (2 split breasts cut in half crosswise, 2 drumsticks, and 2 thighs), trimmed
2	tablespoons vegetable oil
1	onion, chopped fine
5	garlic cloves, minced
1	tablespoon tomato paste
2	teaspoons dried oregano
1	teaspoon ground cumin
½	teaspoon ground cinnamon
3	tablespoons chopped fresh cilantro
	Lime wedges

1. Adjust oven rack to lower-middle position and heat oven to 300 degrees. Place guajillos and anchos on rimmed baking sheet. Bake until fragrant and guajillos are deep red and have curled edges, about 7 minutes. Immediately transfer chiles to bowl and cover with hot water. Let stand until pliable, about 5 minutes.

2. Drain chiles and transfer to blender. Add broth, vinegar, orange juice, sugar, 1¼ teaspoons salt, and ½ teaspoon pepper and process until smooth, 1 to 2 minutes, scraping down sides of blender jar as needed. Set aside adobo.

3. Pat chicken dry with paper towels and sprinkle with remaining ½ teaspoon salt and remaining ½ teaspoon pepper. Heat oil in Dutch oven over medium-high heat until shimmering. Add chicken and cook until well browned, about 4 minutes per side. Transfer to plate.

4. Add onion to now-empty pot and reduce heat to medium. Cook until softened, about 4 minutes. Stir in garlic, tomato paste, oregano, cumin, cinnamon, and orange zest and cook until fragrant, about 30 seconds. Whisk in adobo until combined. Return chicken, skin side up, to pot along with any accumulated juices; bring to simmer. Transfer pot to oven and bake, uncovered, until chicken is tender and breasts register 160 degrees and drumsticks/thighs register 175 degrees, 35 to 40 minutes.

5. Transfer chicken to platter. Stir sauce to combine and season with salt and pepper to taste. Pour sauce over chicken and sprinkle with cilantro. Serve with lime wedges.

CHICKEN POT PIE WITH SPRING VEGETABLES

WHY THIS RECIPE WORKS This classic comfort food typically requires a major time commitment. We wanted an easier way and found our trusty Dutch oven to be just the ticket to get us there. Boneless, skinless chicken thighs, cut into bite-size pieces, were easy to work with and stayed moist through cooking. We stirred the chicken right into the gravy and turned to two powerhouse ingredients—tomato paste and soy sauce—to boost savoriness without being distinguishable in their own right. To give our pot pie fresh spring flavor, we swapped in leeks for onions and stirred in some asparagus, convenient frozen peas, and tarragon. With our one-pot filling perfected, we turned to the crust. Instead of labor-intensive homemade pastry, we decided to use buttery store-bought puff pastry. Baking the crust on top of the filling inevitably led to sorry, soggy results, but we didn't want to add another dish to the recipe. The solution lay in getting creative with the Dutch oven lid: We turned the lid upside down before covering the pot and baking the pastry on top. A simple egg wash turned the crust a deep golden brown. Once we slid the baked crust onto the filling, our simplified centerpiece was complete.

CHICKEN POT PIE WITH SPRING VEGETABLES

If it were up to me, chicken pot pie would be crowned the comfort food king. Gooey grilled cheese and buttery pasta have their place, but in my opinion, nothing can quite match a great pot pie. Underneath a tender, flaky crust lie flavorful chunks of savory chicken and vegetables swimming in a rich gravy. But as with most comfort foods, a pot pie can just be too rich. Between the butter-laced pie crust and gravy, there is no respite from richness other than an occasional sprinkling of fresh parsley. I set out to revitalize classic chicken pot pie using lighter, brighter ingredients without losing its signature comfort factor. I'd also challenge myself to do it all in the confines of a Dutch oven.

NOTES FROM THE TEST KITCHEN

MAKING A LATTICE TOP

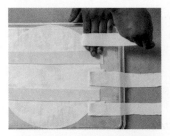

1. Space 5 pastry strips parallel and evenly across parchment circle. Fold back first, third, and fifth strips almost completely.

2. Lay additional pastry strip perpendicular to second and fourth strips, keeping it snug to folded edges of pastry, then unfold strips.

3. Repeat laying remaining 4 pastry strips evenly across parchment circle, alternating between folding back second and fourth strips and first, third, and fifth strips to create lattice pattern.

4. Using pizza cutter, trim edges of pastry following outline of parchment circle.

I started with an existing test kitchen recipe for chicken pot pie that calls for a couple unusual ingredients: tomato paste and soy sauce. Using these glutamate-rich ingredients in moderation would boost the umami flavor of the filling without imparting their distinctive tastes. Cremini mushrooms also added umami depth, and lemon juice perked it all up. The rest of the ingredients—chicken, mirepoix vegetables, and a roux-based gravy—were pretty standard. However, I was intrigued by the "crust" in this recipe, a crumbly mix between biscuit dough and pie crust that is partially baked on a baking sheet before being scattered over the filling and going back in the oven.

This recipe was a good starting point, but it didn't check all the boxes. For starters, it's cooked in a shallow baking dish. I was using a Dutch oven, a much deeper cooking vessel that didn't exactly encourage the crumble topping to brown. And while the lemon juice brightened up the dish, I knew I could transform this pot pie into something more spring-forward. I also wanted to streamline the cooking process even further.

The quickest fix would be reimagining the vegetable element. The recipe I was using featured the classic trio of finely chopped onion, carrots, and celery; savory mushrooms; and quick-cooking peas. I scrapped the mushrooms because their earthiness distracted from the fresh twist I was after. With a sweetness reminiscent of spring, the carrots and peas would stay. Onions were fine, but the more delicate flavor of leeks was even better for a spring-inspired pot pie. Finally, I ditched forgettable celery in favor of perhaps the most quintessential spring vegetable: asparagus.

Up to this point, I had been simmering whole chicken pieces in chicken broth, setting both the broth and chicken aside, shredding the chicken, and finally adding them back to the pot to finish the filling. What if I chopped up the chicken and added it directly to the filling? The benefits of this method were twofold: The chicken quickly absorbed the filling's flavors, and I cut two time-consuming steps. I chose to use chicken thighs, which wouldn't dry out as readily as white meat.

With the filling mostly set, it was time to move to the real Dutch-oven-only challenge: the topping. No matter what I tried, it refused to crisp up in the moist environment of a Dutch oven. I thought a layer of raw puff pastry might sit atop the filling and crisp up, but the pastry sank, turning soggy and making the pie difficult to scoop out and serve. I was just about to break my one-pot rule when, tapping into my resourcefulness, I turned to the lid of the Dutch oven. Jackpot. Using the lid as a guide, I fashioned a lattice pattern on a parchment circle, transferred it to the inverted lid, and let it crisp up for about 30 minutes as the filling underneath bubbled away.

With the pastry and filling separate, I was able to perfect the filling right before serving. Quick-cooking asparagus pieces and peas went in for a few minutes, followed by fresh tarragon, lemon juice, and plenty of lemon zest for brightness. Finally, I plopped the cooked puff pastry right on top of the filling before doling the pot pie out to my tasters. Stodgy and labor-intensive? Not at all. Comfort food? No doubt about it.

—JOSEPH GITTER, *America's Test Kitchen Books*

Chicken Pot Pie with Spring Vegetables

SERVES 6

To thaw frozen puff pastry, let it sit in the refrigerator for 24 hours or on the counter for 30 minutes to 1 hour. We prefer to place the baked pastry on top of the filling in the pot just before serving for an impressive presentation, but you can also cut the pastry into wedges and place them over individual portions of the filling.

1   (9½ by 9-inch) sheet puff pastry, thawed

4   tablespoons unsalted butter

1   pound leeks, white and light green parts only, halved lengthwise, cut into ½-inch pieces, and washed thoroughly

4   carrots, peeled and cut into ½-inch pieces

1⅛   teaspoons table salt, divided

½   cup all-purpose flour

4   garlic cloves, minced

1   teaspoon tomato paste

3   cups chicken broth, plus extra as needed

¼   cup heavy cream

1   teaspoon soy sauce

2   bay leaves

2   pounds boneless, skinless chicken thighs, trimmed and cut into 1-inch pieces

1   large egg, lightly beaten

1   pound asparagus, trimmed and cut on bias into 1-inch lengths

1   cup frozen peas

2   tablespoons chopped fresh tarragon or parsley

1   tablespoon grated lemon zest plus 2 teaspoons juice

1. Cut sheet of parchment paper to match outline of Dutch oven lid and place on large plate or upturned rimmed baking sheet. Roll puff pastry sheet into 15 by 11-inch rectangle on lightly floured counter. Using pizza cutter or sharp knife, cut pastry widthwise into ten 1½-inch-wide strips.

2. Space 5 pastry strips parallel and evenly across parchment circle. Fold back first, third, and fifth strips almost completely. Lay additional pastry strip perpendicular to second and fourth strips, keeping it snug to folded edges of pastry, then unfold strips. Repeat laying remaining 4 pastry strips evenly across parchment circle, alternating between folding back second and fourth strips and first, third, and fifth strips to create lattice pattern. Using pizza cutter, trim edges of pastry following outline of parchment circle. Cover loosely with plastic wrap and refrigerate while preparing filling.

3. Adjust oven rack to lower-middle position and heat oven to 400 degrees. Melt butter in Dutch oven over medium heat. Add leeks, carrots, and 1 teaspoon salt and cook until vegetables are softened, about 5 minutes. Stir in flour, garlic, and tomato paste and cook for 1 minute.

4. Slowly stir in broth, scraping up any browned bits and smoothing out any lumps. Stir in cream, soy sauce, and bay leaves. Bring to simmer and cook until mixture is thickened, about 3 minutes. Stir in chicken and return to simmer.

5. Off heat, cover pot with inverted lid and carefully place parchment with pastry on lid. Brush pastry with egg and sprinkle with remaining ⅛ teaspoon salt. Transfer pot to oven and bake until pastry is puffed and golden brown, 25 to 30 minutes, rotating pot halfway through baking.

6. Remove pot from oven. Transfer parchment with pastry to wire rack; discard parchment. Remove lid and discard bay leaves. Stir asparagus into filling and cook over medium heat until crisp-tender, 3 to 5 minutes. Off heat, stir in peas and let sit until heated through, about 5 minutes. Adjust filling consistency with extra hot broth as needed. Stir in tarragon and lemon zest and juice. Season with salt and pepper to taste. Set pastry on top of filling and serve.

AIR-FRYER CHICKEN NUGGETS

✓ **WHY THIS RECIPE WORKS** These homemade nuggets are tender and juicy, not gristly and spongy. And they're convenient if made ahead and frozen, ready to be popped into the air fryer at short notice. A 15-minute brine seasoned the white meat and guarded against dryness even after freezing. Two dipping sauces completed the picture.

When I think of nostalgic comfort food—the kind of food that takes me straight back to my childhood—I think of chicken nuggets. Nothing gets a kid excited for dinner quite like a plate piled high with tender chicken pieces coated in golden-brown bread crumbs. So when I was tasked with creating a recipe for chicken nuggets that could be made in an air fryer (a device that's gained massive popularity in the past few years because it can produce crispy "fried" foods with a tiny fraction of the amount of oil called for in conventional deep-frying recipes), I instantly knew I wanted to make something kid-friendly that adult family members would enjoy as well. Also, if I was going to the trouble to make chicken nuggets from scratch, I wanted a recipe that would make a lot, so extra nuggets could be frozen for future rushed weeknight dinners. And finally, I wanted something at least a little leaner than the standard supermarket or fast food chicken nuggets.

To start with, I focused on the chicken. I wanted my nuggets to be made from whole chicken pieces, not fast food–style ground chicken parts. I pounded chicken breasts, which would cook up quick and tender, to an even thickness before cutting them into bite-size pieces to ensure that they cooked evenly in the air fryer. I knew that the nuggets' bread-crumb coating and their short cooking time should protect them from drying out too much, but I still wanted to test whether a brining step might enhance their flavor and texture. I brined batches of chicken pieces in a solution of cold water, salt, and sugar for varying amounts of time before covering them in bread crumbs and adding them to the air fryer. I found that just a short 15-minute brine noticeably bumped up the flavor and juiciness of the chicken.

Now that I had the chicken just right, I turned my attention to what really gives a nugget its identity: the breading. It needed to be both light and crunchy, seasoned just enough to complement the chicken flavor but not so much that it was off-putting to kids, and to adhere well to the chicken. I kept my seasonings simple: just a little bit of onion powder, garlic powder, salt, and pepper would highlight the chicken's natural savoriness without overdoing it. For simplicity's sake, I stirred the spices directly into the egg mixture that I would use to bind the bread crumbs to the chicken. And as for the bread crumbs, I had a couple options: traditional-style crumbs, which generally have a fine texture, and panko bread crumbs, which are typically larger and crunchier. Traditional-style bread crumbs were quickly ruled out as an option; they gave the nuggets a dusty, sandy texture, and tasters thought they tasted stale. That left me with panko, which I tried two ways: leaving the crumbs whole, or pulsing them in a food processor to achieve a texture somewhere between those of traditional-style crumbs and whole panko crumbs. I liked the extra-crispy texture of whole panko crumbs, and they adhered well to the chicken despite their larger size, so I went with them.

There was just one last problem to tackle. The air fryer was cooking my nuggets quickly and easily—cooking them in two batches ensured that the air-fryer basket wasn't overcrowded—but they just weren't turning the classic golden-brown color I was after. Oil is instrumental in promoting browning, and even though I had sprayed the basket with vegetable oil spray before adding the nuggets, there simply wasn't enough to brown them adequately. I was stumped until I remembered a test kitchen trick we've used in the past to achieve crispy brown breading on food baked in an oven: Before coating the chicken with the panko, I tossed the bread crumbs with olive oil in a small bowl and then microwaved them until they were light golden brown. Pretoasting the crumbs this way meant that my nuggets now emerged from the air fryer crunchy and evenly browned every time.

Chicken nuggets and ketchup are a classic combination, but I'm all about having options, so before calling it quits, I whipped up two easy sauces that I hoped might appeal to both adults and kids. I now had a foolproof recipe for chicken nuggets that could be made ahead of time, frozen, and warmed up any time I wanted a fast, no-fuss dinner or quick snack. I was also pleased that they happened to contain a bit less fat than traditional deep-fried nuggets. The kid in me just couldn't wait to dig in.

—LAWMAN JOHNSON, *America's Test Kitchen Books*

Air-Fryer Chicken Nuggets

MAKES 36 NUGGETS; SERVES 4

You can skip the freezing step, if desired. Simply reduce the cooking time to 10 to 12 minutes. Serve with one of our dipping sauces (recipes follow), if desired.

    4 (8-ounce) boneless, skinless chicken breasts,
       trimmed
    3 tablespoons sugar, for brining
    3 tablespoons table salt, for brining
    3 cups panko bread crumbs
    ¼ cup extra-virgin olive oil
    3 large eggs
    3 tablespoons all-purpose flour
    1 tablespoon onion powder
    1 teaspoon table salt
    ¾ teaspoon garlic powder
    ¼ teaspoon pepper

1. Pound chicken to uniform thickness as needed. Cut each breast diagonally into thirds, then cut each piece into thirds. Dissolve sugar and 3 tablespoons salt in 2 quarts cold water in large container. Submerge chicken in brine, cover, and let sit for 15 minutes.

2. While chicken brines, toss panko with oil in bowl until evenly coated. Microwave, stirring frequently, until light golden brown, about 5 minutes. Transfer to shallow dish and let cool slightly. Whisk eggs, flour, onion powder, 1 teaspoon salt, garlic powder, and pepper together in second shallow dish.

3. Set wire rack in rimmed baking sheet. Remove chicken from brine and pat dry with paper towels. Working with several chicken pieces at a time, dredge in egg mixture, letting excess drip off, then coat with panko mixture, pressing gently to adhere; transfer to prepared rack. Freeze until firm, about 4 hours. (Frozen nuggets can be transferred to zipper-lock bag and stored in freezer for up to 1 month.)

4. Lightly spray base of air-fryer basket with vegetable oil spray. Place 18 nuggets in prepared basket. Place basket in air fryer, set temperature to 400 degrees, and cook for 6 minutes. Transfer nuggets to clean bowl and gently toss to redistribute. Return nuggets to air fryer and cook until chicken is crispy and registers 160 degrees, 6 to 10 minutes. Repeat with remaining 18 nuggets. Serve.

Honey-Dijon Dipping Sauce

MAKES ¾ CUP

The sauce can be refrigerated for up to four days; bring to room temperature before serving.

    ½ cup Dijon mustard
    ¼ cup honey

Whisk mustard and honey together in bowl; season with salt and pepper to taste.

Sweet-and-Sour Dipping Sauce

MAKES ABOUT ¾ CUP

The sauce can be refrigerated for up to four days; bring to room temperature before serving.

    ¾ cup apple jelly
    1 tablespoon distilled white vinegar
    ½ teaspoon soy sauce
    ⅛ teaspoon garlic powder
       Pinch ground ginger
       Pinch cayenne pepper

Whisk all ingredients together in bowl; season with salt and pepper to taste.

THAI-STYLE FRIED CHICKEN

✓ **WHY THIS RECIPE WORKS** For a crispier and lighter version of classic fried chicken, we used rice flour and cornstarch, plus baking powder for extra lightness, as the base of a tempura-like batter. We marinated cut-up chicken thighs in a flavorful, deeply savory mixture of fish sauce, soy sauce, garlic, white pepper, and red pepper flakes. Just 30 minutes was plenty of time for the marinade to season the chicken, and then we added both the chicken and the marinade to the batter for more depth of flavor. We fried the chicken pieces until golden before letting them cool and tossing them with fresh herbs and a sauce that echoed the flavors of the tempura batter for a fresh, seriously seasoned flavor punch.

THAI-STYLE FRIED CHICKEN

Let's get one thing straight: I would never throw shade on a good piece of classic Southern-style fried chicken. But I do like to dress it up from time to time.

Fried chicken can be so much more than the Southern standard—there are countless varieties belonging to cuisines around the United States and the world. And after my editor described the fantastic Thai-style fried chicken that made him swoon on a recent trip to Seattle, I knew I had to try to make my own version.

My editor's lowdown on the key components of this rendition? Tender dark-meat chicken (either bone-in or boneless) aggressively seasoned with garlic, chiles, soy sauce, and deeply savory fish sauce, all coated in an ultracrispy, ultracrunchy crust made with lightly sweet rice flour. As if that wasn't enough, the chicken is served with fresh herbs plus sweet chile sauce to spoon on top. Wow. I was up for the challenge.

For the chicken, I decided off the bat to use boneless thighs: They cook more quickly than bone-in parts, require less oil to fry, and are easier to eat. For the marinade, I knew that haphazard use of potent ingredients such as soy sauce and fish sauce can be dangerous; while these sauces add tons of savory flavor, they can also make your food taste out of whack or too salty if not used judiciously. I found that a balanced combo of the two—3 tablespoons of soy sauce and 2 tablespoons of fish sauce—mixed with a good dose of minced garlic and red pepper flakes was best for 2 pounds of boneless thighs; this formula provided strong but balanced flavor. After just 30 minutes in the marinade, this seasoned chicken was ready to fry.

The coating was more challenging. An all-purpose flour coating, the kind used for classic craggy fried chicken, was not in play here; I was after a smoother, crunchier crust. Straight rice flour fried up plenty crunchy but was hard and tough to bite through. After several days of playing around with different flours and ingredients, I landed on a tempura-like batter made with 1 cup each of rice flour, cornstarch, and water, plus some baking powder for lightness. You can find rice flour with the alternative flours in the supermarket; it makes for an incredibly crispy coating.

After weeks of testing, I landed on an easy process. Just marinate the chicken in a zipper-lock bag for convenience, stir together the batter in a bowl, dump the chicken and its marinade into the batter, and toss to coat. From there the chicken went right into the hot oil for

about 5 minutes of frying, then onto paper towels set on a wire rack to absorb excess oil, and then straight onto the serving platter.

The chicken was supercrunchy, but I hoped to crank up the flavor just one more notch. Eyeing the sweet chili sauce I had planned to use for dipping, I decided to boost its flavor by stirring in a little of the soy and fish sauces I was already using in the marinade, plus a glug of mild rice vinegar for extra brightness. Perfect.

—ALLI BERKEY, *Cook's Country*

Thai-Style Fried Chicken

SERVES 4 TO 6

Boneless, skinless chicken breasts can be substituted for the chicken thighs; cut breasts in half horizontally before slicing crosswise into 1-inch pieces. We developed this recipe using Bob's Red Mill white rice flour.

3½ tablespoons fish sauce, divided
3 tablespoons plus 1 teaspoon soy sauce, divided
7 garlic cloves, minced, divided
2½ teaspoons white pepper, divided
1½ teaspoons red pepper flakes, divided
2 pounds boneless, skinless chicken thighs, trimmed and sliced crosswise into 1-inch-thick strips
5 tablespoons Asian sweet chili sauce, plus extra for serving
2 tablespoons rice vinegar
1 cup white rice flour
1 cup cornstarch
1 cup water
1 teaspoon baking powder
3 quarts peanut or vegetable oil, for frying
2 tablespoons chopped fresh cilantro
2 tablespoons chopped fresh basil

1. Combine 2 tablespoons fish sauce, 3 tablespoons soy sauce, 6 garlic cloves, 2 teaspoons white pepper, and 1 teaspoon pepper flakes in 1-gallon zipper-lock bag. Add chicken to marinade, seal bag, and turn to distribute marinade. Refrigerate chicken for at least 30 minutes or up to 1 hour.

2. Meanwhile, combine chili sauce, vinegar, remaining 1½ tablespoons fish sauce, remaining 1 teaspoon soy sauce, remaining 1 garlic clove, remaining ½ teaspoon white pepper, and remaining ½ teaspoon pepper flakes in large bowl. Set aside.

3. Whisk flour, cornstarch, water, and baking powder in second large bowl until smooth. Add chicken and marinade to batter and stir to coat.

4. Set wire rack in rimmed baking sheet and line with triple layer of paper towels. Add oil to large Dutch oven until it measures about 2 inches deep and heat over medium-high heat to 375 degrees.

5. Working with one-third of chicken, 1 piece at a time, remove from batter, allowing excess to drip back into bowl, and add to hot oil. Cook until deep golden brown, about 5 minutes, stirring gently as needed to prevent pieces from sticking together. Adjust burner, if necessary, to maintain oil temperature between 350 and 375 degrees. Transfer chicken to prepared rack. Return oil to 375 degrees and repeat with remaining chicken in 2 batches.

6. Add chicken, cilantro, and basil to bowl with reserved chili sauce mixture and toss to combine. Transfer chicken to serving platter. Serve with extra chili sauce.

BONELESS TURKEY BREAST WITH GRAVY

✔ **WHY THIS RECIPE WORKS** Some Thanksgiving cooks find themselves surrounded by those who like only white meat. For those occasions, we wanted to create a recipe for a showstopping turkey breast roast that would please all the white-meat lovers. We started at the butcher's counter, selecting a bone-in, skin-on turkey breast instead of deboned turkey breast halves. We found that split breasts varied greatly in size, even when they were packaged together. Deboning a full breast at home ensured consistency in the size of the two turkey breast halves. Plus, this step gave us a turkey breastbone that we could roast and use as the base for a flavorful gravy to serve on the side. Since white-meat turkey breast is prone to drying out if cooked too long, we salted the breast halves a couple hours in advance of roasting them to lock in more moisture and then roasted them in a low 275-degree oven. Tying the two breast halves together helped ensure even cooking and made for a roast with a celebration-worthy presentation. A quick sear in a skillet on the stovetop before the turkey went into the oven jump-started the exterior's photo-worthy bronzed hue.

When it comes to eating the Thanksgiving turkey, my family has a preference for white meat. That suits me fine, as it means there's always plenty of rich, silky dark meat for me. But this year I decided to put my own preferences aside and prepare a turkey breast roast for the family. The turkey breasts would be a breeze to carve, and I wouldn't have to face the usual challenge of bringing the white and dark meat to perfect doneness at the same time.

The white meat of a turkey breast is less flavorful than the dark meat, so I'd need to crank up the flavor. Since it's lean, I'd have to take care not to dry it out. I was confident I'd be able to clear these hurdles, but I was worried about the gravy. How do you make a superflavorful gravy with minimal turkey drippings and no turkey neck? And even though I knew my roast wouldn't present like a classic Norman Rockwell bird, I still wanted it to look worthy of a holiday.

Now, you can buy boneless, skinless turkey breasts, but I ruled them out from the start because I wasn't willing to forgo crispy turkey skin. That left me with bone-in, skin-on breasts, which are sold both split into halves and together as a full breast sharing the same breastbone. But the breast halves I was getting were inconsistent in size; it was better, I found, to eliminate the size variable and buy one bone-in full breast.

Eyeing the big full breast on the counter, I had a thought: What if I took both halves of the breast off the bone and used that bone to make a flavorful stock for the gravy? I removed the breast meat from the bone, taking care to leave the skin intact. I then roasted the bone until it was well browned, which took about an hour, and simmered it with carrot, onion, celery, and herbs. After straining this rich stock, I used a roux of butter and flour to thicken it into a silky gravy. Even better, the stock and gravy can be made a day ahead.

With the gravy taken care of, I turned to roasting the now boneless but skin-on turkey breast halves. The juiciest meat was cooked to an internal temperature of 160 degrees in a low 275-degree oven, which took about 2½ hours. Roasting the turkey at such a low temperature ensured that it cooked evenly. With 15 minutes of resting time, the meat was perfect. But somehow, bringing two roasted breast pieces to the table felt less than festive. I needed a proper centerpiece.

After a bit of trial and error, I found that I could tie the breast halves together with the skin sides facing out before roasting them. To make the joining easier, a coworker suggested I use a loaf pan to hold the breasts together while I tied them (see "Key Steps for Making Roast Turkey Breast and Gravy"). And to add more seasoning and flavor, I sprinkled the breast halves liberally with a mixture of salt, pepper, and rosemary before tying them together. Refrigerating the rubbed, tied turkey for at least a couple hours ensured that the seasoning penetrated deep into the meat. And to render the extra fat in the skin and give the exterior a photo-worthy bronzed hue, I found that a quick stove-top sear in a skillet before roasting was just the thing.

As a dark-meat lover, I admit that I was skeptical about roasting only the breast. But this recipe quickly won me over. The tender, deeply seasoned meat; crispy skin; and rich gravy look and feel special on the table—and, if you're lucky, in sandwiches a few hours later.

—MORGAN BOLLING, *Cook's Country*

Boneless Turkey Breast with Gravy

SERVES 8 TO 10

Plan ahead: The salted turkey needs to be refrigerated for at least 2 hours before cooking. We prefer a natural (unbrined) turkey breast here, but both self-basting and kosher also work well. Omit the salt in step 1 if you buy a self-basting or kosher turkey breast. You can make soup with the excess turkey stock, if desired.

TURKEY

- 1 (5- to 7-pound) bone-in turkey breast, trimmed
- 1 tablespoon kosher salt
- 2 teaspoons minced fresh rosemary
- ½ teaspoon pepper
- 1 tablespoon vegetable oil

TURKEY STOCK

- 1 onion, chopped
- 1 carrot, peeled and chopped
- 1 celery rib, chopped
- 6 sprigs fresh rosemary
- 1 bay leaf

GRAVY

- 4 tablespoons unsalted butter
- ¼ cup all-purpose flour
- ⅓ cup dry white wine
- 1½ teaspoons kosher salt
- ½ teaspoon pepper

NOTES FROM THE TEST KITCHEN

KEY STEPS FOR MAKING ROAST TURKEY BREAST AND GRAVY

1. Use sharp knife to slice down along both sides of breastbone to remove meat, keeping skin intact.

2. Use loaf pan to keep breast halves in compact, manageable shape when you tie them together.

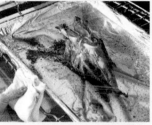

3. Roast breastbone in 450-degree oven until well browned (browned bones make more flavorful stock).

4. Make turkey stock with roasted bone, water, and aromatics; use finished stock for gravy.

1. FOR THE TURKEY: Position turkey breast skin side up on cutting board. Using sharp knife, remove each breast half from bone by cutting through skin on top of breast on either side of center bone. Continue to work knife along bone until each breast half is removed. Reserve breastbone for stock. Combine salt, rosemary, and pepper in bowl. Sprinkle breasts all over with salt mixture.

2. Lay two 24-inch pieces of kitchen twine crosswise in middle of 8½ by 4½-inch loaf pan, about 1 inch apart. Arrange 1 breast half skin side down in pan on top of twine. Position remaining breast half over first, skin side up, with thick end over tapered end. Tuck turkey into edges of pan to fit if necessary. Tie twine tightly to secure. Remove turkey from pan and continue to tie at 1-inch intervals. Wrap in plastic wrap and refrigerate for at least 2 hours or up to 24 hours.

3. FOR THE TURKEY STOCK: Meanwhile, adjust oven rack to middle position and heat oven to 450 degrees. Line rimmed baking sheet with aluminum foil. Place reserved breastbone on prepared sheet and roast until well browned, about 1 hour. Let sit until cool enough to handle, about 15 minutes.

4. Place breastbone in large saucepan (if necessary, use kitchen shears to break down bone to fit). Add onion, carrot, celery, rosemary sprigs, and bay leaf. Add water to cover by 1 inch and bring to boil over high heat. Reduce heat to medium-low and simmer for 1 hour. (Bone should remain covered with water throughout simmer.)

5. Discard breastbone. Strain turkey stock through fine-mesh strainer set over large bowl. Using spoon, press on solids to extract liquid; discard solids. Reserve turkey stock to make gravy when ready.

6. Three hours before serving, adjust oven rack to middle position and heat oven to 275 degrees. Set wire rack in rimmed baking sheet. Heat oil in 12-inch nonstick skillet over medium-high heat until just smoking. Add turkey and cook until well browned on all sides, about 10 minutes. Transfer turkey to prepared wire rack. Roast until turkey registers 160 degrees, 2¼ to 2¾ hours. Transfer turkey to carving board and let rest for 15 minutes.

7. FOR THE GRAVY: Meanwhile, melt butter in large saucepan over medium heat. Whisk in flour until smooth. Cook, whisking frequently, until color of peanut butter, about 5 minutes. Slowly whisk in 3 cups turkey stock until no lumps remain. (Remaining stock can be refrigerated for up to 2 days or frozen for up to 2 months.) Whisk in wine, salt, and pepper and bring to boil. Reduce heat to medium-low and simmer until slightly thickened and reduced to about 2½ cups, 8 to 10 minutes. Off heat, season with salt and pepper to taste. Cover and keep warm.

8. Slice turkey ½ inch thick, removing twine as you slice. Serve, passing gravy separately.

PAN-SEARED SWORDFISH STEAKS

✔ **WHY THIS RECIPE WORKS** Mildly flavored but meaty swordfish steaks are best when cooked quickly over high heat, where they acquire a golden-brown crust. Slow cooking gives their enzymes the time to break down the proteins in these dense steaks, rendering them unappealingly mushy. To speed up cooking, we seared them in a hot skillet, flipping them frequently so that they cooked from both the bottom up and the top down. To keep each bite juicy, we made sure to remove the steaks from the heat when they reached 130 degrees and let carryover cooking bring them up to the desired temperature of 140 degrees.

It seems funny to admit that a fish was once my nemesis, but there was a spell back when I was a line cook when that was exactly the case. For five straight nights, I carefully prepared what appeared to be pristine swordfish steaks and began to plate them up, only to find that they were soft and mushy. The restaurant waitstaff then had to inform the diner that his or her entrée choice had been taken off the menu for the evening. Back then, I didn't know what to attribute the poor—not to mention wasteful—results to, and we ultimately stopped serving swordfish altogether. But I've long wondered why the texture of swordfish can sometimes be perfect—meaty, juicy, and tender—and other times so unpleasant. It was time to use a scientific approach to figure out why—and come up with a solution.

It would be a worthwhile effort: I knew that swordfish, unlike silky salmon or flaky halibut, at least had the potential to offer a unique dense meatiness. This distinctive texture, combined with a sweet, mild flavor, could excite even a staunch carnivore. In fact, swordfish steaks are similar enough to beef steaks that I decided to start my investigation by looking to one of the test kitchen's favorite methods for cooking steak.

We call it reverse searing: First, we gently cook the meat in the oven until it's perfectly juicy and tender, and then we transfer it to the stovetop to brown the exterior quickly. I seasoned four 8-ounce swordfish steaks with salt and cooked them gently in a 300-degree oven for about 45 minutes, until they were a few degrees shy of 140 degrees, a temperature that the test kitchen likes for white fish. Next, I briefly seared the fish steaks in an oil-slicked nonstick skillet until they

PAN-SEARED SWORDFISH STEAKS

acquired a golden-brown crust and let them rest for a few minutes. They looked gorgeous, but I knew all too well that a good-looking swordfish exterior often hides a disappointing interior. Sure enough, although some tasters charitably described the fish as "too tender," most reported that it had the soft, tacky, almost mushy texture of canned tuna.

After consulting with our science editor, I understood what was going on. Just like meats, fish contains enzymes called cathepsins. If the circumstances are right, the cathepsins will snip the proteins that give swordfish its sturdy texture, turning it soft. Although they're ultimately destroyed by heat, cathepsins are increasingly active at low cooking temperatures. By slowly bringing the swordfish steaks up to 140 degrees, I was giving the cathepsins plenty of time to take the flesh from meaty to mushy.

Clearly, I needed to speed up the cooking. The fastest way to cook these (or any) steaks indoors would be to sear them in a skillet. The metal in the pan would conduct heat to the fish more rapidly than even the hottest oven or broiler. In a skillet, flipped once halfway through cooking, the steaks were done in just 16 to 18 minutes. Tasters agreed that this was a step in the right direction: Each bite was firmer since the enzymes hadn't been given much time to act. But I wasn't going to get off that easy. The swordfish was dry and tough just beneath the well-browned crust.

It made sense that the portions of the swordfish that had been nearest to the hot skillet were overcooked. The part of the fish that's in contact with the pan heats up very quickly because of the skillet's ability to transfer heat. That portion of the flesh must in turn transfer that heat to the layers adjacent to it. And most food, swordfish included, doesn't transfer heat quickly. The upshot is that as the interior slowly heats up, the exterior overcooks. But if gentle cooking turned these steaks to mush and a hard sear—necessary for preserving their texture—left them wrung out, where did that leave me?

I had flipped the steaks only once during cooking. What if I flipped them more frequently? After the first flip, the steaks would cook from both sides. Simultaneously, the top side would get a reprieve from the hot pan, which could minimize overcooking.

When my oiled skillet began to smoke, I added the swordfish steaks. I flipped them every 2 minutes, and after about 10 minutes, they hit 140 degrees. This significantly cut the cooking time, and the steaks were much improved. They were cooked throughout and sported golden-brown crusts, and each bite was dense and meaty. There was just one problem: The fish oozed juices as it rested. A quick temperature check revealed the reason. The aggressive cooking had caused the fish to carry over to 150 degrees. And at such a high temperature, the proteins shrank and squeezed out juices. I seared another batch, this time pulling the steaks from the skillet when they registered just 130 degrees. That did the trick: During a 10-minute rest, they climbed to the target temperature of 140 degrees.

Though the rich, meaty, juicy steaks were great with just a squeeze of lemon, I wanted to celebrate the conquering of my nemesis (how I wish I knew then what I know now!) with a couple of sauces. One was a classic Italian swordfish accompaniment, an *agrodolce*-style relish based on piquant capers and sweet currants; the other was an ultragarlicky sauce with the unique addition of dried mint.

—LAN LAM, *Cook's Illustrated*

Pan-Seared Swordfish Steaks

SERVES 4

For the best results, purchase swordfish steaks that are ¾ to 1 inch thick. Look for four steaks that weigh 7 to 9 ounces each or two steaks that weigh about 1 pound each. If you purchase the latter, cut them in half to create four steaks. Serve with Caper-Currant Relish or Spicy Dried Mint–Garlic Sauce (recipes follow), if desired.

 2 **teaspoons vegetable oil**
 2 **pounds skinless swordfish steaks,**
    ¾ to 1 inch thick
1½ **teaspoons kosher salt**
    Lemon wedges

1. Heat oil in 12-inch nonstick skillet over medium-high heat until shimmering. While oil heats, pat steaks dry with paper towels and sprinkle both sides with salt.

2. Place steaks in skillet and cook, flipping every 2 minutes, until golden brown and centers register 130 degrees, 7 to 11 minutes. Transfer to serving platter or individual plates and let rest for 10 minutes. Serve with lemon wedges.

Caper-Currant Relish
MAKES ABOUT ½ CUP

Golden raisins can be substituted for the currants.

- 3 tablespoons minced fresh parsley
- 3 tablespoons extra-virgin olive oil
- 2 tablespoons capers, rinsed and chopped fine
- 2 tablespoons currants, chopped fine
- 1 garlic clove, minced
- 1 teaspoon grated lemon zest plus 2 tablespoons juice

Combine all ingredients in bowl. Let stand at room temperature for at least 20 minutes before serving.

Spicy Dried Mint–Garlic Sauce
MAKES ABOUT ½ CUP

This sauce gets its spiciness from the raw garlic. If you are not using a garlic press, use a fork to bruise the minced garlic when stirring the sauce together.

- 4 teaspoons dried mint
- ¼ cup extra-virgin olive oil
- 2 tablespoons red wine vinegar
- 4 garlic cloves, minced
- ⅛ teaspoon table salt

Place mint in fine-mesh strainer and use spoon to rub mint through strainer into bowl. Discard any solids left in strainer. (You should have about 1 tablespoon mint powder.) Add oil, vinegar, garlic, and salt to mint powder and stir to combine.

NOTES FROM THE TEST KITCHEN

SWORDFISH BASICS

SHOPPING Swordfish steaks typically have a bloodline—a dark muscle rich in myoglobin—running through them. Since we found that the bloodline has an unpleasant mineral taste, we recommend looking for steaks with as minimal a bloodline as possible.

PREP Thick, rubbery swordfish skin tightens up more than the flesh during cooking and can cause the steak to buckle. You can either ask your fishmonger to remove it for you or trim it off yourself using a thin, sharp knife.

SAUTÉED TILAPIA

✔ **WHY THIS RECIPE WORKS** We quickly cooked mild-tasting tilapia in a nonstick skillet over high heat to maximize flavorful browning without overcooking and drying out the fillets. We found that this fish is firm and resilient enough to cook over aggressive heat without falling apart. Dividing each fillet into a thick and a thin portion and sautéing them separately allowed for more precise cooking and even browning. Finishing with a cilantro chimichurri sauce added flavor and richness to this lean fish.

Until recently, tilapia was not a fish that ever came up in our weekly discussion of potential recipes to develop. We had a vague idea of it as being a second-rate, predominantly farm-raised fish with a muddy taste, so why even go there? Then we learned that tilapia is now the fourth most consumed seafood in the United States (after shrimp, tuna, and salmon) and decided that it was time to take a closer look. A tilapia fact-finding mission ensued: My fellow test cooks and I scoured the internet for information and started experimenting in the test kitchen. Boy, were we ever wrong about this fish. Tilapia has a whole lot going for it: It's low in fat and high in protein, most of it is responsibly raised, and it even has a strong recommendation from a leading consumer watchdog group.

The flesh of tilapia, a freshwater fish, is firm and moist, with a clean, mild—not at all muddy—flavor, sort of a cross between trout and flounder. In fact, tilapia is so appealing that when we included it in a blind tasting of five types of white fish, it landed in second place, only one point shy of tying with haddock for the win. Given that stellar showing and the fact that tilapia is so reasonably priced—it runs only about $8.95 per pound—we saw no good reason not to cook with it.

I dove right in, eager to file my first tilapia recipe. I knew that flavorful browning would enhance the fillets' delicate taste, so a simple stovetop sauté seemed like the best way to go. Because it had been a while since we developed a recipe for relatively thin white fish fillets, I wondered if I should apply lessons we've learned from cooking salmon. These days we usually brine or salt salmon before cooking; it seasons the flesh and helps it retain moisture, which benefits even a fatty fish.

SAUTÉED TILAPIA

Indeed, when I quickly sautéed both unsalted tilapia and tilapia that I'd salted for 15 minutes, the latter was moister and better seasoned.

With that question answered, I was ready to cook the fish. I salted another batch of fillets and blotted them dry with paper towels before giving each one a dip into all-purpose flour, a technique we commonly use to accelerate browning. As I proceeded to cook the lightly coated fish in two batches in an oil-slicked nonstick skillet over medium heat, I noticed yet another likable trait: Whereas most thin fish fillets are fragile and demand a gentle touch, denser tilapia didn't flake apart, so it was easy to maneuver in the pan.

Unfortunately, moderate heat failed to brown the fish in the few short minutes it took to reach 130 degrees, the doneness temperature we found ideal for tilapia. In a subsequent test, I cranked the heat up to high and was pleased to find that the sturdy tilapia could withstand this aggressive approach. After just 2 to 3 minutes per side, some deep golden browning developed. But it wasn't uniform.

Only half of each fillet was taking on color; the other half emerged from the pan pale as could be. That's because tilapia are small, so a single fillet is a whole side of the fish. Half the fillet is the thinner belly portion, and the other half is the thicker portion beneath the dorsal fin. The thick half was resting flat on the pan and browning nicely, but the thin half, tilted up by the thick side, hardly made contact at all, making it impossible to brown.

As I stared at four more fillets on my cutting board, an answer presented itself. A natural seam runs the length of each fillet, separating the thin belly from the thicker portion. I ran my knife along the seams to split the fillets. Then, still working in two batches, I sautéed the four thick halves together before proceeding with the four thin halves. That did the trick: Freeing the thin pieces gave them full contact with the pan, allowing them to turn a deep golden brown, and cooking the thick and thin halves separately let me tailor the cooking time to suit the thickness of each.

But the high heat I was using caused a problem: As I browned the first batch of fillets, they shed a bit of the flour into the skillet. By the time the second batch went in, those flour particles were starting to burn, producing scorched flavors and smoking up the kitchen. I didn't want to have to wipe out a hot pan between batches (or set off the fire alarm), so I ran a quick test without the flour dredge to see if it was really necessary. It wasn't: The high heat alone was sufficient to get the fillets remarkably browned and even lightly crispy in spots. The fish was top-notch with just a squeeze of lemon, but I felt that a rich finishing touch would give it a little more oomph. To add that richness, I came up with a garlicky olive oil–based chimichurri featuring fresh cilantro and parsley. Spooned onto the hot-from-the-pan tilapia, the chimichurri added aromatic pops of flavor.

At long last, here is a great recipe for tilapia. We're sorry we waited so long.

—STEVE DUNN, *Cook's Illustrated*

Sautéed Tilapia

SERVES 4

You can use fresh or frozen tilapia in this recipe (if frozen, thaw before cooking). There is no need to take the temperature of the thin halves of the fillets; they will be cooked through by the time they are golden brown. Omit the lemon wedges and serve the fish with Cilantro Chimichurri (recipe follows), if desired.

4 (5- to 6-ounce) skinless tilapia fillets
1 teaspoon kosher salt
2 tablespoons vegetable oil
   Lemon wedges

1. Place tilapia on cutting board and sprinkle both sides with salt. Let sit at room temperature for 15 minutes. Pat tilapia dry with paper towels. Using seam that runs down middle of fillet as guide, cut each fillet in half lengthwise to create 1 thick half and 1 thin half.

2. Heat oil in 12-inch nonstick skillet over high heat until just smoking. Add thick halves of fillets to skillet. Cook, tilting and gently shaking skillet occasionally to distribute oil, until undersides are golden brown, 2 to 3 minutes. Using thin spatula, flip fillets. Cook until second sides are golden brown and tilapia registers 130 to 135 degrees, 2 to 3 minutes. Transfer tilapia to serving platter.

3. Return skillet to high heat. When oil is just smoking, add thin halves of fillets and cook until undersides are golden brown, about 1 minute. Flip and cook until second sides are golden brown, about 1 minute. Transfer to platter and serve with lemon wedges.

Cilantro Chimichurri

SERVES 4

Briefly soaking the dried oregano in hot water and vinegar before combining it with the remaining ingredients helps soften it and release its flavor. Top Sautéed Tilapia with ¼ cup of chimichurri before serving and pass the remaining chimichurri separately.

2	tablespoons hot water
2	tablespoons red wine vinegar
1	teaspoon dried oregano
½	cup minced fresh parsley
¼	cup minced fresh cilantro
3	garlic cloves, minced
1	teaspoon kosher salt
¼	teaspoon red pepper flakes
¼	cup extra-virgin olive oil

Combine hot water, vinegar, and oregano in medium bowl; let stand for 5 minutes. Add parsley, cilantro, garlic, salt, and pepper flakes and stir to combine. Whisk in oil until incorporated.

SHRIMP MOZAMBIQUE

✔ **WHY THIS RECIPE WORKS** Shrimp Mozambique is a bracing dish of shrimp bathed in a buttery, garlicky, peppery sauce (think spicy shrimp scampi) with roots in southeast Africa, where Portuguese colonists cultivated the *piri-piri* pepper that traditionally gives this dish its heat. We wanted our version to come together quickly and have all the character and flavor of the original. As a stand-in for the hard-to-find piri-piri pepper, we turned to our favorite all-purpose hot sauce, Frank's RedHot Original Cayenne Pepper Sauce. Like many of the imported piri-piri sauces we tried, this cayenne pepper sauce is a puree of peppers, salt, vinegar, and oil. To give it the body and balance of those piri-piri sauces, we blended the Frank's with olive oil, garlic, parsley, paprika, and torn bread. After sautéing some onion and a healthy dose of garlic, we added white wine for acidity. We then added the shrimp, and when they were just opaque, we stirred in our pepper sauce and a couple of tablespoons of butter to bring everything together.

Shrimp Mozambique is a deeply satisfying dish in which shrimp are coated with a rich, spicy sauce. It can be found in households and restaurants in Portuguese communities such as Fall River and New Bedford, both in Massachusetts. It's a sophisticated but simple dish, suitable as an appetizer or light main course, and it comes together quickly.

The Mozambique moniker grows from Portugal's history in southeast Africa, where Portuguese colonists cultivated the *piri-piri* pepper in the late 15th century. But this pepper, known for its beautiful bright red hue and complex flavor (fresh, fruity, and hot but not screaming hot), can be hard to find in the United States. When I set out to make my own version of shrimp Mozambique, I knew this would be the first issue I'd need to sort out. I tried to find a substitute for piri-piri by testing various canned, fresh, and dried peppers but came up short.

During my research, I came across one recipe that suggested subbing cayenne peppers for the piri-piris. While a straight swap wasn't perfect (cayenne peppers are a bit milder), they are easier to find and have a similar flavor. Another aha moment came when reading labels: Our favorite all-purpose hot sauce, Frank's RedHot Original Cayenne Pepper Sauce, contains vinegar, cayenne peppers, salt, water, and canola oil. Since a good fresh piri-piri sauce is basically a puree of the peppers with vinegar, salt, garlic, and oil, maybe we could just doctor up the Frank's a bit.

Pureeing the hot sauce with olive oil, garlic, seasonings (parsley and paprika), and torn bread to thicken and help bind the sauce resulted in bright and balanced flavors. But would it taste right in the finished dish? There was only one way to find out.

The first step was to soften some onion and garlic in a skillet and then add white wine to reduce by half (I tested beer, which many shrimp Mozambique recipes call for, but I preferred the crisp acidity that white wine provided). Next into the skillet: shrimp.

When the shrimp were just opaque (this took only 4 minutes), a healthy slosh of our pepper sauce and 2 tablespoons of butter brought everything together. Salt, pepper, and a sprinkling of chopped parsley finished the dish. I had a dish that was exciting, flavorful, complex, and supereasy.

—ELLE SIMONE SCOTT WITH MATTHEW FAIRMAN,
Cook's Country

Shrimp Mozambique

SERVES 4

We prefer to use untreated shrimp—those without added salt or preservatives such as sodium tripolyphosphate (STPP). Salt-treated shrimp are fine in a pinch, but we've found that STPP-treated shrimp have a chemical flavor and mushy texture. Most frozen E-Z peel shrimp have been treated (the ingredient list should tell you). If you're using treated shrimp, do not sprinkle the shrimp with salt in step 2. Do not omit the white sandwich bread from the sauce; it gives the sauce body. Serve with crusty bread or over white rice.

SAUCE

- 2 tablespoons Frank's RedHot Original Cayenne Pepper Sauce
- 2 tablespoons extra-virgin olive oil
- 2 tablespoons water
- ¼ slice hearty white sandwich bread, torn into small pieces
- 1 tablespoon chopped fresh parsley
- 2 garlic cloves, chopped
- 2 teaspoons paprika
- ½ teaspoon pepper

SHRIMP

- 2 pounds extra-large shrimp (21 to 25 per pound), peeled, deveined, and tails removed
- ¼ teaspoon pepper
- 1 teaspoon table salt, divided
- 1 tablespoon extra-virgin olive oil
- ½ cup finely chopped onion
- 3 garlic cloves, sliced thin
- 1 cup dry white wine
- 2 tablespoons unsalted butter, cut into 2 pieces
- 2 tablespoons chopped fresh parsley

1. FOR THE SAUCE: Process all ingredients in blender until smooth, about 2 minutes, scraping down sides of blender jar as needed.

2. FOR THE SHRIMP: Sprinkle shrimp with pepper and ½ teaspoon salt; set aside. Heat oil in 12-inch nonstick skillet over medium heat until shimmering. Add onion and remaining ½ teaspoon salt and cook until softened, about 5 minutes. Add garlic and cook until fragrant, about 1 minute. Add wine and bring to boil. Cook until reduced by half, about 4 minutes.

3. Add shrimp and cook, stirring occasionally, until opaque and just cooked through, about 4 minutes. Stir in butter and sauce and cook until butter is melted and sauce is heated through, about 1 minute. Season with salt and pepper to taste. Sprinkle with parsley and serve.

THAI PANANG SHRIMP CURRY

✔ **WHY THIS RECIPE WORKS** Panang curry is a sweeter, more full-bodied version of Thai red curry that's often enriched with ground peanuts and seasoned with sugar, fish sauce, deeply fragrant makrut lime leaves, and a touch of fiery chile. And unlike more familiar curries, which are typically brothy, panang curry has a thick, velvety consistency (from a judicious amount of coconut milk) that steadfastly clings to the shrimp. To start, we sizzled a few tablespoons of homemade curry paste in vegetable oil; blooming the paste ensured that the fresh aromatics and spices reached their full flavor potential despite the dish's short cooking time. This is a departure from traditional recipes that call for frying the paste in coconut cream that has been "cracked"—that is, simmered until its oil separates out. We've found that coconut milks from different brands yield varying amounts of cream, so the vegetable oil method was more foolproof. Peanut is a final key flavor component; scattering finely chopped roasted peanuts over the top before serving gave the dish subtle nuttiness as well as a nice crunch.

For what is, at its heart, a simple dish—crisp-tender vegetables and a protein coated in a warm, aromatic sauce—Thai curry can seem intimidating. Traditional recipes often call for a long list of ingredients in order to achieve that signature balance of flavor and heat. And recipes that call for store-bought curry paste certainly simplify the process but can deliver disappointing results. I was determined to create a recipe for a Thai curry that was every bit as flavorful as a restaurant version without being overly complicated.

I chose to make panang curry, a lesser-known cousin of red curry that's distinctive for including peanuts, with a subtle background heat and a sauce that coats the vegetables like a warm blanket. Deciding on the vegetables I would use was easy; sugar snap peas and bell pepper would cook in just minutes while maintaining their crisp texture, giving each bite a pleasing light crunch. Shrimp could be stirred directly into the sauce and would be perfectly done in even less time than the vegetables, making this a quick one-pan dinner. The tricky part, I knew, would be the curry.

Store-bought and homemade curry paste each have pros and cons. Store-bought is superconvenient, requiring nothing more than opening a jar or can and spooning out the proper amount. However, brands vary in spiciness and flavor profile, making it hard to know exactly how the finished curry will taste, and they lack the fresh punchiness of homemade curry paste. But while homemade curry paste is a flavor powerhouse, making it entails adding several additional ingredients and steps to a recipe. I wanted a recipe that was versatile enough to use either: store-bought curry paste for when I was in a rush and wanted a quick way to satisfy a curry craving, and homemade for when I had the time to make something special.

One simple step coaxed maximum flavor out of whatever curry paste I was using: toasting the paste in a skillet for several minutes until it turned a dark brick red and filled the kitchen with its spicy aroma. Doing so bloomed the spices in the paste and produced richer, fuller flavor than I got from stirring raw paste directly into coconut milk. I experimented with blooming the paste in coconut cream, as many traditional recipes dictate, but in the end I discovered that using vegetable oil was easier and made no difference in the final flavor of the curry.

Once my curry paste was toasted, the rest of the dish came together in a snap. I stirred in coconut milk and fish sauce (for depth of flavor) and let the sauce simmer until it was thick enough to coat the back of a spoon. I then added my vegetables and, a few minutes later, my shrimp, and finished the dish with a combination of mint and basil. The full ½ cup of fresh herbs brightened the rich sauce. After sprinkling some chopped roasted peanuts over the top, I tasted my creation. I was well on my way, but I wondered if I could do even better.

My initial recipe called for two 14-ounce cans of coconut milk, which resulted in a sauce that was almost too rich, muting the brighter flavors of the spices and herbs. I tried the recipe with just one can of coconut milk and had a revelation: This sauce was still rich, but much more balanced, allowing the layers of flavor in the panang spice paste to take the spotlight.

Lastly, I turned to developing my own curry paste blend. Although toasting store-bought paste improved its flavor immensely, making my own meant that the aromatic elements would be even fresher, and I could control the spice level. I started with just four spicy Thai bird chiles, which I ground fine along with coriander and cumin. I left the spices untoasted since they would later be toasted in the paste. I soon decided four chiles wasn't enough even for relatively mild panang curry. Test by test, the amount rose, until finally I settled on 20 chiles—five times my starting amount. Now I had a curry paste that made its presence pleasantly known. As for the other ingredients, garlic added a peppery bite, tomato paste and a bit of brown sugar added subtle sweetness and darker color, and lemon grass and makrut lime leaves contributed citrusy notes. I tried leaving out or using substitutions for the makrut lime leaves, which can be hard to find, but in the end I decided their unique flavor made them well worth the trouble to seek out.

After tasting the final product, I was confident that I'd created something great—and judging by how fast the rest disappeared, my colleagues agreed. Now that I knew how easy it was to achieve the warm, vibrant flavors of panang curry at home, I'd be getting my curry on a lot more often.

—LEAH COLINS, *America's Test Kitchen Books*

PURCHASING AND PREPPING SHRIMP

This recipe calls for peeled and deveined large shrimp, which are also known as "26/30s" because that's how many shrimp of this size make a pound. Peeling shrimp is easy to do by hand; many supermarkets carry E-Z peel shrimp, which have been split open along the back and deveined.

To do it yourself, peel the shell away from the flesh starting at the swimming legs, and then gently pull the meat from the tail. To remove the vein (which is actually the shrimp's digestive tract), use a paring knife to make a ¼-inch incision along the back of the shrimp and then use the tip of the paring knife to get under the vein and gently pull it free.

Thai Panang Shrimp Curry

SERVES 4

We prefer to use our homemade Thai Panang Curry Paste here (recipe follows), but you can substitute store-bought Thai red curry paste if you wish. Thai basil can be hard to find, but feel free to substitute it for the Italian basil if you have some on hand. For a spicier curry, use the larger amount of curry paste.

- 2 tablespoons vegetable oil
- 2–4 tablespoons Thai Panang Curry Paste (recipe follows)
- 1 (14-ounce) can coconut milk
- 2 tablespoons fish sauce
- 6 ounces sugar snap peas, strings removed
- 1 red bell pepper, stemmed, seeded, and cut into ¼-inch-wide strips
- 1½ pounds large shrimp (26 to 30 per pound), peeled, deveined, and tails removed
- ¼ cup chopped fresh mint
- ¼ cup chopped fresh basil
- ⅓ cup dry-roasted peanuts, chopped

1. Heat oil in 12-inch nonstick skillet over medium heat until shimmering. Add curry paste and cook, stirring frequently, until paste is fragrant and darkens in color to brick red, 5 to 8 minutes. Whisk in coconut milk and fish sauce, bring to simmer, and cook until sauce is slightly thickened, 10 to 12 minutes.

2. Add snap peas and bell pepper and simmer for 3 minutes. Add shrimp, cover, and cook, stirring occasionally, until shrimp are opaque throughout and vegetables are crisp-tender, about 4 minutes. Off heat, stir in mint and basil. Sprinkle with peanuts and serve.

Thai Panang Curry Paste

MAKES ABOUT ½ CUP

This red paste balances sweet and spicy aromatic flavors. The makrut lime leaves (sometimes sold as kaffir lime leaves) are worth seeking out, but you can substitute one 3-inch strip each of lemon and lime zest.

- ½ ounce (about 20) bird chiles, stemmed
- 1 teaspoon coriander seeds
- ½ teaspoon cumin seeds
- 2 lemon grass stalks, trimmed to bottom 6 inches and sliced thin
- 6 tablespoons water
- 8 garlic cloves, smashed and peeled
- 2 tablespoons packed dark brown sugar
- 2 makrut lime leaves
- 1 tablespoon tomato paste
- 1 teaspoon grated fresh ginger

1. Process bird chiles, coriander seeds, and cumin seeds in spice grinder until finely ground, about 30 seconds; transfer to blender.

2. Microwave lemon grass and water in covered bowl until steaming, about 2 minutes; transfer to blender with spices. Add garlic, sugar, lime leaves, tomato paste, and ginger and process until smooth paste forms, about 4 minutes, scraping down sides of blender jar as needed. (Paste can be refrigerated in airtight container for up to 1 week.)

SALT-BAKED WHOLE BRANZINO

✔ **WHY THIS RECIPE WORKS** The tradition of baking whole fish in a thick salt crust goes back at least as far as fourth-century-BC Sicily. Why (beyond presentation) would we do this? We found that baking branzino in a salt crust not only seasoned the fish throughout—and perfectly—but it also cooked the entire body evenly for some of the most succulent fish we've tasted. In fact, when we compared a salt-crusted fish to a whole fish baked directly on a baking sheet, the fillet touching the sheet was overcooked by 30 degrees by the time the top fillet was just done; the insulated salt-encased fish cooked evenly.

SALT-BAKED WHOLE BRANZINO

The process of salt-baking fish is essentially just what it sounds like: A whole fish is encased in a salt crust and baked before being cracked out of the crust and served, either whole or in fillets. But why would you go through the trouble of salt-baking when you could bake and season the fish normally? I was determined to find out. As it happens, the technique dates back thousands of years and was common in many regions across the Mediterranean and Asia. Today, salt-baked whole fish remains a popular, impressive-looking dish in restaurants. Eye-catching presentation aside, this technique has stood the test of time because the salt allows the fish to bake evenly without drying out, resulting in fillets of fish that are unparalleled in their succulence. I wanted to experience this for myself, so I set out to create my own recipe.

To get my bearings, I gathered as many recipes as I could dig up. The sheer number of recipes available was overwhelming. There were those that kept to the basics—fish, salt, maybe some lemon for serving—and others that called for a wide variety of spices, herbs, and flavoring agents to add to the crust or stuff inside the fish itself. I even dug up some recipes for salt-baked chicken to see how the methods compared. After sifting through a stack of the most promising recipes, I narrowed the group down to four. Each recipe called for a different type of fish, different oven temperatures and baking times, and varying amounts of salt and added liquid. They also differed in flavor profiles. After testing all four as written, I took all that I learned about what worked—and what definitely didn't—and got to work.

First, I needed to nail down the salt coating. While most traditional recipes called for sea salt, I opted to use kosher salt for its lower price and lower moisture content (after all, I'd be adding liquid of some sort to my coating anyway). For now, I decided to work with branzino, which had been my favorite fish of those called for in the recipes I'd tested. To serve four people, I would need two whole fish, and I found that 8 cups was the minimum amount of salt I'd need to cover both fully. One of the recipes I'd tested called for using salt alone with no binder. This method gave me a fish that was dried out and difficult to hold together, so I knew I needed a liquid component. Next, I tried combining the salt with equal parts water, mixing them together until I had a paste. I mounded two portions of the paste on a baking sheet before patting the mounds down into rectangles of equal size. Then I laid one fish on top of

each rectangle and packed the remaining paste on top of both fish, leaving the heads and tails exposed (I wouldn't be eating them, so there was no need to waste any coating there). After baking, I found that this was a definite improvement on the salt-only crust, but this coating cracked early on in baking and the fish was still drier than I would have liked. I next tried swapping in egg whites for the water as some recipes recommended, hoping it would fortify the coating and prevent early cracking, but this paste was too dry and not malleable enough to coat the fish properly. Just about out of options, I tried mixing equal parts water and egg whites in with the salt. This, thankfully, worked well: The paste was workable, neither too dry nor too loose, and perfectly coated the fish. It had also solved the problem of cracking in the oven which led to dried-out fish. But to achieve true perfection, I needed to experiment with different oven temperatures and cooking times to find the best combination.

To find the ideal oven temperature, I decided to coat three fish in my salt mixture and test them at 250, 325, and 400 degrees. The fish baked at 250 degrees seemed almost uncooked after 45 minutes in the oven, and I wasn't interested in a recipe that would take much longer than that. On the other end of the spectrum, the fish baked at 400 degrees grew too firm too quickly, and its dry flesh was a far cry from the characteristic moistness of salt-baked fish. In the end, 325 degrees was the true sweet spot. After about 40 minutes in the oven, the fish registered 135 degrees. After letting the fish rest for a few minutes, I cracked the crust with the back of a large spoon and tried a piece of the branzino. It was firm and meaty but also perfectly tender, moist, and silky. It was evenly cooked and thoroughly seasoned throughout in a way I'd never seen in a whole fish that was simply seasoned and baked, or in a plain baked fish fillet.

Branzino had worked well in my recipe and I liked its mild, almost sweet flavor, but to see how other types of fish would fare, I tested this method using red snapper and sea bass. I was pleased to find that both fish worked perfectly with my method and each had its own distinct flavor.

Finally, I wanted to incorporate some simple, classic flavoring agents into my recipe. The fish already had such extraordinary innate flavor brought out by the salt crust that I didn't want to smother it with other ingredients, so I would have to be judicious with additional flavorings. I placed only lemon slices and a little bit of garlic into cavities I'd cut into the fish before baking. This way the flavor would infuse into the flesh while the fish cooked; I squeezed a bit more lemon over the fish after cooking. This fish had so much going for it beyond its impressive presentation; its foolproof even cooking, delicate texture, and superior seasoning were enough to convince me that this was a dish worth making at home. To put it simply, my salt-baked fish blew standard baked fish right out of the water.

—JOSEPH GITTER, *America's Test Kitchen Books*

Salt-Baked Whole Branzino
SERVES 4

Traditionally sea salt is used here, but we found that affordable kosher salt worked just fine. We developed this recipe using Diamond Crystal kosher salt. If using Morton kosher salt, the weight equivalence for 8 cups is 4½ pounds. Avoid fish weighing more than 2 pounds. Red snapper and sea bass are good substitutes for branzino. To take the temperature of the branzino, insert the thermometer into the fillets through the opening by the gills.

    8 cups (3 pounds) kosher salt
    ⅔ cup water, plus extra as needed
    4 large egg whites
    2 (1½- to 2-pound) whole branzinos, about 16 inches
       long, scaled, gutted, fins snipped off with scissors
    3 garlic cloves, minced, divided
    1 lemon, sliced thin, divided, plus lemon wedges
       for serving

1. Adjust oven rack to upper-middle position and heat oven to 325 degrees. Line rimmed baking sheet with parchment paper. Stir salt, water, and egg whites in large bowl until well combined. (Mixture should hold together when squeezed; if necessary, continue to stir, adding extra water, 1 tablespoon at a time, until mixture holds.)

2. Rinse branzinos under cold running water and pat dry inside and out with paper towels. Working with 1 branzino at a time, open cavity, spread half of garlic on flesh, and stuff with half of lemon slices.

3. Divide 3 cups salt mixture into 2 even mounds on prepared sheet. Pat mounds into 10 by 4-inch rectangles, spaced about 1 inch apart. Lay 1 branzino lengthwise

across each mound. Gently pack remaining salt mixture evenly around each branzino, leaving head and tail exposed. Roast until branzinos register 135 degrees, 40 to 45 minutes, rotating sheet halfway through roasting. Transfer sheet to wire rack and let branzinos rest for 5 minutes.

4. Using back of serving spoon, gently tap top and sides of salt crusts to crack into large pieces; discard crusts. Using spatula, transfer branzinos to cutting board and brush away excess salt. Fillet each branzino by making vertical cut just behind head from top of fish to belly. Make another cut along top of branzino from head to tail. Starting at head and working toward tail, gently slide spatula between top fillet and bones to separate; transfer fillet to serving platter skin side up. Gently lift tail and peel skeleton and head from bottom fillet; discard head, skeleton, and lemon slices. Transfer second fillet skin side up to platter; discard skin. Serve with lemon wedges.

NOTES FROM THE TEST KITCHEN

PREPARING SALT-BAKED WHOLE BRANZINO

1. Divide 3 cups salt mixture into 2 even mounds on prepared sheet. Pat mounds into 10 by 4-inch rectangles.

2. Lay 1 branzino lengthwise across each mound.

3. Gently pack remaining salt mixture evenly around each branzino, leaving head and tail exposed.

PERUVIAN FISH CEVICHE WITH RADISHES AND ORANGE

✔ **WHY THIS RECIPE WORKS** To create a flavorful yet balanced "cooking" liquid for our Peruvian fish ceviche, we made what's known as a *leche de tigre* by blending lime juice, *ají amarillo* chile paste, garlic, extra-virgin olive oil, and a small amount of fish. Once strained, the liquid was an intensely flavorful and silky-textured emulsion. We then soaked thinly sliced and briefly salted fish (red snapper, sea bass, halibut, and grouper were all good options) in the *leche* for 30 to 40 minutes until it was just opaque and slightly firm. To complete the dish, we added sweet oranges; crisp, peppery radishes; and chopped cilantro. We served the ceviche with corn nuts and popcorn, which provided salty crunch.

Ceviche is a Latin American dish in which pieces of raw fish are "cooked" in an acidic marinade until the flesh firms and turns opaque. In the summer, it is one of my go-to dinners for three big reasons: It's quick and easy to prepare, it doesn't require turning on the stove or oven or even firing up the grill, and it's a dish that truly allows the fresh, clean, delicate flavor of seafood to shine.

Full disclosure: When I make ceviche at home, I don't normally use a recipe. I juice some limes, cut up the fish (usually a firm-fleshed white variety such as sea bass, snapper, or halibut—whatever is freshest at the market), and let the fish marinate in the lime juice until it just begins to turn opaque. Then I add minced garlic and chiles, chopped cilantro, some thinly sliced onion, creamy diced avocado, a glug of olive oil for some richness, and a generous pinch of salt. Some crunchy garnishes go in a bowl to be served on the side. When I started researching traditional recipes, I quickly realized how simplistic my understanding of ceviche was. Plenty of versions took an approach similar to mine, but the Peruvian recipes opened my eyes to a more sophisticated take.

Many Peruvian recipes call for blending the marinade ingredients—citrus juice, aromatics, and olive oil—before adding the seafood. But there's another component: fish. Some recipes call for a concentrated fish broth; others call for adding a small portion of fish before blending and straining. In both cases, the added seafood brings savory depth to the marinade, which is called *leche de tigre* ("tiger's milk"). This *leche* is sometimes poured over the marinated fish before serving, like a sauce, or drunk as a beverage, either on its own or mixed into a cocktail.

With its creamy, rich consistency and balanced, nuanced flavor, the blended marinade is akin to an emulsified vinaigrette. Thanks to that emulsification, the silky marinade coats and clings to each piece of fish. (This was a sharp contrast to my usual unblended marinade, which always runs right off the fish, causing individual bites to feature too much sharp lime juice or an abundance of greasy oil.)

I began working on my version by slicing 1 pound of skinless red snapper into small pieces. To make the leche, I poured ½ cup of fresh lime juice into a blender along with two garlic cloves, ¼ cup of chopped cilantro, a couple of teaspoons of salt, and 2 tablespoons of olive oil. For some heat, I added some *ají amarillo* chile paste, which is made from a fruity yellow pepper of the same name and is a traditional ingredient in many Peruvian ceviches (a seeded habanero chile can be substituted in a pinch). Finally, I added ⅓ cup of sliced snapper. After blending, I strained out any remaining solids.

The resulting leche had the creamy consistency I was aiming for, but the lime was so muted that I could barely taste it. Plus, blending the green cilantro with the yellow chile paste turned the leche an unappealing muddy brown. There was nothing to do but try again. I made a new batch with ¾ cup of lime juice and no cilantro (I would add it as a garnish). This bright yellow leche had silky, rich body and bright, balanced flavor. It was time to figure out how long to "cook" my fish in this new marinade.

The acid in a ceviche marinade denatures (unravels) and coagulates (clumps together) proteins, giving the fish an opaque appearance and a slightly firm—yet still tender—texture. When fish is marinated in pure lime juice, it turns opaque at the edges almost instantly and goes from tender to firm in minutes. In contrast, the leche's more tempered acidity affects the fish more slowly, providing a wider window of time for serving. For my snapper, I found 30 to 40 minutes to be the ideal marinating time. At around the 30-minute mark, it's just beginning to turn opaque and its texture is firm but easily yields as you bite into it. Those who prefer ceviche with a texture closer to that of fully cooked fish can marinate the fish for 45 minutes to 1 hour, though beyond that I found the texture dry and chalky.

Before cooking, my fellow test cooks and I often season proteins, including fish, with salt and then let them sit for a while to season them throughout. Was this step necessary here, considering I had sliced the fish thin and exposed more surface area to the marinade? I tossed my next batch of sliced snapper with 1 teaspoon of kosher salt and refrigerated it while I made my leche. After a 30-minute soak, I tasted the presalted ceviche alongside an unsalted version (I still seasoned each batch before serving). The results were clear: Salting enhanced the flavor of the fish; it stood out against the other bold flavors in the ceviche. Further testing showed that a mere 10 minutes was all it took for the salt to have a noticeable effect on the small pieces of fish.

With the fish settled, all that was left was sorting out the mix-ins: It's the layering of flavors and textures that makes a great ceviche. I liked the bright lime from the leche de tigre, but I thought it would be nice to bring in another citrus, so I added orange segments for sweet notes. Thinly sliced radishes added crisp texture and colorful contrast to the yellow leche and green cilantro. For salty, crunchy garnishes, I made a batch of popcorn (much to the delight of my colleagues) and set out a bowl of corn nuts. Both are traditional accompaniments to ceviche in Latin America.

Now that I've experienced this whole new world of elegant-yet-easy ceviches made with leche de tigre, I know what I'm making for dinner the next time it's too hot to cook.

—ANDREW JANJIGIAN, *Cook's Illustrated*

Peruvian Fish Ceviche with Radishes and Orange

SERVES 4 TO 6 AS A MAIN DISH OR 6 TO 8 AS AN APPETIZER

It is imperative that you use the freshest fish possible in this recipe. Do not use frozen fish. Sea bass, halibut, or grouper can be substituted for the snapper, if desired. *Ají amarillo* chile paste is fruity and moderately spicy; it can be found in the Latin section of grocery stores. If you can't find it, you can substitute 1 stemmed and seeded habanero chile. A citrus juicer will allow you to get the maximum amount of juice from each lime; we recommend the Chef'n FreshForce Citrus Juicer. Serving the popcorn and corn nuts separately allows diners to customize their ceviche to suit their taste. Serve the ceviche no longer than 1 hour after combining it with the sauce, or the acid will make the fish too dry.

1 pound skinless red snapper fillets, ½ inch thick
3½ teaspoons kosher salt, divided
¾ cup lime juice (6 limes)
3 tablespoons extra-virgin olive oil, divided
1 tablespoon ají amarillo chile paste
2 garlic cloves, peeled
3 oranges
8 ounces radishes, trimmed, halved, and sliced thin
¼ cup coarsely chopped fresh cilantro
1 cup corn nuts
1 cup lightly salted popcorn

1. Using sharp knife, cut fillets lengthwise into ½-inch-wide strips. Slice each strip crosswise ⅛ inch thick. Set aside ⅓ cup (2½ ounces) snapper pieces. Toss remaining snapper with 1 teaspoon salt and refrigerate for at least 10 minutes or up to 30 minutes.

2. While snapper refrigerates, process reserved snapper pieces, lime juice, 2 tablespoons oil, chile paste, garlic, and remaining 2½ teaspoons salt in blender until smooth, 30 to 60 seconds. Strain mixture through fine-mesh strainer set over large bowl, pressing on solids to extract as much liquid as possible. Discard solids. (Sauce can be refrigerated for up to 24 hours. It will separate slightly; whisk to recombine before proceeding with recipe.)

3. Cut away peel and pith from oranges. Holding fruit over bowl, use paring knife to slice between membranes to release segments. Cut orange segments into ¼-inch pieces. Add oranges, radishes, and salted snapper to bowl with sauce and toss to combine. Refrigerate for 30 to 40 minutes (for more-opaque fish, refrigerate for 45 minutes to 1 hour).

4. Add cilantro to ceviche and toss to combine. Portion ceviche into individual bowls and drizzle with remaining 1 tablespoon oil. Serve, passing corn nuts and popcorn separately.

PERUVIAN FISH CEVICHE WITH RADISHES AND ORANGE

CHAPTER 6

BREAKFAST, BRUNCH, AND BREADS

AMISH CINNAMON BREAD

✓ **WHY THIS RECIPE WORKS** Recipes for this sweet, cinnamony bread traditionally include two oddball ingredients: a sourdough starter shared among friends and vanilla pudding mix. Testing revealed that there was almost no flavor difference between breads baked with and without starter; the bread's decadent sweetness and substantial cinnamon flavor rendered any tang from the starter undetectable. Rather than use packaged vanilla pudding mix, we increased the sugar and added extra vanilla extract. Stirring in a generous dose of vegetable oil resulted in a bread with a soft, moist crumb without any gumminess. A cinnamon-sugar coating sprinkled into the pan and on top of the batter before baking gave the finished bread a crackly, sweet crust. To continue the tradition of sharing, we designed our recipe to make two loaves, so you'll have one to give to a friend.

Like those of many native Midwesterners, my best childhood memories revolve around food. One whiff of the intoxicating aroma of Amish cinnamon bread and I'm instantly transported back to my mom's kitchen—she spent the better part of my high school years baking the stuff. This is comfort food in the best sense: humble, heartwarming, and soul-soothing.

The premise of this sweet bread is simple: A neighbor or friend gives you a bag of special sourdough starter (a gooey, fermented mixture of flour, sugar, milk, and yeast) along with instructions to care for it over the course of 10 days. You use some of the starter, along with flour, sugar, milk, and, in many heirloom recipes, a package of vanilla pudding mix, to make a batch of bread. Then you portion off a bit of the starter to share with another friend, who repeats the process—think of it as an edible chain letter.

After I'd baked several existing recipes, my tasters and I thought that this bread, with its sweet, moist crumb and crackly cinnamon-sugar crust, tasted more like a quick bread than like most starter-based breads. But 10 days is anything but quick. I set out to develop a streamlined recipe that would capture the flavor, texture, and spirit of the original without a starter.

Yeasty starters generally have two main roles: leavening and providing a tangy flavor similar to that of sourdough. But since none of the recipes I found called for letting the dough (really a batter) rest or rise before baking, I knew that the yeast was doing little in the way of leavening. The recipes all called for baking powder and baking soda for lift. So I turned my attention to flavor: Was the starter adding any?

To find out, I baked two batches of bread—one with starter and one without. Surprisingly, we found almost no difference in flavor. The bread's decadent sweetness, along with a substantial shot of cinnamon, rendered any tang undetectable. With the starter in my rearview mirror, I set my sights on the next mystery ingredient: that instant pudding mix.

Several recipes I found called for adding a package of instant pudding mix to the batter, presumably for flavor. A call to my mom confirmed that it was, in fact, a standard ingredient. Don't get me wrong, I love instant pudding, but all things being equal, I'd rather not use too many prefab ingredients. Was it really necessary here?

I tried subbing in a bit more sugar and cornstarch—the two key ingredients in instant pudding mix—but I was disappointed to find out that unlike the modified starch found in many such mixes, which can contribute moistness to cakes in some recipes, the regular cornstarch dried things out.

So I ditched the cornstarch, increased my liquid (in this case milk for its rich, creamy flavor), and added a generous dose of vegetable oil (easier than butter) to give the bread a soft, moist crumb without a hint of gumminess. Bumping up the vanilla added another note to the bread's beautiful aroma.

I had achieved my goal of easy and quick cinnamon bread. The last thing to do was give a nod to friendship. After all, this bread is a perfect expression of how food should bring people together. So my recipe yields two loaves: one for you and one for a friend.

—HEATHER TOLMIE, *Cook's Country*

Amish Cinnamon Bread

MAKES 2 LOAVES

We developed this recipe using an 8½ by 4½-inch metal loaf pan. If you use a glass loaf pan, increase the baking time in step 3 to 1¼ hours to 1 hour 20 minutes; if you use a 9 by 5-inch loaf pan, start checking for doneness 5 minutes early. If you own only one loaf pan, refrigerate half the batter and set aside half the coating so you can bake a second loaf after turning out the first onto a wire rack to cool in step 4. Be sure to clean the loaf pan and brush it with oil before baking the second loaf.

AMISH CINNAMON BREAD

CINNAMON-SUGAR COATING

½ cup (3½ ounces) sugar

1 teaspoon ground cinnamon

2 teaspoons vegetable oil

BREAD

3¾ cups (18¾ ounces) all-purpose flour

3 cups (21 ounces) sugar

1 tablespoon ground cinnamon

1½ teaspoons baking powder

¾ teaspoon baking soda

¾ teaspoon table salt

1¾ cups milk

1⅓ cups vegetable oil

3 large eggs, lightly beaten

2 teaspoons vanilla extract

1. FOR THE CINNAMON-SUGAR COATING: Combine sugar and cinnamon in bowl. Brush two 8½ by 4½-inch loaf pans evenly with oil (1 teaspoon per pan). Add 2 tablespoons cinnamon-sugar coating to each prepared pan and shake and tilt pans until bottoms and sides are evenly coated. Set aside remaining ¼ cup cinnamon-sugar coating.

2. FOR THE BREAD: Adjust oven rack to middle position and heat oven to 325 degrees. Whisk flour, sugar, cinnamon, baking powder, baking soda, and salt together in large bowl. Whisk milk, oil, eggs, and vanilla together in second bowl. Stir milk mixture into flour mixture until just combined (batter will be lumpy).

3. Divide batter evenly between prepared pans (about 3¾ cups or 2¼ pounds batter per pan). Sprinkle remaining cinnamon-sugar coating evenly over top of batter (2 tablespoons per pan). Bake until paring knife inserted in centers of loaves comes out clean, 1 hour 5 minutes to 1 hour 10 minutes.

4. Let bread cool in pans on wire rack for 1 hour. Run paring knife around edges of pans to thoroughly loosen loaves. Working with 1 loaf at a time, tilt pan and gently remove bread. Serve warm or at room temperature. (Cooled bread can be wrapped in aluminum foil and stored at room temperature for up to 3 days.)

PITA BREAD

✓ **WHY THIS RECIPE WORKS** Our recipe creates tender, chewy pitas with perfect pockets, every time. We started with high-protein bread flour, which encouraged gluten formation and increased the pita's chew. A high hydration level and a generous amount of oil helped keep the pita tender, and honey added a touch of sweetness. After quickly making the dough in the food processor, we shaped it into balls and let them proof overnight in the refrigerator to develop complex flavor. We then rolled the dough balls into thin, even disks before baking them on a hot baking stone placed on the lowest oven rack, which ensured that they puffed up quickly and fully.

If your only experiences of pita have been the dry, flavorless rounds from the supermarket, you might wonder how this ancient bread—which dates back thousands of years—has persisted. But I can think of several reasons. The first being that good, fresh pita is a revelation: soft, tender, and pleasantly elastic, with flavor that's both faintly sweet and reminiscent of the hearth on which it was baked. It's got broad functionality, too: Tear it apart and use it as a vehicle for swiping up dips, wrap it around sandwich fillings, or take advantage of its built-in pocket and stuff it with falafel (see our recipe on page 64). And compared to the precision and skill required for other breads, making pita is a low-tech, casual endeavor—basically, you flatten a swath of dough into a thin disk, toss it onto a ripping-hot stone, and watch it puff.

Despite these compelling reasons to make pita at home, the bread's one drawback is that its soft, tender chew is extremely ephemeral. Within hours of being baked, the rounds turn dull and dry—hence the lackluster options at most supermarkets. Maybe there was a way to prolong some of that fresh-baked tenderness and moisture. I also discovered when I tried out a few recipes that pita's inherent simplicity leaves room for pitfalls such as breads that lack complexity and don't reliably puff. I would look for tricks for overcoming those issues, too.

Since pita is a form of flatbread like pizza, I wondered if the dough for our Thin-Crust Pizza would also work here. Using roughly the same ratios with some tweaks to bump up the dough's flavor—after all, I wouldn't be topping every inch of it with sauce and cheese—I combined bread flour, yeast, and honey (more complex-tasting than sugar) in a food processor and then added olive oil and ice-cold water, mixing briefly to form a dough. A 10-minute rest allowed the flour to hydrate and gluten formation to begin, at which point I added the salt (delaying this addition ensures good gluten development) and processed until a smooth dough formed, which took just minutes. I shaped the dough into eight balls, placed them on an oiled baking sheet, and let them proof overnight in the refrigerator. This long fermentation not only is convenient—you can make the dough one day and bake it the next—but also lets the yeast develop complex flavors without producing too much gas, which would result in an overly bubbly dough. It also makes for a less elastic dough that's easier to work with. Those bubbles lead to weak spots when the dough is rolled out—and, as I soon learned, weak spots are an enemy of properly pocketed pitas. The next day, I rolled out my pitas and baked them on a stone in a 425-degree oven for just a few minutes per side, until they had tanned and puffed.

Correction: until most of them had puffed, since several never did. Even those that did inflate were dry, so I took the surest route to increasing the perception of moisture: adding more fat. Starting cautiously, I doubled the 2 teaspoons I had been using and was rewarded with bread that stayed moist noticeably longer than my previous attempts. Encouraged, I kept going until I'd enriched the dough with ¼ cup of oil. Twenty-four hours later, the bread was still nicely moist and reheated impressively well, but its texture was not optimal in other ways. All that fat had compromised the dough's gluten development—that is, its ability to form a structural network—so much that the rounds lacked even a gentle chew, and my already-mediocre success rate with pitas that puffed dropped even lower.

Clearly, I'd overdone it. But backing down on the oil would mean losing the benefits of its rich flavor and moisture, so instead, I balanced its tenderizing effect by adding more water. Doing so made the flour proteins more mobile and increased the gluten's ability to form a stronger network during mixing. More water also created more steam once the breads were in the oven, which helped them puff—though only somewhat more reliably than previous batches had.

I couldn't solve the puffing problem until I figured out what causes the dough to inflate in the first place. The gist is that the oven's heat causes the dough's exterior to form a "skin" while steam from water in the dough causes the interior to expand. If the raw dough is perfectly smooth and taut, the skin that forms during baking is strong enough to withstand the steam pressure, and the dough expands like a balloon. But if the dough has creases, thin patches, or other imperfections, as mine often did, they create weak spots where air can escape, preventing the signature puff.

Knowing that, I was careful to roll the proofed dough balls into flat, smooth, evenly thick disks. If the dough was insufficiently or unevenly coated with flour, it would stick to the counter or the rolling pin and could easily crease. I found a better way of thoroughly coating the dough with flour: Instead of dusting the counter with flour, I put the flour in a bowl and turned the dough in it (see "A New Way to Coat Your Dough"). That way, the dough was completely coated with flour even before it hit the counter. I still needed to use additional flour on the counter, too, since the dough becomes sticky again as it is rolled out.

But even my perfectly smooth dough rounds wouldn't always puff properly; some would inflate halfway and then frustratingly collapse, as if the top layer was too heavy for the steam to lift. When I examined the collapsed pitas, I saw that the top skins were quite thick—likely the result of baking too quickly. So I moved the baking stone from the middle rack to the lowest rack, which created more space between the pitas and the reflected heat at the top of the oven.

At last, every single round puffed beautifully in just 4 minutes or less—and all were gobbled up minutes after I pulled them from the oven. With a recipe this simple, there's no reason to reach for those bland supermarket pitas again.

—ANDREW JANJIGIAN, *Cook's Illustrated*

NOTES FROM THE TEST KITCHEN

A NEW WAY TO COAT YOUR DOUGH

To ensure that the dough is thoroughly coated in flour before it's rolled out, we add flour to a bowl and turn each dough ball in it, brushing the excess right back into the bowl.

Pita Bread

We recommend weighing the flour and water. We prefer King Arthur bread flour for this recipe because of its high protein content. If using another bread flour, reduce the amount of water in the dough by 2 tablespoons (1 ounce). If you don't have a baking stone, bake the pitas on an overturned and preheated rimmed baking sheet. The pitas are best eaten within 24 hours of baking. Reheat leftover pitas by wrapping them in aluminum foil, placing them in a cold oven, setting the temperature to 300 degrees, and baking for 15 to 20 minutes.

2⅔ cups (14⅔ ounces) King Arthur bread flour
2¼ teaspoons instant or rapid-rise yeast
1⅓ cups (10½ ounces) ice water
¼ cup extra-virgin olive oil
4 teaspoons honey
1¼ teaspoons table salt
    Vegetable oil spray

1. Whisk flour and yeast together in bowl of stand mixer. Add ice water, oil, and honey on top of flour mixture. Fit stand mixer with dough hook and mix on low speed until all flour is moistened, 1 to 2 minutes. Let dough stand for 10 minutes.

2. Add salt to dough and mix on medium speed until dough forms satiny, sticky ball that clears sides of bowl, 6 to 8 minutes. Transfer dough to lightly oiled counter and knead until smooth, about 1 minute. Divide dough into 8 equal pieces (about 3⅜ ounces each). Shape dough pieces into tight, smooth balls and transfer, seam side down, to rimmed baking sheet coated with oil spray. Spray tops of balls lightly with oil spray, then cover tightly with plastic wrap and refrigerate for at least 16 hours or up to 24 hours.

3. One hour before baking pitas, adjust oven rack to lowest position, set baking stone on rack, and heat oven to 425 degrees.

4. Remove dough from refrigerator. Coat 1 dough ball generously on both sides with flour and place seam side down on well-floured counter. Use heel of your hand to press dough ball into 5-inch circle. Using rolling pin, gently roll into 7-inch circle, adding flour as necessary to prevent sticking. Roll slowly and gently to prevent any creasing. Repeat with second dough ball. Brush both sides of each dough round with pastry brush to remove any excess flour. Transfer dough rounds to unfloured peel, making sure side that was facing up when you began rolling is faceup again.

5. Slide both dough rounds carefully onto stone and bake until evenly inflated and lightly browned on undersides, 1 to 3 minutes. Using peel, slide pitas off stone and, using your hands or spatula, gently invert. (If pitas do not puff after 3 minutes, flip immediately to prevent overcooking.) Return pitas to stone and bake until lightly browned in center of second side, 1 minute. Transfer pitas to wire rack to cool, covering loosely with clean dish towel. Repeat shaping and baking with remaining 6 pitas in 3 batches. Let pitas cool for 10 minutes before serving.

EASIEST-EVER BISCUITS

✓ **WHY THIS RECIPE WORKS** We wanted to combine the ease of cream biscuits (which eliminate the step of cutting cold fat into dry ingredients) with the ease of drop biscuits (which skip the rolling and cutting) to create the easiest biscuits ever. But the most obvious solution—increasing the amount of cream in a cream biscuit recipe until the dough had a droppable consistency—produced greasy biscuits that spread too much. Instead of increasing the amount of cream, we found a way to increase its fluidity: We heated it to between 95 and 100 degrees, which melted the solid particles of butterfat dispersed throughout. This made a dough that was moister and scoopable and that rose up instead of spreading out in the oven, producing biscuits that were appropriately rich and tender but not greasy.

A fresh, warm biscuit instantly doubles the coziness quotient of practically anything you serve it with: chicken stew, vegetable soup, fried eggs, or—my favorite accompaniment—another fresh, warm biscuit. But mastering the traditional biscuit-making technique takes some practice.

First, you combine flour with salt, baking powder, and maybe a bit of sugar and then toss in cubes of cold butter, which you crumble and flatten until precisely the right amount of tiny butter flakes are strewn evenly throughout the flour. Next, you stir in cold milk or buttermilk until the mixture forms a shaggy dough. Finally, you transfer the mass of dough to the counter,

EASIEST-EVER BISCUITS

gently roll or pat it out, and cut out rounds with a sharp biscuit cutter before transferring them to the oven and baking them for about 15 minutes.

It's not difficult, but there are rules that must be followed, and all that mashing of the butter and rolling and cutting can get messy. Happily, there are shortcuts.

Want to skip cutting in the butter? Make cream biscuits: Replace both the butter and the milk with heavy cream. Thanks to the cream's generous butterfat content, the biscuits will be plenty rich and tender. This formula makes a pretty stiff dough, so you'll still have to roll and cut.

Want to skip the rolling and cutting? Make drop biscuits: Start by cutting the butter into the dry ingredients in the traditional way, but add extra buttermilk or milk so that the dough has a wetter consistency. Simply drop scoops of the soft dough onto the baking sheet and bake.

Cream biscuits tend to be more uniform and have a subtly layered structure, while drop biscuits are more craggy, with a beautifully tender, cake-like crumb. Why couldn't I have the benefits of both styles and make a dropped cream biscuit, aka "dream biscuit"? As that nickname suggests, it would be the easiest biscuit ever. I wondered if things could be as simple as adding more cream to a cream biscuit dough until it was loose enough to drop.

I whisked together 3 cups of all-purpose flour, a tablespoon of baking powder, and a teaspoon of salt and then experimented with adding enough cream to make a scoopable dough, which turned out to be 3 cups. I then deposited scoops of dough on a parchment-lined baking sheet and baked them in a 400-degree oven.

Sounds so easy that it makes you wonder why cookbooks aren't bursting with dropped-cream-biscuit recipes, right? Here's why: It didn't work. The dough mounds spread as they baked and came out looking like bland, lumpy cookies. They had a pleasantly milky flavor, a tender crumb, and a crisp exterior, but they left thick, greasy spots on the parchment and a slick on my fingers.

Clearly, the additional moisture and fat from the extra cream were the source of these problems. But I couldn't reduce the amount of cream—that would bring me right back where I'd started, with an overly dry dough. Maybe I was asking for the impossible: a dough that was moist and scoopable before baking but that acted like a drier, less fatty dough in the oven, rising instead of spreading out. And I was expecting that a single ingredient, cream, would perform this miracle.

That was when I had a revelation. Cream isn't a single ingredient, it's two: water (with a little protein and sugar mixed in) and solid fat. The fat particles in cream are so minute that we don't perceive them as solid, and they were stowing away in the cream only to melt in the heat of the oven, making the biscuits greasy and, in combination with the water in the cream, causing them to spread.

A new thunderbolt struck: What if I melted the fat by warming the cream before I mixed it into the dough? That sound you just heard was the collective gasp of generations of horrified Southern bakers, but hear me out: Maybe heating the cream would increase its fluidity enough to enable me to make a scoopable dough with less of it. If so, that could potentially fix both the spreading and the greasiness.

My first attempt failed pretty spectacularly. I heated 2 cups of cream to 160 degrees, and as I stirred it into the dry ingredients, its heat and moisture activated the baking powder, causing the dough to expand so boisterously that it defied my frantic attempts to shovel it into the 1/3-cup measuring cup. By the time the dough mounds went into the oven, the baking powder was spent, so the biscuits didn't rise. But they didn't spread either, and they weren't objectionably fatty.

A bit of research revealed that the fat in cream liquefies between 90 and 95 degrees and the acids in baking powder are activated at about 140 degrees. Maybe all I had to do was make sure the cream was above 95 degrees but below 140 degrees.

I cautiously heated the cream only to body temperature and then stirred it into the dry ingredients. The dough came together easily, neither too dry nor too wet, and with no riotous inflation. I scooped and I baked. And I prevailed. Mostly.

These biscuits held their shape beautifully; were fluffy, not flat; and were pleasantly rich without being greasy. Their flavor, however, was a bit bland. Having already flouted the most sacred law of biscuit making by introducing a warm ingredient, I took a firm stand on the side of sugar and added a little to the dry ingredients. I also added a bit of baking soda, not for lift but for its slightly mineral-y tang.

You can serve biscuits with almost anything, and with a recipe this quick and easy, why wouldn't you?

—ANDREA GEARY, *Cook's Illustrated*

Easiest-Ever Biscuits

SERVES 10

These biscuits come together very quickly, so start heating your oven before gathering your ingredients. We like to brush the biscuits with melted butter, but if you're serving the biscuits with a rich accompaniment such as sausage gravy, you can skip this step.

- 3 cups (15 ounces) all-purpose flour
- 4 teaspoons sugar
- 1 tablespoon baking powder
- ¼ teaspoon baking soda
- 1¼ teaspoons table salt
- 2 cups heavy cream
- 2 tablespoons unsalted butter, melted (optional)

1. Adjust oven rack to upper-middle position and heat oven to 450 degrees. Line rimmed baking sheet with parchment paper. In medium bowl, whisk together flour, sugar, baking powder, baking soda, and salt. Microwave cream until just warmed to body temperature (95 to 100 degrees), 60 to 90 seconds, stirring halfway through microwaving. Stir cream into flour mixture until soft, uniform dough forms.

2. Spray ⅓-cup dry measuring cup with vegetable oil spray. Drop level scoops of batter 2 inches apart on prepared sheet (biscuits should measure about 2½ inches wide and 1¼ inches tall). Respray measuring cup after every 3 or 4 scoops. If portions are misshapen, use your fingertips to gently reshape dough into level cylinders. Bake until tops are light golden brown, 10 to 12 minutes, rotating sheet halfway through baking. Brush hot biscuits with melted butter, if using. Serve warm. (Biscuits can be stored in zipper-lock bag at room temperature for up to 24 hours. Reheat biscuits in 300-degree oven for 10 minutes.)

NOTES FROM THE TEST KITCHEN

WHY WE "MELT" THE CREAM IN OUR BISCUITS

Fridge-cold cream is a combination of water, protein, and sugar, with tiny particles of solid butterfat suspended throughout. By warming the cream just enough to melt the fat particles (but not enough to activate the baking powder when the cream is mixed into the dry ingredients), we turn it into pure liquid. This means we can use less cream to create a dough that is still loose enough to scoop and drop but that doesn't spread too much or bake up greasy.

CHALLAH

✓ WHY THIS RECIPE WORKS To make challah dough that was moist but malleable, we combined a short rest before kneading with a long rising time; this built a sturdy but stretchy gluten network that made the dough easy to handle. We also employed an Asian bread-baking technique called *tangzhong* by incorporating a cooked flour-water paste into the dough; this bound up water in the dough so that it was moist but not sticky. Pointing the four dough strands in different directions, rather than arranging them parallel to one another, made them easier to keep track of during braiding. Brushing an egg wash—lightly salted to make the eggs more fluid—over the braided dough encouraged browning as the loaf baked.

I think I speak for all my colleagues when I say we occasionally doubt our ability to add value to a cooking technique. But challah was the assignment that really gave me pause.

That's partly because the enriched, glossy braid is a cultural heavyweight. More than just a fixture at Ashkenazi Jewish holiday tables, it's a biblically significant bread steeped in age-old rituals, symbolism, and strong opinions. When I polled a few well-versed colleagues and experts about what qualities challah should have, I received a flurry of disparate answers: The crumb should be fluffy or densely chewy. It should taste rich and sweet or only slightly so. It should have raisins—or definitely not have raisins.

There's also the fact that countless challah recipes have been published, and even more get passed through the diaspora via word of mouth and muscle memory. So I wasn't sure what I—someone who really enjoys challah but didn't grow up making it—could contribute to the conversation.

But as it turned out, my inexperience was an asset. When I shaped and baked a few loaves to familiarize myself with the process, I zeroed in on challenges that might not faze a seasoned challah baker. For example: the relationship between the workability of the dough and the texture of the baked bread. Moist doughs sagged and stuck together, making a messy braid but resulting in a soft, tender crumb. Recipes that tried to solve the problem produced drier doughs that were easy to handle but baked up dense and a bit tough. Then there was the braiding technique itself: Even the simplest weave takes practice, and the loaf might still bake up misshapen.

CHALLAH

What I wanted was a plush, resilient crumb that struck that perfect—but rarely achieved—balance of moderate sweetness and richness; a tall, tidy braid; and a recipe that would win over rookies and experts alike.

As breads go, challah isn't difficult to make. All you do is combine bread flour, instant yeast, eggs and/or egg yolks, water, sugar, salt, and vegetable oil in a mixer. Once you have a cohesive mass, knead the dough until it is smooth and pliable and then cover it and let it rise until doubled in size—the visual cue that the yeast has consumed sugars in the dough and released gas that causes the dough to expand. Then you press out the air, which eliminates large air bubbles, encourages a fine crumb, and redistributes the yeast and sugars so they can continue their activity during the second rise. Finally, you divide the dough into even lengths that you roll into long ropes. You braid the strands, let the dough rise again, brush the surface with an egg wash, and bake it until the crust shines like polished mahogany.

Hoping that three whole eggs and ¼ cup of oil would amply enrich the dough, I homed in on my main focus: how to turn this moist dough into something more workable. The consistency of a dough is measured in percent hydration—the amount of water relative to the amount of flour. During baking, the water turns to steam, which acts as a leavening agent by opening up the crumb so that the bread is light and soft. The hydration levels of the recipes I found ranged from 45 percent to more than 60 percent, or about 4.5 to 6 parts water to every 10 parts flour. Doughs at the low end of that range were drier than your average bagel dough, presumably to make them easy to handle, but nobody wants challah with bagel-like density. The nicest loaves I made came in at 55 to 60 percent, so I considered that my benchmark and got to work on a seemingly impossible task: making a moist dough handle like a drier, firmer dough.

I started by asking myself what helps a dough become less sticky so it's easier to handle. Part of the answer was a stronger gluten network, the mesh of interlinked proteins that forms when water and flour are combined, giving bread its structure. Up to a point, the more extensive and tightly organized this mesh is, the firmer and less sticky the dough. With this in mind, I introduced a French bread-baking trick called autolyse, a brief rest between mixing and kneading that we often use in bread doughs. During this rest, enzymes in the flour snip the gluten proteins, helping them uncoil so that they can more efficiently line up and link together.

With the autolyse, my dough was firmer but not very extensible; when I rolled out the lengths for braiding, they snapped back or even tore if I applied too much pressure. So I next looked closely at the dough's first rise, known as bulk fermentation. This long rest is crucial for building structure because more gluten develops. However, resting times vary, and I had admittedly tried a relatively quick 1-hour rest. When I tacked on another 30 minutes, there was no more snapping back or tearing. But the dough was still sticky.

This might have been the point where I conceded that challah is better left to the experts. But I realized that the qualities I wanted in the dough—malleable but moist—were the same ones we'd wanted in our recipes for Fluffy Dinner Rolls and Sticky Buns. And the solution in those cases—an Asian bread-baking technique called *tangzhong*—couldn't have been further from challah tradition.

Free water that hasn't been absorbed by starch is what makes dough sticky. The gist of the tangzhong method is to cook some of the water in the recipe with some of the flour. Heat causes the starch molecules to separate from each other and absorb more water than they would at room temperature. The resulting gel is then added to the dough. The water trapped in the gel won't contribute to stickiness, and the upshot is a dough that feels drier and is easier to handle.

Mixing the gel into the dough made it much easier to handle, and when I tried again after removing two of the egg whites (a source of water), the dough firmed up even more. I also decided to see if I could decrease the oil, which softens the dough, and found I could go down by half and still produce challah that was cotton-candy plush. (But about those raisins: They robbed the dough of its moisture, turning the baked crumb dry. They were officially out.)

For a bakery-worthy braid, I started by rolling the dough into four long, even ropes. Then, using a technique I learned from veteran challah baker Mike Lombardo at Rosenfeld's Bagels in Newton, Massachusetts, I pointed the dough strands in different directions and started braiding—this method made it easy to keep track of the strands and produced an intricate-looking loaf (see "How to Braid Challah," page 192).

I lightly covered the braid with plastic wrap to prevent it from drying out during its second rise. When it was fully proofed, I moved it to a rimmed baking sheet, brushed it with a lightly salted egg wash, and baked the challah in a 350-degree oven for half an hour. The braid was tall, but the underside of the loaf was too dark. Going forward, I baked the bread on a pair of nested baking sheets, which created an air gap that insulated the underside from burning.

The statuesque, burnished braid hid a crumb that was golden, fluffy, and gently elastic—perfect for slicing thick and slathering with butter. (Leftovers, if there are any, make exceptional French toast or stuffing). Maybe the challah-baking tradition has room for this new-school baker after all.

—LAN LAM, *Cook's Illustrated*

Challah

MAKES 1 LOAF

We strongly recommend weighing the flour for this recipe. This dough will be firmer and drier than most bread doughs, which makes it easy to braid. Some friction is necessary for rolling and braiding the ropes, so resist the urge to dust your counter with flour. If your counter is too narrow to stretch the ropes, slightly bend the pieces at the 12 o'clock and 6 o'clock positions. Bake this loaf on two nested baking sheets to keep the bottom of the loaf from getting too dark.

NOTES FROM THE TEST KITCHEN

HOW TO BRAID CHALLAH
Our unconventional braiding method is easier to follow than those of most recipes and produces a loftier loaf.

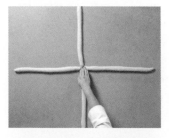

1. Arrange ropes in plus-sign shape, with 4 ends overlapping in center by ½ inch. Firmly press center of cross into counter to seal ropes to each other and to counter.

5. Lift rope at 3 o'clock and, working toward yourself, bring over braid and place in 8 o'clock position.

2. Lift rope at 12 o'clock, bring over center, and place in 5 o'clock position.

6. Adjust ropes so they are at 12, 3, 6, and 9 o'clock positions. Repeat steps 2 through 6.

3. Lift rope at 6 o'clock, bring over center, and place in 12 o'clock position.

7. Continue braiding, working toward yourself, until you can no longer braid. Loaf will naturally list to 1 side.

4. Lift rope at 9 o'clock, bring over center, and place in 4 o'clock position.

8. Pinch ends of ropes together. Tuck both ends under braid.

FLOUR PASTE

½ cup water

3 tablespoons bread flour

DOUGH

1 large egg plus 2 large yolks

¼ cup water

2 tablespoons vegetable oil

2¾ cups (15⅛ ounces) bread flour

1¼ teaspoons instant or rapid-rise yeast

¼ cup (1¾ ounces) sugar

1 teaspoon table salt

Vegetable oil spray

EGG WASH

1 large egg

Pinch table salt

1 tablespoon sesame seeds or poppy seeds (optional)

1. FOR THE FLOUR PASTE: Whisk water and flour in bowl until no lumps remain. Microwave, whisking every 20 seconds, until mixture thickens to stiff, smooth, pudding-like consistency that forms mound when dropped from end of whisk into bowl, 40 to 80 seconds.

2. FOR THE DOUGH: In bowl of stand mixer, whisk flour paste, egg and yolks, water, and oil until well combined. Add flour and yeast. Fit stand mixer with dough hook and mix on low speed until all flour is moistened, 3 to 4 minutes. Let stand for 20 minutes.

3. Add sugar and salt and mix on medium speed for 9 minutes (dough will be quite firm and dry). Transfer dough to counter and lightly spray now-empty mixer bowl with oil spray. Knead dough briefly to form ball and return it to prepared bowl. Lightly spray dough with oil spray and cover bowl with plastic wrap. Let dough rise until about doubled in volume, about 1½ hours.

4. Line rimmed baking sheet with parchment paper and nest in second rimmed baking sheet. Transfer dough to counter and press into 8-inch square, expelling as much air as possible. Cut dough in half lengthwise to form 2 rectangles. Cut each rectangle in half lengthwise to form 4 equal strips of dough. Roll 1 strip of dough into 16-inch rope. Continue rolling, tapering ends, until rope is 18 inches long. Repeat with remaining dough strips. Arrange ropes in plus-sign shape, with 4 ends overlapping in center by ½ inch. Firmly press center of cross into counter to seal ropes to each other and to counter.

5. Lift rope at 12 o'clock, bring over center, and place in 5 o'clock position. Lift rope at 6 o'clock, bring over center, and place in 12 o'clock position.

6. Lift rope at 9 o'clock, bring over center, and place in 4 o'clock position. Lift rope at 3 o'clock and, working toward yourself, bring over braid and place in 8 o'clock position. Adjust ropes so they are at 12, 3, 6, and 9 o'clock positions.

7. Repeat steps 5 and 6, working toward yourself, until you can no longer braid. Loaf will naturally list to 1 side.

8. Pinch ends of ropes together and tuck both ends under braid. Carefully transfer braid to prepared sheets. Cover loosely with plastic and let rise until dough does not spring back fully when gently pressed with your knuckle, about 3 hours.

9. FOR THE EGG WASH: Thirty minutes before baking, adjust oven rack to middle position and heat oven to 350 degrees. Whisk together egg and salt. Brush loaf with egg wash and sprinkle with sesame seeds, if using. Bake until loaf is deep golden brown and registers at least 195 degrees, 35 to 40 minutes. Let cool on sheets for 20 minutes. Transfer loaf to wire rack and let cool completely before slicing, about 2 hours.

BAGEL BREAD

WHY THIS RECIPE WORKS We absolutely love bagels, with their dense but soft interiors surrounded by chewy exteriors. But we don't love that they don't fit in some toasters and don't lend themselves well to sandwich making. Given those drawbacks, we were after a sliceable bread loaf with the signature chewy exterior and dense but soft interior of a bagel. After poking around online, we landed on bagel bread. To develop our version, we started with a basic bagel dough made with bread flour. We kneaded this dough for 10 minutes in a stand mixer to develop gluten and ensure a chewy texture. Then came the odd part: Boiling the risen, not-yet-baked loaf in a solution of water, baking soda, and corn syrup helped the bread achieve a lovely brown crust and gently set its exterior so that when the dough continued to rise in the oven, it had a chewy crumb. Making slashes across the top of the dough allowed steam to escape as it baked and expanded, and coating the dough with a homemade "everything" topping brought it to a place of bagel-like bliss.

BAGEL BREAD

There's nothing better than a fresh bagel—a dense but soft interior surrounded by a chewy exterior. But many bagels fall short on two important physical challenges: fitting into a toaster and creating a sandwich that you can actually fit into your mouth. We set out to find a work-around and, after a few clicks online, came across the idea of bagel bread.

The promise was simple: a sliceable loaf with all the qualities of a fresh bagel, including that signature chewy exterior. The versions we saw were adorable, like a stack of bagels turned sideways. And following existing recipes, which called for boiling chunks of yeasted, risen dough and then lining those up on their sides in a loaf pan to bake, gave us great-looking results.

But as the saying goes, you can't always judge a book by its cover. The bread was certainly camera-ready, but when we sliced into it, we discovered that its texture ranged from bready (good) to pasty and gray (not good) at the seams where the separate chunks met. We wanted the good looks but a more consistent crumb all the way through the loaf.

We started back at the beginning, with a basic bagel dough made with bread flour and a bit of corn syrup. To develop the gluten we needed for chewiness, we kneaded the dough in the stand mixer for a full 10 minutes. Next, we shaped the dough into a loaf and let it rise for an hour.

And then, rather than pinch off individual chunks of dough and boil them separately, we did something shocking: We boiled the entire loaf. Yes, it felt weird, but it got us the exterior "skin" we needed. This boiling step also gently sets the exterior so that when the bread continues to rise in the oven, it rises into a tighter, chewier crumb. Eventually, we settled on 1½ minutes in boiling water bolstered with baking soda and corn syrup to help the loaf achieve a lovely brown exterior.

Postboil, the loaf looked absurd—mangled and odd. But once it was tucked into a loaf pan (with the help of a pair of slotted spoons or a spider skimmer), we said a short prayer and slid it into the oven. The loaf quickly recovered its dome, rising in the oven's heat to create a classic sandwich-bread loaf shape. Tasting the baked-and-cooled bread assured us we were on the right track: The bread was chewy and just dense enough, with an even texture throughout.

But it lacked that handsome appearance we'd fallen in love with. To achieve it, we decided to slash the loaf between boiling and baking to create a series of peaks and valleys across the top. Just shallow slashes would suffice, since they would grow deeper during that oven-spring moment.

Bonus: This slashing step wasn't just for the sake of good looks; it also created more surface area to catch our "everything" topping: sesame seeds, poppy seeds, dried minced garlic, dried onion flakes, and kosher salt.

A simple egg wash applied before baking helped the topping stick; we also dusted the pan with more of the topping for complete coverage (some of it stuck to the pan, but we were willing to sacrifice a few seeds if it meant 360-degree coverage).

The final tests: slicing, toasting, and building sandwiches. Tasters agreed: This bread had the flavor and texture of a first-rate bagel as well as the flexibility of a sandwich loaf.

—MORGAN BOLLING AND KATIE LEAIRD,
Cook's Country

Bagel Bread

MAKES 1 LOAF

We prefer bread flour here; its higher protein content gives this loaf a chewy yet light texture. We developed this recipe using King Arthur Unbleached Bread Flour, but Gold Medal Bread Flour will also work. The test kitchen's preferred loaf pan measures 8½ by 4½ inches; if you use a 9 by 5-inch loaf pan, start checking for doneness 5 minutes early.

TOPPING

- 2 teaspoons sesame seeds
- 2 teaspoons poppy seeds
- 2 teaspoons dried minced garlic
- 2 teaspoons dried onion flakes
- 2 teaspoons kosher salt

BREAD

- Vegetable oil spray
- 3 cups (16½ ounces) bread flour
- 2¼ teaspoons instant or rapid-rise yeast
- ¼ cup light corn syrup, divided
- 1½ tablespoons kosher salt
- 1½ teaspoons baking soda
- 1 large egg, lightly beaten

1. FOR THE TOPPING: Combine all ingredients in bowl; set aside.

2. FOR THE BREAD: Spray 8½ by 4½-inch loaf pan with oil spray. Whisk flour and yeast together in bowl of stand mixer. Fit stand mixer with dough hook. Add 1¼ cups (10 ounces) water and 2 tablespoons corn syrup. Mix on medium-low speed until dough comes together and no dry flour remains, about 2 minutes. Turn off mixer, cover bowl with dish towel or plastic wrap, and let dough stand for 10 minutes.

3. Add salt to dough and knead on medium speed until dough is smooth and elastic, about 10 minutes. Turn out dough onto clean counter and form into ball by pinching and pulling dough edges under so top is smooth. Flip dough smooth side down.

4. Pat dough into 6-inch square and position parallel to edge of counter. Fold top edge of dough down to midline, pressing to seal. Fold bottom edge of dough up to meet first seam at midline and press to seal. Fold dough in half so top and bottom edges meet; pinch together to seal. Flip dough seam side down and roll into 8-inch log.

5. Transfer dough, seam side down, to prepared pan. Spray top of dough lightly with oil spray, then cover loosely with plastic. Let sit in warm place until dough rises to lip of pan, about 1 hour.

6. Adjust oven rack to middle position and heat oven to 350 degrees. Line large plate with clean dish towel. Bring 2 quarts water to boil in Dutch oven. Once boiling, add baking soda and remaining 2 tablespoons corn syrup.

7. Gently tip dough out of pan onto counter. Lift dough, gently lower into boiling water, and cook for 45 seconds per side. Using spider skimmer or 2 slotted spoons, transfer dough to prepared plate. Gently fold dish towel over dough to wick away excess moisture on top. Let sit until cool enough to handle, about 2 minutes.

8. Respray now-empty pan with oil spray. Add 2 tablespoons topping to pan and shake until bottom and sides of pan are evenly coated. Transfer dough, seam side down, to prepared pan, pushing it in at edges to fit if necessary.

9. Using paring knife, make six ¼-inch-deep slashes crosswise along surface of dough, about 1 inch apart. Brush dough with egg, then sprinkle with remaining 4 teaspoons topping. Bake until golden brown and loaf registers at least 200 degrees, about 45 minutes. Let bread cool completely in pan, about 2 hours. Remove from pan, slice, and serve, toasted if desired.

ENGLISH MUFFINS

✔ **WHY THIS RECIPE WORKS** For quicker English muffins that didn't sacrifice flavor or the requisite nooks and crannies, we needed to employ a few tricks. We used honey and warm milk for flavor and to help jump-start the yeast, speeding up the rising process. Bread flour provided some extra protein, resulting in chewier muffins. Finally, we seared the muffins on both sides in a skillet before finishing them in the oven. Be sure not to slice these open with a knife; you want to split them with a fork to ensure the perfect interior texture.

Time to bust a myth: English muffins are not hard to make at home. You don't need special equipment or even much time to turn out English muffins that are fresher and better than any that you could buy at the supermarket.

To develop the best recipe, I first had to survey existing recipes for English muffins. The basic process was this: Mix flour, yeast, salt, and milk, and then let the dough rise. Shape it into muffins, dust them with cornmeal, and let them rise again. Next, sear the muffins in a pan before finishing them off in the oven.

But there was a lot of variance in the details among recipes. Some call for letting the dough rise in the refrigerator for two days to develop extra yeasty flavor and big air pockets; others call for complex shaping techniques you'd need to be a pastry chef to understand. I hoped to streamline the process without shortchanging the flavor or texture.

While I wasn't happy with any of the recipes I tried, a few did have elements worth borrowing. One recipe included honey in the usual mix of ingredients; the honey boosted the flavor and gave the muffins a nice golden color. Another employed warm milk to help jump-start the yeast and thus reduce the rising time—a great idea. And finally, some recipes called for bread flour, which has more protein than all-purpose flour and thus results in chewier baked goods, a definite bonus here.

In terms of streamlining the recipe, I was hoping to avoid two rises (one before portioning the dough and one after), but it turned out that both rises were necessary for nicely pocketed muffins that were light yet chewy. The good news was that each rise needed to be only 1 hour (although the second one can be longer if you refrigerate the dough).

Another trick I came up with: after the first rise, using a greased ¼-cup measuring cup to simultaneously scoop, portion, and shape the dough into squat cylinders that rise into the signature English muffin shape.

To give the outsides the proper brown hue, I seared the muffins in a nonstick skillet (the dough stuck to traditional steel skillets, and it was too hard to regulate the temperature in cast iron). Once they were browned, I transferred the muffins to a baking sheet and baked them in a 350-degree oven for just 10 minutes.

After working out the details over 40 tests, I was finally pleased with my easy method and fantastic results. One word to the wise: For the best interior texture, don't use a knife. Use the tines of a fork to separate the halves before toasting.

—ASHLEY MOORE, *Cook's Country*

English Muffins

MAKES 8 MUFFINS

For the best texture, use a fork to split the muffins. Don't heat the milk higher than 110 degrees; doing so will kill the yeast and result in squat muffins.

2¾	cups (15⅛ ounces) bread flour
1	tablespoon instant or rapid-rise yeast
1¼	teaspoons table salt
1	cup plus 6 tablespoons (11 ounces) warm whole milk (110 degrees)
2	tablespoons honey
5	tablespoons cornmeal, divided
2	tablespoons unsalted butter, cut into 2 pieces, divided

1. Combine flour, yeast, and salt in large bowl. In second bowl, whisk warm milk and honey together. Add milk mixture to flour mixture and stir until no pockets of dry flour remain. Cover bowl with plastic wrap and let dough rise in warm place until doubled in size, about 1 hour.

2. Line rimmed baking sheet with parchment paper and spray with vegetable oil spray. Sprinkle prepared sheet with ¼ cup cornmeal. Using greased ¼-cup dry measuring cup, divide dough into 8 heaping ¼-cup portions. Using your lightly greased hands, gently cup each portion of dough and shape into even 2- to 2½-inch-diameter round about 1 inch tall, then place

NOTES FROM THE TEST KITCHEN

MAKING ENGLISH MUFFINS AT HOME ISN'T HARD— HERE'S HOW WE DO IT

1. PORTION THE DOUGH
Using greased ¼-cup dry measuring cup, make 8 dough rounds.

2. BROWN ON THE STOVE
Cook dough rounds in butter in skillet until both sides are browned.

3. BAKE IN THE OVEN
Place browned muffins on baking sheet and bake in 350-degree oven.

4. CHECK FOR DONENESS Use digital thermometer to see if muffins register 205 to 210 degrees.

FRESH MUFFINS FOR BREAKFAST

Do you want to make the dough rounds ahead so that all you have to do when you wake up is cook and then toast them? Here's how.

The Night Before
Make dough, let it rise, portion and shape dough, place on rimmed baking sheet, cover sheet with plastic wrap, and let rounds rise for at least 12 hours in refrigerator.

In the Morning
Brown both sides of chilled rounds in butter in nonstick skillet, then finish cooking (about 10 minutes) in oven. Let muffins cool before toasting.

on prepared sheet. Sprinkle tops of rounds with remaining 1 tablespoon cornmeal. Cover sheet loosely with greased plastic and let rounds rise in warm place until puffy and nearly doubled in size, about 1 hour.

3. Adjust oven rack to middle position and heat oven to 350 degrees. Melt 1 tablespoon butter in 12-inch nonstick skillet over medium heat. Add 4 dough rounds and cook until deep golden brown on first side, about 2 minutes, moving rounds as needed for even browning. Flip muffins and cook until deep golden brown on second side, about 2 minutes, pressing down lightly with spatula if muffins begin to rise unevenly. Transfer muffins to clean baking sheet. Wipe skillet clean with paper towels and repeat with remaining 1 tablespoon butter and remaining 4 dough rounds.

4. Bake muffins until centers register 205 to 210 degrees, 10 to 12 minutes. Let muffins cool completely on wire rack. Using fork, split muffins. Toast and serve.

TO MAKE AHEAD: In step 2, let dough rounds rise in refrigerator for at least 12 hours, until nearly doubled in size (you can refrigerate them for up to 48 hours). When ready to bake, proceed with step 3.

OATMEAL-RAISIN BREAD

✔ **WHY THIS RECIPE WORKS** Flavored with oatmeal and sweet raisins, this bread is great toasted for breakfast or perfect with coffee for an afternoon snack. Our first goal was to get the oat flavor to really shine. Mixing the oatmeal into the dough toward the end of kneading was the perfect way to incorporate it without creating big clumps of oats. We tried adding oat flour to the dough as well, but the flour absorbed so much water that the loaf turned out dry. Replacing a small amount of the bread flour with whole-wheat flour complemented the earthy flavor of the oats and ensured that the crumb stayed light and moist. We found that the raisins provided all the sweetness the bread needed, so we left out the sugar in the dough. For a pretty finish, we misted the loaf with water and then sprinkled more oats on top. Baking the bread in a preheated Dutch oven created a beautifully even crumb and a bronzed crust without the need for specialty equipment.

Why bake bread in a Dutch oven? As it turns out, it's all about steam. When bread first goes into the oven, it undergoes one last rapid rise as the heat activates the yeast. The yeast produces gas, which gets trapped as air bubbles in the dough, giving it lift and opening up its structure. At the same time, the outside of the loaf is cooking faster than the inside. If the exterior cooks too quickly, it can stiffen enough to prevent the dough from expanding past a certain point, limiting its rise. Adding steam during the first few minutes of baking keeps the crust soft for longer, allowing for a higher rise and a more open crumb. Some of the steam also condenses in tiny droplets on the surface of the bread, dissolving some of the natural sugars present in the dough. When the steam evaporates, it leaves behind these sugars, which harden and caramelize to produce that characteristic artisan-style shatteringly crisp crust.

Bakeries have professional-grade bread ovens that can inject steam directly into the oven during baking, but home bakers have to do without. Some bread recipes call for creating your own steam by misting the oven with a spray bottle or by filling a baking sheet with water and placing it beneath the dough on the lower oven rack, but these methods can be tricky to get just right. That's where the Dutch oven comes in. A Dutch oven's tight-fitting lid is perfect for trapping the steam that rises from the baking dough, creating a steamy oven-within-an-oven.

The test kitchen has used this bread-baking method before, but I wanted to take it in an unexpected direction. Inspired by my love of oatmeal-raisin bread, I set out to see if I could create a bakery-style version in my Dutch oven.

My first step was to nail down the dough. I wanted to infuse my bread with as much oat flavor as possible. The obvious way to do this was by using more oats, but there was a limit: Using too many would interfere with the bread's gluten formation and result in a stodgy, dense loaf. Using bread flour as a base, I determined that I could add up to ¾ cup of oats to the dough without interfering with its structure. An additional ¼ cup of oats pressed onto the outside of the loaf added visual appeal and a nutty-tasting crust.

Still, I wanted my bread to have a stronger oat flavor. Instead of adding more oats to the dough, I experimented with other whole grains. I tried replacing some of the bread flour with whole-wheat flour, wheat germ, or oat flour. The wheat germ was too pungent, and oat

OATMEAL-RAISIN BREAD

flour made the bread dry. Whole-wheat flour delivered the nutty flavor I'd been lacking, and I found that I could replace up to ½ cup of the bread flour with it without changing the texture of the bread. Enriching the dough with butter and whole milk gave the crumb an appealing tenderness and a richer flavor without making it crumbly.

It was time to try out my recipe in a Dutch oven. This proved to be trickier than I'd anticipated. Getting the temperature of the Dutch oven just right was imperative. It needed to be hot enough to produce steam quickly, but not so hot that the bottom of the loaf scorched. Starting the dough in a cold oven meant that it didn't rise very much, resulting in a squat, heavy loaf. Next, I tried preheating the Dutch oven before placing the dough inside. I baked the dough covered for 15 minutes before removing the lid to allow the steam to escape and the crust to dry out. This time it rose beautifully, but the bottom burned. After further trials, I wondered if the temperature of the Dutch oven wasn't to blame for the burnt bottom. My original recipe called for 2 tablespoons of brown sugar, but contact with the hot Dutch oven made the added sugar caramelize and burn. Leaving it out in my next trial turned out just fine; in fact, I found that the raisins added all the sweetness I wanted. And this time, the bottom was just browned, not burnt. The crackly crust rose high over a hearty but light crumb dotted with raisins. This bread was pure, simple goodness, ready to be smeared with butter or jam or eaten on its own.

—ANNE WOLF, *America's Test Kitchen Books*

NOTES FROM THE TEST KITCHEN

MIXING AND KNEADING THE DOUGH

1. Whisk dry ingredients together in bowl of stand mixer. Whisk wet ingredients in 2-cup liquid measuring cup.

2. With mixer on low speed, slowly add wet ingredients to dry ingredients and mix until cohesive dough starts to form and no dry flour remains.

3. Increase speed to medium-low and knead until dough is smooth and elastic. Add raisins, then add oatmeal and mix until incorporated. Transfer to lightly greased large bowl or container and cover with plastic wrap.

4. After dough has risen for 30 minutes, use greased bowl scraper to fold dough over itself by gently lifting and folding edge of dough toward middle. Turn bowl 45 degrees and repeat folding 7 more times.

Oatmeal-Raisin Bread

MAKES 1 LOAF

Do not substitute quick or instant oats in this recipe.

- 1 cup (3 ounces) old-fashioned rolled oats, divided
- ¾ cup (6 ounces) water, room temperature
- 2 cups (11 ounces) bread flour
- ½ cup (2¾ ounces) whole-wheat flour
- 2 teaspoons instant or rapid-rise yeast
- 1½ teaspoons table salt
- 1 cup (8 ounces) whole milk, room temperature
- 3 tablespoons unsalted butter, melted
- ½ cup raisins

1. Microwave ¾ cup oats and room-temperature water in large bowl, covered, stirring occasionally, until oats are softened and water is completely absorbed, about 5 minutes; let cool completely.

2. Whisk bread flour, whole-wheat flour, yeast, and salt together in bowl of stand mixer. Whisk milk and melted butter together in 2-cup liquid measuring cup. Fit stand mixer with dough hook and mix on low speed, slowly adding milk mixture to flour mixture, until cohesive dough starts to form and no dry flour remains, about 2 minutes, scraping down bowl as needed.

3. Increase speed to medium-low and knead until dough is smooth and elastic and clears sides of bowl, about 6 minutes. Reduce speed to low and slowly add raisins, then add oatmeal, 2 tablespoons at a time, and mix until mostly incorporated, about 3 minutes. Transfer dough to lightly greased large bowl or container, cover tightly with plastic wrap, and let rise for 30 minutes.

4. Using greased bowl scraper (or your fingertips), fold dough over itself by gently lifting and folding edge of dough toward middle. Turn bowl 45 degrees and fold dough again; repeat turning bowl and folding dough 6 more times (total of 8 folds). Cover tightly with plastic and let rise for 30 minutes. Repeat folding and letting rise every 30 minutes, 2 more times. After third set of folds, cover bowl tightly with plastic and let dough rise until nearly doubled in size, 45 minutes to 1¼ hours.

5. Place 18 by 12-inch sheet of parchment paper on counter and spray with vegetable oil spray. Transfer dough to lightly floured counter. Using your lightly floured hands, press and stretch dough into 10-inch round; deflate any gas bubbles larger than 1 inch.

6. Working around circumference of dough, fold edges toward center until ball forms. Flip dough ball seam side down and, using your cupped hands, drag in small circles on counter until dough feels taut and round and all seams are secured on underside of loaf. Mist loaf with water on all sides and sprinkle with remaining ¼ cup oats, pressing gently to adhere.

7. Place loaf, seam side down, in center of prepared parchment and cover loosely with greased plastic. Let rise until loaf increases in size by about half and dough springs back minimally when poked gently with your knuckle, 30 minutes to 1 hour.

8. Thirty minutes before baking, adjust oven rack to lower-middle position, place Dutch oven (with lid) on rack, and heat oven to 500 degrees. Holding sharp paring knife or single-edge razor blade at 30-degree angle to loaf, make two 5-inch-long, ½-inch-deep slashes in swift, fluid motion along top of loaf to form cross. Discard any exposed raisins on top of loaf.

9. Carefully transfer pot to wire rack and uncover. Using parchment as sling, gently lower dough into pot. Cover, tucking any excess parchment into pot, and return to oven. Reduce oven temperature to 425 degrees and bake for 15 minutes. Uncover and continue to bake until loaf is deep golden brown and registers 205 to 210 degrees, about 20 minutes longer.

10. Using parchment sling, remove loaf from pot and transfer to wire rack; discard parchment. Let cool completely, about 3 hours, before serving.

BLUEBERRY CORNBREAD

✓ WHY THIS RECIPE WORKS Our aim was simple: a slightly sweet, blueberry-packed rendition of moist and airy cornbread. We quickly discovered that just throwing a few handfuls of blueberries into the batter of our favorite cornbread wasn't the answer. Other recipes produced cornbread that was either dry and dense or too sweet. In some versions, the blueberries sank to the bottom. To make our bread more cakey than the average cornbread and to help keep the blueberries afloat, we opted for a higher ratio of flour to cornmeal. Using a full 2 cups of fresh blueberries ensured that each bite was packed with juicy fruit. And a bit of sugar sprinkled on before baking melted in the oven to give the cornbread a lightly sweet, golden top.

My sister and I used to beg our mother to take us to our local market when we were young—not because we thought that the young man working the fish counter was cute (although that didn't hurt) and not even for the floor-to-ceiling bulk candy bins. We were after the market's signature blueberry cornbread. A far cry from savory, dense, and crumbly cornbread, this was fluffy and sweet, rich with butter, and loaded with juicy blueberries. My mom would buy it for dessert, but my sister and I would eat it any time of day.

When I started developing a recipe inspired by this cornbread, I discovered that our small North Carolina grocer wasn't alone in making it. I uncovered blueberry cornbread recipes from a variety of sources all over the country. I baked six versions for my colleagues to try, and we were surprised to find that the cornbreads ran the gamut from a dry, salty version with a pitiful sprinkling of blueberries to something akin to a sweet, vanilla-flavored blueberry quick bread.

Our favorite from this initial round had a moderate sweetness, so I used it as a jumping-off point. This cornbread followed the standard procedure: stirring a mixture of melted butter, eggs, and milk into the dry ingredients. Then the blueberries were folded in and the batter was poured into a round cake pan and baked.

Right off the bat, my tasting team clamored for more berries, so I doubled the amount to a full 2 cups. We also thought that the cornbread, which contained equal parts cornmeal and flour, was a bit too dense. In the end, we determined that a ratio of 1 cup cornmeal to 1½ cups flour made for the best texture. And while the

BLUEBERRY CORNBREAD

cup of cornmeal was enough to deliver sweet corn flavor, I sprinkled a bit more cornmeal into the greased cake pan before pouring in the batter for an additional burst of cornmeal flavor and crunch.

The cornbread was delicious, but I found two simple ways to make it even better. First, I sprinkled the batter with a tablespoon of sugar before baking. The sugar melted in the oven, turning the top lightly sweet, crunchy, and golden. As a final flourish, I prepared a stir-together honey butter that made this delicious cornbread even more irresistible.

—MORGAN BOLLING, *Cook's Country*

Blueberry Cornbread

SERVES 8

We developed this recipe using commonly available Quaker Yellow Corn Meal. If you're using our favorite cornmeal, Arrowhead Mills Organic Yellow Cornmeal, you will need to use 1¼ cups to yield 5 ounces for the batter. If you use a dark-colored cake pan, reduce the baking time in step 3 to 35 to 40 minutes. You can use frozen blueberries here; if doing so, leave the berries in the freezer until the last possible moment and toss them with 2 tablespoons of all-purpose flour before stirring them into the batter. Then, increase the baking time to 45 to 50 minutes. Serve with Honey Butter (recipe follows), if desired.

1½ tablespoons cornmeal, plus 1 cup (5 ounces), divided
1½ cups (7½ ounces) all-purpose flour
¾ cup (5¼ ounces) plus 1 tablespoon sugar, divided
2 teaspoons baking powder
¾ teaspoon table salt
1 cup whole milk
12 tablespoons unsalted butter, melted
2 large eggs
10 ounces (2 cups) blueberries

1. Adjust oven rack to middle position and heat oven to 375 degrees. Grease light-colored 9-inch round cake pan, then dust pan with 1½ tablespoons cornmeal.

2. Whisk flour, ¾ cup sugar, baking powder, salt, and remaining 1 cup cornmeal together in large bowl. Whisk milk, melted butter, and eggs together in second bowl (butter may form clumps; this is OK). Stir milk mixture into flour mixture until just combined. Stir in blueberries until just incorporated. Transfer batter to prepared pan and smooth top with rubber spatula. Sprinkle remaining 1 tablespoon sugar over top.

3. Bake until golden brown and paring knife inserted in center comes out clean, 40 to 45 minutes. Let cornbread cool in pan on wire rack for 20 minutes. Run paring knife between cornbread and side of pan. Remove cornbread from pan and let cool on wire rack for 20 minutes. Serve warm.

Honey Butter

MAKES ABOUT ⅓ CUP

This honey butter also tastes great on roasted root vegetables, boiled corn, pork chops, pancakes, muffins, biscuits, and dinner rolls.

4 tablespoons unsalted butter, softened
2 tablespoons honey
¼ teaspoon table salt
   Pinch cayenne pepper

Using fork, mash all ingredients in bowl until combined.

TRIPLE-CHOCOLATE STICKY BUNS

✅ **WHY THIS RECIPE WORKS** To take sticky buns over the top, we added three types of chocolate: bittersweet and milk chocolate in the filling and cocoa powder in the sticky caramel topping. To ensure that the buns were ultratender, we microwaved a portion of the dough's flour and milk, turning it into a gel-like paste, before adding it to the rest of the dough ingredients. This paste made the dough soft without it becoming overly sticky and difficult to work with. For an easy filling with complex flavor, we microwaved butter and bittersweet chocolate to form a ganache that we spread over the rolled-out dough. We then sprinkled on milk chocolate chips: Rolled up in the dough, they delivered just the right amount of sweetness. For the easiest-ever caramel, we simply stirred together melted butter, brown sugar, corn syrup, and cocoa powder for another dose of chocolate. We then poured it into a metal baking pan and nestled the buns on top. The mixture cooked into caramel as the buns baked.

Sticky buns—soft, yeasted spirals of dough dripping with gooey caramel and studded with crunchy nuts—are already a perfect sweet treat. But as far as I'm concerned, perfection is just a starting point. I wanted to take these over the top with chocolate.

First, some context: Like cinnamon rolls, sticky buns start as buttery dough rolled into a log with cinnamon sugar inside; the dough is sliced into buns and allowed to rise before being baked in a rich pool of caramel. Once they're finished, you invert them like an upside-down cake so that the gooeyness drapes over the buns and sinks into their coils.

I'm not the first person to try adding chocolate to the mix; I found a handful of recipes in my research. They ranged from relatively austere (with just chocolate chips rolled up inside) to more daring (melted chocolate in the center, cocoa in the dough). But none had the perfect balance of sweet, gooey caramel and luxurious chocolate over soft, pull-apart dough.

For the dough, I turned to a bread-making technique that some of my coworkers have used for ultratender buns. The method, called *tangzhong*, produces a super-hydrated dough, so the buns stay moist. And it's remarkably simple: You just microwave a portion of the flour and milk to form a gel-like paste, which locks in moisture. Once the paste is incorporated, the dough becomes very easy to handle. And it yielded soft, tender buns. Tasted next to buns made the traditional way (which were also delicious), we chose the more foolproof tangzhong route.

On to the chocolate. I assembled every variety: cocoa powder, bar chocolate, and chocolate chips; semisweet, bittersweet, and milk. Then I got to experimenting.

Cocoa powder in the dough was the first casualty; it turned the dough dry and chalky. I moved on to bar chocolate, creating a simple ganache (melted chocolate with cream or butter) in the microwave to spread (once cooled) onto the dough before rolling it up. I loved the complex flavor of bittersweet chocolate for the ganache, but it just wasn't sweet enough. After spreading the ganache onto the dough, I sprinkled milk chocolate chips across the surface; once the dough was rolled up, cut, and baked, these made for delightful pockets of sweet, creamy flavor.

I was ready to tackle the chocolate and caramel topping, which starts out, of course, on the bottom of the pan. While caramel traditionally involves cooking sugar on the stovetop—a notoriously fussy affair—I knew I could sidestep this process by simply stirring together the caramel ingredients (brown sugar, corn syrup, butter, and a bit of water and salt) and pouring this mixture into a 13 by 9-inch metal baking pan before adding the buns on top. In the oven, the mixture transformed into a sweet, sticky caramel sauce; the moisture from brown sugar and corn syrup (a liquid sugar) kept it soft and pliable even after the buns cooled. To really seal the deal on the chocolate flavor, I returned to my can of cocoa powder, adding a tablespoon to the stir-together caramel.

When I inverted this final batch out of the pan, the buns glistened with drippy, dark caramel. A sweet bakery aroma saturated the air, drawing coworkers from the farthest corners of the kitchen. Once in a while, there is a recipe in the test kitchen that leaves our entire company begging for leftovers. This was it.

—CECELIA JENKINS, *Cook's Country*

Triple-Chocolate Sticky Buns

SERVES 12

These buns take about 4 hours to make. One packet of rapid-rise or instant yeast contains 2¼ teaspoons of yeast. Be sure to use a metal, not glass or ceramic, baking pan here. The tackiness of the dough aids in flattening and stretching it in step 7, so resist the urge to use a lot of dusting flour. Rolling the dough cylinder too tightly in step 8 will result in misshapen rolls. Buns baked according to the make-ahead instructions will be shorter than buns baked after the second proofing.

FLOUR PASTE

⅔ cup whole milk

¼ cup (1¼ ounces) all-purpose flour

DOUGH

⅔ cup whole milk

1 large egg plus 1 large yolk

3¼ cups (16¼ ounces) all-purpose flour

2¼ teaspoons instant or rapid-rise yeast

3 tablespoons granulated sugar

1½ teaspoons table salt

6 tablespoons unsalted butter, cut into
    6 pieces and softened

TOPPING

- ¾ cup packed (5¼ ounces) brown sugar
- 6 tablespoons unsalted butter, melted
- ¼ cup dark corn syrup
- 2 tablespoons water
- 1 tablespoon unsweetened cocoa powder
- ¼ teaspoon table salt

FILLING

- 4 ounces bittersweet chocolate, chopped fine
- 4 tablespoons unsalted butter
- 1 cup (6 ounces) milk chocolate chips

1. FOR THE FLOUR PASTE: Whisk milk and flour in small bowl until no lumps remain. Microwave, whisking every 25 seconds, until mixture thickens to stiff paste, 50 to 75 seconds. Whisk until smooth.

2. FOR THE DOUGH: In bowl of stand mixer, whisk flour paste and milk until smooth. Add egg and yolk and whisk until incorporated. Add flour and yeast. Fit stand mixer with dough hook and mix on low speed until mass of dough forms and all flour is moistened, 1 to 2 minutes. Turn off mixer, cover bowl with dish towel or plastic wrap, and let dough stand for 15 minutes.

3. Add sugar and salt to dough. Knead on medium-low speed for 5 minutes. Add butter and continue to knead until incorporated, scraping down dough hook and bowl as needed (dough will be sticky), about 5 minutes longer.

4. Transfer dough to lightly floured counter and knead briefly to form ball. Transfer, seam side down, to greased large bowl, cover tightly with plastic, and let rise at room temperature until doubled in size, about 1 hour.

5. FOR THE TOPPING: Meanwhile, whisk all ingredients in bowl until combined. Spray 13 by 9-inch metal baking pan with vegetable oil spray. Pour topping into prepared pan and use rubber spatula to spread to edges of pan; set aside.

6. FOR THE FILLING: About 30 minutes before dough is done rising, microwave bittersweet chocolate and butter in bowl at 50 percent power, stirring occasionally, until melted and combined, about 2 minutes. Refrigerate until matte and firm, 30 to 40 minutes.

7. Transfer dough to lightly floured counter and lightly flour top of dough. Roll and stretch dough to form 18 by 15-inch rectangle with long side parallel to counter's edge. Stir bittersweet chocolate mixture with rubber spatula until smooth and spreadable (mixture

KEY STEPS TO THE BEST BUNS

1. Microwave mixture of flour and milk to make stiff paste.

2. Mix paste with more milk, egg and yolk, yeast, and flour in mixer. Let dough stand for 15 minutes, then add sugar and salt.

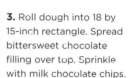

3. Roll dough into 18 by 15-inch rectangle. Spread bittersweet chocolate filling over top. Sprinkle with milk chocolate chips.

4. Carefully roll dough into even log, then pinch seam to seal. Position log seam side down on counter.

5. Cut log into 12 equal portions and place buns, cut side down, on top of caramel topping in pan. Let rise.

6. Bake buns. Run knife around edge of pan, cover with rimmed baking sheet, and carefully invert. Let cool and serve.

should have similar texture to frosting). Using offset spatula, spread mixture over entire surface of dough, leaving 1-inch border along top edge. Sprinkle evenly with chocolate chips.

8. Beginning with long edge nearest you, loosely roll dough away from you into even log, pushing in ends to create even thickness. Pinch seam to seal. Roll log seam side down and slice into 12 equal portions. Place buns, cut side down, in prepared pan in 3 rows of four, lightly reshaping buns into circles as needed. Cover tightly with plastic and let rise at room temperature until buns are puffy and touching one another, about 1 hour.

9. Adjust oven racks to lowest and lower-middle positions and heat oven to 375 degrees. Place rimmed baking sheet on lower rack to catch any drips. Discard plastic and bake buns on upper rack until golden brown on top, about 20 minutes. Cover loosely with aluminum foil and continue to bake until center buns register at least 200 degrees, about 15 minutes longer.

10. Carefully remove foil from pan (steam may escape) and immediately run paring knife around edge of pan. Place large platter or second rimmed baking sheet over pan and carefully invert pan and sheet. Remove pan and let buns cool for 15 minutes. Serve.

TO MAKE AHEAD: Follow recipe through step 8, then refrigerate buns for at least 8 hours or up to 24 hours. When ready to bake, let buns sit on counter for 30 minutes before proceeding with step 9. Increase uncovered baking time by 10 minutes.

NOTES FROM THE TEST KITCHEN

GOOD THINGS COME IN THREES, INCLUDING CHOCOLATE
Could we have simply added some cocoa powder to the dough or drizzled some melted chocolate over the top of these buns and called it a day? Sure—if we didn't care about making a knockout recipe. After testing every kind of chocolate in each component, we ended up keeping the bun dough chocolate-free, but we added cocoa powder to the caramel topping, used bittersweet chocolate in the filling, and then sprinkled milk chocolate chips on top of that. The result is a multifaceted chocolate flavor that makes these buns a mind-blowing treat.

EVERYDAY FRENCH TOAST

✔ **WHY THIS RECIPE WORKS** We started our easy French toast recipe by whisking together eggs, sugar, salt, cinnamon, and vanilla and then stirring in melted butter and milk. Instead of dipping the bread in the custard mixture one slice at a time, we poured the custard into a rimmed baking sheet that we'd generously sprayed with vegetable oil spray. We placed all the bread slices in the custard and then flipped each slice. The bread soaked up just enough egg mixture to ensure a creamy, custardy center, but not so much that it cooked up flat and soggy. We baked the slices on the lowest oven rack to brown their bottoms and then turned on the broiler to brown and crisp their tops.

I thought my days as a short-order cook were long behind me, but in recent months I've been logging a lot of hours on the test kitchen's breakfast line. It all started with my recipe for Easy Pancakes, in which I prioritized pantry-friendly ingredients and minimal effort so that the flapjacks could be thrown together anytime. That got me thinking about an equally simple formula for that other breakfast mainstay, French toast. Soaking bread in custard and browning the slices in a pan until they're golden on the outside and custardy within doesn't take long, but all that dipping, flipping, and batch cooking is fussy business, especially if you're trying to serve a crowd. And the custard-to-bread ratio rarely works out just right: Either you're short on custard and the last slices are dry, or you're left with an excess of custard that gets poured down the drain.

So back to the breakfast station I went with my sights set on a recipe for French toast that could transform ordinary sandwich bread into a creamy, crisp-crusted treat. No fuss. No mess. No waste.

I mixed up a basic custard—just eggs, milk, and sugar flavored with vanilla, cinnamon, and salt—but quickly realized that simply dumping all the ingredients into a bowl and whisking wasn't the best approach if I wanted the custard to be homogeneous. To break up the eggs, I had to whisk vigorously, which caused milk to slosh out of the bowl while stubborn clumps of yolk slid past the tines of the whisk. Going forward, I held back the milk, adding it once I had beaten the eggs with the vanilla, sugar, salt, and cinnamon until they were completely smooth. At that point, the milk could simply be stirred in.

EVERYDAY FRENCH TOAST

I proceeded with the conventional dip-and-fry approach, dunking each slice into the custard and browning a few slices at a time in a hot skillet. The custard's flavor needed tweaking—it lacked richness and depth. Whisking a couple of tablespoons of melted butter into the custard made it more luxurious, and I found that adding the butter to the egg mixture before the milk prevented the butter from clumping. Meanwhile, switching from granulated to brown sugar and adding more vanilla (a full tablespoon) boosted the custard's flavor.

Calibrating exactly how long the bread should soak was trickier. A quick dip yielded toast that was dry in patches, while fully saturating the slices left them downright soggy. With some trial and error, I figured out the ideal scenario: The custard needed to penetrate ¼ inch into each slice, leaving a slim "backbone" of dry bread in the center that supported the weight of the custard to ensure that each piece cooked up creamy, not soggy.

I know what you're thinking: No one would go to the trouble of measuring the soaking depth of the custard for French toast. But I did. And happily, those tests helped me figure out a really simple way to get each slice perfectly saturated.

I poured the custard into a rimmed baking sheet, which caused it to spread into an even layer. Then I laid out the bread slices like tiles on the custard-covered surface. By the time the last slice was in place, the first side of the first slice had soaked up just the right amount of custard. I flipped each slice, and in barely a minute I was rewarded with eight perfectly soaked slices of bread and no excess custard in the sheet.

The only problem was that the custard-laden slices were too delicate to transfer to the skillet. But maybe I didn't need a skillet. Why not bake the slices instead?

There were two potential advantages to baking: The saturated slices would stay intact, and they could be cooked in a single batch (no need to worry about keeping the first batch warm while the remaining slices cooked). For the next batch, I coated the baking sheet generously with vegetable oil spray to prevent the bread from sticking during baking, poured in the custard, added the bread, flipped it, and placed the sheet on the lowest rack of a 425-degree oven. The bottoms of the slices browned in about 10 minutes.

I was about to flip each slice to brown the second side when I had a better idea: Instead of painstakingly turning each slice (and potentially burning my fingers), I could broil the toast. All I had to do was move the baking sheet to a rack set about 5 inches below the broiler and switch the oven from bake to broil. Three minutes later, the custardy toast was browned on both sides. The crisp broiled surface contrasted beautifully with the toast's creamy center—even after I doused it with maple syrup.

This recipe for French toast is so quick and easy that you can make it in your sleep—or at least while the coffee is brewing.

—LAN LAM, *Cook's Illustrated*

NOTES FROM THE TEST KITCHEN

A BETTER WAY TO WHISK CUSTARD

Mixing up custard the usual way—by whisking all the ingredients together at once—tends to slosh liquid out of the bowl and yields a broken custard that cooks up streaky on French toast. We found that whisking the ingredients into the eggs in stages blends the mixture more thoroughly and without making a mess. First we beat the sugar, cinnamon, and salt into the eggs and vanilla; the gritty particles of the dry ingredients help break up the egg yolks. At that point, it's easy to thoroughly incorporate the melted butter and milk.

MIXED ALL AT ONCE   MIXED IN STAGES

STAGGERING MAKES IT SMOOTH
For a homogeneous custard, first whisk the dry ingredients into the eggs to break up the yolks, and then stir in the liquids.

FRENCH CONNECTION? MAYBE NOT

French toast is about as French as French dressing—which is to say, not very. Many sources claim that the tradition of soaking bread in sweet, spiced liquid (such as wine, milk, or fruit juice) and frying it has long been a tradition in numerous countries from England to Germany to India. Among these other fried eggy breads: German toast, Bombay toast, and poor knights of Windsor.

Everyday French Toast

SERVES 4

We developed this recipe to work with presliced supermarket bread that measures 4 by 6 inches and is ¾ inch thick. Our favorite is Arnold Country Classics White Bread. Be sure to use vegetable oil spray here; it contains lecithin, which ensures that the oil stays well distributed, preventing the toast from sticking. Top with maple syrup or confectioners' sugar, if desired.

- 3 large eggs
- 1 tablespoon vanilla extract
- 2 teaspoons packed brown sugar
- ½ teaspoon ground cinnamon
- ¼ teaspoon table salt
- 2 tablespoons unsalted butter, melted
- 1 cup milk
- 8 slices hearty white sandwich bread

1. Adjust 1 oven rack to lowest position and second rack 5 to 6 inches from broiler element. Heat oven to 425 degrees. Generously spray bottom and sides of 18 by 13-inch rimmed baking sheet with vegetable oil spray. Whisk eggs, vanilla, sugar, cinnamon, and salt in large bowl until sugar is dissolved and no streaks of egg remain. Whisking constantly, drizzle in melted butter. Whisk in milk.

2. Pour egg mixture into prepared sheet. Arrange bread in single layer in egg mixture, leaving small gaps between slices. Working quickly, use your fingers to flip slices in same order you placed them in sheet. Let sit until slices absorb remaining custard, about 1 minute. Bake on lower rack until bottoms of slices are golden brown, 10 to 15 minutes. Transfer sheet to upper rack and heat broiler. (Leave sheet in oven while broiler heats.) Broil until tops of slices are golden brown, watching carefully and rotating sheet if necessary to prevent burning, 1 to 4 minutes.

3. Using thin metal spatula, carefully flip each slice. Serve.

SCRAMBLED EGGS WITH PINTO BEANS AND COTIJA CHEESE

✔ WHY THIS RECIPE WORKS To tenderize and provide richness without adding moisture to the eggs, we skipped dairy and other watery liquids in favor of extra-virgin olive oil. We cooked the eggs quickly in more olive oil over medium-high heat, stirring constantly to create large curds. For Mexican flair, we then folded in jarred jalapeños, canned pinto beans, and cilantro once the curds were well established but still a little wet; this helped the eggs set up around the beans to create a cohesive scramble. We topped the eggs with more cilantro and cotija cheese.

When I'm running low on time, energy, groceries, or all three, I like to whip up my "emergency eggs": I just chop up whatever leftover cooked vegetables are stashed in the refrigerator, toss them in a hot skillet with beaten eggs, and stir until curds form. Whether they're for breakfast, brunch, or dinner, these healthful scrambles always satisfy, even if they are a little rough around the edges. But I knew that if I gave them some attention, I could come up with recipes worth repeating.

My fresh take on scrambled eggs meant staying away from heavy add-ins such as meat and cheese and mundane vegetables such as onions and bell peppers. As I experimented with more contemporary options, I nixed leafy greens such as spinach and Swiss chard; they tended to weep after cooking, making the eggs watery. Superdelicate greens, such as baby arugula, were also out: They liked to clump, which made them difficult to disperse evenly.

Perhaps I needed to think further outside the box or, more accurately, outside the fridge: Gazing into the pantry, I spotted a can of pinto beans. Beans are often served alongside Mexican egg dishes such as huevos rancheros or *migas*, so why not put them directly into the eggs?

For a bit of personality, I sizzled a couple cloves of minced garlic and some chopped jarred jalapeños in olive oil in a nonstick skillet before adding the rinsed beans along with a few tablespoons of chopped fresh cilantro. I cooked the mixture for a minute or so until any moisture evaporated, transferred it to a bowl, and then wiped the skillet clean with paper towels so I could use it to cook the eggs.

But before I did that, I wanted to ensure that the eggs would be tender. Eggs get tough when their proteins bond too tightly. One way around that is to dilute them with liquid, which prevents the proteins from linking up too quickly and closely. The test kitchen likes to add half-and-half, which makes fantastic classic scrambled eggs. But for this fresher take, I really wanted to use extra-virgin olive oil. Its grassy savoriness would be an ideal complement to the earthy pintos. Two tablespoons of oil for eight eggs kept them loose and lubricated.

Since I was already beating oil into the eggs, I also used a couple of teaspoons to cook them. The test kitchen's method for producing large, billowy curds has two stages: Start the eggs over medium-high heat, folding them gently but constantly for about a minute to form large curds. Then, reduce the heat to low to gently finish cooking them and to provide ample time to remove them from the skillet before they overcook and become rubbery. It was important to return the beans to the pan when the curds were well established but still a little wet so the eggs could set up around them to create a cohesive dish.

I now had large, tender egg curds studded with creamy pink beans and flecks of chopped cilantro and jalapeños. I didn't want to overload the eggs with gobs of cheese, but I thought that a bit of cotija—a dry, crumbly, salty Mexican cheese—might be a worthy addition. Indeed, just an ounce of it perked things up (if you can't find cotija, crumbled feta makes for a fine substitute). Sprinkled with more chopped cilantro and served with a stack of warm tortillas and a bottle of hot sauce, these eggs made a fine, fresh, anytime meal.

—ANDREW JANJIGIAN, *Cook's Illustrated*

Scrambled Eggs with Pinto Beans and Cotija Cheese

SERVES 4

This recipe calls for olive oil instead of milk or cream for its distinctive flavor and tenderizing effect on eggs. If cotija cheese is unavailable, you can substitute feta. This recipe can easily be halved, if desired; use a 10-inch skillet. We like to serve these eggs with warm tortillas and hot sauce.

- 8 **large eggs**
- 3 **tablespoons extra-virgin olive oil, divided**
- ¼ **teaspoon table salt**
- ¼ **cup jarred sliced jalapeños, chopped coarse**
- 2 **garlic cloves, minced**
- 1 **(15-ounce) can pinto beans, rinsed**
- ¼ **cup chopped fresh cilantro, divided**
- 1 **ounce cotija cheese, crumbled (¼ cup)**

1. In medium bowl, beat eggs, 2 tablespoons oil, and salt with fork until no streaks of white remain. Heat 1 teaspoon oil, jalapeños, and garlic in 12-inch nonstick skillet over medium heat until fragrant, about 1 minute. Add beans and 3 tablespoons cilantro and cook, stirring frequently, until moisture has evaporated, about 1 minute. Transfer bean mixture to small bowl and set aside. Wipe skillet clean with paper towels.

2. Heat remaining 2 teaspoons oil in now-empty skillet over medium-high heat until shimmering. Add egg mixture and, using rubber spatula, constantly and firmly scrape along bottom and sides of skillet until eggs begin to clump and spatula just leaves trail on bottom of skillet, 30 to 60 seconds. Reduce heat to low and gently but constantly fold eggs until clumped and just slightly wet, 30 to 60 seconds. Fold in bean mixture. Transfer to serving dish, sprinkle with cotija and remaining 1 tablespoon cilantro, and serve.

NOTES FROM THE TEST KITCHEN

TESTING 12-INCH NONSTICK SKILLETS

In the test kitchen, we reach for our nonstick skillets when we're cooking delicate foods that stick, such as eggs or fish. We also like these pans for stir-fries because the browned bits don't stick as much, so they're less likely to burn.

Our ideal nonstick skillet is easy to handle, is durable, has great release, and cooks food evenly. We evaluated the market and chose the top seven pans from major manufacturers. We prefer 12-inch skillets, but we included two 11-inch models because they were the largest skillets offered by two major manufacturers. We set a $60.00 price limit because nonstick pans wear faster than other pans, so we don't think they're worth a major investment.

After cooking and abuse tests, we found our new winner: the **OXO Good Grips Non-Stick 12-Inch Open Frypan** ($39.99). It cooked and released food perfectly, its stay-cool handle was flawless, and other than some light knife marks, it emerged from testing unscathed.

SCRAMBLED EGGS WITH PINTO BEANS AND COTIJA CHEESE

EGGS IN SPICY TOMATO AND ROASTED RED PEPPER SAUCE (SHAKSHUKA)

✓ **WHY THIS RECIPE WORKS** The North African dish *shakshuka* (eggs poached in a tomato sauce flavored with peppers, spices, and garlic) makes a great meal any time—if you can get the eggs to cook properly. For the sauce, we blended whole peeled tomatoes and jarred roasted red peppers for a mix of sweetness, smokiness, and acidity. Adding pita bread helped prevent the silky-smooth sauce from weeping. A combination of garlic, tomato paste, and ground spices created the distinct flavor profile we were after. To ensure that the eggs cooked perfectly, we added them to the skillet off the heat, cooked them in a smooth rather than chunky sauce for more even heat transfer, and covered the whites with sauce to help speed their cooking. Covering the skillet created a steamy environment that quickly cooked the eggs from both above and below. Chopped fresh cilantro, crumbled feta, and sliced kalamata olives on top provided brightness, texture, and contrasting flavor.

Forgive me while I take a minute to gush like a perfectly poached egg about why I love *shakshuka*. This dish features eggs gently poached in a bright, savory tomato sauce fragrant with warm spices and spiked with red pepper and pops of fresh herbs. The runny yolks mingle with the sauce, and everything gets scooped up with pita or crusty bread. It is often customized with additions such as crumbled cheeses, olives, sausage, or ground lamb—making it an excellent breakfast-for-dinner option—and may be further enlivened by condiments such as harissa, zesty herb sauce, or even tahini.

I'm not alone in my devotion: This North African dish has long been a favorite across the Middle East and Europe, and in recent years its popularity has spread to the United States. As if all this isn't enough, there's also a practical reason to love shakshuka: A basic version comes together quickly from staples you're likely to have on hand. Chopped tomatoes (canned work well), red bell peppers, aromatics, and spices get cooked in a skillet until the flavors blend and the sauce thickens; you then crack in the eggs, cover the pan, and cook until they're done.

The only downside to shakshuka is that if you're making enough to serve four, getting eight eggs perfectly poached—with gently set whites and thickened but still runny yolks—in a single skillet can be a challenge. But if there was ever a dish I was inspired to make foolproof, it was this one.

I first focused on the sauce. In a 12-inch skillet, I softened red bell pepper that I'd cut into ½-inch pieces and then added four cloves of sliced garlic. When the garlic turned golden and fragrant, I added a tablespoon of tomato paste for savory depth and bloomed a few ground spices in oil: coriander, smoked paprika, cumin, and cayenne. Once the tomato paste had darkened, in went canned tomatoes, which I intentionally left chunky.

After a 10-minute simmer, the sauce had thickened slightly, so I quickly cracked eight eggs into the pan, covered it, and waited. After a few minutes, I peeked. Things had already gone awry. The eggs I'd added first were cooking faster than the others. The eggs nestled deeply into the sauce had hard yolks, while eggs near the surface had runny yolks but watery whites. The sauce wasn't great either; its flavor was nondescript, and though the pepper's texture was pleasing, I couldn't taste it through all the tomato.

I made a couple of changes. First, I swapped the fresh bell pepper for smoky, sweet jarred roasted ones. I also doubled the spices. When it came time to add the eggs, I removed the skillet from the burner to eliminate the urgency of adding them over heat and to help them cook at a more even rate. These were all improvements, but the eggs still sank into the sauce to varying degrees, so they remained unevenly cooked. I also realized that there were watery patches in the sauce.

When eggs are poached in water, they are completely submerged in a thin liquid of uniform consistency. But here, the eggs were sitting in a chunky liquid. Was that the cause of the uneven cooking?

I tried processing the tomatoes and half the red peppers in a blender and then adding the remaining red peppers, finely chopped, for just a little texture. The results were encouraging. The yolks were evenly contained and surrounded by the smooth sauce. They were also more evenly cooked. Our science research editor explained that chunks in a sauce impede convection currents, whereas a smoother, more fluid sauce carries heat more evenly. I was thrilled to have worked out the yolks' cooking, but I still had loose whites and a weepy sauce to deal with.

Traditional gazpacho, in which vegetables are pureed until smooth, can also separate this way. But Spanish cooks have a solution: Add bread. Would that work here? I added a slice of white sandwich bread to the blender with a batch of tomatoes and red peppers. The resulting sauce was silky, smooth, and stayed homogeneous after cooking. Moving forward, I swapped in pita, which I'd be serving with the dish anyway.

The yolks were perfect, but I still needed to speed up the cooking of the egg whites. Plopping the eggs into the sauce neatly contained the yolks and cooked them from underneath and around the sides, but the whites flowed freely over the surface of the sauce. I wondered if I could use the sauce to help the whites cook faster.

Once I added the eggs (making slight indentations in the sauce with the back of a spoon helped map out where to drop each one), I spooned some of the sauce over the whites so they were more contained and submerged in the hot sauce, hoping it would transfer heat to them faster than the air above them in the covered skillet would. Sure enough, in my next batch, by the time the yolks were soft and golden, the whites had set.

NOTES FROM THE TEST KITCHEN

HOW TO POACH EGGS IN THICK SAUCE
Poaching eggs directly in a thick sauce can be particularly challenging. Here's how to do it successfully.

1. OFF HEAT, CREATE INDENTS Moving the pan off the heat allows the sauce to cool slightly so the eggs cook at an even rate. The indents hold the yolks in place.

2. ADD EGGS TO INDENTS Creating indents ensures that the eggs are evenly spaced around the pan.

3. TOP WHITES WITH SAUCE Spooning sauce over the whites just after adding the eggs provides immediate direct heat to help the whites set faster.

It was time for the garnishes: chopped fresh cilantro, sliced kalamata olives, and crumbled feta were all simple but potent. (But if you're interested in creating a truly knockout dish, whip up a batch of *zhoug*, a spicy green sauce of fresh herbs and chiles that's often served alongside shakshuka.)

With this satisfying, richly flavored version featuring perfectly oozy, creamy eggs, I fell in love with shakshuka all over again.

—ANNIE PETITO, *Cook's Illustrated*

Eggs in Spicy Tomato and Roasted Red Pepper Sauce (Shakshuka)
SERVES 4

Served with a green salad, this dish makes a satisfying brunch, lunch, or dinner. Use a glass lid if you have it. If not, feel free to peek at the eggs frequently as they cook. Top with Spicy Middle Eastern Herb Sauce (Zhoug) (recipe follows), if desired.

- 4 (8-inch) pita breads, divided
- 1 (28-ounce) can whole peeled tomatoes, drained
- 3 cups jarred roasted red peppers, divided
- ¼ cup extra-virgin olive oil
- 4 garlic cloves, sliced thin
- 1 tablespoon tomato paste
- 2 teaspoons ground coriander
- 2 teaspoons smoked paprika
- 1 teaspoon ground cumin
- ½ teaspoon table salt
- ¼ teaspoon pepper
- ¼ teaspoon cayenne pepper
- 8 large eggs
- ½ cup coarsely chopped fresh cilantro leaves and stems
- 1 ounce feta cheese, crumbled (¼ cup)
- ¼ cup pitted kalamata olives, sliced

1. Cut enough pita bread into ½-inch pieces to equal ½ cup (about one-third of 1 pita bread). Cut remaining pita breads into wedges for serving. Process pita pieces, tomatoes, and half of red peppers in blender until smooth, 1 to 2 minutes. Cut remaining red peppers into ¼-inch pieces and set aside.

2. Heat oil in 12-inch skillet over medium heat until shimmering. Add garlic and cook, stirring occasionally, until golden, 1 to 2 minutes. Add tomato paste, coriander, paprika, cumin, salt, pepper, and cayenne and cook, stirring constantly, until rust-colored and fragrant, 1 to 2 minutes. Stir in tomato–red pepper puree and reserved red peppers (mixture may sputter) and bring to simmer. Reduce heat to maintain simmer; cook, stirring occasionally, until slightly thickened (spatula will leave trail that slowly fills in behind it, but sauce will still slosh when skillet is shaken), 10 to 12 minutes.

3. Remove skillet from heat. Using back of spoon, make 8 shallow dime-size indentations in sauce (seven around perimeter and one in center). Crack 1 egg into small bowl and pour into 1 indentation (it will hold yolk in place but not fully contain egg). Repeat with remaining 7 eggs. Spoon sauce over edges of egg whites so that whites are partially covered and yolks are exposed.

4. Bring to simmer over medium heat (there should be small bubbles across entire surface). Reduce heat to maintain simmer. Cover and cook until yolks film over, 4 to 5 minutes. Continue to cook, covered, until whites are softly but uniformly set (if skillet is shaken lightly, each egg should jiggle as a single unit), 1 to 2 minutes longer. Off heat, sprinkle with cilantro, feta, and olives. Serve immediately, passing pita wedges separately.

Spicy Middle Eastern Herb Sauce (Zhoug)
SERVES 12

This warm-spiced, garlicky chile-herb sauce takes *shakshuka* to the next level.

- 2 cups fresh cilantro leaves and stems
- 4 Thai chiles, stemmed
- 3 garlic cloves, peeled
- ½ teaspoon ground coriander
- ½ teaspoon ground cumin
- ½ teaspoon table salt
- ½ cup extra-virgin olive oil

Pulse cilantro, Thai chiles, garlic, coriander, cumin, and salt in food processor until coarsely chopped, 8 to 10 pulses. Transfer to small bowl. Add oil and stir until sauce has consistency of loose paste. Season with salt to taste. (Sauce can be refrigerated in airtight container for up to 2 weeks. Let come to room temperature before serving.)

SOUS VIDE SOFT-POACHED EGGS

✓ **WHY THIS RECIPE WORKS** The sous vide method is perfect for cooking eggs. It's hands-off and easily scalable, and it gently cooks eggs to a set temperature. Typically, sous vide eggs are cooked at a low temperature (around 145 degrees Fahrenheit/63 degrees Celsius) for at least an hour. This will give you yolks that are slightly thickened but still runny and barely set whites. We found the whites to be too loose when cooked at this temperature. Some recipes call for cracking "63-degree eggs" such as these into simmering water to better set the whites. We wanted to ditch that extra step and still produce a perfectly poached egg, so we opted to cook at a higher temperature for a shorter time to set more of the white. This method produced a traditional poached egg—right out of the shell. And with the ability to make these eggs ahead of time, this recipe is perfect for brunch.

At America's Test Kitchen, we've devised countless ways to make egg cookery easier, from poaching eggs in salted water with vinegar to hard-cooking eggs in a steamer basket. But bringing sous vide into the equation changes things. Eggs are a perfect candidate for the sous vide method because they're a self-contained vessel (so you don't need to seal them off in a bag, as in other sous vide methods) and they're essentially an entry-level task for anyone learning about sous vide or cooking in general. Cooking eggs in a low-temperature water bath with a sous vide circulator allows you to cook with a precision absent from traditional methods.

Egg whites begin to thicken at 150 degrees Fahrenheit/65.5 degrees Celsius and fully set at 158°F/70°C, while the yolks begin to thicken at 145°F/62.8°C and fully set at 180°F/82°C. "An egg soft-cooked at 60°C (140°F) is barely jelled throughout; at 62.8°C (145°F), the yolk is actually firmer than the surrounding white," writes food scientist Harold McGee in the introduction to chef Thomas Keller's *Under Pressure* (2008). "Sous vide cooking has opened up new realms of texture and flavor that weren't discernible before and that still aren't fully understood."

But egg cookery isn't just about temperature. It's also about time. Sous vide cooking allows you, the home cook, to play with time in a way that's impossible with traditional cooking methods, giving you the ability to decide exactly what texture you want, without any guesswork.

However you like your eggs, one thing is clear: Each temperature degree difference is distinctive in sous vide cooking. "I can look at an egg at any point that's been cooked low temperature and tell you in this range exactly how hot or cold it was," says Dave Arnold, founder of the Museum of Food and Drink and author of *Liquid Intelligence* (2014). Arnold calls an egg cooked at 145°F/63°C for about an hour an "in-betweener egg"—not totally set but still creamy (perfect for serving on toast). Meanwhile, Dr. Michael Eades, cocreator of the SousVide Supreme water oven, calls an egg cooked at 147°F/64°C for 55 minutes the "perfect custard egg"—a "soft white and a custardy, custardy yolk."

As much as I appreciate the artistry of poaching such an egg, I wanted my recipe to be a bit more approachable for sous vide beginners. I decided to steer away from the runny-white eggs you might see in a restaurant—atop a flatbread pizza or Asian-style rice bowl—and opted instead for a more traditional type, similar to those you'd be served at the diner down the street: an egg soft at the edges but with a firmer white and a semirunny yolk.

The variables in cooking eggs are fairly straightforward. I had to play with time and temperature to achieve the poached eggs I was after. Egg whites become firm at a higher temperature than egg yolks do, so the challenge in poaching an egg is to balance the cooking of the whites and the yolks. The lower the temperature, the longer it takes for the white to begin to set. To get my bearings, I started my testing at 140 degrees, cooking the eggs in a large container with my sous vide circulator for 90 minutes until the whites began to set. From there, I worked up degree by degree, adjusting the cooking time accordingly. It didn't take long for me to realize I'd need to crank up the temperature significantly to bring the cooking time down and set the whites quickly without allowing the yolks to become too firm and fudgy. The temperature-time sweet spot turned out to be 167 degrees for 12 minutes. After cooling for about a minute in an ice bath, these eggs were easy to crack right out of their shells. They emerged with whites that were set enough to handle and yolks that were just barely firmed up, runny enough to mop up with a crusty piece of toast. I also found that I was able to poach and store my eggs to be served up to five days later by simply chilling and refrigerating them and then reheating them in a warm water bath. This make-ahead potential makes them perfect for serving in big batches, so you can skip the Sunday morning trip to the diner and bring the brunch crowd right into your own kitchen.

—TIM CHIN, *America's Test Kitchen Books*

Sous Vide Soft-Poached Eggs

MAKES 1 TO 16 EGGS

Be sure to use large eggs that have no cracks and are cold from the refrigerator. Fresher eggs have tighter egg whites and are better suited for this recipe. Serve with crusty bread or toast.

1–16 large eggs, chilled

1. Using sous vide circulator, bring 4 inches water to 167 degrees Fahrenheit/75 degrees Celsius in 7-quart container. Using slotted spoon, gently lower eggs into prepared water bath, cover, and cook for 12 minutes.

2. While eggs cook, fill large bowl halfway with ice and water. Using slotted spoon, transfer eggs to ice bath and let sit until cool enough to handle, about 1 minute. To serve, crack eggs into individual bowls and season with salt and pepper to taste.

TO MAKE AHEAD: Eggs can be rapidly chilled in ice bath for 10 minutes and then refrigerated for up to 5 days. To reheat, lower eggs into water bath set to 140 degrees Fahrenheit/60 degrees Celsius and cook until heated through, at least 15 minutes or up to 60 minutes. Crack into bowls as directed.

NOTES FROM THE TEST KITCHEN

TESTING SOUS VIDE MACHINES

Whether or not you're familiar with sous vide, chances are you've eaten food prepared this way. In the past decade, this method of cooking food in a temperature-controlled water bath has made its way from Michelin-starred restaurants to popular chains, and it's now making a splash in home kitchens. To find the best sous vide machine, we evaluated seven models marketed for home use, with prices ranging from $129.99 to $274.95. We used each to prepare eggs, salmon, flank steak, pork loin, and beef short ribs. Three of the models were Wi-Fi-enabled with accompanying mobile apps. Our favorite circulator, made by **Joule** ($199.00), was lightweight and accurate, and its smartphone app was intuitive and simple to use.

BREAKFAST TACOS

BREAKFAST TACOS

✓ **WHY THIS RECIPE WORKS** We love tacos for lunch and dinner, so we set out to make tacos that could be eaten for breakfast, too. First we had to nail down the tortillas. A tortilla should be tender and chewy yet sturdy enough to hold the substantial fillings, with a clean, non-distracting flavor. Unfortunately, most store-bought flour tortillas are loaded with calories, fat, sodium, and carbohydrates. Store-bought corn tortillas, which are whole grain, made a great and easy substitute. With the tortillas squared away, we focused on the filling. We kept it healthy (but still flavorful) by scrambling eggs with a splash of low-fat milk; we then folded in a bit of cheddar cheese to boost the flavor. As for the rest of the filling, we ditched the typical greasy processed breakfast meats in favor of something lighter-tasting. Pico de gallo and avocado slices made for refreshing and healthy garnishes. A few bright cilantro leaves on top completed these perfect breakfast tacos.

Waffles, pancakes, and cereal all have their place, but sometimes I wake up craving a hearty, savory breakfast to start my day. That inevitably means eggs of some kind, often paired with bacon, sausage, or even fried potatoes in the form of hash browns. One of my favorite ways to enjoy a savory breakfast is to turn it into a breakfast taco by wrapping everything in a flour tortilla and throwing some cheese on top. But while some might argue that this high-protein approach to breakfast is healthier than starting the day with sugary waffles or cereal, it's still loaded with fat, salt, and calories. I wanted to be able to enjoy a couple of filling tacos for breakfast without feeling weighed down for hours afterward. That's why, when I was charged with developing a recipe for *The Complete Diabetes Cookbook*, I was excited to see if I could craft one for breakfast tacos that cut way down on calories without cutting down on flavor.

The most common pitfall for health-focused recipes is the tendency to eliminate "unhealthy" elements, such as fatty meat or extra salt, without considering the impact these elements have on the dish and how their absence will affect the recipe's final flavor. Fat and salt are both extremely flavorful and useful ingredients. In addition to adding richness and aiding in browning, fat often affects the texture and mouthfeel of food. Salt draws out and amplifies the flavors of other ingredients,

making the overall dish taste bolder and more complex than it would with no added salt. As a result, dishes that simply leave out these two elements usually taste bland and uninspiring and often get pushed around the plate rather than eaten.

Luckily, I had a plan for how to approach my healthier breakfast tacos. I would indeed eliminate the greasy sausage and salty bacon from the filling, but to compensate I would also incorporate more fresh, bold flavors in the form of a homemade pico de gallo. The acidity and spice of this chunky salsa would add extra layers of flavor to my tacos so that they would taste far from boring.

But first, there was the issue of the tortillas. Store-bought flour tortillas are calorie dense and sodium heavy—clearly not the right choice to pair with my healthier filling. I could try to make my own tortillas, but mixing up a dough from scratch, rolling out the tortillas, and toasting them in a pan was more effort than I was willing to put in for a simple, quick breakfast. That left me with store-bought corn tortillas. These are not only convenient but also contain fewer calories, less fat, and less salt than flour tortillas. Plus, their subtle corn taste would be a welcome addition to the flavor profile of my tacos.

Next, the eggs. While eggs do contain some fat, they're also full of protein, which helps you feel full for longer after eating. I opted to simply beat my eggs with some low-fat milk and a pinch of salt, which was just enough to make the flavor of the eggs shine. Scrambling them in a skillet until they were just slightly wet before transferring them to a bowl meant that they wouldn't overcook. I then stirred some shredded cheddar cheese directly into the eggs. I could have left cheese out altogether, but my tasters agreed that the richness it added to the tacos was very welcome, and by carefully controlling the portion, I was able to ensure that I didn't add too much fat back to my recipe.

For my pico de gallo, I sought to combine the freshest and most flavorful ingredients I could find. A shallot provided a bit of bite while fresh lime juice contributed acidic brightness. Some minced jalapeño was sure to wake up my tastebuds with a spicy kick, and cilantro and a juicy tomato brought everything together.

I was ready to assemble my tacos. I divided the egg mixture evenly over four warmed tortillas before topping them with the pico de gallo. Some sliced avocado added healthy fat and complemented the creamy texture of the eggs. After sprinkling on a little more cilantro, I had four amply filled tacos, enough for two substantial servings. I wouldn't be going hungry in the morning with a breakfast like this. And my tastebuds wouldn't be disappointed either: Every bite contained a mixture of crisp vegetables, creamy eggs, bright acidity, and a slight hit of spice. This was healthy done right.

—LAWMAN JOHNSON, *America's Test Kitchen Books*

Breakfast Tacos

SERVES 2

Do not substitute skim milk here. Be sure to remove the eggs from the skillet as soon as they are done to prevent them from overcooking.

 1 plum tomato, cored and chopped fine
 ¼ cup fresh cilantro leaves, divided
 1 shallot, minced
 1 tablespoon minced jalapeño chile
 1 tablespoon lime juice
 2 pinches table salt, divided
 4 large eggs
 2 tablespoons 1 percent low-fat milk
 1 teaspoon canola oil
 1 ounce cheddar cheese, shredded (¼ cup)
 4 (6-inch) corn tortillas, warmed
 ½ avocado, sliced ¼ inch thick

 1. Combine tomato, 2 tablespoons cilantro, shallot, jalapeño, lime juice, and pinch salt in bowl; set aside pico de gallo.

 2. Beat eggs, milk, and remaining pinch salt with fork in bowl until eggs are thoroughly combined and color is pure yellow; do not overbeat.

 3. Heat oil in 10-inch nonstick skillet over medium-high heat until shimmering, swirling to coat skillet. Add egg mixture and, using rubber spatula, constantly and firmly scrape along bottom and sides of skillet until eggs begin to clump and spatula just leaves trail on bottom of skillet, 45 to 75 seconds. Reduce heat to low and gently but constantly fold eggs until clumped and just slightly wet, 30 to 60 seconds. Quickly fold in cheddar, then immediately transfer eggs to medium bowl.

 4. Divide egg mixture among tortillas and top with pico de gallo, avocado, and remaining 2 tablespoons cilantro. Serve immediately.

CHEWY GRANOLA BARS WITH WALNUTS AND CRANBERRIES

✓ **WHY THIS RECIPE WORKS** Most store-bought granola bars are too sweet, contain mostly filler, and are soft instead of chewy. They're also prone to falling apart. For wholesome bars that were satisfyingly chewy and stayed intact, we combined toasted oats, nuts, and seeds with a mixture of pureed apricots, brown sugar, oil, and water and pressed the mixture firmly into the baking pan before baking it. Small chunks of dried fruit provided pops of bright flavor and extra chew while airy rice cereal lightened the bars and provided a crisp texture. The nuts, seeds, and fruit can be swapped out to make bars that suit a variety of tastes.

Every adult I know goes through the same mental checklist before leaving the house in the morning: Keys? Phone? Wallet? Granola bar? Okay, maybe that last one is just me.

But granola bars should be on your must-have list because they're tasty and easy to eat on the go. And because they contain fiber, protein, and healthy fats, they make great snacking alternatives to hastily grabbed cookies or chips. That said, buying granola bars can be disappointing. Many commercial bars are so sweet that they're really just undercover candy, and most are pretty light on hearty additions such as nuts, seeds, and dried fruit. Such stinginess is especially annoying because granola bars are pricey, even though most are largely composed of inexpensive oats.

I decided that the best way to be sure the granola bars in my bag were packed with satisfying nuts, seeds, and fruit; had just the right amount of sweetness; and kept costs in check was to make them myself. Mine would be of the chewy variety. Crunchy granola has its place (on top of Greek yogurt), but chewy bars are less likely to fall apart in my hand, and the physical act of chewing them reinforces the feeling that I've eaten something substantial. And I'm not alone: When I polled our readers on Facebook, 72 percent of respondents preferred chewy bars.

The first recipes I tried followed a similar procedure: Mix oats, nuts, seeds, and, in some cases, chunks of dried fruit with a combination of sugar and a liquid sweetener—usually honey or maple syrup. Most recipes called for stirring in some oil or butter; many also called for peanut butter or almond butter. I spread the mixtures in pans and baked them. So far, so easy. It was only when I tried to cut the cooled slabs into individual bars that things literally fell apart.

Most of the resulting bars were unacceptably sticky to the touch yet, paradoxically, they refused to stick together. These bars were tender all the way through and were too yielding to be called chewy. Other bars were drier and left my hands cleaner, but they were too hard and were prone to shattering into messy chunks. I wanted to make cohesive granola bars with varied textures, balanced sweetness, and plenty of chew, ideal for on-the-go snacking.

I started my own baseline recipe by toasting 2½ cups of oats, 1 cup of sunflower seeds, and 1½ cups of chopped walnuts in the oven to bring out their flavors. I transferred everything to a bowl and stirred in 1 cup of dried cranberries for pops of brightness. One cup of brown sugar and ½ cup each of peanut butter and honey made up my "glue." Because it's high in saturated fat, butter seemed antithetical to the granola bar concept, so I mixed in ½ cup of vegetable oil instead. (A bonus: Using oil instead of butter would allow the bars to keep longer at room temperature.) I pressed the mixture firmly into a foil-lined, greased baking pan and baked it for about 25 minutes. These bars tasted pretty good but, like many in my initial round of testing, were both tacky and crumbly.

Thinking that smaller particles might absorb some of the stickiness and hold together better, I coarsely ground the toasted oats and nuts in the food processor before mixing the next batch. This granola was more cohesive, which made it easier to cut into bars, but the bars felt grainy and pasty in my mouth and bore an unsettling resemblance to those blocks of compressed seeds you hang out for the birds when the weather turns cold. So the oats would have to stay whole. But having the food processor out reminded me of another technique I had seen: binding the bars with pureed dried fruit.

While my next batch of oats, nuts, and seeds toasted, I ground 1 cup of dried apricots with the brown sugar in the food processor. I added peanut butter, honey, and oil as the machine ran, and then I mixed the promisingly viscous mixture with the warm oat mixture and the cranberries. I also added some crisped rice cereal. I suspected that firm compression of the mixture before

HOW WE PUT THE "CHEW" IN OUR CHEWY GRANOLA BARS

"Too tender." "Too soft." "Too dense." We were dedicated to getting the perfect chewy texture in our granola bars, so each bite would meet with satisfying resistance. How did we achieve it? A mix of pureed dried apricots, brown sugar, oil, and water helped the ingredients cohere. Using just the right amount of moisture was key: We added enough to make the bars tender and to hold them together when they were bent or bitten—but not so much that they became soft and lost their chew.

A BENDY BAR
Properly chewy bars should flex, not break, when bent.

baking was going to be important for cohesion, so I hoped that the airy cereal would provide tiny pockets of lightness. After baking and cooling, these bars stood up to cutting better than any previous batches, but they were still rather tender and crumbly when I ate them. I was aiming for a bar so resilient that I could bend it into a shallow arc; this bar simply broke in two.

I knew that fat tenderizes baked goods. Was it possible that my formula was simply too high in fat? If so, I had two options: Nix the vegetable oil or nix the peanut butter. I decided to eliminate the latter so I could devise a nut-free variation later on.

Now I was getting somewhere: Without the peanut butter, the bars were distinctly chewy and definitely cohesive. They even passed the bend test.

I knew I was getting close, but without peanut butter's salty richness, the bars were a bit too sweet and the honey flavor was especially obtrusive. Discouragingly, a batch made without honey was too dry and crumbly. I considered using corn syrup, which has very little flavor, in place of the honey because it seemed like some form of syrup was the key to chewy, moist, cohesive bars. But was it?

Syrups are mostly sugar and water. In some cases, they're added to recipes, such as caramel, to inhibit crystallization, but that wasn't important in my granola bars. So maybe it wasn't a syrup that was the magic ingredient. Maybe it was something I had never seen in a granola bar recipe: water.

The ½ cup of honey had been contributing water, so I added a small amount to the next honey-free batch, streaming it into the food processor with the oil. Three tablespoons of water worked beautifully, producing bars that were chewy and cohesive without being sticky. The tart cranberries, nutty toasted oats, and crunchy walnuts were balanced by the sweetness of the apricots and brown sugar.

I was so happy with this recipe that I used it as a template for a hazelnut, cherry, and cacao nib bar so sophisticated that a box of them would make a luxurious gift, as well as a richly seeded, nut-free version.

—ANDREA GEARY, *Cook's Illustrated*

Chewy Granola Bars with Walnuts and Cranberries

MAKES 24 BARS

We like the sweetness of Mediterranean or Turkish apricots in this recipe. Be sure to use apricots that are soft and moist, or the bars will not hold together well. Avoid using extra-thick rolled oats here. Light and dark brown sugar will work equally well in this recipe.

- 1½ cups walnuts
- 2½ cups (7½ ounces) old-fashioned rolled oats
- 1 cup raw sunflower seeds
- 1 cup dried apricots
- 1 cup packed (7 ounces) brown sugar
- ¾ teaspoon table salt
- ½ cup vegetable oil
- 3 tablespoons water
- 1½ cups (1½ ounces) Rice Krispies cereal
- 1 cup dried cranberries

1. Adjust oven rack to middle position and heat oven to 350 degrees. Make foil sling for 13 by 9-inch baking pan by folding 2 long sheets of aluminum foil; first sheet should be 13 inches wide and second sheet should be 9 inches wide. Lay sheets of foil in pan perpendicular to each other, with extra foil hanging over edges of pan. Push foil into corners and up sides of pan, smoothing foil flush to pan. Lightly spray foil with vegetable oil spray.

2. Pulse walnuts in food processor until finely chopped, 8 to 10 pulses. Spread walnuts, oats, and sunflower seeds on rimmed baking sheet and toast until lightly browned and fragrant, 12 to 15 minutes, stirring halfway through toasting. Reduce oven temperature to 300 degrees.

3. While oat mixture is toasting, process apricots, sugar, and salt in now-empty processor until apricots are very finely ground, about 15 seconds. With processor running, add oil and water. Continue to process until homogeneous paste forms, about 1 minute longer. Transfer paste to large, wide bowl.

4. Add warm oat mixture to bowl with paste and stir with rubber spatula until well coated. Add cereal and cranberries and stir gently until ingredients are evenly mixed. Transfer mixture to prepared pan and spread into even layer. Place 14-inch sheet of parchment or waxed paper on top of granola and press and smooth very firmly with your hands, especially at edges and corners, until granola is level and compact. Remove parchment and bake granola until fragrant and just beginning to brown around edges, about 25 minutes. Transfer pan to wire rack and let cool for 1 hour. Using foil overhang, lift granola out of pan. Return granola to wire rack and let cool completely, about 1 hour.

5. Discard foil and transfer granola to cutting board. Using chef's knife, cut granola in half crosswise to create two 6½ by 9-inch rectangles. Cut each rectangle in half to make four 3¼ by 9-inch strips. Cut each strip crosswise into 6 equal pieces. (Granola bars can be stored at room temperature for up to 3 weeks.)

VARIATIONS

Chewy Granola Bars with Hazelnuts, Cherries, and Cacao Nibs

Substitute blanched hazelnuts for walnuts and pulse until finely chopped, 8 to 12 pulses. Substitute chopped dried cherries for cranberries. Stir in ½ cup cacao nibs with cereal in step 4.

Nut-Free Chewy Granola Bars

Omit walnuts and cranberries. Toast 1 cup raw pepitas, ¼ cup sesame seeds, and ¼ cup chia seeds with oats in step 2. Increase cereal to 2 cups.

CHEWY GRANOLA BARS WITH HAZELNUTS, CHERRIES, AND CACAO NIBS

TORTA CAPRESE

✓ **WHY THIS RECIPE WORKS** *Torta caprese* is an Italian flourless chocolate cake that contains finely ground almonds, which subtly break up the fudgy crumb. In our version, we included melted butter and bittersweet chocolate as well as vanilla, cocoa powder, and salt to boost the chocolate's complexity. Instead of grinding almonds in a food processor, we used commercial almond flour (commercial almond meal, which may or may not be made from skin-on nuts, also worked well). All flourless chocolate cakes are aerated with whipped eggs instead of chemical leaveners, and we found that whipping the whites and yolks separately in a stand mixer, each with half the sugar, created strong, stable egg foams that lightened the heavy batter and prevented it from collapsing after baking. Dusted with confectioners' sugar and served with amaretto- or orange-infused whipped cream, this cake is ideal for entertaining. It also tastes great the next day, so it's an excellent make-ahead dessert.

Italian chocolate-almond cake (*torta caprese*) has a storied past—though it's not clear which of the stories (if any) is true. One legend has it that the cake came to be when an Austrian princess visiting the island of Capri longed for a taste of the Sachertorte of her homeland. Not knowing how to make the dense Viennese chocolate layer cake, a local pastry chef added chocolate to his popular almond torte and hoped for the best. According to another tale, it was the accidental invention of an absent-minded baker who forgot to add flour to a chocolate-almond cake he made for a trio of Italian mobsters. And a third story tells of a sleep-deprived cook who confused cocoa powder for flour when he was mixing up almond cake batter.

What is certain: This torte, a classic dessert along the Amalfi Coast, can be a simple, elegant showstopper. When done well, it packs all the richness and depth of flourless chocolate cake, but it features finely ground almonds in the batter that subtly break up the fudgy crumb, making it lighter and less cloying to eat. It's also easy to make: Mix melted butter and chocolate with the ground almonds, lighten the batter with whipped eggs and sugar, pour it into a greased springform pan, and bake it for about an hour. There are no layers to assemble and no frosting to pipe and smooth. All it needs is a dusting of confectioners' sugar and maybe a dollop of whipped cream.

Simple ingredients, simple method. But making a great one takes a precise formula. The recipes I tried during the research phase of this project yielded a motley crew of cakes—some dry and dull like diluted cocoa, others as wet and dense as fudge—which made clear how important it would be to nail down just the right ingredient ratios and mixing method.

Butter and chocolate are typically the foundation of flourless chocolate cakes, and this one is no different. I melted 12 tablespoons of butter and 6 ounces of bittersweet chocolate in the microwave (easier than and just as foolproof as melting chocolate over a traditional water bath). Next came the eggs: Some recipes call for whipping just the whites with sugar, others for whipping the whites and yolks separately (both with sugar), and still others for whipping whole eggs with the sugar until the mixture is thick and pale. I tried the last, simplest route first. Finally, I blitzed sliced almonds to a fine meal in the food processor, blended them with the chocolate mixture, gently folded in the whipped eggs, poured the batter into the prepared pan, and baked it in a 325-degree oven.

The chocolate flavor was flat, but that was an easy fix with additions such as vanilla, salt, and cocoa powder to boost complexity. The bigger issue was the cake's consistency, which was downright dense.

The tricky thing about flourless chocolate cakes is that they don't contain chemical leaveners such as baking powder or baking soda. That's because the air created by a chemical leavener is useless unless it is trapped within the pastry's structure, typically by the gluten networks formed by flour. With no flour in the torta, the task of aerating my butter-, chocolate-, and nut-laden batter fell entirely to the eggs. The whipped whole eggs weren't providing enough lift or structure, so I made a couple more cakes in which I varied how I incorporated the eggs.

Whipping just the whites with sugar and folding them into the batter after I had whisked in the yolks didn't cut it either; the cake exited the oven proud and puffed but quickly collapsed as it cooled. Only when I beat the whites and yolks separately in the stand mixer, each with half the sugar, were the two components able to work together to aerate the heavy batter. Mixed this way, the center of the cake was moist, tender, and just a tad dense, just as a flourless cake should be. And though the cake sank slightly as it cooled, it held its stature.

TORTA CAPRESE

The other good news: The whipped yolks were so thick and stable that I discovered I could pour the chocolate-butter-almond mixture directly over them and mix everything in the stand mixer rather than by hand in a separate bowl as I had been doing. Even better, mixing the batter mechanically allowed me to incorporate a small portion of the whipped whites, which had been difficult to do with a spatula because of the batter's heft. But with the mixer's help, I was able to lighten the heavy, stiff batter just enough that I could then very gently fold in the rest of the whipped whites, preserving as much of their volume and aerating effect as possible.

To make the cake's crumb just a tad tighter, I tried cutting back on the almond meal by 25 percent, which did the trick without noticeably affecting the flavor of the cake. While I was at it, I also discovered that commercial almond meal worked just as well as nuts I had ground myself—and it saved me the trouble of hauling out the food processor.

Dusted with confectioners' sugar, the torta looked festive and elegant—a dessert fit for a princess, a mobster, or your favorite dinner guest. Serving it with infused whipped cream (I made one with amaretto and another with orange liqueur and orange zest) brought it a step closer to its Italian roots and gave it further distinction from a typical flourless chocolate cake. And if you happen to have leftovers, you're in luck: It tastes great the next day.

—STEVE DUNN, *Cook's Illustrated*

NOTES FROM THE TEST KITCHEN

ALMOND FLOUR VERSUS ALMOND MEAL
There are no official labeling standards for these products, but almond flour is typically made from blanched (skinless) nuts, while almond meal is most often ground from skin-on nuts. Luckily, both work equally well in our *torta*.

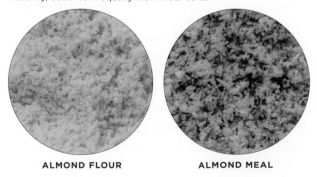

ALMOND FLOUR   ALMOND MEAL

Torta Caprese
SERVES 12 TO 14

For the best results, use a good-quality bittersweet chocolate and Dutch-processed cocoa here. We developed this recipe using our favorite bittersweet chocolate, Ghirardelli 60% Cacao Bittersweet Chocolate Premium Baking Bar, and our favorite Dutch-processed cocoa, Droste Cacao. Either almond flour or almond meal will work in this recipe; we used Bob's Red Mill. Serve this cake with lightly sweetened whipped cream or with Amaretto Whipped Cream or Orange Whipped Cream (recipes follow).

12	tablespoons unsalted butter, cut into 12 pieces
6	ounces bittersweet chocolate, chopped
1	teaspoon vanilla extract
4	large eggs, separated
1	cup (7 ounces) granulated sugar, divided
2	cups (7 ounces) almond flour
2	tablespoons Dutch-processed cocoa powder
½	teaspoon table salt
	Confectioners' sugar (optional)

1. Adjust oven rack to middle position and heat oven to 325 degrees. Lightly spray 9-inch springform pan with vegetable oil spray.

2. Microwave butter and chocolate in medium bowl at 50 percent power, stirring often, until melted, 1½ to 2 minutes. Stir in vanilla and set aside.

3. Using stand mixer fitted with whisk attachment, whip egg whites on medium-low speed until foamy, about 1 minute. Increase speed to medium-high and continue to whip, slowly adding ½ cup granulated sugar, until whites are glossy and thick and hold stiff peaks, about 4 minutes longer. Transfer whites to large bowl.

4. Add egg yolks and remaining ½ cup granulated sugar to now-empty mixer bowl. Whip on medium-high speed until thick and pale yellow, about 3 minutes, scraping down bowl as needed. Add chocolate mixture and mix on medium speed until incorporated, about 15 seconds. Add almond flour, cocoa, and salt and mix until incorporated, about 30 seconds.

5. Remove bowl from mixer and stir few times with large rubber spatula, scraping bottom of bowl to ensure almond flour is fully incorporated. Add one-third of egg whites to bowl, return bowl to mixer, and mix on medium speed until no streaks of white remain, about

30 seconds, scraping down bowl halfway through mixing. Transfer batter to bowl with remaining whites. Using large rubber spatula, gently fold whites into batter until no streaks of white remain. Pour batter into prepared pan, smooth top with spatula, and place pan on rimmed baking sheet.

6. Bake until toothpick inserted in center comes out with few moist crumbs attached, about 50 minutes, rotating pan halfway through baking. Let cake cool in pan on wire rack for 20 minutes. Remove side of pan and let cake cool completely, about 2 hours. (Cake can be wrapped in plastic wrap and stored at room temperature for up to 3 days.)

7. Dust top of cake with confectioners' sugar, if using. Using offset spatula, transfer cake to serving platter. Cut into wedges and serve.

Amaretto Whipped Cream
SERVES 12 TO 14 (MAKES 2 CUPS)

For the best results, chill the bowl and the whisk attachment before whipping the cream.

 1 **cup heavy cream, chilled**
 2 **tablespoons amaretto**
 1 **tablespoon confectioners' sugar**

Using stand mixer fitted with whisk attachment, whip cream, amaretto, and sugar on medium-low speed until foamy, about 1 minute. Increase speed to high and whip until soft peaks form, 1 to 3 minutes.

Orange Whipped Cream
SERVES 12 TO 14 (MAKES 2 CUPS)

For the best results, chill the bowl and the whisk attachment before whipping the cream. You can substitute Grand Marnier for the Cointreau, if desired.

 1 **cup heavy cream, chilled**
 2 **tablespoons Cointreau**
 1 **tablespoon confectioners' sugar**
 ¼ **teaspoon grated orange zest**

Using stand mixer fitted with whisk attachment, whip all ingredients on medium-low speed until foamy, about 1 minute. Increase speed to high and whip until soft peaks form, 1 to 3 minutes.

CLEMENTINE CAKE

✔ **WHY THIS RECIPE WORKS** To achieve the maximum amount of bright, floral clementine flavor in our Clementine Cake, we put clementines both inside and on top of the cake. For the batter, we relied on the standard creaming process but added clementines that we had softened in the microwave and pureed. We baked the cake in a greased springform pan to ensure that it baked up tall. And while it was baking, we quickly candied some sliced clementines in a sugar syrup. For a showstopping white glaze that set off the bright-orange candied fruit slices, we whisked together confectioners' sugar, water, and a pinch of salt.

Clementine cakes are almost always tender single-layer cakes made with ground clementines. They can be upside down or right side up and are typically dusted with confectioners' sugar or covered with a glaze (chocolate or sugar) and decorated with candied slices of their namesake fruit. It seems odd, but the pulverized clementines add just the right amount of sweet, sour, and floral citrus flavor to every bite.

I began by baking five clementine cake recipes. Each one was unique, but they all called for ground almonds as the base of the cake (a few added a bit of flour, too). The clementine flavor in the best of these cakes was surprisingly sweet, with just a hint of pleasant bitterness. But those recipes called for cooking the whole clementines in water for 2 hours (to tame the rind's bitterness and soften the fruit) before pulverizing them in a food processor. Was cooking them for that long really necessary?

Thankfully, through a few days of testing, I discovered that while the clementines did need to be softened before grinding, a long boiling time wasn't necessary. Microwaving the fruit in a covered bowl for just a few minutes did a splendid job of softening it and getting rid of most of the bitterness.

As for the cake itself, my tasters loved the rich flavor provided by the ground almonds (sliced almonds that I had buzzed in a food processor), but using all ground almonds made the texture gritty and dense. Cutting the almonds with some flour made for a sturdier, lighter cake. I also discovered that a well-greased springform pan was necessary to get the best result—it's important that this single-layer cake be tall, and a springform pan has taller sides than a cake pan.

CLEMENTINE CAKE

For the top of the cake, we loved the version with a thick white glaze draped over the cake, so it was just a matter of finding the ratio of confectioners' sugar to water (plus a pinch of salt) for the perfect consistency. We also fell for the beautiful slices of candied clementines that adorned some versions. To get consistent ¼-inch-thick slices, I found that it helped to chill the fruit and then use a mandoline; from there, all it took was a stint in boiling sugar water to candy the fruit nicely. The candied clementines looked amazing when laid atop the white glaze—they tasted great, too, adding a sweet-tart citrus punch.

Having worked through all the elements, I baked and assembled one last cake. I then listened to my coworkers ooh and aah as I sliced into the finished cake. Let's just say there weren't any leftovers.

—ASHLEY MOORE, *Cook's Country*

Clementine Cake

SERVES 8

Use clementines measuring about 2 inches in diameter (about 1¾ ounces each). We recommend using a mandoline to get consistent slices of clementine to arrange on top of the cake; you can also use a chef's knife. We found it easier to slice the clementines when they were cold. You will have a few more candied clementine slices than you will need; use the nicest-looking ones for the cake's top.

CAKE

9	ounces clementines, unpeeled, stemmed (about 5 clementines)
2¼	cups (7½ ounces) sliced blanched almonds, toasted
1	cup (5 ounces) all-purpose flour
1¼	teaspoons baking powder
¼	teaspoon table salt
10	tablespoons unsalted butter, cut into 10 pieces and softened
1½	cups (10½ ounces) granulated sugar
5	large eggs

CANDIED CLEMENTINES

4	clementines, unpeeled, stemmed
1	cup water
1	cup (7 ounces) granulated sugar
⅛	teaspoon table salt

GLAZE

2	cups (8 ounces) confectioners' sugar
2½	tablespoons water, plus extra as needed
	Pinch table salt

1. FOR THE CAKE: Adjust oven rack to middle position and heat oven to 325 degrees. Spray 9-inch springform pan with vegetable oil spray, line bottom with parchment paper, and grease parchment. Microwave clementines in covered bowl until softened and some juice is released, about 3 minutes. Discard juice and let clementines cool for 10 minutes.

2. Process almonds, flour, baking powder, and salt in food processor until almonds are finely ground, about 30 seconds; transfer to second bowl. Add clementines to now-empty processor and process until smooth, about 1 minute, scraping down sides of bowl as needed.

3. Using stand mixer fitted with paddle, beat butter and sugar on medium-high speed until pale and fluffy, about 3 minutes. Add eggs, one at a time, and beat until combined, scraping down bowl as needed. Add clementine puree and beat until incorporated, about 30 seconds.

4. Reduce speed to low and add almond mixture in 3 additions until just combined, scraping down bowl as needed. Using rubber spatula, give batter final stir by hand. Transfer batter to prepared pan and smooth top. Bake until toothpick inserted in center comes out clean, 55 minutes to 1 hour. Let cake cool completely in pan on wire rack, about 2 hours.

5. FOR THE CANDIED CLEMENTINES: While cake cools, line baking sheet with triple layer of paper towels. Slice clementines ¼ inch thick perpendicular to stem; discard rounded ends. Bring water, sugar, and salt to simmer in small saucepan over medium heat and cook until sugar has dissolved, about 1 minute. Add clementines and cook until softened, about 6 minutes. Using tongs, transfer clementines to prepared sheet and let cool for at least 30 minutes, flipping halfway through cooling to blot away excess moisture.

6. FOR THE GLAZE: Whisk sugar, water, and salt in bowl until smooth. Adjust consistency with extra water as needed, ½ teaspoon at a time, until glaze has consistency of thick craft glue and leaves visible trail in bowl when drizzled from whisk.

7. Carefully run paring knife around cake and remove side of pan. Using thin metal spatula, lift cake from pan bottom; discard parchment and transfer cake to serving platter. Pour glaze over cake and smooth top with offset spatula, allowing some glaze to drip down sides. Let sit for 1 hour to set.

8. Just before serving, select 8 uniform candied clementine slices (you will have more than 8 slices; reserve extra slices for another use) and blot away excess moisture with additional paper towels. Arrange slices around top edge of cake, evenly spaced. Serve. (Cake can be wrapped in plastic wrap and stored at room temperature for up to 2 days.)

STRAWBERRY SHORTCAKE TRIFLE

WHY THIS RECIPE WORKS We wanted strawberries to be the star of our trifle. To extract the most flavor out of the berries, we tossed them with a bit of sugar and let them sit for a spell, which intensified their sweetness and created a lightly sweet syrup. For a festive, grown-up vibe, we added orange liqueur to the syrup. Inspired by strawberry shortcake, we opted to use fluffy, tender shortcake biscuits instead of the typical cake component. To construct the trifle, we layered pieces of the biscuits followed by some of the syrup and the strawberries. Next came a healthy dose of vanilla pastry cream (which we'd prepared and refrigerated before making the other components) and some whipped cream. After repeating those layers twice, we decorated the top with sliced strawberries.

Resplendent in appearance but made up of humble parts, a sweet fruit trifle works just as well as a casual weekend dessert as it does as a holiday centerpiece.

A trifle's architecture usually goes like this: A layer of sponge cake or ladyfingers doused in sweet wine such as sherry or Marsala forms the base; it's followed by a layer of fruit (often jam), a layer of rich chilled pastry cream, and a layer of whipped cream. The layers repeat one or more times, depending on the depth of the vessel. Each layer sinks slightly into the next as the trifle grows taller, gradually melding the flavors and textures to form a delightful mess.

For when strawberry season is in full swing, I wanted to create a trifle with strawberries as the star. To get the most out of my berries, I chopped them, tossed them with a bit of sugar, and let them sit for a spell; this resting period intensified their sweetness while leaving behind a slightly sugared syrup. For the booze element, I chose orange liqueur; its subtle citrus flavors contributed a festive, grown-up vibe.

My trifle needed a base with enough structure to stand up to the strawberry juice and support the layers above, but the obvious pastry options—angel food cake, pound cake, or chiffon cake cut into cubes—were either too soft, too dense, or too time-consuming.

Inspired by another favorite dessert, strawberry shortcake, I decided to use quick-and-easy shortcake biscuits. Fluffy and tender, they provided just the right texture (soft but not mushy) and a pleasant buttery flavor.

Pastry cream, a vanilla-flavored custard, is an essential component of a trifle. It isn't difficult to make but requires some time and attention. And it must be made first because it needs to be refrigerated for at least 3 hours before you can use it.

Once I'd whipped the cream, I was ready for construction. I lined the bottom of my trifle dish with chunks of the biscuits and then added a bit of strawberry juice, followed by some of the berries. Next came a dollop of pastry cream and some whipped cream, and then I started all over again. Once I'd completed this process three times, I covered my dish with plastic wrap and stuck it in the fridge to let the flavors meld.

An hour or so later, I decorated the top with a few sliced strawberries and called my tasters. They were entranced by the bold look of the trifle and delighted by the range of sweet, nuanced flavors. "Only one thing is missing," said a colleague. "Champagne."

—ALLI BERKEY, *Cook's Country*

Strawberry Shortcake Trifle

SERVES 12

We call for a 3½-quart trifle dish for this recipe; however, a 4-quart bowl can be used in its place. Individual trifles can also be made in twelve 1-cup jars or cups.

PASTRY CREAM

- 5 large egg yolks
- ½ cup (3½ ounces) sugar, divided
- 3 tablespoons cornstarch
- 2 cups whole milk
   Pinch table salt
- 4 tablespoons unsalted butter, cut into
   4 pieces and chilled
- 1½ teaspoons vanilla extract

BISCUITS

- 2 cups (10 ounces) all-purpose flour
- 2 teaspoons baking powder
- ½ teaspoon baking soda
- 1 teaspoon sugar
- ¾ teaspoon table salt
- ½ cup whole milk, chilled
- ½ cup heavy cream, chilled
- 8 tablespoons unsalted butter, melted

STRAWBERRIES

- 3 pounds strawberries, divided
- ½ cup sugar
- ¼ cup Grand Marnier
-   P.nch table salt

WHIPPED CREAM

- 1½ cups heavy cream, chilled
- 2 tablespoons sugar
- ½ teaspoon vanilla extract

1. FOR THE PASTRY CREAM: Whisk egg yolks, 2 tablespoons sugar, and cornstarch in medium bowl until mixture is pale yellow and thick, about 1 minute; set aside. Combine milk, salt, and remaining 6 tablespoons sugar in medium saucepan and bring to simmer over medium heat, stirring occasionally to dissolve sugar.

2. Gradually whisk half of milk mixture into yolk mixture to temper. Return milk-yolk mixture to saucepan. Return to simmer over medium heat and cook, whisking constantly, until mixture is thickened and 3 or 4 bubbles burst on surface, about 3 minutes. Off heat, whisk in butter and vanilla. Transfer mixture to clean bowl, press parchment paper directly onto surface, and refrigerate until set, at least 3 hours.

3. FOR THE BISCUITS: While pastry cream sets, adjust oven rack to middle position and heat oven to 450 degrees. Line baking sheet with parchment. Whisk flour, baking powder, baking soda, sugar, and salt together in large bowl. Stir milk, cream, and melted butter together in small bowl (butter will form clumps).

4. Add dairy mixture to flour mixture and stir with rubber spatula until just combined. Using greased ¼-cup dry measuring cup, drop 12 scant scoops of batter 1½ inches apart on prepared sheet. Bake until biscuit tops are golden brown, about 12 minutes, rotating sheet halfway through baking. Transfer biscuits to wire rack and let cool completely, about 20 minutes.

FOUR STEPS TO PERFECT PASTRY CREAM

1. Whisk yolks, sugar, and cornstarch in bowl until mixture is pale yellow and thick.

2. Bring milk, salt, and remaining sugar to simmer in saucepan, stirring occasionally to dissolve sugar.

3. Gradually whisk half of milk mixture into yolk mixture to temper.

4. Simmer milk-yolk mixture, whisking constantly, until thickened, then whisk in butter and vanilla off heat.

---

5. FOR THE STRAWBERRIES: Set aside 6 strawberries. Hull remaining strawberries and cut into ½-inch pieces. Combine cut strawberries, sugar, Grand Marnier, and salt in large bowl. Let sit at room temperature for 30 minutes.

6. FOR THE WHIPPED CREAM: Using stand mixer fitted with whisk attachment, whip cream, sugar, and vanilla on low speed until foamy, about 1 minute. Increase speed to high and whip until stiff peaks form, 1 to 3 minutes. Refrigerate until ready to use.

7. Drain strawberries in colander set in bowl, reserving juice. Whisk pastry cream to recombine. Break 4 biscuits into 1-inch pieces and arrange on bottom of

PAVLOVA WITH FRUIT AND WHIPPED CREAM

3½-quart trifle dish. Pour one-third of reserved strawberry juice over biscuits. Top with one-third of strawberries, followed by one-third of pastry cream. Spread 1 cup whipped cream evenly over pastry cream. Repeat layers twice. Cover dish with plastic wrap and refrigerate for at least 1 hour or up to 24 hours. Hull reserved strawberries and slice thin, then arrange decoratively on top of trifle. Serve.

PAVLOVA WITH FRUIT AND WHIPPED CREAM

✓ **WHY THIS RECIPE WORKS** For foolproof pavlova, we switched from the typical French meringue—which requires precise timing when adding the sugar to the egg whites—to a Swiss meringue, which is made by dissolving the sugar in the egg whites as they are heated over a simmering water bath and then whipping the mixture to stiff peaks. Adding cornstarch and vinegar to the mixture produced a meringue that had a marshmallowy interior, a crisp exterior, and a slight chew where the two textures met. We shaped the meringue into a wide, flat disk, baked it, and then let it dry in a turned-off oven for 1½ hours. Lightly sweetened whipped cream and tart fresh fruit balanced the meringue's sweetness and made for a beautiful presentation of colors and textures. Letting the finished meringue sit for a few minutes before serving softened the crust for neater slices.

Anna Pavlova was known as the "incomparable" ballerina, captivating audiences across the world at the turn of the 20th century. It's no wonder, then, that chefs at the time immortalized her in recipes, including frogs' legs à la Pavlova in France, Pavlova ice cream in the United States, and most famously, the glamorous meringue, whipped cream, and fruit confection that's simply called pavlova.

Unlike meringue cookies, which are uniformly dry and crunchy throughout, the meringue for pavlova (which can be baked in a single large round or smaller individual disks) offers a crispy outer shell; a tender, marshmallowy interior; and a pleasant chew where the two textures meet. The meringue's sweetness is balanced by whipped cream and tart fresh fruit, which makes for a gorgeous jumble of flavors and textures—and a lightness that is ideal at the end of a rich meal.

Because of its dramatic appearance, you might think that pavlova is a real project. But in fact it calls for only a handful of ingredients, and the meringue base can be baked in advance, leaving only cream to be whipped and fruit topping to be prepped before serving. Pavlova's unfussiness is part of its allure. More often than not, its shape is rustic and a few cracks are unavoidable, but there's beauty in these imperfections.

That said, there is one part of the process that can be intimidating: producing just the right texture for the meringue. So that's where I started my testing.

Most pavlova recipes start with a French meringue, which is made by whipping raw egg whites and sugar to stiff peaks and then folding in cornstarch and an acid, usually white vinegar (more on these ingredients later), along with a flavoring such as vanilla. The meringue is spread into a disk on a parchment-lined baking sheet and baked in a low oven until the outside is crisp. The oven is then turned off, and the meringue is left to continue drying out until the inside is no longer wet but still soft.

A French meringue is tricky because it requires adding the sugar to egg whites at just the right moment: too soon and the meringue won't inflate properly; too late and the meringue can be gritty.

To avoid that guesswork, I decided to switch to a Swiss meringue, where the sugar is dissolved from the start. It's made by gently warming the whites and sugar in a bowl set over simmering water until the sugar is dissolved and then whipping the mixture to stiff peaks.

I heated six egg whites and 1 cup of sugar to 140 degrees; whipped the mixture to stiff peaks; added cornstarch, vinegar, and vanilla; and spread the meringue into a round. Unfortunately, it baked up with a pitted, coarse interior.

Our science research editor explained: Egg white proteins start out as separately wound little molecules, like balls of yarn. When heated and whipped, as in a Swiss meringue, the balls uncoil into linear strands (denature) and then slowly start to knit together (coagulate) at about 140 degrees.

As the meringue bakes, the knitted proteins firm and contract, squeezing out water, which then evaporates. The more loosely knit the proteins are, the more they're pushed apart by the escaping steam, which can result in a coarse-textured dessert. Cooking the whites to a higher temperature—160 degrees—before baking would cause more coagulation. With the proteins knit into a finer, more cohesive mesh, the structure would not be as disrupted by escaping steam and the final product would be smoother.

When I thought about it, it made sense that I needed to alter the standard Swiss meringue. It's most often used as the base for buttercream frosting, not baked for pavlova. Sure enough, when I brought the whites and sugar to 160 degrees, I was rewarded with a smooth, fine texture.

However, the exterior of the meringue was soft rather than crispy because it contained too much free water after baking. Adding sugar is the time-tested way to make sure a meringue crisps up: It draws water from the egg whites, so they dry out during baking.

For my next set of tests, I made three batches of meringue with increasing amounts of sugar: 1 cup, 1¼ cups, and 1½ cups for six egg whites. The smaller amounts all resulted in meringues with soft exteriors, so I moved forward with 1½ cups of sugar, which resulted in a dry, crispy shell.

Now, back to the vinegar and cornstarch. Many meringue recipes call for acid to be added to the egg whites. Pavlova meringue is unusual in that cornstarch is also typically mixed in and the vinegar is added after—not before—whipping. Recipes suggest that this combination is responsible for the meringue's tender yet chewy texture.

To determine whether the presence of vinegar and cornstarch was dictated by tradition or function, I made five batches of meringue: one with just egg whites and sugar, one with cornstarch, one with vinegar, one with cream of tartar (an acidic powder), and one with both vinegar and cornstarch. The plain sample seemed wet and slick on the inside. The starch-only interior was all chew, like a nougat, while the vinegar- and cream of tartar–based meringues were superdelicate and tender within. Only the batch made with acid and starch was just right: chewy at the edge and marshmallowy inside. Since cream of tartar and vinegar performed identically, I stuck with tradition and called for vinegar since it's what most cooks keep on hand.

I spread a thick layer of lightly sweetened whipped cream onto the cooled meringue disk. For a festive finish, I topped the whipped cream with sliced oranges, tart cranberries soaked in sugar syrup to cut their bitterness (for sparkle, I rolled some in sugar), and fresh mint. Slicing pavlova can be a slightly messy affair, which is part of the fun, but letting the dessert sit for just 5 minutes softened the meringue's crust just enough to make cutting easier.

Ladies and gentlemen, I present to you: the incomparable pavlova!

—ANNIE PETITO, *Cook's Illustrated*

Pavlova with Fruit and Whipped Cream
SERVES 10

Because eggs can vary in size, measuring the egg whites by weight or volume is essential to ensure that you are working with the correct ratio of egg whites to sugar. Open the oven door as infrequently as possible while the meringue is inside. Don't worry when the meringue cracks; it is part of the dessert's charm. The inside of the meringue will remain soft.

NOTES FROM THE TEST KITCHEN

PAVLOVA: A TRIO OF FUN-TO-EAT TEXTURES
Whereas a traditional meringue cookie is dry and crunchy throughout, the meringue for pavlova boasts three unique textures that keep things interesting as you eat.

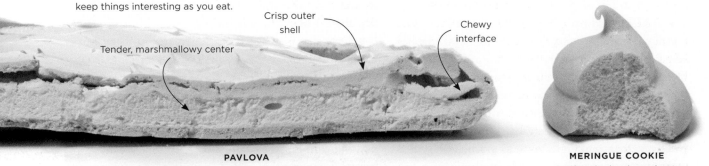

Crisp outer shell

Chewy interface

Tender, marshmallowy center

PAVLOVA
Crisp, chewy, and tender

MERINGUE COOKIE
Uniformly dry throughout

MERINGUE

1½ cups (10½ ounces) sugar

¾ cup (6 ounces) egg whites (5 to 7 large eggs)

1½ teaspoons distilled white vinegar

1½ teaspoons cornstarch

1 teaspoon vanilla extract

WHIPPED CREAM

2 cups heavy cream, chilled

2 tablespoons sugar

1 recipe Orange, Cranberry, and Mint Topping (recipe follows)

1. FOR THE MERINGUE: Adjust oven rack to middle position and heat oven to 250 degrees. Using pencil, draw 10-inch circle in center of 18 by 13-inch piece of parchment paper. Combine sugar and egg whites in bowl of stand mixer and place bowl over saucepan filled with 1 inch simmering water, making sure that water does not touch bottom of bowl. Whisking gently but constantly, heat until sugar is dissolved and mixture registers 160 to 165 degrees, 5 to 8 minutes.

2. Fit stand mixer with whisk attachment and whip mixture on high speed until meringue forms stiff peaks, is smooth and creamy, and is bright white with sheen, about 4 minutes (bowl may still be slightly warm to touch). Stop mixer and scrape down bowl with spatula. Add vinegar, cornstarch, and vanilla and whip on high speed until combined, about 10 seconds.

3. Spoon about ¼ teaspoon meringue onto each corner of rimmed baking sheet. Press parchment, marked side down, onto sheet to secure. Pile meringue in center of circle on parchment. Using circle as guide, spread and smooth meringue with back of spoon or spatula from center outward, building 10-inch disk that is slightly higher around edges. Disk should measure about 1 inch high with ¼-inch depression in center.

4. Bake meringue until exterior is dry and crisp and meringue releases cleanly from parchment when gently lifted at edge with thin metal spatula, 1 to 1½ hours. Meringue should be quite pale (a hint of creamy color is OK). Turn off oven, prop open door with wooden spoon, and let meringue cool in oven for 1½ hours. Remove sheet from oven and let meringue cool completely before topping, about 15 minutes. (Cooled meringue can be wrapped tightly in plastic wrap and stored at room temperature for up to 1 week.)

5. FOR THE WHIPPED CREAM: Before serving, whip cream and sugar in chilled bowl of stand mixer fitted with whisk attachment on low speed until small bubbles form, about 30 seconds. Increase speed to medium and whip until whisk leaves trail, about 30 seconds. Increase speed to high and continue to whip until cream is smooth, thick, and nearly doubled in volume, about 20 seconds longer for soft peaks. If necessary, finish whipping by hand to adjust consistency.

6. Carefully peel meringue away from parchment and place on large serving platter. Spoon whipped cream into center of meringue. Top whipped cream with fruit topping. Let stand for at least 5 minutes or up to 1 hour, then slice and serve.

Orange, Cranberry, and Mint Topping
SERVES 10 (MAKES 4½ CUPS)

You can substitute tangelos or Cara Cara oranges for the navel oranges, if desired. Valencia or blood oranges can also be used, but since they are smaller, increase the number of fruit to six.

1½ cups (10½ ounces) sugar, divided

6 ounces (1½ cups) frozen cranberries

5 navel oranges

⅓ cup chopped fresh mint, plus 10 small leaves

1. Bring 1 cup sugar and 1 cup water to boil in medium saucepan over medium heat, stirring to dissolve sugar. Off heat, stir in cranberries. Let cranberries and syrup cool completely, about 30 minutes. (Cranberries in syrup can be refrigerated for up to 24 hours.)

2. Place remaining ½ cup sugar in shallow dish. Drain cranberries, discarding syrup. Working in 2 batches, roll ½ cup cranberries in sugar and transfer to large plate or tray. Let stand at room temperature to dry, about 1 hour.

3. Cut away peel and pith from oranges. Cut each orange into quarters from pole to pole, then cut crosswise into ¼-inch-thick pieces (you should have 3 cups). Just before serving, toss oranges with nonsugared cranberries and chopped mint in bowl until combined. Using slotted spoon, spoon fruit in even layer over pavlova. Garnish with sugared cranberries and mint leaves. Before serving, drizzle pavlova slices with any juice from bowl.

BROWNED BUTTER BLONDIES

✓ **WHY THIS RECIPE WORKS** For a blondie that's chewy and not too sweet, we found that you can't simply swap in a cookie dough or a brownie batter. Using melted rather than softened butter made for a blondie that was characteristically dense and chewy instead of cakey, and browning the butter boosted the blondie's bland flavor with incredible nutty complexity. Brown sugar was a must for its underlying caramel notes, and its moisture helped keep the bars chewy. To tone down the sweetness, we replaced a portion of the sugar with corn syrup. A full 2 tablespoons of vanilla brought more complexity to the bars, and a generous amount of salt in the batter brought all the flavors into focus. Chopped pecans and milk chocolate chips complemented the butterscotch flavor without overwhelming it.

Do blondies have more fun? Compared with brownies, which get far more attention than their fairer counterpart, I'm not so sure. While you have to look hard to find a truly bad brownie, pale, cloying blondies seem to be more the rule than the exception. That's too bad, because those times I've run across a blondie that was moist, chewy, slightly dense, and full of complex butterscotch goodness, I've always thought that it could hold its own next to any baked treat. I wanted to perfect this bar and give it the respect it deserves.

Before I got down to serious testing, I decided to experiment with two popular notions—that blondies are simply brownies stripped of chocolate, or they're chocolate chip cookies pressed and baked in a pan.

I took recipes for chewy brownies and chewy chocolate chip cookies, eliminated the chocolate in the former, and patted the dough for the latter into a 13 by 9-inch pan. Not surprisingly, each confection was a dud.

The brownie-based bars were gummy, greasy, and sickeningly sweet. As for the chocolate chip cookie bars, which I baked long enough to ensure that the dough at the center of the pan wasn't gooey, they were mostly dry and tough, particularly the edge pieces. They also lacked the nice toffee notes that cookies gain from browning when they are baked individually.

Clearly, a blondie has its own identity, and I'd have to treat it that way to create a successful version. The first decision I faced was the mixing method. Creaming the butter and sugar incorporated air that resulted in a cakey texture, so I settled on mixing melted butter, sugar, and eggs before adding the dry ingredients, which led to a denser, chewier bar.

Most blondie recipes call for light brown sugar, but I wondered if using dark brown sugar instead would help boost butterscotch flavor. I ran a quick side-by-side test. Interestingly, most tasters panned the dark brown sugar for making the blondies taste more like molasses than butterscotch; they also preferred the more golden color of the bars made with light brown sugar.

But I did have something more promising in mind to try: Instead of just melting the butter, I would brown it to create warm, toasty, nutty flavors. So for my next batch of bars, I cooked the butter in a skillet until the milk solids had turned a dark golden brown and had a nutty fragrance, combined it with the other ingredients, and then baked the batter in a 13 by 9-inch pan in a 350-degree oven until lightly golden. This was a big step in the right direction: The blondies tasted decidedly more nutty and rich.

Another idea: Since vanilla extract's earthy, woodsy notes mirror and complement butterscotch flavors, why not try more of it? Doubling the amount of vanilla worked so well to deepen the warm caramel flavor in the bars that I kept going and tripled it.

Increasing the vanilla gave me the idea to increase another ingredient: the salt. Salt is included in most sweet applications because it helps sharpen flavors. When I doubled it from ½ teaspoon to 1 teaspoon, the nutty, buttery flavors stood out a little more in my blondies and the sweetness a little less.

But I wanted to cut back even more on the sweetness. When I decreased the sugar, the results were a good reminder that sugar is never merely a sweetener in baking; it plays multiple roles—and messing with its proportions has consequences. Because brown sugar adds moisture and, like all sugar, is hygroscopic (it attracts and retains moisture), even ¼ cup less made the bars drier. Sugar also acts as a tenderizer by interfering with the flour proteins' ability to form gluten, and less of it made the bars a little tough.

I needed a sweetener that performed all the positive actions of sugar but wasn't too sweet, so I turned to corn syrup. Unlike the extremely sweet high-fructose corn syrup used to make soda, regular corn syrup is actually less sweet than sugar: Made by breaking down starch into glucose molecules and small glucose chains, corn syrup is about 50 percent less sweet than white

BROWNED BUTTER BLONDIES

and brown sugars. I subbed in ⅓ cup for ¼ cup of the brown sugar. Even though the corn syrup's volume was greater, the blondies tasted noticeably less sweet.

I had the flavor right where I wanted it, but I wasn't quite done. I scaled up my recipe by 25 percent to create thicker bars and found that I had to double the baking time. This had the unintended but happy consequence of drying out the top of the batter, so it browned more deeply and had even more nutty, caramelized flavor while the interior remained moist and chewy.

It was time to add complementary elements such as nuts and chips. For nuts I chose buttery pecans. For chips, I opted for milk chocolate morsels, whose mild dairy sweetness didn't overpower the caramel flavor.

As a final touch, I crumbled flaky sea salt over the batter before it went into the oven. After the bars cooled completely, I cut them into squares. These blondies were exactly as I'd envisioned: moist, chewy, wonderfully complex and butterscotch-y, and not too sweet. The nuts and chocolate played nicely with the browned butter, and the crunchy pops of flaky salt made for an appealing contrast. I was equally thrilled to find that the bars kept very well—for close to a week—at room temperature. Though I doubted they'd last that long.

—ANNIE PETITO, *Cook's Illustrated*

NOTES FROM THE TEST KITCHEN

SECRETS TO SUPERIOR BLONDIES
For properly moist, chewy blondies, you can't get around using a lot of sugar. But our bars have so many other nutty, buttery, caramel-y flavors that the sweetness stays in check. Here's how we created an ideal version.

BROWNED BUTTER Melted butter contributes to chewy texture. Browning it darkens the milk solids to create toasty, nutty depth.

BROWN SUGAR + CORN SYRUP Brown sugar contributes toffee notes, and both sweeteners enhance chewy texture. Corn syrup is also less sweet than other sugars.

LOTS OF VANILLA Two full tablespoons of vanilla enhance caramel-like flavors.

PLENTY OF SALT More than the usual amount of salt in the batter (plus more on top) brings all the flavors into focus.

COMPLEMENTARY MIX-INS Pecans add buttery richness; milk (versus dark) chocolate chips don't overwhelm the butterscotch notes.

Browned Butter Blondies
MAKES 24 BLONDIES

We developed this recipe using a metal baking pan; using a glass baking dish may cause the blondies to overbake. Toast the pecans on a rimmed baking sheet in a 350-degree oven until fragrant, 8 to 12 minutes, stirring them halfway through toasting.

2¼	cups (11¼ ounces) all-purpose flour
1¼	teaspoons table salt
½	teaspoon baking powder
12	tablespoons unsalted butter
1¾	cups packed (12¼ ounces) light brown sugar
3	large eggs
½	cup corn syrup
2	tablespoons vanilla extract
1	cup pecans, toasted and chopped coarse
½	cup (3 ounces) milk chocolate chips
¼–½	teaspoon flake sea salt, crumbled (optional)

1. Adjust oven rack to middle position and heat oven to 350 degrees. Make foil sling for 13 by 9-inch baking pan by folding 2 long sheets of aluminum foil; first sheet should be 13 inches wide and second sheet should be 9 inches wide. Lay sheets of foil in pan perpendicular to each other, with extra foil hanging over edges of pan. Push foil into corners and up sides of pan, smoothing foil flush to pan. Lightly spray foil with vegetable oil spray.

2. Whisk flour, table salt, and baking powder together in medium bowl.

3. Melt butter in 10-inch skillet over medium-high heat. Continue to cook, swirling skillet and stirring constantly with rubber spatula, until butter is dark golden brown and has nutty aroma, 1 to 3 minutes longer. Transfer butter to large heatproof bowl.

4. Add sugar to hot butter and whisk until combined. Add eggs, corn syrup, and vanilla and whisk until smooth. Using rubber spatula, stir in flour mixture until fully incorporated. Stir in pecans and chocolate chips. Transfer batter to prepared pan; using spatula, spread batter into corners of pan and smooth surface. Sprinkle with sea salt, if using. Bake until top is deep golden brown and springs backs when lightly pressed, 35 to 40 minutes, rotating pan halfway through baking (blondies will firm as they cool).

5. Let blondies cool completely in pan on wire rack, about 2 hours. Using foil sling, lift blondies out of pan and transfer to cutting board. Remove foil. Cut into 24 bars. (Blondies can be wrapped tightly in plastic wrap and stored at room temperature for up to 5 days.)

CHEWY PEANUT BUTTER COOKIES

✓ **WHY THIS RECIPE WORKS** We wanted superpeanutty peanut butter cookies with crispy edges and moist, chewy centers, but because peanut butter has a fair amount of starch, more peanut butter in the dough resulted in drier, crumbly, more stunted cookies. So in pursuit of more chew, we examined the dough's fat ratio. In the past, we've found that a ratio of about 30 percent saturated fat to 70 percent unsaturated fat yielded the chewiest cookies, so we've used a combination of butter (mostly saturated) and vegetable oil (mostly unsaturated). Peanut butter, which is mostly unsaturated, replaced the oil here, and melting the butter meant that no mixer was required to combine the ingredients. Dark brown sugar deepened the color of the dough, and honey aided browning as the cookies baked. A half cup of finely chopped dry-roasted peanuts provided another layer of nutty flavor, some visual interest, and a bit of crunch.

I'm a peanut butter fanatic, and I feel uneasy if I don't have an extra jar or two of the stuff stashed away "just in case." So you might be surprised to learn that peanut butter cookies haven't always been my first choice for spur-of-the-moment baking. After all, the cookies' other ingredients are constants in my kitchen, too. But the truth is that I enjoy most peanut butter cookies only when they're warm and fresh. As they cool, so does my enthusiasm for them.

I wanted to think that a solution to these flaws would come easy to a peanut butter devotee such as myself. But after weeks of trying to devise a recipe for cookies with robust peanut flavor and lasting chew, I had to admit that a fix was anything but easy—and was not, as I'd initially hoped, simply a matter of packing more peanut butter into the dough. When I did finally nail a formula that produced soft, chewy, deeply nutty cookies, I humbly realized that the trick boiled down to a subtle but fundamental point of baking: ratios.

I decided to focus on producing a chewy texture first, and luckily I was on familiar ground. Several factors contribute to chewiness in cookies (including adequate amounts of sugar and moisture), but fat is also key. While developing a brownie recipe years ago, I discovered that boxed-mix brownies get their beguilingly chewy texture from a specific ratio of saturated fat to unsaturated fat in the batter: 30 percent saturated to 70 percent unsaturated. Since then, I've applied that fat ratio to recipes for both sugar and oatmeal cookies with great success. So I figured all I had to do was bend the traditional peanut butter cookie formula to fit the chewiness template and I'd be done.

The typical peanut butter cookie recipe I used as a starting point called for 1 cup each of butter (melted for easier mixing) and peanut butter and 2 cups of flour. After whisking the butter and peanut butter together along with granulated sugar, eggs, and vanilla, I stirred in the flour, baking soda, and salt. Next, I scooped equal portions onto a baking sheet, used a fork to imprint the tops with the cookie's signature crosshatch pattern, baked them, and let them cool briefly.

With all that butter, 56 percent of the fat in the dough was saturated, producing a cookie that was tender and short instead of chewy; it also lacked nutty flavor. Most of the fat in peanut butter is unsaturated, though, so replacing ½ cup of highly saturated butter with an additional ½ cup of peanut butter would not only boost peanut flavor but also lower the saturated fat to a more favorable 35 percent.

But by the time I had a cohesive dough, I could tell that this formula wasn't going to work. The mixture was so stiff I was practically kneading it, and the cookies themselves hardly spread at all in the oven and emerged dry and cracked at the edges.

I suspected that the peanut butter–butter swap was to blame for the stiff, dry results. Butter is almost pure fat (it's also about 20 percent water), but peanut butter contains protein and starch. According to Lisa Dean, research food technologist at the U.S. Department of Agriculture's Agricultural Research Service, the protein in peanut butter swells and absorbs added water; this phenomenon was surely drying out my cookies. But this quirk was potentially useful: If I could rely on peanut butter protein and starch instead of some of the flour to give my cookies structure, maybe I could prevent the cookies from drying out and gain more robust peanut flavor in one fell swoop.

CHEWY PEANUT BUTTER COOKIES

But decreasing the flour to 1½ cups got me only part of the way to my goal. The dough was softer, the cookies spread more, and their flavor improved, but biting into the cookies caused them to crumble, and overall they were now more tender than chewy.

It took a few more tests, but I finally figured out that the limit on the ratio of peanut butter to flour was 1 cup to 1½ cups, respectively. Any more peanut butter and the cookies didn't have enough flour for gluten development, which left the cookies too crumbly.

But that satisfying chew still eluded me until I realized that, in general, fat acts as a tenderizer in baked goods. Was it possible that my recipe simply had too much fat overall? To find out, I dropped the butter from ½ cup to ¼ cup. This not only brought the saturated/unsaturated fat ratio back to the ideal 30/70 split but also decreased the ratio of total fat to other ingredients, yielding a supremely chewy cookie.

The chewy cookie lover in me was completely satisfied. The peanut butter fanatic was not, though I wasn't about to touch my carefully calibrated dough formula to pack in more peanut flavor. Instead, I went straight to the source and added ½ cup of finely chopped dry-roasted peanuts to the dough after mixing in the dry ingredients. Their richness and crunch added the depth I was looking for without affecting the fat ratio or interfering with the texture of the dough, but my tasters thought they left the cookies tasting a bit savory. Substituting dark brown sugar for white sugar and adding 2 tablespoons of honey tilted things back in a sweet direction and had the added benefit of enhancing the chewiness a little more.

One final tweak. With the chopped peanuts clearly advertising the cookies' identity, I decided to abandon the crosshatch. While it's up for debate why peanut butter cookies traditionally bear this mark, I've always suspected that it's because the stiff dough needs to be firmly pressed down for the cookies to spread properly. But because my dough was softer than the typical peanut butter cookie dough, it spread nicely if I simply pressed it with my fingers after portioning it on the baking sheet.

Now that I have an easy, truly satisfying peanut butter cookie recipe at the ready, I should probably add another jar or two of peanut butter to my stash. Just in case.

—ANDREA GEARY, *Cook's Illustrated*

Chewy Peanut Butter Cookies

MAKES 24 COOKIES

To ensure that the cookies have the proper texture, use a traditional creamy peanut butter in this recipe; do not substitute crunchy or natural peanut butter. We developed this recipe with Skippy Creamy Peanut Butter. For the best results, be sure to weigh the flour, sugar, and peanut butter. You can substitute light brown sugar for dark, but your cookies will be lighter in color. Our favorite imitation vanilla extract is Baker's Imitation Vanilla Flavor, and our favorite pure vanilla extract is Simply Organic Pure Vanilla Extract.

- 1½ cups (7½ ounces) all-purpose flour
- 1 teaspoon baking soda
- ½ teaspoon table salt
- 1½ cups packed (10½ ounces) dark brown sugar
- 1 cup (9 ounces) creamy peanut butter
- 2 large eggs
- 4 tablespoons unsalted butter, melted and cooled
- 2 tablespoons honey
- 1 teaspoon vanilla extract
- ½ cup dry-roasted peanuts, chopped fine

1. Adjust oven rack to middle position and heat oven to 350 degrees. Line two 18 by 13-inch rimmed baking sheets with parchment paper. Whisk flour, baking soda, and salt together in medium bowl.

2. In large bowl, whisk sugar, peanut butter, eggs, melted butter, honey, and vanilla until smooth. Add flour mixture and stir with rubber spatula until soft, homogeneous dough forms. Stir in peanuts until evenly distributed.

3. Working with 2 tablespoons dough at a time (or using #30 portion scoop), roll dough into balls and evenly space on prepared sheets (12 dough balls per sheet). Using your fingers, gently flatten dough balls until 2 inches in diameter.

4. Bake cookies, 1 sheet at a time, until edges are just set and just beginning to brown, 10 to 12 minutes, rotating sheet after 6 minutes. Let cookies cool on sheet for 5 minutes. Using wide metal spatula, transfer cookies to wire rack and let cool completely before serving.

BELGIAN SPICE COOKIES (SPECULOOS)

✔ **WHY THIS RECIPE WORKS** *Speculoos* are Belgian cookies with a light, crumbly texture and a blend of caramel and warm spice flavors. To achieve the appropriate texture, we rolled the dough thin so it would bake up dry and crispy, used just enough sugar (which absorbs and holds on to water) to lightly sweeten the dough without making the cookies chewy, and added baking powder along with the usual baking soda to produce an open, airy crumb. For a subtle caramel flavor, we chose turbinado sugar rather than molasses-based brown sugar or traditional (but hard-to-find) Belgian brown sugar. To nail the complex spice flavor, we used a large amount of cinnamon and small amounts of cardamom and cloves.

There is a story floating around the internet about a grandmother who gobbled up her grandson's cookies as he slept beside her during a long flight. The motive for the 30,000-foot crime? Biscoff, the signature onboard snack of Delta Air Lines. The tempting cookie dates back to 1932, when a Belgian bakery started selling *speculoos*. Fifty years later, the bakery began manufacturing speculoos for Americans under the name "Biscoff" and its popularity soared.

The speculoos enthusiasm is understandable: The cookies boast warm spice notes, nuanced caramel flavor, and an open texture that crumbles easily. Imagine something between a delicate graham cracker and a hard gingersnap that nearly melts in your mouth.

I wanted to use the one-of-a-kind texture of Biscoff as a model for homemade speculoos. I also intended to mimic their caramel taste and improve the spice flavor—one place I found the packaged version lacking.

Speculoos recipes are straightforward: Simply cream sugar and softened butter in a stand mixer, add an egg (or not), and then mix in flour, spices, baking soda, and salt. Traditional recipes call for pressing the dough into shallow molds that serve the dual purpose of leaving a decorative imprint on the cookies and keeping them from spreading. I'd definitely be taking the more streamlined, modern route of simply rolling the dough thin so that the cookies could bake up dry and crispy.

None of the recipes I tried produced the right texture, so I set out to establish my own. Since the dough would be rolled thin, I wouldn't need a large volume, so I started with just 1½ cups of flour. Most speculoos recipes call for roughly half as much butter as flour by weight, and sure enough, this made the cookies appropriately crumbly; any more butter made them too fragile. I kept the sugar in check so as to avoid the slight oversweetness of packaged Biscoff, and this also got me closer to the ideal texture. That's because sugar is hygroscopic, meaning that it holds on to water, which creates chewiness in cookies. In the end, I landed on 1½ cups of flour, 8 tablespoons of butter, just ¾ cup of brown sugar, and 1 egg, which bound the dough without adding a lot of extra moisture.

As for the leavener, I started with ¼ teaspoon of baking soda, which didn't do much to enhance the texture since it requires acid to react—and these cookies had only the slight acidity of brown sugar. Switching to baking powder successfully opened the internal structure. However, without the baking soda, the cookies lacked a certain savoriness, so I added it back in.

With the crumb of my speculoos just right, I investigated the sugar flavor. Most American speculoos recipes call for brown sugar, which is made by combining refined white sugar with molasses. But authentic speculoos are sweetened with Belgian brown sugar, which is made by adding caramelized sugar to refined white sugar, so it has a cleaner taste, with none of the bitterness of molasses.

I wondered if turbinado sugar would make an effective substitute for Belgian brown sugar, since turbinado sugar is easily available and it has the appropriate caramel-like notes. My next batch of cookies was closer in flavor, but turbinado crystals are larger than those of other sugars, so it gave the speculoos an underlying grittiness. My fix was to grind the turbinado in the food processor. With that, the cookies had the right honeycomb texture along with caramel undertones.

NOTES FROM THE TEST KITCHEN

GET A DECORATIVE EDGE
The fluted pastry wheel that we use to give our *speculoos* a scalloped edge can also be used to cut fresh pasta or ravioli dough, lattice strips for pie, cracker dough, or dough for turnovers, empanadas, or other filled pastries.

Now, how to nail the spice flavor? I was using a sizable 5 teaspoons of cinnamon, but something was missing. After some experimenting, I found that 1 teaspoon of cardamom and ¼ teaspoon of cloves made the cinnamon sing with warmth and sweetness without calling attention to themselves.

To finish, I rolled the just-mixed dough between sheets of parchment and then chilled it before cutting and baking. This was easier than having to either roll and cut a soft dough straightaway or wait for a disk of dough to chill to a workable consistency. After rolling the dough thin—⅜ inch was just right—I copied Biscoff's scalloped edges by using a fluted pastry wheel to cut it into rectangles. Finally, I gently baked the cookies in a 300-degree oven, which gave them ample time to thoroughly dry and crisp.

I had one more thought: Since I already had the food processor out to grind the turbinado, could I also use it to prepare the dough? To find out, I prepared the recipe in a stand mixer and in a food processor. Happily, the resulting cookies were identical; I would stick with the food processor.

With that, there was just one thing left to do: Step across the border to Holland, where speculoos are stamped with windmills and have almonds baked into the underside. I wasn't about to carve miniature windmills in individual cookies, but it was easy enough to roll sliced almonds into the bottom of my dough. With or without nuts, one thing was for certain: These speculoos were topflight.

— ANDREW JANJIGIAN, *Cook's Illustrated*

Belgian Spice Cookies (Speculoos)

MAKES 32 COOKIES

For the proper flavor, we strongly recommend using turbinado sugar (commonly sold as Sugar in the Raw) here. If you can't find it, use ¾ cup plus 2 tablespoons (6 ounces) of packed light brown sugar and skip the sugar grinding in step 2. In step 3, use a rolling pin and a combination of rolling and a smearing motion to form the rectangle. If the dough spreads beyond the rectangle, trim it and use the scraps to fill in the corners; then, replace the parchment and continue to roll. Do not use cookie molds or an embossed rolling pin for the speculoos; they will not hold the patterns. We like Morton & Bassett Spices Ground Cinnamon.

1½ cups (7½ ounces) all-purpose flour
5 teaspoons ground cinnamon
1 teaspoon ground cardamom
¼ teaspoon ground cloves
¼ teaspoon baking soda
¼ teaspoon baking powder
¼ teaspoon table salt
¾ cup (6 ounces) turbinado sugar
8 tablespoons unsalted butter, cut into
  ½-inch pieces and chilled
1 large egg

1. Whisk flour, cinnamon, cardamom, cloves, baking soda, baking powder, and salt together in bowl. Using pencil and ruler, draw 10 by 12-inch rectangle in center of each of 2 large sheets of parchment paper, crisscrossing lines at corners. (Use crisscrosses to help line up top and bottom sheets as dough is rolled.)

2. Process sugar in food processor for 30 seconds (some grains will be smaller than granulated sugar; others will be larger). Add butter and process until uniform mass forms and no large pieces of butter are visible, about 30 seconds, scraping down sides of bowl as needed. Add egg and process until smooth and paste-like, about 10 seconds, scraping down sides of bowl as needed. Add flour mixture and process until no dry flour remains but mixture remains crumbly, about 30 seconds, scraping down sides of bowl as needed.

3. Transfer dough to separate bowl and knead gently with spatula until uniform and smooth, about 10 seconds. Place 1 piece of parchment on counter with pencil side facing down (you should be able to see rectangle through paper). Place dough in center of marked rectangle and press into 6 by 9-inch rectangle. Place second sheet of parchment over dough, with pencil side facing up, so dough is in center of marked rectangle. Using pencil marks as guide, use rolling pin and bench scraper to shape dough into 10 by 12-inch rectangle of even ⅜-inch thickness. Transfer dough with parchment to rimmed baking sheet. Refrigerate until dough is firm, at least 1½ hours (or freeze for 30 minutes). (Rolled dough can be wrapped in plastic wrap and refrigerated for up to 5 days.)

4. Adjust oven racks to upper-middle and lower-middle positions and heat oven to 300 degrees. Line 2 rimless baking sheets with parchment. Transfer chilled dough to counter. Gently peel off top layer of parchment from dough. Using fluted pastry wheel (or sharp knife or pizza cutter) and ruler, trim off rounded edges of dough that extend over marked edges of 10 by 12-inch rectangle. Cut dough lengthwise into 8 equal strips about 1¼ inches wide. Cut each strip crosswise into 4 equal pieces about 3 inches long. Transfer cookies to prepared sheets, spacing them at least ½ inch apart. Bake until cookies are lightly and evenly browned, 30 to 32 minutes, switching and rotating sheets halfway through baking. Let cookies cool completely on sheets, about 20 minutes. (Cookies can be stored at room temperature for up to 3 weeks.)

VARIATION

Belgian Spice Cookies (Speculoos) with Almonds
Once dough has been rolled into rectangle in step 3, gently peel off top layer of parchment. Sprinkle ½ cup sliced almonds evenly over dough. Using rolling pin, gently press almonds into dough. Return parchment to dough, flip dough, and transfer with parchment to sheet. Proceed with recipe as directed.

GOOEY BUTTER CAKE BARS

✔ **WHY THIS RECIPE WORKS** Our unique Gooey Butter Cake Bars, which are based on a favorite St. Louis dessert, top the charts with three layers of sweet goodness. The buttery shortbread crust gives the bars structure and a slight crunch, and it serves as the foundation for a decadent filling of butter, cream cheese, eggs, and sugar. Poured on top of the crust before the bars are baked on the upper oven rack, the filling transforms into two layers: a gooey, buttery middle layer and a perfectly cracked, meringue-like top.

Gooey butter cake, the pride of St. Louis, is well-known as a soft, sweet, and, well, gooey dessert. But when one of my colleagues encountered a different riff on the concept—gooey butter cake bars—my interest was piqued anew.

The sweet treat had several distinct layers: a solid, not-too-sweet bottom crust; a slightly softer second layer of crust; a buttery layer of gooey pudding; and finally a thin and delicate meringue-like crackle on top. Thanks to the sturdy base, it's just as easy to walk around with a bar in hand as it is to eat one with a fork. I set out to perfect each layer before joining them into one harmonious stacked bar.

Early experiments steered me toward a single layer of crust. If I could find the right construction, it would have just as much impact but be much easier than making two. After considering graham cracker crust (too flimsy) and pie crust (too dull), I headed toward a shortbread crust. A few tests gave me a dead-simple method: Just stir together melted butter, sugar, flour, and salt; press the mixture into a 13 by 9-inch pan; and bake it. The trick was adding just enough salt to balance out the sweetness of the bars. Three-quarters of a teaspoon was just right.

The custard filling was trickier. The main ingredients are butter and sugar, but like most custard recipes, this one also calls for eggs, which can be vexing. Most custard recipes suggest cooking the filling over a double boiler so the delicate eggs can be carefully supervised to prevent scrambling, but that kind of fussiness didn't seem right for these rustic bars. I wanted to stir the filling together, dump it over the partially baked (and cooled) crust, and then return it to the oven to cook.

The answer was to replace some of the butter with cream cheese. This helped create a smooth and cohesive filling that, even though it contained two eggs plus two yolks (the extra yolks added richness and contributed to the pale yellow color), needed no prebaking and had just the right pudding-like consistency—think cheesecake but with a bit more jiggle. It also added a lovely tangy flavor to counter the sweetness. And for that gorgeous, crackly, meringue-like top? The egg whites managed to create that all by themselves in the oven, with no extra nudge from me.

If you have a sweet tooth like I do, these bars hit all the creamy, tangy, sweet notes you crave. And they're almost too pretty to eat. Almost.

—ALLI BERKEY, *Cook's Country*

Gooey Butter Cake Bars
SERVES 10 TO 12

A 2-pound bag of confectioners' sugar will yield enough for both the crust and filling with leftovers for dusting. Do not use a glass or ceramic baking dish here. Scrape down the sides and bottom of the mixer bowl with a rubber spatula as often as needed to make sure all the ingredients are fully combined.

GOOEY BUTTER CAKE BARS

CRUST

2½ cups (12½ ounces) all-purpose flour

¾ cup (3 ounces) confectioners' sugar

¾ teaspoon table salt

12 tablespoons unsalted butter, melted

FILLING

8 ounces cream cheese, softened

8 tablespoons unsalted butter, softened

4 cups (1 pound) confectioners' sugar, plus extra for dusting

2 large eggs plus 2 large yolks

2 tablespoons vanilla extract

¼ teaspoon table salt

1. Adjust oven rack to upper-middle position and heat oven to 350 degrees. Make foil sling for 13 by 9-inch baking pan by folding 2 long sheets of aluminum foil; first sheet should be 13 inches wide and second sheet should be 9 inches wide. Lay sheets of foil in pan perpendicular to each other, with extra foil hanging over edges of pan. Push foil into corners and up sides of pan, smoothing foil flush to pan. Spray foil with vegetable oil spray.

2. FOR THE CRUST: Combine flour, sugar, and salt in bowl. Add melted butter and stir with rubber spatula until evenly moistened. Crumble dough over bottom of prepared pan. Using bottom of dry measuring cup, press dough into even layer. Using fork, poke dough all over, about 20 times. Bake until edges are light golden brown, about 20 minutes. Transfer pan to wire rack and let crust cool completely, about 30 minutes.

3. FOR THE FILLING: Combine cream cheese and butter in bowl of stand mixer fitted with paddle. With mixer running on low speed, slowly add sugar and mix until fully combined, about 1 minute, scraping down bowl as needed. Increase speed to medium-high and mix until light and fluffy, about 2 minutes.

4. Reduce speed to low; add eggs and yolks, one at a time, and mix until incorporated. Add vanilla and salt and mix until incorporated, about 20 seconds, scraping down bowl as needed. Increase speed to medium-high and mix until light and fluffy, about 2 minutes (mixture should have consistency of frosting). Spread filling evenly over cooled crust. Gently tap pan on counter to release air bubbles.

5. Bake until top is golden brown, edges have cracked, and center jiggles slightly when pan is gently shaken, about 30 minutes. Transfer pan to wire rack and let bars cool completely, at least 3 hours.

6. Using foil overhang, lift bars out of pan. Cut into 12 pieces. Dust with extra sugar and serve. (Bars can be stored in airtight container at room temperature for up to 3 days.)

CHOCOLATE FUDGE

✔ **WHY THIS RECIPE WORKS** We were after a creamy, rich, ultrachocolaty fudge that didn't take hours or an arm workout to put together. Brown sugar offered a deep, caramel-y flavor that enhanced the chocolate, and cooking the sugar to 234 degrees (what candymakers call "softball stage") ensured that the fudge was firm yet pliable after cooling. Marshmallows guaranteed a smooth, melt-in-your-mouth texture. Bittersweet, rather than milk or unsweetened, chocolate struck the perfect balance—still sweet enough to taste like candy but also deeply and satisfyingly chocolaty.

Growing up, I thought it more practical to bribe Santa with a plate of chocolate fudge than a squad of gingerbread men. At its best, fudge is soft (but not too soft), sweet (but not too sweet), and rich (but not too . . . oh, who are we kidding? It's a holiday!). To return to this tradition, I began researching recipes in cookbooks and online. Many old-style recipes follow an exhausting formula: Boil sugar, butter, and cream until it reaches a specific temperature, and then add chocolate and stir for upwards of an hour for a smooth consistency.

That's fine for a fudge shop with specialty equipment, but I wasn't up for that much labor. So I looked for recipes with special ingredients that promised to make the process easier, from sweetened condensed milk to Velveeta cheese (no kidding). I tested a dozen existing recipes but found the results unexciting, gummy, and more sugary than chocolaty. The closest contender was one made with marshmallow crème, but the fudge came out much too soft.

After a bit more research and testing, I knew that my fudge would achieve the correct texture only if I cooked the sugar mixture to a temperature between 234 and

238 degrees (what candymakers call "softball stage"). When the temperature is within this range, enough water has been driven off from the cooked sugar that it will hold its shape yet remain pliable once cooled.

More kitchen tests showed me that marshmallows, rather than marshmallow crème, were a better route to the creamy-but-firm texture I needed, thanks to the small amount of cornstarch that coats each marshmallow. (They're also easier to work with.) I learned that canned evaporated milk was the best choice for dairy, as whole milk gave me inconsistent results, heavy cream's richness masked the chocolate flavor, and sweetened condensed milk was just too sweet.

Next I experimented with the chocolate—I tried milk, bittersweet, and unsweetened. Unsweetened was too bitter and milk chocolate too sweet. Bittersweet was just right; it paired satisfyingly rich chocolate flavor with enough sweetness to balance it out.

One of the fudges I made during my initial tests called for brown sugar, which gave it a slightly more complex flavor, more like the nostalgic, candy-store quality I was after. My tasters preferred the cleaner flavor of light brown sugar to dark brown here.

While many chocolate fudge recipes call for vanilla extract, after extensive testing I decided to leave it out; my tasters noted that it confused the chocolate flavor. But we did find that just a bit of salt really amplified it.

I finally had a solid recipe that was perfect for my holiday gift giving. But why stop there? I decided to create a few variations, including chocolate toffee and—especially for Santa—chocolate peppermint.

—MORGAN BOLLING, *Cook's Country*

Chocolate Fudge

MAKES ABOUT 3 POUNDS

You will need a digital or candy thermometer for this recipe. We developed this recipe using Kraft Jet-Puffed Marshmallows. With this brand, 21 marshmallows yield 5 ounces. Be sure to use evaporated milk here, not sweetened condensed milk. We developed this recipe using Ghirardelli 60% Cacao Bittersweet Chocolate Premium Baking Bar. You can substitute semisweet chocolate bars or bars labeled "dark chocolate," but we do not recommend using chocolate that's 85 percent cacao or higher. If you're using an electric stove, the mixture will likely take longer than 5 minutes to reach 234 degrees in step 2.

3   cups packed (21 ounces) light brown sugar
12 tablespoons unsalted butter, cut into 12 pieces
⅔   cup evaporated milk
½   teaspoon table salt
12 ounces bittersweet chocolate, chopped
5   ounces large marshmallows (about 3 cups)
1½ cups walnuts, toasted and chopped coarse (optional)

1. Make foil sling for 8-inch square baking pan by folding 2 long sheets of aluminum foil so each is 8 inches wide. Lay sheets of foil in pan perpendicular to each other, with extra foil hanging over edges of pan. Push foil into corners and up sides of pan, smoothing foil flush to pan. Spray foil with vegetable oil spray.

2. Combine sugar, butter, evaporated milk, and salt in large saucepan. Bring to boil over medium-high heat, stirring frequently. Once boiling, reduce heat to medium-low and simmer, stirring frequently, until mixture registers 234 degrees, 3 to 5 minutes.

3. Off heat, add chocolate and marshmallows and whisk until smooth and all marshmallows are fully melted, about 2 minutes (fudge will thicken to consistency of frosting). Stir in walnuts, if using. Transfer mixture to prepared pan. Let cool completely, about 2 hours. Cover and refrigerate until set, about 2 hours.

4. Using foil overhang, lift fudge out of pan. Cut into 1-inch cubes. Let sit at room temperature for 15 minutes before serving. (Fudge can be stored in airtight container at room temperature for up to 2 weeks.)

VARIATIONS

Chocolate Peppermint Fudge

Omit walnuts. Add 1 teaspoon peppermint extract with chocolate and marshmallows in step 3. After transferring fudge to prepared pan, sprinkle with ¼ cup crushed soft peppermint candies before letting fudge cool.

Chocolate Toffee Fudge

Omit walnuts. Add 1½ tablespoons instant espresso powder with chocolate and marshmallows in step 3. Stir ¼ cup Heath Toffee Bits into fudge before transferring to prepared pan. After transferring fudge to prepared pan, sprinkle with additional ¼ cup toffee bits before letting fudge cool.

PISTACHIO GELATO

✔ **WHY THIS RECIPE WORKS** To make homemade pista-chio gelato, we first had to figure out the ideal ratio of milk to heavy cream for the base. We found that using mostly whole milk with just a bit of cream gave us the dense, rich texture we were looking for. For deep pistachio flavor, we ground raw pistachios and steeped them in warm milk and cream to release their flavorful oils. We then strained the mixture through cheesecloth to ensure a velvety-smooth texture. From there we thickened our base with cornstarch, as well as egg yolks for rich creaminess. We also added a surprise ingredient: corn syrup. Like the cornstarch, corn syrup helped absorb excess water and slow the formation of ice crystals, keeping the custard smooth. After 6 hours in the freezer, the gelato had reached the ideal tempera-ture for serving; any longer and we needed to temper the frozen gelato in the refrigerator until it warmed to 10 to 15 degrees. This creamy, intensely pistachio-flavored treat instantly transported us to a sunny afternoon in Sicily.

If you've ever been to Italy, you've surely had the life-changing experience of tasting Italian-standard gelato. My favorite, hands down, is pistachio. At once subtly sweet and savory with the distinct nuttiness of real pistachios, this flavor is especially remarkable in Sicily, where the nuts are abundant and of exceptional quality. Gelato shops are popular in cities far and wide in the United States; some of them boast bona fide gelato, but, sadly, others peddle poorly disguised impos-tors. American-made gelato tends to be higher in fat and lighter on flavor; it straddles the line between true gelato and standard ice cream and, in my opinion, is much less satisfying than either of the two. Real gelato should be lighter in density and deliberately intense in flavor. In short, it should taste just like the flavor it claims to be, rather than like a mere imitation. I decided it was time to put the fakers in their place and bring genuine gelato with outstanding pistachio flavor into the home kitchen.

To begin, I considered everything I know about both ice cream and gelato. A fundamental difference between the two is their respective butterfat contents. American ice cream contains about 12 to 14 percent butterfat, while Italian gelato contains about 3 to 8 per-cent. We can all agree that ice cream's decadent creaminess is what makes it irresistible—the high fat

content there is earned. But gelato doesn't suffer from its relative leanness. With less fat to coat the tongue, the flavors come through with more intensity and pre-cision. I also learned that gelato is typically served at a warmer temperature than ice cream is, which changes the way we perceive its flavor.

After some more research, I selected a handful of existing recipes and tested them all side by side. Recipes called for varying quantities of pistachios, either toasted or raw. The standout recipe called for an unusual (to me) ingredient: pistachio paste. With a consistency similar to that of Nutella, this paste imparted smooth, strong, salty-sweet pistachio flavor to the gelato. The problem? While this ingredient is revered and easily available in Italy—specifically in Sicily, where pistachio is a hugely popular gelato flavor—pistachio paste isn't easy to come by in the States. Home cooks would need to order it online or search for it in an Italian specialty market. I decided to make my recipe more accessible by re-creating this concentrated pistachio flavor using the nuts alone.

Creating a working base for my gelato was rather straightforward. Gelato is made from both milk and cream in varying amounts, but all the recipes I'd found in my research called for a higher ratio of milk to cream. Taking my cues from the most promising of these recipes, I settled on 3¾ cups of whole milk and ⅓ cup of heavy cream to churn out a quart of gelato. I whisked the dairy together with sugar and then intro-duced some corn syrup, which I knew from previous ice cream recipes would help smooth out the mixture and prevent an icy, crystallized texture.

Gelato doesn't always contain egg yolks, but I decided to include them. Transforming the mixture from liquid to custard, I whisked in five egg yolks, loving the cream-iness they brought without tipping the scales to ice cream–level richness. I brought the mixture to a sim-mer on the stove and cooked it until it registered 190 degrees, about 5 minutes. I'd learned that some gelato recipes include cornstarch, which acts as both a thickener and a stabilizer. My mixture still looked a little thin, so I whisked some cornstarch into the cus-tard and cooked it for just 30 seconds more to thicken. Then I set the custard in an ice bath and chilled it for about an hour and a half. Finally, I whisked the custard to recombine and churned it in my ice cream maker to a thick soft-serve consistency.

PISTACHIO GELATO

Gelato base handled, it was time to refocus on my main objective: pistachio flavor. I'd found that tasters preferred recipes that called for raw nuts as opposed to toasted. Although the toasted pistachios brought strong nuttiness, their flavor was overpowering and just too . . . toasty. Raw nuts brought a clean pistachio taste. But still, I would need to work to get the most out of their flavor. Grinding the nuts in a food processor helped them thoroughly release their flavorful oil. Taking every opportunity to maximize pistachio punch, I decided to steep the ground nuts in some of the dairy-sweetener mixture that would be the base of the custard. After an hour, the nuts had turned the milk a subtle yellow-green hue—nothing like the artificial minty green of supermarket pistachio ice cream.

I could have used the entire nut-liquid mixture in the gelato, but I decided instead to strain it through a cheesecloth, removing the bits of nuts and holding on to all the nutty flavor from the oil. This would produce the smooth, velvety texture and clean, deep flavor I was after. I then added the egg yolks, cooked the custard on the stove, and finally added the cornstarch, which I whisked with a little bit of the milk to make it easy to incorporate. After chilling the custard and then churning it in my ice cream maker, I popped it into the freezer. Homemade ice cream usually needs an overnight freeze, but gelato should be served at a warmer temperature and the texture should be softer. After 6 hours, the gelato was the perfect temperature and thickness. At last, I served myself a scoop of pure pistachio perfection. With its intensity and creaminess, one spoonful was all it took to transport me right to sunny Sicily.

—AFTON CYRUS, *America's Test Kitchen Books*

Pistachio Gelato

MAKES ABOUT 1 QUART

If you're using a canister-style ice cream maker, be sure to freeze the empty canister for at least 24 hours and preferably for 48 hours before churning. If using a self-refrigerating ice cream maker, prechill the canister by running the machine for 5 to 10 minutes before pouring in the custard. Instead of chilling the custard in an ice bath in step 4, you can cover and refrigerate it for at least 6 hours or up to 24 hours before continuing with step 5.

2½ cups (11¼ ounces) shelled pistachios
3¾ cups whole milk, divided
¾ cup (5¼ ounces) sugar
⅓ cup heavy cream
⅓ cup light corn syrup
¼ teaspoon plus ⅓ cup table salt, divided
5 teaspoons cornstarch
5 large egg yolks

1. Process pistachios in food processor until finely ground, about 20 seconds. Combine 3½ cups milk, sugar, cream, corn syrup, and ¼ teaspoon salt in large saucepan. Cook over medium-high heat, stirring frequently, until tiny bubbles form around edge of saucepan, 5 to 7 minutes. Off heat, stir in pistachios; cover and let steep for 1 hour.

2. Line fine-mesh strainer with triple layer of cheesecloth, with extra cheesecloth hanging over edges, and set over large bowl. Strain pistachio mixture through prepared strainer and press on pistachio pulp to extract as much liquid as possible. Gather sides of cheesecloth around pulp and gently squeeze remaining liquid into bowl; discard pulp.

3. Whisk cornstarch and remaining ¼ cup milk together in small bowl; set aside. Return pistachio-milk mixture to clean saucepan. Whisk in egg yolks until combined. Bring to gentle simmer over medium heat and cook, stirring occasionally and scraping bottom of saucepan with rubber spatula, until custard registers 190 degrees, 4 to 6 minutes.

4. Whisk cornstarch mixture to recombine, then whisk into custard. Cook, stirring constantly, until custard thickens, about 30 seconds. Immediately pour custard into bowl and let cool until no longer steaming, about 20 minutes. Fill large bowl with 6 cups ice, ½ cup water, and remaining ⅓ cup salt. Set bowl with custard over ice bath and chill, stirring frequently, until custard registers 40 degrees, about 1½ hours.

5. Whisk custard to recombine, then transfer to ice cream maker and churn until mixture resembles thick soft-serve ice cream and registers 21 degrees, 15 to 30 minutes. Transfer gelato to airtight container, pressing firmly on gelato to remove any air pockets, and freeze until firm, about 6 hours. Serve. (Gelato can be frozen for up to 5 days; if frozen for longer than 6 hours, let gelato sit in refrigerator for 1 to 2 hours until it registers 10 to 15 degrees before serving.)

PEACH TARTE TATIN

✔ **WHY THIS RECIPE WORKS** The classic tarte Tatin is an upside-down caramelized apple tart. We wanted to create a peach version, but simply swapping fruits produced a cloying tart that was awash in juice. To make wetter, sweeter, more fragile peaches work, we had to tweak the recipe. We started by layering butter, sugar, salt, and peaches in a cold skillet. After cooking the filling on the stovetop until the peach juice was browned, we removed the skillet from the heat, slid a disk of pie dough on top, and baked it. When the crust was browned and crisp, we let the tart cool for 20 minutes before pouring off the excess juice and inverting the tart onto a plate. Reducing the juice with a bit of bourbon and then brushing the mixture over the peaches gave this tart extra shine while keeping its flavors cohesive.

If you've got peaches, you should make a peach tarte Tatin. You say your peaches aren't quite ripe? You're allergic to long ingredient lists? You always fret that you've added the wrong amount of thickener to fruit pie filling? Excellent: This is the dessert for you.

Tarte Tatin is traditionally made with apples, which are cooked on the stovetop with butter and sugar, topped with a disk of puff pastry or pie dough, baked in the oven, and then inverted to display the burnished, caramelized apples. While apple tarte Tatin has its charms, I was after a summer dessert, so I was eager to try a few of the many recipes I found in which peaches were substituted for the apples. They followed the same procedure: caramelize the peaches, cover with pastry (I opted for convenient store-bought puff), bake, and flip. But each one turned out too sweet, mushy, and/or flooded with watery juice. Simply swapping peaches for apples wasn't going to cut it.

I got the caramelization process underway, smearing a cold skillet with 3 tablespoons of softened butter and then sprinkling it with ½ cup of sugar (and a pinch of salt). Hoping that a thickener might bind up the extra liquid, I tossed peeled, pitted, and quartered peaches with cornstarch. I spiraled the peaches snugly on top of the sugar and placed the skillet over high heat. Ten minutes later, the butter, sugar, and peach juice had combined to make a rich caramel. I popped the puff pastry disk on top and placed the skillet in a 400-degree oven. Sadly, the cornstarch produced a gelled texture instead of the lightly sticky peaches I envisioned.

But without a thickener, the watery failures continued. Steam vents cut into the puff pastry proved ineffective. Withholding the pastry until later in the baking process allowed for some evaporation—but not enough. As each tart emerged from the oven, I quantified my failure by placing an inverted plate on top of the pastry and tilting the skillet over a liquid measuring cup. Each time almost a full cup of liquid poured out.

Instead of thickening the liquid, how about getting rid of it before the peaches went into the oven? I tossed the peaches with 1 cup of sugar and let them sit while the sugar pulled out juice via osmosis. After 45 minutes, the peaches released ¾ cup of liquid, which I reserved. I proceeded with the caramelizing and baking, and while the tart was in the oven, I reduced the juice to a syrup, which I planned to brush onto the baked tart. To my dismay, the postbake "tilt and drain" test still yielded almost ¾ cup of juice. Belatedly, I realized that much of what I had drained off before baking had been liquefied sugar, and indeed, after I brushed the syrupy reduction onto the tart, it was far too sweet. I considered halving the macerating sugar, but that would mean halving the osmotic force exerted on the peaches, so even less liquid would be released. It didn't seem worthwhile.

It occurred to me that my tilting and draining move might be good for something beyond measuring my failures: I decided to skip macerating and simply bake the tart, drain off the accumulated juice, and then reduce the liquid and brush it onto the peaches.

Having taken no preemptive measures to decrease the excess liquid, I knew this tart would be a real slosh-fest when it came out of the oven. So with safety in mind, I transferred it to a wire rack to cool for 20 minutes before draining the juice. After I'd drained the juice, the tart, for once, was not drowning. And when brushed with the reduced juice, the peaches were pretty much perfect: soft but not too soft, with a lovely balance of sweetness and caramel-y bitterness.

Now that I had sorted out the juice problem, I could no longer ignore the fact that, except at the very edges, the underside of the puff pastry was kind of raw. So for my next test, I parbaked the pastry on a baking sheet while I caramelized the peaches and then married the two for a final bake.

But they remained very separate. The crust stayed awkwardly flat instead of molding itself around the peaches, and I never got that velvety interface where

PEACH TARTE TATIN

the fruit and crust met. And though the puff pastry expanded majestically in the oven, it collapsed under the fruit when I inverted the tart, so even though it was fully baked, it seemed dense and tough.

Given the special requirements of a peach Tatin, pie dough was a better option. I simply rolled out a disk of dough, folded the edge underneath itself to form a bit of a rim to contain the peaches, cut a few vents, and placed the pastry on top of the caramelized fruit. I brushed the dough with water and sprinkled it with sugar, so it would become extra-crunchy when baked. As the tart baked, the pie crust absorbed more steam than the less-porous puff pastry had and did it without getting soggy, so there was a little less juice to drain.

Sensing that I was nearing the end of my quest, I celebrated by adding a splash of bourbon—for a little more complexity—to the reducing juice before brushing the mixture over the peaches for a glossy, lightly sticky finish. Now that I have a summery peach version, I can make tarte Tatin all year round.

—ANDREA GEARY, *Cook's Illustrated*

Peach Tarte Tatin

SERVES 8

Refrigerate the dough for at least 2 hours before rolling it. Firm peaches are easier to peel and retain their shape when cooked, so we prefer them here; yellow peaches are also preferable to white peaches. When pouring off the liquid in step 7, the peaches may shift in the skillet; shaking the skillet will help redistribute them.

CRUST

- **10 tablespoons unsalted butter, chilled, divided**
- **1¼ cups (6¼ ounces) all-purpose flour, divided**
- **1 tablespoon sugar**
- **½ teaspoon table salt**
- **¼ cup ice water, divided**

FILLING

- **3 tablespoons unsalted butter, softened**
- **½ cup (3½ ounces) plus 2 tablespoons sugar, divided**
- **¼ teaspoon table salt**
- **2 pounds ripe but firm peaches, peeled, pitted, and quartered**
- **1 tablespoon bourbon (optional)**

1. FOR THE CRUST: Grate 2 tablespoons butter on large holes of box grater and place in freezer. Cut remaining 8 tablespoons butter into ½-inch cubes.

2. Pulse ¾ cup flour, sugar, and salt in food processor until combined, 2 pulses. Add cubed butter and process until homogeneous paste forms, about 30 seconds. Using your hands, carefully break paste into 2-inch chunks and redistribute evenly around processor blade. Add remaining ½ cup flour and pulse until mixture is broken into pieces no larger than 1 inch (most pieces will be much smaller), 4 to 5 pulses. Transfer mixture to medium bowl. Add grated butter and toss until butter pieces are separated and coated with flour.

3. Sprinkle 2 tablespoons ice water over mixture. Toss with rubber spatula until mixture is evenly moistened. Sprinkle remaining 2 tablespoons ice water over mixture and toss to combine. Press dough with spatula until dough sticks together. Transfer dough to sheet of plastic wrap. Draw edges of plastic over dough and press on sides and top to form compact, fissure-free mass. Wrap in plastic and flatten to form 5-inch disk. Refrigerate dough for at least 2 hours or up to 2 days. Let chilled dough sit on counter to soften slightly, about 10 minutes, before rolling. (Wrapped dough can be frozen for up to 1 month. If frozen, let dough thaw completely on counter before rolling.)

4. Invert rimmed baking sheet and place sheet of parchment paper or waxed paper on top. Roll dough into 10-inch circle on lightly floured counter. Roll dough loosely around rolling pin and gently unroll it onto prepared sheet. Working around circumference, fold ½ inch of dough under itself and pinch to create 9-inch round with raised rim. Cut three 2-inch slits in center of dough and refrigerate until needed.

5. FOR THE FILLING: Adjust oven rack to middle position and heat oven to 400 degrees. Smear butter over bottom of 10-inch ovensafe skillet. Sprinkle ½ cup sugar over butter and shake skillet to spread sugar into even layer. Sprinkle salt over sugar. Arrange peaches in circular pattern around edge of skillet, nestling fruit snugly. Tuck remaining peaches into center, squeezing in as much fruit as possible (it is not necessary to maintain circular pattern in center).

6. Place skillet over high heat and cook, without stirring fruit, until juice is released and turns from pink to deep amber, 8 to 12 minutes. (If necessary, adjust skillet's placement on burner to even out hot spots and encourage even browning.) Remove skillet from heat.

Carefully slide dough over fruit, making sure dough is centered and does not touch edge of skillet. Brush dough lightly with water and sprinkle with remaining 2 tablespoons sugar. Bake until crust is very well browned, 30 to 35 minutes. Transfer skillet to wire rack set in rimmed baking sheet and let cool for 20 minutes.

7. Place inverted plate on top of crust. With 1 hand firmly securing plate, carefully tip skillet over bowl to drain juice (skillet handle may still be hot). When all juice has been transferred to bowl, return skillet to wire rack, remove plate, and shake skillet firmly to redistribute peaches. Carefully invert tart onto plate, then slide tart onto wire rack. (If peaches have shifted during unmolding, gently nudge them back into place with spoon.)

8. Pour juice into now-empty skillet (handle may be hot). Stir in bourbon, if using, and cook over high heat, stirring constantly, until mixture is dark and thick and starting to smoke, 2 to 3 minutes. Return mixture to bowl and let cool until mixture is consistency of honey, 2 to 3 minutes. Brush mixture over peaches. Let tart cool for at least 20 minutes. Cut into wedges and serve.

LEMON–OLIVE OIL TART

☑ **WHY THIS RECIPE WORKS** Most lemon tart recipes feature butter in both the crust and the filling, but here we used extra-virgin olive oil instead. It made the crust a snap: We simply mixed the flour, sugar, and salt with the oil and a little water until a soft dough formed; crumbled it into the tart pan; pressed it into the sides and bottom; and baked it right away—no rolling or chilling required. Using olive oil in the filling didn't compromise its sliceability because the filling had plenty of structure from the protein in the eggs. What's more, olive oil allowed the lemons' acidity to come to the fore. That meant we could use a bit less juice and still enjoy plenty of bright lemon flavor.

When you're a test cook, being asked to develop a recipe for a classic item such as lemon tart can be daunting. After all, bakers have been producing handsome, crisp-crusted tarts filled with bracing, just-sliceable curd for centuries without my assistance. What could I possibly contribute? Well, actually, I had an idea: extra-virgin olive oil.

Admittedly, it's counterintuitive: Butter is featured in both the crust and the filling of almost every lemon tart. But developing a recipe for an olive oil cake a couple of years ago reminded me that other fats offer advantages, too. Using a liquid fat in that cake made the mixing process easy and quick: There was no softening of the fat and no creaming until light and fluffy, yet the crumb was beautifully plush and fine and the cake had an intriguing hint of olive oil flavor.

In fact, the olive oil flavor in the cake was so subtle that I had to take care not to obscure it. I added a near-homeopathic dose of lemon zest—just ¼ teaspoon—to boost the oil's fruity, floral notes and left it at that. And readers loved that olive oil cake, but they voiced one small objection: not enough lemon flavor.

They had a point. Olive oil and lemons have such an undeniable affinity that it's a shame not to make the most of it. This lemon tart recipe was my chance to let the fruit side of the pairing shine. And maybe, as with the cake, olive oil would make the recipe even easier.

Years ago I developed a tart dough in which I defied convention by using melted rather than cold butter. I simply stirred 10 tablespoons of melted butter into the dry ingredients until the mixture resembled Play-Doh—no food processor necessary. Then I crumbled it straight into the tart pan and pressed it to an even thickness. There was no chilling or rolling required, and the crust baked up crunchy and rich.

Substituting olive oil for the melted butter seemed like a no-brainer, but it didn't work out quite the way I had envisioned it. Ten tablespoons of oil made the dough shiny with grease, and the baked crust was so tender and crumbly that I couldn't cut it into wedges without it disintegrating. This was because unlike olive oil, butter isn't a pure fat; it's almost 20 percent water. So 10 tablespoons of butter is actually 8 tablespoons of fat and 2 tablespoons of water. That water interacts with the protein in the flour to form gluten, which provides the structure that holds the crust together. An absence of water produces a too-fragile crust.

When I substituted ½ cup of olive oil plus 2 tablespoons of water for the butter, the dough was appropriately moist but not slick, and I had no trouble cutting the baked crust into pristine wedges. There was a mere hint of olive oil flavor in the crust, which seemed perfect. But an empty tart shell, even one that's so easy to make and so satisfyingly crisp, is a forlorn thing. I needed to move on to the filling.

I worried that the olive oil substitution would fail in this recipe because butter is a solid at room temperature and oil is clearly a liquid. How much of the sliceable nature of a lemon tart filling is owed to butter's solidity?

To find out, I made two tart shells, and while they baked, I cooked two batches of filling. Each had 1 cup of sugar, 2/3 cup of lemon juice, 1 tablespoon of zest, three whole eggs, and three yolks. I whisked them over medium-low heat until they were thick, and then I took them off the heat and whisked 1/4 cup of butter into one and 1/4 cup of olive oil into the other. I strained each batch, transferred it to a shell, and returned it to the oven. After 10 minutes, when both fillings had gelled, I set the tarts on the counter to cool.

After 2 hours, I sliced. I was astonished to find that the olive oil version wasn't softer than the butter version. Turns out, most of the firmness of lemon curd comes from the coagulation of the egg proteins, not from the hardening of the butter as it cools. But that's not to say that the two fillings were exactly alike.

The olive oil filling was so tart that it made my forehead perspire, but the butter had softened the acidity in the other filling, leaving it milder but still lemony. Butter contains dairy proteins that bind to the lemon juice in two ways. First, the proteins bind to the acid, muting its sour taste. They also bind to other flavor compounds in lemon, such as limonene, reducing the lemon flavor even more. Since olive oil does not contain dairy proteins, it does not reduce lemon flavor. I grabbed at the excuse to juice one less lemon and decreased the lemon juice in the olive oil version to 1/2 cup. The smaller amount of juice would make the filling just a bit firmer, too.

Finally, I added some starch to the filling to further temper the acidity and also slow down the bonding of the eggs' proteins as they cooked, to prevent curdling. Cornstarch and flour each worked equally well, but because I already had flour in the crust, I went with that. The filling in the final tart was creamy and tender, but it sliced beautifully and each wedge had a perfectly clean point. The crust was crisp and remained so even after the tart was refrigerated for three days. Though there was a tiny bit of olive oil pepperiness on the finish, the tart's flavor was mostly bright and lemony.

But if, by chance, this tart is too lemony for your taste, I have an olive oil cake recipe you might like.

—ANDREA GEARY, *Cook's Illustrated*

NOTES FROM THE TEST KITCHEN

A BETTER WAY TO FORM A PAT-IN-PAN CRUST
Distributing crumbles of dough around the pan before pressing them together means you won't run out of dough before the edge is complete.

1. Crumble three-quarters of dough over bottom of tart pan and press to even thickness.

2. Crumble remaining one-quarter of dough evenly around edge of pan and press into fluted sides.

3. Press dough across bottom of pan until even and smooth.

4. Bake until crust is deep golden brown and firm to touch, rotating pan halfway through baking.

WHAT'S EVOO DOING IN LEMON TART?
Unlike butter, olive oil doesn't require melting to make our pat-in-the-pan crust. As for the filling, olive oil and lemon have a natural affinity, but interestingly, you need less lemon without butter in the picture. That's because dairy proteins in butter bind to flavor compounds in lemon, muting its flavor in curd.

Lemon-Olive Oil Tart

SERVES 8

Use a fresh, high-quality extra-virgin olive oil here. Make sure that all your metal equipment—saucepan, strainer, and whisk—is nonreactive, or the filling may have a metallic flavor.

CRUST

1½ cups (7½ ounces) all-purpose flour
5   tablespoons (2¼ ounces) sugar
½   teaspoon table salt
½   cup extra-virgin olive oil
2   tablespoons water

FILLING

1   cup (7 ounces) sugar
2   tablespoons all-purpose flour
¼   teaspoon table salt
3   large eggs plus 3 large yolks
1   tablespoon grated lemon zest plus ½ cup juice (3 lemons)
¼   cup extra-virgin olive oil

1. FOR THE CRUST: Adjust oven rack to middle position and heat oven to 350 degrees. Whisk flour, sugar, and salt together in bowl. Add oil and water and stir until uniform dough forms. Using your hands, crumble three-quarters of dough over bottom of 9-inch tart pan with removable bottom. Press dough to even thickness in bottom of pan. Crumble remaining dough and scatter evenly around edge of pan, then press crumbled dough into fluted sides of pan. Press dough to even thickness. Place pan on rimmed baking sheet and bake until crust is deep golden brown and firm to touch, 30 to 35 minutes, rotating pan halfway through baking.

2. FOR THE FILLING: About 5 minutes before crust is finished baking, whisk sugar, flour, and salt in medium saucepan until combined. Whisk in eggs and yolks until no streaks of egg remain. Whisk in lemon zest and juice. Cook over medium-low heat, whisking constantly and scraping corners of saucepan, until mixture thickens slightly and registers 160 degrees, 5 to 8 minutes.

3. Off heat, whisk in oil until incorporated. Strain curd through fine-mesh strainer set over bowl. Pour curd into warm tart shell.

4. Bake until filling is set and barely jiggles when pan is shaken, 8 to 12 minutes. Let tart cool completely on wire rack, at least 2 hours. Remove outer metal ring

of tart pan. Slide thin metal spatula between tart and pan bottom, then carefully slide tart onto serving platter. Cut tart into wedges, wiping knife clean between cuts if necessary, and serve. (Leftovers can be wrapped loosely in plastic wrap and refrigerated for up to 3 days.)

VIRGINIA PEANUT PIE

✅ **WHY THIS RECIPE WORKS** The contrasting flavors and textures of this Virginia specialty are easy to love. The pie is simultaneously sweet and salty, with a creamy filling tucked beneath a crunchy top. It's a lot like pecan pie but easier to make. The recipes we tried turned out pies that were too busy with added flavors and spices, were too sweet, or had nuts that didn't feel integrated with the filling. For our version, we settled on a mix of light corn syrup and brown sugar as the sweetener, limited our flavorings to just vanilla and salt, and doubled the amount of peanuts called for in most recipes. We also found a way around precooking the filling and prebaking the crust. And when it came to choosing the peanuts, we found that any type except Spanish redskin peanuts will work.

If you're lucky enough to visit Wakefield, Virginia, you can order a slice of "World Famous Peanut Pie" at the bustling Virginia Diner. Sounds great. I had just one question: What the heck is peanut pie?

The simplest answer is that peanut pie is like a pecan pie made with—you guessed it—peanuts. According to Virginia food writers, this pie should be a celebration of contrasting flavors and textures: sweet and salty, crunchy and creamy. I pored over cookbooks to find a handful of promising recipes to make. The pies were all built using a similar formula: A mixture of sweet syrup (Lyle's Golden Syrup, maple syrup, or corn syrup), brown sugar, eggs, butter, flavorings (vanilla, cayenne, and/or cinnamon), salt, and peanuts was cooked in a saucepan and then poured into a prebaked pie shell and baked. While we generally liked these initial pies, they didn't quite add up: Some were overly sweet or overwhelmed by nuts, while others called for so many spices and flavorings that the flavor was muddied.

First, I decided that using corn syrup was the way to proceed since Lyle's can be hard to find and the distinctive flavor of maple syrup competed with the peanuts. Second, my tasters thought that vanilla and plenty of

VIRGINIA PEANUT PIE

salt were all the seasoning this pie needed. Finally, we agreed that something called "peanut pie" ought to pack a ton of peanut flavor, so I used a full 2 cups of nuts, twice the amount called for in some recipes, to ensure that the peanuts were the uncontested star of the show. Crushing the peanuts made the filling more cohesive and easier to eat. The pie tasted great, but I hoped to make the process easier.

As for the filling, did I have to cook it on the stovetop before baking the pie? I hoped I could skip that fussy-seeming step and just stir together all the ingredients and bake—after all, many pecan pie fillings aren't precooked. Sure enough, the uncooked filling turned out great in the baked pie, not noticeably different from the cooked version.

As for the crust, could I do away with the parbaking? We often parbake a crust before adding a liquid filling to prevent it from becoming soggy. But because I'd packed this filling chock-full of crushed peanuts, it was thicker than most. I poured the peanut mixture into a raw crust and baked it until browned. The risk was happily rewarded with a crisp, layered crust.

I love serving this pie as a special summertime treat, but who's to say that, come holiday-time, it won't end up on my family's table?

—KATIE LEAIRD, *Cook's Country*

Virginia Peanut Pie

SERVES 8 TO 10

Cocktail or honey-roasted peanuts can be substituted for the salted dry-roasted peanuts. Do not use Spanish redskin peanuts. Inspect the peanut packaging to be sure the ingredient list includes only peanuts, salt, and oil (plus sweetener if using honey-roasted peanuts). You can use light or dark brown sugar in the filling. Crush the peanuts in a zipper-lock bag using a rolling pin or meat pounder; you want peanut pieces, not dust. Serve with vanilla ice cream, if desired.

CRUST

- 1¾ cups (8¾ ounces) all-purpose flour
- 1 tablespoon granulated sugar
- ¾ teaspoon table salt
- 12 tablespoons unsalted butter, cut into ½-inch pieces and chilled
- ½ cup ice water

FILLING

- ¾ cup light corn syrup
- ¾ cup packed (5¼ ounces) brown sugar
- 3 large eggs
- 6 tablespoons unsalted butter, melted
- 1 tablespoon vanilla extract
- ½ teaspoon table salt
- 2 cups salted dry-roasted peanuts, crushed

1. FOR THE CRUST: Process flour, sugar, and salt in food processor until combined, about 3 seconds. Scatter butter over top and pulse until mixture resembles coarse crumbs, about 10 pulses. Transfer to bowl. Sprinkle ice water over mixture. Using rubber spatula, stir and press dough until it sticks together.

2. Turn out dough onto lightly floured counter, form into 6-inch disk, wrap tightly in plastic wrap, and refrigerate for 1 hour. Let chilled dough sit on counter to soften slightly, about 10 minutes, before rolling. (Wrapped dough can be refrigerated for up to 2 days or frozen for up to 1 month. If frozen, let dough thaw completely on counter before rolling.)

3. Adjust oven rack to lowest position and heat oven to 350 degrees. Roll dough into 12-inch circle on lightly floured counter. Roll dough loosely around rolling pin and gently unroll it onto 9-inch pie plate, letting excess dough hang over edge. Ease dough into plate by gently lifting edge of dough with your hand while pressing into plate bottom with your other hand.

4. Trim overhang to ½ inch beyond lip of plate. Tuck overhang under itself; folded edge should be flush with edge of plate. Crimp dough evenly around edge of plate using your fingers. Push protruding crimped edge so it slightly hangs over edge of plate. Wrap dough-lined plate loosely in plastic and freeze until dough is firm, about 15 minutes.

5. FOR THE FILLING: Whisk corn syrup, sugar, eggs, melted butter, vanilla, and salt in large bowl until fully combined. Stir in peanuts until incorporated.

6. Place pie plate on rimmed baking sheet. Pour filling into shell. Bake until filling is puffed and set but still jiggles slightly when pie is shaken, 1 hour 5 minutes to 1 hour 10 minutes. Let pie cool completely on wire rack, at least 4 hours or overnight. Serve.

MAKE-AHEAD PUMPKIN PIE WITH MAPLE-CINNAMON WHIPPED CREAM

✓ **WHY THIS RECIPE WORKS** When we set out to develop a recipe for a make-ahead pumpkin pie—one that we could freeze for up to two weeks with no negative effects—we knew that a steep challenge lay ahead of us. Custard pies typically don't survive the freezer because the egg proteins in the custard are damaged during freezing, causing the custard to split into weepy mush once thawed. We discovered that substituting gelatin for the eggs was the answer. The gelatin suspended excess water in a flexible network, so the filling remained smooth and retained its structure after being frozen and thawed. Cream replaced the richness that we lost when we ditched the eggs. Since gelatin sets up in a cool environment, we didn't need to cook the filling before pouring it into the prebaked crust. Best of all, the crust remained crisp and flaky even after being filled, frozen, and thawed. A festive cinnamon-spiced whipped cream was the crowning touch on this game-changing holiday pie.

I love making pies of all kinds. For that reason, I volunteer to make some of my favorites every Thanksgiving for my family's big gathering. And every Thanksgiving I find myself scrambling at the last minute to get the pies made. Sure, sometimes I'm organized enough to make the pies a day ahead of time, but let's face it: The day before Thanksgiving isn't exactly devoid of other tasks to accomplish. What if I could make a pumpkin pie, baked and all, a week or more ahead?

My skeptical coworkers said it couldn't be done. Homemade custards tend to split into mush once thawed; store-bought frozen pies use industrial-strength emulsifiers and stabilizers that prevent the custard from splitting but make the texture weird and spongy. Freezing the parts individually to bake off later wasn't my goal—all I wanted to do on Thanksgiving Day was take the pie out of the freezer and let it thaw. Also, it needed to have a velvety-smooth filling and crisp crust that were just as good as those of a fresh pie.

I started my experimenting with a traditional custard of pumpkin puree, cream, eggs, sugar, and spices cooked in a saucepan. I froze this filling in a plastic container and then thawed it. Sure enough, it was chunky and weepy-wet. Upon investigation, I found that ice crystals were to blame. Eggs and pumpkin puree both contain a lot of water. When that water freezes, it expands and forms sharp ice crystals that damage the protein structure of the egg. Then when the filling thaws, the custard can no longer hold the water in place, so it leaks out. Without eggs, I'd lose structure and richness (bad) but decrease water (good).

I needed something that could do the structural work of the eggs and decrease or at least trap or suspend any excess water. Gelatin has come to the rescue in the past, so I tried it again here. Bonus: Using gelatin instead of eggs meant I wouldn't need to cook the custard.

I dissolved a tablespoon of gelatin in heavy cream (which I hoped would help replace some of the richness lost when I ditched the eggs). I then zapped this mixture in the microwave for a minute and let it rest for a few minutes before stirring it into a mixture of pumpkin puree, sugar, and spices. Sure enough, this filling set up beautifully—without baking.

But would it freeze? Only one way to find out. I spooned it into an already-baked pie shell, wrapped it, and after 24 hours, thawed it out, watching carefully for weeping. I saw none, nor any other obvious damage. When I cut into the pie, I was rewarded with a pumpkin filling that was smooth and silky, with no traces of trouble. Score!

About that prebaked pie shell: I used a test kitchen recipe designed to be made ahead (once shaped, the dough can be frozen for up to a month before baking). This crust stayed crisp and flaky after I added a wet filling and even after I froze and thawed the pie. As I carefully sliced into the frozen-and-thawed pie, I could hear the crunch of the crust.

Topped with a delicious maple-cinnamon whipped cream, this pie, according to my tasters, was "luxurious," "creamy," "festive," and "a total holiday game changer." To me, that last comment was the most gratifying of all.

—CECELIA JENKINS, *Cook's Country*

Make-Ahead Pumpkin Pie with Maple-Cinnamon Whipped Cream
SERVES 8 TO 10

For the best flavor, use a good-quality maple syrup here. We prefer to use granulated sugar in place of pie weights when baking the dough, but raw rice, dried beans, or ceramic pie weights will also work. The sugar can be reused for baking future pie doughs.

MAKE-AHEAD PUMPKIN PIE WITH MAPLE-CINNAMON WHIPPED CREAM

CRUST

- 1½ cups (7½ ounces) all-purpose flour
- 1 tablespoon sugar, plus about 5 cups to use as pie weight
- ½ teaspoon table salt
- 12 tablespoons unsalted butter, cut into ½-inch pieces and chilled
- 6 tablespoons ice water

FILLING

- 1 cup heavy cream
- 1 tablespoon unflavored gelatin
- 1 (15-ounce) can unsweetened pumpkin puree
- ¾ cup (5¼ ounces) sugar
- ¼ cup maple syrup
- 1½ teaspoons ground ginger
- 1 teaspoon table salt
- ½ teaspoon ground cinnamon
- ¼ teaspoon ground nutmeg

TOPPING

- 1 cup heavy cream, chilled
- ¼ cup maple syrup
- ¼ teaspoon ground cinnamon
- Pinch table salt

1. FOR THE CRUST: Process flour, 1 tablespoon sugar, and salt in food processor until combined, about 3 seconds. Scatter butter over top and pulse until irregular large chunks of butter form with some small pieces throughout, about 5 pulses. Add ice water and process until little balls of butter form and almost no dry flour remains, about 10 seconds, scraping down sides of bowl after 5 seconds. Turn out dough onto clean counter and gather into ball. Sprinkle dough and counter generously with flour and shape dough into 6-inch disk, pressing any cracked edges back together. Roll dough into 13-inch circle, reflouring counter and dough as needed.

2. Roll dough loosely around rolling pin and gently unroll it onto 9-inch pie plate, leaving at least 1-inch overhang around edge. Ease dough into plate by gently lifting edge of dough with your hand while pressing into plate bottom with your other hand. Trim overhang to ½ inch beyond lip of plate.

3. Tuck overhang under itself; folded edge should be flush with edge of plate. Crimp dough evenly around edge of plate using your knuckles. Push protruding crimped edge so it slightly hangs over edge of plate.

Pierce bottom and sides of dough all over with fork, about 40 times. Wrap dough-lined plate loosely in plastic wrap and refrigerate until dough is very firm, at least 2 hours or up to 2 days. (After being refrigerated for 2 hours, dough-lined plate can be wrapped tightly in plastic and frozen for up to 1 month. Let dough thaw at room temperature for 25 minutes before using.)

4. Adjust oven rack to lowest position and heat oven to 375 degrees. Line chilled pie shell with aluminum foil and, while pressing into plate bottom with 1 hand to keep foil flush with bottom of plate, work foil around crimped edge with your other hand. Fill foil to lip of plate with sugar. Transfer plate to wire rack set in rimmed baking sheet and bake until edges are dry and light golden brown, about 1 hour. Remove foil and sugar, rotate sheet, and continue to bake until edges of crust are peanut butter–colored and center is golden brown, 20 to 25 minutes longer. Let cool completely.

5. FOR THE FILLING: Whisk cream and gelatin in microwave-safe bowl until all gelatin looks wet (mixture will be slightly lumpy). Let mixture sit until it looks like loose cottage cheese, about 5 minutes.

6. Microwave gelatin mixture until gelatin has melted, about 1 minute, whisking halfway through microwaving. Whisk until smooth and syrupy and no lumps remain. (If lumps persist, microwave in 10-second intervals, whisking after each, until smooth.)

7. Whisk pumpkin, sugar, maple syrup, ginger, salt, cinnamon, and nutmeg in large microwave-safe bowl until combined. Microwave until pumpkin mixture registers 110 degrees, about 2 minutes, stirring halfway through microwaving. Immediately add gelatin mixture to pumpkin mixture and whisk to thoroughly combine.

8. Pour filling into crust. Gently shake pie so filling spreads to edges of crust; let cool for 10 minutes. Spray sheet of plastic wrap with vegetable oil spray and gently press onto filling. Refrigerate for at least 4 hours.

9. FOR THE TOPPING: Using stand mixer fitted with whisk attachment, whip all ingredients on medium-low speed until foamy, about 1 minute. Increase speed to high and whip until soft peaks form, 1 to 3 minutes. (Topping can be refrigerated for up to 24 hours.)

10. Spread topping evenly over pie. Serve.

TO MAKE AHEAD: At end of step 8, pie can be wrapped tightly in plastic wrap, then aluminum foil, and frozen for up to 2 weeks. To serve, completely unwrap pie and let thaw at room temperature for 5 hours. Make topping while pie thaws and spread over pie just before serving.

TEST KITCHEN RESOURCES

** Not all products we tested are listed in these pages. Web subscribers
can find complete listings and information on all products tested and
reviewed at CooksIllustrated.com and CooksCountry.com.*

BEST KITCHEN QUICK TIPS

PLUNGE TOMATO PASTE

Instead of spooning tomato paste from its small can, Gary Schwartz of Lake Elmo, Minn., "plunges" it out. He uses a can opener to cut the lids on both ends, removes the lid from only one side, and uses the freed-up lid on the opposite side to push the paste into a bowl.

TRAVELING TOOL KIT

Noreen McGovern of Biddeford, Maine, likes to make sure she has a well-equipped kitchen when she travels for the holidays or rents a home for vacation. She takes one knife roll (a fabric case with slots to hold knives) packed with her favorite knives and carries a second knife roll loaded with small tools such as a wooden spoon, a spatula, a rasp-style grater, a thermometer, and a pair of tongs. All the tools are neatly packed and easily accessible.

PIN YOUR PLACE IN A RECIPE

To avoid losing her place in a recipe when toggling between reading the text and cooking, Mary Gerber of Brunswick, Maine, clips a clothespin to the page. She moves it down the text as she cooks so she can quickly find her place.

SAVE TIME WITH SPICE KITS

Nancy Immel of Bernalillo, N.M., saves herself prep time in advance by putting together "spice kits" for her favorite dishes. She stores them in small zipper-lock bags to have at the ready when she cooks these recipes.

SOFTEN BUTTER UNDER A HOT GLASS

When Kimberly Bernards of Robbinsdale, Minn., wants to soften a whole stick of butter for a baking recipe, she uses this trick: Stand the stick of butter on its end. Pour boiling water into a heatproof glass, wait 30 seconds, and then discard the water and invert the hot glass over the butter. In about 20 minutes, the butter will be properly softened and ready to use.

MECHANICALLY MASSAGING KALE

Deborah Bernstein of Warwick, N.Y., uses her stand mixer to massage kale for salad. After adding the greens and the dressing to the bowl, she mixes them on low speed using the paddle attachment, which kneads the kale and breaks down its cell walls so that the pieces turn tender.

KEEP SANDWICHES INTACT WITH FROZEN BREAD

When Maureen Stanley of Blacklick, Ohio, was a child, her mother made sandwiches for her school lunchbag using frozen bread. This made it easier to spread fillings such as peanut butter and jelly without tearing the bread, and the sandwiches thawed by lunchtime. Maureen still uses this method when packing her lunch for work.

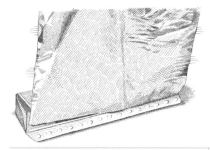

A BETTER WAY TO TEAR FOIL

To neatly tear aluminum foil or plastic wrap, Joy M. Suh of Fremont, Calif., pulls out the length needed from the box, flips the box upside down so the blade is facing the counter, and rips it with confidence. She gets a clean sheet every time.

SPIN YOUR CHICKPEAS DRY

When a recipe calls for rinsing canned beans for a salad (or another application where excess moisture can be an issue), Mary Hardy of Marina del Rey, Calif., rinses them in a salad spinner basket. When the water runs clear, she removes any excess from the beans by spinning the basket.

EASY WAY TO REMOVE SOLIDS FROM STOCK

When Julia Weinberg of Ann Arbor, Mich., is making chicken stock, she places the chicken bones and vegetable scraps in a large pasta pot with an insert. After the stock has simmered for 1 to 2 hours, she just removes the insert to discard the solids.

FRESH BROWNIES IN A FLASH

When Jason Nachowicz of Elgin, Ill., bakes brownies, he lines the pan with an aluminum foil sling for easy removal, per our recipe instructions. The sling also makes it easy to freeze the brownie batter before baking it. After pouring the batter into the foil-lined pan, he freezes it until the batter is solid. He then transfers the frozen batter in the sling to a zipper-lock bag. The next time guests arrive, he can conveniently return the frozen batch to a pan and bake homemade brownies (the frozen batter bakes for the same amount of time as just-made batter).

CUT COLD BUTTER QUICKLY AND CLEANLY

AN EASIER WAY TO CLEAN CORN

When husking fresh corn, Carrol Bailey of Williamsburg, Va., dons clean rubber gloves to remove the clingy silk. The friction from the gloves helps her grab the fine threads, making them easier to pull away.

Cutting cold butter into biscuit or pie dough can be a bit of a mess. Penelope Stygar of Richmond, Va., reduces the mess while achieving just the right size bits of butter by using a rotary grater. She cuts chilled sticks of butter into lengths that fit in the grater; after giving the grater a few turns, she's ready to toss the butter into the flour.

SALAD GREENS BOXES AS STORAGE BINS

Sharon Morris of Austin, Texas, reuses large plastic salad greens containers as bins to consolidate dry goods such as pasta and rice in her pantry. The clear plastic ensures that the contents are visible, and the flat containers can easily be stacked.

HOW TO CLEAN DOUGHY HANDS

Whenever Juli Lederhaus of Petaluma, Calif., needs to clean flour or dough from her hands, she uses cold water instead of hot so the flour doesn't turn into a gluey mess. With cold water, the floury paste slides right off.

BEST KITCHEN QUICK TIPS

A NEW WAY TO PACK A COOLER

Nancy Shannon of Rockford, Ill., discovered that small stackable shelves typically used to add extra tiers to cabinets can also work in coolers. They're great for raising foods such as cheese, fruits, or sandwiches to prevent them from getting wet in melting ice; they can also be used to keep beverages separate.

HOMEMADE UMAMI SEASONING

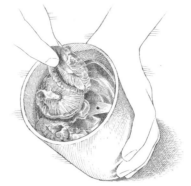

To add deep savory flavor to soups, stews, or even meatloaf, Cheryl Lundgren of Klamath Falls, Ore., grinds cleaned, dried mushrooms in her coffee grinder to a fine powder. She stores the powder in a cheese shaker for easy distribution.

SOCK UP BOTTLE DRIPS

Judy Page of Centerville, Ohio, catches drips of wine or oil by outfitting the bottle with a clean long sock. She cuts a hole in the toe and pulls the narrow opening over the neck of the bottle to absorb any spills.

OIL POUR CONTROL

Mary Jones of El Sobrante, Calif., doesn't tear away the foil seal on a bottle of oil. Instead, she uses a sharp paring knife to cut a V-shaped slit in it. When the narrow part of the V is facing downward, she can pour the oil slowly in a steady stream. When the wide end of the V is facing downward, she can pour the oil more quickly.

MAKESHIFT MEAT POUNDER

Mandy Phillips of Omaha, Neb., doesn't own a meat pounder, so she uses the flat bottom of a small heavy skillet instead. After sandwiching the raw meat between sheets of plastic wrap, she pounds the meat to an even thickness.

STORING BUTTER "ORPHANS"

Whenever Elise Darrow of Denver, Colo., gets to the end of a stick of butter, she stores it in a clean, lidded plastic dairy container. (If the pieces are exact tablespoons, she leaves the measurement-marked wrapper on.) This frees up her butter dish for a new stick, and the "orphans" don't absorb any odors.

EASY-PEEL POTATOES

When peeling a large amount of potatoes, Nate Basinger of Spicewood, Texas, first makes two holes on opposite ends of the potato with the eye remover of a Y-peeler. He then places his thumb and middle finger in the holes and peels. The holes prevent the potato from slipping out of his grip and allow him to easily rotate the potato in his hand while peeling.

A MINIMALLY INVASIVE WAY TO TEST DONENESS

Recipes often suggest testing the doneness and tenderness of dense vegetables such as beets, squash, and potatoes by sliding the tip of a paring knife into the flesh. Christina Boni of Somerville, Mass., prefers to use a metal cake tester, which is slimmer and barely disturbs the flesh.

JUICE POMEGRANATE SEEDS WITH A RICER

To juice a small amount of pomegranate seeds, Gene Simmonds of New York, N.Y., found that a ricer does the trick. Simply load the seeds into the hopper of the ricer and gently press.

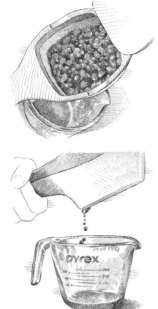

QUICK KIWI PREP

To easily cut up a kiwi, Anita Wood of Westford, Mass., has come up with this fun and effective method: Cut a kiwi in half crosswise. Take a metal beater from a handheld mixer, push it down into the kiwi, and twist. The kiwi separates cleanly from its skin, and you get four neat wedges per half.

GOOD USE FOR THAT LAST BIT OF HONEY

Instead of struggling to extract honey from a near-empty jar, Alicia Connolly of New Britain, Conn., adds warm water (enough to equal the amount of honey left in the jar) and then shakes it up to make a honey "simple syrup." She stores this syrup in the refrigerator and uses it to sweeten cocktails or iced tea.

GOOD TOOL FOR STIRRING PASTA

Megan Bressler of Philadelphia, Pa., likes to keep a chopstick handy to stir pasta while it cooks. Its slender shape helps easily and delicately untangle any noodles that have clumped, and it's less cumbersome to use than a spoon.

BREADING CHICKEN FOR A CROWD

When Abby Kropp of Franklin, Tenn., is breading chicken for a large group, she spreads the bread crumbs or panko on a rimmed baking sheet so she can coat several pieces at once.

SAVING SPILLED SPICES

When measuring spices from the jar, Betsy Dupre of Scituate, Mass., always has some spillage, which is tricky to neatly scoop up and save (instead of simply sweeping into the trash). To save the spillover while measuring, she places the plastic lid of a large yogurt or soup container underneath her spoon to catch any spice that falls. She also cuts a notch in the lid's lip to make a spout. When she's done measuring, she bends the lid like a taco to easily pour the spice back into its container. Plus, the lid can be washed and reused.

CLEAN YOUR KITCHEN WITH DRYER SHEETS

When Geoff Walker of Farmington Hills, Mich., removes an unscented dryer sheet from the laundry, he takes it to the kitchen before throwing it away. The sheet's coarse texture makes it uniquely suited to wiping away grease from kitchen surfaces such as the stovetop, backsplash, and microwave. A quick swipe and into the garbage it goes.

A CARRIER FOR HOT CASSEROLES

When Troy Emerson of Somerville, Mass., brings a hot casserole to a friend's house, he makes it portable by lining a large, heavy-duty cardboard box with cutout handles in the sides (such as a box used for transporting liquor) with a towel and placing the hot dish inside. Besides acting as a trivet inside the box, the towel helps prevent the casserole from sliding around.

TOP 12 GRILLING MISTAKES TO AVOID

Some of the most common practices are also the wrong ones.

LEGEND
C charcoal grills   G gas grills

1. USING LIGHTER FLUID C

Lighter fluid can impart a chemical flavor to the food.

BEST PRACTICE: Light coals in a chimney starter.

METHOD: Place wadded-up newspaper in the bottom chamber and briquettes in the top. Light the newspaper. When the top coals are covered in ash, dump the coals into the grill.

2. PACKING TOO MUCH PAPER INTO THE CHIMNEY C

Too much paper blocks airflow, so the coals will take longer to ignite—or will not ignite at all.

BEST PRACTICE: Don't place more than two sheets of newspaper in the bottom chamber at one time.

3. POURING THE COALS BEFORE THEY ARE FULLY IGNITED C

If the coals aren't hot enough, they won't cook food at the right rate. Or, worse, the fire can die out.

BEST PRACTICE: Don't pour the coals until the top layer is partially covered with ash—a sure sign that they're ready.

4. SKIPPING THE PREHEAT STEP C G

Meat placed on a cooking grate that's not sufficiently hot will stick aggressively because its proteins form a chemical bond with the metal.

BEST PRACTICE: Wait to add food until the metal is very hot. This will break the bonds (which are thermally unstable), preventing sticking. It will also produce much better color and char.

CHARCOAL PREHEAT TIME
About 5 minutes

GAS PREHEAT TIME
About 15 minutes

5. USING ONE FIRE SETUP FOR ALL TASKS C G

The fire setup—how much charcoal or how many burners you're using and where the heat is located in relation to the food—allows you to control the heat level and the rate of cooking. Using the wrong setup can cause food to burn before it's cooked through or cook through without developing any flavorful browning or char.

BEST PRACTICE: Use one of our three favorite fire setups.

SINGLE-LEVEL FIRE

BEST FOR: Small, quick-cooking foods such as sausages, shrimp, fish fillets, and some vegetables.

CHARCOAL SETUP
Distribute lit coals in even layer across bottom of grill.

GAS SETUP
Turn all burners to high, cover, and heat grill until hot. Leave all burners on high.

HALF-GRILL FIRE

BEST FOR: Foods that you want to cook gently but also sear, such as bone-in chicken parts and pork chops.

CHARCOAL SETUP
Distribute lit coals in even layer over half of grill.

GAS SETUP
Turn all burners to high, cover, and heat grill until hot. Leave primary burner on high and turn off other burner(s).

CONCENTRATED FIRE

BEST FOR: Quick-cooking foods on which you want substantial char, such as burgers or thin steaks.

CHARCOAL SETUP
Poke holes in bottom of large disposable aluminum pan, place pan in center of grill, and pour lit coals into pan.

GAS SETUP
Concentrated fire setup is not possible on gas grill. To maximize heat, turn all burners to high.

6. NOT OILING THE COOKING GRATE C G

Most cooking grates are made of steel or cast iron and must be oiled before grilling to keep food from sticking.

BEST PRACTICE: Using tongs, dip a wad of paper towels in vegetable oil and thoroughly wipe the preheated, scrubbed cooking grate before adding food.

7. NOT CHECKING THE PROPANE TANK G

You don't want to end up with an empty propane tank in the middle of grilling—especially in the case of a lengthy project such as brisket or ribs.

HOW TO CHECK THE TANK

If your grill does not have a built-in fuel gauge, you can buy an external one—for example, the intuitive Original Grill Gauge ($13.99). Or try this hot water trick: Boil 1 cup of water and pour it down the side of the tank. Feel the metal with your hand. Where the water has warmed the surface of the tank, it is empty; where the tank remains cool to the touch, there is still propane inside.

8. COOKING ON A GUNKED-UP GRILL C G

Food debris, grease, and smoke residue that build up on various parts of the grill can cause sticking and impart off-flavors to food; full grease traps can ignite; and built-up grease on the interior basin and underside of the grill lid can carbonize and turn into a patchy layer that flakes off and lands on your food.

HOW TO CLEAN YOUR GRILL

Cooking Grate: After preheating the grill, scrape the cooking grate clean with a grill brush.

Interior Basin and Lid: Lightly scrub the cool grill and lid with steel wool and water.

Ash Catcher (charcoal only): Empty the cooled ash regularly.

Grease Traps (gas only): Remove the cool shallow pan from under your grill and scrub it with hot soapy water. To make cleanup easier, line the pan with aluminum foil before use.

WINNING GAS MODEL

Weber Spirit E-310 Gas Grill ($499.00)

Steady heat; sturdy cart; well-angled lid; large, stable grease tray; built-in fuel gauge

UPDATE: We recently discovered that the Weber Spirit E-310 Gas Grill has been replaced with the Weber Spirit II E-310 ($499.00). We ordered and tested the updated model and are happy to report it's our new favorite gas grill.

WINNING CHARCOAL MODEL

Weber Performer Deluxe Charcoal Grill ($399.00)

Maintains heat well; well-positioned vents; push-button gas ignition; roomy cart

9. LEAVING THE LID OPEN G

Because gas grills deliver less heat output than charcoal models, grilling certain foods with the lid up allows too much heat to escape. Note: You should never light a gas grill with the lid down, which can trap gas and cause a dangerous explosion.

BEST PRACTICE: When directed in a recipe, keep the lid closed to trap as much heat as possible.

10. LIFTING THE LID TOO OFTEN C G

This is equivalent to frequently opening the oven door. Heat will escape, which prolongs the grilling time.

BEST PRACTICE: Use a probe thermometer, which allows you to monitor food's doneness without opening the grill.

11. IGNORING THE GRILL VENTS G

If you're not using the vents, you're not controlling the heat output.

HOW GRILL VENTS WORK

Grill vents are like the dials on your stovetop: They allow you to manipulate how hot the fire gets and how the food cooks. Charcoal grills have top vents on the lid and bottom vents on the underside of the basin. (Gas grills have vents, too, but they are not adjustable.) In general, opening the vents completely allows more oxygen to reach the fire so that it burns hotter and faster; partially closing the vents lowers the temperature and prolongs the fire's duration.

12. TURNING THE MEAT TOO SOON C G

Meat will stick to the cooking grate until the meat's surface is hot enough to release (see "Skipping the preheat step"). Lifting meat before it naturally releases from the grate will tear it.

BEST PRACTICE: Sear the meat without moving it until a substantial crust forms around the edges. If the meat doesn't lift easily, continue searing until it does.

EVERYDAY ROASTED VEGETABLES

Roasting is a great way to breathe life into whatever produce is in your crisper drawer. Plus, it's mostly hands-free. Here's a cheat sheet for doing it well.

Something magical happens when you roast vegetables. The oven's dry heat drives off water to concentrate flavor while the fat encourages browning, transforming the raw vegetables into something entirely different. The trick is to use the right method for each vegetable and to keep a couple of simple garnishes in your back pocket so that you never get bored.

FIVE ROASTING RULES

These best practices apply to all vegetables and roasting methods.

1. USE A STURDY RIMMED BAKING SHEET.

Flimsy baking sheets warp in a hot oven, causing oil to pool and food to brown unevenly.

2. EVENLY COAT THE VEGETABLES WITH OIL AND SEASONINGS.

Oil (use any neutral variety) encourages browning because it conducts heat efficiently from the metal of the sheet to the vegetable. Toss the pieces with oil and salt and pepper in a bowl to ensure that they are evenly coated.

3. ARRANGE THE VEGETABLES IN A SINGLE LAYER.

A single layer of vegetables will cook and brown evenly.

4. DON'T CROWD THE SHEET.

Leaving space between the pieces prevents a buildup of steam and encourages browning.

5. DON'T FLIP TOO SOON.

The side touching the sheet should be brown before you flip your vegetable.

THREE EASY ROASTING METHODS

We use three basic methods for roasting most vegetables so that they emerge perfectly cooked on the inside with maximum surface browning.

METHOD 1: PREHEAT BAKING SHEET; ROAST UNCOVERED

Preheating the baking sheet ensures that relatively quick-cooking vegetables will develop flavorful browning by the time they are tender.

Asparagus
SERVES 4 TO 6

Amount and Prep: 2 pounds thick spears, bottom inch of each trimmed, bottom half peeled down to white flesh; 2 tablespoons oil

Oven Rack Position and Temp: Lowest; 500 degrees

Special Instruction: Don't move spears during roasting.

Cooking Time: 8 to 10 minutes

Keys to Success: Trimming and peeling the spears is less wasteful than snapping off the ends. Preheating the sheet on the lowest rack helps the spears sear upon contact; not moving the spears during roasting allows their undersides to brown deeply while the tops remain bright green.

Broccoli
SERVES 4

Amount and Prep: 1 large bunch (about 1¾ pounds), stalks peeled and cut into 2- to 3-inch lengths and each length into ½-inch-thick pieces, each crown cut into 4 to 6 evenly thick wedges; 3 tablespoons oil

Oven Rack Position and Temp: Lowest; 500 degrees

Special Instruction: Add ½ teaspoon sugar to oil.

Cooking Time: 9 to 11 minutes

Keys to Success: Cutting the crowns into wedges maximizes surface contact with the sheet to encourage browning. Adding sugar helps, too.

DRESS UP YOUR ROASTED VEGETABLES

Adding a flavored salt is an easy way to provide even more interest to roasted vegetables. It can enhance any vegetable and the salt can be thrown together while the vegetables are cooking. Our Chili-Lime Salt combines the smoky heat of chili powder with aromatic grated lime zest. It can be refrigerated in an airtight container for up to one week.

Chili-Lime Salt
MAKES 3 TABLESPOONS

2 tablespoons kosher salt

4 teaspoons chili powder

¾ teaspoon grated lime zest

Combine all ingredients in small bowl.

METHOD 2: ROAST UNCOVERED

The simplest roasting method works well for vegetables that will be sufficiently softened by the time their exteriors develop flavorful browning.

Butternut Squash

SERVES 4 TO 6

Amount and Prep: 1 large (2½ to 3 pounds), peeled down to deep orange flesh, halved lengthwise, seeds removed, each half sliced crosswise ½ inch thick; 3 tablespoons oil (or substitute equal amount of melted unsalted butter for richer flavor)

Oven Rack Position and Temp: Lowest; 425 degrees

Cooking Time: 25 to 30 minutes, rotate sheet and roast 6 to 10 minutes longer, flip squash, roast 10 to 15 minutes longer

Key to Success: Peeling the squash thoroughly, to remove not only the tough outer skin but also the fibrous layer of white flesh just beneath, ensures supremely tender results.

Cremini Mushrooms

SERVES 4 TO 6

Amount and Prep: 1½ pounds, trimmed and left whole if small, halved if medium, or quartered if large; 2 tablespoons oil

Oven Rack Position and Temp: Lowest; 450 degrees

Special Instruction: Before roasting, brine mushrooms for 10 minutes in solution of 2 quarts water and 5 teaspoons salt. Dry well.

Cooking Time: 35 to 40 minutes, toss, 5 to 10 minutes longer

Key to Success: Brining the mushrooms seasons them evenly and helps them stay moist during roasting.

METHOD 3: ROAST COVERED, THEN UNCOVERED

Initially covering the baking sheet with foil traps steam that helps dense vegetables soften and cook through. Uncovering the sheet allows moisture to evaporate so that the vegetables can brown.

Brussels Sprouts

SERVES 4

Amount and Prep: 1¼ pounds, trimmed and halved; 2 tablespoons oil

Oven Rack Position and Temp: Middle; 500 degrees

Special Instruction: Add 1 tablespoon water when tossing sprouts with oil, salt, and pepper.

Covered Time: 10 minutes

Uncovered Time: 10 to 12 minutes

Keys to Success: Adding water to the oil helps the sprouts steam during the covered phase. Initially arranging the sprouts cut side down ensures that their flat surface browns deeply.

Cauliflower

SERVES 4 TO 6

Amount and Prep: 1 medium head (about 2 pounds), outer leaves trimmed, stem cut flush with bottom, and head cut into 8 equal wedges so that core and florets remain intact; ¼ cup oil

Oven Rack Position and Temp: Lowest; 475 degrees

Special Instructions: Rub oil, salt, and pepper into each wedge. Line sheet with aluminum foil or parchment paper, pressing liner into corners.

Covered Time: 10 minutes

Uncovered Time: 8 to 12 minutes, flip, 8 to 12 minutes longer

Keys to Success: Leaving the core intact makes it easy to flip the pieces halfway through cooking. Rubbing the oil and seasonings into each piece ensures that the nooks and crannies are evenly coated.

Carrots

SERVES 4 TO 6

Amount and Prep: 1½ pounds, peeled, halved crosswise, and cut lengthwise if necessary to create even pieces; 2 tablespoons oil (or substitute equal amount of melted unsalted butter for richer flavor)

Oven Rack Position and Temp: Middle; 425 degrees

Special Instructions: Line sheet with aluminum foil or parchment paper, pressing liner into corners.

Covered Time: 15 minutes

Uncovered Time: 30 to 35 minutes, stirring twice

Key to Success: Cutting the carrots into batons ensures that they cook evenly. Lining the sheet prevents scorching and makes cleanup easy.

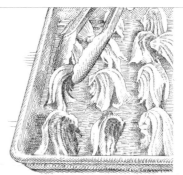

Fennel

SERVES 4 TO 6

Amount and Prep: 3 bulbs, 3 to 3½ inches in diameter, stalks discarded, each bulb cut lengthwise through core (don't remove core) into 8 wedges; 2 tablespoons oil

Oven Rack Position and Temp: Lower-middle; 425 degrees

Covered Time: 15 minutes

Uncovered Time: 10 to 15 minutes, flip, continue to roast until core is tender and side touching sheet is browned, 5 to 10 minutes longer

Keys to Success: Cutting the bulbs lengthwise creates maximum surface area for browning. Leaving the core intact makes the halves easy to flip.

TEN DISCOVERIES THAT CHANGED THE WAY WE COOK

Over the past 26 years, we've performed countless tests in the pursuit of better, faster, easier, and more foolproof recipes. Here are a few of the game changers that transformed how we—and, dare we say, our readers—cook.

1. BEST PRETREATMENT FOR MEAT: SALT THERAPY

You may have missed our Roast Brined Turkey in 1993—the recipe that put brining on the map. But you can't have missed that brining and salting poultry and meat are two of our core techniques. Here's a refresher on why.

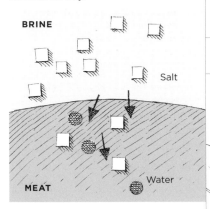

BRINING

Brining adds moisture, which makes it a particularly good choice for lean proteins. The salt in the brine not only seasons the meat but also promotes a change in its protein structure, reducing its overall toughness and creating gaps that fill up with water and keep the meat juicy.

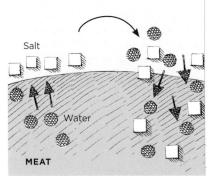

SALTING

Salting helps proteins retain their natural juices and is the best choice for ensuring crispy skin or a crusty exterior. When salt is applied to raw meat, moisture inside the meat is drawn to the surface. The salt then dissolves in the exuded liquid, forming a brine that the meat eventually reabsorbs.

2. DON'T FEEL LIKE SEARING? YOU CAN SKIP IT

While making our Hungarian Beef Stew in 2008, we learned that there's no need to sear the meat if you're making a low-liquid braise that cooks in the oven. Over time, the dry surface of the meat that sits above the liquid will reach a high enough temperature for the meat to brown and form hundreds of new flavor compounds.

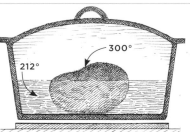

3. THIS GOOP MAKES BETTER BREAD

We didn't believe it either—until we applied the Asian bread-baking technique called *tangzhong* to our 2016 recipe for Fluffy Dinner Rolls and came away with an airy, feathery, ultramoist crumb that remained fresh and soft longer than any bread we'd made the conventional way. Incorporating this goop—a pudding-like paste made by cooking a portion of the recipe's flour with water—into the dough allows you to add more water to the dough than you could by simply combining the dry and wet ingredients. That's because flour can absorb twice as much hot water as cold water. The upshot: a superhydrated dough that bakes up incredibly moist and fluffy.

4. BROWNING MEAT BACKWARD KEEPS IT ROSY

The first step when cooking a steak or roast is to sear it, right? Wrong. When we dug deep into steak cookery in 2007, we realized that the best way to achieve a uniformly rosy interior and a deep crust is to "reverse-sear" the meat by first roasting it in a low oven until nearly done and then browning it in a hot skillet. The oven's gentle heat minimizes the temperature difference between the meat's center and edges, and the hot pan rapidly browns the warm, dry surface, so there's no time for the meat beneath it to overcook.

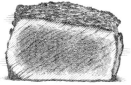

SEARED FIRST

SEARED LAST

5. A "COLD" SKILLET LEADS TO MORE EVEN COOKING

Adding food to a ripping-hot skillet will quickly brown the exterior. But in 2004 we realized that if you want to brown a food that requires more than a flash of blazing heat to cook through or render fat—a pork chop, a skin-on chicken breast or salmon fillet, dense Brussels sprouts—it's best to place the food in a "cold" (not preheated) skillet and then turn on the heat. That way, the food has more time to gently cook through (or render its fat) before the exterior burns.

6. AMP UP MEATINESS WITHOUT MEAT

When we added a few anchovies (per tradition) to our Daube Provençal in 2005, we didn't know exactly why it made the dish taste more complex. We later learned that anchovies are uniquely rich in compounds called glutamates and nucleotides, which individually enhance savory depth, or umami, in food but amp it up even more when present together. Nowadays we routinely slip anchovies into stews, soups, chilis, and even meatballs to boost meaty flavor. For vegetarian dishes, we turn to tomato paste, soy sauce, or Parmigiano-Reggiano; to get that synergistic effect, we sometimes also add dried mushrooms.

GLUTAMATE-RICH	Parmigiano-Reggiano
	Soy sauce
	Tomato paste
NUCLEOTIDE-RICH	Dried porcini mushrooms
GLUTAMATE- AND NUCLEOTIDE-RICH	Anchovies
	Dried shiitake mushrooms

7. OVERCOOKED DARK MEAT CHICKEN SEEMS JUICIER

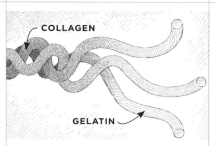

COLLAGEN

GELATIN

A cardinal rule of preparing chicken: Don't overcook it, or the meat will be dry and stringy. But while developing a braised chicken thighs recipe in 2015, we realized that dark-meat poultry is the exception to the rule. While it is safe to eat at 160 degrees and moderately tender at 175, it tastes exceptionally juicy and tender when cooked to 195 degrees. That's because it's loaded with connective tissue, which dissolves into gelatin as the meat cooks, rendering it tender and especially juicy. Slowly cooking the meat to 195 degrees maximizes collagen breakdown so that it's not just tender but downright silky and succulent.

8. BAKING SODA ISN'T JUST FOR BAKING

Of course we use baking soda as a leavening agent. But page through the *Cook's Illustrated* archive and you'll see that it has a slew of other applications that can all be attributed to its alkaline properties.

TENDERIZES MEAT: Briefly soaking ground beef or thin slices of meat destined for a stir-fry in a solution of baking soda and water raises the pH on the meat's surface, making it more difficult for the proteins to bond excessively, which keeps the meat tender and moist when it's cooked.

HASTENS BROWNING: Whether it's stirred into pancake batter or rubbed onto the surface of meat, baking soda creates a high-pH environment in which browning reactions occur more readily.

RAPIDLY SOFTENS VEGETABLES, GRAINS, AND CHICKPEAS: Adding just a pinch to vegetables, grains, or chickpeas during cooking weakens their cell walls so they break down and soften more quickly.

BOOSTS FLAVOR: Baking soda adds a salty, mineral flavor to baked goods and pancakes.

9. A MARINADE'S MOST IMPORTANT INGREDIENT IS SALT

Other recipes may call for soaking bland, chewy cuts in a marinade in the hope that the flavorful liquid will tenderize the meat or infuse flavor to the bone. Not ours. After dozens of in-house and independent lab tests, we declared in 2009 that marinades don't tenderize and most seasonings won't penetrate the meat, no matter how long the soak.

The one ingredient that does make a big difference? Salt. As in a brine, salt in an overnight marinade is able to penetrate deep into the food to season the meat and enhance its juiciness. Other marinade must-haves include glutamate-rich soy sauce; water-soluble flavorings such as garlic and onion; and sweeteners, which add complexity and also encourage flavorful browning. While these ingredients won't penetrate as deep into meat as salt does, given enough time, they will move beyond its surface. Finally, oil dissolves the fat-soluble flavor compounds in most herbs and spices, allowing them to flavor the meat's exterior.

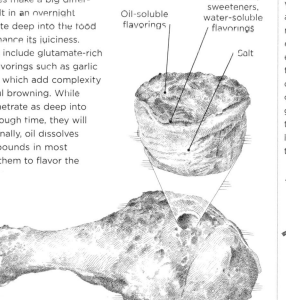

Oil-soluble flavorings

Glutamates, sweeteners, water-soluble flavorings

Salt

10. THE GENTLEST WAY TO COOK? NO HEAT

In 2008, we roasted an eye round for 24 hours at 130 degrees to see how tender this lean cut could be if cooked ultralow and slow. The results were exceptional, so we devised a faster, equally effective approach: cooking food partway at a moderate temperature and then shutting off the heat. As the heat of the cooking environment—an oven or a covered pot on the stovetop—declines, the temperature of the food gradually rises. In lean proteins, gentle heat prevents muscle fibers from getting too hot and squeezing out moisture and, in certain cases, can even increase enzymatic activity that helps tenderize the meat.

Hot   Ambient temperature

Cold   Food internal temperature

DWINDLING HEAT EQUALS TENDER MEAT

GETTING THE MOST OUT OF YOUR MOST IMPORTANT KNIFE

A good chef's knife is indispensable for all cutting tasks, from precision work such as mincing a shallot to heavy-duty jobs such as breaking down a butternut squash. Here's how to make sure you use it to its best advantage.

START WITH A GOOD KNIFE

We believe that all kitchen tasks go better and more easily when you use well-designed equipment, and this maxim is especially true of a chef's knife. It's imperative to have a good one. Our two favorites merge the knife traditions of the East and West: curved cutting edges that encourage the rocking motion favored by most Western cooks and slimmer blades like those common on Japanese knives, which can more deftly move through food.

VICTORINOX SWISS ARMY FIBROX PRO 8" CHEF'S KNIFE ($39.95)

Our Swiss-made longtime favorite continually beats out the competition with its 15-degree cutting edge (versus the 20-degree angle of classic Western chef's knives) that slides effortlessly through food yet is sturdy enough to easily cut through butternut squash. We also love its good edge retention and textured, secure grip—not to mention its bargain price.

WHY EIGHT IS THE MAGIC NUMBER

Chef's knives range in length from 8 to 10 inches. We find that 8 inches is long enough to maneuver through a wide roast or a hefty watermelon but short enough to allow for good control of the blade.

MASAMOTO VG-10 GYUTOU, 8.2" ($136.50)

For those willing to fork over more for a chef's knife, this knife's asymmetrical cutting edge (21 degrees on one side, 9 degrees on the other) cuts through anything it encounters like a dream, including butternut squash and chicken cartilage. With a blade more curved than that of a typical Japanese knife, it also assists a rocking motion that cleanly minces herbs. Its edge retention is excellent.

HOW TO HOLD THE KNIFE

The first step to making efficient cuts is holding the knife appropriately.

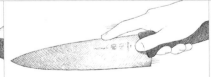

PINCH GRIP

Pinch the blade where it meets the handle with your thumb and forefinger. This grip, our go-to for most cutting tasks, allows you to choke up on the blade to get leverage over the whole length of the knife.

FINGER GRIP

Rest your thumb on the side of the blade and your forefinger on the spine. This grip is useful for precision tasks in which you're mainly using the tip of the blade and don't need to put a lot of force behind it, such as filleting fish.

HANDLE GRIP

Grasp the knife firmly where the handle meets the blade. While this grip can often feel the most secure for inexperienced cooks, it doesn't offer the control over the tip that is needed to make precision cuts. We recommend using this grip only when honing the blade or when mincing herbs.

THE "CLAW"

Not a knife grip but the position of your hand holding the food. Curve your fingers into a claw on top of the food, tucking your thumb behind them and pressing down to hold the food in place. This position allows your knuckles to help guide the side of the blade while your fingertips stay out of harm's way. With practice, your claw will move back in even increments after each cut, guiding the knife to make even slices.

THREE CUTS EVERY COOK SHOULD KNOW

The goal when cutting any food is to avoid crushing or bruising it and to create even-size pieces that cook at the same rate and/or ensure even flavor distribution throughout the dish. With practice, executing the proper motions—all of which rely on a pushing or pulling action rather than a straight downward cut—will make your prep work go much more smoothly and quickly.

1. SLICING

Create flat, stable surface by cutting food in half or removing thin slice from bottom. Hold food with claw grip.

For small items, keep tip down: Using pinch grip and with tip of knife on cutting board and middle of blade resting on food, push down and forward, using length of blade to cut through food. As you cut, blade follows rocking motion; As heel of knife goes down, knife slices forward; then, blade slides back as heel is lifted up.

For large items, lift blade up: To slice large items such as eggplant, use pinch grip and lift entire blade off board to start each cut. Starting with front part of blade on food, push down and forward. As you cut, blade follows same rocking motion as with small item.

WHAT IT'S USED FOR: Most vegetable and fruit prep

2. MINCING

Start by roughly chopping food using pinch grip and slicing cut. Then gather food into small pile. While steadying tip of knife with your nondominant hand and using handle grip, rock knife up and down with slight pivoting motion, without lifting knife tip off cutting board, until food is evenly minced.

WHAT IT'S USED FOR: Herbs, garlic cloves, citrus zest

3. TIP CUT

This precision cut uses only the knife tip. Using pinch grip, place tip of knife on food and draw it through or across food with gentle downward pressure.

WHAT IT'S USED FOR: Cutting meat from around bones or crosshatching fat on meat

KEEPING YOUR CHEF'S KNIFE SHARP

A sharp knife is a precise, efficient tool, while a dull knife is an accident waiting to happen. That's because a dull blade requires more force to do the job and has a higher chance of slipping and missing the mark. The result most often is food that's crushed or bruised. And it doesn't take months or weeks for a knife to lose its edge. Even a few minutes of cutting dense or hard foods can dull a blade. To maintain your knife, you should hone it or sharpen it regularly.

HONING VERSUS SHARPENING

Honing a knife with a honing steel (also referred to as a sharpening steel—a misnomer) repositions (or "trues") the edge of a blade that is slightly out of alignment to restore sharpness. Sharpening trims and reshapes the blade by removing metal that is blunted or too far out of alignment for honing to work.

TAKE THE SHARPNESS TEST

Hold a sheet of paper by one end and drag your knife, from heel to tip, across it. If the knife snags or fails to cut the paper, it needs to be honed or sharpened.

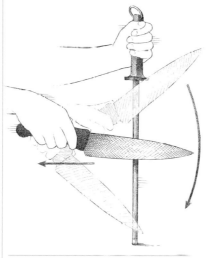

HOW OFTEN SHOULD YOU HONE?

A good rule of thumb is to use a honing steel every time you start to cook. If you are doing a lot of heavy cutting work, such as butchering a chicken or slicing a lot of onions, it's a good idea to also hone while you are working. Regular maintenance will prolong the time between sharpening sessions.

1. Using handle grip, place tip of honing steel on counter and heel of blade against its top, pointing knife tip slightly upward. Hold blade at consistent angle away from steel (15 to 20 degrees depending on the knife).

2. Maintaining light pressure and consistent angle, sweep blade down length of steel, pulling knife toward your body so that entire edge of blade makes contact with steel.

3. Repeat this motion on other side of blade. Four or 5 strokes on each side of blade (total of 8 to 10 alternating passes) should realign edge.

HOW OFTEN SHOULD YOU SHARPEN?

If you cook often, you should check your knife weekly for sharpness using the sharpness test (see "Take the Sharpness Test"). If it fails the test, try honing first. If that doesn't work, run it through a sharpener.

TWO GREAT SHARPENERS

MANUAL: Chef'sChoice Pronto Manual Diamond Hone Asian Knife Sharpener ($49.99)

Comments: Tall walls hold the knife steady so that a 15-degree blade can be drawn through the chamber with even pressure. The slim body is easily stowed in a drawer.

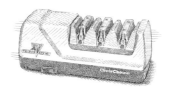

ELECTRIC: Chef'sChoice Trizor XV Knife Sharpener ($149.99)

Comments: The aggressive first slot can quickly repair extensive damage and narrow a 20-degree Western knife to a sharper 15-degree edge. Use the fine slot to gently resharpen a slightly dull knife.

HOW TO MAKE A GREAT GREEN SALAD

It starts with skipping packaged greens and returning to the classic way of making salad—using crisp, mature head lettuces.

Opening a box of baby greens is a fine way to make a salad. But this delicate produce can't compete with mature head lettuces, whose crisp, flavorful, bristling leaves also offer a sturdier base to support add-ins like cheeses, fruits, and vegetables that contribute interest and character to a salad. We have also found that seemingly small tweaks—such as how thoroughly you dry your greens, the way you prep add-ins, the order in which you add ingredients to the serving bowl, and the extra effort of emulsifying your dressing—can make the difference between a good salad and a truly memorable one.

GET YOUR HEAD IN THE GAME

Familiar head lettuces such as Bibb, romaine, and red or green leaf are salad stalwarts. We use them to provide most of the bulk in the bowl, and their relatively mild flavors make them extremely versatile. Think of them as a functional base layer that you can accessorize with more assertive accent greens, herbs, and other vegetables.

BIBB (ALIASES: BUTTER, BOSTON)

PROFILE: Tender, smooth, grassy

TIP: For longer shelf life, leave root intact until ready to use.

ROMAINE (ALIAS: COS)

PROFILE: Crunchy; mild, slightly bitter spine

TIP: Its cup-shaped leaves and sturdy spine hold up well when paired with thick, creamy dressings.

RED/GREEN LEAF

PROFILE: Earthy; tender edges, crisp spine

TIP: The leaves' uneven surfaces and ruffled edges are great at capturing mix-ins and flaky salt.

STRONG ACCENTS

A generous handful of any of these spicy, bitter, crunchy, or frilly greens will make your salad pop.

RADICCHIO

PROFILE: Bitter, crunchy

TIP: Discard wilted outer leaves, but don't bother washing the rest. It is rare for dirt to get into the tightly packed head.

ARUGULA

PROFILE: Peppery, tender

TIP: Mature arugula can be very sandy, so wash it in several changes of water.

FRISÉE

PROFILE: Bitter, crisp

TIP: Trim away the green parts and use the yellow and white parts.

WATERCRESS

PROFILE: Juicy, spicy, tender

TIP: Like arugula, watercress bunches harbor grit and must be washed thoroughly.

DOUBLE-DRY YOUR GREENS

Excess moisture that's left on lettuces and herbs will dilute your dressing. After washing the greens, dry them as much as possible in a salad spinner (our favorite is the OXO Good Grips Salad Spinner, $29.99) and then blot away any remaining water with paper towels.

THE BEST WAY TO STORE GREENS

Store washed, dried leaves as well as intact heads of lettuce wrapped in moist paper towels in a partially open plastic produce bag or zipper-lock bag. Never store lettuce in the refrigerator without any protection, as it will rapidly go limp.

DON'T TOSS WILTED LETTUCE, SOAK IT

Lettuce wilts because it loses water, so the key to reviving it is to put the water back in. A 30-minute soak in ice water will usually restore crispness.

HERBAL ESSENCES

Herbs are greens, too, and they pack much more flavor than basic lettuces. We like to add whole leaves of tender fresh herbs (parsley, cilantro, basil, chervil, tarragon, mint, or dill) or 1-inch pieces of fennel fronds to the bowl. (Save woodier herbs such as rosemary, thyme, and sage for cooking.) And if you have to go the supermarket mesclun route, herbs are a great way to improve a packaged mix.

PREP AND ADD YOUR ADD-INS PROPERLY

Nobody likes carrot chunks or wads of goat cheese that sink to the bottom of the bowl. Follow these guidelines to prepare your add-ins so that they distribute evenly in the salad.

DRESS AND SEASON THE SALAD RIGHT

Add the dressing in increments. Toss the salad, tasting as you go, to ensure that the greens aren't over- or underdressed

VEGETABLES: Shave or thinly slice them (a peeler or mandoline is helpful here) so they mix evenly with the greens.

FRUITS: Thinly slice and drain wet varieties (such as citrus) so that they don't dilute the dressing.

CHEESE: Crumble soft varieties into ¼- to ½-inch pieces; shave small slivers of hard cheeses.

LEAVE SOME FOR THE TOP: Reserve half of heavier nuts and cheeses to sprinkle over the dressed salad.

SEASON THE SALAD, TOO: The measured amounts of salt in a dressing may not be enough, so we like to season the salad to taste with kosher or flake sea salt just after dressing it. This also creates appealing pops of salty crunch.

SALAD BY THE NUMBERS

3:1	2-3	3:1	¼
Ratio of head lettuce to accent greens (approx.)	Add-ins	Ratio of oil to vinegar	Cup dressing per 10 cups greens

A BETTER KIND OF CROUTON

By soaking bread cubes in a little water and then frying them in olive oil, we made croutons that are crispy on the outside and chewy in the middle—a far cry from dry supermarket varieties.

Place 5 cups ¾-inch bread cubes (ciabatta or other crusty, rustic loaf) in large bowl. Sprinkle with ¼ cup water and ¼ teaspoon table salt. Toss, squeezing gently so bread absorbs water. Heat ¼ cup extra-virgin olive oil and soaked bread cubes in 12-inch nonstick skillet over medium-high heat, stirring frequently, until browned and crisp, 7 to 10 minutes.

TWO ROUTES TO A WELL-DRESSED SALAD

Using high-quality oil and vinegar (or lemon juice) beats a bottled dressing any day. But the way you add these components to your salad affects how quickly it wilts. Here are two routes to ensure that your greens stay crisp.

QUICK ROUTE: LAZY PERSON'S VINAIGRETTE

Drizzling oil and vinegar over your greens is fast and perfectly fine—as long as you add them in the right order. We found that tossing the salad first with the vinegar and again after adding the oil prevented the leaves from wilting too quickly. Why? Lettuce leaves have a protective waxy cuticle layer that helps keep out water-based liquids (such as vinegar), but oil easily penetrates this film. Vinegar helps block the oil so it doesn't penetrate the cuticle and wilt your lettuce.

BEST ROUTE: EMULSIFIED VINAIGRETTE

An emulsified vinaigrette works best for keeping the salad crisp because the vinegar surrounds droplets of oil, trapping them and preventing contact with the greens. (Not to mention that an emulsified vinaigrette will guarantee balanced flavor in every bite.) The mustard and mayonnaise in our Foolproof Vinaigrette contain emulsifying agents that help the oil and vinegar combine into a unified sauce and stay that way for more than an hour.

Foolproof Vinaigrette
SERVES 4 (MAKES ¼ CUP)
TOTAL TIME: 10 MINUTES

Here are our favorite supermarket vinegars: Napa Valley Naturals Organic White Wine Vinegar, Pompeian Gourmet Red Wine Vinegar, Bertolli Balsamic Vinegar of Modena, and Napa Valley Naturals Reserve Sherry Vinegar.

- **1 tablespoon balsamic, sherry, or wine vinegar or lemon juice**
- **1½ teaspoons very finely minced shallot**
- **½ teaspoon mayonnaise**
- **½ teaspoon Dijon mustard**
- **⅛ teaspoon table salt**
- **3 tablespoons extra-virgin olive oil**

1. Combine vinegar, shallot, mayonnaise, mustard, and salt in small bowl and season with pepper to taste. Whisk until mixture looks milky and no lumps of mayonnaise remain.

2. Whisking constantly, very slowly drizzle oil into vinegar mixture. If pools of oil are gathering on surface as you whisk, stop addition of oil and whisk mixture well to combine, then resume whisking in oil in slow stream. Vinaigrette should be glossy and lightly thickened, with no pools of oil on surface.

GARNISHES WE CAN'T LIVE WITHOUT

There's no better way to fend off dinner doldrums than to keep a variety of ultraquick and vibrant sauces, seasonings, and toppings on hand.

Every cook needs an arsenal of finishing touches—tangy chutneys, piquant pastes, rich dressings, earthy spice blends, and seasoned salts—that can breathe new life into chicken breasts, jazz up vegetables, and add visual, textural, and flavor contrast to make a dish pop. Behold a larder's worth of our favorites, both familiar classics and modern riffs. We've organized them by flavor and texture and offered suggested uses, but these are just starting points; use your imagination.

TANGY

Green Tomato Chutney

YIELD: 2 CUPS

What it is: Sweet-sour preserve

Serve with: Rich meat, sausage, cheese, sandwiches

Total time: 3 hours

Bring 2 pounds green tomatoes, cored and cut into 1-inch chunks; ¾ cup sugar; ¾ cup distilled white vinegar; 1 teaspoon coriander seeds; 1 teaspoon table salt; and ½ teaspoon red pepper flakes to simmer in saucepan. Cook until thickened, about 40 minutes. Let cool completely, about 2 hours. Stir in 2 teaspoons lemon juice just before serving.

TIP: To expedite cooling, spread the chutney into an even layer in a shallow dish.

Tangy Hoisin Sauce

YIELD: ½ CUP

What it is: Vinegary, gingery Asian soybean sauce

Serve with: Pork, chicken, rice, noodles, eggs

Total time: 5 minutes

Stir ½ cup hoisin sauce, 2 thinly sliced scallions, 4 teaspoons rice vinegar, and 1 teaspoon grated fresh ginger in bowl until smooth.

ONE-INGREDIENT FINISHERS

These minimalist seasonings enhance food without distracting from its flavor. Just be sure to use fresh, high-quality ingredients.

- **Citrus zest:** Grate over vegetables, chicken, fish
- **Grilled lemon halves:** Squeeze over meat and seafood
- **Extra-virgin olive oil:** Drizzle over soup, salad, seafood, steak, pasta, grains
- **Parmesan or Pecorino Romano cheese:** Grate or shave over soup, salad, pasta, grains
- **Vinegar:** Drizzle a few drops over soup, stew, sauces, fried food

CREAMY

Preserved-Lemon Aioli

YIELD: 1 CUP

What it is: Tangy garlic mayonnaise

Serve with: Vegetables, seafood, sandwiches

Total time: 5 minutes

Process ¼ cup chopped preserved lemon, 3 large egg yolks, 1 tablespoon water, and 1 minced garlic clove in blender until well combined, about 30 seconds, scraping down sides of blender jar as needed. With blender running, slowly drizzle in ½ cup vegetable oil until emulsified and thickened, about 45 seconds, then drizzle in 1 tablespoon lemon juice and 2 tablespoons water.

Tahini Sauce

YIELD: ⅓ CUP

What it is: Middle Eastern sesame sauce

Serve with: Vegetables, French fries, falafel, grains, chicken, lamb

Total time: 5 minutes

Whisk 2 tablespoons tahini, 2 tablespoons extra-virgin olive oil, 1 tablespoon lemon juice, 2 teaspoons honey, and pinch table salt together in small bowl.

FRESH

Tarragon-Lemon Gremolata

YIELD: ¼ CUP

What it is: Italian herb garnish

Serve with: Soup, pasta, fish, vegetables

Total time: 5 minutes

Combine 2 tablespoons minced fresh tarragon, 2 tablespoons minced fresh parsley, 2 teaspoons grated lemon zest, and 1 minced garlic clove in bowl.

Mint Persillade

YIELD: 1 CUP

What it is: French herb sauce

Serve with: Meat, fish, vegetables

Total time: 5 minutes

Pulse 1 cup fresh mint leaves; 1 cup fresh parsley leaves; 3 peeled garlic cloves; 3 anchovy fillets, rinsed and patted dry; 1 teaspoon grated lemon zest; ½ teaspoon table salt; and ⅛ teaspoon pepper in food processor until finely chopped, 15 to 20 pulses. Add 1 tablespoon lemon juice and pulse to combine. Transfer to bowl and whisk in ⅓ cup extra-virgin olive oil.

Cilantro-Mint Chutney

YIELD: 1 CUP

What it is: Bright, subtly spicy Indian herb sauce

Serve with: Grilled or roasted fish, Indian curries

Total time: 5 minutes

Process 2 cups fresh cilantro leaves; 1 cup fresh mint leaves; ½ cup water; ¼ cup toasted sesame seeds; 1 (2-inch) piece ginger, peeled and sliced thin; 1 stemmed, seeded, and sliced jalapeño chile; 2 tablespoons vegetable oil; 2 tablespoons lime juice; 1½ teaspoons sugar; and ½ teaspoon table salt in blender until smooth, about 30 seconds, scraping down sides of blender jar as needed.

SPICY

Harissa

YIELD: ½ CUP

What it is: North African chile-spice paste

Serve with:
Vegetables, eggs, lamb, soup

Total time: 5 minutes

Combine 6 tablespoons extra-virgin olive oil, 6 minced garlic cloves, 2 tablespoons paprika, 1 tablespoon ground coriander, 1 tablespoon ground dried Aleppo pepper, 1 teaspoon ground cumin, ¾ teaspoon caraway seeds, and ½ teaspoon salt in bowl and microwave until bubbling, about 1 minute, stirring halfway through microwaving. Let cool completely.

Korean Chile Sauce

YIELD: ⅔ CUP

What it is: Sweet and spicy sauce

Serve with: Stew, chili, rice bowls, noodles, macaroni and cheese, eggs

Total time: 5 minutes

Whisk ¼ cup gochujang, 3 tablespoons water, 2 tablespoons toasted sesame oil, and 1 teaspoon sugar together in small bowl.

TIP: Store in a squeeze bottle for easy drizzling.

CRISPY/CRUNCHY

Crispy Bread-Crumb Topping

YIELD: 2 TABLESPOONS

What it is: Seasoned panko bread crumbs

Serve with: Vegetables, meat, fish, pasta

Total time: 10 minutes

Grind 2 tablespoons panko bread crumbs using spice grinder or mortar and pestle to medium-fine crumbs. Transfer panko to 12-inch skillet, add 1 tablespoon vegetable oil, and stir. Toast over medium-low heat for 5 to 7 minutes. Off heat, add ¾ teaspoon kosher salt, ¼ teaspoon pepper, and ¼ teaspoon red pepper flakes.

Pistachio Dukkah

YIELD: ½ CUP

What it is: Egyptian nut, seed, and spice blend

Serve with: Olive oil as dip for bread, soup, seafood

Total time: 5 minutes

Coarsely grind 1½ tablespoons toasted sesame seeds using spice grinder or mortar and pestle; transfer to bowl. Finely grind 1½ teaspoons toasted coriander seeds, ¾ teaspoon toasted cumin seeds, and ½ teaspoon toasted fennel seeds in grinder. Transfer to bowl with sesame seeds. Stir in 2 tablespoons shelled pistachios, toasted and chopped fine; ½ teaspoon table salt; and ½ teaspoon pepper.

Za'atar

YIELD: ⅓ CUP

What it is: Earthy, bright Middle Eastern spice blend

Serve with: Dips, meatballs, kebabs, roasted potatoes

Total time: 5 minutes

Grind 2 tablespoons dried thyme and 1 tablespoon dried oregano using spice grinder or mortar and pestle until finely ground and powdery. Transfer to bowl and stir in 1½ tablespoons sumac, 1 tablespoon toasted sesame seeds, and ¼ teaspoon table salt.

Candied Bacon Bits

YIELD: ¼ CUP

What it is: Sugar- and vinegar-glazed bacon bits

Serve with: Creamy soup, salad, pasta, eggs, dips

Total time: 10 minutes

Cook 4 slices bacon, cut into ½-inch pieces, in 10-inch nonstick skillet over medium heat until crispy, 5 to 7 minutes. Remove bacon from skillet and discard fat. Return bacon to skillet and add 2 teaspoons packed dark brown sugar and ½ teaspoon cider vinegar. Cook over low heat, stirring constantly, until bacon is evenly coated. Transfer to plate and let cool completely.

COMPOUND BUTTERS

Stirring seasonings into softened butter is an easy way to make a rich, flavor-packed condiment for meat, fish, and vegetables that can be refrigerated for up to three days or frozen indefinitely. It's also a great way to use up ingredients such as a single scallion, the last spoonful of honey, or stray bits of cheese. Here are a few suggestions.

Combine 4 tablespoons softened unsalted butter with one of the following flavor combinations.

BASIL AND LEMON BUTTER	4 teaspoons shredded fresh basil, 2 teaspoons minced fresh parsley, ¾ teaspoon finely grated lemon zest, ¼ teaspoon table salt, ⅛ teaspoon pepper
THAI CHILE BUTTER	1 minced garlic clove, 1½ teaspoons thinly sliced scallion (green part only), 1 tablespoon chopped fresh cilantro, 2 teaspoons Asian chili-garlic paste, ½ teaspoon red curry paste
BLUE CHEESE–CHIVE BUTTER	⅓ cup crumbled mild blue cheese, 2 tablespoons minced fresh chives, 1 minced garlic clove, ¼ teaspoon pepper
LATIN-SPICED BUTTER	4 teaspoons minced fresh cilantro, 2 teaspoons minced fresh parsley, ¾ teaspoon minced canned chipotle chile in adobo sauce, ¼ teaspoon finely grated orange zest, ¼ teaspoon table salt

FRESH MOZZARELLA

Mozzarella can be found in a variety of forms, but when we want the milkiest, richest flavor and a tender, soft texture, we turn to balls of "fresh" high-moisture mozzarella. To find the best one, we sampled eight fresh mozzarellas plain (twice, to control for variability), in our Cherry Tomato Caprese Salad, and melted onto miniature toasts. Tasters preferred balanced mozzarellas that were moderately salty (with 85 to 95 milligrams of sodium per serving) and slightly tangy, with delicate grassy, floral notes. We sent samples of each to an independent lab to have pH, moisture, fat, and protein levels calculated. Sodium level and type of acid were taken from ingredient labels. Sodium levels were standardized for comparison, using a serving size of 1 ounce. The top seven cheeses are listed below in order of preference.

RECOMMENDED

BELGIOIOSO Fresh Mozzarella
PRICE: $7.99 for 8 oz ($1.00 per oz)
PACKAGE: Shrink-wrapped
INGREDIENTS: Pasteurized milk, vinegar, enzymes, salt
SODIUM: 85 mg
TYPE OF ACID: Vinegar
pH: 6.0 **MOISTURE:** 60.3%
COMMENTS: This mozzarella was "pillowy" and "tender," with a "melt-in-your-mouth" richness that tasters loved. It had a moderate amount of sodium and "balanced tang" as well as a flavor that was "buttery," "creamy," and "fresh."

LIONI Fresh Mozzarella
PRICE: $4.99 for 8 oz ($0.62 per oz)
PACKAGE: Shrink-wrapped
INGREDIENTS: Pasteurized whole milk, starter, cheese cultures, vegetable rennet, salt
SODIUM: 95 mg
TYPE OF ACID: Cheese culture
pH: 5.9 **MOISTURE:** 61.2%
COMMENTS: This mozzarella was "tender but not too squishy" and "firm but not too dry." It had "the perfect amount of salt," and tasters also picked up on "grassy" notes of "cultured" milk. Its texture was "springy" and "soft," and we loved its "luxurious," "buttery" richness.

FRIGO Fresh Mozzarella Cheese
PRICE: $3.99 for 8 oz ($0.50 per oz)
PACKAGE: Shrink-wrapped
INGREDIENTS: Pasteurized milk, cheese cultures, salt, enzymes
SODIUM: 110 mg
TYPE OF ACID: Cheese culture
pH: 6.1 **MOISTURE:** 55.9%
COMMENTS: This "bold" mozzarella had plenty of sodium; most tasters found it "balanced," but a few thought it was "overseasoned." Its texture was "springy," "bouncy," and "smooth," and it had a "mild," "sweet" milkiness that contrasted with its more "savory" notes.

GALBANI Fresh Mozzarella
PRICE: $4.59 for 8 oz ($0.57 per oz)
PACKAGE: Shrink-wrapped
INGREDIENTS: Pasteurized milk, vinegar, salt, enzymes
SODIUM: 100 mg
TYPE OF ACID: Vinegar
pH: 5.9 **MOISTURE:** 57.9%
COMMENTS: This mozzarella was "soft" and "chewy," with a "buttery dairy flavor." Its "shaggy" texture reminded a few tasters of "hand-pulled mozz." However, it was "a bit too salty and tangy" for some tasters.

RECOMMENDED WITH RESERVATIONS

BOAR'S HEAD Fresh Mozzarella Cheese
PRICE: $4.99 for 8 oz ($0.62 per oz)
PACKAGE: Shrink-wrapped
INGREDIENTS: Pasteurized milk, vinegar, sea salt, rennet
SODIUM: 90 mg
TYPE OF ACID: Vinegar
pH: 5.8 **MOISTURE:** 58.3%
COMMENTS: This cheese, which was more "yellow" than the stark white we're used to with mozzarella, had a "buttery" and "fairly salty" flavor. Tasters were split on its texture, which was "soft" and "almost spreadable" when uncooked. While this cheese would be fine for a margherita pizza, it was a little atypical for a Caprese salad or for serving plain because of its softer texture.

CALABRO Fior Di Latte Ovolini
PRICE: $4.99 for 8 oz ($0.62 per oz)
PACKAGE: Brine
INGREDIENTS: Pasteurized milk, starter, rennet, salt
SODIUM: 90 mg
TYPE OF ACID: Cheese culture
pH: 5.8 **MOISTURE:** 59.5%
COMMENTS: One of the two brine-packed cheeses in our lineup, this mozzarella was "moist" and "tender," with "vegetal," "fresh dairy" notes. Its interior was "soft" and "creamy" but a bit "loose," almost like "cottage cheese," likely because of its lower pH. This also meant that the cheese was more acidic, and many tasters noted "a hint of sourness," which they were divided on.

CRAVE BROTHERS Farmstead Classics Fresh Mozzarella Cheese
PRICE: $5.99 for 16 oz ($0.37 per oz)
PACKAGE: Shrink-wrapped
INGREDIENTS: Pasteurized milk, lactic/citric acid, salt, enzymes
SODIUM: 55 mg
TYPE OF ACID: Lactic and citric acids
pH: 6.2 **MOISTURE:** 48.8%
COMMENTS: With the lowest moisture content of any cheese in our lineup, this mozzarella was "firm" and "chewy"—more like low-moisture shredding mozzarella than fresh. Tasters also thought it was "a bit bland" and "slightly sweet" as a result of its low levels of salt and acid. Still, many tasters applauded this cheese's subtle "fresh," "milky" flavors.

AMERICAN PROVOLONE

Provolone is unfairly regarded as the middle child of Italian cheeses: neither as punchy as Parmigiano-Reggiano nor as mild and widely used as mozzarella. Yet iconic sandwiches such as the Philadelphia cheesesteak and the New Orleans muffuletta would be incomplete without slices of this aged cow's-milk cheese. For this tasting, we focused on sliced domestic provolone (either packaged or from the deli) since we use slices more often than wedges in our recipes. We chose five products from top-selling, nationally available cheese brands—four packaged presliced and one that we had sliced at the deli. We tasted the cheeses plain, in stromboli, and in quesadillas. Results from the stromboli tasting were not included in the final results because it was too hard for tasters to single out the flavor and texture of the provolone, since the stromboli was bready and included boldly flavored salami. Ultimately, we can recommend all the provolones in our lineup; they were all smooth and pliable in texture and melted easily. While they varied a bit in flavor, none tasted bad. Our favorite cheeses were aged for two months and had more sodium. Sodium amounts and ingredient lists were taken from nutritional labels, and manufacturers provided information on aging. Sodium is reported per 21-gram serving. Scores from the plain and quesadilla tastings were averaged, and the cheeses are listed below in order of preference.

RECOMMENDED

ORGANIC VALLEY Provolone Cheese Slices
PRICE: $6.89 for 6 oz ($1.15 per oz)
INGREDIENTS: Organic cultured pasteurized part skim milk, salt, vegetarian enzyme, calcium chloride
AGED: 2 months
PACKAGING: Presliced
SODIUM: 190 mg
COMMENTS: Our winning provolone was "pleasantly tangy," with "subtle sharpness" and "nutty," "grassy" notes. This cheese was "richer than all the others" thanks to its big hit of salt.

KRAFT Sliced Provolone Cheese
PRICE: $4.00 for 8 oz ($0.50 per oz)
INGREDIENTS: Pasteurized milk, cheese culture, salt, enzymes, natural smoke flavor
AGED: Proprietary
PACKAGING: Presliced
SODIUM: 166 mg
COMMENTS: This cheese, which has natural smoke flavor added, had a "meaty," "smoky" quality and an "unexpected," "earthy aroma." The smoke flavor was subtle—so much so that some tasters barely noticed it, calling this cheese "fresh," "mild," and "milky." A few thought the cheese's flavor was more reminiscent of gouda than of provolone.

APPLEGATE Naturals Provolone Cheese
PRICE: $4.99 for 8 oz ($0.62 per oz)
INGREDIENTS: Pasteurized milk, cheese cultures, salt, and enzymes (non-animal)
AGED: 2 months
PACKAGING: Presliced
SODIUM: 177 mg
COMMENTS: Tasters found this cheese "creamy" and "a bit sharp," "a little like Swiss cheese." Many picked up on a slightly "bitter" minerality, which they felt "added some character." Overall, this is a "milky," "earthy" cheese that's "great for both snacking and melting."

RECOMMENDED (continued)

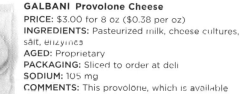

SARGENTO Sliced Provolone Cheese
PRICE: $3.49 for 8 oz ($0.44 per oz)
INGREDIENTS: Pasteurized milk, cheese culture, salt, enzymes, natural smoke flavor
AGED: 2 weeks
PACKAGING: Presliced
SODIUM: 149 mg
COMMENTS: Tasters thought this cheese—which is one of two products in our lineup that have natural smoke flavor added—was "nutty," "buttery," and "subtly smoky." Though the added smoke helped punch up the flavor, a few tasters thought this cheese was "a little too mild," likely due to its lack of aging.

GALBANI Provolone Cheese
PRICE: $3.00 for 8 oz ($0.38 per oz)
INGREDIENTS: Pasteurized milk, cheese cultures, salt, enzymes
AGED: Proprietary
PACKAGING: Sliced to order at deli
SODIUM: 105 mg
COMMENTS: This provolone, which is available sliced from the deli, was "mild" and "buttery" with a "sweet," "milky" flavor. However, it had the lowest salt content of any cheese in the lineup, and some tasters found it a bit "dull." One taster noted that it might "play well" with bolder ingredients but "wasn't a star on its own."

BASMATI RICE

We love basmati rice for its fluffy, long, fragrant grains. To find the perfect product, we bought eight basmati rices: six grown in India (one is also sourced from Pakistan) and two grown in the United States. We cooked them according to the stovetop directions provided on each package and tasted them plain; we also tasted them in our recipes for Basic Rice Pilaf and Chicken Biryani. Tasters sampled them blind, rating the flavor, aroma, texture, and overall appeal of each rice. We liked products with fluffy, intact grains and a pleasing aroma; we also found that, like a fine wine or cheese, our higher-ranking rices were aged. The products were purchased in Boston-area supermarkets and online, and prices shown are what we paid. Information about origins and aging methods was obtained from manufacturers. We calculated the average length-to-width ratio (how much longer a grain is than it is wide) of cooked grains. Scores from the three tastings were averaged, and the top six rices are listed below in order of preference.

RECOMMENDED

DAAWAT Basmati Rice
PRICE: $17.98 for 10 lb ($1.80 per lb)
AGED: 12 to 18 months SOURCE: India
LENGTH-TO-WIDTH RATIO OF COOKED
GRAIN: 8.04
AVERAGE GROWTH PERCENTAGE WHEN
COOKED: 94%
COMMENTS: With "pleasantly chewy," "long, elegant, distinct, intact grains" with a "nice bite," this long-aged Indian-grown rice was "fragrant and tender, perfect" when eaten plain and in pilaf. When cooked in Chicken Biryani, "it contributes an earthy flavor and the grains are very long, elegant, and toothsome." One taster simply wrote: "My favorite."

GOYA Basmati Rice
PRICE: $19.99 for 11 lb ($1.82 per lb)
AGED: At least 1 year SOURCE: India
LENGTH-TO-WIDTH RATIO OF COOKED
GRAIN: 6.11
AVERAGE GROWTH PERCENTAGE WHEN
COOKED: 81%
COMMENTS: "Fluffy, tender/firm, [and] aromatic," with "long and slender," "very distinct" grains that tasted "nutty" and "toasty," this rice was "very fragrant," with a "buttery" aftertaste when eaten plain. In pilaf, this rice was "beautifully tender" and had "full flavor," but tasters noted that it seemed a little more "mellow," even a bit "bland," in biryani.

ROYAL Basmati Rice
PRICE: $23.16 for 10 lb ($2.32 per lb)
AGED: At least 1 year SOURCE: India
LENGTH-TO-WIDTH RATIO OF COOKED
GRAIN: 5.76
AVERAGE GROWTH PERCENTAGE WHEN
COOKED: 58%
COMMENTS: "Gently fragrant," with "mild flavor" and "nice distinct grains," this rice was a bit "chewy" and "firm" when eaten plain. In pilaf, tasters enjoyed its "nice al dente texture" and "delicate" flavor with "grassy" notes, but some found that the "long, slim" grains had a "rough," "coral-like" surface. Cooked in biryani, this rice became a little too soft, and while some tasters enjoyed its "earthy" flavor, a few mentioned that it came across as a little "bland."

RECOMMENDED (continued)

TILDA Basmati Rice
PRICE: $24.00 for 20 lb ($1.20 per lb)
AGED: A few months SOURCE: India
LENGTH-TO-WIDTH RATIO OF COOKED
GRAIN: 8.45
AVERAGE GROWTH PERCENTAGE WHEN
COOKED: 108%
COMMENTS: With "long grains that are distinct without seeming dry," our previous winner didn't perform quite as well this time. Tasters praised its "clean flavor" but found it "a bit soft." In biryani, "it meshed nicely with the chicken" and had "a pleasant flavor on its own; it's not flavorless."

PRIDE OF INDIA Extra Long Indian White Basmati Rice
PRICE: $8.99 for 1.5 lb ($5.99 per lb)
AGED: 2 years SOURCE: India
LENGTH-TO-WIDTH RATIO OF COOKED
GRAIN: 8.80
AVERAGE GROWTH PERCENTAGE WHEN
COOKED: 117%
COMMENTS: Despite tasters' praise for its "crazy-long grains!" and "floral" scent, this long-aged rice came in last in our plain tasting due to its "mushy" texture; we'd followed the package directions, which called for too much water. (We later tried tweaking the rice-to-water ratio, with minimal improvement.) But it was truly stellar in our Chicken Biryani, where tasters raved: "Delicious, slightly nutty flavor," and "Wow! I had no idea rice could be this flavorful." Our takeaway? We recommend it—but only if you ignore the package instructions.

RECOMMENDED WITH RESERVATIONS

RICESELECT Texmati White Premium Rice
PRICE: $5.99 for 2 lb ($3.00 per lb)
AGED: No SOURCE: Texas
LENGTH-TO-WIDTH RATIO OF COOKED
GRAIN: 3.71
AVERAGE GROWTH PERCENTAGE WHEN
COOKED: 42%
COMMENTS: Tasters found this rice "chewy and slightly sticky. A little neutral in flavor, and texture is more like a short-grain rice." "Mildly fragrant, nutty, but also not remarkable." One wrote: "Are you sure this is basmati? The grains are short and fat. It looks like regular long-grain generic stuff." In pilaf and biryani, comments were similar, noting the "plumper, shorter, softer grains" that were "short and sticky for basmati," with a "mild, noncompeting flavor."

UNSALTED BUTTER

We go through 30 to 40 pounds of unsalted butter a week as we bake cakes and cookies, make frostings and pancake batter, and cook pan sauces, roast chicken, and sautéed vegetables. We tasted seven unsalted butters, all sold in individually wrapped ¼-pound sticks. Tasters sampled them in three blind tastings: plain, in pound cake, and in sugar cookies. While cultured butters have their place, we preferred the simple, straightforward taste of sweet cream butter, with Challenge Unsalted Butter leading the pack. Information on wrappers, ingredients, and the cows' diets was obtained from manufacturers and/or product packaging. Fat is reported per 1-tablespoon serving. Scores from the tastings were averaged, and the top six unsalted butters are listed below in order of preference.

RECOMMENDED

CHALLENGE Unsalted Butter
PRICE: $4.49 per lb
INGREDIENTS: Pasteurized cream (milk), natural flavoring
FAT: 11 g
WRAPPER: Foil
STYLE: Sweet cream
COMMENTS: Made in California and well-known on the West Coast, this butter is now available in all 50 states. Its "clean" dairy flavor made it a "crowd-pleaser" when sampled plain. Describing pound cake made with this product, one taster said, "I can't imagine a better version." The sticks are wrapped in aluminum foil, which may protect them from picking up off-flavors during shipping and storage. The natural flavoring is lactic acid, which acts as a preservative.

KATE'S CREAMERY 100% Pure Butter, Unsalted
PRICE: $5.99 per lb
INGREDIENTS: Grade A cream, natural flavors developed by healthy dairy cultures
FAT: 11 g
WRAPPER: Foil
STYLE: Sweet cream
COMMENTS: We loved the "good, fresh, slightly sweet flavor" of this Maine-made butter. Desserts made with it tasted "just about perfect." Lactic acid, which acts as a preservative, is derived from cultured milk and listed on the label as "natural flavors." However, no actual cultures are added to the butter; it's a sweet cream butter. It's wrapped in parchment-coated aluminum foil that may protect the butter's flavor, and though the foil doesn't have measurement markings on it, the edge of the box does, serving as a ruler.

LAND O'LAKES Unsalted Butter
PRICE: $4.99 per lb
INGREDIENTS: Sweet cream, natural flavoring
FAT: 11 g
WRAPPER: FlavorProtect Wrapper (a proprietary coated parchment paper)
STYLE: Sweet cream
COMMENTS: This recognizable product, which is made in California and Pennsylvania, wasn't boldly flavored, and that was fine with us. We enjoyed its "familiar," straightforward flavor in all three tastings. It produced "great, classic" pound cake and "rich, delicious" cookies. Although the coated-parchment wrapper sounds like a gimmick and the company wouldn't disclose details about it, the butter had no off-flavors.

RECOMMENDED (continued)

KERRYGOLD Unsalted Pure Irish Butter
PRICE: $7.58 per lb
INGREDIENTS: Cultured pasteurized cream
FAT: 12 g
WRAPPER: Parchment
STYLE: Cultured
COMMENTS: The sole European import we tasted, this Irish butter was a noticeably deeper yellow color than the other butters in our lineup. It's likely that the cows ate a lot of fresh grass rich in the yellow pigment beta-carotene (a Kerrygold representative told us that the cows "graze outdoors for up to 300 days"). The combination of the cows' feed and the cultures resulted in an especially flavorful butter. Tasters called out "complex," "grassy" notes and a "tangy," "cheesy" quality.

ORGANIC VALLEY Cultured Unsalted Butter
PRICE: $6.99 per lb
INGREDIENTS: Pasteurized organic sweet cream (milk), microbial cultures
FAT: 11 g
WRAPPER: ButterLock (a proprietary coated parchment paper)
STYLE: Cultured
COMMENTS: Like Kerrygold, this butter is both dark yellow (which indicates that the cows ate a lot of grass) and cultured. It was rich in "grassy," "vegetal," and "floral flavors" and tasted strongly of rich, tangy cream. The ButterLock coated-parchment wrapper, which is unique to Organic Valley, likely helped protect the butter's flavor.

CABOT CREAMERY Unsalted Butter
PRICE: $4.99 per lb
INGREDIENTS: Cream (milk), natural flavoring
FAT: 11 g
WRAPPER: Parchment
STYLE: Sweet cream
COMMENTS: For the most part, this sweet cream butter was "unremarkable but acceptable." Desserts made with it struck the balance of butter flavor and vanilla-y sweetness that we wanted. But some tasters noticed off-flavors and a "plasticky" aftertaste, likely due to inferior parchment wrappers that let in odors. As one taster said, it "tastes like the box it was packaged in—or the fridge."

VANILLA EXTRACT

Vanilla, the world's most popular flavor and fragrance, comes in two forms: pure vanilla extract, which is derived from the seed pods of vanilla orchid vines, and synthetic vanilla, which is manufactured in a lab. Just 1 percent of the world's vanilla flavor is "real"; the rest is imitation. To find out if the pricier pure vanilla is worth it, we tasted 10 top-selling vanillas, including seven pure vanilla extracts and three imitation vanilla products. Tasters tried each one in our Classic Vanilla Pudding and Quick and Rich Vanilla Frosting. Then we tried the top extract and top imitation product in our Vanilla Icebox Cookies and Fluffy Yellow Layer Cake—surprisingly, the imitation product won both times. Overall, our tasters favored simple vanilla flavor over busier-tasting products. An independent lab measured vanillin levels in grams per 100 milliliters; ingredient and bean origin information was taken from product packaging or confirmed by company representatives. The vanilla extracts are listed below in order of preference.

RECOMMENDED

BAKER'S Imitation Vanilla Flavor
WINNING IMITATION

PRICE: $0.98 for 8 fl oz ($0.12 per fl oz)
STYLE: Imitation   **VANILLIN:** 0.58 g
INGREDIENTS: Water, propylene glycol, vanillin, caramel color, 0.1% sodium benzoate (added as a preservative), phosphoric acid, and ethyl vanillin
COMMENTS: This was the only imitation product to use two different kinds of synthetic vanillin, and tasters approved. "Good vanilla presence, lovely overall flavor," said one. "Rich but not too powerful," said another. Tasters noted some nuance, but overall comparisons were minimal: just "classic vanilla flavor here."

SIMPLY ORGANIC PURE VANILLA EXTRACT
WINNING PURE EXTRACT

PRICE: $12.99 for 4 fl oz ($3.25 per fl oz)
STYLE: Pure (Madagascar)   **VANILLIN:** 0.08 g
INGREDIENTS: Organic vanilla bean extractives in water, organic alcohol
COMMENTS: This bold extract had its friends and its foes. First off, it was boozy. "Too much alcohol, not enough bean," said one taster. Another disagreed: "Very expensive- and original-tasting, like pudding from a fancy restaurant." But overall, this extract earned praise for an "elegant, interesting, and complex" flavor.

MCCORMICK Pure Vanilla Extract

PRICE: $12.38 for 2 fl oz ($6.19 per fl oz)
STYLE: Pure (Madagascar)   **VANILLIN:** 0.07 g
INGREDIENTS: Vanilla bean extractives in water, alcohol
COMMENTS: This extract had milder vanilla flavor but interesting nuance: slightly nutty, toasty, oaky, and floral, with notes of anise, rose water, and warm spices. "Tastes richer, more nuanced, almost smoky," said one taster.

PENZEYS Vanilla Extract Single-Strength

PRICE: $11.95 for 2 fl oz ($5.98 per fl oz)
STYLE: Pure (Madagascar)   **VANILLIN:** 0.05 g
INGREDIENTS: Water, alcohol, sugar, vanilla bean extractives
COMMENTS: This product had a classic vanilla flavor with some additional complexity in a supporting role. It was "a touch bitter in a good way" and "slightly floral," with warmer notes of caramel and a "hint" of booziness, in the vein of rum and bourbon.

SIMPLY ORGANIC Non-Alcoholic Vanilla Flavoring

PRICE: $15.99 for 4 fl oz ($4.00 per fl oz)
STYLE: Flavoring (Madagascar)   **VANILLIN:** 0.10 g
INGREDIENTS: Organic glycerine, organic vanilla bean extractives in water
COMMENTS: Tasters said this vanilla was "faintly floral," with notes of caramel; it was "not very complex but [had a] nice intensity of warm, sweet, vanilla flavor."

RECOMMENDED *(continued)*

FRONTIER Organic Vanilla Extract, Indonesia

PRICE: $8.87 for 2 fl oz ($4.44 per fl oz)
STYLE: Pure (Indonesia)   **VANILLIN:** 0.10 g
INGREDIENTS: Water, organic alcohol, organic vanilla bean extractives
COMMENTS: This pure extract was fruity and evocative. Tasters compared its flavor to those of bananas and bubble gum. Some appreciated the robust combination of flavors; others wished for more classic vanilla flavor.

MCCORMICK Vanilla Flavor—Premium

PRICE: $3.99 for 2 fl oz ($2.00 per fl oz)
STYLE: Imitation   **VANILLIN:** 0.32 g
INGREDIENTS: Water, alcohol (26%), natural flavorings (including extractives of cocoa and tea), vanillin and other artificial flavorings, corn syrup, caramel color
COMMENTS: Tasters described this product as "caramel-y" and "boozy." Some tasters found the vanilla notes to be "a touch weak."

RECOMMENDED WITH RESERVATIONS

WATKINS Original Gourmet Baking Vanilla with Pure Vanilla Extract

PRICE: $4.99 for 2 fl oz ($2.50 per fl oz)
STYLE: Imitation and pure (Madagascar and Indonesia)   **VANILLIN:** 0.64 g
INGREDIENTS: Water, sugar, propylene glycol, vanilla extract (water, alcohol, extractives of vanilla beans), alcohol, artificial flavors, fruit juice (color)
COMMENTS: This extract sang one note—VANILLA!—and sang it loudly. Some tasters thought its bold flavor was a heady foil that balanced butter and sugar in desserts; others found it "fake," like "vanilla invented in a lab."

NIELSEN-MASSEY Madagascar Bourbon Pure Vanilla Extract

PRICE: $19.99 for 4 fl oz ($5.00 per fl oz)
STYLE: Pure (Madagascar)   **VANILLIN:** 0.05 g
INGREDIENTS: Water, alcohol (35% minimum), vanilla bean extracts
COMMENTS: Tasters picked out notes of caramel, rum, flowers, cherries, warm spices, and almonds in this product. Almost everyone wished the classic vanilla notes were stronger.

MORTON & BASSETT SPICES Pure Vanilla Extract

PRICE: $19.99 for 4 fl oz ($5.00 per fl oz)
STYLE: Pure (Madagascar and Uganda)   **VANILLIN:** 0.03 g
INGREDIENTS: Water, alcohol (35% minimum), sugar, vanilla bean extractives
COMMENTS: This extract had the lowest vanillin level; it made pudding and frosting taste sweeter without bold vanilla flavor. Some found its booziness "harsh."

TOMATO PASTE

We deploy the concentrated sweetness and savory umami flavor of tomato paste to bring depth and complexity to both classic applications and unexpected ones. Historically, tomato paste has been sold in cans in the United States, but in the past decade, tubed pastes from Italy have popped up on supermarket shelves. To find out if one packaging style reigns supreme, we tasted eight tomato pastes—three made in Italy and sold in tubes and five made in the United States and sold in cans—plain, lightly cooked, and in a simple marinara sauce in which we halved the amount of crushed tomatoes and doubled the amount of tomato paste. While we can recommend every product we tasted, we prefer the convenience of the Italian-made tubed pastes. Sodium amounts were taken from product packaging and are reported based on a 33-gram serving size. The tomato pastes are listed below in order of packaging and price.

Tubed Tomato Pastes

RECOMMENDED

CENTO Double Concentrated Tomato Paste
PRICE: $2.59 for 4.56 oz ($0.57 per oz)
ORIGIN: Italy
INGREDIENTS: Tomatoes, salt
SODIUM: 70 mg
COMMENTS: This Italian paste had "intense, roasty tomato flavor"; it was "sweet at first, with a tart finish." "Like it was dried under the Italian sun," said one taster. In sauce, it was "intensely tomatoey," with "good acidity" and "very concentrated flavor."

MUTTI Double Concentrated Tomato Paste
PRICE: $3.49 for 4.5 oz ($0.78 per oz)
ORIGIN: Italy
INGREDIENTS: Tomatoes, salt
SODIUM: 113.4 mg
COMMENTS: This paste, like the other Italian pastes, was looser and redder than the American ones. When eaten plain, it was "sharp," "acidic," and "surprisingly complex," "with a depth and tomatoeyness behind it." "I could eat a whole jar of this," said one taster. In sauce, it had "robust tomato flavor" and pronounced acidity.

AMORE Tomato Paste
PRICE: $3.49 for 4.5 oz ($0.78 per oz)
ORIGIN: Italy
INGREDIENTS: Tomatoes
SODIUM: 22 mg
COMMENTS: This paste was "tangy," "sweet," "jammy," and "pleasant," with "a sun-dried tomato flavor." In sauce, it was "richly tomatoey," "balanced and warm." "This could really up the savoriness of a dish," said one taster.

Canned Tomato Pastes

RECOMMENDED

CENTO Tomato Paste
PRICE: $0.74 for 6 oz ($0.12 per oz)
ORIGIN: United States
INGREDIENTS: Tomatoes, citric acid
SODIUM: 20 mg
COMMENTS: Like all the American pastes, this one was thick. It was "savory, with good fruity flavors," and "bright and acidic but not in a bitter/harsh way." In sauce, tasters found it "fruity," "earthy," and "sweet but not too sweet," with "acidic undertones" that contributed complexity.

CONTADINA Tomato Paste
PRICE: $0.99 for 6 oz ($0.17 per oz)
ORIGIN: United States
INGREDIENTS: Tomatoes, citric acid
SODIUM: 20 mg
COMMENTS: This paste was "very savory" and "meaty," with "bright" tomato flavor and some fruitiness. It made thicker sauce that had "beautifully nuanced tomato flavor, with balanced sweetness and acidity."

GOYA Tomato Paste
PRICE: $0.99 for 6 oz ($0.17 per oz)
ORIGIN: United States
INGREDIENTS: Tomatoes
SODIUM: 25 mg
COMMENTS: Tasters described this paste as "tart" but a bit "flat," with a "concentrated sweetness." It was dense and smooth and made slightly thicker sauce that had "roasty tomato flavor" and leaned "slightly acidic."

HUNT'S Tomato Paste
PRICE: $1.19 for 6 oz ($0.20 per oz)
ORIGIN: United States
INGREDIENTS: Tomatoes, citric acid
SODIUM: 20 mg
COMMENTS: This thicker paste was fine, if not underwhelming: "Kind of bland and flat," remarked one taster. In sauce, it was "mellow" and "acceptable," with some "sweet-tart tomato flavor."

MUIR GLEN Organic Tomato Paste
PRICE: $3.39 for 6 oz ($0.57 per oz)
ORIGIN: United States
INGREDIENTS: Tomatoes, citric acid
SODIUM: 35 mg
COMMENTS: This paste was thicker, with a "concentrated tomato flavor" and a "jammy sweetness." "Like a Fruit Roll-Up," said one taster. In sauce, it was "nicely balanced between sweet and savory," with "real tomato earthiness."

BLACK PEPPERCORNS

Ground black pepper is one of the most ubiquitous and well-loved spices in the world. It holds a place of honor next to salt on restaurant tables and at kitchen workstations and appears in at least 2,000 of our recipes, from *cacio e pepe* to steak au poivre. No matter the recipe, we love its balanced heat and earthy, toasty flavor. To find our favorite, we sampled 10 nationally available whole black peppercorns ground and mixed into white rice and egg salad. We used brand-new grinders—one per product—to grind the peppercorns for each tasting (including the two products that came with built-in grinders). Eight were top-selling nationally available products, and two were mail-order products. While you'll get good results with almost any of the whole black peppercorns we tasted, we preferred our winner for its mild spiciness and fragrant, citrusy notes. The black peppercorns are listed in below order of preference.

RECOMMENDED

TONE'S Whole Black Peppercorns
PRICE: $2.43 for 2.13 oz ($1.14 per oz)
ORIGIN: Proprietary mix
COMMENTS: Our top-ranked product was "mild" and "floral," with a "subtle, lingering heat." Tasters liked the "fragrant" "citrus" notes, which slowly "bloomed" into a "buzzy," "pleasant" spiciness. A bonus: It's the cheapest product in our lineup.

PENZEYS Whole Tellicherry Indian Peppercorns
PRICE: $6.49 for 2.2 oz ($2.95 per oz)
ORIGIN: India
COMMENTS: This mail-order Tellicherry pepper had a "robust," "perfumy" aroma, "woodsy" "warm spice" notes, and a heat that "builds slowly." Tasters particularly liked it in egg salad, where it added "just the right amount of zing."

MCCORMICK Whole Black Peppercorns
PRICE: $6.49 for 3.5 oz ($1.85 per oz)
ORIGIN: Proprietary mix
COMMENTS: Tasters loved this product's "warm, buzzy, toasted peppery flavor" and "mild heat." Some picked up on a "sweet" fruitiness that was reminiscent of "fresh green peppercorns."

OLDE THOMPSON Tellicherry
PRICE: $9.94 for 7.4 oz ($1.34 per oz)
ORIGIN: India
COMMENTS: Another Indian Tellicherry pepper, this product was "earthy," with a "slight acidity." The heat was a bit more "numbing" than we're used to with black pepper, but overall this pepper was "bright" and "vibrant."

MORTON & BASSETT Whole Black Peppercorns
PRICE: $6.99 for 2.1 oz ($3.33 per oz)
ORIGIN: Vietnam
COMMENTS: This supermarket product was "zippy," with "pops of spice" and a "lingering heat." Some tasters thought its spiciness was a bit too prominent, but most appreciated its "fragrant," "woodsy" notes.

RECOMMENDED *(continued)*

MORTON Pepper Grinder
PRICE: $2.49 for 1.24 oz ($2.01 per oz)
ORIGIN: Brazil, India, Indonesia, Vietnam, and Malaysia
COMMENTS: This product was "punchy," "bright," and "slightly sweet." It's available only in a container with a built-in grinder, but the peppercorns can be removed if you want to use them in your own pepper mill.

SPICE ISLANDS Tellicherry Peppercorns
PRICE: $9.22 for 2.4 oz ($3.84 per oz)
ORIGIN: India
COMMENTS: The most expensive product in the lineup, this supermarket pepper had "vibrant," "woodsy" notes but lacked heat. Many tasters found the flavor "a bit flat."

BADIA Whole Black Pepper
PRICE: $3.39 for 2 oz ($1.70 per oz)
ORIGIN: Proprietary mix
COMMENTS: This supermarket pepper had a "nice kick of heat" and "strong spiciness" but lacked a more nuanced aroma. Those who could pick up on some of this pepper's fragrance noted a slight "vegetal," "almost minty" earthiness.

SIMPLY ORGANIC Whole Black Peppercorns
PRICE: $5.49 for 2.65 oz ($2.07 per oz)
ORIGIN: India and Vietnam
COMMENTS: This product was "mild," with "muted heat" and subtler "herby" notes. It was a bit "too dull" for some tasters, but we liked its "woodsy" aroma and slight "earthiness."

RECOMMENDED WITH RESERVATIONS

KALUSTYAN'S Tellicherry Indian Black Peppercorns
PRICE: $6.99 for 2.5 oz ($2.80 per oz)
ORIGIN: India
COMMENTS: This Tellicherry pepper, which was once a test kitchen favorite, received low marks for its "overly earthy," "mushroomy" notes and "duller heat." While some tasters liked the "deeper fragrance" of these peppercorns, others thought they tasted a bit "musty" and "smoky," "almost burnt."

POTATO CHIPS

Potato chips were invented in America and remain one of the country's favorite snacks. In 2017, we spent $7.3 billion on them—considerably more than we spent on pretzels, corn chips, or popcorn. So which potato chip is the best? To find out, we tasted nine best-selling potato chip products, both plain and dipped into creamy French onion dip, which helped us gauge the chips' sturdiness and compatibility with thick, flavorful dips. Our lineup included five thick kettle-style chips and four traditional thinly sliced chips. Our overall top scorer was a kettle chip, but a regular chip was close on its heels. We think they're ideal representatives of their styles—kettle chips are thicker and described as "crunchy," while regular chips are thinner and described as "crispy"—and we enthusiastically recommend both. The top eight potato chips are listed below in order of preference.

RECOMMENDED

UTZ Kettle Classics, Original
BEST KETTLE-STYLE POTATO CHIP
PRICE: $3.79 for 8-oz bag ($0.47 per oz)
STYLE: Kettle
OIL: Peanut
AVERAGE THICKNESS: 1.47 mm
COMMENTS: Our new favorite kettle chip took the top spot overall, due in large part to its "nicely thick and crunchy" texture. The chips were "supercrunchy" and, in the words of one taster, "perfect." Unlike other products in the lineup, they're fried in peanut oil.

HERR'S Crisp 'N Tasty Potato Chips
BEST REGULAR POTATO CHIP
PRICE: $2.99 for 9.5-oz bag ($0.31 per oz)
STYLE: Regular
OIL: Corn, cottonseed, soybean, and/or sunflower
AVERAGE THICKNESS: 1.06 mm
COMMENTS: These "very thin," "crisp" chips were our favorite made in the regular style. Tasters raved that they were "delicate" but not too weak or filmsy. Even in thick French onion dip, they held up. These "classic," "traditional" potato chips had tasters asking for "more, please!"

LAY'S Kettle Cooked, Original
PRICE: $3.49 for 8-oz bag ($0.44 per oz)
STYLE: Kettle
OIL: Sunflower, corn, and/or canola
AVERAGE THICKNESS: 1.59 mm
COMMENTS: These had "a thick, homemade kind of crunch" and a particularly "dense" structure. The ratio of folded and curled chips was especially high; we counted 16 in our randomized sample of 25 chips. But they were lower in sodium, and our tasters missed that extra salt.

LAY'S Classic Potato Chips
PRICE: $4.29 for 10-oz bag ($0.43 per oz)
STYLE: Regular
OIL: Sunflower, corn, and/or canola
AVERAGE THICKNESS: 1.08 mm
COMMENTS: The chips in the iconic glossy yellow bag were familiar to many on our panel. They were "very thin" and "light" but still satisfyingly crisp. Even when dragged through thick dip, most didn't crack or crumble. (Only one chip broke.) They were fairly high in sodium but didn't taste overly salty.

RECOMMENDED (continued)

CAPE COD Kettle Cooked Potato Chips, Original
PRICE: $3.79 for 8-oz bag ($0.47 per oz)
STYLE: Kettle
OIL: Canola, safflower, and/or sunflower
AVERAGE THICKNESS: 1.31 mm
COMMENTS: These kettle chips were "perfectly balanced: thick and crunchy but not too hard." We counted a lot of folded chips (8 out of 25), which "added to the crunch" and reminded us of good homemade chips. They also tasted nicely salty.

WISE Golden Original Potato Chips
PRICE: $3.99 for 9-oz bag ($0.44 per oz)
STYLE: Regular
OIL: Corn, cottonseed, sunflower, soybean, and/or canola
AVERAGE THICKNESS: 1.13 mm
COMMENTS: These regular chips were particularly light and delicate, which gave them an "all-American," "standard cookout snack" feel. Some tasters wanted a bit more heft, even from a regular chip. They had "great potato flavor" and plenty of salt.

RECOMMENDED WITH RESERVATIONS

UTZ Original Potato Chips
PRICE: $4.29 for 9.5-oz bag ($0.45 per oz)
STYLE: Regular
OIL: Cottonseed
AVERAGE THICKNESS: 1.02 mm
COMMENTS: These chips tasted great despite their low sodium level, but they had an "insubstantial air to them." Tasters thought they were too "delicate" and had to daintily dunk them in French onion dip to keep them from breaking.

KETTLE BRAND Potato Chips, Sea Salt
PRICE: $3.99 for 8.5-oz bag ($0.47 per oz)
STYLE: Kettle
OIL: Safflower and/or sunflower and/or canola
AVERAGE THICKNESS: 1.71 mm
COMMENTS: The "very thick, very crunchy" texture of these kettle chips stood out from the rest. In fact, they were "downright hearty." They lost points because they had a "somewhat greasy" quality and a "lingering" oil flavor.

PACKAGED STUFFING

Homemade stuffing isn't particularly difficult to make, yet Americans still spend $258 million on packaged versions each year. Part of the appeal is how easily and quickly the boxed stuffing comes together, and the rest is nostalgia. For Thanksgiving dinner or a quick weeknight meal, which store-bought stuffing is best? To figure that out, we identified six top-selling brands of packaged stuffing; to narrow down each brand's offerings, we held preliminary tastings; the top-scoring stuffing from each brand was included in our final lineup. These six stuffings included two chicken-flavored stuffings and four "traditional" or "seasoned" options. Tasters sampled the stuffings prepared on the stovetop according to package directions. We rated each product on flavor, texture, and overall appeal. We're able to fully recommend just one product, which had "good, moist texture" and big, bold flavor. We don't think it will convert people who are used to homemade stuffing, but if you like the ease and familiarity of the packaged stuff, this is the one to buy. Ingredients and nutrition information were taken from product packaging; the latter represents a 28-gram serving (roughly ½ to ⅓ cup) of each dry stuffing mix. The packaged stuffings are listed below in order of preference.

RECOMMENDED

STOVE TOP Stuffing Mix—Chicken
PRICE: $2.29 for 6-oz package ($0.38 per oz)
SODIUM: 390 mg
SUGAR: 2 g
COMMENTS: This iconic packaged stuffing was the runaway favorite. It had "pretty classic stuffing flavor" and tasted intensely "savory," like "poultry seasoning." This bold taste was likely due to umami boosters such as monosodium glutamate. It was one of just two products to achieve the right amount of moisture, with fully hydrated pieces of bread that formed a "cohesive" stuffing that wasn't mushy or dry.

RECOMMENDED WITH RESERVATIONS

BETTY CROCKER Homestyle Stuffing—Chicken
PRICE: $1.65 for 6-oz package ($0.28 per oz)
SODIUM: 390 mg
SUGAR: 2 g
COMMENTS: Our runner-up also had "a good amount of moisture" and wasn't too mushy or too firm. We liked that it felt cohesive and didn't fall apart when we scooped up bites with a fork. Although it's chicken-flavored, it was "very herby," and some tasters found the flavor overwhelming. Others thought it had an "artificial" quality and likened it to the flavoring packets that come with instant ramen.

NOT RECOMMENDED

BELL'S Traditional Stuffing Mix
PRICE: $2.99 for 14-oz package ($0.21 per oz)
SODIUM: 530 mg
SUGAR: 2 g
COMMENTS: "Too mushy," wrote tasters about this product, which for a 12-ounce batch called for almost ½ cup more water and 1 tablespoon more butter than our winner. It was so moist that panelists compared it to "pudding" and "porridge." That's too bad, because tasters loved its seasoned flavor, calling it "chicken-y," "savory," and very "herby."

NOT RECOMMENDED *(continued)*

MRS. CUBBISON'S Herb Seasoned Cube Stuffing
PRICE: $4.14 for 10-oz package ($0.41 per oz)
SODIUM: 263.5 mg
SUGAR: 0.8 g
COMMENTS: The bread mix was a little "bland," and the flavors of the fresh celery and onion called for in the instructions dominated. Although some panelists liked those flavors, most missed the intense savoriness of our top scorers. It was also too dry, like "lightly soaked croutons" with a few "mushy bits."

PEPPERIDGE FARM Herb Seasoned Cubed Stuffing
PRICE: $2.99 for 12-oz package ($0.25 per oz)
SODIUM: 401.1 mg
SUGAR: 1.5 g
COMMENTS: Prepared with chicken broth and sautéed celery and onion, this stuffing still tasted "bland" and "flavorless." In fact, some tasters thought that the vegetables overwhelmed the mildly flavored "sad cubes of bread." The texture was inconsistent. The "bread was soft but somehow still firm" and had a "slimy," "gluey" quality.

ARNOLD Premium Seasoned Stuffing
PRICE: $2.99 for 12-oz package ($0.25 per oz)
SODIUM: 408.3 mg
SUGAR: 1.2 g
COMMENTS: One taster asked, "Is this plain bread cubes?" We could detect a little salt, but "no herbs or spice came through." This stuffing was not only bland but also too dry. As a result, it was more like a bowl of damp bread cubes than a moist, cohesive stuffing. We could probably gussy it up with fresh vegetables and herbs, but we could also just buy bread and cube it ourselves.

SUPERMARKET BACON

According to a recent report by market research group Mintel, 70 percent of American adults eat bacon regularly. To find out how classic supermarket bacon measured up, we sampled five nationally top-selling bacons in two tastings: plain and in simple BLT sandwiches. For each blind tasting, we cooked the bacon according to our Oven-Fried Bacon recipe. While we unsurprisingly liked every bacon, we found that we preferred products with near-equal amounts of fat and protein and a nice balance of crispiness and chew. Tasters deemed our winner a "truly all-American, supermarket-staple bacon." Nutritional information was taken from product packaging and, when necessary, converted to reflect a 19-gram serving. The bacons are listed below in order of preference.

RECOMMENDED

OSCAR MAYER Naturally Hardwood Smoked Bacon
PRICE: $6.99 for 16-oz package ($6.99 per lb)
WOOD: Maple, birch, and beech
SLICE THICKNESS: 2 mm
FAT: 7 g   PROTEIN: 7 g
SODIUM: 350 mg
CURE INGREDIENTS: Water, salt, sugar, sodium phosphates, sodium ascorbate, sodium nitrite
COMMENTS: This "classic," "textbook bacon" was our favorite both plain and in BLTs. Most tasters loved its "mildly meaty" flavor and "ideal texture," which had a "good balance of chew and crispness," thanks to equal amounts of fat and protein and its extra-thin slices.

SMITHFIELD Hometown Original Bacon
PRICE: $5.99 for 16-oz package ($5.99 per lb)
WOOD: Hickory
SLICE THICKNESS: 2.6 mm
FAT: 8 g   PROTEIN: 5 g
SODIUM: 360 mg
CURE INGREDIENTS: Water, salt, sugar, sodium phosphates, sodium erythorbate, sodium nitrito
COMMENTS: Although many tasters thought it "could be smokier," especially when eaten plain, the thickest bacon in the lineup was acclaimed for its "hearty," "substantial" chew and good porky flavor. Its distinctive savory, tangy cured flavor reminded some tasters of prosciutto or ham.

HORMEL Black Label Original Bacon
PRICE: $10.39 for 16-oz package ($10.39 per lb)
WOOD: Proprietary
SLICE THICKNESS: 2.3 mm
FAT: 7.4 g   PROTEIN: 6.3 g
SODIUM: 422 mg
CURE INGREDIENTS: Water, salt, sugar, dextrose, sodium erythorbate, sodium nitrite
COMMENTS: Tasters appreciated this well-marbled, "visually appealing," "ultrasavory" bacon with "mild smoke" and "nice porkiness" that really "stands up in [a] sandwich." At 422 milligrams of sodium per serving, it was "a little on the saltier side," but it had "the best crunch of the bunch."

RECOMMENDED *(continued)*

FARMLAND Hickory Smoked Classic Cut Bacon
PRICE: $4.99 for 12-oz package ($6.65 per lb)
WOOD: Hickory
SLICE THICKNESS: 2.1 mm
FAT: 8.9 g   PROTEIN: 5.1 g
SODIUM: 329 mg
CURE INGREDIENTS: Water, salt, sugar, sodium phosphates, sodium erythorbate, sodium nitrite
COMMENTS: This bacon was particularly enjoyable in BLTs, where its "good smoke" presence and "nice porky flavor" came through loud and clear. Tasters also liked its "moderate chew" and edges that got "nice and crispy," thanks in part to its relatively high fat content.

BAR-S Naturally Smoked Bacon
PRICE: $3.00 for 12-oz package ($4.00 per lb)
WOOD: Hickory
SLICE THICKNESS: 2.1 mm
FAT: 9.5 g   PROTEIN: 5.4 g
SODIUM: 380 mg
CURE INGREDIENTS: Water, salt, sugar, smoke flavor, sodium phosphates, sodium erythorbate, sodium nitrite
COMMENTS: With small islands of lean meat surrounded by large strips of fat, this bacon reminded some tasters of English-style back bacon. The relatively high fat content made it a bit greasy. A few tasters also noted a slightly "artificial" smoky aftertaste, but most enjoyed the "strong" "grilled" flavor.

YELLOW MUSTARD

In the condiment world, yellow mustard is often considered the Robin to ketchup's Batman, relegated to a supporting role on burgers and hot dogs. But it's much more than a sidekick. Its pungency and relatively low spice level make it highly versatile, ideal for adding tang and flavor to hot dogs, potato salad, barbecue sauce, marinades, salad dressings, and more. When we heard that our favorite yellow mustard from our last tasting (Annie's Organic Yellow Mustard) had been reformulated, we decided to retest. To find the ideal yellow mustard, tasters blindly sampled seven nationally available products, both plain and on pigs in a blanket. We evaluated these products for both flavor and texture. A number of factors determined good mustard flavor, including tanginess, sweetness (which helped balance the acidity), and saltiness. We preferred mustards that were mellower, with a moderate acidity that didn't dominate other flavors. Our two favorite mustards had sweet notes that nicely balanced their acidity. Sodium levels ranged from 25 to 80 milligrams per serving, with the former being the low-sodium option from Boar's Head. While none of the mustards tasted strikingly salty or underseasoned, this low-sodium product fell to the bottom of our rankings, as tasters found it less flavorful, spicier, and sharper than a typical yellow mustard. Texture-wise, our favorite products had a moderately creamy texture and enough body to cling nicely to pigs in a blanket. Tasters were averse to one product's grainy, thick texture, which reminded them of whole-grain mustard; on the opposite end of the spectrum, an "ultrasmooth" mustard seemed aerated and foamy to some tasters. Our favorite mustard was creamy and moderately tangy, with "a hint of sweetness." Nutritional information and ingredients were taken from product labels and are per 1-teaspoon serving. The yellow mustards are listed below in order of preference.

RECOMMENDED

HEINZ Yellow Mustard
PRICE: $1.99 for 14 oz ($0.14 per oz)
SODIUM: 60 mg
COMMENTS: We liked this mustard's "nice sweetness" and "good acidity," which gave it "some zing," as well as its smooth texture and "old-fashioned," "iconic" flavor. As one taster noted, it "tastes like classic mustard on a ballpark hot dog."

FRENCH'S Classic Yellow Mustard
PRICE: $3.19 for 20 oz ($0.16 per oz)
SODIUM: 55 mg
COMMENTS: Our runner-up had many of the characteristics we liked: a "hint of sweet" and "acidic bite" combined with a "creamy texture." Some tasters detected a slightly "earthy," "herby" flavor when tasting the mustard plain, but it was less noticeable on pigs in a blanket.

KOOPS' Original Yellow Mustard
PRICE: $5.95 for 18 oz ($0.33 per oz)
SODIUM: 60 mg
COMMENTS: Overall, we liked this product's thicker texture, which was "a little coarser," with a "grainy" consistency. It also had an "acidic" bite that paired nicely with food, though tasters deemed its mustard flavor "neutral" and "nondescript."

WOEBER'S Yellow Mustard
PRICE: $1.30 for 16 oz ($0.08 per oz)
SODIUM: 80 mg
COMMENTS: Not everyone liked this mustard's "very vinegary" flavor, but some loved its tartness and thicker consistency. Tasters compared it to both pickles and brined olives, but some thought it was too "sour." It also lost points with some tasters for having a "thick and grainy" consistency.

RECOMMENDED *(continued)*

GULDEN'S Yellow Mustard
PRICE: $2.50 for 12 oz ($0.21 per oz)
SODIUM: 55 mg
COMMENTS: Some tasters thought this "punchy" mustard had an "earthy aftertaste." The "herbal taste" was evident even on pigs in a blanket, but overall we liked this product's "sharp and tangy" "dill pickle flavor" and "smooth," "creamy" texture.

ANNIE'S Organic Yellow Mustard
PRICE: $3.99 for 9 oz ($0.44 per oz)
SODIUM: 50 mg
COMMENTS: Tasters picked up on "funky," "musty" notes, but overall this mustard's flavor was deemed milder and "missing a little complexity." Most tasters also liked the silky texture of this product, but some found it "foamy."

BOAR'S HEAD 54% Lower Sodium Yellow Mustard
PRICE: $3.39 for 9 oz ($0.38 per oz)
SODIUM: 25 mg
COMMENTS: The only yellow mustard available from Boar's Head, this low-sodium product had more heat than flavor and was sharper and thicker than the others. Tasters described it as "sharp" and "more viscous," like whole-grain mustard.

VANILLA ICE CREAM

Vanilla ice cream is a classic, but it's also the purest expression of ice cream—there's nowhere for inferiority to hide. So which product is best? To find out, we tasted 17 nationally available vanilla ice creams to determine a final lineup of eight. We sampled each product in our final lineup plain in a blind, randomized tasting. We preferred products with 20 grams of sugar or less per ½-cup serving—the eliminated products had anywhere from 21 to 24 grams of sugar per serving and were too sweet, with muted vanilla flavor. Ice creams with balanced sweetness and prominent, rich vanilla flavor received top marks. Regarding texture, we looked at overrun, the amount of air in each product (ice cream with 100 percent overrun is half air). Ice creams with low overrun percentages are typically dense and silky, while those with high overrun percentages are lighter. In the products we tasted, overrun ranged from 21 percent to 117 percent, a huge difference. Tasters were split on whether they preferred high- or low-overrun ice cream. Overrun percentages were calculated by an independent laboratory. All ingredient and nutritional information was taken from product labels, and nutritional information is based on a ½-cup serving size. The top six vanilla ice creams are listed below in order of preference.

RECOMMENDED

TURKEY HILL Original Vanilla Premium Ice Cream
PRICE: $2.99 for 1.5 qt ($1.00 per pint)
INGREDIENTS: Milk, cream, corn syrup, sugar, whey, nonfat milk, cellulose gel, cellulose gum, natural and artificial flavors, mono and diglycerides, carrageenan, annatto color
OVERRUN: 97% **FAT:** 7 g **SUGAR:** 12 g
TYPE OF SUGAR: Corn syrup and sugar
COMMENTS: Tasters loved this "silky," "creamy" ice cream, which had "rich" vanilla flavor. It was "spoonable" and "airy," thanks to its relatively high overrun percentage, but still "velvety" due to the use of viscous corn syrup.

BEN & JERRY'S Vanilla Ice Cream
PRICE: $4.99 per pint
INGREDIENTS: Cream, skim milk, liquid sugar (sugar, water), water, egg yolks, sugar, guar gum, vanilla extract, vanilla beans, carrageenan
OVERRUN: 21% **FAT:** 16 g **SUGAR:** 20 g
TYPE OF SUGAR: Liquid sugar and sugar
COMMENTS: This premium ice cream had the lowest overrun percentage in the lineup, and its texture was "silky," "creamy," and "almost luxurious." While most tasters loved the "rich" flavor and texture of this product, a few thought the ice cream was a bit "dense," and some picked up on slightly unpleasant "boozy" notes from the vanilla extract.

EDY'S Slow Churned Classic Vanilla Ice Cream (also sold as Dreyer's Slow Churned Classic Vanilla Ice Cream)
PRICE: $5.99 for 1.5 qt ($2.00 per pint)
INGREDIENTS: Non-fat milk, cane sugar, cream, buttermilk, tapioca starch, carob bean gum, natural flavor, guar gum, annatto color
OVERRUN: 117% **FAT:** 3 g **SUGAR:** 14 g
TYPE OF SUGAR: Cane sugar
COMMENTS: We were surprised to find that tasters couldn't distinguish this product, which is marketed as a light ice cream, from the full-fat ice creams. A fair amount of sugar and a high overrun percentage ensured that this product had a "creamy," "airy" texture that tasters loved. A few tasters thought it was a bit too "whipped," and some commented on its "lackluster vanilla flavor."

RECOMMENDED *(continued)*

HÄAGEN-DAZS Vanilla Ice Cream
PRICE: $3.99 per pint
INGREDIENTS: Cream, skim milk, cane sugar, egg yolks, vanilla extract
OVERRUN: 38% **FAT:** 15 g **SUGAR:** 18 g
TYPE OF SUGAR: Cane sugar
COMMENTS: Another premium product, this ice cream had the shortest ingredient list in our lineup, and tasters appreciated its "familiar," "sweet" taste. Many tasters noted that it had the "strongest" vanilla flavor, but some disliked the "booziness" of the vanilla extract. The texture was "thick," "creamy," and "a little bit chewy."

BREYER'S French Vanilla Ice Cream
PRICE: $4.99 for 1.5 qt ($1.66 per pint)
INGREDIENTS: Milk, cream, sugar, corn syrup, egg yolks, whey, vegetable gums (carob bean, tara, guar), mono and diglycerides, natural flavors, annatto (for color), salt
OVERRUN: 53% **FAT:** 7 g **SUGAR:** 14 g
TYPE OF SUGAR: Sugar
COMMENTS: Though this wasn't the only product with added egg yolks, tasters picked up a "rich," "prominent" eggy flavor that reminded some of "eggnog." While a few thought this ice cream was a bit too eggy, most loved its "thick," "custardy" texture. We wished it had a bit more vanilla flavor.

BLUE BELL Homemade Vanilla Ice Cream
PRICE: $7.89 for 2 qt ($1.97 per pint)
INGREDIENTS: Milk, cream, sugar, skim milk, high-fructose corn syrup, natural and artificial vanilla flavor, cellulose gum, vegetable gums (guar, carrageenan, carob bean), salt, annatto color
OVERRUN: 82% **FAT:** 9 g **SUGAR:** 19 g
TYPE OF SUGAR: Sugar and high-fructose corn syrup
COMMENTS: Tasters praised this product's "supercreamy" and "smooth" texture, but some thought its sweetness was "overpowering." Many picked up on "butterscotch" and "caramel" notes that were pleasant but more reminiscent of a "sugar cookie" than of vanilla ice cream. Though this brand (a regional powerhouse around Texas) is available in grocery stores in only about 20 states, we were able to order it over the phone.

DIGITAL INSTANT-READ THERMOMETERS

If you cook or bake regularly, you should have a food thermometer. A good one takes the guesswork out of cooking, telling you exactly what's going on inside your food. The old dial-faced ones are slow and imprecise: Digital is the only way to go. We've highly recommended the ThermoWorks Thermapen Mk4, but at about $99, it's expensive; we wanted to see if newer, cheaper models could top our old favorite. To find out, we tested 11 digital thermometers. We ran a series of accuracy and speed tests and evaluated each model's comfort, ease of use, and durability while making caramel, roasted beef, seared steaks, and grilled chicken. Ultimately, the Thermapen Mk4 took the top spot yet again. The top four thermometers are listed below in order of preference.

HIGHLY RECOMMENDED	PERFORMANCE	TESTERS' COMMENTS
THERMOWORKS Thermapen Mk4 MODEL: THS-234-457 (blue) PRICE: $99.00 AVERAGE MARGIN OF ERROR IN TESTING: 0.13° at 32°F, 0.07° at 125°F AVERAGE READ TIME: 2.2 sec RANGE: −58°F to 572°F PROBE LENGTH: 4.3 in FEATURES: Adjustable automatic rotating screen (1, 2, or 4 ways), automatic backlight, sleep mode, auto wake-up, calibration, waterproof (39 in for 30 min)	ACCURACY ★★★ SPEED ★★★ EASE OF USE ★★★ DURABILITY ★★★	This thermometer is dead accurate, fast, and so streamlined and simple that it's a breeze to use. It does just what we want: "Tell me the temp; get out of my way," as one tester put it. Its long handle gave us plenty of room to maneuver, allowing for multiple grips, and a ring of slightly tacky silicone kept our hands confidently secured. The rotating screen is handy for lefties and righties needing different angles. The auto wake-up function is extremely useful; you don't have to stop and turn the thermometer on again midtask. The digits were large and legible, and it's waterproof in up to 39 inches of water for up to 30 minutes. It's also calibratable, promising years of accuracy.

RECOMMENDED

	PERFORMANCE	TESTERS' COMMENTS
OXO Good Grips Thermocouple Thermometer MODEL: 11204300 PRICE: $99.95 AVERAGE MARGIN OF ERROR IN TESTING: 0.0° at 32°F, 0.3° at 125°F AVERAGE READ TIME: 3.85 sec RANGE: −58°F to 572°F PROBE LENGTH: 4.25 in FEATURES: Automatic 2-way rotating screen, 225-degree probe rotation, illuminated digits for visibility	ACCURACY ★★★ SPEED ★★★ EASE OF USE ★★½ DURABILITY ★★★	This thermometer was accurate and relatively fast. In addition to having a rotating display like other models, it has a probe that opens 225 degrees instead of the typical 180 degrees. This meant we could hold it at an offset angle in both our right and left hands, keeping us even farther away from the heat. There were a few downsides, though. It doesn't have an auto wake-up feature, and the probe is a bit stiff. It also comes with a dial that's meant as a hands-free way to access the probe, but it was too stiff to be convenient. Lastly, while it had a large, comfortable handle, it was a bit too slick, especially when we were frying greasy steaks.
LAVATOOLS Javelin PRO Duo MODEL: PX1D PRICE: $49.99 AVERAGE MARGIN OF ERROR IN TESTING: 0.13° at 32°F, 0.52° at 125°F AVERAGE READ TIME: 3 sec RANGE: −40°F to 482°F PROBE LENGTH: 4.35 in FEATURES: Automatic 2-way rotating screen, manual backlight, sleep mode, auto wake-up, hold, max, min, magnet for storage	ACCURACY ★★★ SPEED ★★★ EASE OF USE ★★½ DURABILITY ★★★	This thermometer wasn't quite as good as the Mk4 or the OXO model, but it gave them a real run for their money. It was fast and accurate and had a large handle that kept us safely away from the heat, although it was slightly slick. The big, clear display rotates two ways, and the long probe worked great at various angles. It turned on automatically when we opened the probe and turned off when we closed it. It also automatically wakes up with a touch if you leave the probe open. Its one button operates a hold feature and min/max functions; we found the latter unnecessary, but the former is quite useful. The button wasn't perfectly responsive, and loading three functions on one button was a bit confusing, but overall the design was pleasantly minimalist.
THERMOWORKS ThermoPop MODEL: TX-3100-PK PRICE: $29.00 AVERAGE MARGIN OF ERROR IN TESTING: 0.07° at 32°F, 0.29° at 125°F AVERAGE READ TIME: 3 sec RANGE: −58°F to 572°F PROBE LENGTH: 4.5 in FEATURES: Manually operated screen rotation, manual backlight	ACCURACY ★★★ SPEED ★★★ EASE OF USE ★★ DURABILITY ★★★	Our former inexpensive winner had another strong showing. It was dead accurate and extremely fast. Compared with fancier models, this model felt like driving a standard car. The display does rotate and has a backlight, but you have to stop and press a button for both functions. You have to be more careful when holding its small lollipop-shaped head, but it makes the best of its size with a grippy, ergonomic design that's reasonably secure and easy to push and pull out of dense foods. Because the head is so small, this model did put our hands a little closer to the heat.

DUTCH OVENS

Is there anything you can't do with a Dutch oven? We use these large, heavy-duty pots for boiling, searing, frying, braising, and baking food and for sous vide cooking. We turn them into smokers, steamers, coolers, and panini presses. They might just be the busiest pots in our kitchen. To find our favorite Dutch oven, we selected 11 models and put them to the test, rating each pot on the quality of its food, how easy it was to use and clean, and how durable it was. The top five Dutch ovens are listed below in order of preference.

	PERFORMANCE	TESTERS' COMMENTS

HIGHLY RECOMMENDED

LE CREUSET 7¼ Quart Round Dutch Oven
MODEL: LS2501-28
PRICE: $367.99
MATERIALS: Enameled cast iron, phenolic knob
WEIGHT: 13.7 lb
COOKING SURFACE DIAMETER: 9 in
INTERIOR COLOR: Light
INTERIOR HEIGHT: 4.5 in

COOKING ★★★
EASE OF USE ★★★
DURABILITY ★★★

This perfect, pricey pot bested the competition again. It was substantial enough to hold and distribute heat evenly without being unbearably heavy. The light-colored interior combined with low, straight sides gave us good visibility and made it easy to monitor browning and thermometer position. The broad cooking surface saved us time since we could cook more food at once. The lid was smooth and easy to clean. This pot is expensive, but it was exceptionally resistant to damage.

RECOMMENDED

CUISINART Chef's Classic Enameled Cast Iron Covered Casserole `BEST BUY`
MODEL: CI670-30CR
PRICE: $83.70
MATERIAL: Enameled cast iron
WEIGHT: 16.7 lb
COOKING SURFACE DIAMETER: 10.0 in
INTERIOR COLOR: Light
INTERIOR HEIGHT: 4.38 in

COOKING ★★★
EASE OF USE ★★½
DURABILITY ★★½

With an exceptionally broad cooking surface and low, straight sides, this 7-quart pot had the same advantageous shape as the Le Creuset. It was a little bit heavier but not prohibitively so. The looped handles were comfortable to hold, though slightly smaller than was ideal. The rim and lid chipped cosmetically when we repeatedly slammed the lid onto the pot, so it's slightly less durable than our winner.

CROCK-POT 7 Quart Round Cast Iron Dutch Oven with Lid
MODEL: 69144.02
PRICE: $79.99
MATERIALS: Enameled cast iron, stainless-steel knob
WEIGHT: 14.35 lb
COOKING SURFACE DIAMETER: 8.88 in
INTERIOR COLOR: Light
INTERIOR HEIGHT: 5.19 in

COOKING ★★★
EASE OF USE ★★
DURABILITY ★★★

This pot had large looped handles that were easy to grab even with oven mitts on. It also had a light interior so we could make sure our food didn't burn. The medium weight was hefty enough to conduct heat nicely without being burdensome. It had taller sides and a slightly smaller cooking surface; this combination made it harder to maneuver in and was slower at times, as we had to sear beef in three batches instead of two. But it made great food and was resistant to chipping.

LAVA Signature 7 Qt. Enameled Cast Iron Round Dutch Oven
MODEL: LV Y TC 28 K2 BLU
PRICE: $134.95
MATERIALS: Enameled cast iron, stainless-steel knob
WEIGHT: 15.5 lb
COOKING SURFACE DIAMETER: 9.75 in
INTERIOR COLOR: Dark
INTERIOR HEIGHT: 4.31 in

COOKING ★★★
EASE OF USE ★½
DURABILITY ★★★

With an especially broad cooking surface, this pot got through its searing stages faster than other models. We liked the looped handles, though they weren't as roomy as some. The low, straight sides let us see and work inside the pot without craning our necks or hitching our elbows awkwardly. However, the dark interior made it harder to monitor browning and position our thermometer probe. The lid had spikes designed to drip moisture back into the pot (we didn't notice a difference in the food) and a deep ridge around the underside, a design element that comes from the days of cooking with coals, as the ridge would cradle the coals a bit; both features made the lid harder to clean. This model was very resistant to damage.

STAUB Cast Iron 7 Qt Round Cocotte
MODEL: 1102806
PRICE: $279.99
MATERIALS: Enameled cast iron, stainless-steel knob
WEIGHT: 14.95 lb
COOKING SURFACE DIAMETER: 9.38 in
INTERIOR COLOR: Dark
INTERIOR HEIGHT: 5.13 in

COOKING ★★★
EASE OF USE ★½
DURABILITY ★★★

This very durable pot was heavy enough to conduct heat well, and it had a nice broad cooking surface, which saved us time when we were browning in batches; however, the dark interior made it harder to see what was going on inside. The knob on its lid frequently became wiggly, though it was easy to tighten. The handles were looped, which we liked, but a little small. The lid had spikes designed to cycle moisture back into the food (though we saw no measurable benefit) and a deep ridge; both made it harder to clean.

METAL SPATULAS

A metal spatula is an essential component of any cook's toolkit. We use it to flip or transfer foods whenever we're working with metal cookware or bakeware. It had been a while since our last review, and we wanted to know if our old favorite from Wüsthof still held up to the competition. We tested 10 metal spatulas, using them to flip and remove eggs, pancakes, burgers, fried fish, and home fries from a variety of cookware and to transfer sugar cookies from a baking sheet to a wire rack. We also had users of different dominant hands and hand sizes flip and transfer pancakes with each model. Models were evaluated on their overall performance, as well as their head design and handle design. The top five spatulas are listed below in order of preference.

HIGHLY RECOMMENDED	PERFORMANCE	TESTERS' COMMENTS

WÜSTHOF Gourmet 12" Fish Spatula
MODEL: 4433
PRICE: $49.95
AVERAGE HEAD DIMENSIONS: 2.2 x 5.5 in
HEAD SURFACE AREA: 12.1 sq in
HEAD THICKNESS: 0.9 mm
HANDLE LENGTH: 4.75 in
HANDLE CIRCUMFERENCE: 2.75 in
HANDLE MATERIAL: Polyoxymethylene
(high-density plastic)

PERFORMANCE ★★★
HEAD DESIGN ★★★
HANDLE DESIGN ★★½

Our former winner continues its reign: Its perfectly proportioned head supported foods of all shapes and sizes and maneuvered nimbly even in tight spaces. And because it's also moderately thin and flexible, it excelled at getting under food. The head's pronounced curve provided extra leverage for prying up food and kept our hands high above hot pans. Its handle was easy to hold, though some testers wished the otherwise comfortable plastic were grippier.

RECOMMENDED

MIU FRANCE Flexible Fish Turner–Slotted `BEST BUY`
MODEL: 90011
PRICE: $16.57
AVERAGE HEAD DIMENSIONS: 2.2 x 5.5 in
HEAD SURFACE AREA: 12.1 sq in
HEAD THICKNESS: 0.8 mm
HANDLE LENGTH: 4.5 in
HANDLE CIRCUMFERENCE: 2.6 in
HANDLE MATERIAL: Polyoxymethylene
(high-density plastic)

PERFORMANCE ★★★
HEAD DESIGN ★★½
HANDLE DESIGN ★★½

This fish spatula was nearly identical to our winner, with one small but important difference: Its head was almost flat, lacking the curvature that would allow users to summon extra leverage and keep their hands higher above hot surfaces. It still excelled at every task we gave it and was comfortable to hold, although its handle, like the one on our winning model, was a bit too smooth.

VICTORINOX 3 x 6-Inch Chef's Slotted Fish Turner
MODEL: 40415
PRICE: $19.20
AVERAGE HEAD DIMENSIONS: 2.25 x 5.5 in
HEAD SURFACE AREA: 12.4 sq in
HEAD THICKNESS: 0.9 mm
HANDLE LENGTH: 4.75 in
HANDLE CIRCUMFERENCE: 2.75 in
HANDLE MATERIAL: Walnut

PERFORMANCE ★★★
HEAD DESIGN ★★★
HANDLE DESIGN ★★

Like our winner, this fish spatula had a nicely curved, well-proportioned head of moderate thickness and flexibility, which allowed it to effortlessly flip, transfer, and support foods of all sizes. But testers were mixed on its handle: While the textured wood surface helped us keep our grip on the spatula when handling greasy, splattering foods, a rough metal edge stuck out from that wood, digging into our hands and making the spatula unpleasant to hold.

MERCER CULINARY Hell's Handle High Heat 6" x 3" Fish Spatula
MODEL: M33183
PRICE: $17.57
AVERAGE HEAD DIMENSIONS: 2.25 x 5.5 in
HEAD SURFACE AREA: 12.4 sq in
HEAD THICKNESS: 0.8 mm
HANDLE LENGTH: 5 in
HANDLE CIRCUMFERENCE: 3.4 in
HANDLE MATERIAL: Polypropylene (plastic)

PERFORMANCE ★★★
HEAD DESIGN ★★★
HANDLE DESIGN ★★

This fish spatula's head was well proportioned, moderately thin and flexible, and gently curved, allowing it to perform every task well. We liked the grippy plastic material of its handle, which was easy to hold even when covered in grease. The only problem? The handle itself was quite thick, which made it slightly harder for even larger-handed testers to hold comfortably for extended periods.

KUHN RIKON Flexi Spatula, 11"
MODEL: 2165
PRICE: $17.95
AVERAGE HEAD DIMENSIONS: 2.07 x 5.25 in
HEAD SURFACE AREA: 10.9 sq in
HEAD THICKNESS: 0.8 mm
HANDLE LENGTH: 4 in
HANDLE CIRCUMFERENCE: 2.3 in
HANDLE MATERIAL: Stainless steel

PERFORMANCE ★★½
HEAD DESIGN ★★½
HANDLE DESIGN ★★

While this turner performed ably in every task, its head and handle were a touch undersized next to those of the other fish spatulas in the lineup. Because the spatula had a smaller surface area, it felt less secure when flipping or transferring larger items such as pancakes. The metal handle was a bit short, narrow, and slick, which made it slightly harder to hold.

BURR GRINDERS

If you want the freshest, most full-flavored cup of coffee, we always recommend grinding your own coffee beans. Home grinders come in two styles: blade and burr. While a blade grinder has one chamber where you load, grind, and dispense the beans, a burr grinder consists of three components: a hopper where you feed the beans, the grinding chamber, and a removable container that holds the grounds. Burr grinders also allow you to choose your grind setting, giving you the option to grind coarse, medium, and fine coffee. To find the best burr grinder, we purchased 10 products and used each to grind coffee beans until we found the grind setting on each that produced the highest percentage of medium-size pieces. We then brewed coffee using grinds from the least even and most even coffee grinders (keeping every other variable the same), and asked 21 tasters to sample the coffees in a blind tasting. Surprisingly, each made a good cup of coffee, though we preferred grinders that produced an even grind. Six users tried the top four coffee grinders and gave feedback about grind size and ease of use. We removed the burrs from all the grinders, inspecting their shape and size; measured the capacity of each bean hopper using whole beans; and measured the capacity of each grounds container using ground coffee. Our favorite grinders were intuitive and easy to use; had roomy, sturdy plastic grounds containers that could withstand a morning drop; and ground cleanly without making messes of our kitchens. The top four grinders are listed below in order of preference.

RECOMMENDED	PERFORMANCE	TESTERS' COMMENTS
BARATZA Encore MODEL: 485 PRICE: $139.00 NUMBER OF GRIND SETTINGS: 40 BURR TYPE: Conical CAPACITY OF GROUNDS CONTAINER: 5.5 oz HIGHEST PERCENTAGE OF MEDIUM PIECES: 88%	EASE OF USE ★★ GRINDING ★★★ CLEANUP ★★½	This grinder is pretty bare-bones, with only a pulse button and (confusingly) two on/off buttons. You adjust the grind size by turning the hopper clockwise for a finer grind and counterclockwise for a coarser grind. There's no electronic interface, no timer, and no automated dosing—you turn the grinder on, and it mills beans until you turn it off. It was too minimal for our novice testers, who wanted a little more guidance, but this product's no-fuss design is perfect for more-experienced users. It doesn't include a scale, so you need to weigh your beans prior to grinding.
CAPRESSO Infinity Conical Burr Grinder, Black `BEST BUY` MODEL: #560.01 PRICE: $99.99 NUMBER OF GRIND SETTINGS: 16 BURR TYPE: Conical CAPACITY OF GROUNDS CONTAINER: 4 oz HIGHEST PERCENTAGE OF MEDIUM PIECES: 69%	EASE OF USE ★★ GRINDING ★★½ CLEANUP ★★½	Another grinder without any bells or whistles, this product had only 16 grind settings, but we liked that each was clearly labeled as extra-fine, fine, medium, or coarse. It ground consistently and evenly, and for those who don't want to weigh their beans, it has a dial timer that doses the correct amount of coffee for the number of cups you're making. It was a bit tricky to get the right amount for just one cup, as the dial would often snap automatically to off, but it provided an accurate amount of coffee for two cups or more. Its mushroom-shaped grounds container was on the small side and a bit awkward to hold and clean, but those are minor quibbles for an otherwise simple and intuitive grinder.
DE'LONGHI Dedica Stainless Steel Conical Burr Grinder MODEL: KG 521.M PRICE: $158.99 NUMBER OF GRIND SETTINGS: 18 BURR TYPE: Conical CAPACITY OF GROUNDS CONTAINER: 5.5 oz HIGHEST PERCENTAGE OF MEDIUM PIECES: 67%	EASE OF USE ★½ GRINDING ★★½ CLEANUP ★★★	This model had a mostly digital interface that helped take the guesswork out of selecting a setting. However, its digital display was hard for our shorter testers to read—the numbers were visible only when looking from directly overhead—and it took us a few extra glances at the manual to figure out what the odd symbols on the display denoted. It kept the coffee neatly contained, and we liked the shape and size of its grounds container and the fact that it came with a lid.
BREVILLE The Smart Grinder PRO MODEL: BCG820BSSXL PRICE: $199.95 NUMBER OF GRIND SETTINGS: 60 BURR TYPE: Conical CAPACITY OF GROUNDS CONTAINER: 5.5 oz HIGHEST PERCENTAGE OF MEDIUM PIECES: 73%	EASE OF USE ★★ GRINDING ★½ CLEANUP ★★★	Even novice testers felt comfortable and confident using this machine, which has a digital display that guides you through choosing a grind setting for your preferred brew method. Once set, it automatically dispenses the right amount of coffee based on your flavor preferences (strong or light) and the number of cups you're making. We found that its presets didn't give quite enough coffee right out of the box, but the grinder is easily programmable. When programmed, it remembers your favorite settings and adjusts the grind accordingly when you want more than one cup. However, its settings for "coarse" grinding were much finer than what we're used to—even on the coarsest setting, the coffee still looked like a medium-fine grind.

12-INCH STAINLESS-STEEL SKILLETS

We love stainless-steel skillets in the test kitchen. While cast-iron, carbon-steel, and even nonstick skillets have been elbowing them out of the limelight, they're still our top choice for achieving golden, uniform browning and developing flavorful fond, the secret weapon of chefs. We purchased seven skillets that measured about 12 inches in diameter. All are fully clad pans made of bonded layers of steel and aluminum. We evaluated their cooking performance, ease of use, and cleanup and how well they stood up to routine use. We also conducted abuse testing to evaluate construction and durability. Our favorite models were sturdy (without being too heavy), had a simple design, and encouraged even browning. The top six skillets are listed below in order of preference.

HIGHLY RECOMMENDED	PERFORMANCE	TESTERS' COMMENTS
ALL-CLAD d3 Stainless Steel 12" Fry Pan with Lid MODEL: 41126 PRICE: $119.95 **WEIGHT:** 2.8 lb COOKING SURFACE DIAMETER: 9.5 in BOTTOM THICKNESS: 3 mm HEIGHT OF SIDES: 2 in **LID:** Yes	PERFORMANCE ★★★ EASE OF USE ★★★ CLEANUP/DURABILITY ★★★	Our longtime favorite skillet still beats all newcomers, with a clean design that includes no unnecessary frills. We appreciate the wide cooking surface and low, flaring sides that encourage excellent browning and evaporation; a steel handle that stays cool on the stovetop and won't rotate in your hand; and an overall weight and balance that hit the sweet spot between sturdiness and maneuverable lightness. It resisted warping and withstood thermal shock and outright abuse with nary a scratch or dent.

RECOMMENDED		
ALL-CLAD d5 Stainless Steel 12" Fry Pan MODEL: SD55112 PRICE: $200.00 **WEIGHT:** 3.1 lb COOKING SURFACE DIAMETER: 9.25 in BOTTOM THICKNESS: 3 mm HEIGHT OF SIDES: 2 in **LID:** No	PERFORMANCE ★★½ EASE OF USE ★★½ CLEANUP/DURABILITY ★★★	This is a five-layer version of our favorite skillet, sporting a central layer of stainless steel sandwiched by two layers of aluminum and two more of steel. While it shares the shape of our winner, it's a bit heavier and smaller and performs a little more sluggishly, which stands to reason since it's thicker and contains more steel. For $80.00 more and with no lid, we don't see the point of choosing this model over the d3 pan. Note: All-Clad sells a flat universal lid in its TK (Thomas Keller) line for $59.99; you need the 15-inch lid for this 12-inch pan.
HESTAN NanoBond 12.5" Open Skillet MODEL: 60031 PRICE: $400.00 **WEIGHT:** 3.4 lb COOKING SURFACE DIAMETER: 9.5 in BOTTOM THICKNESS: 3.1 mm HEIGHT OF SIDES: 2 in **LID:** No	PERFORMANCE ★★★ EASE OF USE ★★½ CLEANUP/DURABILITY ★★½	The lustrous gunmetal finish of this pricey three-layer skillet is truly lovely, and the pan browns evenly and deeply, but it was harder to monitor the color of fond against the darker finish. Low, flaring sides helped evaporate steam and reduce pan sauces. Some testers objected to the offset angle of its handle, which didn't feel like a natural extension of their arms. The shiny finish became marred every time we cooked, but an included bottle of proprietary liquid cleanser restored it.
LE CREUSET Stainless Steel Fry Pan 12" MODEL: SSP2000-30 PRICE: $100.00 **WEIGHT:** 2.8 lb COOKING SURFACE DIAMETER: 9.5 in BOTTOM THICKNESS: 2.5 mm HEIGHT OF SIDES: 2 in **LID:** No	PERFORMANCE ★★★ EASE OF USE ★★½ CLEANUP/DURABILITY ★★½	This three-layer pan mostly browned well, due to its roomy cooking surface and low, flaring sides. We liked that it's light and maneuverable, but we found its handle a little too round and slippery. It sometimes cooked a bit unevenly, and its shiny surface developed black spots that were difficult to remove. It also dented and warped slightly during abuse testing.
DEMEYERE Industry 5-Ply 12.5" Stainless Steel Fry Pan with Helper Handle MODEL: 48632 PRICE: $189.99 **WEIGHT:** 4.2 lb COOKING SURFACE DIAMETER: 10 in BOTTOM THICKNESS: 3.3 mm HEIGHT OF SIDES: 2.38 in **LID:** No	PERFORMANCE ★★★ EASE OF USE ★★ CLEANUP/DURABILITY ★★½	This very roomy, sturdy five-layer pan browned well and evenly, despite higher sides than we'd prefer, and its pale silver surface cleaned up easily, especially since the interior has no rivets to trap food. It survived abuse testing with noticeable small dents. But at 4.2 pounds when empty, even with a helper handle, it's very heavy and awkward to maneuver or hold up while scooping food.
ZWILLING Aurora 12.5" Fry Pan MODEL: 66088-320 PRICE: $127.49 **WEIGHT:** 4.25 lb COOKING SURFACE DIAMETER: 10.5 in BOTTOM THICKNESS: 3.3 mm HEIGHT OF SIDES: 2.25 in **LID:** No	PERFORMANCE ★★★ EASE OF USE ★★ CLEANUP/DURABILITY ★★½	This five-layer pan is very roomy, which helped it brown food well, though sometimes less deeply than we'd prefer. It was heavy and had higher sides than was ideal. Its skinny, slightly too-short handle became hot on the stovetop and made the pan feel off-balance. It survived abuse testing with no warping and very minor dents.

INEXPENSIVE 12-INCH STAINLESS-STEEL SKILLETS

A 12-inch stainless-steel skillet is the definition of a kitchen workhorse: It can go from stovetop to oven effortlessly, so it's great for cooking meat and fish, baking skillet pies, and pan-roasting whole chickens. We love our longtime favorite from All-Clad, but we wondered if we could find a comparable option for less than $100. To find out, we purchased eight 12-inch skillets, priced from about $50 to about $100, to compare to our high-end favorite, the All-Clad d3 Stainless Steel 12" Fry Pan with Lid. All models were fully clad pans made of bonded layers of steel and aluminum. We evaluated their cooking performance, ease of use, and cleanup, in addition to how well they stood up to routine use. We also conducted abuse testing to evaluate construction and long-term durability. In the end, no pan could compete with our all-time favorite. The top five skillets are listed below in order of preference.

HIGHLY RECOMMENDED	PERFORMANCE	TESTERS' COMMENTS
ALL-CLAD d3 Stainless Steel 12" Fry Pan with Lid MODEL: 41126 PRICE: $119.99 WEIGHT: 2.8 lb COOKING SURFACE DIAMETER: 9.5 in BOTTOM THICKNESS: 3.0 mm HEIGHT OF SIDES: 2 in	PERFORMANCE ★★★ EASE OF USE ★★★ CLEANUP/DURABILITY ★★★	Our longtime favorite skillet still beats the cheaper competition. We appreciate the broad cooking surface and low, flaring sides that encourage excellent browning and evaporation; a steel handle that stays cool on the stovetop and won't rotate in your hand; an overall weight and balance that hits the sweet spot between sturdiness and maneuverable lightness; and durable construction that resists warping while withstanding thermal shock and outright abuse with nary a scratch or dent.

RECOMMENDED WITH RESERVATIONS		
MADE IN 12" Fry Pan MODEL: COOK-12-FRY-SS PRICE: $85.00 WEIGHT: 3 lb COOKING SURFACE DIAMETER: 8.75 in BOTTOM THICKNESS: 2.8 mm HEIGHT OF SIDES: 2 in	PERFORMANCE ★★★ EASE OF USE ★★½ CLEANUP/DURABILITY ★★	This pan's moderate weight, good balance, well-shaped handle, and low, flaring sides made it easy to use, and it had just enough surface area to cook a whole chicken or four strip steaks without crowding. It created a deep sear on both sides of our steaks, browned onions and chicken evenly, and left flavorful fond for pan sauce. Its simple lines were easy to swipe around with a spatula and to scrub clean, and it came with a proprietary cleansing powder, similar to Bar Keeper's Friend, which helped scrub away stains. Its flaw? Even when the pan is new, its bottom doesn't sit flat, and it warped more during testing. This is barely detectable on a gas stove, but for induction or glass-topped electric stoves, it's not the best choice.
TRAMONTINA Gourmet Tri-Ply Clad 12-Inch Fry Pan with Helper Handle MODEL: 80116/057DS PRICE: $69.95 WEIGHT: 3.2 lb COOKING SURFACE DIAMETER: 8.38 in BOTTOM THICKNESS: 2.8 mm HEIGHT OF SIDES: 2 in	PERFORMANCE ★★ EASE OF USE ★★½ CLEANUP/DURABILITY ★★½	This sturdy pan barely dented and didn't warp, which makes it a good choice, especially if you own a flat-topped stove. Its cooking surface was the narrowest in the lineup, so four steaks or eight pieces of chicken were crowded and didn't cook as evenly. We like its low, flaring sides to promote evaporation during browning, but for a pan weighing just over 3 pounds, it felt surprisingly heavy and a bit awkward.
CUISINART Multiclad Pro 12" Skillet with Helper Handle & Cover MODEL: MCP22-30HCN PRICE: $69.95 WEIGHT: 3.75 lb COOKING SURFACE DIAMETER: 10 in BOTTOM THICKNESS: 2.8 mm HEIGHT OF SIDES: 2.13 in	PERFORMANCE ★★½ EASE OF USE ★★½ CLEANUP/DURABILITY ★★	Despite a generous cooking surface, which made for very good browning and plenty of space to move food around, this pan warped early in routine cooking and wobbled noticeably, even on a gas stove. It felt a bit heavy and harder to hold up with one hand, though the handle was easy to grip. We liked that it came with a lid.
OXO Good Grips Stainless Steel Pro 12" Open Frypan MODEL: CW000974-003 PRICE: $79.99 WEIGHT: 3.2 lb COOKING SURFACE DIAMETER: 9.5 in BOTTOM THICKNESS: 2.7 mm HEIGHT OF SIDES: 2.13 in	PERFORMANCE ★★ EASE OF USE ★★½ CLEANUP/DURABILITY ★★	We liked the cooking surface and flaring sides of this skillet, and it was well balanced. Browning was slightly uneven but acceptable. Testers complained that the handle felt a bit shorter than preferred and seemed "fat" and a bit slippery. Though the pan didn't warp, it became moderately dented and the handle loosened during abuse testing. The shiny steel surface took extra effort to scrub clean, even with Bar Keeper's Friend.

8-INCH NONSTICK SKILLETS

An 8-inch nonstick skillet is perfect for making a couple of fried eggs, for recipes scaled down for one or two people, and for toasting nuts, spices, garlic, and more. To find the best model, we tested eight widely available 8-inch non-stick skillets. Four of the pans had traditional PTFE nonstick coatings, and four had ceramic nonstick coatings. To evaluate nonstick ability, we made eggs over-easy with no fat in each new pan, cooking the eggs one after another, stopping either when they began to stick (a sign that the coating was starting to fail) or when we reached 50 eggs; we repeated this at the end of testing to assess the durability of each pan's nonstick coating. In between, we cooked scalloped potatoes and omelets and had a series of users scramble eggs in each pan and provide feedback. We also conducted a series of abuse tests: scraping a metal spatula across each pan 50 times, heating the pans to 400 degrees and shocking them in an ice bath, and banging each one three times on a concrete ledge. In the end, our winner was from the same manufacturer as our favorite 12-inch model. It has a durable PTFE nonstick surface and comfortable, secure handle. The top five skillets are listed below in order of preference.

HIGHLY RECOMMENDED

OXO Good Grips Hard Anodized Pro Nonstick 8-Inch Fry Pan
MODEL: CW000958-003
PRICE: $29.95
STYLE: PTFE nonstick
OVENSAFE TO: 430°F
CAPACITY: 4.4 cups

PERFORMANCE
NONSTICK ABILITY ★★★
EASE OF USE ★★★
CAPACITY ★★★
DURABILITY ★★★

TESTERS' COMMENTS
This little OXO skillet bested the rest for three simple reasons: superior nonstick ability, a comfortable handle, and a nicely shaped body. It cruised through 50 eggs at the beginning and end of testing, indicating a slick, durable nonstick coating. Testers found its rounded, brushed-steel handle "grippy" and liked that it gave "options for where to hold." Construction-wise, it was "lightweight but sturdy" and perfectly balanced, which made it especially pleasing to cook with.

RECOMMENDED

ALL-CLAD Stainless Steel Nonstick 8" Fry Pan
MODEL: 4108NS
PRICE: $109.95
STYLE: PTFE nonstick
OVENSAFE TO: 500°F
CAPACITY: 4.4 cups

PERFORMANCE
NONSTICK ABILITY ★★★
EASE OF USE ★★½
CAPACITY ★★★
DURABILITY ★★★

TESTERS' COMMENTS
This pricey pan had a great nonstick surface; it released 50 eggs easily at both the beginning and the end of testing. It was also notably well constructed and durable. Yet while testers called the pan nicely "balanced," a few took issue with the handle, which felt "stable" but "uncomfortable," thanks to a concave metal shape with hard edges that dug into some testers' hands.

LE CREUSET 8" Nonstick Fry Pan
MODEL: TNS2200-20
PRICE: $99.95
STYLE: PTFE nonstick
OVENSAFE TO: 500°F
CAPACITY: 3.8 cups

PERFORMANCE
NONSTICK ABILITY ★★★
EASE OF USE ★★½
CAPACITY ★★★
DURABILITY ★★★

TESTERS' COMMENTS
This expensive pan performed well: The nonstick coating released eggs just as cleanly at the end of testing as it did at the beginning. The handle was longer and heavier, which made some testers feel that the balance was a bit out of whack; "it's a little clunky," said one tester, who explained, "I feel like I'm a mile from the pan." But overall, it felt "well constructed" and durable.

T-FAL Professional Total Nonstick Thermo-Spot Heat Indicator Fry Pan, 8-Inch, Black
MODEL: E93802
PRICE: $17.99
STYLE: PTFE nonstick
OVENSAFE TO: 400°F
CAPACITY: 3.2 cups

PERFORMANCE
NONSTICK ABILITY ★★★
EASE OF USE ★★½
CAPACITY ★★
DURABILITY ★★★

TESTERS' COMMENTS
This pan released eggs perfectly and stayed notably scratch-free, likely due to its five layers of nonstick coating (the rest of the PTFE pans we tested had three). The handle was "comfortable and grippy," and the rivets were coated in nonstick, which made them particularly easy to clean. The pan's rim was uncoated and got stained, but our major gripe was capacity: Unless we were cooking just one or two eggs, it was too small. "I'm afraid I'm going to lose some," said one tester midscramble, and scalloped potatoes overflowed in the oven.

RECOMMENDED WITH RESERVATIONS

SCANPAN Classic 8" Frypan
MODEL: 20001200
PRICE: $47.95
STYLE: Ceramic
OVENSAFE TO: 500°F
CAPACITY: 3.8 cups

PERFORMANCE
NONSTICK ABILITY ★★★
EASE OF USE ★★½
CAPACITY ★★★
DURABILITY ★½

TESTERS' COMMENTS
The only ceramic model to stay nonstick throughout testing, this little pan was divisive. We liked that there weren't any rivets on the inside, which allowed us to swoop around with a spatula and made it easier to clean. But the handle was shorter and was set low on the pan, which put it closer to the heat; most testers wanted a cooler handle and more clearance underneath so they could grab it more easily. This pan also sustained the most scratches, and its handle wiggled a bit by the end of testing.

HEAVY-DUTY CUTTING BOARDS

For some cooks, the ultimate cutting board is a thick, solid model made of wood or bamboo. Compared to a lightweight plastic board, a wood board is an investment. You'll have to spend more money and perform regular maintenance, but for that money and effort, you get a board that can potentially last a lifetime. It had been a while since we last tested cutting boards, and we wanted to know if our former winner, the Teakhaus by Proteak Edge Grain Cutting Board, was still the best heavy-duty option available. So we pitted it against six other wood and bamboo models. The boards we chose measured at least 20 inches long and 15 inches wide and were made from bamboo or one of four types of wood (maple, birch, teak, or hinoki, a Japanese cypress). We minced parsley, chopped onions, sliced loaves of bread, pounded chicken cutlets, and cleaved pounds of bone-in chicken parts on them. We chopped chipotle chile in adobo on them, washed them, and then checked for stains and odors. We also washed each board by hand more than 100 times, maintaining the boards with mineral oil as needed. In addition to conducting rounds of user testing in the kitchen, we sent copies of the boards home with staffers for some real-life testing in their kitchens. We also evaluated the durability, stability, ease of use, and maintenance of all the boards. The top five cutting boards are listed below in order of preference.

HIGHLY RECOMMENDED	PERFORMANCE	TESTERS' COMMENTS
TEAKHAUS BY PROTEAK **Edge Grain Cutting Board** MODEL: 107 PRICE: $104.95 MATERIAL: Teak DIMENSIONS: 18 x 24 x 1.5 in WEIGHT: 15 lb	DURABILITY ★★½ STABILITY ★★½ EASE OF USE ★★★ MAINTENANCE ★★★	This cutting board required the least amount of maintenance and resisted cracking, warping, and staining. It was light enough to lift comfortably but heavy enough to be stable for most tasks, though a few users noted that it wobbled occasionally. While the moderately hard teak did take on some scars from the cleaver, testers loved cutting on its surface, which felt luxuriously satiny under the knife.
BOARDSMITH Maple Carolina **Slab 2 x 16 x 22 in** MODEL: n/a PRICE: $214.72 MATERIAL: Hard maple DIMENSIONS: 16 x 22 x 2.9 in WEIGHT: 19.4 lb	DURABILITY ★★★ STABILITY ★★★ EASE OF USE ★★ MAINTENANCE ★★½	This roomy model showed no signs of wear and tear. It sat securely on the counter and was easy to lift using the gap created by its plastic feet. Some thought that its ultrasmooth maple surface was a touch hard on the knife, and it was too tall for shorter users.
JONES CUTTING BOARDS **Maple End Grain 2.5"** **Butcher Block with Feet** MODEL: 2018/2.25 PRICE: $190.00 MATERIAL: Hard maple DIMENSIONS: 15 x 20 x 2.6 in WEIGHT: 14.25 lb	DURABILITY ★★★ STABILITY ★★★ EASE OF USE ★★½ MAINTENANCE ★★	With a good weight and plastic-coated feet, this beautiful end-grain board was stable and fairly easy to pick up; having arrived preseasoned, it showed almost no wear after the full course of testing apart from the occasional stain. Like the other end-grain boards, it sucked up water and oil readily, requiring a bit more care to maintain. It's also on the tall side, which makes it less ideal for shorter users, and it's a little less spacious than some of the other boards.
RECOMMENDED		
TOTALLY BAMBOO Big Kahuna **24" Bamboo Cutting Board** MODEL: 20-3100 PRICE: $134.00 MATERIAL: Bamboo DIMENSIONS: 18 x 24 x 3 in WEIGHT: 20.3 lb	DURABILITY ★★½ STABILITY ★★★ EASE OF USE ★★ MAINTENANCE ★★½	Large and in charge, this footed bamboo board provided tons of workspace and was unbudgeable on the counter, if a real bear to lift. Some testers found its hard, slightly rough surface less enjoyable to cut on. But that hardness meant it showed only a few minor knife marks at the conclusion of testing, and stains disappeared after a few washes. Perhaps because it was so big, it required a little more oil than other edge-grain boards; it was also too tall for shorter testers.
KISO HINOKI Extra Large **Cutting Board** MODEL: KS5000 PRICE: $238.57 MATERIAL: Hinoki DIMENSIONS: 18 x 24 x 1.5 in WEIGHT: 11.5 lb	DURABILITY ★★ STABILITY ★★ EASE OF USE ★★★ MAINTENANCE ★★½	Made with hinoki, a Japanese cypress, this satiny-smooth edge-grain board was roomy and quite soft, providing a luxurious, plush cutting experience (though also sustaining the deepest scarring). Because it was the lightest board in the lineup, it was easy to pick up, but while it was stable for most tasks, it did slip a bit more frequently than other models.

LARGE COOLERS

A cooler is an indispensable tool for the traveling cook, handy for camping, beach trips, long car rides, parties, and tailgating. To find a durable option that kept food cool, we tested eight products from five top-selling, well-known brands, with capacities of about 50 quarts. To evaluate cold retention, we loaded each with 32 pounds of ice and measured its daily ice loss until none remained. We also filled the coolers with ice packs and soda cans, tracking how long the sodas stayed below 50 degrees. We tested ease of use by attempting to stuff a weekend's worth of groceries into each cooler and to carry or wheel the full coolers across concrete, asphalt, gravel, and grass; up and down stairs; and in and out of the back of a car. We also performed abuse tests: We pushed full coolers out of the back of an SUV five times and operated all handles, latches, and hinges a minimum of 100 times. The top four coolers are listed in order of preference.

RECOMMENDED	PERFORMANCE	TESTERS' COMMENTS
YETI Tundra 45 MODEL: 45 PRICE: $299.99 WEIGHT: 25 lb WHEELS: No INSULATED LID: Yes THICKNESS OF INSULATION: 1.3 to 2.2 in DENSITY OF INSULATION: 35 mg/cu cm	COOLING ★★★ PORTABILITY ★½ EASE OF USE ★★★ DURABILITY ★★★	This ultradurable cooler outpaced every other model in cooling and durability, but it's a bit heavy for the average person. Ice lasted a whole week, and when we placed sodas and ice packs inside, the cooler kept our beverages below 50 degrees for more than five days. We also loved its rubber latches, which were easy to close, and its durable rope handles. The cooler's weight did make it fairly difficult for one person to carry when full, and it didn't fit all our groceries or soda cans (it could fit only 24 cans, along with ice packs). However, if you're looking for a smaller cooler that holds all the essentials, this is an excellent option.
YETI Tundra 65 MODEL: 65 PRICE: $349.99 WEIGHT: 30 lb WHEELS: No INSULATED LID: Yes THICKNESS OF INSULATION: 1.4 to 2.25 in DENSITY OF INSULATION: 35 mg/cu cm	COOLING ★★★ PORTABILITY ★ EASE OF USE ★★★ DURABILITY ★★★	Another model by Yeti that excelled at cooling, this larger cooler held it all—but it was difficult for even two people to carry. Ice lasted six days, and when we placed sodas and ice packs inside, the cooler kept our beverages below 50 degrees for more than five days. This cooler had the same rubber latches and rope handles we loved in the smaller version. Our biggest frustrations were the cooler's weight and shape: At 30 pounds and over 2 feet long, it was impossible for one person to carry when it was full—and still heavy for two people. But we think this is a fair trade-off given the cooler's standout performance.
COLEMAN 50 QT Xtreme Wheeled Cooler BEST BUY MODEL: 3000005153 PRICE: $45.99 WEIGHT: 12 lb WHEELS: Yes INSULATED LID: Yes THICKNESS OF INSULATION: 0.7 to 1.6 in DENSITY OF INSULATION: 43 mg/cu cm	COOLING ★★½ PORTABILITY ★★★ EASE OF USE ★★½ DURABILITY ★½	This budget-friendly model did a decent job of cooling, keeping ice for six days—longer than any other product priced under $100.00. Its wheels made it more portable, and its roomy interior easily held a weekend's worth of groceries. We liked that the side handles were molded into the body, which prevented them from breaking when we dropped the cooler. The telescoping handle you use to roll the cooler (like a luggage handle) wasn't so durable, though; one of the poles dented after we dropped the cooler, which prevented us from pushing the handle down and obstructed the lid from opening fully.
PELICAN Elite 45QW Wheeled Cooler MODEL: 45QW PRICE: $379.95 WEIGHT: 38 lb WHEELS: Yes INSULATED LID: Yes THICKNESS OF INSULATION: 2 to 3 in DENSITY OF INSULATION: 40 mg/cu cm	COOLING ★★★ PORTABILITY ★½ EASE OF USE ★★ DURABILITY ★★★	A premium option from a company known for manufacturing professional camera cases, this cooler was well constructed, with up to 3 inches of foam on all sides. It kept ice for eight days and sodas frosty for four days. Testers struggled with its considerable weight, though: It weighed 38 pounds empty. Though the wheels helped a bit, they were no use when trying to move the full cooler up and down stairs or in and out of a car. The wheel wells also took up space in the body of the cooler, creating awkward spots where we had to fit food like puzzle pieces.

LOAF PANS

Loaf pans give baked goods a tall, rectangular shape that would be impossible to achieve with any other piece of equipment. They're a must-have when baking zucchini and banana breads, sandwich loaves, and pound cake. To find a loaf pan that released food easily, was easy to maneuver, and produced beautiful breads and cakes, we tested 10 models. Our lineup included nonstick metal, silicone, and glass models. Testers used each pan to bake pound cake, sandwich bread, and lasagna. We weighted baked good appearance more heavily than easy cleanup. When performance was identical, we rated less expensive pans higher. The top seven loaf pans are listed below in order of preference.

RECOMMENDED	PERFORMANCE	TESTERS' COMMENTS
USA PAN Loaf Pan, 1 lb Volume MODEL: 1140LF PRICE: $14.95 MATERIAL: Aluminized steel DIMENSIONS: 8⅝ x 4½ x 2¾ in CAPACITY: 1.5 L DISHWASHER-SAFE: No	BAKED GOOD APPEARANCE ★★★ CLEANUP ★★½ DURABILITY ★★½	This folded metal pan produced tall, picture-perfect pound cake and sandwich bread with crisp corners. Like all folded pans, it lacked handles and had crevices in the corners that trapped food. We had to clean it very carefully. The corrugated pattern on the metal didn't affect the appearance of the baked goods. It still scratched slightly.
CHICAGO Metallic Commercial II Nonstick 1 lb Loaf Pan MODEL: 59042 PRICE: $17.99 MATERIAL: Aluminized steel DIMENSIONS: 8½ x 4½ x 2¾ in CAPACITY: 1.48 L DISHWASHER-SAFE: Yes	BAKED GOOD APPEARANCE ★★★ CLEANUP ★★½ DURABILITY ★★½	This folded pan produced straight-sided baked goods with sharp edges that released cleanly and browned evenly. But as with all the folded pans in our lineup, its inside corners had small crevices and we had to wash them carefully. The pan became slightly scratched in our abuse testing.
WILLIAMS SONOMA Goldtouch Nonstick Loaf Pan, 1 lb MODEL: 1983915 PRICE: $22.95 MATERIAL: Aluminized steel DIMENSIONS: 8⅝ x 4½ x 2¾ in CAPACITY: 1.44 L DISHWASHER-SAFE: Yes	BAKED GOOD APPEARANCE ★★★ CLEANUP ★★½ DURABILITY ★★½	In evaluations of baking performance, our old winner was still excellent. We love the crisp corners and straight walls it creates on cakes and breads. It became lightly scratched during abuse testing. The small crevices in each corner trapped food, so we had to pay close attention to them when we cleaned the pan.
OXO Good Grips Non-Stick Pro 1 Lb Loaf Pan MODEL: 11160300 PRICE: $16.95 MATERIAL: Aluminized steel DIMENSIONS: 8½ x 4½ x 2¾ in CAPACITY: 1.58 L DISHWASHER-SAFE: No	BAKED GOOD APPEARANCE ★★ CLEANUP ★★★ DURABILITY ★★½	This pan's rounded corners created baked goods with rounded edges that lacked the polish and refinement of foods baked in higher-ranking pans. The trade-off is that it's much easier to clean. The raised bumps at the bottom of the pan deflected and concealed knife marks, though the inside walls still scratched slightly.
SIMPLY CALPHALON Nonstick Bakeware Medium Loaf Pan MODEL: 1758084 PRICE: $12.01 MATERIAL: Carbon steel DIMENSIONS: 8½ x 4½ x 2⅝ in CAPACITY: 1.52 L DISHWASHER-SAFE: Yes	BAKED GOOD APPEARANCE ★★ CLEANUP ★★★ DURABILITY ★★½	This pan, which was exactly 8½ by 4½ inches across the top, performed well across our tests. It produced evenly browned baked goods with the rounded edges characteristic of molded loaf pans. The loaves still tasted great, but they weren't as attractive. The pan scratched slightly.
PYREX Easy Grab 1.5-qt Loaf Pan MODEL: 5300092 PRICE: $15.75 MATERIAL: Glass DIMENSIONS: 8¼ x 5⅛ x 3 in CAPACITY: 1.54 L DISHWASHER-SAFE: Top rack only	BAKED GOOD APPEARANCE ★½ CLEANUP ★★★ DURABILITY ★★★	We liked the even browning of pound cake and sandwich bread baked in this iconic pan. Unfortunately, it was significantly wider than we wanted and its baked goods looked chubby and squat. It was heavier than metal and silicone pans, but it had helpful handles and was easy to clean. It didn't scratch, but overall we preferred metal pans, which are less likely than glass to shatter or crack.
OXO Good Grips Glass 1.6 Qt Loaf Baking Dish MODEL: 11176000 PRICE: $8.99 MATERIAL: Glass DIMENSIONS: 8¼ x 5½ x 3⅛ in CAPACITY: 1.74 L DISHWASHER-SAFE: Yes	BAKED GOOD APPEARANCE ★½ CLEANUP ★★★ DURABILITY ★★★	This glass pan is wider than our top-rated models. Baked goods were a bit round; we preferred sharp, distinct rectangular loaves. The pan didn't scratch, and it was easy to clean. Although it was heavy and fragile, we liked its big handles.

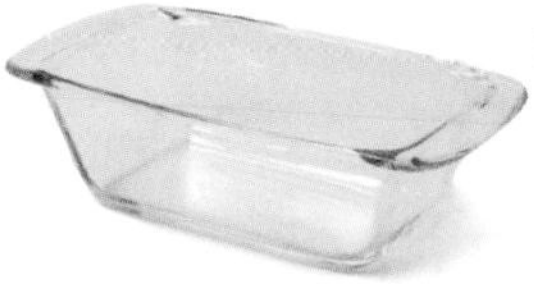

LONG-SLOT TOASTERS

Recently, a handful of "long-slot" toasters—those with extra-long, extra-wide bread slots that can fit any kind of bread—have appeared on the market. To find our favorite, we purchased eight long-slot toasters and tested them by toasting sandwich bread, artisan loaves, bagels, and both fresh and frozen bread. We liked toasters that produced crisp, uniform, golden toast every time and had intuitive controls; if a toaster had features that made it easier to use, we rated it higher. The top five toasters are listed below in order of preference.

HIGHLY RECOMMENDED	PERFORMANCE	TESTERS' COMMENTS
BREVILLE The Bit More Toaster **MODEL:** BTA730XL **PRICE:** $79.99 **TOASTER DIMENSIONS:** 15.8 x 8 x 7.8 in **SLOT DIMENSIONS:** 10 x 5 in **HEATING ELEMENT:** Wires **FEATURES:** "A Bit More" button, "Lift and Look" lever to check browning **AVERAGE SPEED:** 2 min, 8 sec 	PERFORMANCE ★★½ SPEED ★★★ EASE OF USE ★★★ CLEANUP ★★★	This toaster is large and solid and performed reliably. Its controls are well designed, including an "A Bit More" button (to add a short toasting cycle for slightly darker toast), a bar of lights that indicates progress, and a "Lift and Look" feature to peek at your bread without stopping the cycle. Its stainless-steel exterior stayed cool. Once we'd fiddled a little to find the best settings, this toaster usually produced uniformly, accurately browned toast. Its slots are deep enough for tall breads, but at 10 inches wide, they are slightly tight for two slices of sandwich bread to sit side by side; we'd prefer at least ½ inch more wiggle room.
DASH Clear View Toaster `BEST BUY` **MODEL:** DVTS501 **PRICE:** $36.03 **TOASTER DIMENSIONS:** 15 x 5 x 8 in **SLOT DIMENSIONS:** 10.5 x 5 in **HEATING ELEMENT:** Quartz **FEATURES:** Window, "cancel" button, reheating **AVERAGE SPEED:** 2 min, 12 sec 	PERFORMANCE ★★½ SPEED ★★★ EASE OF USE ★★★ CLEANUP ★★★	The price is right on this model, which made pretty toast without any fuss. We loved its glass window to monitor browning. A "reheat" button lets you warm up cooled toast or add a bit more browning. Its profile is compact, and the exterior stays cool. On the medium setting, toast was too light, but once we pushed the dial higher, it came out reliably golden and uniform on both sides; the highest setting made great "dark" toast. This toaster might have won if it didn't occasionally throw toast onto the counter or floor, which can be comical but unsettling. (A backup copy did the same.)

RECOMMENDED	PERFORMANCE	TESTERS' COMMENTS
RUSSELL HOBBS Glass Accent Long Slot 2-Slice Toaster **MODEL:** TRL9300GYR (stainless steel) **PRICE:** $99.99 **TOASTER DIMENSIONS:** 15 x 5 x 7.1 in **SLOT DIMENSIONS:** 10.25 x 5 in **HEATING ELEMENT:** Wires **FEATURE:** Bun-warming rack **AVERAGE SPEED:** 1 min, 44 sec 	PERFORMANCE ★★½ SPEED ★★★ EASE OF USE ★★½ CLEANUP ★★★	We appreciated this toaster's slim, neat profile; its extra rack for warming buns and croissants; and the way it lifted finished bread a full 2 inches out of the toaster for easy retrieval. It toasted quickly, making golden, appealing toast, but we had a major setback when the toaster died after four pieces of toast. (A replacement copy worked fine.) Finding the best settings required a small learning curve, but then it was reliable, and even on the darkest setting, it didn't scorch. Some testers felt that the plus and minus buttons to set toast color were confusing.
MAGIMIX Vision Toaster **MODEL:** 11526 (chrome) **PRICE:** $249.95 **TOASTER DIMENSIONS:** 15.5 x 7 x 9 in **SLOT DIMENSIONS:** 10.25 x 6.88 in **HEATING ELEMENT:** Quartz **FEATURES:** Windows, "stop" button, bread-lift lever **AVERAGE SPEED:** 1 min, 25 sec	PERFORMANCE ★★ SPEED ★★★ EASE OF USE ★★★ CLEANUP ★★★	This toaster is a pleasure to use, with glass walls and a big "stop" button to let you watch and halt toasting at your ideal color. It makes gorgeous, evenly colored toast, and its exterior stays cool. However, toast browns too much at any setting past the middle of the dial, sometimes burning and smoking. For its price, this toaster should be perfect.
HAMILTON BEACH Keep Warm 4-Slice Long-Slot Toaster **MODEL:** 24810 **PRICE:** $36.85 **TOASTER DIMENSIONS:** 15.75 x 7.5 x 7.75 in **SLOT DIMENSIONS:** 10 x 4.75 in **HEATING ELEMENT:** Wires **FEATURE:** "Keep warm" button **AVERAGE SPEED:** 2 min, 3 sec	PERFORMANCE ★★ SPEED ★★★ EASE OF USE ★★ CLEANUP ★★★	This toaster beeps at the beginning and end of toasting; the first beep didn't seem necessary, but we appreciated the second beep alerting us when our toast was ready. Although it toasted fast, this model kept us fiddling with settings to get our desired color. It performed acceptably with single slices, but consecutive full-capacity batches of toast came out uneven and patchy. It failed twice to toast one half of a bagel, and the slots were just slightly too short for two slices of sandwich bread to sit side by side.

CAN OPENERS

There's no doubt about it: Can openers are a kitchen must-have. There are two styles—traditional and safety. Traditional models puncture and cut the lid inside the rim of the can; safety models cut into the side of the can just beneath the rim so that both the lid and its rim can be removed, creating a smoother, safer edge. We purchased seven can openers and used each model to open two cans of black beans to gauge how intuitive the opener was to operate. Then we opened 16 more cans in a range of sizes and shapes—including four cans of black beans, four cans of tuna, four cans of tomato paste, and four cans of whole tomatoes—to assess how easy it was to attach, operate, and detach each model. We hand-washed each can opener (per manufacturer instructions) five times to test ease of cleanup and durability and asked three users to open a can of black beans with each model to get additional feedback on ease of use. We opened an additional 25 cans of black beans with the winning model to test durability. The top six can openers are listed below in order of preference.

HIGHLY RECOMMENDED	PERFORMANCE	TESTERS' COMMENTS
EZ-DUZ-IT Can Opener MODEL: 89 PRICE: $10.00 STYLE: Traditional DRIVING HANDLE LENGTH: 3½ in	EASE OF USE ★★★ COMFORT ★★★ DURABILITY ★★★	Our favorite can opener required almost no thought to operate—it was intuitive and easy to use in all respects. It had the longest driving handle of any opener we tested, which made it easier and more comfortable to rotate. Can opening was smooth and effortless.

RECOMMENDED

SWING-A-WAY Portable Can Opener MODEL: 407BK PRICE: $7.99 STYLE: Traditional DRIVING HANDLE LENGTH: 3¼ in	EASE OF USE ★★★ COMFORT ★★½ DURABILITY ★★★	We liked how easy this opener was to use, but testers felt that it was a little less comfortable than our winner. Though this model was similar in appearance to our winner, the "turning mechanism is not as smooth." Testers noted that its slightly shorter driving handle required more force to turn. Overall, however, it was intuitive and a cinch to attach to and remove from cans.
OXO Good Grips Soft-Handled Can Opener MODEL: 28081 PRICE: $13.95 STYLE: Traditional DRIVING HANDLE LENGTH: 3 in	EASE OF USE ★★★ COMFORT ★★★ DURABILITY ★★	This traditional model was intuitive and "very quick" to use, and we also liked its bulbous, comfortable driving handle. Our testers thought it was "lovely" and simple to operate, but we docked durability points because one of the handle covers became loose during testing; we found that we could pull it off entirely with minimal effort.

RECOMMENDED WITH RESERVATIONS

ZYLISS Lock 'n Lift Can Opener MODEL: 20362 PRICE: $13.95 STYLE: Traditional DRIVING HANDLE LENGTH: 3 in	EASE OF USE ★★ COMFORT ★★½ DURABILITY ★★★	This model was fine overall, but its handle had an annoying button that we had to press both to attach it to and remove it from a can, thereby making a simple process overly complicated. Once we had it attached to the can, testers thought it was "very smooth" to operate, but "the one thing is just remembering to press the button down to unlock it again and release it."
FISSLER Magic Can Opener MODEL: 020-081-18-000 PRICE: $43.95 STYLE: Safety DRIVING HANDLE LENGTH: 3¼ in	EASE OF USE ★½ COMFORT ★★ DURABILITY ★★★	Our previous winner still has a sleek design and prevents sinking lids, but it wasn't easy to tell when we had successfully attached it to cans, and its driving handle was more difficult to rotate than those of our top-ranked models. It also wasn't easy to remove the opener; users didn't know they had to rotate the handle backward when done circling the can. We liked it more once we got the hang of it, but testers still struggled to determine whether the opener was cutting into the can.

NOT RECOMMENDED

RÖSLE Can Opener with Pliers Grip MODEL: 12757 PRICE: $54.99 STYLE: Safety DRIVING HANDLE LENGTH: 2⅞ in	EASE OF USE ★ COMFORT ★ DURABILITY ★★★	This stainless-steel model was far more impressive in appearance than in performance. It was hard to attach to cans, owing to the blade's location on the underside of the opener, hidden from view, and it was "very tight, very hard to turn." Plus, we couldn't always tell when the opener had completed its revolution around the can, so some users "had to go around several times." The bird-beak-like pliers "weren't very easy to use," so we often just removed lids with our hands.

NUTRITIONAL INFORMATION FOR OUR RECIPES

We calculate the nutritional values of our recipes per serving; if there is a range in the serving size, we used the highest number of servings to calculate the nutritional values. We entered all the ingredients, using weights for important ingredients such as meat, cheese, and most vegetables. We also used our preferred brands in these analyses. We did not include additional salt or pepper for food that's "seasoned to taste."

RECIPE	CALORIES	TOTAL FAT (G)	SAT FAT (G)	CHOL (MG)	TOTAL CARBS (G)	PROTEIN (G)	FIBER (G)	SODIUM (MG)
CHAPTER 1: SOUPS, SALADS, AND STARTERS								
Pasta e Fagioli	441	13	4	17	58	22	9	785
Hearty Cabbage Soup	240	11	2	40	18	17	5	430
Thai Hot and Sour Noodle Soup with Shrimp (Guay Tiew Tom Yum Goong)	318	5	1	104	47	23	4	1642
Thai Chili Jam (Nam Prik Pao)	81	6	0	0	5	0	0	161
Fregula with Clams and Saffron Broth	330	8	1	45	29	28	0	1100
Mexican Corn Salad (Esquites)	176	11	3	17	16	5	1	229
Beet Salad with Goat Cheese and Arugula	164	8	3	8	16	7	5	468
Pan-Roasted Pear Salad	271	18	5	20	20	5	3	265
Potato, Green Bean, and Tomato Salad	437	27	3	1	43	7	8	702
Cauliflower Salad with Golden Raisins and Almonds	280	20	2	0	23	5	6	522
Cauliflower Salad with Apricots and Hazelnuts	266	22	2	0	14	5	5	500
Cauliflower Salad with Cranberries and Pistachios	281	21	2	0	22	5	6	492
Spanish-Style Meatballs in Almond Sauce (Albóndigas en Salsa de Almendras)	545	40	11	129	15	25	2	657
Easy Egg Rolls	660	63	7	25	16	9	1	510
Soy-Vinegar Dipping Sauce	40	0	0	0	4	4	0	1840
Smoky Shishito Peppers with Espelette and Lime	75	7	0	0	4	1	1	167
Shishito Peppers with Fennel Pollen, Aleppo, and Lemon	77	7	1	0	3	1	1	151
Shishito Peppers with Mint, Poppy Seeds, and Orange	77	7	1	0	3	1	1	167
Shishito Peppers with Mustard and Bonito Flakes	76	7	0	0	3	1	1	168
Baked Goat Cheese	139	9	4	11	7	6	2	266
Whipped Feta Dip	109	9	4	25	1	4	0	262
Whipped Feta and Roasted Red Pepper Dip	110	9	4	25	1	4	0	261
Whipped Feta Dip with Dill and Parsley	120	11	5	25	2	4	0	260
CHAPTER 2: VEGETABLE SIDES								
Caesar Brussels Sprouts	282	21	3	5	17	7	6	346
Charred Sichuan-Style Okra	360	28	2	0	18	3	4	770
Crunchy Broccoli and Cheese Casserole	352	25	15	73	19	15	0	362
Sautéed Mushrooms with Red Wine and Rosemary	97	4	2	8	8	5	1	198
Sautéed Mushrooms with Mustard and Parsley	88	4	2	8	8	5	2	240
Sautéed Mushrooms with Soy, Scallion, and Ginger	97	4	1	8	11	4	3	496

RECIPE	CALORIES	TOTAL FAT (G)	SAT FAT (G)	CHOL (MG)	TOTAL CARBS (G)	PROTEIN (G)	FIBER (G)	SODIUM (MG)
CHAPTER 2: VEGETABLE SIDES (continued)								
Skillet-Charred Green Beans	100	7	0.5	0	8	2	3	150
Skillet-Charred Green Beans with Crispy Bread-Crumb Topping	140	11	1	0	10	2	3	220
Skillet-Charred Green Beans with Crispy Sesame Topping	114	7	0	0	11	3	4	310
Grilled Zucchini with Red Pepper Sauce	111	7	1	0	9	3	3	561
Roasted Delicata Squash	148	7	2	10	22	1	3	201
Basque-Style Herb Sauce (Tximitxurri)	84	9	1	0	0	0	0	41
Goat Cheese and Chive Sauce	31	2	1	5	0	2	0	47
Spicy Honey	50	0	0	0	12	0	0	100
Cheddar Scalloped Potatoes	459	31	18	107	30	14	2	648
Crushed Red Potatoes with Garlic and Herbs	211	11	7	30	24	3	2	29
Crushed Red Potatoes with Garlic and Smoked Paprika	229	13	1	0	24	3	2	28
Crushed Red Potatoes with Oregano and Capers	214	11	7	30	25	3	3	62
German Potato Salad	305	15	5	25	32	8	4	347
Air-Fryer Parmesan, Rosemary, and Black Pepper French Fries	240	10	2	10	31	8	2	340
Whole Romanesco with Berbere and Yogurt-Tahini Sauce	300	25	12	50	16	7	5	230
CHAPTER 3: PASTA, PIZZA, SANDWICHES, AND MORE								
Falafel	440	35	4	5	34	11	1	570
Tomato-Chile Sauce	60	5	0.5	0	4	1	1	400
Sliders	293	17	5	18	17	15	0	327
Croque Monsieur	780	50	28	172	38	44	3	1894
Croque Madame	900	59	31	363	39	51	3	1966
Philly Tomato Pie	439	13	1	0	71	10	4	651
Pizza al Taglio with Arugula and Fresh Mozzarella	593	32	9	39	54	20	2	651
Pizza al Taglio with Potatoes and Soppressata	771	42	13	56	67	29	4	1115
Pizza al Taglio with Prosciutto and Figs	505	20	3	10	64	15	3	559
Crispy Tacos (Tacos Dorados)	650	41	8	70	48	27	2	980
Three-Cheese Ravioli with Browned Butter–Pine Nut Sauce	619	43	20	181	35	22	1	405
Cheesy Stuffed Shells	549	25	13	121	53	27	4	777
Agnolotti	450	27	12	240	24	22	1	360
Pork, Fennel, and Lemon Ragu with Pappardelle	559	26	11	93	49	29	3	648
Pasta alla Gricia (Rigatoni with Pancetta and Pecorino Romano)	496	20	7	34	57	17	2	390
Hot Sesame Noodles with Pork	597	28	5	27	64	19	4	695
Sichuan Chili Oil	227	23	1	0	4	0	1	2
Shrimp Risotto	388	12	6	118	47	16	3	1188
Stuffed Portobello Mushrooms	460	40	10	20	15	13	3	870
CHAPTER 4: MEAT								
Beef Top Loin Roast with Potatoes	783	44	16	184	42	51	5	1412
Korean Marinated Beef (Bulgogi)	562	35	12	92	31	28	3	997
Texas Barbecue Brisket	470	14	5	235	1	79	0	1160
Bacon-Wrapped Filets Mignons	551	31	10	207	0	65	0	604
Gorgonzola Vinaigrette	361	35	9	21	4	6	1	385

RECIPE	CALORIES	TOTAL FAT (G)	SAT FAT (G)	CHOL (MG)	TOTAL CARBS (G)	PROTEIN (G)	FIBER (G)	SODIUM (MG)
CHAPTER 4: MEAT *(continued)*								
Hamburger Steaks with Onion Gravy	507	34	15	138	12	34	1	303
Sous Vide Butter-Basted Rib-Eye Steaks	1060	74	22	290	2	92	0	870
Sous Vide Butter-Basted Rib-Eye Steaks with Green Peppercorn–Star Anise Butter	1070	74	22	290	3	92	1	870
Sous Vide Butter-Basted Rib-Eye Steaks with Rosemary-Orange Butter	1060	74	22	290	2	92	0	870
Vietnamese Grilled Pork Patties with Rice Noodles and Salad (Bun Cha)	406	16	6	54	46	17	2	1641
Braised New Mexico–Style Pork in Red Chile Sauce (Carne Adovada)	439	26	9	133	8	38	0	141
Tuscan Grilled Pork Ribs (Rosticciana)	204	19	4	28	0	5	0	124
Sweet-and-Sour Baby Back Ribs	216	9	1	19	26	6	0	608
Pork Tenderloin Roulade with Bacon, Apple, and Gruyère	358	18	6	130	6	39	1	558
Grilled Bone-In Leg of Lamb with Charred-Scallion Sauce	650	50	16	160	3	44	1	796
Spiced Lamb Pot Roast with Figs	400	18	7	120	10	38	2	520
CHAPTER 5: POULTRY AND SEAFOOD								
Best Grilled Chicken Thighs with Gochujang Paste	377	26	7	155	4	27	0	595
Best Grilled Chicken Thighs with Mustard-Tarragon Paste	362	26	7	155	2	26	0	212
Kung Pao Chicken	339	18	2	106	16	28	3	715
Skillet-Roasted Chicken Breasts with Garlicky Green Beans	577	32	8	166	11	58	3	1146
Skillet-Roasted Chicken Breasts with Harissa-Mint Carrots	575	30	7	159	19	54	5	1253
Braised Chicken with Mustard and Herbs	563	35	9	207	5	50	0	726
Braised Chicken with Basil and Tomato	564	35	9	207	5	50	0	725
Indian Butter Chicken (Murgh Makhani)	454	30	16	220	12	33	1	782
Cast Iron Oven-Fried Chicken	860	43	9	315	44	68	1	2040
Chicken Scampi	727	47	12	145	41	28	2	782
Chicken in Adobo	904	60	15	257	20	67	4	1192
Chicken Pot Pie with Spring Vegetables	600	28	14	205	50	42	6	1090
Air-Fryer Chicken Nuggets	671	24	4	305	48	61	2	221
Honey-Dijon Dipping Sauce	280	2	0	0	67	3	3	919
Sweet-and-Sour Dipping Sauce	113	0	0	0	27	0	0	37
Thai-Style Fried Chicken	719	43	4	142	46	33	2	1663
Boneless Turkey Breast with Gravy	260	10	4	140	4	36	0	720
Pan-Seared Swordfish Steaks	350	17	4	150	0	45	0	600
Caper-Currant Relish	450	42	6	0	18	2	3	410
Spicy Dried Mint–Garlic Sauce	190	20	2	0	1	0	0	85
Sautéed Tilapia	212	9	1	77	0	31	0	382
Cilantro Chimichurri	130	14	2	0	2	0	0	290
Shrimp Mozambique	375	18	5	301	9	32	1	1487
Thai Panang Shrimp Curry	548	38	20	255	13	42	4	980
Thai Panang Curry Paste	7	0	0	0	2	0	0	6
Salt-Baked Whole Branzino	292	6	1	116	1	55	0	397
Peruvian Fish Ceviche with Radishes and Orange	324	20	2	27	18	20	4	67

RECIPE	CALORIES	TOTAL FAT (G)	SAT FAT (G)	CHOL (MG)	TOTAL CARBS (G)	PROTEIN (G)	FIBER (G)	SODIUM (MG)
CHAPTER 6: BREAKFAST, BRUNCH, AND BREADS								
Amish Cinnamon Bread	359	15	1	27	51	3	0	165
Pita Bread	251	8	1	0	36	5	1	227
Easiest-Ever Biscuits	347	20	12	71	35	5	1	223
Challah	275	7	0	46	43	8	1	227
Bagel Bread	274	3	0	23	51	8	1	253
English Muffins	305	6	3	14	52	9	1	324
Oatmeal-Raisin Bread	210	4	2.5	10	35	6	2	300
Blueberry Cornbread	440	19	11	95	61	7	2	360
Honey Butter	134	11	7	30	8	0	0	57
Triple-Chocolate Sticky Buns	495	23	14	61	66	7	2	320
Everyday French Toast	316	13	6	160	34	12	2	394
Scrambled Eggs with Pinto Beans and Cotija Cheese	384	22	5	379	23	21	6	538
Eggs in Spicy Tomato and Roasted Red Pepper Sauce (Shakshuka)	463	27	6	378	38	20	6	739
Spicy Middle Eastern Herb Sauce (Zhoug)	88	9	1	0	1	0	0	64
Sous Vide Soft-Poached Eggs	38	2	0	98	0	3	0	37
Breakfast Tacos	440	26	7	390	33	20	6	430
Chewy Granola Bars with Walnuts and Cranberries	143	7	0	0	18	2	1	83
Chewy Granola Bars with Hazelnuts, Cherries, and Cacao Nibs	205	11	1	0	24	3	2	85
Nut-Free Chewy Granola Bars	178	10	1	0	19	4	2	87
CHAPTER 7: DESSERTS								
Torta Caprese	310	22	9	79	26	5	2	106
Amaretto Whipped Cream	70	6	4	20	2	0	0	0
Orange Whipped Cream	70	6	4	20	2	0	0	0
Clementine Cake	777	31	11	154	117	12	4	257
Strawberry Shortcake Trifle	510	30	18	166	51	6	2	350
Pavlova with Fruit and Whipped Cream	460	17	11	55	75	4	2	45
Browned Butter Blondies	218	10	4	39	29	2	0	123
Chewy Peanut Butter Cookies	174	9	2	20	19	4	1	91
Belgian Spice Cookies (Speculoos)	69	3	1	12	9	0	0	33
Belgian Spice Cookies (Speculoos) with Almonds	78	3	1	12	9	1	0	33
Gooey Butter Cake Bars	540	26	16	135	68	6	0	280
Chocolate Fudge	304	15	8	23	43	2	1	90
Chocolate Peppermint Fudge	300	14	9	23	44	1	1	90
Chocolate Toffee Fudge	317	15	9	28	46	1	1	97
Pistachio Gelato	480	28	8	140	48	14	4	140
Peach Tarte Tatin	350	18	11	50	44	3	2	220
Lemon–Olive Oil Tart	437	22	3	69	54	5	0	243
Virginia Peanut Pie	600	36	15	110	61	12	2	330
Make-Ahead Pumpkin Pie with Maple-Cinnamon Whipped Cream	480	31	19	90	48	4	2	380

CONVERSIONS & EQUIVALENTS

Some say cooking is a science and an art. We would say that geography has a hand in it, too. Flour milled in the United Kingdom and elsewhere will feel and taste different from flour milled in the United States. So, while we cannot promise that the loaf of bread you bake in Canada or England will taste the same as a loaf baked in the States, we can offer guidelines for converting weights and measures. We also recommend that you rely on your instincts when making our recipes. Refer to the visual cues provided. If the bread dough hasn't "come together in a ball," as described, you may need to

add more flour—even if the recipe doesn't tell you so. You be the judge.

The recipes in this book were developed using standard U.S. measures following U.S. government guidelines. The charts below offer equivalents for U.S., metric, and imperial (U.K.) measures. All conversions are approximate and have been rounded up or down to the nearest whole number. For example:

1 teaspoon	=	4.929 milliliters, rounded up to 5 milliliters
1 ounce	=	28.349 grams, rounded down to 28 grams

VOLUME CONVERSIONS

U.S.	METRIC
1 teaspoon	5 milliliters
2 teaspoons	10 milliliters
1 tablespoon	15 milliliters
2 tablespoons	30 milliliters
¼ cup	59 milliliters
⅓ cup	79 milliliters
½ cup	118 milliliters
¾ cup	177 milliliters
1 cup	237 milliliters
1¼ cups	296 milliliters
1½ cups	355 milliliters
2 cups	473 milliliters
2½ cups	591 milliliters
3 cups	710 milliliters
4 cups (1 quart)	0.946 liter
1.06 quarts	1 liter
4 quarts (1 gallon)	3.8 liters

WEIGHT CONVERSIONS

OUNCES	GRAMS
½	14
¾	21
1	28
1½	43
2	57
2½	71
3	85
3½	99
4	113
4½	128
5	142
6	170
7	198
8	227
9	255
10	283
12	340
16 (1 pound)	454

CONVERSIONS FOR INGREDIENTS COMMONLY USED IN BAKING

Baking is an exacting science. Because measuring by weight is far more accurate than measuring by volume, and thus more likely to achieve reliable results, in our recipes we provide ounce measures in addition to cup measures for many ingredients. Refer to the chart below to convert these measures into grams.

INGREDIENT	OUNCES	GRAMS
Flour		
1 cup all-purpose flour*	5	142
1 cup cake flour	4	113
1 cup whole-wheat flour	5½	156
Sugar		
1 cup granulated (white) sugar	7	198
1 cup packed brown sugar (light or dark)	7	198
1 cup confectioners' sugar	4	113
Cocoa Powder		
1 cup cocoa powder	3	85
Butter†		
4 tablespoons (½ stick, or ¼ cup)	2	57
8 tablespoons (1 stick, or ½ cup)	4	113
16 tablespoons (2 sticks, or 1 cup)	8	227

* U.S. all-purpose flour, the most frequently used flour in this book, does not contain leaveners, as some European flours do. These leavened flours are called self-rising or self-raising. If you are using self-rising flour, take this into consideration before adding leavening to a recipe.

† In the United States, butter is sold both salted and unsalted. We generally recommend unsalted butter. If you are using salted butter, take this into consideration before adding salt to a recipe.

OVEN TEMPERATURES

FAHRENHEIT	CELSIUS	GAS MARK (imperial)
225	105	¼
250	120	½
275	135	1
300	150	2
325	165	3
350	180	4
375	190	5
400	200	6
425	220	7
450	230	8
475	245	9

CONVERTING TEMPERATURES FROM AN INSTANT-READ THERMOMETER

We include doneness temperatures in many of our recipes, such as those for poultry, meat, and bread. We recommend an instant-read thermometer for the job. Refer to the table above to convert Fahrenheit degrees to Celsius. Or, for temperatures not represented in the chart, use this simple formula:

Subtract 32 degrees from the Fahrenheit reading, then divide the result by 1.8 to find the Celsius reading.

EXAMPLE:

"Roast chicken until thighs register 175 degrees."
To convert:

175° F − 32 = 143°
143° ÷ 1.8 = 79.44°C, rounded down to 79°C

INDEX

B